FOR VICTORY IN PEACEFUL COMPETITION
WITH CAPITALISM

FOR VICTORY
IN PEACEFUL
COMPETITION
WITH CAPITALISM

With a Special Introduction Written
For the American Edition

Nikita S. Khrushchev

E. P. DUTTON & CO., INC.
NEW YORK   1960

First published in the United States of America, 1960
by E. P. Dutton & Co., Inc.

All rights reserved. Printed in the U.S.A.

Library of Congress Catalog Card Number: 60-6004

FOR VICTORY IN PEACEFUL COMPETITION WITH CAPITALISM

Эта книга не предназначалась специально для американского читателя. Она представляет собою сборник выступлений и заявлений, сделанных на протяжении 1958 года по различным вопросам международного положения и внешней политики Советского Союза. Читатель может познакомиться с тем, что волновало нас, советских людей, в течение этого периода, как воспринимали и оценивали мы важнейшие международные события.

Во всех странах, в том числе в Соединенных Штатах, выходит немало книг о Советском Союзе, о коммунизме, его целях и принципах. Немало авторов в поте лица своего трудится над тем, чтобы извратить истинные цели советской политики, намерения социалистических государств. Поэтому особенно важно, чтобы читатель узнал правду о советской стране, о ее внешней политике, о коммунизме.

Открытое и честное изложение взглядов – первейшее условие достижения взаимопонимания между народами, а стало быть и установления сотрудничества между ними. В особенности это необходимо в современной международной обстановке. Человечество подошло к такому моменту, когда народы стоят перед выбором: либо мирное сосуществование государств с различным социальным строем, либо катастрофическая ядерная война.

В предлагаемой вниманию американского читателя книге главное место принадлежит обоснованию необходимости и возможности мирного сосуществования и мирного соревнования государств с различным социальным строем – социалистическим и капиталистическим. Различные общественные системы существуют на земле и никуда нельзя уйти от этого факта. И поскольку это так, сохранение мира возможно лишь на основе мирного сосуществования и сотрудничества государств, независимо от имеющихся между ними идеологических разногласий.

Ни один народ не хочет войны. Особенно страстно стремится к миру советский народ. Война противна нашим убеждениям, гуманистической природе социалистического строя. Как я теперь могу судить по личным наблюдениям, громадное большинство американского народа также настроено миролюбиво и стремится избежать войны.

INTRODUCTION TO THE AMERICAN EDITION

This book is a collection of speeches and statements made in the course of 1958 on various questions relating to the international situation and foreign policy of the Soviet Union. Although it was not especially intended for American readers, they will be able to learn from it what we Soviet people were preoccupied with during that period, and how we reacted to and evaluated the most important international events.

Quiet a few books on the Soviet Union, on communism and its objectives and principles, are published in all countries, including the United States. Quite a few authors are working feverishly to distort the true aims of the Soviet foreign policy and the intentions of the socialist states. It is especially important, therefore, that the reader should learn the truth about the Soviet Union and her foreign policy, and about communism.

A forthright and honest exposition of views is the first and foremost condition for reaching understanding between nations and, consequently, for establishing cooperation between them. This is especially necessary in the contemporary international situation. Mankind has approached a time when the peoples are faced with a choice—either peaceful coexistence of states with different social systems, or a disastrous nuclear war.

This book offered for the attention of the American reader is mainly devoted to the substantiation of the necessity and possibility of peaceful coexistence and peaceful competition between states with different social systems—socialist and capitalist. Different social systems exist on earth, and one cannot get away from this fact. And since this is so, the preservation of peace is possible solely on the basis of peaceful coexistence and the cooperation of states, irrespective of ideological differences that exist between them.

No nation wants war. The desire for peace is particularly strong with the Soviet people. War is alien to our convictions, to the humane nature of the socialist system. As I can now judge by my personal observations, the overwhelming majority of the American people are also peace-minded and are striving to avoid war.

Instead of military conflicts between states, we offer the prospect of peaceful competition, primarily in the economic field, but also in scientific, technical, cultural and all other fields. We stand for honest competition in peaceful pursuits, without some countries' interfering in the internal affairs of others. Who will produce more goods for peaceful needs? Who will create better conditions for the development of technology, science and culture? Which social system offers greater opportunities for developing the productive forces and for meeting the spiritual needs of the people? Whose people will have higher living standards? This is, in the main, the essence of the competition. Such competition does not at all rule out cooperation between countries, but on the contrary, implies it. Competition in the development of economy, technology and culture harms no one.

With each retaining its convictions, we can find a broad field for cooperation wherein our interests coincide. The averting of a nuclear war, the development of international trade without any discrimination, the exchange of achievements in the sphere of science and culture—is it not a noble field for cooperation? We are firmly convinced that in the long run common sense will prevail in international relations. Peaceful coexistence of states with different social systems is in our day both an imperative necessity dictated by the correlation of forces at present in the international arena, and the only reasonable course for all mankind. It is time to pass in international affairs from the thousands of years old, savage ways of behavior based on violence, to new forms of relations between states worthy of the intellect of contemporary man and of his magnificent achievements in harnessing the forces of nature.

The Soviet Government is doing all it can for the sake of preserving peace and developing cooperation among states on the basis of peaceful coexistence. Expressing the interests of the entire nation, the Soviet Government is striving for the improvement of relations and for the development of friendly cooperation with all states, irrespective of their social systems. It is with these aims that we submitted our proposals on general and complete disarmament, and we will spare no effort so that genuine disarmament may become a fact.

Is there any need to prove how important it is that our countries—the Soviet Union and the United States of America—and our peoples, the Soviet and American peoples, should better understand and trust each other? This is necessary if we want to live in peace, cooperating to the mutual benefit of our nations. Mutual distrust, suspicion and fear are poor advisers not only in relations between individuals, but still more so in relations between states.

Recently, a number of good and useful steps have been made which are contributing to a rapprochement between the USSR and the USA. I believe that the exchange of visits between the Chairman of the Council of Ministers of the USSR and the President of the United States will contribute to the improvement of relations between our two countries and also to the improvement of the international atmosphere as a whole. It is with pleasure that I recall the days of my stay in the United States when I came to know still better the enterprising and industrious American people.

I hope that this book will help the American readers to understand better the noble and peaceful aims of the foreign policy of the Soviet state.

Moscow   N. KHRUSHCHEV
November, 1959

N. S. KHRUSHCHEV'S SPEECH
FOLLOWING HIS RETURN TO MOSCOW

N. S. KHRUSHCHEV'S SPEECH
FOLLOWING HIS RETURN TO MOSCOW

The following is the full text of the speech made by N. S. Khrushchev at a meeting of the working people of Moscow in the Palace of Sports in Moscow on September 28, 1959.

Dear comrades, we have only just left the plane which completed a non-stop flight from Washington to Moscow. We have come straight to you, dear Muscovites, to share with you our impressions and to tell you about the results of our visit to the United States of America undertaken at the invitation of the President of the United States, Dwight D. Eisenhower.

In accepting his invitation, we proceeded from the fact that the international situation and the relations between our states, two Great Powers—the Soviet Union and the United States, have long been in a state of tension.

To continue this state of affairs means to perpetuate a situation fraught with all kinds of surprises, with grave consequences for our peoples and the peoples of all the world. This is why the most farsighted statesmen of several countries have come to realize the need of making some sort of effort to end the "cold war," to do away with the tension which has developed in international relations, to clear the atmosphere and create more or less normal relations among states. Then the nations would be able to live and look into the future without fearing for their destinies.

The twentieth century is a century of the greatest flourishing of human thought and genius. In our time people create with their own hands the things that mankind dreamed of for centuries, expressing these dreams in tales, which seemed to be sheer fantasy.

Must we, in this period of the flourishing of human genius which is penetrating the secrets of nature and harnessing its mighty forces, put up with the preservation of relations that existed between people when man was still a beast?

If in those distant times these relations could be explained by man's being in the first stage of his development and differing but little from animals, today, when man has reached an unparalleled level in the development of his scientific knowledge and subordinates, step by step, the forces of nature to his will, making them serve society, today nothing can justify the preservation of such relations as existed between primitive people.

Our time can and should become a time of the realization of great ideals, a time of peace and progress.

The Soviet Government realized this long ago. Precisely for this reason we have repeatedly offered the Great Powers to arrange a summit meeting so as to exchange views on urgent international problems. When we made these proposals, we believed in man's reason. We believed that, given a wise approach, the proponents of various political views, countries with different social systems, will be able to find a common language so as to resolve correctly and in the interests of consolidating peace the contemporary problems that alarm all mankind.

In our age of great technical progress, in conditions when there are states with different social systems, international problems cannot be resolved successfully otherwise than on principles of peaceful coexistence. There is no other way.

Those people who say they do not understand what peaceful coexistence is and are fearful of it contribute, willingly or unwillingly, to the further development of the cold war which will certainly extend if we do not interfere and stop

xiv

it. It will reach a pitch where a spark might result capable of producing a world war.

Much would perish in this war. It would be too late to discuss what peaceful coexistence means when the talking will be done by such frightful means of destruction as atomic and hydrogen bombs, as ballistic rockets which are practically impossible to locate and which are capable of delivering nuclear warheads to any part of the globe. To disregard this is to shut one's eyes, stop one's ears and bury one's head as the ostrich does when in danger.

But if we people imitate the ostrich and hide our head in sand, the question will arise: What is the use of having this head if it is unable to avert the threat to its very life?

No, we must display the reason of man, confidence in this reason, confidence in the possibility of reaching agreement with statesmen of different countries, and mobilize people by joint efforts to avert the war danger. It is necessary to have the will power and courage to go against those who persist in continuing the cold war. It is necessary to bar the road to it, to thaw the ice and normalize international relations.

I must say from this high platform to the Muscovites, to all our people, the government and the Party: that President Dwight Eisenhower of the United States has displayed wise statesmanship in assessing the present international situation, that he has displayed courage and will power.

Despite the complexity of the situation which prevails in the United States, he, the person who enjoys the full confidence of his people, has come out with a proposal to exchange visits between the heads of government of our two countries. We give our due to this important initiative aimed at consolidating peace.

Undertaking this step, he was confident that we would accept the hand he offered us, since we have repeatedly approached both President Eisenhower and the other heads of government on this question. And the President of the United States was not mistaken.

Dear comrades, I report to you with satisfaction that we have fulfilled a part of the agreement with President Eisenhower on the exchange of visits. Availing ourselves of the President's kind invitation, we have undertaken a trip to the United States and have had important meetings and talks there.

I should like to share with you my impressions of this trip and speak briefly about its results.

I think it is best to tell you everything as it was. The truer the account, the better it will be for the strengthening of relations between the people of our two countries. It would be incorrect to say that all outstanding questions are resolved after our tour of some American cities, after our meetings and talks with many Americans. Only a politically blind person could think that it will be as he says.

No, one visit or one tour is not enough to resolve questions of such importance; this calls for great efforts.

Many more meetings will be necessary to achieve full understanding, to achieve what always has been the aim of our Party, our people, our Soviet state—to insure peaceful coexistence between states with different ways of life and to insure the security of the peoples on the basis of noninterference in each other's internal affairs.

I want to tell you how we felt when we first set foot on the soil of the United States of America.

To tell you frankly, my feelings were mixed. The point is that immediately after the announcement of an exchange of visits, many press organs and some leaders in the United States launched a propaganda campaign against my coming to the United States. They created an atmosphere that did not warm me even though the temperature in the United States is considerably higher than in Moscow. They wanted to meet me with a cold shower.

I was particularly disappointed when, flying from Moscow to Washington, I read Vice President Nixon's statement timed for my visit. He had chosen an audience which, seemingly, could not be suspected of any belligerency. It was the American Dental Association. However, Mr. Nixon's speech was by no means of medical significance. He, so to say, added cold to the toothache. It seems that he was afraid lest a thaw should really set in, lest the cold war should really end. I do not understand why this was needed.

However, when we arrived in Washingon, we were given a welcome which was worthy of our great country, our great people. President Eisenhower must be given his due: he did everything that had to be done for a welcome at this level. You certainly have read in the papers what a welcome was given to us in the United States capital and what a speech was made by the President.

I am not going to repeat myself: it was a warm welcome.

Shortly after our arrival in Washington I met the President at the White House. Also present were Vice President Nixon and Secretary of State Herter. I have a somewhat restless character and I am a blunt man, so I asked in our very first conversation—though it may not perhaps have been very diplomatic—why the Vice President had found it necessary to make such a statement on the eve of my arrival. I will not speak of the unfriendly statements and articles by people of lesser standing.

The President said he had not read Nixon's statement. I told him then that it need not be read as it was already a matter of the past. This is one small thing which shows in some measure the preparations made to receive the guest from across the sea.

Another thing. You Muscovites, as indeed all Soviet people —the Russians, Ukrainians, Byelorussians, Uzbeks, Georgians, Kazakhs, Armenians, all peoples—always give a worthy welcome to your guests. Whatever country your guest may represent, whatever his political convictions may be, we meet him with bread and salt because he is our guest, and we show him inner, and not merely outward, respect. But there, in the United States, I witnessed the following thing on the first day: We were riding in a car with the President. There were huge crowds of people. Some raised their hands and waved but—I saw this—jerked the hands back quickly as if from a live wire.

It was difficult for me to understand this at first. I decided to look more attentively at the faces of the people standing along both sides of our route. I began to greet people by slight nods and many of them replied. What was the matter then?

I was told afterward that ten minutes before we drove with the President to the White House, an unknown automobile had passed along our route with a poster saying, "Welcome the guest worthily, politely, but without applause or greetings."

Afterward I asked the President's representative, Mr. Lodge, who accompanied me during the tour of the United States, whether that was true. It was explained that there actually had been such a car, but it was allegedly unknown to whom it belonged. You see, it had broken through the police cordon. When the officials gave me this explanation, I told them I could not imagine how the police, which guarded me so well, failed to notice the car carrying such a poster.

I am sure that the President did not know anything about this and that all this was done contrary to the wishes of the President and the others who organized our welcome. However, as the saying goes, words cannot be cut out from a song. From the very first steps on American soil I was so closely guarded that it was absolutely impossible to contact the ordinary Americans. This guarding turned into a sort of house arrest. I was taken around in a closed car and could see the people welcoming us only through its window. But the people waved and shouted, though very often they could not see me. I am far from taking all the feelings of friendship which were expressed by the American people as referring to myself or even to our Communist ideology.

The Americans told us in these greetings that, like us, they held by the positions of struggle for peace, for friendship between our peoples.

I am not going to speak in detail about all our meetings with the Americans. You apparently know about them from the papers. We visited Washington and then New York, where I had the honor to submit to the United Nations, on behalf of the Soviet Government, a plan for general and complete disarmament.

From New York we went to the West Coast of the United States, to Los Angeles and San Francisco, and then to Iowa and to Pittsburgh, a major industrial center in Pennsylvania. Finally, we returned to Washington. It was a big trip. We saw various parts of the United States and met people of various stripes. We had many good meetings and frank conversations. But there also were meetings of a different kind.

On the first half of our trip we noticed that the same record was played over and over again. Speakers everywhere asserted that I had once said that we would "bury the capitalists." At first, I patiently explained that I really had said this, that we would "bury capitalism" in the sense that socialism would inevitably supersede this moribund social form as capitalism, in its time, had superseded feudalism. But then I saw that the people who stubbornly repeated these questions did not need explanations. They had a definite aim, that of using communism to intimidate people who had only a vague notion of what it is.

I finally had to speak my mind when at a reception in Los Angeles, the Mayor of the city, who was no worse than the other mayors but less diplomatic perhaps, started to say the same thing all over again.

I said: "Do you want to organize an unfriendly demonstration for me in every city, at every meeting? If you are going to receive me in this way then, as the Russian saying goes, 'It is not hard to turn back from the gate.' If you are not yet ready for talks, if you have not yet realized the need for liquidating the cold war and fear lest it should be liquidated, if you want to continue, we can wait; the wind is not blowing in our faces either. We have both enough patience and enough wisdom. Things are going well in our country. Our people have time and again displayed such reason, such strength, such will and such ability to overcome the difficulties that it will be able to stand up for the country and for the cause of peace. They will reply worthily if the forces of aggression attempt to test us by the bayonet."

I had to enter into diplomatic negotiations then. I asked the Minister of Foreign Affairs, Comrade Gromyko, to go and tell the President's representative, Mr. Lodge, who was accompanying me, that if things were not righted I would not find it possible to continue the trip and would have to return to Washington and then to Moscow.

All this seemed to have produced its effect. Mr. Lodge told me through Gromyko that he recommeded that I go on to San Francisco and other cities on our itinerary and that the local authorities would take measures to prevent any recurrence of this.

I must tell you that these negotiations through Comrade Gromyko took place at night, and when I awoke in the morning, everything had indeed changed.

And when we left Los Angeles for San Francisco, I was, figuratively speaking, "uncuffed" and permitted to leave the railroad coach and meet people. People shook my hands, and I replied to their handshakes, they applauded and smiled just as you Muscovites smile when welcoming guests, rejoicing at their arrival and doing everything possible to make the guests feel as one should.

When we came to San Francisco, the sun shone brightly and it was a fine day, the kind we have in summer. The climate of this remarkable city was absolutely different—we were warm from the sun, but even warmer from the cordial unrestrained welcome given us.

We are exceptionally thankful to the Mayor of San Francisco, Mr. Christopher; to the Governor of California, Mr. Brown; the people of San Francisco, all those who approached with understanding our visit, the visit of peace and friendship between our two peoples, among the peoples of all countries.

We were given every opportunity to meet and talk with the common people. True, we did not have enough strength for this, but this was due to the short duration of our stay. Honestly speaking, this dispelled our suspicions about the evil intentions of the local authorities. We immediately established good contacts with the residents of that big and beautiful city.

I wish to note particularly the meeting with the longshoremen. The head of the Pacific Coast Longshoremen's Union, Mr. Bridges, invited me and my companions to come and converse with the dockers. This was a heartfelt meeting. Among the longshoremen, ordinary and sincere people that they are, I felt as though I was among Soviet workers. The greetings I conveyed to them from the Soviet workers were received with enthusiasm, and they asked me to convey their greetings in reply.

I also remember the visit to a factory producing calculating machines in San Jose, near San Francisco. Its manager, Mr. Watson, the workers and employees met us cordially and showed us all the complex production processes, making all explanations in Russian—a touching forethought. The factory itself, its layout and the organization of production made a very good impression.

One of the people making the explanation had a slight Ukrainian accent, and I asked him (in Ukrainian): "And what is your name?"

He replied: "Marchenko."

I said: "How do you do. Are your parents living?"

He said: "Yes."

"My best regards to them."

He thanked me.

But our stay in hospitable San Francisco was drawing to a close and we were to fly to another American city, Des Moines, in Iowa. It is one of the main centers of agricultural production in the United States.

After a warm meeting with the governor of the state, the mayor of the city and representatives of business and public circles, we went out of town to the corn fields, so dear to my heart. And I must tell you that the Americans know how to grow corn. It is all planted in squares and the fields are in good condition.

True, even there, on the farm of a great authority on corn, my old acquaintance (Roswell) Garst, I found some shortcomings. The corn was planted too densely in clusters and I, of course, called his attention to this, friendly like.

We enjoyed the lavish hospitality of our host, Mr. Garst,

who arranged for us an interesting meeting with farmers. There we also met the noted Democratic leader Adlai Stevenson, who had come from Chicago, and our conversation with him was very frank and friendly.

Another thing comes to mind. When we arrived at the University (of Iowa), one of the young people gave me a student newspaper. It carried a big article in which the students, as I was told, welcomed our arrival. It said, however, that the students would meet us without enthusiasm, without cheers. But what happened? The students in whose name the article had been written, those young people thirsting for life, displayed as much enthusiasm as our youth.

They shouted, applauded and expressed their feelings in a most lively way. There were shouts, "Comrade Khrushchev," "Nikita" and other simple words coming from the heart.

I must also tell you about the warm welcome given us by the people of one of America's biggest industrial centers, the city of metallurgists and machine builders, the people of Pittsburgh.

They displayed a great friendliness and respect for us. I even felt a little uncomfortable when I drove from the airport to the city. We arrived in Pittsburgh at midnight. The night was dark, but as we went to the city, there were cars standing along the entire route, there were people, and I saw their smiles and heard their greetings.

In Pittsburgh we visited a machine-building plant of the Mesta Company.

We felt that the plant's management did everything to show us this undertaking, to let us see the working conditions there. We made the rounds of the plant and conversed with workers. I wish to stress one thing: When we entered, the greetings were restrained. However, the more we talked to the workers, the warmer the meeting became, and the workers loudly expressed their sentiments of respect for us, representatives of the Soviet Union, of the Soviet people.

I also carried away the memory of my meeting with the business men and intellectuals of Pittsburgh, which was held at the local university. As usual a dinner was given there during which speeches were made that differed from the others, and in which, as it seemed to me, the need for the establishing of friendly relations between our two countries was presented with a more realistic understanding.

Listening to my speech, some people may think that in describing these friendly meetings Khrushchev has drawn the curtain on hostile demonstrations. No, I do not intend to hush up facts of hostile or unfriendly attitudes toward us. Yes, there were such facts. You should know that just as the American newsmen were my "sputniks" during the tour of the United States, fascist refugees from different countries moved from city to city, flourishing their few miserable posters. We have also met hostile and grim American faces.

There were very many good things, but the bad should not be forgotten either. This worm, and a big one for that matter, is still alive and may show its vitality in the future, too.

Why do I say this? Is it that I wish to cool the relations between the Soviet Union and the United States? No.

I speak of this because you ought to know the truth, so that you should see not only the side that is pleasant to us, but also the other, behind-the-scenes, side, which should not be concealed. There are forces in the United States working against us and against the easing of tension, for the continuation of the cold war. To disregard this would mean showing weakness in the struggle against these evil forces, against these evil spirits.

No, they must be exposed, they must be shown to the world,

publicly whipped, they must be subjected to the torments of Hades. Let those who want to continue the cold war be angry. They will not be supported by the common people of the world, they will not be supported by reasonable people.

The trip to Pittsburgh rounded off our tour of the United States.

Concluding my account of the trip across that country, I should like to express our sincere gratitude to the mayors of the cities and the governors of the states that we visited, representatives of the business quarters and intellectuals, personnel of enterprises and universities, workers and farmers, all the representatives of public organizations. I should like to note, particularly, the splendid work done by the Mayor of New York, Mr. Wagner; the Mayor of San Francisco, Mr. Christopher; the Mayor of Pittsburgh, Mr. Gallagher; the Governor of Pennsylvania, David Lawrence; rector of Pittsburgh University, Mr. Litchfield; rector of Iowa University, Edward Hilton; representatives of the business quarters, Eric Johnston, Robert Dowling, Cyrus Eaton, Thomas Watson, Frank Mesta, Roswell Garst and others.

The numerous gifts presented to us were a remarkable manifestation of respect for our country, its great people. The Mayors of New York and Pittsburgh presented us with symbolic keys of their cities.

By the way, I told them: "I accept these keys as a symbol of trust. You can rest assured, I promise you, that these keys will never be used without the permission of the masters."

The International Harvester Company presented us with a film on the mechanization of corn growing, President Eisenhower presented us with a pedigreed calf from his private farm, Admiral Strauss with a calf and steer, farmer Coolidge with a pedigreed hog. We received many other presents, for which we are grateful.

I wish to note that in the main the American press, radio and television covered our stay in the United States without bias. Of course, there were unfriendly sallies of individual newsmen, but they did not set the tone in the American press.

During the tour of the United States, my companions and I were accompanied by Mr. Lodge, personal representative of the United States President; Mr. Buchanan, State Department chief of protocol; Mr. Thompson, the United States Ambassador to the USSR; their wives and other officials. I must thank them, and particularly Mr. Lodge. He went out of his way to make our trip pleasant and to acquaint us with the life of the great people of the United States.

I jokingly said to Mr. Lodge: "If I, a representative of the working class, of the Communist Party of the Soviet Union, and he, a representative of the capitalist world, were, by chance, abandoned on an uninhabited island, we would find a common language and insure peaceful coexistence there. Why, then, cannot the states with different social systems insure coexistence? Our states are also, so to say, on an island: After all, with the present-day means of communication, which have brought the continents so close together, our planet really resembles a small island, and we should realize this. Having understood the need of coexistence, we should pursue a peaceful policy, live in friendship, cease brandishing arms and destroy them.

Comrades, on Sept. 25 we again met with the United States President at the White House and left with him by helicopter for his country residence, which is called Camp David. We stayed there for Sept. 25, 26 and 27. We had frank, friendly talks and explained the positions of our governments on basic international problems as well as on questions related to the improvement of Soviet-American relations. Taking part in these meetings and conversations were

Mr. Herter, Secretary of State of the United States, and Comrade Gromyko, the Soviet Foreign Minister, as well as the other comrades that accompanied me. And they surely did a useful piece of work.

The chief outcome of the exchange of views with the United States President is recorded in the joint communiqué, which was published by today's papers. There can be no doubt that this document will be received with satisfaction by all those who are interested in consolidating peace.

It should be taken into account, however, that we could not, of course, clear out with the President in one try all the cold-war rubble that has piled up during many years. It will take time to clear out this rubbish, and not only clear it out, but destroy it. Things dividing us are still too fresh in the memory. Sometimes it is difficult for certain statesmen to give up the old positions, the old views and formulas.

But I will tell you with all frankness, dear comrades, that I got the impression from the talks and discussions of concrete questions with the United States President that he sincerely wants to end the state of cold war, to create normal relations between our two countries, to promote the improvement of relations among all states.

Peace is indivisible now, it cannot be ensured by the efforts of two or three countries only. So we must fight for peace in such a way that all the nations, all the countries, are drawn into this struggle.

We exchanged views with the United States President on questions of disarmament. He said that the United States Government was studying our proposal and that the United States, just as we, wanted complete disarmament under due control.

It seems that there is now no reason for delaying the solution of this question but, on the other hand, the question of disarmament is so serious that we should not press our partners for its solution. The question must be studied, of course, so as to find a solution, which would really create an atmosphere of trust and insure disarmament and peaceful coexistence among states.

So let us not make hurried statements, let us be patient and give the statesmen time to consider our proposals. But we shall not sit on our hands, we shall advocate the need of complete universal disarmament.

We regard our proposals as a basis for agreement. We are ready to discuss any amendments to our document, to our proposals. We are ready to discuss other proposals, too, if they are submitted for the purpose of attaining the same goals as ours.

We exchanged views with the President on the German question also, on the question of concluding a peace treaty. We tried to prove, and I think we were successful in this, that our proposals concerning the peace treaty were incorrectly interpreted in the West.

Some people tried to stir up unnecessary excitement by saying that they are an ultimatum, etc. Those who acted in this way were obviously guided by a desire to prolong the cold war. They went so far as to claim that our proposals on the peace treaty with Germany were something short of a declaration of war. It surely takes some nerve to distort the peaceloving position of the Soviet Union in such a way.

We also exchanged views on the holding of a summit meeting. Both President Eisenhower and I set forth the positions of our two governments and agreed that this meeting is necessary and useful.

We discussed with the United States President the date of his reply visit to the Soviet Union.

At first, the President planned to come to the Soviet Union

at the end of October this year. However, he asked me what was the best time for travelling in our country. I began thinking. We Muscovites like Moscow the year round.

But for us, as for all people, spring is the most pleasant time of the year, because it is the time of joy, of the lush flourishing and awakening of life. So, I told him that, to my mind, it was best to come here at the end of May or early in June. It would be good if the President took along with him his wife, son, his son's wife, and grandchildren. We should be happy also to welcome the President's brother, who came to our country together with Mr. Nixon.

The President was kind enough to invite me to his farm. He showed me his corn fields, I could not miss the chance of seeing the President's corn, of course. I also was shown the heifers and steers at the President's farm. Handsome animals they were. I must say, however, that it is not a large farm for the President to have, considering the greatness and wealth of his country. It is not a rich farm and the soil there is not too good. But the President said he wanted to put some work into it, to improve the soil and leave something behind to be remembered for.

At the farm I made friends with the President's grandchildren and held a conference with them. I asked them whether they wanted to come to Russia. They all, big and small, declared they wanted to come to Russia. The President's oldest grandson is 11 years old and the smallest granddaughter is 3 or 4 years of age. So I have won their support.

I told the President jokingly that it was easier to agree on a reply visit with his grandchildren than with him because his grandchildren have a good environment while he, obviously, is confronted with some obstacles which do not allow him to realize this desire of his in the spirit and at the time he prefers.

I wish to tell you, dear comrades, that I do not doubt the President's intention to exert his will and efforts to reach agreement between our two countries, to create friendly relations between our nations and to solve the urgent problems in the interests of consolidating peace.

At the same time I got the impression that there are forces in America which do not work in the same direction as the President.

These forces are for the continuation of the cold war and for the arms race. I would not be in a hurry to say whether these forces are large or small, influential or not influential, and whether the forces supporting the President—and he is backed by the absolute majority of the American people—can win.

Time is a good adviser, or as the Russian people say, "Take counsel of one's pillow." This is a wise saying. Let us do this, the more so since we have arrived in the afternoon and it is in the evening that I am speaking now. It will take perhaps several such counsels before we clear this up. But we shall not rest idle while waiting for the dawn, we shall not wait to see which way the international relations tilt.

For our part we shall do everything we can to tilt the barometer's hand away from "Storm" and even from "Changeable" to show "Fine."

I am confident, comrades, that in the present conditions, when the forces of peace have grown immensely, when the socialist camp has some one billion people and tremendous productive potential, when the Soviet Union has reached great heights in industry and agriculture, science, technology and culture, we can do a lot for the sake of peace.

In our actions we rely on reason, on truth, on the support of all the people. Moreover, we rely on our great potential.

And let it be known to those who want to continue the

cold war so as to turn it sooner or later into a shooting war, that in our time only a madman can start a war and he himself will perish in its flames.

The people must strait-jacket these madmen. We believe that sound statesmanship and human genius will triumph. Citing Pushkin: "Hail reason, down with obscurity!"

Dear Muscovites! We are boundlessly happy to return home, to see the faces of the Soviet people which are so dear to our hearts.

Long live the great Soviet people, who are successfully building communism under the leadership of the glorious Leninist party!

Long live Soviet-American friendship!

Long live friendship among all the peoples of the world!

FOR VICTORY IN PEACEFUL COMPETITION
WITH CAPITALISM

CONTENTS

Page

Introduction to the American Edition . . . . *vii*

N. S. Khrushchev's Speech Following His Return to Moscow . *xiii*

Exchange of Letters Between C. Rajagopalachari and N. S. Khrushchov 9

Replies to Questions Put by V. Sinnbeck, Editor of *Dansk Folkestyre*, Journal of Youth Organization of Danish Venstre Party 21

Some Aspects of International Situation. Speech at Conference of Front-Rank Agricultural Workers of Byelorussian Republic, *January 22, 1958* 30

Interview Given to Axel Springer, West German Publisher, and Hans Zehrer, Editor of *Die Welt, January 29, 1958* . . . 67

Interview Given to I. McDonald, Foreign Editor of *The Times, January 31, 1958* 85

Replies to Questions Put by Manuel Mejido, Correspondent of Mexican Newspaper *Excelsior, February 21, 1958* . . . 106

Letter to Bertrand Russell, *March 5, 1958* 111

Replies to Questions Put by *Trybuna Ludu, March 10, 1958* . 137

Speech at Meeting of Electors of Kalinin Constituency, Moscow, *March 14, 1958* 155

Interview Given to Correspondent of *Le Figaro, March 19, 1958* 193

Interview Given to Eric Ridder, Owner and Publisher of *Journal of Commerce,* and Its Editor Heinz Luedicke, *March 22, 1958* 213

Replies to Questions Put by Giuseppe Palozzi, *Il Tempo* Correspondent, *March 24, 1958* 231

Speech at Budapest Airport on Arrival of Soviet Party and Government Delegation in Hungary, *April 2, 1958* 248

Speech at Meeting in Budapest in Celebration of 13th Anniversary of Hungary's Liberation, *April 3, 1958* 251

Speech at Mass Meeting in Budapest During Stay in Hungary of Soviet Party and Government Delegation, *April 4, 1958* . 268

Speech at Meeting in Cegléd During Stay in Hungary of Soviet Party and Government Delegation, *April 7, 1958* 280

Speech at Mass Meeting in Tatabánya During Stay in Hungary of Soviet Party and Government Delegation, *April 8, 1958* 290

Speech at Soviet Embassy Reception in Budapest During Stay in Hungary of Soviet Party and Government Delegation, *April 8, 1958* 300

Speech at Academy of Sciences of Hungarian People's Republic During Stay in Hungary of Soviet Party and Government Delegation, *April 9, 1958* 302

Speech at Meeting of Csepel Iron and Steel Works During Stay in Hungary of Soviet Party and Government Delegation, *April 9, 1958* 314

Speech on Departure from Budapest of Soviet Party and Government Delegation, *April 10, 1958* 329

Speech at Meeting on Return of Soviet Party and Government Delegation from Hungarian People's Republic, *April 10, 1958* 332

Speech at Embassy Reception of Polish People's Republic on Occasion of 13th Anniversary of Soviet-Polish Treaty of Friendship, Mutual Assistance and Post-War Co-operation, *April 21, 1958* 347

Speech at Luncheon in Honour of Gamal Abdel Nasser, President of United Arab Republic, *April 30, 1958* 352

Replies to Questions Put by Greek Newspaper Publisher Ch. Lambrakis 360

Speech at Reception at Embassy of the United Arab Republic in Honour of Gamal Abdel Nasser, President of U.A.R., *May 14, 1958* 371

Speech at Meeting of Friendship Between Peoples of the Soviet Union and the United Arab Republic, *May 15, 1958* . . . 375

Speech at Luncheon in Honour of Finnish President, Dr. Urho Kekkonen, *May 23, 1958* 389

Speech at Meeting of Political Consultative Committee of Warsaw Treaty, *May 24, 1958* 394

4

Message to Central Committee of Italian Communist Party,
    May 31, 1958 434

Speech at 7th Congress of Bulgarian Communist Party, *June 3,
    1958* 435

Reply to Mr. Cyrus S. Eaton 467

Speech at Meeting of Sofia Working People to Mark Conclusion
    of 7th Congress of Bulgarian Communist Party, *June 7, 1958* 469

Replies to Questions Put by Editor of Melbourne *Herald,* John
    Waters, *June 11, 1958* 477

Speech at Luncheon of Ambassadors of Bandung Conference
    Countries in Honour of the King and Queen of Nepal,
    June 23, 1958 500

Speech Welcoming Antonín Novotný, First Secretary of Central
    Committee of Communist Party of Czechoslovakia and Presi-
    dent of Czechoslovak Republic, *July 2, 1958* 502

Speech at Grand Kremlin Palace Dinner in Honour of Comrade
    Antonín Novotný, President of Czechoslovakia, *July 2, 1958* 505

Speech at U.S.S.R.-Czechoslovakia Friendship Meeting in
    Leningrad, *July 4, 1958* 508

Speech on Arrival in Berlin of C.P.S.U. Delegation to 5th Con-
    gress of Socialist Unity Party of Germany, *July 8, 1958* . . 516

Speech at Mass Meeting in Halle During Stay of C.P.S.U.
    Delegation to 5th Congress of Socialist Unity Party of
    Germany in German Democratic Republic, *July 8, 1958* . . 519

Speech at Meeting Held in Palace of Culture of Bitterfeld
    Electro-Chemical Works During Stay in G.D.R. of C.P.S.U.
    Delegation to 5th Congress of Socialist Unity Party of
    Germany, *July 9, 1958* 524

Speech at 5th Congress of Socialist Unity Party of Germany,
    July 11, 1958 544

Speech at Soviet-Czechoslovak Friendship Meeting of Moscow
    Working People, *July 12, 1958* 584

Speech at Luncheon in Honour of Government Delegation of
    Austrian Republic, *July 22, 1958* 606

Speech at Reception at Embassy of Polish People's Republic on
    14th Anniversary of Day of National Renascence, *July 22, 1958* 609

Replies to Questions Put by Kingsbury Smith, Vice-President and General Director of United Press International Agency, *July 22, 1958* 615

Speech at Dinner Given by Embassy of Austrian Republic, *July 23, 1958* 618

Speech at Kremlin Reception in Honour of Government Delegation of Austrian Republic, *July 24, 1958* 620

Speech on Departure from Moscow of Government Delegation of Austrian Republic, *July 28, 1958* 623

Interview with Indian Journalists, *July 29, 1958* 625

Replies to Questions of *Pravda* Correspondent on Ending of Nuclear Weapons Tests 644

Replies to Questions Submitted by A. E. Johann, West German Writer and Journalist, *September 20, 1958* 651

Replies to Questions Put by *Pravda* Editorial Board Concerning Events in France 661

Replies to Questions Put by Murilo Marroquim de Souza, Brazilian Journalist, *October 3, 1958* 670

Reply to Question of TASS Correspondent 676

Speech at Reception by Vice-President of United Arab Republic, Marshal Abdul Hakim Amer, *October 21, 1958* 679

Speech at Grand Kremlin Palace Reception in Honour of Participants of Afro-Asian Writers' Conference in Tashkent, *October 22, 1958* 686

Speech at Kremlin Reception in Honour of Vice-President of United Arab Republic, Marshal Abdul Hakim Amer, *October 23, 1958* 690

Speech Welcoming Polish People's Republic Delegation in Moscow, *October 25, 1958* 694

Speech at Kremlin Dinner in Honour of Polish People's Republic Delegation, *October 25, 1958* 696

Speech at Luncheon Given by Comrade Wladyslaw Gomulka, Chairman of Polish People's Republic Delegation, *October 27, 1958* 698

Speech at Baltic Works Meeting During Stay in Leningrad of Polish People's Republic Delegation, *November 3, 1958* . . 701

Speech at Soviet-Polish Friendship Meeting of Leningrad Working People, *November 4, 1958* 712

Speech at Grand Kremlin Palace Reception in Honour of 41st Anniversary of the Great October Socialist Revolution, *November 7, 1958* 722

Speech at Friendship Meeting of Polish People's Republic and the Soviet Union, *November 10, 1958* 727

Speech on Departure from Moscow of Polish People's Republic Delegation, *November 11, 1958* 747

Some Questions Concerning International Situation. From Speech at Reception of Graduates of Military Academies, *November 14, 1958* 749

Proposals of the Soviet Government on the Berlin Question. Press Conference in Kremlin Held by N. S Khrushchov, Chairman of the U.S.S.R. Council of Ministers, *November 27, 1958* 758

Replies to Questions Put by Hans Kempski, Chief Correspondent of *Süddeutsche Zeitung*, German Federal Republic 772

EXCHANGE OF LETTERS
BETWEEN C. RAJAGOPALACHARI
AND N. S. KHRUSHCHOV

In November and December 1957 C. Rajagopalachari, Indian public leader, and N. S. Khrushchov, First Secretary of the Central Committee of the C.P.S.U., exchanged letters, the texts of which we publish below.

C. RAJAGOPALACHARI'S LETTER TO N. S. KHRUSHCHOV

Your Excellency may remember the conversation we had in Madras when you and Mr. Bulganin visited this city. The frank and clear statements I had the honour of hearing you and Mr. Bulganin make in answer to my queries during that quiet private talk in the Governor's house, and the events that have happened since then encourage me to approach you with a proposition which I trust you will not reject out of hand as merely idealistic. It is a practical move of creative power that I am suggesting, one emerging from the very special nature of the present moment.

Now that you have established beyond doubt the definite superiority of your technical achievement and potentialities, which have left the opposite party dumbfounded, no gesture on your part of a peace-seeking nature can possibly be misconstructed as arising out of a desire to cover weakness. I submit therefore that the supreme occasion for you has arrived to declare on behalf of your country that you not merely ask for an agreed ban on nuclear weapons, but you will unilaterally abjure the use of those weapons in warfare. This unqualified declaration will give the start for the moral law to work out its chain reactions in the field of the human spirit even as the split atom does in your atomic plants.

It is not pacifism that I am asking you to declare, but only the abjuring of nuclear weapons. It is this new development that has robbed war of all its gradualness which had been the all-important automatic safeguard for peace, humanity and civilization to survive in spite of what would otherwise be an unqualified evil. It is therefore this type of war and these weapons of destruction that have to be abjured for the sake of civilization. There is a point at which man's instruments unfortunately and without his knowing it become his master instead of being his inanimate instrument. That dangerous point has been almost reached in the case of nuclear weapons. It is necessary to halt before it is too late and to restore man's control over his tools and prevent his becoming a helpless victim of his own invention.

It is needless for you to point out to me the lapses of the Western Powers. I know them all and I have been pointing them out publicly. But a supreme moment has now arrived when your republic can attain undying glory by a great and historic step whose moral force will be irresistible, a glory not less than Russia's heroic defence against the might and ferocity of Hitler when she bore the whole brunt of his attack. If this qualified and absolute declaration I am suggesting be forthcoming from you, the West will have to bow in awe and reverence before your moral height. It would be an achievement in the spiritual field no less than what you have demonstrated in technology which has extorted the admiration and envy of the West. As you recently said in your jubilee speech in Moscow, the pattern of competition in the future will change from one of destruction to the unravelling of the mysteries of nature and the promotion of human welfare if you take this great creative unilateral step without caring what others may do or not do.

I have made appeals for unilaterally abjuring nuclear weapons to America and to Britain in the columns of the *New York Times* and the *Manchester Guardian*. This appeal I make to you, may I say, I make with greater hope? For as I have said already, you are in a position of great and demonstrated strength which gives you the status and power to make such a proud declaration.

With highest regards,

Yours sincerely,

C. RAJAGOPALACHARI

Madras-17, Tyagaroyanagor,
Bazlullah Road, 60

N. S. KHRUSHCHOV'S REPLY TO C. RAJAGOPALACHARI'S
LETTER

Madras

Your Excellency,

I was very happy to receive your letter which brought back pleasant memories of my stay in your wonderful country, of our talks in Madras. I remember the talk we had during a concert, when even the superb folk dances of India could not divert us from discussing the important problems that preoccupy all who sincerely want to safeguard peace.

I read your letter very carefully and I am most grateful to you for it. I should like in replying to set out certain considerations regarding the proposal it contains.

We regard your suggestion that the Soviet Union contribute its share to the establishment of a lasting peace among nations as evidence of your lofty convictions, of the great concern for peace of a prominent public leader and statesman, whose life and energies are devoted to the struggle for the great cause of peace.

In your letter you speak in flattering terms of our country, of our people, of the progress they have made and, in particular, of the achievements of Soviet science and technology. I will not deny that we are proud of these achievements, for they show the progress made by a people that has won its freedom from capitalist slavery. You know, of course, that the overwhelming majority of the population of tsarist Russia was illiterate, that Russia was a backward peasant country with an underdeveloped industry. In the 40 years that have elapsed since the Soviet system was set up our people have given free rein to their energy and talent; they built an up-to-date industry, reorganized agriculture along the most modern lines and trained their own intellectuals and their own scientists in all spheres. The construction and launching of the world's first earth satellites was a striking demonstration of the achievements of our people. All this is for us a source of pleasure and inspires us to renew our efforts to attain the great goal set by the Communist Party—to build a communist society in our country, a society in which men will really be brothers, in which everyone will work for himself and for others to the best of his ability and in which all the people's requirements will be met in full. The Soviet people are sparing no effort to build such a social system.

We appreciate that concern for the destinies of the world with which your letter is imbued. Mankind is threatened with a catastrophic war of extermination on an unprecedented scale, a war which, if it breaks out, will take a toll of many millions of lives. This prospect is particularly absurd today, when science is advancing rapidly, when man has far greater opportunities to ease his toil and employ the world's natural resources to meet the requirements of all the peoples inhabiting our planet. It is today perfectly possible therefore to ensure progress and prosperity for every country and every nation on the basis of peaceful co-existence between all states, friendly co-operation and mutual assistance.

Today more than ever before, every honest person, and society as a whole, must strive to find ways not only of postponing war, but also of abolishing it for ever. This problem cannot be completely and finally solved until mankind has established a society in which there will no longer be rich and poor, in which all will be equal and all derive equal benefit from the blessings of collective labour. It will be what we call a communist society. We are convinced that in the long run mankind will build such a just social system. But that still requires a great deal of effort, because the peoples are at different stages of development and there still are many countries where the forces that would dominate others and live on their labour are still strong.

Our common duty today is to prevent war. If we cannot at the moment abolish it for ever, we can and should create conditions enabling the peoples to live in peace, without fear that a war of extermination will be suddenly launched in accordance with the desires of a few madmen.

You propose that, to promote international confidence and save mankind from the threat of a disastrous atomic war, the Soviet Union declare its unilateral renunciation of the use of nuclear weapons for military purposes. We greatly appreciate the confidence that you show in us by submitting this proposal to the Soviet Union, and we wish we could take your advice. The Soviet Union firmly advocates the condemnation and prohibition of the use of atomic and hydrogen weapons as means of mass destruction and calls for their removal from national armouries. We still insist on this; we are prepared to conclude an appropriate agreement with other Powers at any time. It is now up to the Governments of the United States and Britain to decide.

I should also like to draw your attention to the fact that at the jubilee session of the Supreme Soviet of the U.S.S.R. in Moscow on November 6 last it was solemnly declared on behalf of the Soviet Government and the Communist Party of the Soviet Union that our people had never thought, nor would ever think, of using any means of destruction unless our country was attacked by imperialist states. I believe that that declaration is to a considerable extent in line with the idea expressed in your letter. Would it not be a major step towards eliminating the threat of a new war if the U.S. and British governments were in their turn to make similar official declarations?

As for the renunciation of the use of nuclear weapons by one Power only—the Soviet Union—irrespective of the stand taken by the other Powers possessing such weapons, while we fully appreciate the motives underlying your proposal, prompted by deep faith in the good that is inherent in every person, we cannot forget that there are facts and circumstances that necessitate the utmost prudence in considering this matter.

You presume that, by unilaterally declaring that it renounces nuclear weapons, the Soviet Union would set off a moral "chain reaction" in the world and that the West would have to do the same. I must tell you quite frankly, however, that the facts do not warrant so optimistic a presumption.

In this connection I cannot but mention the perfectly correct idea, expressed in one of your articles, that the United States cannot expect the Soviet Union to take unilateral action aimed at ceasing nuclear weapons tests unless it itself intends to take similar action. This is still more true as regards the renunciation of the use of nuclear weapons.

Can we, aware of the great responsibility we bear for the welfare and security of the peoples of the Soviet Union, disregard actions by the Governments of the Western Powers such as the establishment of a network of U.S. military bases along the frontiers of the Soviet Union and of countries friendly to it, a network covering territory belonging to dozens of European, Asian and African countries? Have we the right to ignore the fact that the United States and its West European allies in the NATO military bloc are doing their utmost to make atomic and hydrogen weapons the key element in their armouries, and indeed say so officially?

It is well known, furthermore, that the chief item to be discussed by the forthcoming December meeting of the NATO Council is the roles that the members of the bloc will have to play in preparing an atomic and hydrogen war. The Governments of the United States, Britain and other Western countries persist in rejecting even such measures as the immediate and unconditional suspension of atomic and hydrogen weapons tests on terms equal for all parties.

As we think of all this we fear that if the Soviet Union

were to declare its unilateral renunciation of nuclear weapons, those governments with evil intentions vis-à-vis our country, far from following suit, blinded by their hatred for our new system and all that we are creating, would be tempted to take advantage of the resultant weakening of the Soviet Union's defences. They might attack our country with atomic and hydrogen weapons in order to wipe out the socialist gains which the Soviet people have achieved as a result of their tremendous exertions. We consider the achievements of the Soviet people to be not only our achievements, but also those of all progressive mankind, of all those who want to build human relations on the principles of equality, mutual assistance and respect.

Well knowing that once the Soviet Union has pledged its word it keeps it faithfully and never goes back on it, the aggressive circles of the Western Powers would react to our unilateral commitment to refrain from the use of nuclear weapons by building up their stocks of such weapons even more vigorously in order to gain superiority and then confront the Soviet Union with claims amounting to an ultimatum.

If, on the other hand, the Soviet Union were compelled by the actions of the Western Powers to reconsider its attitude after having once declared its unilateral renunciation of the use of nuclear weapons, it would tend to undermine the people's faith in our pledged word and cause confusion among those who are fighting for peace and whose support we value highly. Such a turn of events would do a great deal of harm to world peace, a cause which you and we have in common, and a great deal of moral harm to the idea of peaceful co-existence. This, in its turn, would complicate the struggle for universal disarmament and for the prohibition of atomic and hydrogen weapons; it would increase international mistrust and lead to an acceleration in the arms race and the stockpiling of the means of mass extermination.

All this would clearly benefit not those who champion peace, but those who advocate a policy "from positions of strength." Needless to say, we do not in the least want events to take such a turn, and I am sure you do not want it any more than we do.

As you see, your proposal gives rise to complex and difficult problems that substantially affect the interests of Soviet security and world peace. An exchange of views was held among the leaders of our Party and Government on the question raised in your letter. Having weighed and considered your proposal, we concluded that, to our regret, the circumstances do not at the moment allow the Soviet Government, for the reasons listed above, to commit itself unilaterally in the manner suggested in your letter. As long as the Governments of the Western Powers show no desire to adopt practical disarmament measures and to renounce atomic and hydrogen weapons, we can apparently do nothing but continue our efforts for peace, revealing to the peoples the disastrous character of the policy being pursued by imperialist groups today. We cannot be reconciled to a situation in which everybody is threatened with a terrible atomic war and in which an increasing share of human labour goes to produce weapons of extermination and destruction instead of to create material values and raise standards of living. We are confident that the peoples will bring greater pressure to bear on those governments whose policies run counter to the interests of peace, and will in the end make them lend ear to the voice and demands of millions upon millions of people and find such a solution as will preclude military catastrophe once and for all.

In conclusion allow me, dear Mr. Rajagopalachari, to wish you good health and success in your activity for the benefit of peace, friendship and co-operation among peoples.

Sincerely yours,

N. KHRUSHCHOV

December 3, 1957

C. RAJAGOPALACHARI'S LETTER TO N. S. KHRUSHCHOV

Dear Mr. Khrushchov,

Mr. Peter Petrov, First Secretary in your Embassy in Delhi, brought an "unofficial translation" of Your Excellency's letter of December 3 and gave it to me personally at Madras in my little room. I am grateful to him for the courtesy shown and trouble taken.

A private person like me has reason to be proud when a letter from him is given earnest and such full consideration by Your Excellency and your Government. The subject is of such momentous importance that I am grateful for the thought I have been able to provoke, whatever may be your reaction to my proposal. I thank you for this.

You said to Mr. Hearst on November 2 last:

"Let us put an end to the cold war." The very pith and substance of the cold war is suspicion. The very nature of the cold war—this suspicion—prevents hope for any "agreement" that can end the cold war. It can be put an end to only by one party or the other beginning with its own unilateral step. There is no way to end the cold war except by taking a first voluntary unilateral step in the conviction that it must lead to a good reaction on the other side. This necessarily involves risk. But the cold war cannot be ended by any process that does not involve risk. The cold war is going on developing a terrible risk by itself. We have to compare one risk with the other. Ending the cold war means suspending our suspicions.

The argument against any step towards it is suspicion itself. We are therefore in a terribly vicious circle. The more I think of it, the clearer it is to me that unless we produce the miracle in the shape of unilateral action, we cannot hope to end this cold war before it bursts into a flame, and I fear this is relentlessly approaching. The strikingly strong position Russia is now in, induced me to appeal to you.

If the step I suggested is unequivocally taken, the U.S.A. will be drawn as by a steel chain to follow suit. There can be no imputation of breach of faith if by aggression the other party forfeits the benefit of the pledge and disgraces itself. If we begin this way the time will arrive when the apprehension will wear away, and, as you have said, everybody can sink these weapons in the sea. My appeal differs from your standing offer for an agreement in that no condition is attached to the declaration. You need not fear reproach if by aggression, which will be universally condemned, the other party invites annihilation.

I have written this letter without waiting for Your Excellency's original letter to arrive. My highest regards and greetings for the New Year.

Yours sincerely,

Madras
December 10, 1957

C. RAJAGOPALACHARI

N. S. KHRUSHCHOV'S REPLY TO C. RAJAGOPALACHARI'S LETTER

Madras

Your Excellency,

I have received your letter of December 10, 1957, which points out the danger of the cold war with a sincere anxiety that is only too understandable and calls for its cessation through unilateral action on the part of the Soviet Government. Trusting in the force of moral influence, you hold that the Soviet Union's unilateral renunciation of nuclear weapons would oblige the United States and its allies to follow suit and would lead to the cessation of the cold war and the arms race.

I fully agree with you that the continuation of the cold war in itself increases the danger of a new war that would wipe out millions of human beings. We must remember that there is not a single country or people left for whom the cold war now being waged does not mean a growing threat of atomic war and a further increase in the burden of military spending.

By virtue of the socialist nature of its system, the Soviet Union has not and cannot have any vested interest in maintaining an atmosphere of cold war and suspicion. In fact, we have been doing our best to restore trust and eliminate tension. To those who voiced their suspicions we held out a friendly hand and repeatedly took specific unilateral action of the kind you suggest in the sphere of disarmament, expecting others to follow suit. During the last two or three years we have reduced our armed forces by nearly two million. But no one has followed our example.

You know that on December 10 the Soviet Government answered a message from Mr. Jawaharlal Nehru, the Prime Minister of India, who called on the Governments of the United States and the Soviet Union to cease nuclear weapons tests. We responded readily to Mr. Nehru's message, informing him that the Soviet Government was prepared solemnly to declare that, as from January 1, 1958, the Soviet Union would not carry out any atomic tests, provided the United States and Britain declared that they were ready to do likewise regarding the tests they were preparing. In signifying our readiness to assume this serious international obligation, we devoutly hoped that the United States and its partners would show good will and follow suit.

Unfortunately, on this occasion too, our hopes were not realized. In reply to Mr. Nehru's message and to the concrete proposal of the Soviet Government, the President of the United States declared that the U.S.A. deemed it necessary to continue nuclear weapons tests.

You admit in your letter that unilateral renunciation of nuclear weapons would constitute a great risk for our country and would not preclude aggression, but you trust that the United States will not choose war and will follow our example. You can see, however, that we are again faced with facts that convince us that the risk would be much too great and would be highly detrimental not only to the security of the Soviet Union, but also to universal peace. Judge for yourself whether we can reasonably expect the unilateral action by the Soviet Union that you have in mind to yield the results we desire at a time when the United States openly confirms that it does not propose to stop improving these deadly weapons.

You are probably aware that U.S. bombers carrying atomic and hydrogen weapons are flying above Britain and other West European countries day and night. These flights are intended to demonstrate U.S. preparedness to begin an atomic war at any moment. The fact that in the United States preventive war is being more and more insistently advocated and that there are those who recommend the U.S. Government to adopt a military policy based on the doctrine of preventive war, that is, open aggression against the peace-loving countries, induces us in the Soviet Union to be particularly vigilant in order to deal properly with any contingency.

I will not here reiterate the considerations I set out in my previous letter. You must certainly know of the proposals made by the Soviet Government in its recent messages to the Governments of the United States, Britain and other countries, as well as of the session of the Supreme Soviet of the U.S.S.R., which passed an important foreign policy resolution a few days ago. I should merely like to point out that the Supreme Soviet of the U.S.S.R. has instructed the Soviet Government to consider the question of a further cut in the armed forces of the Soviet Union. Regarding this resolution as a new and important step towards promoting peace and creating an atmosphere of international confidence, we look forward to the Governments of the United States, Britain and France likewise reducing their armed forces in the interest of genuine international security.

We are certain that if the unilateral steps taken by us were supported with similar efforts by the Western Powers, the international situation would be improved and, moreover, the road would be laid open to further steps towards freeing mankind from the arms race and the threat of an atomic war that would of necessity have dire consequences for mankind.

We fully appreciate your sincere desire to help in ending the cold war. It fortifies our confidence that those who have the destinies of the world at heart will become more and more vocal and that the growing might of the peace-loving forces will eventually triumph and bring the peoples a durable and lasting peace.

I thank you for your good wishes for the New Year. I send you New Year's greetings and sincerely wish you happiness and success in your noble work in defence of peace.

Sincerely yours,

December 31, 1957   *N. KHRUSHCHOV*

REPLIES
TO QUESTIONS PUT BY V. SINNBECK,
EDITOR OF *DANSK FOLKESTYRE*,
JOURNAL OF YOUTH ORGANIZATION
OF DANISH VENSTRE PARTY

Mr. V. Sinnbeck, editor of *Dansk Folkestyre*, a journal published by the youth organization of the Danish Venstre Party, asked N. S. Khrushchov, the First Secretary of the Central Committee of the Communist Party of the Soviet Union, to reply to some questions.

Below we publish Mr. Sinnbeck's questions and N. S. Khrushchov's replies.

Question: Do you think that the deployment of atomic rockets in Denmark and Norway would cause substantial harm to the relations between Scandinavia and the Soviet Union?

Answer: I do not doubt that the deployment of atomic and rocket weapons on Danish and Norwegian territory would do considerable harm to relations between the Soviet Union and these countries. After all, the NATO leaders do not in fact conceal that these weapons of mass annihilation are intended for use against the Soviet Union and other peace-loving countries.

The deployment of atomic and rocket weapons in Denmark and Norway would, of course, lay these countries open to a retaliatory blow, while the other countries of Northern Europe might also be confronted by a serious threat, inasmuch as the danger of an atomic war spreading throughout this traditionally peaceful area would increase. If the North Atlantic Alliance were to establish atomic and rocket weapons bases in Denmark and Norway, and attempt to use them for launching rockets into Soviet territory over the territories of Finland and neutral Sweden, it would directly affect the security of Sweden and Finland and would infringe their sovereign rights. It is doubtful that the peoples of Sweden and Finland could be indifferent to this prospect.

Now it is planned to deploy rockets with atomic warheads in all the NATO countries. Much anxiety is being expressed in this connection by the peoples of the countries on whose territories the war bases are being established. They are well aware that the establishment of bases and rocket launching sites creates a threat to their security. Therefore they are protesting against the building of bases for atomic and rocket weapons. In order to mislead the peoples, the leaders of the Western Powers manoeuvre: they allege that they are deploying rockets without atomic war-heads, rockets with conventional explosives. But this subterfuge cannot mislead anyone, because it is amply clear that a conventional explosive can easily be replaced by an atomic war-head. Thus, the situation is not changed by the fact that the NATO member-countries are being lavishly supplied with rockets without atomic warheads.

We note with satisfaction the statements by the Danish Prime Minister, Mr. Hansen, and the Norwegian Prime Minister, Mr. Gerhardsen, who, prompted by the national interests of their countries, have refused to accept atomic weapons and the building of rocket launching sites. This cannot but be welcomed, for this step will not only promote the improvement of relations between our countries but will also contribute to the improvement of the whole international situation.

Question: Would you like to indicate the measures which the Soviet Union will take in the event of this deployment being effected under any circumstances?

Answer: The present attitude of the Governments of Denmark and Norway gives grounds for hoping that in the future this question will be a purely academic one. But if the Governments of Denmark and Norway yield to pressure from outside and agree to the deployment of atomic and rocket weapons on their territories, the Soviet Union will, naturally, be compelled to take appropriate measures.

Question: Would you and Chairman of the Council of Ministers Bulganin accept a possible invitation to pay an official visit to Denmark as an expression of friendship for the Scandinavian countries? Should the reply be in the affirmative, we should like to know when would you be able to pay this visit?

Answer: We have already expressed our favourable attitude to a visit by Soviet statesmen to Denmark, and also to Sweden and Norway. The question of the date for such a visit is a matter for agreement between the parties concerned.

Question: Do you think that the launching of the two Russian artificial earth satellites has radically altered the balance of forces between the socialist countries in the East, on the one hand, and the Western countries, on the other?

Answer: The launching of the Soviet sputniks above all demonstrates the outstanding successes achieved by the Soviet Union in the development of science and technology, and also the fact that the U.S.S.R. has outstripped the leading capitalist country—the United States—in the field of scientific and technical progress.

The launching of the sputniks undoubtedly also shows that an important change in favour of the socialist states has taken place in the balance of forces between the socialist and capitalist countries.

Balance of forces is a broad concept which includes political, economic and military factors. The Soviet Union and the other socialist states are consistently pursuing a policy of peace and call for the peaceful co-existence of states with different social systems, for the ending of the arms race that is leading to a new war, and the prohibition of the use, production and testing of atomic and hydrogen weapons. The Soviet Union supports the just national-liberation struggle of the peoples against colonialism. This peace-loving and humane policy is near and dear to all honest people and can be understood by them. It cannot fail to win sympathy for the Soviet Union and cannot but increase its weight and influence in international affairs, as the facts daily demonstrate.

As for the economic factor, the Soviet Union and other socialist countries have achieved—and this is no longer denied by anyone—great successes in economic development and are rapidly altering the balance of forces in their own favour. In peaceful economic competition we do not doubt in the least that the task set by V. I. Lenin of economically overtaking and surpassing the most advanced capitalist countries—that is to say, in per capita production—will be successfully carried out by the Soviet people. It can be said that our plans already outline measures for the practical solution of this task. As for the military side of the problem, the successful launching of the Soviet sputniks with the help of the intercontinental ballistic rocket speaks for itself and scarcely needs any extensive comments.

However, I want to emphasize that the change in the balance of forces in favour of the socialist states is an important factor strengthening peace. Owing to their very nature, the socialist states do not pursue, and cannot pursue, any aggressive aims. The Soviet Union is directing all its efforts towards the relaxation of international tension, towards the development of friendly relations with all states on the basis of peaceful co-existence and strengthening confidence between all countries, and it will continue to do so.

Question: How long do you think it will take the Soviet Union to reach the living standard of the United States?

Answer: The living standard means the degree to which man's material and spiritual requirements are satisfied. It includes food, footwear, clothing and other consumer goods, housing, education, medical services, sports facilities, guaranteed work, rest and leisure, conditions for the development of man's finest gifts and the like.

The living standards of the Soviet people have recently increased considerably. In all important spheres such as education, medical services, facilities for sport, the organization of rest and leisure, etc., we are already second to no capitalist country, including the United States. The Americans themselves, for instance, recognize our successes in education.

As for food and consumer goods, the Soviet people have set themselves the task of overtaking the United States in the per capita production of these commodities within the next few years. We have already made definite progress in housing, and are confident that within the next ten or twelve years, or perhaps sooner, the housing problem will be completely solved in our country.

In comparing the situation in the Soviet Union and the United States, it must not be forgotten that the living standard is determined, not so much by the quantity of goods produced for the population, as by the level of their consumption, which depends on effective demand. In the conditions of capitalism there is an extremely big gap between the level of consumption by people with high and low incomes. The Soviet Union provides much greater equality in living standards, since it has no exploiting classes, socialism is already built and the Soviet people are now engaged in building a communist society. I shall not touch in detail on such a question as the existence of a large standing army of unemployed in the United States and other capitalist countries. The Soviet Union has known no unemployment for a long time now, because unemployment has been done away with for good.

Question: Do you think that the so-called youth festivals are an ideal form of East-West youth meetings? Have you in mind any other forms of meetings which could strengthen peaceful co-existence between states?

Answer: The World Festivals of Youth and Students are, of course, not the only form of meetings between the young people of the East and the West. Other useful forms of contacts are also possible.

It is said, for instance, that Scandinavia has a rather widespread network of international work and tourist camps and youth hostels, that forms of international seminars are often used there, etc. These forms of meetings between young people of different countries are very useful. I have been informed that our youth organization also intends to organize an international work camp in the Soviet Union this year and to arrange an international "atoms for peace" seminar and other international events.

At the same time, I cannot but note that World Youth Festivals have rather important merits too. They have become a good tradition and have won wide recognition and approval among the young people. You probably know that six of these festivals have been held in the past ten years. The last—the Sixth World Festival—held in Moscow, was attended by 34,000 people from 130 countries in all continents. There were many more who wanted to come, but were unable to do so.

We still hear assertions that World Youth Festivals are a "communist idea." It is said that many of those who took part in the Moscow Festival were suspicious at the beginning and harboured a certain mistrust, but having got to know one another better, they understood that there was nothing to fear: No one wished to foist his way of thinking or his way of living on others, but everyone wanted the same thing—to live in peace and friendship, to enjoy the blessings of science and culture, to help the peoples to advance along the road of progress and prosperity. People of various countries differ in their way of life and thinking. Now there are two different systems; there are socialist and capitalist countries. The peoples living in these states have no other alternative but to live peacefully side by side, not to interfere in one another's internal affairs, and respect the opinions of others. I think the World Youth Festivals help people to understand this by bringing the representatives of the young people of different nations closer together.

In any case, all forms of meetings are good if they lead to the desired end—to the establishment of mutual understanding, confidence and friendship, to the strengthening of peace.

Question: Do you have any proposals to make regarding ties between the young people of the Soviet Union and Scandinavia?

Answer: During the stay of the Danish Prime Minister, Mr. Hansen, in Moscow in March 1956, a satisfactory solution was found to several practical questions concerning cultural and scientific contacts between our two countries. The question of exchanging students and of reciprocal invitations to professors and instructors for scientific work and lecturing was also settled.

At the present time there are favourable conditions for extending and consolidating friendly ties between the young people of the Soviet Union and Denmark. Regional meetings of the young people of Baltic states, exchanges of delegations of the leaders of youth organizations, reciprocal visits by groups of children for holidays during school vacations, tourist travel, etc., could be very useful in strengthening friendship between our countries. Everything depends on enterprise and sincere desire. The young people must themselves put forward concrete proposals regarding the best ways of strengthening friendship between the youth of the U.S.S.R. and the Scandinavian countries. The Soviet young people will undoubtedly respond with cordiality and sincerity to any good initiative coming from the young people of Scandinavia.

Question: How do you assess relations between Scandinavia and the Soviet Union today?

Answer: The existing possibilities in relations between the Soviet Union and the Scandinavian countries are far from being fully utilized.

The development of friendly relations between the U.S.S.R. and the Scandinavian countries can undoubtedly be furthered by our common interest in strengthening peace in the Baltic area. This community of interests assumes particularly great significance if we take into consideration the fact that the ruling circles of the leading NATO countries, disregarding the peaceful traditions and national interests of the Scandinavian countries, are persistently striving to carry out their plans for militarizing Scandinavia and the Baltic area, thereby aggravating the situation in the region.

These actions by the ruling circles of the leading countries of the North Atlantic bloc and—let us not hide the fact —some Scandinavian statesmen too, run counter to the task of strengthening peace in the Scandinavian and Baltic Sea area. It is our belief that such actions as Denmark's participation in the plans for establishing a joint Baltic naval command with West Germany and Britain are scarcely compatible with this aim.

Correctly understood, the national interests of the Scandinavian countries in our view demand that no artificial barriers be placed in the way of improving mutual understanding between the Baltic countries. It is necessary to encourage the consolidation of friendly ties between them in every way.

For its part, the Soviet Union is ready to develop all-round friendly ties with the Scandinavian countries on the basis of mutual respect for national sovereignty, non-interference in one another's internal affairs, and equality. We stand for the extensive development of mutually beneficial trade with Scandinavia, without any discrimination, and for the establishment of the closest scientific, technical and cultural ties. We believe that the strengthening of contacts between the U.S.S.R. and Scandinavia would greatly benefit the peoples of our countries, and in the final analysis help to turn Northern Europe into a zone of genuinely lasting peace.

Replies sent on January 4, 1958.

Pravda, January 15, 1958

SOME ASPECTS OF INTERNATIONAL SITUATION

Speech at Conference
of Front-Rank Agricultural Workers
of Byelorussian Republic

January 22, 1958

Comrades, you all know how the international situation has changed, how it has improved compared with what it was a year ago. At the end of 1956, as a result of mistakes made by the former Hungarian leadership the events took place in Hungary which you all know about. Counter-revolutionary elements, supported by international reaction, made an attempt to overthrow the people's power in Hungary and to restore the capitalist, fascist system. There were certain difficulties in some other People's Democracies as well, primarily in Poland.

The imperialist Powers were doing everything possible to make use of this for their own ends against the socialist countries. The reactionary vultures, in transports of joy, were croaking for all the world to hear that the disintegration, the crisis of communism had begun, that the Soviet Union and the People's Democracies had come up against difficulties which they would not be able to cope with.

The aggressive forces of the Western Powers decided that the moment was propitious for them to change the situation in the Middle East, to strengthen their colonial positions there, which were shaken by the growth of the national-liberation movement, by the growth of the forces of the world socialist system. The then Governments of Britain, France and Israel started a military gamble against Egypt. You all know how that imperialist adventure ended.

The plans of the imperialists, who staked on the forces of counter-revolution in Hungary, failed. The Revolutionary Workers' and Peasants' Government of the Hungarian People's Republic, led by Comrade János Kadar, mobilized the working class, the working peasantry and the progressive intellectuals of Hungary against the counter-revolutionary forces. It requested the Soviet Union for assistance, and we gave this fraternal assistance. Literally within three days the counter-revolutionary bands were smashed and revolutionary order restored. The Soviet Union and all the other socialist countries helped the Hungarian people, as friends, to restore and further develop the country's economy. Naturally, Hungary still has some serious economic difficulties caused by counter-revolutionary activities and the people feel them and have to pay for the harm done to the country's economy by the fascist rebels.

In the Polish People's Republic, where not a few difficulties still exist, measures are being taken to strengthen the people's democratic system. As you may have seen in the press, I spent three days in the Polish People's Republic recently at the invitation of the First Secretary of the Central Committee of the Polish United Workers' Party, Wladyslaw Gomulka, and Chairman of the Council of Ministers Jozeph Cyrankiewicz and had cordial talks with the Polish leaders. In these talks I derived the impression that by making a correct use of its strength and potentialities, the Polish United Workers' Party, led by Comrade Gomulka, will succeed in overcoming the existing difficulties and will achieve new successes in developing the country's socialist economy and raising the living standards of the people.

The imperialist "prophecies" concerning the Soviet Union and the strength and stability of our socialist system have misfired miserably. Our enemies claimed that we would come up against new domestic difficulties because in the Soviet Union the number of people with a secondary and higher education was increasing every year and therefore they would undoubtedly turn against the communist system and strive for a "free" system, as our enemies understand it, that is to say, the capitalist system.

As the saying goes: "A hungry man dreams of buns." The capitalists in the same way dream of the collapse of the socialist system, the collapse of communism. But neither they, nor their grandchildren or great grandchildren will live to see it. (*Applause.*)

When we criticized the shortcomings in our agriculture, the imperialists started clamouring about a "crisis" of Soviet agriculture, saying that this time the Bolsheviks would not be able to get away with it. Today anyone can see how we have got out of that "crisis." Our Party not only boldly criticized the shortcomings we had, but worked out specific measures for the rapid expansion of socialist agriculture. It organized the work in such a way that a six-year programme for increasing the output of a number of the most important livestock products has been successfully fulfilled in three years. Today, even representatives of capitalism who come to our country no longer speak of a "crisis" in our agriculture, but draw attention instead to its great achievements.

Later, when we raised the question of reorganizing the system of management in industry and construction, the capitalists again began to declare that industry in the Soviet Union was in a bad way and that the Bolsheviks would not cope with the difficulties of industrial development. But only six months have gone by and these forecasts of our opponents have also come to nothing.

The favourite idea of the imperialists, of which they tried to convince themselves and others, was that the socialist system was not conducive to the development of science and culture, that it stifled man's efforts. They spread other fantastic fabrications as well and became so proficient in this that they came to believe those fabrications themselves. It does happen that a man tells a lie once, twice, thrice, and then comes to believe that he is telling the truth, so accustomed has he become to his own story.

But this bourgeois fabrication, too, came to a sorry end. The Soviet Union launched an intercontinental ballistic missile, the testing of which yielded positive results. We can now send a missile to any point on the globe, carrying, if necessary, a hydrogen war-head. Our announcement to this effect was greeted with disbelief and regarded as an attempt by the Soviet leaders to instil confidence in their own people and intimidate the Western governments. But then the Soviet Union, using the intercontinental ballistic missile, launched an artificial earth satellite, and when it started circling the globe and when everyone—unless he was blind—could see it by looking up into the sky, our opponents became silent. They thought at first they would get off with a slight shock. One American general even said that the launching of a satellite did not require much brain and that anyone could take a piece of metal and throw it into the sky. Well, why don't you do it if you are so clever and so strong? (*Animation in the hall. Applause.*) This silly statement by an American general was ridiculed by the Americans themselves, not to mention others.

A month after the launching of the first satellite, a second Soviet sputnik, weighing more than 508 kilograms, was sent up. After this, even the most hidebound sceptics were left without a basis for spreading fabrications about the development of Soviet science, culture and technology.

What was there left for the Americans to do? They said: "We too shall send up a satellite." And they announced the date on which they intended to launch an earth satellite the size of an orange and weighing about one and a half kilograms. They also said that their satellite would be so small that it would not be visible. And they did indeed try to launch an earth satellite, but nothing came of it. A film is now being shown of how their sputnik exploded without leaving the ground and burned up with the rocket.

Then there was nothing left for them to do but admit that the Soviet Union had indeed surpassed the U.S.A. in science and engineering, that the Soviet Union was every year training three times as many engineers as the United States. But this time too some wiseacres started a hue and cry, alleging that the Russians had stolen the plans for the satellite from the Americans. But the Americans themselves asked them: If the Russians did steal our plans and, with their help, built a rocket and launched earth satellites, why cannot we ourselves, using our own designs, build such a rocket and launch such satellites? Thus, the Americans themselves are ridiculing this stupidity too.

A new story then appeared. Some people began to claim that Germans had helped the Russians to build a ballistic rocket. The Russians, it was alleged, had captured German scientists and engineers and made use of their knowledge and experience. But reasonable people again asked: If Germans helped the Russians, why don't they help the U.S.A.? After all, American troops captured the laboratory of the German research institute and the chief designer of the V-2 rocket and took him to America, where he is now working on rockets.

It is no secret that a small group of Germans did work in our country for a time and, on the expiry of their contracts, have either returned, or are returning to Germany. When they returned and told what they knew, the Americans believed that they had reliable information about the stage reached by the Soviet Union in rocket building. When we launched an artificial earth satellite, the Americans complained afresh:

"We have been fooled again. The Germans who came

to us know nothing about what the Russians are doing. It turns out that the Germans did not take part in developing the rocket."

The Soviet Union has demonstrated by deeds that the Soviet system, the socialist system, is the most progressive system, giving great scope to the development of all branches of the national economy and creating the most favourable conditions for the development of science, culture and the arts. Our country has made great headway in the 40 years of Soviet power. In a number of key branches of science our country has outstripped the most highly developed capitalist country—the United States of America. The world's first artificial earth satellites were developed and successfully launched in the Soviet Union. And this, of course, is by no means the last word of Soviet science and technology, of our socialist industry. All the world was amazed by the fact that Sputnik II was over six times heavier than Sputnik I and weighed more than half a ton. But even this is not the limit. We can double and more than double the sputnik's weight, because the Soviet intercontinental rocket is immensely powerful, making it possible for us to launch a still heavier sputnik to a still greater height. And that is what we shall do, perhaps. (*Stormy applause.*)

The imperialists are seriously worried by our achievements in rocketry, in the use of atomic energy for peaceful purposes and in the development of jet aircraft. For more than two years the TU-104 jet plane developed by the outstanding Soviet designer Academician Tupolev has been flying on passenger routes in the Soviet Union. The Americans plan to produce such a plane only in 1959. Other capitalist countries have no such planes either. But we have produced an even more powerful aircraft—the TU-114, as well as new and powerful aircraft by other eminent Soviet designers.

In the spring of 1956, when we were in London and had talks with Messrs. Eden, Lloyd, Macmillan, Butler and other British statesmen, we told them frankly that we had rockets of various ranges. Later, when Israel, Britain and France attacked Egypt, the Soviet Government stated in a message to the British Prime Minister: What would be the position of Britain herself if she were attacked by stronger states possessing modern destructive weapons of all kinds? And such countries, the message said, could even do without sending a navy or an air fleet to British shores, but could use other means, for instance rocketry.

This statement by the Soviet Government evidently influenced them. Previously they had apparently thought that we were simply bluffing when we openly said that the Soviet Union possessed powerful rockets. But then they saw that we really had such rockets. And this had its effect. (*Applause.*)

Now the imperialists are trying to intimidate the Soviet Union and other peace-loving countries by building atomic bases and rocket launching sites on the territories of countries which belong to NATO and other aggressive blocs. But as yet they have no rockets for those bases and only intend to develop them in the future. This means that it will take them two or three years before they will be able to supply these sites with the necessary rockets. But we already today have rockets which could be delivered to any part of the globe to administer a crushing blow to the aggressors if they attempt to unleash a new war. So the imperialists will not succeed in intimidating us. Soviet people are not of the timid kind and those who love military adventures would do better to think about themselves. We have whatever is needed to defend the honour, freedom, independence and great achievements of the Soviet people. (*Stormy applause.*)

Comrades, the U.S. Secretary of State, Mr. Dulles, is especially active in extolling the "policy of strength." He keeps repeating that the United States can talk with the

Soviet Union only when it considers that it has absolute superiority in strength over the Soviet Union—that is, talk in the language of ultimatums and the *diktat*. But we have always contended that this is a stupid policy. The U.S. ruling circles have always thought they are stronger than we are. Our opinion on this subject is different. After the launching of the Soviet sputniks all the world said that the Soviet Union had forged ahead of the United States in many fields of science and technology. The Americans themselves were also compelled to admit: Yes, we have been outstripped.

We have always said and continue to say now. Let us improve our relations, let us trade, let us develop scientific, cultural and sports contacts. Let us meet and discuss pressing international problems in a business-like manner. We have proposed and we propose now that an end be put to the cold war and the arms race, that the "policy of strength" be renounced, that the policy of intimidation by war be abandoned, and that our relations be built on the basis of peaceful co-existence. Now the U.S. rulers declare: First we must catch up with the Soviet Union, and when we match its scientific achievements we shall be able to talk.

The untenability of such a policy is obvious. It is a foregone conclusion that the Soviet Union will not mark time while they are catching up with us. We shall not sit around drinking tea. It is a foregone conclusion that we shall also be doing something to prevent them from catching up with us. And so this senseless policy of the imperialists can have only one result—an endless arms race with all the consequences that it would entail.

The monopolies do not want any reduction of international tension; they refuse to discard the policy of cold war, and in every possible way hinder the settlement of urgent international problems by negotiations. They wax fat in an atmosphere of war hysteria, squeeze huge taxes out of the population, and make fabulous profits out of the manufacture of aircraft, guns, rockets, warships and atomic weapons.

Such, in general outline, is the international situation. On the one hand, there is a universal growing desire on the part of the peoples for the consolidation of peace and international security. There is a further growth of the national-liberation movement and a strengthening of the solidarity of the peoples of Asia and Africa in their struggle against the colonialists. The Cairo Solidarity Conference of Asian and African Countries clearly demonstrated that the peoples are now full of strength and the desire to struggle against colonialism and imperialist reaction. The peoples want to put an end to the cold war, to halt the arms race, ban atomic and hydrogen weapons, and free mankind from the threat of a new world war.

On the other hand, we see the obvious intention of the aggressive circles of the imperialist Powers to aggravate international tension, to continue the arms race for the enrichment of a handful of monopolists at the expense of millions of taxpayers, to intensify the cold war on the basis of the "policy of strength," to halt the disintegration of the colonial system of imperialism and strangle the national-liberation movement of the peoples for freedom and independence. The ruling circles of the imperialist countries are pursuing a policy of further strengthening military blocs, and trying to unite all the aggressive blocs such as NATO, the Baghdad Pact and SEATO, into a single aggressive military bloc led by the United States of America. Is not this policy of the present-day claimants to world domination reminiscent of that pursued by Hitler and Mussolini when they based their policy on strength and built the notorious Anti-Comintern Pact, the Berlin-Rome-Tokyo Axis?

But everyone knows how this fascist scheme ended. Hitler, Mussolini and other fascist bosses have long ceased to keep the world at fever pitch by their criminal adventures, while the Soviet Union is developing and becoming stronger. Today the Soviet Union is not alone in its advance toward communism. This road has been firmly and irrevocably taken by the peoples of many countries in Europe and Asia. Today the world socialist system exists as a powerful factor for peace.

The Soviet Union has been consistently pursuing a peace policy. The Soviet Government, desirous of ensuring world peace, has put forward new concrete proposals to ease international tension. The Soviet Government has sent messages to the President of the United States of America, Mr. Eisenhower, the Prime Minister of Britain, Mr. Macmillan, the Prime Minister of France, M. Gaillard, the Chancellor of the Federal Republic of Germany, Herr Adenauer, to all the Heads of Government of the NATO member-states, and also to the governments of all countries which are members of the United Nations.

As you are well aware, the Soviet Union has proposed that within the next two or three months a conference of representatives of a number of socialist and capitalist states be called on the highest level, that is, a conference of responsible statesmen of these countries to discuss the most important and urgent international problems. Why are we proposing such a conference? We have done this primarily because talks, a calm and reasonable settlement of the present differences between the Great Powers, or at least some of these differences, are the only way which we can all take if we want peace and if we do not want the alternative—war.

We consider it necessary to focus the attention of a conference of leading statesmen above all on the most urgent problems, in order to lay the foundations for an improvement in the entire international climate. This is our position: A meeting must be organized to discuss issues that can be settled today, for there are such issues, some of them very important ones. We propose the convening of such a conference, prompted by the desire to achieve positive results. This should lead to a relaxation of tension and create conditions for the complete elimination of the cold war. The examination of other problems could be postponed to a later stage in the talks. Such a gradual, stage-by-stage examination of pressing international issues is most realistic and reasonable.

But, unfortunately, the ruling circles of the Western countries, which do not want a relaxation of tension, the elimination of the cold war and the ending of the arms race, put forward for discussion above all issues on which it is more difficult or even impossible to reach agreement and, moreover, do it virtually in a form of an ultimatum. They declare that if the questions they put forward are not settled, it is useless to hold a meeting, since, they allege, it is impossible to reach agreement with the Soviet Union.

Why is this being done? People who approach the convening of a conference in this way not only do not want to ease international tension, but are doing everything to intensify that tension and to foment war hysteria in order to make it easier for themselves to use that tension and the peoples' fear of war for their own ends, for the purpose of making profits. We, who are champions of peace, want to hold a meeting on the highest level without delay, to solve all urgent problems—provided, of course, there is willingness on both sides—and thereby to create a certain atmosphere of warmth in relations between states. Such an atmosphere of warmth would help the light spring breezes grow stronger and melt the ice, creating the conditions in which new shoots would spring up on the warmed soil with greater speed, so that there would be greater confidence among states and the cause of peace would develop and grow stronger.

It can scarcely be doubted that it is not only the peoples of the Soviet Union, but also the peoples of the United States of America, Britain, France, Germany and all the other countries as well who are concerned to ease international tension. That is why world public opinion and the governments of a number of countries have received with approval the new peace proposals of the Soviet Government.

In his reply to the message of the Soviet Government, the Indian Prime Minister, Mr. Jawaharlal Nehru, declared that they agree with us that a summit meeting is both desirable and necessary, that they would welcome such a conference regardless of whether it will be attended by a small or a large number of participants.

In his speech in the Danish Parliament the Danish Prime Minister, Mr. Hansen, said:

"We, on the Danish side, favour the holding of a summit conference between East and West and I think everyone will agree with me on this. Of course, no one at the moment can have any idea about which countries will participate in such talks. But if the problem becomes of immediate concern to us, I believe there will be no objections to our positive answer to a possible invitation to take part in such a conference."

The Prime Minister of Afghanistan, Mr. Daoud, says:

"The Government of Afghanistan, supporting the proposal of the Soviet Government for personal contacts between the Heads of the Great Powers, considers them to be a useful and wise step designed to eliminate international tension and settle most of the existing difficulties."

The replies of the governments of a number of other states express a similar positive attitude towards the idea of convening a conference at a high level, although the replies contain various shades of opinion.

How did the leaders of the Western Powers react to the proposals of the Soviet Union? The U.S. President's Message to Congress on the State of the Union says:

"This is the spirit of what we Americans would like to say:

"In the last analysis, there is only one solution to the grim problems that lie ahead. The world must stop the present plunge toward more and more destructive weapons of war, and turn the corner that will start our steps firmly on the path toward lasting peace.

"Our greatest hope for success lies in a universal fact: the people of the world, as people, have always wanted peace and want peace now.

"The problem, then, is to find a way of translating this universal desire into action.

"This will require more than words of peace. It requires works of peace."

And there lies the crux of the problem. Mr. Eisenhower has hinted at something with which I shall deal presently.

One can agree with Mr. Eisenhower's words when he says that what is needed are not only words of peace but works of peace as well. But this should be done by both sides and not only by the Soviet side. The Soviet Union is demonstrating its desire for peace by its deeds. Our Government has unilaterally reduced its armed forces by 1,800,000 men. We have carried out a number of actions in the field of foreign policy in order to ease international tension and put an end to the cold war, we have abolished our military bases in Porkkala-Udd and in Port Arthur, reduced our armed forces in the German Democratic Republic by more than 30,000 men, settled peaceful relations with Austria, put an end to the state of war with Japan, and done much to strengthen peace. Meanwhile, the Governments of the United States, Britain and France have thus far done practically nothing in response to these concrete peace moves of the Soviet Union.

What then are the works of peace that the President has in mind? It is true that the world is awaiting the moment when the Governments of the United States, Britain, France and West Germany will at last make their contribution and begin their works of peace which will facilitate the ending of the cold war and the establishment of lasting world peace. That is paramount. (*Applause.*)

The Soviet Union continues to prove by its works its sincere desire to strengthen peace and international security. In accordance with a decree of the Supreme Soviet of the U.S.S.R., the Soviet Government has resolved further to reduce its armed forces by 300,000 men, including the withdrawal of more than 41,000 troops from the German Democratic Republic and more than 17,000 from Hungary.

Are not these works of peace, Mr. Eisenhower, Mr. Dulles and the other gentlemen on whom depends the ending of the cold war and the easing of international tension?

But I want to stress once again that such works of peace must be performed not only by the Soviet Union and other peace-loving countries, but by all the Western countries as well. It will then be possible to say with certainty that the problems disturbing the minds of people throughout the world will really be solved successfully.

In his reply to the message of the Soviet Government dated December 10, 1957, the President of the United States expressed agreement with the Soviet Government's proposal that a conference of statesmen of the West and East be convened.

His message says:

"I am ready to meet with the Soviet leaders to discuss the proposals mentioned in your letter and the proposals which I make, with the attendance as appropriate of leaders of other states which have recognized responsibilities in relation to one or another of the subjects we are to discuss."

But Mr. Eisenhower proposes that a Foreign Ministers' conference be convened to discuss the substance of international problems before a summit conference is held. His message puts forward the proposal that before a summit conference is called "these complex matters should be worked on in advance through diplomatic channels and by our Foreign Ministers, so that the issues can be presented in a form suitable for our decisions and so that it can be ascertained that such a top-level meeting would, in fact, hold good hope of advancing the cause of peace and justice in the world."

It would appear that everything was going well. In his message Mr. Eisenhower gives the following "solemn and categorical assurances":

"1. Never will the United States lend its support to any aggressive action by any collective defence organization or any member thereof;

"2. Always will the United States be ready to move toward the development of effective United Nations collective security measures in replacement of regional collective defence measures."

These pronouncements by Mr. Eisenhower cannot but be welcomed, but how are they to be equated with the President's demands that such a conference discuss the question of the countries of Eastern Europe—that is to say, the People's Democracies—and also that the problem of reunifying Germany be discussed in order to do away with the German Democratic Republic?

The Soviet Union has repeatedly made clear its attitude both on the question of the European People's Democracies, whose peoples have freely chosen their path of development, and also on the German problem.

The President of the United States is aware of the Soviet Government's attitude on these issues. Nevertheless, in his message in reply, Mr. Eisenhower writes:

"I know that your Government is reluctant to discuss these matters or to treat them as a matter of international concern. . . . This was another matter taken up at our meeting in Geneva in 1955. You then took the position that there were no grounds for discussing this question at our conference and that it would involve interference in the internal affairs of the Eastern European states.

"But have not subsequent developments shown that I was justified in my appeal to you for consideration of these matters? Surely, the Hungarian developments and the virtually unanimous action of the United Nations General Assembly in relation thereto show that conditions in Eastern Europe are regarded throughout the world as much more than a matter of purely domestic scope. I propose that we should now discuss this matter. There is an intrinsic need of this in the interests of peace and justice, which seems to me compelling."

What is it, then, that Messrs. Eisenhower and Dulles want? Apparently they want to meet us and talk about abolishing the socialist system in the Soviet Union and the people's democratic system in the People's Democracies. They apparently want us to abandon the building of socialism and restore the capitalist system. Some go so far as to demand a popular referendum in the socialist countries on whether they are for socialism or for capitalism.

I must tell these gentlemen that they must have forgotten their history. The peoples of the Soviet Union have already had occasion to confront the United States of America, Germany, France, Britain, Japan and other countries on these issues. What did the governments of these countries do when Soviet government was established in our country and when the peoples of the Soviet Republic renounced war and, under the guidance of the Communist Party and its great leader, V. I. Lenin, embarked upon the peaceful building of socialism? They sent their troops to our country to throttle the newly born Soviet state in its cradle. Britain landed troops in Arkhangelsk, Murmansk and in the South of our country. The United States did the same in Arkhangelsk, Murmansk and in the Far East; Japan in Vladivostok; France in Odessa and in the North; Germany occupied vital areas of the Ukraine; the Poland of Pilsudski sent her troops against Kiev. The troops of 14 capitalist states attacked the young and weak Soviet state. That is when the popular referendum on who supported the restoration of capitalism and who supported the gains of the working class and the working peasantry began. (*Stormy applause.*)

That popular referendum lasted three years. And what was the result? The Soviet people, shedding their blood and suffering untold hardships—famine, cold, privations—arms in hand voted unanimously for their own Soviet government. They crushed the internal Russian counter-revolution and drove the foreign invaders who had assailed the freedom and independence of our country from their sacred soil. (*Stormy, prolonged applause.*)

Is not that sufficient for the imperialists, the supporters and followers of that policy? Have our people not clearly demonstrated whether they are for socialism or for capitalism? Who was it who then sent those troops to our country? The British Government was then headed by Lloyd George, and Winston Churchill was Secretary for War; Poincaré was President of France and Clemenceau was Prime Minister and War Minister; Woodrow Wilson was President of the United States (I have forgotten who succeeded him and who it was with whom the Soviet people brought to an end the "talks" he started); Pan Pilsudski was in power in Poland. Many of the gentlemen who attempted to hold such "talks" with the Soviet people are no longer alive, but some still are. Let the present advocates of "referendums" consult those who organized the intervention against the Republic of the Soviets, and ask them how such "talks" and "referendums" end. (*Stormy applause.*)

Later, when the fascists came to power in some countries, they also attempted to organize a similar "referendum." Hitler declared war on communism, announcing that he would destroy it. He began to prepare for war as soon as he had seized power in Germany. He was helped by monopoly groups in the United States and some other countries. They tried hard to incite Hitler Germany against the Soviet Union. The fascists made a vile and perfidious attack on our country. We must remind Herr Adenauer of this, since he may have forgotten that it was fascist Germany that made a gangster-like attack on the Soviet Union. Hitler, Göbbels and others proclaimed that the Soviet Union was a colossus with feet of clay. Some Western politicians hinted to the fascist ringleaders that the German tanks would cut through the Soviet state like a knife through butter. Such a policy encouraged and incited Hitler's predatory acts. And the German fascists when they attacked the Soviet Union thought that their armies would have something in the nature of a pleasant stroll.

Taking advantage of surprise and other factors which were then not in our favour, the German troops reached the approaches to Moscow and Leningrad and got to Stalingrad. But how did it all end? With the complete defeat of the German fascist state. The Soviet Armed Forces and the entire Soviet people, who rose up in the sacred Patriotic War, broke the backbone of the fascist beast, defeated the Hitler armies and thus once again demonstrated the fate in store for those who base their adventurist hopes on the "instability" of the socialist system.

When the Soviet army was waging bitter battles against Hitler's armies, the peoples of the countries occupied by the German invaders began guerilla warfare against fascism. At a certain stage in the struggle against fascism the Soviet Armed Forces were joined by the working class and working peasantry of Poland, Albania, Yugoslavia, Czechoslovakia, Bulgaria, Rumania and Hungary who, under the guidance of their Communist parties, made a great contribution to the rout of the Hitler hordes. As a result of the defeat of fascism, as a result of the people's democratic revolutions in a number of European states, the peoples established the system of people's democracy in their countries. Was not that a vote, comrades? Was not that a popular referendum in the European countries whose peoples have firmly rallied under the banner of Marxism-Leninism and are successfully developing their economy, their people's states and their society on socialist principles? (*Prolonged applause.*)

What kind of "referendum" do the imperialist gentlemen now want? Was not this a convincing expression of the peoples' will? Apparently, they want to impose the capitalist system on the peoples of the socialist countries by force.

But they tried this kind of "referendum" in our country. Remember 1919, when Kolchak, after having seized almost all of Siberia, started moving towards Moscow, when Yudenich threatened revolutionary Petrograd, and when the White armies of Denikin, after having seized Orel, were approaching Tula and thrusting towards Moscow. Then only a small part of the Soviet land was free. But as a result of the efforts of our Party, which headed the struggle of the working class and the working peasantry, the Republic of Soviets beat back the onslaught of the interventionists and the internal counter-revolution. The Soviet people, like the warrior of ancient legend, squared their mighty shoulders, routed the counter-revolutionary forces and expelled the armies of the interventionists from their native soil.

The entire people took part in the struggle against the enemy. The great leader of our Party and of our people, V. I. Lenin, armed the Party and the people with a clear idea, and showed the working class and all the working people how to struggle for their freedom, for the building of a new life without capitalists and landlords. The working class and all the people supported Lenin's idea, supported Lenin's aspirations and followed our Communist Party along the road of Marxism-Leninism. That is how our people in the struggle for their freedom settled the question of choosing their way forward and their state system.

In the conditions of peaceful development the working people of the Soviet Union and the People's Democracies, being as they are the exclusive masters of their destinies, the builders of a new life, the creators of the most democratic society, elect the organs of power in conformity with their constitutions by a free expression of their will. Voting in the elections to the organs of state power, for the finest sons and daughters of their peoples, the

working people place great trust in them and instruc
them to serve the cause of the building of communism
with loyalty and devotion.

And now, when our people are enjoying the fruits of
their victories gained in the 40 years of Soviet power,
the imperialist gentlemen want to divert them from this,
the only correct, tried and tested road. But, gentlemen,
times have changed and events have taken a different
course. (*Stormy applause.*)

The question of a political system in any country is
the domestic concern of the people of that country. Obviously, this is a question which is quite different from, say,
that of abolishing the cold war or ending the arms race. If
some statesmen of the Western Powers want to raise the
question of the socialist system in the People's Democracies, the representatives of the socialist countries have the
right to say: Perhaps, in that case, we should also discuss
the question of whether the imperialists in the capitalist
countries will rule for a long time or whether it is not
time for them to hand over power to the working people?
(*Applause.*)

Why Mr. Eisenhower and Mr. Dulles, do you believe
that you can raise the question of the socialist system in
the European People's Democracies and in the Soviet
Union while not wanting to grant other countries an equal
right to raise the same question with regard to the capitalist countries? But we do not raise and are not going to
raise the question of the social system in one country or
another for discussion at international meetings, inasmuch as each people settles this matter as it wishes. We
support the principle of non-intervention by one state in
the internal affairs of others.

And we say to the representatives of the Western Powers: Let us pursue a policy of peaceful co-existence and
not interfere in one another's internal affairs. Intervention by one state in the internal affairs of other states,
as history has shown, inevitably leads to conflicts and

armed clashes. History also shows that the imperialists' attempts to impose their will upon peoples that have won liberation from capitalist oppression have ended in shameful failure for the imperialists. (*Applause.*)

This is our opinion on the question.

Now let us turn to the German question. As soon as the desirability of a summit conference is mentioned, the governing circles of certain Western Powers consider it necessary to push the so-called German question into the foreground and demand that precisely this issue be discussed by an international conference. But what is the German question in present-day conditions? It is, above all, the question of relations between the two sovereign states with different social systems now existing on German soil. It is the problem of contact, *rapprochement* and unification in one form or another of the two states, with the aim of restoring the national unity of Germany as a single peace-loving and democratic state.

The Soviet Union has more than once set out its views on this question, declaring that the German question can be solved only by the German people themselves. The Soviet Union, for its part, will do everything to help the reunification of Germany. On what basis must such reunification be effected? I think that the Germans themselves will decide this matter. Obviously Herr Adenauer will not want the economy of West Germany to be rebuilt along socialist lines. It is also obvious that the working people of the German Democratic Republic will not want to abolish their socialist gains and will not agree to restore capitalism. Therefore it is necessary to recognize the historical fact that two states with different social systems exist in Germany—the socialist German Democratic Republic and the capitalist Federal Republic of Germany. With the aim of peacefully unifying the country, the Government of the German Democratic Republic has made a reasonable proposal first to create a German confederation, which would be a union by treaty of two sovereign states, in order to pursue a common policy on a definite range of external and internal questions.

Ignoring all the previous declarations of the Soviet Government on the German question and the very fact of the existence of two sovereign German states, Mr. Eisenhower in his message again urges "that we now proceed vigorously to bring about the reunification of Germany by free elections, as we agreed...."

But it is common knowledge that there was never any such agreement! A great deal is being written on this subject in the Western bourgeois press, including American newspapers and magazines. This, for instance, is what the American historian, F. Schuman, wrote:

"I am at a loss to understand what purpose can be served beyond obfuscation by editorial and official misrepresentation of Soviet policy toward Germany. Why keep repeating that the rulers of Russia consented at Geneva in 1955 to the reunification of the Reich and later repudiated their pledge?

"At the summit conference it was agreed that the reunification of Germany by means of free elections shall be carried out in conformity with the national interests of the German people and the interests of European security. At Geneva, and long before Geneva, and ever since Geneva, in hundreds of policy statements and diplomatic Notes the men of Moscow who govern the land which suffered the most appalling losses of any of the belligerents in two world wars unleashed by German aggression, have defined 'European security' in terms of the demilitarization and neutralization of Germany.

"We may concur or dissent. But we do no good, it seems to me, to hurl accusations of 'bad faith.'"

We have declared and declare now that we are not going to meet to discuss the question of the People's Democracies and the German question in the manner proposed by Messrs. Eisenhower, Dulles and Adenauer. On these questions our position is clear.

In his message Mr. Eisenhower puts forward, "as the most important problem which faces the world today," the demand to ban the use of outer (interplanetary) space for testing war missiles and to end the manufacture of weapons which involve the use of outer space.

So that is the question they are interested in! We say: Let us ban the testing of atomic and hydrogen weapons. These weapons are manufactured in the United States, in Britain, in the Soviet Union, and it is also said that France will soon be manufacturing them. Agreement on the prohibition of tests of these weapons could be reached on the basis of equality. To control the implementation of this agreement would not be difficult since, given the present level of techniques, it is not possible to keep explosions of atom and hydrogen bombs secret.

But we are told: Let us establish control. We have already expressed our willingness to accept reasonable control which would preclude the possibility of staging secret explosions. The Western Powers, however, obstructing a solution of the problems involving the prohibition of atomic and hydrogen weapons, now raise quite another question: the prohibition of the use of outer (interplanetary) space—that is to say, in fact, the banning of intercontinental ballistic rockets. But, pray, the Soviet Union has such rockets and the Western Powers have not. Thus, the United States Government wants to single out from the general problem of disarmament only one question—the intercontinental rocket—without wishing to take any practical steps towards banning weapons of mass annihilation. What the United States intends by such a proposal is to ban weapons which can threaten the territory of the United States, but to retain all the other types of weapons with the help of which the United States would like to terrorize all the world. That means it wants to ban what it has not got, while continuing to arm. No, gentlemen, things are never like that!

Of course, one cannot deny the importance of the question of control over the use of outer space, but this question must be regarded as part of the general problem of disarmament, including the prohibition of atomic and hydrogen weapons. In the interests of strengthening peace, with the object of reaching agreement on disarmament, the Soviet Union would also be willing to discuss the question of the intercontinental ballistic rocket, if the Western Powers consent to the prohibition of atomic and hydrogen weapons, the discontinuation of tests and the closing down of the military bases with which the United States has ringed the Soviet Union and other socialist countries.

The imperialist circles of the United States want to retain their military bases, to set up sites for launching rockets from the territory of countries on our border and thus to threaten us daily, declaring that they can wipe out the towns of the Soviet Union. For it is a fact that it is not we who are threatening the United States with our bases (we have no military bases whatsoever in any country), but the Western Powers that are setting up many such bases. But we say: If the American military bases lie near the frontiers of the Soviet Union, then, vice versa, the Soviet Union lies near these bases. And should the aggressors launch military operations, the Soviet Union already has a tested and highly efficient weapon, not only to destroy those bases but also to deal crushing retaliatory blows at more remote objectives.

So let us not frighten one another, but show common sense and agree on a mutually acceptable basis to end the cold war and the arms race, to create conditions of peaceful co-existence between states, to promote world peace. (*Prolonged applause.*)

I should like to say a few words in connection with Mr. Eisenhower's allegations that it is difficult to come to terms with the Soviet Government because it consists of atheists, godless men, while the Governments of the Western Powers are allegedly guided by a morality based on religious principles. Therefore, they ask, how can one negotiate with a government which is not bound by religious morality?

Mr. Eisenhower insists that the future does not belong to the idea of a regimented godless state, but to people who are God-fearing, to the peace-loving people of the world.

Mr. President clearly wants to compromise us in some way in the eyes of public opinion, wishing to stress that it is impossible to reach agreement with the Soviet leaders because they do not believe in God. He seems to say that a government which adheres to atheistic views does evil, while a government which believes in God allegedly does good.

Mr. Eisenhower is himself well aware that this is far from the truth. I wish to draw your attention to the facts, and the facts show the following:

People who say that they believe in God and are allegedly guided by divine principles began the aggressive war against Egypt. It was not the atheists, not the Soviet Government that started the war, but the Prime Minister of Britain, Sir Anthony Eden, and the Prime Minister of France, M. Guy Mollet, who after saying their prayers, gave orders to British and French troops to bomb Cairo and kill civilians, women, old men and children.

Meanwhile the Soviet Union, whose leaders are atheists, together with other peace-loving states, exerted great efforts to stop that war. And, as is common knowledge, the Soviet Union's contribution was great. Consequently the war was started by people who consider themselves religious and declare that they are performing works acceptable to God, while the Soviet Government, made up of atheists, did everything to stop it. The question therefore arises, whose morality is sounder and whose morality is more humane?

But to proceed. The leaders of some governments who constantly appeal to God were energetically inciting Turkey to an aggressive war against Syria. A new and bloody war was to have been unleashed in that area. The Soviet Union did everything it could to avert a new war. It should be frankly said that this is greatly to the credit of the Soviet Union and the Soviet Government.

Regardless of creed or colour, the Soviet people are guided by the interests of strengthening peace.

Or take yet another case: governments headed by people who declare that they believe in God are today waging a bloody war in Algeria. The forces of these governments, which are made up of people who "believe" in God, even have among them priests who give their blessing to the killing of people and pray for the victory of the arms which kill defenceless Arabs in Algeria.

There, gentlemen, is your belief in God!

Other governments, also made up of religious people, declare that they are guided by divine principles, but do not do anything to put an end to this extermination of human beings. In this way, "religious" governments kill people, using the Cross and their belief in God as a screen. Is that justice? British planes bomb the villages of the tiny state of Yemen, killing children and old folk, and this is not regarded as a violation of religious morality because it is "coloured" people who die.

Maybe the President will recall that people professing their piety did everything to remove and expel from Guatemala a government they did not like and a President whom they did not want, organizing intervention in the interests of the profits of a handful of monopolists. All this was also done in the name of strengthening faith in the Lord.

I must mention, Mr. President, the fact that the atheistic Government of the Soviet Union insists on banning atomic and hydrogen weapons, while statesmen who start and finish their speeches with invocations to God wish to retain these death-dealing weapons and engage in every imaginable subterfuge to prevent an agreement to ban these weapons. If God really existed, would He not condemn these statesmen who take His name in vain?

And who was it who gave orders to drop the first atom

bombs over Hiroshima and Nagasaki, which killed thousands upon thousands of people, including defenceless women, old men and children? The man who gave these orders, we know, was the then president of the United States. Mr. Truman considers himself a pious man and always concluded his speeches with an invocation to God. He was lavish with words about peace, humanity and brotherhood. But you, Mr. President, have nowhere censured these cruel actions on the part of Mr. Truman.

You, Mr. President, like every unbiased man, clearly realize that the Soviet Government has always faithfully fulfilled its obligations. You are aware also that many statesmen, while professing their belief in God, often act directly to the contrary. Please recall how some governments went back on their obligations to hold free elections in Viet-Nam. I could cite numerous other similar instances. Therefore, Mr. Eisenhower, let us not rake up religious issues.

We stand for religious freedom and respect for the religious views of every man and every people. But at the same time we hold that no one should kill people using religion as a screen or utilize belief in God to the detriment of other peoples. Let us not make these matters a subject for dispute.

Comrades, in reply to the proposals of the Soviet Government, messages have been received from Mr. Macmillan, the Prime Minister of Britain, M. Gaillard, the Prime Minister of France, Herr Adenauer, the Chancellor of the Federal Republic of Germany, and the Heads of Government of a number of other states.

Mr. Macmillan has agreed with the Soviet Government's opinion on the usefulness of personal contacts between the statesmen of the Soviet Union and the Western Powers. He writes:

"You say that personal contacts between Soviet statesmen and Western statesmen could in your view contribute greatly towards the achievement of mutual understanding. I agree that such meetings do have their part to play in reaching the settlements we all desire."

The Prime Minister of Britain stated that the Soviet Government's proposal for a summit conference was being studied by the British Government and that a reply would be sent later.

We express the hope that the British Government will eventually conclude that the solution of the most pressing international problems above all requires the convocation of a summit conference.

It will be recalled that Mr. Macmillan submitted a proposal to conclude a pact between the NATO and Warsaw Treaty countries.

The Soviet Government took a positive view of Mr. Macmillan's statement on the conclusion of a non-aggression pact between the countries concerned.

Unfortunately Mr. Macmillan, apparently influenced by certain forces, later departed somewhat from his original proposal. In this context the question arises: Are not some circles afraid of the very idea of a non-aggression pact, the conclusion of which the Soviet Union has been consistently advocating—an idea which is being increasingly supported by all the peace-loving peoples and the governments of a number of states?

Mr. Macmillan defends the North Atlantic Alliance and the present foreign policy of the Western Powers, attempting at the same time to shift the responsibility for the breakdown of the disarmament talks on to the Soviet Union. Ignoring the concrete plan for disarmament proposed by the Soviet Union, and specifically the plan for the ending of nuclear tests and the prohibition of nuclear weapons as the first step towards disarmament, Mr. Macmillan again brings the Western Powers' plan which we have already rejected to the fore as a basis for disarmament talks. He is in effect opposed to the proposal to set up an atom-free zone in Europe.

Mr. Macmillan's message does not reply to a number of

questions raised in the Soviet Government's message of December 10; in particular nothing is said about the Soviet proposals for the Middle East, about the reduction of foreign armed forces in Germany and the ending of war propaganda by press and radio, which gives rise to mutual distrust and suspicion.

M. Gaillard, the Prime Minister of France, in his reply opposes the Soviet Government's concrete proposals for easing international tension. He explains his disagreement with the Soviet proposals on the renunciation of the use of nuclear weapons by saying that such a measure would not help to reduce the danger of war but, on the contrary, would only increase it. The possession of nuclear weapons by certain Powers, he alleges, can of itself halt any aggression.

Such assertions can hardly be accepted by ordinary people who wish to live in peace and are fighting against the threat of another war. Indeed, is it possible to live calmly when aircraft carrying atomic and hydrogen bombs fly overhead every day and every hour? Does this not resemble the position of a man, doomed to execution, over whose head hangs the knife of the guillotine? And this man has to lie and wait, not knowing when the knife will fall and cut off his head. It is a terrible position to be in. Statesmen, particularly those of the Great Powers, on whom depends the decision to prohibit atomic and hydrogen weapons, must see to it that this problem is solved as soon as possible in order to free mankind from the terrible threat and relieve it of this burden.

M. Gaillard questions the effectiveness of the proposal to set up an atom-free zone in Europe on the grounds that it allegedly ignores the political aspect of the European problem.

He also rejects the Soviet proposal for the conclusion of a non-aggression pact between the NATO and Warsaw Treaty countries.

But at the end of M. Gaillard's message there are remarks with which one cannot but agree. He points out, among other things, that our governments should be guided in their behaviour by a spirit of mutual understanding and loyalty, that "the agreement, promoting even a partial settlement of concrete issues ... would be accompanied by a solemn reaffirmation of the will of the contracting parties never to resort to aggression."

The message expresses readiness to "study ways and means of examining afresh the problems dividing us" in disarmament and to "resume the discussion on the specific problems of Europe," including the projects put forward by the Soviet Government.

While agreeing with the principle of holding a conference of Heads of Government, M. Gaillard makes it contingent on a preliminary conference of Foreign Ministers in order to define properly the programme for a possible summit conference, making the reservation that the Foreign Ministers would not have competence to discuss the question in substance.

This stand of the French Government differs from that of the United States Government, which, it will be recalled, insists on the convening of a Foreign Ministers conference to discuss the substance of international problems.

I must dwell on the attitude of the Government of the Federal Republic of Germany. In his January 15 broadcast, Herr Adenauer, Chancellor of the Federal Republic of Germany, described the Soviet Government's message as a carefully prepared manoeuvre which made no serious effort to reach mutual understanding. He made an unsubstantiated statement to the effect that the "Soviets are now seeking above all to create confusion in the world." Let us leave such groundless assertions to Herr Adenauer's conscience.

The convening of a conference, says Herr Adenauer, will yield nothing because, if not crowned with success, it will only further worsen the situation. Nevertheless the proposal for a conference should be accepted, with the reservation that not too many participants should be invited, and that careful diplomatic preparation should establish whether mutual understanding is possible.

Herr Adenauer also opposes the plan for setting up an atom-free zone in Central Europe.

In his official reply to the Soviet Government's message, Herr Adenauer sets out the Soviet Government's stand on the reunification of Germany incorrectly. He asserts that the Heads of Government of the Four Powers at the Geneva Conference allegedly reached agreement on the reunification of Germany. I have already said that such an assertion is not in accordance with reality and is at variance with the facts.

The attitude of Herr Adenauer's Government has aroused disappointment and censure, not only on the part of world opinion, but also in West Germany herself. The Social-Democratic Party group in the Bundestag stated that Herr Adenauer's reply "in general is not conducive to any progress in disarmament or in reunification, because it is confined either to rejecting accusations or to repeating well-known reproaches to Moscow. Concrete possibilities to advance the cause of disarmament are rejected." The Free Democratic Party group in the Bundestag also censures the fact that the "Federal Government categorically rejects the idea of setting up an atom-free zone in Europe."

Comrades, the Soviet Government believes that the time is ripe to convene a conference of leading statesmen on a high level with the participation of Heads of Government. We are ready to take part in such a conference at any time.

Are there at present any definite international problems which demand **urgent** solution and which can be solved today? There can only be one answer: Yes, there are such questions, and they are not few in number.

Can statesmen who have even the slightest concern for the destinies of the peoples remain indifferent and tolerate the present state of affairs when the race, growing like an avalanche to produce weapons of ever-increasing destructive power, creates the danger of the catastrophe of war?

Can we tolerate the fact that the cold war atmosphere brings this danger increasingly close and makes it increasingly real?

The Soviet Government has already officially informed all the Powers of its views on the questions which should be discussed first of all. Here are a number of them:

What prevents agreement on **the immediate ending of atomic and hydrogen weapons tests**, in order to put an end to the hazards to health resulting from tests? Is this question not ripe for the most urgent discussion? It is!

Is it not high time to agree at last on **the ending of the so-called cold war**? For more than 10 years the world has been living in an atmosphere of cold war, which is keeping the peoples at fever pitch. On its basis the enemies of peace have been systematically cultivating enmity and hatred among the peoples and fanning war hysteria. The cold war and the arms race, plunging the world further and further down the slope to atomic war—all these are things that are closely interconnected. Is it not high time to put an end to the cold war? It is!

The same should be said of putting **an end to war propaganda** which is carried on day in and day out in some Western countries and which is becoming increasingly unrestrained. Who can deny that there are civilians and military men in the United States who make systematic and open calls for war, including atomic war? It is high time to recognize that propaganda exercises of this kind have become far too dangerous under present conditions for them to be allowed to continue!

We also believe that it is high time to reach agreement on **the reduction of the number of foreign troops stationed in Germany and other European states**. When we say of the reduction of these forces, we mean that this must be only the beginning, only the first stage, because eventually all foreign troops must be withdrawn from the territories of other countries. Would not this be natural in peacetime? Is it not high time today to agree at least on the need for the Powers concerned to take this important step?

Reality prompts the need for solving the important problem of **the setting up in Central Europe of a zone free from every type of nuclear weapon** and embracing such states as the German Democratic Republic, Poland, Czechoslovakia and the Federal Republic of Germany. It is common knowledge that three of these countries have already expressed their consent to the setting up of such a zone. There is no need to prove the exceptional importance and value to the cause of peace of the implementation of this proposal put forward by the Polish Government.

Some foreign leaders declare that appropriate control is needed for the setting up of an atom-free zone in Europe. The Soviet Union is ready to examine this proposal and to accept the establishment of the necessary control.

The question of **the situation in the Middle East** is also pressing. All of us have in recent years more than once seen how, now in one, now in another part of this region, dangerous hotbeds of war have emerged which threatened to plunge all mankind into the abyss of war. That is why we regard it as a duty of the Great Powers to agree as soon as possible on the renunciation of the use of force in settling Middle East issues and of intervention in the affairs of the countries of the area.

Finally, who can deny the need for doing away with such ugly phenomena **in international economic relations** as discrimination, all kinds of black lists and similar artificial obstacles to international trade? It can with confidence be said that all these barriers to the free development of international trade erected during the cold war do not even benefit the states which have created them, but only poison the international atmosphere and provide grist for the mill of the enemies of peace.

In fact, trade discrimination was created in order to

poison the atmosphere. If the rulers of some countries expected to weaken the military potential of the Soviet Union in this way, they have failed. Some probably thought that if sales of strategic goods to the Soviet Union were permitted it would in some measure help to strengthen the military might and promote the advance of the military science and technology in our country. But reality has shown the utter bankruptcy of such views. It is common knowledge that the Soviet Union, despite restrictions and discrimination in trade, relying on the development of national science and technology and the might of its industry, has designed the best types of armaments —a fact which the Western Powers themselves have admitted. We do not speak of trade in armaments—let the Western Powers not sell arms, just as we do not intend to sell our arms. Nor do we plan to purchase arms. The issue is quite different—it is a question of normal trade between countries.

Why are such restrictions and discrimination in international trade necessary? They are necessary in order to keep the world in a state of tension, to trouble the waters and to fish in them, as the saying goes. It is clear that the rulers of the Western Powers are not prompted by business considerations, but by other, quite different. considerations.

I have cited as instances only some questions which in our opinion can be regarded as ripe for immediate discussion at a conference of leading statesmen. We do not exclude other important questions which could be discussed at the summit meeting and definite, positive results achieved.

It goes without saying that, given the desire on both sides, agreement on many questions is possible. But for a summit conference to yield positive results, the *status quo* must be recognized, that is to say, the fact that there are two systems of states in the world—the capitalist and the socialist systems. The principle of peaceful co-existence should be recognized, and there should be no interference in the affairs of other states. If all this is recognized and the ruling circles of the Western countries do not seek a solution of international problems through war against the socialist countries, it will not be at all difficult to reach agreement on urgent international problems in the interests of consolidating peace.

If the *status quo* is not recognized, if the socialist states are ignored, their sovereign rights violated and their domestic affairs made the object for interference, then it is, of course, absolutely impossible to agree. Such a policy is nothing but the policy of "positions of strength," a policy of war. But this has already been tried against the Soviet Union and it is well known that the lovers of such a policy suffered total defeat. Such was the case when the Soviet Union was the only socialist country. What can the imperialists hope for now, when the Soviet Union is no longer the only socialist state, when the great Chinese People's Republic and all the socialist countries of Europe and Asia stand with it in the mighty camp of socialism, when this camp unites about 1,000 million people? Only madmen and adventurers can ignore this and hope for a solution of international problems through war. If the imperialists unleash another war it will inevitably lead to the destruction of those who start it. The peoples will do away for ever with a system which brings mankind untold suffering and bloody wars.

The Soviet Government is ready to discuss any questions designed to strengthen peace and establish greater confidence among the states, to discuss these questions with its partners. Mr. Eisenhower, for instance, recently put forward in one of his speeches the idea of pooling the efforts of the Soviet Union and the United States to combat such scourges of mankind as cancer, tuberculosis and malaria. We believe that one can agree with this. One could list many other questions, such as the struggle against poliomyelitis, locusts, glanders and foot-and-mouth disease. We are successfully co-operating with Iran and Afghanistan in combating locusts. There are many other matters regarding which, far from hindering co-operation, we are doing our utmost to extend it. Although not all these problems are acute or dangerous to our country, we are nevertheless ready to co-operate with countries where such problems are particularly pressing. We shall be pleased to pool our efforts with those of other countries in solving such problems.

But I hope you will understand me correctly, Mr. President; these are not the issues on which mankind awaits agreement between the Great Powers. It is with hope and anxiety that the peoples of all countries watch for the solution of the fundamental problems in the relations between states. They expect, above all, a relaxation in international tension, so that people are not threatened with a war of extermination, so that when they go to bed they need not fear lest they never wake up again, so that they need not fear losing their husbands, fathers, children, wives and mothers in this war.

We should above all bear this in mind, because people all over the world, all mankind, are waiting with anxiety and hope for a solution to these vital problems. (*Prolonged applause.*)

Comrades, the Soviet Government and the Central Committee of our Party have always stood, and firmly stand by the Leninist positions of peace and friendship among the peoples, by the positions of peaceful co-existence between states with different social systems. We want absolute non-intervention in the internal affairs of other states. We have strictly observed, and shall continue to observe this inviolable rule. It is also imperative that all states, big and small, should respect the independence and sovereignty of other states, that an improvement in the relations between the Great Powers should not be brought about at the expense of the interests of the small states.

For our part we shall continue to do everything to attain these noble aims.

The forces for peace and friendship among the peoples have grown immeasurably and continue steadily to grow. In the forefront of these forces are the peoples of the Soviet Union, the Chinese People's Republic, all the socialist countries of Europe and Asia, the Communist and Workers' parties of all countries. The Peace Manifesto, adopted at the Meeting of the Communist and Workers' Parties in Moscow, has found an echo in the hearts of men and women all over the world. The call "Peace to the World!" has become a genuine expression of the aspirations and hopes of the peoples of all the continents of the world.

That is why the ruling circles of certain states have been compelled to disguise their real aims. Fostering their aggressive schemes, they often resort to peaceable phrases in order to lull the vigilance of the peoples.

In these circumstances the peoples must show great organization and cohesion in the struggle for peace, staunchness and persistence in the maintenance and strengthening of world peace.

The Soviet people, taking pride in their country which is implementing its great plans for building communism, are confidently marching from victory to victory with unshaken faith in their inexhaustible strength. We are led along the Leninist road to the triumph of communism by the great Communist Party of the Soviet Union. (*Stormy, prolonged applause. All rise. Cries of* "Glory to our Communist Party!" *followed by further prolonged applause. Cries of* "Long live the Leninist Central Committee of our Party! Hurrah!". *Further stormy, prolonged applause.*)

INTERVIEW GIVEN TO AXEL SPRINGER, WEST GERMAN PUBLISHER, AND HANS ZEHRER, EDITOR OF *DIE WELT*

January 29, 1958

The West German publisher, Axel Springer, and the editor of the Hamburg newspaper *Die Welt*, Hans Zehrer, requested an interview with N. S. Khrushchov, First Secretary of the Central Committee of the Communist Party of the Soviet Union.

They were received by Khrushchov on January 29 and had a long talk with him. Below we publish the text of the interview.

Springer: Mr. Khrushchov, we thank you very much for having received us. We have come to ask you a few questions which agitate us in view of the grave international situation and the situation in Germany. Allow me to start with the first question right away.

Would it not be a welcome initiative and, at the same time, a contribution to the easing of international tension if discussion of the possibility of restoring the unity of Germany were started?

Answer: This is my first meeting with representatives of the press of the Federal Republic of Germany concerning issues which are of interest to public opinion in West Germany. It was natural to expect that my interviewers would not pass over a question which, it seems, is on the tip of everyone's tongue in Germany, whether in the western or the eastern part. That is the question of the possibilities for restoring the national unity of the country. I must say at once that the key to the solution of this problem about which all Germans are concerned is to be sought in Bonn and Berlin rather than in Moscow, Washington, Paris or London.

This, of course, is not due to any lack of concern in the Soviet Union for a settlement of the German issue or any lack of understanding and sympathy for the desire of the Germans to unite their country. We Russian Communists, as Marxist-Leninists, have always championed the right of nations to self-determination and the formation of independent national states, and that is why we cannot remain indifferent to the fact that the people of one single nation are living on different sides of a frontier running across their country, to the fact that economic ties between various parts of Germany which have grown up through the ages have been disrupted and that German families in their everyday life suffer from the abnormal conditions resulting from the division of their country. The Soviet Union is prepared to continue to do everything it can to put an end to this unnatural situation in Germany, which arose in spite of the Soviet Union's efforts to preserve the unity of a German state renovated on a peaceful and democratic basis after the war.

Question: How do you understand the changing of this unnatural situation—the division of the German people?

Answer: I can tell you that it would be a profound mistake to expect that the unity of your country can be introduced by anyone from outside, or that the intermediary role of any governments can replace the efforts of the German people themselves. Unity can only be the product of *rapprochement* and agreement between the German Democratic Republic and the Federal Republic of Germany. More than eight years have elapsed since the administrative functions in Germany were transferred from the Four Powers to the Germans themselves. During that time two independent German states have been established, with their own parliaments and governments responsible for the development of Germany and the future of the German nation.

I have twice had occasion to visit the German Democratic Republic in recent years and I have seen for myself the striking changes that have taken place there since the war. I think that you too will not deny that today each of the German states is separated from the other by a deep gulf and in order to bridge that gulf to achieve their unification one should, first and foremost, draw the necessary conclusions from the obvious fact that the German Democratic Republic and the Federal Republic of Germany are not merely states where people of one nationality, speaking the same language, live and work, but that they are also states with different economic foundations and with different political and social systems.

We do not, of course, intend to impose on anyone our recipes for a solution of the German problem. Besides, it is hardly possible that anyone other than the states directly concerned can put forward any viable proposals which would adequately take stock of the diversity and complexity of the problems arising and give grounds for hope that the existing serious obstacles can be overcome.

In its recent letter to Federal Chancellor Adenauer the Soviet Government noted the unique conditions in which the problem of German reunification has to be solved, namely, that what is involved here is not a problem that is common in international practice, or a movement along a beaten track that has been tried and tested, but the task of peacefully uniting two sovereign states with different social and economic systems—a task which has arisen for the first time in history. Will there be any hope of success in solving such a problem if we act in accordance with patterns developed in the past and try mechanically to merge two states developing in such widely divergent directions?

Question: We are aware of the Soviet Government's view that the problem of German reunification can be solved only by direct negotiations between the two German governments. How do you see the achievement of such understanding in practice?

Answer: It would appear quite natural that the unification of Germany is a two-sided process which cannot be accomplished without the participation of both German states. But the Government of one of them, namely, the Government of the Federal Republic of Germany, pretends that there is no other German state on the map, that is to say, that part of Germany with which, if we are to believe its statements, it wishes to unite. It is difficult not to observe that this attitude of the West German Government is at variance with common sense. Does it not indicate a desire to remain aloof from the search for ways leading to German reunification, and to justify its own inaction by an emphatically hostile attitude towards the only possible partner in an agreement? Was this not the idea behind the allegation that the German Democratic Republic needs "recognition" from the Government of the Federal Republic of Germany? I have no doubt that the German Democratic Republic is not concerned about "recognition" by the Federal Republic of Germany to any greater extent than the Federal Republic of Germany is concerned about "recognition" by the German Democratic Republic. But that is not the point. The point is whether the two German states will work together to solve the national problems of the German people, or whether the cause of unification is to mark time while the German Democratic Republic and the Federal Republic of Germany continue to draw apart.

When I am asked about the possible ways of achieving a *rapprochement* between the two German states and the unification of the country, I can only say with complete conviction that I do not see—and apparently there do not exist—any other proposals designed to solve the problem which promise success, apart from that put forward by the Government of the German Democratic Republic for a confederation of the two German states—that is to say, for a union by treaty of the German Democratic Republic and the Federal Republic of Germany with the aim of pursuing a common policy on a definite range of domestic and external issues, and primarily bringing about their *rapprochement* on the basis of joint action to ease tension in the relations between states and remove the danger of a new war.

Question: The German problem depends in some measure on a relaxation of international tension. On the other hand, that relaxation hinges to some extent on a settlement of the German issue. What could the Federal Government do, for its part, actively to help solve both these issues?

Answer: It is a good thing that people in West Germany are seeking an answer to this very vital question. We have repeatedly expressed our conviction that Germany in general, and the Federal Republic of Germany in particular, has had, and still has, great opportunities for exerting an influence on the situation in Europe and elsewhere. It would be no exaggeration to say that if the Federal Republic of Germany combined its efforts with those of the Soviet Union and other states in order to ease international tension and prevent a new war, peace on the European continent would be assured. With this in mind, the Soviet Government, you will recall, has repeatedly approached the Federal Government with proposals which have gone beyond the framework of relations between our two countries and which concerned the settlement of a wide range of international problems which are the source of tension and friction in relations between states.

Unfortunately there is no evidence as yet of the Federal Government's readiness to act in that direction. So far the Federal Government seems to have preferred to ignore the proposals which have been made to it and which have been designed to safeguard peace, rather than respond to them. It has at the same time declined to take the initiative itself.

Question: What are the proposals you have in mind?

Answer: To be more precise about the decisions now confronting the Federal Republic of Germany, I should like to dwell, primarily, on a question which opens up wide avenues for peace, namely, the idea of creating an atom-free zone in Europe. You will recall that this idea emerged in connection with the fact that Europe, being already an area of dangerous tension, was increasingly becoming, not so much a powder magazine as an atomic arsenal. Apprehensive of these developments, statesmen and public men in many countries are seeking a solution. The Polish Government has shown valuable initiative in putting forward the idea of creating an atom-free zone in Europe which, in its opinion, could, together with Poland, include Czechoslovakia, the German Democratic Republic and the Federal Republic of Germany. The Governments of Czechoslovakia and the German Democratic Republic have already agreed to participate in such a zone, and in order for it to be established this zone now in fact needs only the support of the West German Government.

We are aware that in West German political circles there are both supporters and opponents of the Federal Republic's participation in an atom-free zone. As far as I am aware, you are among those who support the inclusion of the Federal Republic of Germany in such a zone, inasmuch as this would help to solve the German problem. But I must add that to make the establishment of the zone dependent on the solution of other issues on which there is no agreement is to complicate the reaching of agreement on the atom-free zone, whose benefits for the Federal Republic of Germany you recognize.

It seems that those who take a negative view of Poland's proposal underestimate the importance of an atom-free zone to the security of West Germany, ignoring an effective means of warding off the danger of destructive weapons being used against Germany. Of course, one can turn one's back on reality and shut one's eyes to the danger, but that does not make it any the less.

Persons who hold important positions in West Germany and are responsible for her policy say that such a zone would be "illusory" because, they say, there are no guarantees that an atomic war will not be unleashed on the territories of the states that will belong to an atom-free zone. What can be said about such objections? In my opinion, such arguments are either the result of unwillingness to see the real meaning of the proposal to set up an atom-free zone, or of unwillingness to do anything useful in general to prevent an atomic war in Europe.

In fact, the Soviet Government, it will be recalled, has proclaimed its readiness to act jointly with other Powers to provide reliable international guarantees for the atomic neutrality of the member-states of an atom-free zone in order to preclude the possibility of such weapons being used in the zone. In addition, the Soviet Union believes it to be possible for the states concerned to agree on broad forms of control over measures involved in creating an atom-free zone. All this proves that assertions about the "illusory" nature of the atom-free zone are, to say the least, contrived.

The Federal Republic is now faced with yet another vital issue. I refer to the stationing of American atomic bases and rocket launching sites in West Germany.

I am aware that as soon as we raise the subject of atomic and rocket bases, a hue and cry is raised in West Germany about some kind of threat from us. I should like to see the West understand, at long last, that we have not been threatening anyone nor do we intend to do so and that there is nothing more alien to the Soviet state than a "positions of strength" policy, a policy that indeed does involve intimidation and pressure. But we have always spoken of the disastrous consequences which could arise as a result of the preparation of atomic war, and we consider it our duty to continue to do so in the future. The peoples must be told the whole truth about what awaits them if war breaks out. They must have their eyes open when governments and parliaments make decisions increasing the danger of an atomic war.

Our warnings to the Government and population of West Germany contain nothing but the objective facts of modern science and engineering, well-considered and authoritative conclusions dictated by the existing situation. Indeed, many scientists and military specialists in your own country who have some degree of access to information about modern weapons and the nature of military operations in modern conditions, have issued serious warnings about the mortal danger to which the Federal Republic of Germany is being subjected by NATO plans to make West Germany a launching site for American atomic and rocket weapons.

I hope that I have made myself clear: If the Federal Republic intends to make its contribution to easing international tension, it should first and foremost dissociate itself from the plans to involve it in the preparation of an atomic war—the stationing of American atomic and rocket bases on its territory and the equipping of the Bundeswehr with atomic weapons.

The efforts of the Federal Government could also be directed towards solving the question of the conclusion of a non-aggression pact, in one form or another, between the NATO and the Warsaw Treaty member-countries— a question of importance to peace.

One would expect that the Federal Republic of Germany, whose territory abuts on the line dividing these military groupings, would be no less interested in the conclusion of such an agreement than, let us say, the Soviet Union or Britain. It would be strange if the Federal Government, whose members frequently claim that there exists some sort of threat to West Germany from the Soviet Union, were to refuse to receive an undertaking regarding non-aggression from the Warsaw Treaty Organization.

As far as I am aware, much attention is being paid in West Germany to the Soviet Government's proposals for a gradual reduction and subsequently the complete withdrawal of foreign troops from the territories of all North Atlantic Alliance and Warsaw Treaty Organization states and the simultaneous dismantling of foreign military bases, beginning the implementation of these measures in Germany. It would seem that such a proposal, which is in complete accord with the national interests of the German people, should have been regarded favourably by the Federal Republic of Germany. With the present concentration of troops and military equipment in Germany, which is abnormal in peacetime, the disengagement of the armed forces of the Great Powers which are in contact there would also be conducive to the strengthening of security in Europe.

The Federal Government's well-known opposition to the proposal to reduce, and subsequently to withdraw, foreign troops from Germany is naturally not conducive to the solution of a problem which is of such importance to the easing of international tension.

It is also obvious that the Federal Government's refusal to normalize its relations with many countries of Eastern Europe and Asia, including countries which were victims of Hitler's aggression, is likewise at variance with the interests of easing international tension. It is no secret that the Federal Government is entirely responsible for the fact that its relations with these countries are not built on a normal peacetime basis. The Government of the Federal Republic of Germany very recently committed an act of hostility against Yugoslavia by severing diplomatic relations with her, thus introducing a new element of exacerbation into the situation on the European continent.

In short, given the desire, the Federal Republic of Germany has a most extensive field for activities which would contribute to a relaxation of international tension: in the sphere of disarmament, in the sphere of strengthening security in Europe, and in the sphere of improving relations with other states. It is at least necessary that the Federal Republic should refrain from steps which increase the war danger and international tension.

Since you have asked me for advice on ways in which the Federal Republic of Germany could help to ease international tension, here is what I can say: Statesmen who are responsible for the policy of the Federal Republic of Germany would do better to be less concerned about adhering to the "positions of strength" policy and should be guided in their activities by what one might call a "positions of reason" policy—that is to say, they should be guided by their own national interests and the interests of strengthening peace.

Question: Is it not time, Mr. Khrushchov, to consider the question of ending the temporary status which Germany has now had for 12 years and start drawing up a peace treaty?

Answer: We are aware that the problem of a peace treaty profoundly agitates the minds of Germans. And that is understandable. More than 12 years have elapsed since the end of the Second World War, but the German people are still without a peace treaty which would write *finis* to the war and its consequences. The problem of a peace treaty is the problem of restoring Germany's complete sovereignty and independence, the problem of her frontiers and of the withdrawal of foreign troops from her territory. It is therefore natural that no *ersatz* agreements, such as the Paris Agreements, can take the place of a peace treaty. Such decisions can only be of a transitory nature, because they do not spring from the national interests of the two German states and are in direct conflict with the interests of the security of a number of states, above all, those that took part in the war against Nazi Germany.

But it is one thing to end the state of war with Germany, which has also been done by the Soviet Government in view of the Western Powers' opposition to the conclusion of a peace treaty with Germany, and another to conclude a peace treaty, which defines the external conditions, through the observation of which Germany's entire development could be protected from every kind of extraneous interference. During the entire post-war period the Soviet Government has been working for a fundamental settlement of the German problem through the conclusion of a peace treaty with Germany.

Many facts of the post-war period—I refer to the Paris Agreements and similar agreements between the United States and a number of other countries and Japan —indicate that in present-day circumstances, when the struggle between the capitalist countries for world markets, sources of raw materials and spheres for capital investment has been further sharpened, a defeated state does not find it easy to secure for itself a just and democratic peace treaty.

After the First World War the Governments of the United States, Britain and France divided the world into victors and vanquished, leaving the aggressive militarist forces that had unleashed the war in power in Germany. You will recall that the Soviet Union opposed the predatory Versailles Treaty. The aftermath of Versailles is well known. It helped to establish the Hitler régime in Germany and in no small degree helped to unleash the Second World War.

After the First World War international imperialist circles incited Germany to turn to the East, mainly by economic and diplomatic means. Today, they want to conscript West Germany's military and industrial potential, her manpower and also the creative genius of her scientists into the service of an exclusive military grouping—the North Atlantic bloc—directed, as everyone knows only too well, against the Soviet Union and other peace-loving states and against world peace. The Governments

77

of the United States, Britain and France, having imposed the Paris Agreements on the Federal Republic of Germany, are in fact trying to organize post-war relations in Europe on a historically outdated basis similar to the Versailles Treaty. This is profoundly mistaken and can lead to much more disastrous results.

Bearing in mind that there are two sovereign states in Germany today—the German Democratic Republic and the Federal Republic of Germany—it is important not to postpone the drawing up of a draft peace treaty, in order to give the German people a clear idea of Germany's prospects for future development. Needless to say, the Germans themselves—the German Democratic Republic and the Federal Republic of Germany—must take part in the drawing up of such a draft treaty. And here again, in my opinion, it is the proposal of the Government of the German Democratic Republic to set up a German confederation that offers the most realistic possibilities for the conclusion of a peace treaty with Germany. In that event, a peace treaty could be concluded both with the organs of the confederation and with the governments of the states within that confederation.

Question: What is your idea of the military status of the future Germany?

Answer: Intrinsically this problem must be governed by the peace treaty with Germany and must form a component part of it. Inasmuch as we stand for the preparation of a peace treaty with Germany, we are naturally also in favour of Germany's military status being defined now. Taking into consideration the special importance attached to the problem of military status by wide sections of public opinion in West Germany, the Soviet Union is prepared to consider this question independently, irrespective of other provisions of the peace treaty.

In this connection I should like to draw your attention to the fact that the Government of the German Democratic Republic has put forward a number of proposals and carried out practical steps which, as we see it, constitute a suitable foundation for a future agreement on Germany's military status.

We know, in particular, that the German Democratic Republic has, of its own free will, restricted the strength of its armed forces to 90,000 men. In the German Democratic Republic, in contrast to West Germany, conscription has not been introduced, and finally, the armed forces of the German Democratic Republic are under national command. The fact that the Government of the German Democratic Republic does not raise the question of equipping its forces with atomic and rocket weapons but, on the contrary, is making every effort to ensure that there shall be no atomic and rocket weapons—German or foreign—on German soil is of particular importance. Moreover, it is common knowledge that the Government of the German Democratic Republic has proclaimed its readiness to withdraw from the Warsaw Treaty Organization if the Federal Republic of Germany withdraws from NATO, and also to reach an agreement with the Government of the Federal Republic to establish a limit to the size of the armed forces of the two German states.

It seems to me that these proposals of the Government of the German Democratic Republic, and what it has already done in practice in order to find, jointly with the Government of the Federal Republic, ways for the unification of Germany, contain real and important elements of the agreement you have in view when you speak of Germany's military status. One should take into account the fact that Germany's military status consists of two parts, as it were, and that an agreement on this problem depends primarily on those measures of a military nature which are currently being carried out by each of the German states.

Can it be said that the Federal Republic, for its part, is doing everything necessary for an agreement on Germany's military status to be translated into reality? Not at all. In contrast to the German Democratic Republic, the Federal Republic of Germany has introduced conscription. The military units organized there are being placed at the disposal of the NATO Command. The Government of the Federal Republic of Germany refuses to discuss an agreement with the German Democratic Republic establishing levels for the armed forces of the two German states.

At the same time the intention of the Government of the Federal Republic to secure atomic and rocket weapons for the West German Bundeswehr and to take part in research to produce the latest weapons is becoming increasingly evident. The action of the Government of the Federal Republic, which are directed towards the use of the territory of West Germany for American nuclear weapon dumps and launching sites for rocket and nuclear weapons, is also incompatible with the definition, now or in the future, of the military status of Germany.

It should be added that not once has the Government of the Federal Republic shown that it has been prepared to abstain, in the interests of re-establishing national unity, from any of the military measures envisaged by the NATO military and strategic plans. Moreover, it goes out of its way to stress that it attaches special importance to the implementation of the military commitments it has assumed under the Paris Agreements. Flaunting its loyalty to NATO, the Federal Government has proclaimed its complete solidarity with the plans repeatedly put forward by the three Western Powers at international conferences for including the whole of Germany in this military bloc, although such demands can relate only to the realm of fiction.

I should like to stress that inasmuch as the question has been posed on a purely military plane, I am taking precisely this aspect of the German problem. But even if, for the purpose of clarifying the essence of the question you have raised, we should confine ourselves to these somewhat conventional restrictions, even such an abstract approach reveals that a solution to the problem of Germany's military status acceptable to the parties concerned can be found only in a *rapprochement* and mutual understanding between the German Democratic Republic and the Federal Republic of Germany.

We believe that both German states must unconditionally renounce all kinds of weapons of mass destruction, that is to say, renounce both their own production of atomic, hydrogen and rocket weapons and also the equipping of their armed forces with foreign-made weapons of this kind, and prevent the building of atomic and rocket bases belonging to other Powers on their territory. Both German states, after embarking on the road of re-establishing national unity, must renounce membership of the military groupings of the Powers to which they belong at the present time. And lastly, the levels of the armed forces of the two German states must be established in conformity with their requirements for self-defence and for ensuring internal security, through an agreement between the Governments of the German Democratic Republic and the Federal Republic of Germany.

Question: Would it not in your opinion be a good beginning if the movement towards the reunification of the German people were to start with the normalization of the situation in Berlin?

Answer: Indeed, the present situation in Berlin cannot be regarded as normal. Berlin is, we know, the capital of the German Democratic Republic, while the western part of the city, namely, the American, British and French sectors, represent a kind of island within the German Democratic Republic.

The military authorities of the Western Powers in Berlin in every way stress their prerogatives as occupation authorities. Whereas in West Germany some of the restrictions of the occupation régime which affect the Germans most have been lifted, in West Berlin these restrictions are still in force. It is also well known that West Berlin is being extensively used for subversive activities against the German Democratic Republic and other socialist countries. I must say frankly that as a result of the policy of the United States, Britain and France, and also of the Federal Republic of Germany, West Berlin has become one of the most painful sores of the cold war. It seems to us that in the interest of the population of Berlin it is necessary to remove the present tension in the relations between the German authorities of East and West Berlin and to achieve co-operation between them, both in municipal administration and in other spheres.

I think that, given a desire on the part of the Government of the Federal Republic and the West Berlin *Magistratur* to find a solution to the Berlin problem acceptable both to themselves and to the German Democratic Republic, such a decision could be found, and the Soviet Union would only welcome such a development.

Question: Mr. Khrushchov, normal diplomatic relations between the Soviet Union and the Federal Republic of Germany have already existed for over two years. Do you think that these relations have brought our peoples closer to each other? And how do you assess the prospects for the development of these relations?

Answer: More than two years have elapsed since diplomatic relations between the Soviet Union and the Federal Republic of Germany were established. Was that step a useful one? The answer to this question is definitely in the affirmative. I believe that the leaders of the Federal Republic of Germany, too, have no reason to take a different view. The governments of the two countries now have far greater possibilities for studying and correctly understanding each other's views and intentions and for bringing out factors tending to achieve a *rapprochement* between the U.S.S.R. and the Federal Republic of Germany in the interests of strengthening world peace. Some progress has been achieved in trade. Exchanges in science, technology and culture are getting under way. A beginning has been made in sport and tourism. But all these things are simply initial, and I would say, timid steps. Of course, the beginning is always difficult. But it seems to me that this is not the only point. Much greater results could have been achieved had there been no artificial restrictions on the development of contacts, as was the case, for instance, when the authorities of the Federal Republic refused to issue entry visas to a group of Soviet circus artistes.

For our part, we always try to give every assistance to measures facilitating a closer mutual acquaintance with the material and spiritual riches of both peoples. It is to be hoped that in this matter, which is in the interests of both parties, we shall meet with reciprocity on the part of the Government of the Federal Republic. It is well known that Germany's well-being has always been accompanied by the activization of mutual relations and the extension of economic and other co-operation with the East, and primarily with Russia in the past and with the Soviet Union at present.

We attach considerable importance to the successful completion of the current talks now being held in Moscow between the government delegations of the U.S.S.R. and the Federal Republic of Germany, which, as has been agreed by the two Governments, are aimed at improving relations between our countries. If we are to judge the prospects of the talks by the results achieved up to date, there is every reason to expect that they will lead to positive results on all problems under discussion.

I should like to ask you, Herr Springer, to tell West German readers that the Soviet Union will make earnest and consistent efforts to achieve *rapprochement* and mutual understanding between the U.S.S.R. and the Federal Republic of Germany. We should like all the remnants of mistrust and suspicion in the relations between our countries to be completely removed. In my opinion, the necessary turning-point in the relations between our countries towards their improvement could be achieved, in particular, by the establishment of contacts between the parliaments and also between individual statesmen and public leaders and by the ending of ill-intentioned propaganda.

Springer: We are very grateful for having been given the opportunity to have a talk with you. Forgive us for having taken so much of your time.

Khrushchov: It has also been a great pleasure to meet you and have a talk with you. Such meetings undoubtedly help to establish better mutual understanding, which is in the interests of the peoples of our countries.

Pravda, February 8, 1958

INTERVIEW GIVEN TO I. McDONALD, FOREIGN EDITOR OF *THE TIMES*

January 31, 1958

On January 31, N. S. Khrushchov granted an interview to Mr. Iverach McDonald, foreign editor of *The Times.* Below we publish a record of the interview.

McDonald: This is my seventh visit to the Soviet Union and it has been a very interesting trip.

Khrushchov: We are glad when Western representatives pay us several visits and have an opportunity to see for themselves the stages of our development.

McDonald: Yes, indeed. I have seen great changes taking place in recent years. I first came here 26 years ago. At that time I made a trip down the Volga, visited the North Caucasus and the Ukraine. It was a bad year for agriculture. During my present visit I have been pleasantly surprised at the enormous progress made in the countryside, particularly in the last two or three years.

Now let me ask you the following:

I have read with great care the Soviet Government's statement on the international situation published on January 8. Naturally, I have also read your Minsk speech. I shall take up one point. As the second item for discussion at a summit conference the Soviet Government proposes the problem of banning atomic and hydrogen weapons. But further on, the same statement says that since the Governments of the United States and Great Britain do not wish at the present time to agree to ban nuclear weapons and destroy stockpiles, "there is nothing else to be done but to postpone the problems pertaining to a radical solution of atomic disarmament to a later stage of the talks." In view of this I should like to know what results the Soviet Government hopes to achieve by raising the issue for examination at a top-level conference at this stage.

Khrushchov: This should be regarded as a desire on our part to achieve a radical solution of disarmament problems. We favour the eventual abolition of armies and the adoption of a system of militia, that is to say, to have no armed forces in the country but militia forces to maintain order. As a matter of fact, in the period before the October Revolution and immediately following it our Party intended to organize a people's militia instead of a permanent army. At that time we believed the Western countries would not attack us. But things took quite a different turn; the actual state of affairs gave the problem a new aspect. "We could not exist," said Lenin, "without the armed defence of the Socialist Republic." Winston Churchill gave us an object lesson by organizing the attack against the Soviet Union. Churchill once told Stalin jokingly: You should have awarded me an Order because I was the first to help train your young Soviet army in the art of war by organizing intervention against the Soviet Union! Of course, I am not quoting Churchill verbatim, but that is the gist of what he said.

McDonald: I regret having to use an interpreter but my knowledge of Russian is insufficient.

Khrushchov: I know Ukrainian pretty well, but I must admit I also want people to slow down when they speak too fast. One naturally finds it easier to speak one's native tongue.

Generally speaking, Mr. Churchill has a pungent sense of humour. He once told our Ambassador during a meeting at Chequers: There was a time when I received the white-guard Savinkov and had a talk with him in this very room. We helped him in the struggle against the Soviet state. Now you and I are talking here. . . .

Indeed, Britain, and Mr. Churchill personally, were largely responsible for forcing our country to organize its own strong army and defend the Soviet state against its enemies. But I want to stress that the existence of a standing army did not spring from our convictions but was the result of a definite situation. We are internationalists and believe in the friendly co-operation of all peoples. Our aim is peace and not war.

You know that Hitler and the Nazis preached their nationalistic and chauvinistic philosophy, which was really no philosophy at all, but the ravings of a madman. They preached the concept that the "Aryans," that is to say, the German nation, were superior to all other nations, the idea of the enslavement of all peoples by the Germans. We Marxists say that all men and women, all peoples, regardless of their colour, creed, nationality and language, have equal rights to exist and should organize their lives after their own fashion. Therefore, all peoples should co-operate and live in peace with each other on the basis of the principles of peaceful co-existence.

If we pay great attention to our army it is only because we are forced to. Since capitalist countries cannot think of existing without armies we must also have an army, and if we must have it, it must be an army capable of opposing any force threatening us.

I am elaborating on this issue because in my opinion it explains the essence of our attitude to all armed forces in all countries. We are accused of trying to maintain large armed forces and of wanting to use them to impose our will on others; we are accused of wanting to impose our ideology on other peoples by force. Mr. Dulles excels in this respect. But it is nonsense. I think that Mr. Dulles himself does not believe what he says and if he persists in saying it, it is only for propaganda purposes, hoping to stir up hatred for the Soviet Union.

It is sometimes pointed out that in my speeches I express the conviction that our cause, that is to say, the cause of communism, will triumph all over the world. And on these grounds our opponents declare that the Soviet Union wants to have large armed forces to achieve its aim by force, that is to say, to dominate the world. That is also nonsense.

When we speak of the triumph of communism all over the world, we have in mind, first and foremost, the inevitable victory of communist ideas and the triumph of the Marxist-Leninist philosophy, the development of countries in accordance with objective laws that are independent of our will, laws which Marx and Lenin discovered. No armed forces—either conventional, or, still less so, atomic armaments—are necessary for the triumph of progressive ideas expressing the urgent demands of social development. If a theory is correct and reflects the laws of social development, it inevitably wins the minds of millions upon millions of people and becomes a mighty force in the struggle for the new and progressive. Socialist society offers better material and spiritual opportunities for the development of all men, and every man wishes only for the best. It is clear then that the ideas of socialism attract the working people.

We do not have to teach the British, for example, to effect a revolution and establish the socialist system in their country. They will do it themselves when they come to realize that the system which we have here, in the Soviet Union and in other socialist countries, presents greater advantages to the peoples than the capitalist system, that the socialist system offers unlimited possibilities and people are better able to show their worth.

Such is our point of view. Of course, the establishment of the socialist system does not proceed simultaneously, the various countries have their own peculiarities and there are different stages that depend on the level of development of this or that state. Besides, not only material but other factors are of great importance. We believe this to be the internal affair of every nation; the peoples themselves will decide the problems of social development. If the peoples decide to take the socialist road, let them do so and we shall only welcome it and sympathize with their wish, but if they have no such wish and prefer to retain the old forms of social life on a capitalist basis, we shall not make this an issue for war, nor can it be a source of conflict between the peoples.

We willingly maintain and shall continue to maintain friendly relations and business contacts beneficial to our people and to countries with a social system different from that of the Soviet Union. This is common knowledge and needs no proof. Our foreign policy, however, is at times crudely distorted. This is not due to misunderstanding but because there is a deliberate desire to misrepresent it. But truth is inescapable, truth is truth. Good and vigorous seed, even if it falls on bad soil and finds it hard to break through, will nevertheless break a way for itself and sprout. Not an army but peace is required to advance communist ideas, disseminate them and establish them in the minds of men.

Yes, we are convinced that our ideas will triumph. But victory for these ideas will not be won by war but by a higher standard of living under socialism and a higher level of culture, science and art, of everything required for the life and not for the death of man. Hydrogen bombs and rockets are powerless against this; neither Atlantic nor Baghdad pacts can hinder dissemination of the ideas of scientific communism, because the logic of life is inculcating them in the minds and hearts of men. When everyone sees that people in socialist countries live well, enjoy equal rights, have good housing—and we have now set ourselves the task of solving the housing problem within the next 10-12 years—that they are well fed and have the shortest working day because they are the owners of their plants and factories and no one exploits them; when people see that science develops faster and more successfully in these countries, that everyone who wishes can obtain higher education and finds application for his abilities in any sphere of mental or physical labour, that people enjoy every material benefit; when they see that as a result of the higher productivity of labour and the shorter working day man will have increasingly more free time to develop his talents and abilities and to take up the arts according to his inclination, then only an idiot, pardon the word, will oppose this.

This is the basis of our confidence and conviction in the inevitable triumph of communism. All people will inevitably come to this, but it is hard to say when. It is a long path and one must not advance towards communism by sowing death. On the contrary, communism is the most humane and the most philanthropic ideology. If the triumph of communism were to be gained by aggressive wars and the extermination of people, in that case I personally would oppose communism. We are intent on creating conditions of prosperity for the people, for the flourishing of material and spiritual culture, and we strive to preclude the possibility of wars between states and conflicts among people.

Soviet and British people live in different conditions; but why should we be hostile to the British or the Germans, or to the Negroes? Every nation and people create material and spiritual values and have specific features of development. The British are strong in their own sphere and manufacture goods that are needed by other countries, including ours; we also can and do produce goods in the manufacture of which we are superior to the British. Both they and we need these goods and thus there is absolutely no cause for hostility on those grounds.

When all the peoples, or most of them, reach communism there will be some kind of distribution of labour and duties among the peoples. This will not be competition but friendly co-operation and a rational distribution of forces, so as to produce, with the minimum expenditure, more goods to satisfy the vital needs of society and man. That is our ideal and purpose. Is war between nations necessary to achieve this aim?

But since the ruling circles of the Western Powers, blinded by hatred for our country and the other socialist countries and for our communist ideas, wish to destroy us, we are compelled to maintain armed forces to protect the gains of the peoples of our country. And if anyone attacks us it will be no easy military jaunt. If the attack against our country did not end in success for Mr. Churchill in 1918 and if it ended in disaster for Hitler and his régime, now that the Soviet Union is not alone and the mighty socialist camp, embracing almost 1,000 million people, is growing stronger, hopes of destroying the socialist countries by force are pure delirium. This is out of the question.

That is why we maintain powerful armed forces—they serve to cool the ardour of the imperialist madmen.

Some bourgeois politicians plan to impose a still more acute cold war on the Soviet Union, thereby make it spend more on armaments, and in this way weaken its economic potential and impede its development along peaceful lines. Despite the cold war policy, however, our country's rate of economic development greatly exceeds that of capitalist countries and will continue to exceed it. This is convincingly shown by the facts. The time is not far off when we shall overtake the most advanced capitalist states and outstrip them in per capita output. Everything now points to this, and when it has been achieved the indisputable superiority of the socialist system will be even more obvious to everyone.

Consequently, proceeding from the actual state of affairs and forecasts for the future, the Soviet Union is not interested in the arms race and the continuation of the cold war policy. We are for ending the cold war policy, for the establishment of the most sincere and friendly relations with all countries, for complete disarmament and the abolition of armed forces. But this, apparently, is something our partners are not yet prepared to do.

Figuratively speaking, policy-making reminds one of natural phenomena. It is 20 degrees below zero in Moscow today, for instance, but in some places in our country the temperature is even 50 or 60 degrees below zero. With the approach of spring, of course, the temperature rises gradually, the sun becomes hotter, little by little the snow melts and the spring floods begin, and this does not usually result in any calamities. But just imagine what would happen were the mercury to jump suddenly from 60 below zero to 25 above. There would be something like the "Deluge" and even good swimmers would be in danger of drowning.

In politics one must also sometimes abide by the rule of gradual transition and settle questions in several stages. Pressing problems of lesser complexity can be solved first, and later, when the "thaw" has set in, when conditions of greater confidence between states have been established, you can go on to the next stage, gradually introducing complete disarmament and establishing friendly relations between our countries. This is what our proposals amount to.

We stand for the complete and radical solution of disarmament problems, but we are aware that our partners are obviously not yet ready for this. Although we favour the establishment of friendly relations, we realize that it is impossible to rely on a mere word of honour. We do not trust our Western partners in everything, just as they do not have complete trust in us. Let us wait and see, let us pay each other more frequent visits, develop trade and thus prove that we are not "cannibals," that we partake of the same food as our partners.

I am replying so exhaustively to this first question because I regard it as a point of departure for others.

McDonald: I am very grateful for your exceptionally clear and exhaustive introduction.

Khrushchov: Please don't think I want to make a Communist of you, although I should regard it as a good deed if I were to succeed. I want you, who represent a different conception, a different philosophy, to understand us correctly and not to distort our views and our positions. That outstanding American journalist, John Reed, paved the way in 1917 to the objective understanding and description of our life in the West, and his book *Ten Days that Shook the World* was highly appreciated by Lenin and has now become very popular. This book will live on in the centuries.

It is a good thing when bourgeois journalists, engineers, writers and intellectuals of other circles accept communist views. But it is also very useful when honest-minded people from among the bourgeoisie—and there are a lot of them—correctly understand matters and objectively explain our policy. That is important and valuable for the establishment of proper understanding between countries with different social systems.

McDonald: Permit me to go over to the second question. The Soviet Government's statement says that suspension of nuclear tests does not involve any intricate control measures. However, Western statesmen insist that nuclear explosions can now be effected in such a way that their detection is impossible, and that strict control is therefore indispensable. Do you believe, Mr. Khrushchov, that nuclear bombs or other explosive mechanisms can be fired without this being noticed from a distance?

Khrushchov: I think it impossible because explosions will always be detected. And not only because explosions cause an earth tremor but also because an atom or hydrogen bomb explosion creates a very characteristic fall-out that shifts in the atmosphere as the earth rotates and leaves traces polluting the air. This makes it possible with the aid of special instruments, to find out what your neighbour is doing. When the first hydrogen bomb was exploded in the Soviet Union, the Americans correctly determined that it was not an atom but a hydrogen bomb. The scientists are well aware of this.

If the other countries believe that it is necessary to establish a control system when agreement is reached on ending nuclear tests, we are prepared to agree to this. But it is necessary to site the control posts wisely, both on our territory and in other countries, so as to deprive those who are against the elimination of the cold war of their argument that we oppose control because we want to continue clandestine nuclear weapons tests.

The Americans speak a great deal about the "clean" bomb. Frankly speaking, these statements do not promote the cause of disarmament and the ending of the cold war, but have the purpose of continuing the "positions of strength" policy. Honest-minded scientists of America, Britain and other countries have refuted the possibility of developing a "clean" hydrogen bomb. Scientists say that there can be no "clean" bomb since radioactive combustion products remain and these products of the disintegration of radioactive substances have a deadly effect on the human organism. Some time ago the Labour M.P.s in the House of Commons cleverly cornered the acting Prime Minister, Mr. Butler (whom we met during our British tour and with whom we were sure a reasonable understanding could be reached through negotiations). Mr. Butler said that if a plane accidentally releases a hydrogen bomb it will not explode since it is not charged. Then Mr. Bevan asked Mr. Butler whether it was possible to charge the hydrogen bomb in the air. Of course, Mr. Butler could not give an affirmative reply to this question for, indeed, how can an airman charge the hydrogen bomb in the air if he has no access to the bomb racks? A hydrogen bomb can be taken up only ready for action. Why fly with it at all if you have to land for charging? It is a dreadful thing to fly with "cocked" hydrogen bombs over peaceful cities! And yet, some influential quarters, even in your country, do not wish to solve the disarmament problem and are misleading public opinion.

I think that a policy associated with the flights of bombers laden with hydrogen bombs over Britain is, bluntly speaking, a stupid policy which it would be difficult even for such wise people as Mr. Butler to defend.

McDonald: I must say that in its articles our paper has opposed the flights of American bombers over our country.

Khrushchov: Such flights are dreadful. And arguments about the "clean" hydrogen bomb are inventions of the cold war proponents.

McDonald: With your permission I shall take up the third question. Would the Soviet Government be inclined to agree to a postponement of a summit conference to a later date than the one it proposed, "within the next two or three months," if this would make the conference more probable?

Khrushchov: We said "within the next two or three months" tentatively. If it is worth while, the date could be postponed. In this connection I recall the following incident: When a young man I worked as a fitter. At that time employers paid wages very irregularly—sometimes once in two or three months. I remember a notice posted up at one of the mines: "Pay at the end of the month"— without specifying in which year and which month.

And so we are anxious that a summit conference, too, should not be fixed for "the end of the month" without specifying either the month or the year.

McDonald: The fourth question. Would you still object, Mr. Khrushchov, to a Foreign Ministers' conference, even if such a conference were to confine itself to preparatory work for a summit meeting? Is it not a fact that some preparatory work is certainly necessary?

Khrushchov: Personally I have not denied and do not deny now the need for good preparation of a summit meeting. It would seem logical that the purpose of Foreign

Ministers is to deal with international problems. But if you have a baby you naturally want a good nurse, so that the baby does not injure its eyes or hands or does not develop bad habits. You choose a nurse with whom your baby will be safe. But if you were recommended a nurse who cannot guarantee the safety of your child, would you entrust its fate to her? Or, if you love flowers and employ a gardener to grow them, you would naturally try to get a gardener who is not only good at the job but also loves flowers and would lovingly tend and care for them.

Unfortunately, among Foreign Ministers there are some "gardeners" and "nurses" who make you fear for the fate of the flowers, for the fate of the child. In other words, we fear lest a summit meeting should die before it is born. Then it would not be the birth of a baby but a miscarriage. And that is what we fear. It is necessary to find such ways of preparing a summit meeting that would ensure against this happening. Perhaps a meeting should be prepared through diplomatic channels?

If the Foreign Ministers are to be regarded as midwives who should help bring the child into the world—and, as we understand it, such a child is the strengthening of peace, the elimination of international tension and cold war, greater mutual understanding and confidence among states—we have reasons to fear that among these midwives there are those who are not interested in the birth of a child that all mankind is awaiting.

McDonald: I should like to make one point finally clear. When you said before that in general you did not object to a Foreign Ministers' conference, did you mean that you did not object to such a conference despite the existence of bad "gardeners" and bad "nurses"?

Khrushchov: You do not understand me rightly. That is precisely what we want to avoid, we want to preclude the influence of those who oppose the establishment of a new spirit in the relations between countries. We want to provide conditions for the organization of a meeting and for the solution of problems which are urgent today. The solution of these problems could be a good beginning for the complete elimination of the cold war in the future. I am not sure that if the preparation of a summit meeting is entrusted to Foreign Ministers the solution of this question would not be prevented. So what should we do? Confront public opinion with such an outcome? That would be too hard on all the peoples, because they are awaiting good results and not the confirmation of evil.

McDonald: I raised this question, because it seemed that I had not understood you rightly. But even after a summit meeting, the Foreign Ministers evidently will have to get together anyhow, to carry out directives drawn up by the Heads of Government. Is it not possible that the results might be sabotaged even after the conference?

Khrushchov: Yes, it is possible in general. Even after a summit meeting the decisions reached could be sabotaged. But in physics there is the law of inertia. When, say, a ball is at rest one must apply a certain force to overcome the state of inertia and start the ball rolling. And once the ball is rolling, it is necessary to apply a certain force to stop it. We want a summit meeting to be that force which would move international relations out of their present state, because this would offer greater hope for the achievement of positive decisions. After a summit meeting the Ministers could continue their work, but then it would be more difficult for them to raise obstacles, they would have to reckon with public opinion.

If the peoples decide that the cold war must be eliminated, no power on earth will be able to prevent that and a solution to this problem will certainly be found. Those who object to the elimination of the cold war are well aware of this and that is why they fear a meeting of Heads of Government, they fear the achievement of positive results at a summit meeting. It is a fact that public opinion would grasp at the initial positive results and would exert still stronger pressure in order to ensure a continuous improvement in international relations. The enemies of peace, in contradiction to the facts, continually present the Soviet Union as some kind of evil spirit, allege that the Soviet Union does not keep its word, that it cannot be trusted, etc. But the peoples are sick of such talk, they are beginning to ignore it. Obviously a summit meeting will definitely take place.

McDonald: In this connection, Mr. Khrushchov, I should like to ask you a question about the Rapacki plan. As is known, the Soviet Government is in favour of establishing an "atom-free zone" in Europe, which would include both parts of Germany as well as Poland and Czechoslovakia. Do you mean that rockets for short-range fighting, tactical rockets, as well as rockets with a longer range, the so-called intermediate-range rockets, would also be banned in this zone? If so, could this plan be combined with an agreement to reduce conventional armed forces in this zone, in order to achieve a more equal distribution of armed forces in both parts of Germany, or should this plan be regarded quite separately, having in view tactical atomic weapons—missiles and rockets?

Khrushchov: We do not preclude that. The idea is to solve not a narrow but a broader range of problems. We stand for full disarmament, and the further we advance in that direction at the first stage, the easier it would be to attain the final objectives. So this is no problem to us. We are ready to agree to the complete banning of atomic and hydrogen weapons, to complete disarmament, to a complete withdrawal of troops and the closing down of foreign bases on the territories of other states. We know that our partners are not prepared for such a solution and for this reason we have proposed that these problems be solved gradually, by stages. As regards the stage our partners are ready to go to, you must ask them; we do not know As for us, we are prepared to discuss and solve disarmament problems in their broadest aspect.

To make my point more clear I would say the following:

the doctors at first treat a man emaciated by a grave illness gradually and prescribe food for him in small doses. If more were given the patient, it might kill him. And so we want to begin disarmament not with a full dose, although we are prepared even for a full dose. I have said already that the Western Powers have shown great distrust of us and we, too, do not trust them in everything. And so, in order not to wreck something of great and vital importance to mankind—disarmament—we suggest beginning not with a cardinal but with a gradual solution of disarmament problems, beginning with what offers hope, inspires confidence. Thus, step by step, gradually, it would be possible to reach the main goal, that is, the full solution of the disarmament problem.

McDonald: I fully agree that this is really the only way to solve the problem.

Now I should like to ask a question about the Middle East. Does Mr. Khrushchov think that a one- or two-year moratorium on arms deliveries to this area from all sources would be useful as a preliminary step to the relaxation of tension? We made this point in our paper.

Khrushchov: That is a reasonable way. When we were in London, in a personal conversation with Mr. Lloyd, and also at a press conference, we spoke of the expediency of discontinuing arms deliveries to the Middle East by both sides. We had that conversation with Mr. Lloyd in a car on the way to Chequers. But evidently our conversations failed to make a proper impression on British statesmen and the British Government did not change its opinion. The outcome, as you know, was the unpleasant incident if you may call it such, which occurred in Suez and which had tragic consequences for the people.

Evidently there must not only be a moratorium on arms deliveries to the Middle East but also an agreement on non-intervention in the affairs of Arab states so that their sovereignty and independence be recognized. All this must be done in such a way as not to make the Arab countries think that we are proclaiming a moratorium in order to leave them unarmed and permit the aggressive forces of other states to interfere in the internal affairs of Arab states or attack them with impunity and deprive them of their independence. That would be a bad and harmful act. This should be foreseen and precluded.

McDonald: Do you mean a moratorium conditional upon an agreement on non-aggression and the renunciation of hostile actions of any kind?

Khrushchov: Exactly. If we simply proclaim a moratorium the Arabs might think that the Soviet Union has changed its policy and is renouncing the principles we have proclaimed and are unwaveringly carrying out. Our principles stem from the United Nations Charter: we stand for the sovereignty and independence of the Arab states, for non-interference of other states in the internal affairs of these countries, and so forth.

McDonald: Does Mr. Khrushchov think that the Soviet Union could at present contribute to the establishment of peace between the Arab states and Israel, or that the moment is not propitious?

Khrushchov: We think that if the Great Powers would not interfere, the Arab countries and Israel themselves would more quickly achieve mutual understanding and reach agreement on their relations. This would help bring peace to this area and help find ways to eliminate the tension now existing there. If any outside interference were attempted now, it would hardly be useful because relations there are exceptionally strained. Obviously, Israeli statesmen themselves should give more thought to the concrete conditions existing there, should take into account the interests of the Arab world, interests which Israel not only frequently does not consider but even openly ignores, adopting an arrogant attitude towards the Arab countries.

McDonald: When the Soviet Government in its statement of January 8 speaks about the need for eliminating all kinds of interference in the internal affairs of the Middle Eastern countries, does it regard the functioning of oil companies as interference?

Khrushchov: We believe that if it is done on a mutually profitable commercial basis, it is, naturally, a business deal. Therefore, far from being a hindrance, it is inevitable. We said so in London during our talks with Sir Anthony Eden, Mr. Lloyd, Mr. Butler and other British statesmen. When Sir Anthony Eden spoke about the importance of oil for Britain, our attitude to the question was one of understanding. And today we also realize full well that the British economy cannot do without oil. This would retard the development of British economy, affect Britain's vital interests and lower the living standard of the British people. This is not what we want. We have never thought of preventing Britain from obtaining raw materials, including oil, from the countries of the Middle East or from other countries. And we ourselves are ready to trade with you on a broader basis. The only question is—on what basis?

McDonald: Now a question concerning the internal development of the Soviet Union. Would Mr. Khrushchov be so kind as to explain what seems to us to be the increased role which is assigned here to the Central Committee of the Party. Does the appointment of a greater number of secretaries of the Party indicate the increasing role of the Central Committee of the Communist Party?

Khrushchov: You understand this question correctly. Yes, the changes you have mentioned indicate the constantly growing role of the Communist Party in the life of our country and, obviously, this role will continue to grow. In the Soviet Union a certain change is taking place in the ways and means of administrative ties that formerly existed between districts, regions and republics. At the same time the ideological ties between regions and republics are being extended and strengthened making for a further consolidation of the unity of the Soviet people. A decisive role in this belongs to the Communist Party and the role of the Party is increasing. The peoples of our country form a single closely-knit family, welded together by unity of political views, unity of political aims, by common vital interests. Each Soviet Republic, proceeding from the common tasks confronting the Soviet Union, solves its own problems with due consideration paid to its own specific features. In our opinion, the solution of economic and administrative problems is the internal affair of each republic, each people.

The mutual relations between the peoples of our country are in a state of continuous development. Changes are also occurring in the various functions of the state. The process of change in these functions results from our concepts, from the theoretical postulates of Marxism-Leninism on the state. When the conditions for the transition to communist society are created in our country, many organs of state administration will gradually wither away. Thus the army, the court, the Prosecutor's office and other organs will wither away.

The court is obviously destined to outlive the army and other bodies of administrative control. The court will continue to exist, in a different form, of course, because there will still be conflicts of different kinds between people and there must be some kind of arbiter to settle these conflicts.

I do not intend to forecast changes in our society over a lengthy period, but already today social life is developing precisely along the lines that emerge from the theoretical principles of Marxism-Leninism. And so, under these conditions, in order to make the most rational use of available material and other resources, the Party's role is increasing. The Party has a stronger foundation than the government bodies. It grew up and exists not as a result of some obligations of a legislative kind. Its development is conditioned by the political views of people, that is, from propositions of a moral factor. And humanity will always need moral factors.

McDonald: Finally, my last question. Is Mr. Khrushchov satisfied with the progress of the reorganization of management in industry and building? Has this stimulated in practice greater initiative on the part of Party members on the spot?

Khrushchov: I am more than satisfied. I am delighted. It has far surpassed our boldest hopes and expectations.

McDonald: I have had many talks in Moscow and Irkutsk with representatives of economic councils. These talks make it clear that they are very much satisfied. Besides, I have seen for myself that things are going well.

Khrushchov: As a result of the reorganization of management in industry and building, our forces have grown considerably, and industry and agriculture are now operating much better than before. Now that we are reorganizing the machine and tractor stations, we shall ensure better incentives for the development of our economy, particularly agriculture.

All this is easily explained. Previously work of industrial undertakings and agriculture in this country was influenced chiefly by administrative action. The forces of the Party, trade unions and the Young Communist League did not operate with all the energy of which they are capable. Now, with decentralization of industrial management the guidance of industry and construction has been transferred to the localities, nearer to the plants and the building sites. That is why the impact of Party, trade-union and Y.C.L. organizations on the work of enterprises has grown immeasurably. These organizations have become more active and are showing greater initiative and their responsibility for the fulfilment of the plans has increased. Besides, the plans themselves are being drawn up with the obligatory participation of the enterprises concerned. This is a subject on which much can be said. But to make it short I must stress that we have had exceptionally good results from the measures taken to reorganize management in industry and building. It is naturally very difficult to manage the industry of the whole country from one centre, from a Ministry in Moscow. A Minister had to be greater than God because he had to know everything and see everything that was being done, for example, in Sakhalin, Kamchatka, Baku or Armenia. That is impossible. Now we have transferred the solution of these problems of operating plants to the localities, and this is all to the good.

McDonald: The improvements in your agriculture are really tremendous.

Khrushchov: They will be even greater. We overcame stagnation in agriculture by taking certain steps in September 1953. Then we amended certain laws and created better conditions for agricultural development, and it began to develop rapidly and grow.

The same goes for international affairs. If we succeed in overcoming the stalemate in the current relations between our states, and primarily between the Soviet Union, the United States, Britain, France and other countries, if we begin to develop mutually advantageous trade, improve cultural, sports and other ties between the countries, it will have a favourable effect on the improvement of relations between countries as well as on the internal situation in those countries. A reduction in the armed forces and in expenditures on armaments will create greater possibilities for raising living standards. If we succeed in moving the relations between our countries out of the deadlock in which they now stand, and succeed in turning them towards eliminating the cold war, this alone will be a great thing. Naturally, there will at first be no agreement on complete disarmament. But I foresee that the tendency towards unilateral disarmament could be strengthened because when people realize that the danger of war has passed, states possessing large armed forces will strive to reduce them, to release manpower and vast material resources to develop their economy, in order to prove the advantages of this or that state system in peaceful competition, in competition to raise living standards in their countries. This is a very good road—without blood, without fear for the people. This is what every man and mankind as a whole live for.

McDonald: I would like to thank you sincerely, Mr. Khrushchov, for your detailed and comprehensive replies to my questions. I fear that I have taken up an enormous amount of your time. I thank you once again for having been given the opportunity to talk with you, and assure you that everything you have said will be highly useful for the development of understanding between our countries.

Khrushchov: I am glad that you are satisfied with the interview. Commercially speaking, I hope that the time spent on the interview will yield high interest.

In conclusion I should like to stress once again that we wish to be correctly understood—we firmly stand for peace and peaceful co-existence.

McDonald: I hope to have the honour, Mr. Khrushchov, of seeing you once again in London or at a summit conference in Geneva. I hope that such a conference will be held.

Khrushchov: I also hope that such a conference will certainly be held.

Pravda, February 16, 1958

REPLIES
TO QUESTIONS PUT BY MANUEL MEJIDO, CORRESPONDENT OF MEXICAN NEWSPAPER *EXCELSIOR*

February 21, 1958

Manuel Mejido, correspondent of the Mexican newspaper *Excelsior,* submitted a series of questions to N. S. Khrushchov, First Secretary of the Central Committee of the Communist Party of the Soviet Union. On February 21, N. Khrushchov received Mr. Mejido and replied to his questions.

The questions and answers are printed below.

Question: How do you envisage the conclusion of economic agreements between the Soviet Union and the Latin American countries—goods exchange, loans or only direct purchases? What other forms of economic exchange might there be with these countries? If there is trade with some of them, what is its scale, can it be increased, and how?

Answer: The trade policy of the Soviet Union derives from the necessity for the all-round development of international economic contacts since these are important not only from the standpoint of normal trade between countries, but above all because they facilitate normal political relations and promote confidence between states.

We are for any of the forms of economic exchange practised in international trade, provided the principle of equality and mutual benefit is observed and all forms of restriction and discrimination rejected. So, given good will and the desire on both sides, it should be easy to find forms of economic relations acceptable alike to the Soviet Union and the Latin American countries. The point is not the form, but the essence; the main thing is the desire to conduct trade on conditions of equality and mutual benefit.

At the moment we are trading with a number of Latin American countries. And although there has been some expansion since the war, the level is still not satisfactory. Many opportunities for expansion remain unused. In particular, the Soviet Union could supply these countries with a wide range of machines and plant needed for their industrialization, as well as raw materials, in exchange for the traditional Latin American exports.

Our greatest trade in Latin America at present is with Argentina and Uruguay. The Soviet Union has concluded pertinent trade and payment agreements with these countries. I can tell you, for example, that trade between the U.S.S.R. and Argentina during the past four years was in the vicinity of $180 million. We could have had an equal volume of trade with other Latin American countries given favourable conditions—normal diplomatic and trade relations.

Question: Has the Soviet Union any plan to effect a closer rapprochement with the Latin American nations in the trade, cultural and political spheres, and also in the spheres of economy and tourist travel?

Answer: The Soviet Union on the basis of its policy of peace and the principle of peaceful co-existence, is willing to establish normal diplomatic, trade, cultural and other relations with those countries with which, for one reason or another, such relations have not yet been established.

Our people are keenly interested in the rich and ancient culture of the Latin American nations. We are ready to enter into the broadest cultural contacts with them, ready to extend our sports contacts, tourist travel, etc.

Question: Will not the economic competition which, as I understand it, peaceful co-existence presupposes, endanger the successful realization of this international peaceful co-existence?

Answer: When we speak of peaceful co-existence we

have in mind co-existence between the socialist and capitalist countries. And this not only admits but also presupposes the solution of differences and contradictions between them by means of peaceful competition and, first and foremost, economic competition, or if you like, contest. What does economic competition imply? We understand it as competition in the sphere of peaceful production, a contest between the two systems—socialism and capitalism—in making life better for the people, in raising living standards.

What can hinder peaceful co-existence? Here, I think, there can be no two opinions: war and the preparation of war. The cold war, arms drive, propaganda of war, enmity and hatred between nations, trade discrimination and undermining of world commerce—all add to the danger of another devastating war and, consequently, endanger peaceful co-existence between the nations. You, of course, realize that should the imperialists resort to war, then, in view of the nature of modern armaments, the consequences for the people would be calamitous. As matters stand at present there is no place in the world where the population can be sure they will be immune from military action, not only the belligerent armies will suffer, but peaceful cities with a peaceful population will suffer as well.

We in all sincerity say to the capitalist countries, let us compete not in making the largest number of H-bombs and missiles, for that is a competition which bodes no good to the peoples, but in building more houses, schools and hospitals, produce more grain, milk, meat, clothes and other consumer goods. That is the kind of competition the people want. Instead of the slogan "Let us arm!" we proclaim "Let us trade!"

Although the Soviet Union has made significant progress in all spheres, and in raising the standard of living of the people as well, it has set itself the goal of producing more consumer goods than any capitalist country. And we are confident that under these conditions we shall achieve a still higher standard of living. How can this endanger peaceful co-existence of nations? The imperialists fear such a competition, while we are eager that each system—socialist and capitalist—should demonstrate its superiority not on the war front, but on the front of peaceful labour.

Far from endangering peaceful co-existence, economic competition would, on the contrary, strengthen it, safeguard the nations against the danger of another war and contribute to the improvement of their living conditions in a state of peace.

Question: What is the attitude of the Soviet Government to the liberation of the countries traditionally colonial?

Answer: We, Soviet people, whole-heartedly sympathize with the yearning of the colonial peoples to throw off the shackles of slavery and the yoke of the imperialist Powers.

The Soviet Union is a multi-national country in which the relations between the peoples are based on equality and friendship; hence, Soviet people simply loathe national oppression. We know the price of freedom: our peoples, particularly in Transcaucasia and Central Asia, were once forced to wage a long and bitter struggle before they won national liberation and established their own national states as equal republics in the Union of Soviet Socialist Republics. It is natural, therefore, that the national-liberation struggle of the colonial nations should evoke the warm sympathy of our peoples.

Today, we see how more than 1,500 million people in Africa and Asia have taken the road of independent development. In some places the colonial Powers, forced under pressure of the national-liberation movement to recognize the formal independence of one or another country, still retain a strong economic grip on them. But this will not be the case for long. Having attained political independence, these young countries are striving to build up their own economy, strengthening their economic independence of the foreign monopolies. True, this process is taking place not without struggle and not without difficulties, but ultimately these countries will triumph over the difficulties.

The Soviet Union deeply sympathizes with all the nations striving to win and uphold their right to independence. And these nations can rest assured that the Soviet Union, without any meddling in their internal affairs, without stipulating any conditions, will help them to strengthen the independence for which they fought so hard. In the economic sphere, for example, they no longer need bow before their former enslavers. They can now get industrial plant, machinery and technical documents on mutually beneficial conditions from the socialist countries. Our country has already extended disinterested help to the Afro-Asian nations in developing their economies and culture, and, furthermore, this help is given without any political or military strings attached. I think that the people of Mexico fully appreciate the difference between this kind of help and the "aid" of the imperialist states which binds the economy of the small countries hand and foot and which leads to the loss of that which is dearest to the nations—their freedom and independence.

And the other nations now battling valiantly against colonial oppression can always rely on our moral and political support, in particular on support within the framework of the United Nations.

Question: Would you care to comment on any other matter?

Answer: I avail myself of this opportunity to convey to the people of Mexico through the medium of your paper my respects and sincere friendship and wish them success and prosperity. The Soviet people have a sympathetic attitude to the courageous people of Mexico and are deeply interested in their unique and ancient culture. We hold the view that the relations between the Soviet Union and Mexico should continue to be further improved and strengthened for the benefit of our peoples and peace.

International Affairs, No. 4, 1958

LETTER TO BERTRAND RUSSELL

March 5, 1958

The British philosopher, Bertrand Russell, addressed an Open Letter to N. S. Khrushchov and President Eisenhower, which was published in the London *New Statesman* of November 23, 1957. Khrushchov's reply was published in the *New Statesman* of December 21, 1957.

Both Russell's Open Letter and Khrushchov's reply were published in No. 1 of *International Affairs* for 1958.

The U.S. Secretary of State, John Foster Dulles, wrote a reply to Bertrand Russell on behalf of the U.S. President which was published in the *New Statesman* of February 8, 1958.

On March 5, 1958, Khrushchov sent a second letter to Bertrand Russell which the *New Statesman* published on March 14.

It is published below.

Mr. KINGSLEY MARTIN, THE EDITOR, *NEW STATESMAN*

Dear Mr. Editor,

On February 8 you published the letter by Mr. Dulles, the U.S. Secretary of State, sent on behalf of the U.S. President in reply to the Open Letter of Professor Bertrand Russell addressed to President Eisenhower and myself.

In so far as Mr. Dulles' letter contains distortions and inaccuracies concerning Soviet foreign policy, and also in so far as Mr. Dulles comments upon a number of points made in my reply to Lord Russell published in your journal in an extremely arbitrary fashion, I felt it necessary to address a second Open Letter to professor Bertrand Russell.

Since many readers of your journal clearly read Lord Russell's letter and my reply, and also that of Mr. Dulles, I would ask you to be so kind as to publish my second letter to Lord Russell.

Yours faithfully,
N. KHRUSHCHOV

March 5, 1958

N. S. KHRUSHCHOV'S LETTER TO BERTRAND RUSSELL

Dear Lord Russell,

I see that the *New Statesman* on February 8 published a letter from Mr. John Foster Dulles, which he wrote on behalf of the U.S. President in reply to your Open Letter addressed to myself and Mr. Dwight D. Eisenhower, President of the United States.

I had no intention of writing you a second letter, as in my letter of December 7 I had already set out my views on the important international problems you had touched upon. However, after carefully reading Mr. Dulles' letter in which he comments extensively and, regrettably, in a most peculiar way, on the Soviet Union's attitude and on my letter to you, the idea occurred to me to write you this letter. Naturally, it will deal with Mr. Dulles' letter.

To read Mr. Dulles' letter and remain silent—would not that be tantamount to agreeing, to some extent, with what he writes? It is, however, impossible to agree—completely impossible—for in the heat of argument Mr. Dulles has been so carried away that he has completely lost any basis of real facts and has begun to build his arguments on his emotions and deductions. But deductions based on emotions, even if they come from a person of such strong convictions as Mr. Dulles, do not acquire the weight of facts.

Emotions are always emotions. The logic of facts is an entirely different matter. I have always been attracted rather by the logic of facts, and not by the logic of emotional deductions.

One cannot but agree with Mr. Dulles that the world in which we live is made of sterner stuff than mere words. So much combustible material has now been accumulated that it needs only a single spark to cause disaster. Such is the situation in the world that as a result of just one absurd incident or a defect in the equipment of a single plane carrying a hydrogen bomb, or the slightest deviation from the normal in the mentality of a pilot at the controls, war can become a fact this very day.

To Mr. Dulles, I should like to say that we are both getting on in years. I don't know about him, but during the Second World War it fell to my lot to see the death of many of my comrades and the devastation of entire towns. Believe me, it was a terrible thing. But that was in wartime. Today, while the British people sleep peacefully in their beds, a horrible death constantly hovers over their heads, borne not by enemy planes but by bombers carrying U.S. atom and hydrogen bombs.

Probably Mr. Dulles regards this circumstance differently from the way I regard it, and it awakens no protest from him; but I—and I am not alone—cannot speak of this without indignation. My entire being protests against such criminal playing with fire. And just think— for the sake of what? They say for the sake of security and as a defence against possible attack. What attack do they have in mind? It turns out that what they are thinking of is defence against a possible Soviet attack.

To such people one can only say:

"Come to your senses, gentlemen—what makes you think that the Soviet Union intends to attack the Western Powers? Why do you deceive your own people?"

I often wonder what kind of logic it is that some of the leaders of the Western countries apply. If the Soviet Union says that there should be an immediate ending of nuclear weapons tests in view of the danger threatening mankind, we are told: "That's propaganda." If the Soviet Union suggests that a summit conference be called to examine urgent problems—we are accused of trying to weaken the Western world. If the Soviet Union proposes the disbanding of all military blocs and the dismantling of all military bases, we are accused of wanting to set the Western allies "against one another," and so on.

In everything connected with the Soviet Union Mr. Dulles tries to see "communist propaganda."

Let us examine calmly and soberly some of the most important aspects of the present international situation.

If we base ourselves on facts, we have to admit that in the world today there are two world systems—the new, socialist system, and the old, capitalist system. Each is developing in accordance with its own inherent laws. And these systems were not born today or yesterday.

Prior to October 1917, one system—the capitalist system—held undivided sway in the world. This system had asserted itself in the struggle against the system of feudal serfdom and had replaced that system practically everywhere on our planet. If you take a look at history you will soon become convinced that the new system was disliked by many at the time. History, however, did its job.

As a result of the victory of the working class in Russia, a new state, a workers' and peasants' state, was born—the Soviet Republic. A new, socialist system was created over one-sixth of our planet. Even those who dislike this system cannot but admit that the people themselves have now become the complete masters of all their country's wealth, with full rights to build their own life.

This is how the new ideology founded by Karl Marx and Vladimir Ilyich Lenin triumphed in practice.

I foresee that Mr. Dulles will once again say: "More propaganda." Please understand me, Lord Russell, I have no intention whatsoever of making propaganda. I am compelled to speak of these things because Mr. Dulles, in interpreting them in his own way, has given them a most peculiar slant.

There was no festive peal of bells to welcome the birth of the new, socialist world in Russia—only volleys from the guns aimed against the victorious people. Fourteen foreign countries launched a bloody crusade against the Land of Soviets. Tell me, on what grounds did they invade our country and attempt to drown the newly-born Soviet socialist state in rivers of blood? They did not like Soviet power and they planned to put a noose round the people's neck. Is it to be wondered at that the peoples of the Soviet land swept the interventionists from their soil, as a good housewife sweeps the rubbish from her home?

And then came the time for peaceful work, to furnish our house in a way that suited our people. And we all worked, oblivious of self, relying on no one, asking help from nobody—doing everything ourselves. It was hard, for we were creating a society never before known in history. Everything was done to hinder us and spanners were thrown into the works, but Soviet men and women went resolutely forward, regardless of everything. For a long time the Soviet Union was the only socialist country.

And then, in 1939, the Second World War broke out. You know how that ended. The peoples in a whole number of countries in Europe and Asia refused to tolerate any longer a system that had brought them war and disaster. They threw out the unwanted governments which had betrayed the peoples, and set up in their countries the system of people's democracy; they followed the socialist path of development.

The Communists, who had devoted their lives to the cause of the people and who had always been in the very midst of the people, flesh and blood of the people—those Communists who, together with their people, had experienced all the hardships and misfortunes and in every respect had set an example of loyal service to their country's interests—naturally proved worthy of the people's great trust. The victorious people of the socialist countries saw in practice that they were worthy of the people's confidence.

What is the strength of the Communists, and where does it come from? Their strength lies in their unbreakable ties with the people. It is well known that, during the February Revolution, our Party had between 40,000 and 45,000 members in tsarist Russia. But the Party grew rapidly. At the time of the April Conference, it already had 80,000 members; in August, by the 6th Congress, 240,000, while on the eve of the October Revolution the Party membership had grown to 400,000. The best sons and daughters of the people joined the Party. What could the Communists have done in a country with a population of more than 100 million, had they not relied on the people, enjoyed their support, and expressed their cherished ideas and aspirations?

The Communist Party was the beacon which illumined the path to victory for the workers and peasants. The Communists helped the people, the disinherited and exploited men and women, to remove the scales from their eyes. The people themselves stepped into the arena of history and proclaimed their legitimate rights.

And eventually this will happen in other countries. This is what will happen both in the United States and in Britain, though there are no Soviet Communists there, nor will there be. Such is the relentless course of historical development, which no one can halt.

We are confident that the ideas of communism will find a way to reach the minds of the peoples, for Marxism-Leninism corresponds to the most vital interests of the working class—and not only of the working class. The working class is more receptive of the ideas of communism because the very conditions of capitalism have prepared it to receive them, but it acts in the interests of the people as a whole, in the interests of historical progress.

Communists enjoy citizenship rights in their country on an equal footing with persons who do not belong to the Party. In times of military misfortunes and hardships they voluntarily bear the brunt of those hardships and misfortunes, setting a personal example of heroism, steadfastness and self-sacrificing work.

That is what Communists are. They are united in the Party by communist ideals and by unshakable belief in the triumph of the communist society, in which there will be no oppression of man by man, or of nation by nation, and where the whole of society will consist of working people enjoying equal rights, in which nations will form one united and harmonious family, regardless of colour of skin or language.

Well, is it the Communists who impose their rule on the peoples, and not the handful of millionaires and billionaires who have concentrated in their own hands all the main wealth of their countries, who have subordinated to their service the state, the army, the law courts, the police, and a mighty propaganda machine in the shape of countless papers and magazines, radio and television, clubs and entertainment establishments?

These are the facts, which Mr. Dulles has forgotten in his letter to you, dear Lord Russell. He prefers to allege that the Communists are imposing their will, their rule, on the people, and to remain silent about facts which are obvious to everyone, such as the fact that the monopolists of a whole number of "democratic" countries not only hold in the grip of their capital the mass of the people in their own countries, but also mercilessly exploit millions upon millions in colonial and dependent countries.

What explanation, other than a desire to mislead the readers, can there be for the fact that Mr. Dulles deliberately confuses questions concerning the class struggle in individual countries with questions concerning relations between the capitalist and socialist countries? I do not think this is the result of ignorance. No! Who knows better than Mr. Dulles that the class struggle in every capitalist country is the result of internal economic and political factors? The U.S. workers' struggle to improve their conditions and defend their rights takes a different course from that of the Italian workers, let us say, or the French. The struggle of the American farmers similarly differs from that of the Spanish peasants, although both are striving for a better life, striving to abolish the glaring injustice whereby the fruits of their labour are appropriated by a small handful of persons possessing power and wealth.

Mr. Dulles distorts Soviet foreign policy, the policy of the Communist Party of the Soviet Union. Who today does not realize that the people of each country decide their own social system? The peoples themselves decide how they are to achieve the triumph of a system in which the men and women who create all the material wealth necessary for the development of society should have the best material and spiritual opportunities for their life, so that the products of their labour be fairly distributed among the workers and not appropriated by owners of enterprises, by financial magnates—that is to say, so that there should be no exploitation of man by man. In the capitalist countries, the working people are waging a struggle against those who exploit and plunder them. They are struggling for the reorganization of society.

In his attempt to mislead people who are insufficiently informed on political questions Mr. Dulles distorts the Declaration of the Communist and Workers' Parties. What does this Declaration say?

"The forms of the transition from capitalism to socialism may vary for different countries. The working class and its vanguard—the Marxist-Leninist Party—seek to achieve the socialist revolution by peaceful means. This would accord with the interests of the working class and the entire people, with the national interests of the country. . . .

"In the event of the exploiting classes resorting to violence against the people, the possibility of non-peaceful transition to socialism should be borne in mind. . . . In this case the degree of bitterness and the forms of the class struggle will depend not so much on the proletariat as on the resistance put up by the reactionary circles to the will of the overwhelming majority of the people, on these circles using force at one or another stage of the struggle for socialism.

"The possibility of one or another way to socialism depends on the concrete historical conditions in each country."

That is what is said in the Declaration which Mr. Dulles interprets so freely and tendentiously. He depicts the ideological class struggle in the capitalist countries as the result of the activity of the Communist Party of the Soviet Union. We have said, and we continue to say, that the Communists in the Soviet Union sympathize with the struggle of the workers in the capitalist countries for their liberation from the yoke of monopoly capital, but we have never imposed our ideology on anyone nor do we intend to do so, least of all by force of arms. Mr. Dulles is fully aware of this and yet he asserts the opposite.

In his speeches, Mr. Dulles had frequently tried, for propaganda purposes, to use the Hungarian events against the Soviet Union. Since he refers to them again in his letter to you, Lord Russell, I must examine this question in substance, at least briefly. The essence of the matter is that in Hungary the Horthy elements, the agents of foreign monopoly capital, tried to overthrow the people's democratic order, to restore the hated fascist régime. The handful of fascist conspirators and imperialist agents were followed by a small number of misguided honest people.

In pursuing their anti-popular aims, the enemies of socialist Hungary took advantage of mistakes made by the former Hungarian leaders. The conspirators provoked a rebellion against the legitimate Government of the Hungarian People's Republic, which the people had elected on a constitutional basis. To declare that these Horthy elements were expressing the will of the people is to present black as white.

The Hungarian Government had every right to appeal for help, and the Soviet Government, on the basis of the agreement existing between our two countries, gave assistance to Hungary—in the interests of the Hungarian people and of all the peoples of Europe and the whole world—to prevent the return of the Horthy régime and to put an end to the fascist violence that had begun in Hungary. The Soviet Union's help to fraternal Hungary was given on legitimate grounds, and it was justified from every point of view. If the counter-revolution had succeeded in establishing a fascist régime in Hungary, it would have been a tremendous disaster for the peoples of Europe—and not of Europe alone, for it could have led to tragic events similar to those which followed the fascist seizure of power in Germany, Italy, Hungary, Austria and Spain, which caused the peoples so much disaster, bloodshed and tears—including the peoples of the United States, Britain and France.

In the last war our countries were allies, fighting jointly against bloody fascism. It is in the interests of the peoples, in the interests of peace, to prevent the rise of fascism.

It is clear that the Hungarian events were dragged in artificially by Mr. Dulles to confirm his argument that the Soviet Union interferes in the internal affairs of other countries.

In discussing the Hungarian events, it must also be pointed out that the old class that has outlived its time does not voluntarily give way to the new. The whole course of history clearly demonstrates this. The feudal system gave way to the capitalist system which replaced it only after a fierce struggle. If we examine, for instance, the history of the rise of the United States of America as an independent state, we shall see that it was born of a fierce struggle for freedom from colonial domination. When they rose up in struggle for their independence, the Americans did not ask the permission of the English. They drove the colonialists out and in the course of this struggle created their own state, the United States of America.

The Soviet Union also arose as the result of the struggle of the peoples of former tsarist Russia against the bankrupt capitalist system. The Soviet people swept away all oppressors and foreign interventionists and, arms in hand, voted for Soviet power. How could the new system be consolidated in our country, in the People's Democracies, without a self-sacrificing struggle by the working people against the power of the capitalists and landlords?

The people of the Soviet Union, of the Chinese People's Republic, of all the People's Democracies, won their freedom in stern struggle; they have become the creators of the new and most democratic society, in which there is no exploitation of man by man. Judge for yourself, Lord Russell, how objective and convincing is Mr. Dulles' assertion that nowhere in the world does the Communist Party maintain its rule except by forcibly imposing that rule upon the majority.

I cannot help but draw attention to Mr. Dulles' exhortation that power should be exercised only when "this reflected the freely given consent of the governed." This is precisely the stand we Communists take, and we fight for this, for it is the people who are the determining force, their will is sacred, it is their interests that the governments should express if they are really worth anything. In our opinion, it is not the people who must serve the government, but the government which must serve the people.

Perhaps I am saying things which Mr. Dulles does not like. However, I prefer speaking sharply but truthfully to speaking politely but falsely.

Take the Government of the Soviet Union, let us say, or any other socialist country, and compare its composition with that of the Government of the United States of America or any other capitalist country. Who is in power in the one and in the other? The position is so obvious that I don't think there is any need for me to enlarge upon it. In the Soviet Union and in the other socialist countries the members of the government, the leaders in all bodies of state power, cannot but serve the interests of the people, for the very reason that they come from the people, they form part of the people, have been put forward by the people.

As far as the bodies both of executive and legislative powers in the capitalist countries are concerned, though Mr. Dulles tries to convince us that "the governed entrust them with government," it is just the opposite. Who does not know that "people of capital" and "adherents of capital" rule there? It would be interesting to hear what Mr. Dulles would say if he were to be asked whose interests were defended by the Rockefellers and the men in their service. How can the class interests of the billionaires be the same as the interests of the workers? Who can believe that the "governed," that is the people, elect the bodies of power in the capitalist countries by their own choice, in accordance with their own interests?

One can only wonder how it comes about that, after all these so-called "free elections," it is as a rule not workers who are in power in the capitalist countries, but men of capital, not those who by their toil create the material and spiritual values, but those who possess the money with which to buy these values.

No, Mr. Dulles, such "miracles" do not happen, and

things are fairly simple. You speak of "force and violence" by the Communist parties, but you know far better
what the force of capital, the violence of capital, are. This
is well known by the workers, the small peasants, the
clerks, the handicraftsmen, the entire working people, who
have themselves experienced it, and who, therefore, know
how to measure the sincerity of Mr. Dulles' "indignation"
regarding the "violence" of the Communists.

Mr. Dulles calls for submission to the tenets of the moral law on which his creed is based, and anathematizes
the tenets of the moral law on which the communist ideology is based, particularly that "variety of communism"
which is espoused by the Soviet Communist Party. And
here Mr. Dulles makes reference to Marx, Lenin and Stalin. For this reason I take the liberty of again drawing
your attention to certain facts.

Mankind has continued for 1,957 years since the birth
of Christ alone, but how many thousands of years had it
existed before our system of chronology? And, as long as
mankind has existed, so long have there been wars. They
were waged by men long before the word communism
ever came into existence, let alone the term "dictatorship
of the proletariat."

On what moral law were those wars based? If we were
to follow Mr. Dulles' logic, who but the Communists are
to blame for those wars? But Marxism, as a theory, has
existed for only just over a hundred years, while the first
socialist state created on the basis of communist ideology
has only been in existence for 40 years!

Recall the Crusades. The whole of Europe supplied war-
riors for the armies of the Crusaders. And they went
through the land with fire and sword, carpeting it with
the corpses of the followers of the Christian religion and
the bodies of the infidels. And how true is it that these
men then fought for the tomb of their Lord? Was it not
rather for the rich lands of Asia Minor? Was it not in order
to take these lands from the Moslem and Byzantine feudal

lords and win domination for the European merchants over the trade routes between Europe and Asia that the Crusades were organized by the enterprising zealots of the religion of Christ?

In his letter to you, Mr. Dulles presents the matter as though communism and the Communists are the chief, virtually the only, culprits of wars.

But was it the Communists who organized and waged the 30 years' Wars of the Roses in England? Was it they who kindled the wasteful Hundred Years' War between England and France(1337-1453)? Was it they who sent British, French and other troops to the walls of the Russian city of Sevastopol in 1854, where thousands upon thousands of Russians, British and French gave their lives?

And in the name of what moral law was the First World War started, taking over ten million lives?

When those wars were being fought, priests carrying the cross and holy images marched in the ranks of the warring troops, praying for the triumph of the arms they had blessed.

Is there anyone who does not know that the Second World War was not started by us, was not started by the socialist state? It was started by the governments of the bourgeois countries and by bloody fascism, the offspring of imperialism.

Anyone who follows developments and studies history can discover the crying contradiction between historical facts and Mr. Dulles' statements. And this is only natural, for Mr. Dulles' statements do not conform to historical truth.

It is not communist ideology, but capitalism alone and its highest stage, imperialism, with its irreconcilable contradictions (between the monopoly groups) that gives rise to war. Imperialism has carried the contradictions between the capitalist states to the limit and during the lifetime of just one generation has caused two of the most devastating world wars, inflicting terrible wounds on mankind.

With his characteristic bombast, Mr. Dulles declares that it is not possible to find in the history of the United States any occasion when an effort has been made to spread its creed by force of arms. It is allegedly otherwise with the creed of communism.

Enough of appealing to the history of the U.S.A., Mr. Dulles. Surely you know that at one time the territory of your country was inhabited by numerous brave Indian tribes, valiant hunters and peaceful tillers? Where today are the native inhabitants of America? Can you name just one of them who represents his people in Congress? Can you give us the name of just one Indian who has become a millionaire or billionaire? And where are the tribes themselves? It is said that they have been driven into reservations, and that in some amusement parks, by paying a fee, one can see the descendants of these native inhabitants of America who are put on show. Exterminate completely an aboriginal people, destroy them in the name of capitalist civilization.... One must have a great belief in miracles to appeal to the memory of peoples and say that in the history of the United States there has not been any occasion "when an effort has been made to spread its creed by force of arms."

I don't want to be misunderstood. I have no intention whatever of accusing the forefathers of the present inhabitants of the United States of America of imposing by force of arms their creed of belief in white superiority over the aborigines of America. I am only referring to historical facts, and no more. Possibly Mr. Dulles interprets them otherwise. But that is how I am accustomed to understand them.

Or let me refer to another period in the history of the United States—the period of the wars between the slave-owning South and the North. What creed was being imposed by the slave-owners of the rich plantations in the southern States, who turned millions of people like themselves into disfranchised cattle, just because their skin was black? The whole world knows that it was not then a matter of a single occasion of "an effort made to spread their creed by force of arms," but of the systematic dissemination of the creed of the slave-owners. Of course, Mr. Dulles may forget this, but the facts of history are unbiased. They refute Mr. Dulles' assertions.

But why go into the past? Is it not in our own time that in the United States Negroes are being compelled by force of arms, by flagrant violence, to keep their children from schools where white children are taught? Isn't it in our own time that frenzied racists beat up and kill men with impunity, just because their skins aren't white?

What about the creed of the superiority of the rich, the monopolists, over the workers and farmers? On what does this creed rest if not on the weapons at the disposal of the monopolists, the handful of millionaires and billionaires?

You will of course remember that in his letter to you Mr. Dulles said that for the United States "there is no need to 'abandon' what Lord Russell condemns. On the contrary, it would be abhorrent and unthinkable that there should be introduced into our creed the concept of its maintenance or extension by methods of violence and compulsion."

But let us resort to facts once more.

Let us recall the United States' vile war against Mexico, as a result of which Texas and other territories were forcibly wrested from Mexico. Had Mexico attacked the United States? No, this was the most flagrant aggression by the United States against a weaker neighbour. And what about the Spanish-American war of 1898, unleashed by American imperialism? That was the first war of the epoch of imperialism. As a result, Spanish colonies like Cuba, Puerto Rico, Guam and the Philippines became American colonies. Do you remember those wars, Mr. Dulles?

Or by what concept was the United States guided when

it sent troops to the Far East during the Civil War in Soviet Russia? And how many indirect, camouflaged wars have been waged by aggressive U.S. circles against other countries? Let us just recall Guatemala, where a democratic government, lawfully elected by the people, was destroyed and a President who enjoyed the support and confidence of the people forced to leave the country. Or take such an historical fact as the direct interference by the United States in the internal affairs of China, and the open, completely undisguised military support for the bankrupt Chiang Kai-shek clique, and the ignoring of the great Chinese People's Republic.

If one were to take Mr. Dulles' words in good faith, one might assume that he really does believe in non-interference in the internal affairs of other countries. But again, when we turn to the facts, we see that his words are at variance with reality.

Are the demands of leading statesmen in the U.S.A. that the Great Powers discuss the state structure of the East European countries compatible with the concept of non-interference? Does not such a policy bring to mind the activities of a colonialist, who wants to settle the affairs of another country in the same way as he does those of his own estate?

And what is this Dulles-Eisenhower Doctrine? It also envisages direct and open interference by imperialist states in the internal affairs of the countries of the Middle East under the guise of fighting communism. Everyone very well knows that this doctrine denies the right of the people to decide their own fate for themselves in the way they think necessary, in accordance with their own interests.

The colonial war in Algeria has been in progress for several years now. There is great bloodshed there. Are the Communists, against whom Mr. Dulles breathes thunder and lightning, to blame? No, this war was unleashed by the representatives of French monopoly capital, who do not want a peaceful settlement of the Algerian problem, but who are trying to preserve their colonial supremacy in Algeria by armed force and to extort profits.

What moral laws guide those who send French soldiers and mercenaries to "pacify" the Algerian population, and who gave the order for the bombing of the defenceless Tunisian village of Sakiet Sidi Youssef?

The peoples of the colonial and dependent countries want to break away from the yoke of colonialism. Some peoples have already liberated themselves, others are struggling for their freedom and independence, others again are gathering their strength, in order to stand up in the future and break the chains of colonial slavery. The imperialists are trying to keep their colonies, they want to accumulate still more wealth by exploiting the peoples of the colonial and dependent countries.

That is the essence of events in Algeria, Tunisia and the countries of the Middle East.

Such are the facts. They are stronger than words. What, then, are the moral laws Mr. Dulles is talking about?

Now let us turn to other questions which Mr. Dulles touched upon in his letter. He declares that the U.S.A. rejects the concept of nuclear war. "The United States," Mr. Dulles writes, "not only rejects that concept, but strives earnestly to do something to remove the danger of nuclear war."

These are fine words. We should welcome them with all our heart, if they were followed up with practical deeds. We have often declared and here again declare that the Soviet Union is most sincerely striving to do everything that lies within its power to avert events which can lead to atomic war, the consequences of which will be catastrophic for all countries.

Thus, so far as the desire to avert the danger of atomic war is concerned, our positions seemingly coincide. What, then, is the matter? Why not go from words to deeds, and make it possible for the peoples to breathe, freed from the danger of a new world conflagration which hangs over them like the sword of Damocles? Why not enable the world—to quote your good words, Professor Russell—"to live again in a noonday brightness of hope"?

The Soviet Union is ready to settle the disarmament problem as quickly as is practically possible in the interests of peace and security of the peoples. We have supported and still do support a fundamental solution of the disarmament problem; we have been and still are in favour of the complete and unconditional prohibition of atomic and hydrogen weapons, the ending of their production and testing, the destruction of all existing stockpiles, and a substantial reduction in armed forces, armaments and military expenditures—all with the establishment of reasonable international control.

It is not we who want to hold things up. However, as you know, due to some considerations, the Western Powers, and above all the U.S.A., are evading such a solution of the disarmament problem. If the Western Powers are not ready to accept a maximum programme, then we have suggested a minimum programme, in the belief that it is very important to make a first step, in order then to solve one problem after another, until finally the day that the peoples so long for will be reached, the day when war as a means of solving international problems will be excluded.

I must tell you, dear Lord Russell, that I am becoming more and more convinced that certain people in the West have a biased approach to any Soviet proposals including those on disarmament in which many Western suggestions receive careful consideration; they treat them from the very outset with suspicion and fear, as if they were dealing with a delayed action bomb just about to go off.

Of course, we cannot deny that mutual distrust still exists; we do not trust the Governments of the Western Powers in everything, and there is distrust of the Soviet Union. There's nothing to be done about this: a lot of effort must still be exerted to dispel these suspicions about the Soviet Union's policy, and the Governments of the Western Powers must by their deeds show their desire for world peace and international security. Are we not confronted by yet another phenomenon which prevents us from reaching an understanding? For the policy of the Soviet Union is frequently presented in a distorted form with the deliberate desire of throwing doubt upon it and arousing distrust and suspicion of it.

Judge for yourself, Lord Russell. The U.S. Secretary of State writes, for example, that the Soviet Union has rejected the U.S. proposal for the creation of "an international organ of control over all forms of the use of atomic energy."

But to present the matter in this way is to distort the true facts of the case. In actual fact, when the U.S.A. enjoyed a monopoly of atomic energy, it suggested the establishment of some kind of world pool, known as the Baruch Plan. But the most important question is, for what aims? If it really had been a matter of prohibiting the production and use of atomic energy for military purposes, without doubt all honest people in the world would have warmly welcomed the U.S. Government's step. And we should not now have been faced with these complicated problems, raised by the nuclear arms drive.

But the facts were otherwise. The U.S. representatives proposed a plan which, if it had been carried out, would only have strengthened the United States' monopoly over atomic energy, and would have made the U.S.A. the complete and only master of the secret of the production of atomic bombs—which, of course, could only suit certain monopoly circles, which have laid, and still lay, claim to world domination.

How could such a plan be accepted by the peace-loving countries, when it was clear to everyone that it was based not on concern for peace and international security, but on the selfish aims of the imperialist monopolies? Even the United States itself later repudiated the fundamental principles of its own plan.

We say: Let us act, let us impose a strict prohibition on atomic and hydrogen weapons, immediately cease testing these weapons and establish reasonable control. Let us come to an agreement on conditions which do not trespass on the interests of the parties concerned, which do not strengthen some and weaken others, on conditions which would not lead to states losing their independence and sovereignty, whichever system they may belong to, and on conditions which would not offer advantages to some countries to the detriment of others.

The time is ripe and, before the opportunity is lost, the Soviet Union calls on the Western Powers. It is time to go over from words to deeds, we must act on the basis of equal rights, without dictation—not from a "positions of strength," but from a position of reason.

As I have already written, Lord Russell, in my previous letter to you, man's reason and conscience cannot be reconciled to the dangerous threat of nuclear war, common sense protests against the senseless and—I will speak frankly—criminal waste of national wealth on the invention of ever more terrible means of destruction and devastation. The scientists' wonderful discoveries which have captured man's imagination can bring abundance and happiness to mankind, if they are turned to peaceful aims, to lightening people's work, eradicating disease: in short, to everything that makes man's life on earth joyous and full.

In a situation which is poisoned by the cold war, even the greatest achievements of science, the products of great minds and persistent work by people worthy of respect, are painted in military hues, and adapted for purposes foreign to the spirit of man. You have probably noticed, Lord Russell, that in the United States even the launching of the sputniks was considered by many official spokesmen, and by the press in particular, primarily from the point of view of their military significance. Now

131

we are told by the press that American scientists have been given the task of designing sputniks to be used for reconnaissance purposes.

In his letter to you, Mr. Dulles also touches on the question of outer space. Recalling the well-known proposal made by the President of the United States, Mr. Eisenhower, Mr. Dulles says that the Soviet Union now has "the chance to demonstrate that its words of peace mean something more than a mere effort to lull the non-communist world into a mood of illusory security."

You probably remember, Lord Russell, that the President of the U.S.A. proposed the prohibition of the use of outer (interplanetary) space for testing missiles intended for military use, and also to end the production of weapons which envisage the use of interplanetary space—in short, the prohibition of intercontinental ballistic rockets.

As you know, the Soviet Union has expressed its readiness to examine this question too. The only question is, how? It is proposed that we extract from the general problem of disarmament the question of the intercontinental rocket, leaving other questions of disarmament—for example, that of the prohibition of atomic and hydrogen weapons—unresolved. What is to be done? You must agree that it is unreasonable to focus attention on outer space, on intercontinental ballistic rockets—which, incidentally, the U.S.A. does not yet possess—and leave the question of nuclear weapons and the whole range of disarmament problems as before.

Surely, with such logic and such an approach, even if we were to manage to reach a definite agreement on outer space, the whole question of disarmament would have acquired a kind of ill-omened character: the unlimited production and accumulation of atomic and hydrogen weapons would continue, as well as other kinds of armament, until finally they were brought into use by some evil will.

This is the essence of the question and this is the logical conclusion, if the matter is approached seriously.

We agree to discuss the control of cosmic space, which is in fact the question of intercontinental ballistic rockets. But it must be examined as part of the general disarmament problem, including the question of prohibiting nuclear weapons and winding up the U.S. military bases surrounding the Soviet Union.

We are told that here the Soviet Union is again "presenting conditions," is again tying one disarmament question to another. Yes, we are tying them together in the same way that they are tied together in real life; for if we did otherwise, instead of an end to the arms drive, this drive could develop speeds such as the world has never known. There could be only one result: the moment would come, when, at the behest of imperialist circles, a holocaust would burst upon the world—and then it would be too late to discuss whether or not one disarmament problem is related to another.

The Soviet Union, of course, has weapons against these bases. It also has intercontinental ballistic rockets. And although the United States of America is a considerable distance from the Soviet Union, the Soviet Union now possesses the means of combating the U.S.A., should the latter unleash war against us. The Soviet Union also had these means before in the shape of intercontinental bombers, but the ballistic rocket is, of course, an improved weapon. This is why we can understand the U.S. interest in the problem of outer space. It demands the prohibition of the intercontinental ballistic rocket in order to put itself in a more advantageous position, should war break out. If a sensible approach is to be made, then thought must be given not only to one's own security, but also to the security of other countries in Asia and Europe, where American military bases are sited and which, should war break out, would be subject to retaliatory attacks.

I think therefore, Lord Russell, that you will agree that the question of the control of the use of outer space must be decided simultaneously with the prohibition of atomic and hydrogen weapons, the ending of tests, the dismantling of American military bases sited close to the Soviet Union and other socialist countries and directed against those countries.

The Soviet Union is, therefore, trying to solve the disarmament problem in such a way that its solution will be a threat neither to the U.S.A., nor to the U.S.S.R., nor to any other country and will favour neither the U.S.A., nor the U.S.S.R., to the disadvantage of other countries. Such an approach is, it seems, the only correct and reasonable one. It is, therefore, possible to say in advance that if the leaders in the U.S.A. hope to use pressure and diplomatic evasions to achieve agreements placing the U.S.A. in the position of a protected and invulnerable country, while other countries are rendered defenceless, then they hope in vain.

I have already had occasion to say that if the "policy of strength" towards the Soviet Union was previously unwise and dangerous, then in present-day conditions it is simply adventurist and disastrous for the American people as well.

You very well know, Lord Russell, that modern armaments and atomic and hydrogen bombs will be exceptionally dangerous in wartime not only for the two belligerent states in terms of outright devastation and destruction of human beings; they will also be deadly for states wishing to stand aside from military operations, since the poisoned soil, air, food, etc., will cause terrible torments and the slow annihilation of millions of people. There is in the world today an enormous quantity of atom and hydrogen bombs. According to the scientists' calculations, if they were all to be exploded simultaneously, the existence of almost every living thing on earth would be threatened.

Is it not, therefore, time to think again, to end this duel of words, to eliminate the cold war, which was not begun by the peace-loving peoples, and turn to concrete negotiations in order, in a business-like atmosphere, paying heed to each other's interests, patiently to advance step by step towards the solution of urgent international problems, including disarmament? And for this there is no need for either the Soviet Union or the United States of America to renounce its own ideology.

Mr. Dulles, however, believes that the Soviet Union must reject "at least that part of Soviet communist creed."

Which part, Mr. Dulles, would you want Communists to reject? What if we were to suggest that Mr. Dulles should reject private property and establish public property in his country? I do not think that Mr. Dulles is prepared to do this. And not only he, but others of his persuasion. Therefore we consider it absurd to present the question in this way. Only a person who is not trying to achieve agreement between states, not trying to eliminate the cold war or ease international tension, only a person who is against peaceful co-existence, can present the question in that way.

Certain eminent political figures have adopted the practice of blackening the communist movement, of presenting it in a distorted form as an aggressive teaching, allegedly based on violence and wars, of presenting the matter in such a way that the socialist countries appear as the instigators of international tension. They are guided by the rule: the more you accentuate the atmosphere of distrust among states, the better. Such a policy is understandable. The imperialists exploit the people's fear of a war, so that it is easier for them to extort constantly growing taxes from the population, and waste huge sums on the armaments drive. They are not disturbed that such a policy can lead to war—for war is the most abundant source of enrichment for the monopolies.

We have condemned and still condemn such an ill advised policy, which can lead to no good However much our opponents may slander us, the socialist countries will not disappear, and communism, the most progressive and humanist teaching, will not cease to exist.

How many attempts have been made to destroy communism by force of arms! History has convincingly shown where this leads to. Only short-sighted people can think that the ideas of communism can be destroyed by war. These ideas are reaching the minds and hearts of more and more millions of people, and are spreading far and wide. Everyone remembers how, after the First World War unleashed by the imperialists, and as a result of the October Revolution, the first socialist state in the world was created in Russia, a state in which the people took the power into their own hands. The Second World War, also unleashed by the imperialists, aroused a mighty people's movement and led to the victory of socialism in a number of countries of Europe and Asia, and to the formation of the great camp of the socialist countries.

I think that if imperialism unleashes a new world war, it will perish in it. The peoples will not want to tolerate a system which cannot exist without wars, without the annihilation of millions of people, to enrich a handful of monopolists.

I should like to say once more that ideological questions are not solved in the way Mr. Dulles suggests. Ideological questions and questions of social organization are the internal affairs of the peoples of each country.

These are the questions about which, on learning of Mr. Dulles' letter, I considered it necessary to say a few words. Please excuse the fact that I have had to elucidate in some considerable detail some positions which received such incorrect treatment in Mr. Dulles' letter.

With deep respect,

N. KHRUSHCHOV

March 5, 1958
Kommunist, No. 5, 1958

REPLIES
TO QUESTIONS PUT BY *TRYBUNA LUDU*

March 10, 1958

The editorial board of the Polish newspaper *Trybuna Ludu* requested N. S. Khrushchov, First Secretary of the Central Committee of the Communist Party of the Soviet Union, to answer a number of questions.

On March 10, N. S. Khrushchov received Z. Broniarek, a member of the newspaper's editorial board, and M. Lucki, the paper's permanent correspondent in Moscow, and had a talk with them. Below we publish the questions submitted by the editorial board of *Trybuna Ludu* and N. S. Khrushchov's replies.

Question: What is your estimate, Comrade Khrushchov, of the implementation of the decisions of the 20th Congress of the Communist Party of the Soviet Union during the past two years in developing Soviet national economy, and in particular:

a) in developing Soviet industry and the improvement of methods of industrial management;

b) in developing Soviet agriculture and the forms of agricultural management;

c) in improving the living standards of the Soviet working people?

Answer: I believe there is no need for me to tell the readers of *Trybuna Ludu* of the magnificent prospects for the development of our country's national economy outlined by the 20th Congress of the Communist Party of the Soviet Union. They were extensively reported in your newspaper and in other Polish papers. To put it briefly, the Soviet people, headed by the Communist Party, are firmly resolved not only to overtake but also to outstrip in the near future the leading capitalist countries, including the United States, in per capita output of the most important items.

In the past two years we achieved considerable successes in developing our national economy. Today Soviet industry is working much better and is producing far more goods than it was two years ago. In 1957, industrial output was 22 per cent higher than in 1955, the year preceding the 20th Congress of the C.P.S.U. In those two years steel production increased by 5,800,000 tons, coal by 72 million tons, oil by 27,500,000 tons, cement by 6,400,000 tons and electric power by 39,000 million kilowatt-hours.

So that you may be better able to judge the significance of these figures I must add that **the increase in output for the past two years exceeded the total volume of production in pre-revolutionary Russia for the year 1913: steel by almost 50 per cent, coal by 150 per cent, oil by almost 200 per cent, cement by more than 300 per cent and electric power by 1,900 per cent.**

One of the chief measures implemented in our country in that period was the reorganization of management in industry and building, which may justly be called a revolutionary measure. The reorganization of management in industry and the liquidation of industrial ministries that had played a positive role at a certain stage of development gave wider scope to the initiative of workers and production executives Now the management of factories and construction jobs is concentrated in the economic areas and is effected by the economic councils set up in these areas. The combination of centralized planning with democratic managerial methods is the key to a more efficient application of the advantages accruing from the socialist economic system.

The period following reorganization of our industry has already yielded excellent results. The recently held all-Union conference of chairmen of economic councils and Party and local government leaders has shown how beneficial and timely was the reorganization of management in industry and building. Soviet industry is now working on a higher level and with much fuller use of its resources.

In future the positive aspects of the reorganization of management in industry will unquestionably make themselves felt to a still greater extent and this will result in a further gigantic growth of industrial production in the Soviet Union. We shall speed up the carrying out of our main economic task—to overtake and surpass the leading capitalist countries in per capita industrial production within the shortest period possible.

There have also been considerable achievements in agriculture. The collective-farm system gave the Soviet peasantry the opportunity to radically reorganize agricultural economy and transform life in the Soviet countryside. Today our country produces much more grain, cotton, sugar-beet, meat, milk, butter and other farm produce than ever before. Suffice it to say that in comparison with 1913 the quantity of marketed produce has increased: meat by 100 per cent, milk by more than 200 per cent, and wool also by more than 200 per cent. In the last two years alone the number of cattle in the Soviet Union has increased by 7,900,000, that of pigs by 10,300,000, and that of sheep by 16,800,000. Or take such a fact as the increase in the cropped area. Thanks to the development of virgin and disused lands, the area under crops in the Soviet Union has increased by 36 million hectares in the last four years alone, and this made it possible even under unfavourable weather conditions to grow much more grain last year than in the best harvest years in pre-revolutionary Russia.

Of course, we still have a great deal to do in order to raise annual grain production in the Soviet Union to 11,000 million poods as required by the decision of the 20th Congress of the Party, but we shall unquestionably carry out the task set us by the Party Congress.

As for the prospects for the development of animal husbandry, our task is to overtake the United States in the per capita production of meat, milk and butter within the next few years. This means that, with our present population, we shall have to bring meat output up to 20-21 million tons and that of milk up to 70 million tons. There is every condition for this target, too, to be most certainly reached.

I should like to recall a few facts. Three years ago, at the January 1955 Plenary Meeting of the C.P.S.U. Central Committee, we set a number of targets for the increased output of livestock products in the next six years. Some of these targets, such as, for example, higher milk yields on the collective farms and the increase of sales of milk to the state by 80 per cent, have been fulfilled ahead of schedule, in three years. By 1957 the U.S.S.R. already produced some 55 million tons of milk, that is to say, about 95 per cent of American milk output. As for the total butter output, we have already caught up with the United States.

Trybuna Ludu readers perhaps already know that the recent Plenary Meeting of the C.P.S.U. Central Committee discussed the further development of the collective-farm system and the reorganization of the machine and tractor stations. A nation-wide discussion of the measures proposed by the Central Committee of the Party is now under way. The implementation of measures to reorganize the machine and tractor stations will constitute a major and revolutionary step in the development of Soviet agriculture.

Speaking of the improvement of the living conditions of the Soviet people, one must first of all stress the considerable rise in their living standards and the fuller satisfaction of their constantly growing material and cultural requirements.

The national income, which is the most general index of the people's well-being, has risen in the U.S.S.R. 14-fold per head of population since 1913, whereas in the United States it has risen less than 100 per cent, and in France and Britain about 60 per cent.

In fulfilment of the decisions of the 20th Party Congress we have raised the wages of the lower-paid categories of factory and office workers and reduced the length of the working day on the eve of national holidays and on Saturdays. A seven-hour working day is being introduced, with a six-hour day for underground workers in the coal and ore-mining industries.

The scale of housing construction has been greatly increased in our country. During the past two years alone, houses with a total floor space of 85 million square metres have been built in towns and workers' housing settlements. In the same period, 1,420,000 homes have been built by collective farmers and by intellectuals working in the countryside.

The state allocates huge sums every year for social insurance, benefits, pensions and scholarships, for free education, medical and other services. Last year, for instance, appropriations for these purposes totalled more than 201,000 million rubles, or approximately one-third of the total budget expenditure of the U.S.S.R.

In speaking of the improvement of living conditions, one must mention the expansion of state and co-operative trade. Here are some figures to illustrate this. In 1957, the state and co-operative shops sold to the population 250 per cent more meat and meat products, 260 per cent more butter, milk and dairy products, 220 per cent more sugar, and 180 per cent more fabrics than in 1940.

The Communist Party and the Soviet Government regard it as their main task to work for the further all-round improvement of the living conditions of the working people. And we are firmly convinced that the time is not far off when the citizens of the Soviet Union and of all socialist countries will have much higher living standards than the working people of any capitalist country. After all, the main task of the Communists is to better the life of the people, and the socialist system offers the working people everything necessary for its accomplishment.

This, briefly, is what can be said in reply to your first question.

Question: The great achievements of Soviet science and technology in recent years have attracted public attention.

What do you think of the prospects for the development of science and engineering in the Soviet Union?

Answer: You are right in saying that the recent achievements of Soviet science and technology have attracted the attention of the public. This is no accident. The Soviet Union built the world's first atomic power station, the world's most powerful microparticle accelerator, launched the world's first atomic ice-breaker, and is regularly expanding the application of atomic energy to peaceful purposes. Our scientists were the first to report to an international conference on their work on controlled thermo-nuclear reactions. We were the first to put giant jet air liners into regular passenger service. The discoveries of our geographers in the Arctic and their truly heroic explorations in the Antarctic are widely known. The intercontinental ballistic missile was developed in the Soviet Union. The crowning achievement of Soviet science and technology was the development and successful launching, on October 4, 1957, of the world's first artificial earth satellite, which was soon followed by another.

Let us recall what our opponents in the West have but recently been saying and writing about the scientific and cultural level of the Soviet Union. They were saying that the Soviet Union and the other socialist countries were lagging behind in science and technology; this, they claimed, was because socialism does not provide the scientist and engineer with conditions for creative development.

Everybody can now see what these vicious assertions are worth. The socialist system offers unlimited opportunities for the all-round development of the individual and for creative endeavour. Socialism opens up such great prospects for scientists, engineers and technicians, for the creative work of our intellectuals and of every Soviet man and woman, as the capitalist system is incapable of ever ensuring.

That is why the West now speaks differently about the level of science and technology in the Soviet Union and not only of that. The more sober-minded people there are arriving at conclusions which bring them close to a recognition of the advantages of developing science and technology along socialist lines. But you must have read all this in the bourgeois press yourselves.

The achievements of our science and technology are a striking demonstration of the advantages of the socialist system. Soviet science draws upon the achievements of the whole of our national economy and, in turn, contributes to its development. The Soviet people are interested in the development of science and technology and provide our scientists and engineers with everything necessary for their work, everything necessary to ensure scientific and technological progress. The Communist Party and the Soviet Government regard the development of science as a matter of great importance to the state and give every assistance and support to scientists, inventors and innovators in production.

As regards the prospects for the development of science and technology in the Soviet Union, they are very heartening and encouraging prospects. There is no doubt that our science and technology will continue to develop successfully and that Soviet scientists and engineers will give us the pleasure of witnessing fresh achievements, making their contribution to the building of communism.

Speaking of the further development of science and technology, one must stress the paramount importance of theoretical research, which opens up new paths in science, and of such branches as automation, telemechanics and computing machinery, where achievements, given practical application, greatly lighten people's work.

But the point I want to stress mostly is that Soviet science and technology are developing in close co-operation with science and technology in all the socialist countries. Fraternal mutual assistance and skilful co-ordination of our joint efforts in this field will ensure an even greater flourishing of scientific and technical thought in the socialist countries.

Question: The 20th Congress elaborated the famous theses on the peaceful co-existence of the two systems and the possibility of averting wars in our time.

What are the prospects today for a relaxation in international tension and the development of co-operation between countries with different social systems in the field of economy, and also in the field of scientific and cultural exchanges?

Answer: I would like to point out, first of all, that the proposition of the peaceful co-existence of the two systems was first put forward by our great teacher, V. I. Lenin, who pointed out on more than one occasion that the socialist and the capitalist systems can co-exist peacefully if they do not interfere in each other's internal affairs. The 20th Congress of the C.P.S.U., drawing on Lenin's teaching and summarizing the experience of international relations over a long period, stressed vigorously that in our time, when two world systems—the socialist and the capitalist systems—are in existence, the peaceful co-existence of states with different social systems has become a vital necessity. To think otherwise is to carry matters to the unleashing of war, which modern weapons would make the most frightful and most devastating that mankind has ever known. Today the question presents itself in this way:

either peaceful co-existence or war. The 20th Congress of the C.P.S.U. also stressed that the growth of the peace forces in all countries is such that it is now possible to avert war. .These peace forces can curb any fomenter of war if they display vigilance and if the peaceful peoples of the world make greater efforts in the struggle for peace.

It may safely be said that although certain circles in the imperialist countries are clinging frantically to the bankrupt "positions of strength" policy, the prospects for the relaxation of international tension and the development of economic co-operation and scientific and cultural exchanges between countries with different social systems have now become more favourable. Take, for instance, the agreement on the development of cultural contacts concluded between the Soviet Union and the U.S.A. It is a big step forward. The socialist countries have made definite progress in the development of cultural contacts with the capitalist countries. Indeed, every socialist country is doing its utmost to extend cultural relations with other countries, the Polish People's Republic among others, having done much in this direction. One can only welcome this development of co-operation, this strengthening of friendly ties between peoples, for it leads to better understanding and the consolidation of the cause of peace.

It is well known that the socialist countries have established economic ties with many capitalist countries. Recently, business circles in capitalist countries have been making more frequent statements in favour of the extension of these contacts. Today there are few people in the West who believe in the efficiency of the bankrupt policy of economically blockading the socialist countries. The world socialist economy is able to produce everything needed for its further development, and no bans imposed by the ruling circles of certain countries on trade with the socialist countries can prevent us from continuing to advance as successfully as we are now doing. If anyone stands to lose from these prohibitions, it is the business circles of the Western Powers. Their interests call for the extension of trade with the socialist countries. For our part, we also welcome the expansion of trade between the socialist and the capitalist countries.

The socialist countries have always stood for the all-round development of economic relations with all the other countries. It goes without saying that these relations must be based on the strictest observance of equality, mutual advantage and non-interference in internal affairs.

Thus, there exist objective prerequisites for the extension of economic relations between the capitalist and socialist states. The translation of these objective prerequisites into reality will, undoubtedly, promote peace throughout the world.

There still are and there will continue to be no small number of obstacles and difficulties in the way of the further development of economic, cultural and other relations. But, given the willingness of both sides, these difficulties and obstacles will be overcome.

We can say with confidence that international tension will be further relaxed. This will be brought about, above all, by ending the cold war and renouncing the imperialist "positions of strength" policy, by the establishment of contacts and the achievement of still greater understanding between states.

The Soviet Government, as you know, has recently put forward a proposal to hold a conference at top level with Heads of Government participating. The proposal has received ardent support in all countries of the world.

It can be said in all certainty that if a top-level conference is held and understanding is reached, it will make a great contribution to the further relaxation of international tension and the establishment of greater confidence between states with different social systems.

Question: The question of a conference of Heads of Government is now a very urgent one, and we would like to know how it stands now that the Soviet Government has accepted the French Government's proposal to hold a Foreign Ministers' meeting. If you could reply to this question, Comrade Khrushchov, it would be of great interest to our readers.

Answer: We have set forth our views on this question in the latest message sent by the Soviet Government to President Eisenhower of the United States, and also in our aide-mémoire. These documents were published in our press.

Why do we consider it possible to accept the proposal of the French Foreign Minister, M. Pineau, on a Foreign Ministers' meeting to prepare a summit conference? We are of the opinion that any means are good if they expedite the convocation of a summit conference in the interests of peace. We, therefore, approve of the use of all channels if they really facilitate preparations for this meeting. But we fear that diplomatic channels may be turned into channels for endless correspondence or endless talks and give the peoples the impression that a summit meeting is being prepared (and this is now desired and actually demanded by all nations), while in actual fact there might not be any preparation at all.

Secret talks through diplomatic channels are very handy for politicians who oppose the meeting, since such a system of negotiations prevents the peoples from knowing anything because nothing is released for publication. You know that exchange of messages can be continued for ever, and diplomats are well aware of its possibilities.

I repeat that we do not reject talks through diplomatic channels. In the present instance we are for the kind of negotiations which would be useful for the preparation of a summit conference. If we see, however, that diplomatic channels and the secret form of the talks do not expedite the meeting, but tend to prevent it, to mislead the people, to bury quietly the idea of a meeting, we shall have nothing to do with them. We believe, therefore, that it is better to have a Foreign Ministers' meeting, because it must be scheduled for some specific date and will be watched by the public. If the Ministers' meeting is broken off and no agreement is reached on a mutually acceptable agenda or other questions of procedure, everyone will see that certain Ministers have assembled and that one country has adopted this position and another country that position. Public opinion will then be able to determine and assess who really stands for a top-level conference with the participation of Heads of Government, and who is against it.

We are not dogmatic on this point and do not oppose in principle any meeting of Ministers. True, we do not cherish any illusions, because we know these Ministers. But it is obvious that a Ministers' conference cannot be avoided, and they will have to meet. If the Ministers torpedo the summit conference at their meeting, everyone will see that the Soviet Government representatives were right in warning the public that there was little chance of a Foreign Ministers' conference justifying the hopes placed in it by the peoples. We must, of course, keep in mind the fact that public pressure is now very strong, and that even if some of the Ministers are inwardly against ending the cold war, they will be compelled, by public pressure, to take some positive steps, and if this pressure grows, to reckon with public opinion.

At a Ministers' conference, of course, positive decisions can also be achieved. We, for our part, will spare no efforts to make the Foreign Ministers' meeting successful. We believe, however, that the Ministers should not discuss questions in substance, but should organizationally prepare and ensure the convocation of a top-level conference with the participation of Heads of Government. If all the questions are discussed in substance by the Foreign Ministers' meeting, why have a summit conference at all?

Question: We feel that if you, Comrade Khrushchov and

Comrade Bulganin, were to visit Washington for a meeting at the highest level, it would produce a deep impression.

Answer: We are aware that owing to certain circumstances the United States President has difficulty in leaving his country. We are ready to meet on United States territory for that matter. The distance between Moscow and Washington is not so great: we can breakfast at home, lunch on the plane, and dine in the United States.

For the sake of peace and co-existence we are ready to meet anywhere, if only we are sure that urgent problems will be settled in the way desired by the peoples of all countries.

Question: Please let us know your opinion on the development of relations between the Communist and Workers' parties during the past two years in the light of the decisions of the 20th Congress of the C.P.S.U.

Answer: During the past two years relations between the Communist and Workers' parties have developed and grown stronger, as hitherto, following the principles of proletarian internationalism. The Communist parties are called upon to unite the peoples in the struggle for peace and socialism. That is why the Communist parties strive for close bonds with each other and for unity of action. At the same time every party is absolutely independent politically and organizationally and expresses the interests of its own working class and working people, the national interests of its country. The international and national interests of the working class, as of all working people, do not contradict each other, but on the contrary, blend harmoniously together. The Communist parties have always regarded the strengthening of international proletarian solidarity as their sacred duty, and have always fought resolutely against any attempts to weaken the unity of the international working-class movement.

In the Inaugural Address of the Working Men's International Association Marx wrote: "Past experience has shown how disregard of that bond of brotherhood which ought to exist between the workmen of different countries and incite them to stand firmly by each other in all their struggles for emancipation, will be chastised by the common discomfiture of their incoherent efforts." In their relations the Communist and Workers' parties proceed on the basis of this wise admonition.

Now we can say with satisfaction that the unbreakable unity of the international communist movement, which has been particularly strengthened in the past few years, is the supreme expression of this fraternal union of the workers of all countries. It did not come of itself. The Communist and Workers' parties have forged it in the struggle against the attempts of imperialist reaction and revisionists to split the world communist movement.

The enemies of the working class counted on causing "complications" in relations between the fraternal parties, and particularly between the parties of the socialist states. With this end in view they tried to exaggerate difficulties encountered in building socialism and to take advantage of certain individual misunderstandings and irregularities in relations between the socialist states. These misunderstandings can, of course, occur, since an absolutely new type of relations is taking shape—relations which have no precedent in history. As experience shows, however, all the problems concerning relations between the socialist states are solved, and can be solved, by friendly discussion on the basis of the strict observance of the principles of proletarian internationalism.

This, of course, does not suit our enemies. They would like to see the peoples of the socialist countries at loggerheads. This would make it easier to realize their cherished dream of restoring capitalism in the People's Democracies. It is common knowledge, for instance, that the reactionary imperialist forces wanted to make use of the events in Hungary for their own ends; the same applies to the difficulties encountered in building socialism in Poland. Moreover, they actively interfered in the Hungarian events. The counter-revolutionary forces rushed there to crush socialist Hungary and restore the fascist régime. But the sound forces of the Hungarian people united to repel fascist reaction and, helped by the Soviet Union and the other socialist states, defeated the counter-revolutionary insurgents.

If there were formerly some people who doubted whether the Hungarian events were provoked by the imperialist forces, everyone now sees who inspired and encouraged the fascist thugs in Hungary.

The enemies of socialism have shouted their heads off, and still continue shouting about some sort of "special processes" taking place in Poland, about some sort of tendencies in Poland to depart from the path of socialism. The proverb: "A hungry man dreams of buns," is appropriate here.

Can the working people voluntarily forfeit their socialist gains to their enemies, agree that capitalism be restored in the countries of socialism, that the factories be returned again to a handful of capitalists, and that the land be returned to the landowners and kulaks?

Can the working people of these countries permit the return of unemployment and cruel exploitation of the workers and peasants, and allow the capitalists and landowners to saddle the working people again?

It is absolutely clear how illusory and impracticable are the dreams of representatives of international reaction about the restoration of capitalism in the socialist states.

It is obvious that the working people of Poland will never permit restoration of the rule of capitalists and landowners. Rallied closely around the Polish United Workers' Party and overcoming all difficulties, they will continue confidently along the road of socialist construction. The forward march of a country whose people have chosen the road of socialism and are working to build a new society without rich or poor, without the exploitation of man by man, without unemployment and poverty, cannot be reversed. That is even less possible now that every socialist country relies upon the support and assistance of the whole of the mighty socialist camp.

The working people of every socialist country are deeply concerned with everything that happens in the other fraternal, friendly countries.

The camp of socialism is constantly growing and gaining in strength. This was borne out by the recent Meetings of Representatives of Communist and Workers' Parties in Moscow. The results of these meetings have shown the whole world the ridiculous nature of the assertions of imperialist propagandists about the "crisis of communism." These meetings are a major ideological and political victory for the world communist and working-class movement. The Declaration and the Peace Manifesto, unanimously adopted by the representatives of the fraternal parties, are documents of great mobilizing power, documents testifying to the unanimity and cohesion of the Communist and Workers' parties in the struggle for socialism, for world peace.

Question: What would you, Comrade Khrushchov, like to tell the readers of *Trybuna Ludu* about the new tendencies you see in the development of friendship and co-operation between Poland and the Soviet Union?

Answer: First of all I must stress that friendship and co-operation between People's Poland and the Soviet Union have always developed and are developing on the basis of the Leninist principles of proletarian internationalism and mutual assistance, on the basis of complete equality and respect for each other's interests. We have never thought of any other relations. The friendship between our two countries is cemented by the blood spilt in the common struggle against tsarist autocracy, against the capitalists and landowners, and against the German fascist invaders during the Second World War. This great friendship has endured many stern trials.

Persistently clinging to the evil legacy of the past, the enemies of socialism are searching for aspects of the history of relations between our two countries which would somehow cast a shadow on the friendship between our peoples. What is more, they are speculating on nationalist sentiments and are trying to stir them up. Is there anyone who does not realize the purpose of this? But all the attempts of our enemies to undermine friendship between the peoples of the Polish People's Republic and the Soviet Union are doomed to failure, because the peoples of our countries know full well that only our enemies will stand to gain if there is no friendship between Poland and the Soviet Union.

Certain violations of Leninist principles that occurred in the relations between our countries in the past have been completely eliminated through the consistent implementation of the well-known Declaration of the Soviet Government of October 30, 1956, and the Joint Soviet-Polish Statement of November 18 of the same year. In its relations with Poland as well as with all other socialist countries, the Soviet Union has invariably proceeded on the basis of the great Leninist principles that have been verified by experience. We have always stood, and we now stand for the development of fraternal relations between our countries, for the utmost respect for the interests of the peoples of our countries, for the development of mutually advantageous trade between the Polish People's Republic and the U.S.S.R., for the maximum extension of cultural, sports and other contacts between them, for mutual aid and support in the common struggle for socialism, for the closest co-operation between the Communist Party of the Soviet Union and the Polish United Workers' Party. The peoples of the Soviet Union and Poland are well aware that the stronger the friendship between them, between all countries of the socialist camp, the more impregnable our countries will be to any enemy, the greater will be the might of the new socialist world, and the stronger will be world peace.

We should always remember that the great strength of the socialist camp lies in the friendship and cohesion of the socialist countries.

Co-operation between our countries in the international field is developing fruitfully in the struggle for lasting peace, against the threat of a new world war. This was shown, specifically, by the support given by the Polish Government to the Soviet Union's recent moves in foreign policy and the support given by the Soviet Government to the valuable Polish proposal concerning the establishment of a zone in Central Europe free from atomic and hydrogen weapons.

The recent agreement on cultural co-operation in 1958 concluded between our countries and the Soviet-Polish trade agreement for 1958-60, providing for a considerable increase in trade, will undoubtedly be of major importance for the development of relations between our countries in the coming period.

Allow me to express confidence that the fraternal friendship, mutual assistance and all-round co-operation between Poland and the Soviet Union, and among all socialist countries, will continue to grow and develop for the good of our peoples, for the consolidation of world peace.

I would like to avail myself of this opportunity to convey through your paper fraternal, heartfelt greetings to the Polish people and to wish them new successes in building a socialist Poland.

Pravda, March 12, 1958

SPEECH
AT MEETING OF ELECTORS
OF KALININ CONSTITUENCY, MOSCOW

March 14, 1958

Comrades,

Allow me first of all to thank you, all the electors of the Kalinin constituency in Moscow, for the great trust you have shown me by nominating me your candidate for the U.S.S.R. Supreme Soviet. (*Applause.*)

The confidence of the people is a great and high honour which must be justified by work for the good of the country. I regard the fact that you have again nominated me your candidate as a high estimate of my work and I promise to devote all my energies in future to justifying the confidence of the electors, the confidence of the people. (*Prolonged applause.*)

Elections to the U.S.S.R. Supreme Soviet have become a gala day for the entire Soviet people. In these days Soviet men and women are summing up our country's successes and achievements during the term of office of the Supreme Soviet of the last convocation and are planning what we should do in the next few years.

The results of the work for the past four years are well described in the message addressed by the Central Committee of the Communist Party of the Soviet Union to all electors and in other well-known documents.

We have a right to be proud of the achievements of our socialist homeland. Gross output of Soviet industry has increased by 55 per cent as compared with 1953, including a 61 per cent increase in the output of means of production and a 45 per cent increase in the output of consumer goods.

It should be stressed that the development of industry in the Soviet Union is proceeding at a rapid pace all the time. The recent reorganization of the management of industry and building, bringing the management of industrial establishments and building sites directly to the places where material wealth is produced, has played a tremendous constructive part in improving the work of our country's industry.

Here, for example, is what we expect from our industry this year. Our plans, as you know, are not only being fulfilled but also successfully overfulfilled. According to figures of the Central Statistical Board, the two months' plan for industrial output in January and February was overfulfilled 3.5 per cent, with output increasing 11 per cent as compared with the same period of last year. The 1958 plan calls for the production of 53,600,000 tons of steel and 41,700,000 tons of rolled metal. These are approximately the quantities of steel and rolled metal that were produced during the first 17 years of Soviet power, that is to say, between 1918 and 1934. In order to produce 489,300,000 tons of coal, the figure planned for 1958, the Soviet state required more than 16 years in its early days; in order to extract the planned 112 million tons of oil more than 13 years were needed, and to produce the planned 33,600,000 tons of cement about 19 years were needed. The production of electric power in 1958 is planned at 231,000 million kilowatt-hours. This is approximately as much as was generated in the first 21 years of Soviet rule, that is to say, between 1918 and 1938.

Consider these figures, comrades! It now takes the country's industry only one year to produce as much as it could produce in 15-20 years in the past. This is a qualitative leap which shows convincingly how our country has changed. Today we can tackle any task, however great and complicated it may be. Today, Russia, the Ukraine, Byelorussia, Kazakhstan, Uzbekistan, every republic in Transcaucasia, Central Asia and the Baltic area—all the fraternal republics—have become advanced, industrially developed socialist republics. Every one of them can vie with many capitalist states as regards the level of their economic development. (*Applause.*)

How can we not rejoice, comrades, at the gigantic achievements of our industry—that firm foundation of the economic might and the defence capacity of the Soviet state, the foundation for the constant improvement of the well-being of the Soviet people. These achievements are vivid evidence of the viability and invincibility of the new social system—socialism. (*Applause.*)

The working people of Moscow, including those of the Kalinin constituency, one of the biggest districts of our capital, are contributing greatly to the strengthening of the might of our Soviet country. It is gratifying to note that the working people of Kalinin district fulfilled their 1957 state plan ahead of schedule—as early as December 14—and produced 300 million rubles' worth of goods above target. (*Applause.*) Moscow's industry also fulfilled its state plan ahead of schedule and last year produced several thousand million rubles' worth of goods above target.

Since the reorganization of the management of industry and building, Moscow industrial enterprises, like those of the entire country, have considerably improved their work. Moscow enterprises and Moscow's Economic Council have drafted a long-term plan for the development of the capital's industry in the 1959-65 period. This plan makes provision for a 43.3 per cent increase in industrial output as compared with the 1958 plan; over three-quarters of this increase is to be achieved by higher labour productivity at existing enterprises through the use of more productive equipment and advanced technology, and by expanding specialization and rational co-operation.

This is an excellent and honourable undertaking and I would like, from the bottom of my heart, to wish the working people of Moscow, who have more than once been the initiators of patriotic deeds, success in accomplishing this important economic task. (*Prolonged applause.*)

Comrades, we are implementing a vast programme of capital construction, the volume of which is expanding every year. In the two years that have elapsed since the 20th Congress of the Communist Party of the Soviet Union, 400,000 million rubles (in prices as of July 1, 1955) have been invested in the national economy. And this is more than the total investments made for the First and Second Five-Year Plans and the three and a half pre-war years of the Third Five-Year Plan.

What other state has ever built on such a scale? There never has been such a country. Only for our socialist country and its remarkable people—a people of fighters, a people of pioneers—are such things possible. (*Stormy applause.*)

The development of socialist industry, and first and foremost of heavy industry, has ensured the socialist reconstruction of the entire national economy and the transformation of our country's agriculture. In Soviet times, agricultural output has increased considerably, though the percentage of the population engaged in agriculture has decreased in our country by nearly a half. In some branches of cropping and livestock farming the output of marketable produce is between three and six times greater than that of pre-revolutionary Russia. Particularly great progress has been made in the past four years, following the well-known Party and Government decisions on agriculture.

With the development of virgin and disused lands, grain production has risen substantially. The output of sugar-beet, cotton, flax and other industrial crops is also increasing.

Great successes have been achieved in the development of animal husbandry. In the past four years the cattle population alone has increased by 10,900,000, and there has been a substantial increase in the output of livestock products. In this period meat production, including increases in the herds, has risen by 38 per cent, with an increase of nearly 80 per cent on the collective and state farms; milk production for the country as a whole has risen by 50 per cent, with a more than 100 per cent increase on the collective and state farms. The quantity of milk marketed has risen by 10,000,000 tons in these four years. Let us recall, by way of comparison, that in 1913 milk produced for the market on the present territory of our country amounted to only 7,000,000 tons.

Our country's agriculture is developing at an exceptionally rapid pace. And we are confident that the patriotic movement, launched on the initiative of the foremost collective and state farms, to overtake the United States within the next few years in per capita production of meat, butter and milk, will meet with complete success. (*Prolonged applause.*)

The measures mapped out by the February Plenary Meeting of the Central Committee of the C.P.S.U. for the further consolidation of the collective-farm system and the reorganization of the machine and tractor stations are now being discussed throughout the country. The implementation of these truly revolutionary measures will contribute to still greater progress in all branches of socialist agriculture. The tremendous potentialities and advantages of socialist farming and animal husbandry will now be developed to an even greater extent.

As the country's economy develops the living standards of the Soviet people steadily improve. The national income is growing year by year. Since the last elections the Party and the Government have carried out a number of major measures to raise the standard of living of the working people in our country. I will remind you of some of them.

A new law on state pensions has been passed; the wages of the lower-paid categories of factory and office workers have been raised; the working day has been shortened on the eve of holidays and on Saturdays. The decision of the Party and the Government on the introduction of a seven-hour working day in general and a six-hour working day on underground jobs in the coal and ore-mining industry is being carried out. Social insurance benefits and expenditures for free education, medical and other services for the working people are increasing year by year.

Our country has abolished for all time such a scourge of the working people as unemployment.

The past four years have been marked by new and outstanding achievements of Soviet science and technology and by a further cultural advance. Soviet scientists, engineers, technicians and workers have produced the world's finest jet and turboprop air liners, launched an atomic ice-breaker, developed intercontinental ballistic missiles, made important discoveries in electronics and successfully launched the first artificial earth satellites in the world.

It was not long ago that some conceited representatives of the Western world were spreading all kinds of fables about science and technology in our country lagging behind that of the United States. Now everyone sees that socialism, which has freed man from the fetters of the private property ideology and made the people masters of their own destiny, creates boundless possibilities for daring quests, discoveries, inventions and creative endeavour, for genuine progress in science, technology and culture. (*Prolonged applause.*)

Today the whole world recognizes the great achievements of the Soviet Union. Soviet people are pleased to hear of this recognition. But we must not be conceited and, still less, be complacent and rest on our laurels. We still have a lot to do and still have to work persistently so as to accomplish the main economic task confronting our country, so that in all spheres of life our country may be in the forefront of mankind, may be abreast of the latest achievements of science and technology. We are confident that our achievements in this field, too, will grow and multiply.

The Soviet Union now has everything for the successful solution of the tasks of communist construction—a powerful industry, a large-scale mechanized agriculture, highly developed science and technology, untold natural resources, and highly qualified cadres. Backed by our achievements and utilizing the advantages of the social-ist economic system, our country in the next few years will make a further gigantic stride towards the great goal —the building of communist society. (*Stormy applause.*)

From the materials of the jubilee session of the U.S.S.R. Supreme Soviet devoted to the 40th anniversary of the October Revolution, you know that the Party and the Government have outlined a vast programme of economic construction. This programme envisages a further rapid expansion in the output of the metal, coal, electric power, machine-building, chemical and other branches of industry so that, within the next 15 years, not only to overtake but also outstrip the biggest capitalist countries in per capita output of the main items. This, comrades, is not an easy task. But it is quite feasible and we are confident that it will be successfully accomplished. (*Prolonged applause.*)

Our economic plans reflect the concern of the Commun-ist Party and the Soviet Government for the well-being of the Soviet people. The growth of the decisive branches of economy in the next 15 years to approximately double or treble the present level and a further rapid advance in agriculture will make it possible to raise the living standard of our people and more fully satisfy their ma-terial and cultural requirements.

You know that the Party and the Government have drawn up a big programme of housing construction in order to end the housing shortage in our country within he next 10 or 12 years. And this programme is being translated into reality. Last year Soviet builders achieved notable successes. In 1957, new housing with a total floor space of more than 48 million square metres was completed and occupied. In addition, collective farmers and intelligentsia in the countryside built 770,000 houses last year. This means that in 1957 alone we built considerably more housing than during the whole of the Second Five-Year Plan. (*Applause.*)

To give an idea of the real scale of housing construction in the country I want to remind you that in 1954 we built an average of seven flats per thousand of population, whereas in 1957, the figure was 10.2 flats per thousand. This volume of building is much higher than that of the capitalist countries. According to official statistics, the number of flats built in 1957 per thousand of population was 6.7 in the United States, 5.9 in Britain, and 6.2 in France.

Allow me to give some figures for housing construction in Moscow. Whereas 4,477,000 square metres of housing were made available for occupation from 1950 to 1953, the figure for the period from 1954 to 1957 reached 8,320,000 square metres. Last year alone 71,800 families in Moscow received flats in new, well-appointed buildings, most of them going to workers' families. The long-term (1959-65) plan for the development of the municipal economy of the capital provides for the annual construction of housing with a total floor space of about four million square metres. (*Applause.*)

The task is to increase the rate of building and achieve high quality. The proper distribution of housing is assuming exceptional importance. Although a great deal of housing has been built in Moscow in recent years, the number of people whose housing conditions ought to be improved is still great. Why is that so? There are many reasons, but one of them is the shortcomings in the distribution of dwellings. (*Applause.*)

A procedure should be established whereby the lists of

people who are to receive flats should be carefully examined and approved in advance, so that the people on these lists know when they will get dwellings. (*Applause.*) It is necessary to exercise strict supervision over the distribution of housing and to draw representatives of factories, and offices into this work. (*Applause.*)

It is necessary, at long last, to put an end to the growth of the population in the bigger cities due to the influx of people from other areas. (*Applause.*) Some executives of Moscow industrial establishments complain that they are short of workers for laborious jobs, that it is hard to find people to do "rough" work and therefore, you see, it is necessary to permit the enlistment of labour from other areas. But to present the question in that way means, as it were, to divide people into two categories. It turns out that people from other places should come to do the "rough" work. But that is no way out of the situation. We have to mechanize laborious jobs—that is the main thing. (*Prolonged applause.*)

You have probably seen on more than one occasion how men and women are engaged in chipping ice off the pavements with crowbars. This is unproductive labour. Such a sight really makes one uncomfortable. So much has been done in our country to mechanize complicated production processes, so many machines have been created to make work easier, and the first artificial earth satellites have been developed, but as for replacing the crowbar and shovel with a machine—we have not yet got round to that. (*Animation in the hall. Applause.*) What is it that we lack? I think the main reason is that we pay too little attention to such matters and regard them as trivial. But is this trivial? No, it is such "trivial matters" that constitute the work of many people.

Some foreign visitors who have been to the Soviet Union write: "When you walk through Moscow in winter you see many women working with crowbars and picks." On this basis they claim that women are not held in esteem in our country. There is hardly any need to prove what great esteem is enjoyed by Soviet women, who, not just in words, but in actual fact have equal rights with men in all spheres of public and political life and in production. (*Applause.*) Much has been done in our country to ease the work of women, but this is still not enough. It is high time to take up the mechanization of labour-consuming processes in order to make work easier, particularly where women are employed, and to make it more productive and hence more remunerative. (*Applause.*)

We should also see to easing woman's work in the household in every way. For this purpose, we should build more nurseries, kindergartens, boarding-schools, dining halls, laundries, and other cultural and service establishments. We should do everything necessary in order that cultural and service establishments, enterprises serving the daily needs of the people, should satisfy more fully and better the growing needs of the population. All these are very important questions that concern the life of the Soviet people. The solving of these questions must not be brushed aside.

Labour productivity will continue to rise steadily in connection with the development of technology, further improvement of production, specialization and automation. Under these conditions there will be no shortage of workers in the bigger cities and in some places there may be redundancy. The workers who are released will be fully able to find a use for their labour in other towns.

Many factory and office workers, especially young people, have recently left the bigger cities for work in other areas. Young patriots from Moscow, Leningrad, Kiev and many other cities have responded enthusiastically to the call of the Party and gone to develop new lands, to build factories and other enterprises. We are confident that our splendid Soviet youth will continue to take part even more energetically in accomplishing the great tasks of building communism. (*Prolonged applause.*)

Comrades, I, as a voter, shall also be voting and as a voter I want to make some remarks about the shortcomings in urban building.

Not so long ago much was being said and written about tall buildings. It has been shown that tall buildings are uneconomical and now they are no longer being built. But what type of building should predominate in large-scale urban construction? There are architects who consider that it is necessary to erect many-storeyed residential buildings for the sake of a town's better architectural appearance. They are mistaken. And this can easily be proved by the example of the development of Leningrad, Minsk and many other cities. I did not see the old Minsk, but I have heard that it was an unprepossessing city. I visited Minsk in January and saw that the city has been well built and well planned. When you drive through the main street of Minsk you get the impression that you are on Nevsky Prospekt. What is important in developing a city is not the height of its houses, but purposeful town-planning, the ability to lay out the sections correctly and to utilize relief and landscape effectively. All these factors affect the cost of construction and should be taken into consideration when determining the number of storeys for dwelling-houses.

Isn't it time that the officials in charge of urban building, and especially those in charge of developing Moscow, stopped arguing and arrived at a decision on the economically desirable height for housing developments on a mass scale?

The state is allocating vast sums for housing construction, and government bodies and building organizations are duty-bound to take particular care that these funds are used in the most effective way. At the same time thought should be given to attracting the savings of those sections of the population who have them and are in need of better housing conditions. With that end in view, it is evidently advisable to organize housing co-operatives and to build with their aid. (*Applause.*) People who have savings should be given an opportunity to build country cottages or buy prefabricated houses. (*Applause.*) In this way it will be possible to use spare funds in the possession of the population for housing construction.

In recent years the output of consumer goods has considerably increased in our country—more textiles, clothing and other articles are being produced. People have begun to eat better and dress better. But it must be admitted that we have difficulties in this connection which must be overcome.

We are confronted with the important task of increasing the output of footwear, textiles, clothing and other consumer goods so as to meet the requirements of the Soviet people for these goods in the next five to seven years. How can this task be accomplished? Every year agriculture is turning out more and more natural raw materials for industry. In addition to using natural raw materials, we must secure a considerable increase in the production of textiles, footwear and other goods from artificial fibre and high-quality substitutes for leather, fur and other materials.

The Central Committee of the Party and the Government plan to organize on an extensive scale the production of artificial and synthetic fibres, plastics and other materials and goods made from them, for the purpose of satisfying the requirements of the population and the needs of industry. By using synthetic materials, it is planned to carry out large-scale measures to meet the needs of the population in clothing, footwear and household goods. In addition to a considerable quantitative expansion in the production of textiles, it is planned to bring about a substantial improvement in variety and quality.

It is necessary, by using synthetic materials, to achieve a rapid increase in the output of all kinds of domestic appliances and articles, and also high-quality furniture, building materials and structural components.

The output of consumer goods will be sharply increased in the next few years. It is also necessary to improve the quality of these goods in every way and to manufacture high-quality goods and attractive clothing and footwear.

Our people want to have not only all the essential articles for domestic use and clothing; they also want to dress well and attractively. And is our industry doing everything possible in this field? No, not by a long way.

The measures that are being taken by the Party and the Government will enable us to secure notable changes in this sphere of economic activity too, not only to bring about a still more rapid advance in light industry production and in the output of consumer goods, but also to bring about a radical improvement in the quality of the goods designed to give colour to the life of the people.

Comrades, all the successes of our country have become possible because we are living under socialism, when the people are the complete masters of their country and take a most active part in all spheres of political, economic and cultural life.

The working people of our country are deeply interested in electing as deputies the best and worthiest representatives of the people. It is precisely for this reason that our people regard the elections to the Supreme Soviet as their own vital concern. Almost the entire electorate takes part in the voting.

There is nothing like that in capitalist countries. For instance, during the last congressional elections in the United States only 57.3 per cent of the people who had reached voting age went to the polls, and in the previous elections, in 1954, there were even fewer—42.5 per cent. Or take the elections to the House of Commons in Britain. At the last elections only 26,760,000 of the 34,852,000 electors voted. Don't these figures speak for themselves? The voters in those countries see that no matter what representative of the ruling classes they elect to Congress or Parliament there will be no change in the state of affairs. It makes no difference whether representatives of the Republican or the Democratic Party sit in the United States Congress, they will defend the interests of the ruling classes—the capitalists, bankers, big landowners and big businessmen.

Take the present composition of the United States Congress. Of the 531 congressmen, more than half are lawyers and one quarter are employers and bankers. All of them are representatives of Big Business. How many workers are members of the United States Congress? There are no real workers in the American Congress. Or let us see how many ordinary farmers are members of the American Congress. There are no farmers either. Seventeen and a half million Negroes, or 10.4 per cent of the country's entire population, are citizens of the United States. How many Negroes have been elected to Congress? According to American sources, there are three Negroes in the United States Congress, or 0.56 per cent of the total number of congressmen. Or let us see how many women are members of the United States Congress. In all, 17 women have been elected to Congress, or only three per cent. Consequently the American Congress is actually inaccessible to workers and farmers, to women and to national minorities, who are placed in a position of inequality.

Here you have the so-called "free world," in which the workers, all the working people, are given the right to vote for this or that representative of the ruling classes, but have no right to take part in the activities of the legislative bodies.

In this connection I would like to quote figures which have been provided at my request by comrades in the Central Electoral Commission. In our country 1,378 people have been registered as candidates for the Soviet of the Union and the Soviet of Nationalities. Among them 614 are workers and collective farmers directly engaged in production. which makes up 44.6 per cent of all the candidates. (*Prolonged applause.*) In all, more than 60 per cent of the candidates are workers and peasants by social status. The others are representatives of the working intelligentsia. All the candidates are representatives of the bloc of Communists and non-Party people. Of the candidates nominated for the U.S.S.R. Supreme Soviet 26.4 per cent are women. (*Applause.*) It is not difficult to see in these figures an expression of genuine Soviet democracy.

The strength and merit of our socialist democracy consists not only in the fact that the people themselves take a direct part in determining the composition of the legislative bodies, but also in the fact that all the activities of our state bodies serve the interests of the people. Workers, collective farmers, intellectuals—all the working people of our country—are working to build communist society under the banner of Marxism-Leninism, under the leadership of the Communist Party, founded by the great Lenin. All the activities of the Communist Party prove that it has always served, and continues to serve, its people, confidently leading them to the cherished goal—communism. (*Prolonged applause.*)

It is socialist democracy which has liberated the Soviet people from such "freedoms" as the right to elect their exploiter and be unemployed, the right to die of starvation or to be a wage slave of capital. That is not what our people understand by freedom. In freedom we see the right of the people to a life worthy of man, without exploiters or exploitation; the right to genuine political equality; the right to enjoy all the achievements of science and culture. We understand freedom as the liberation of the people from the horrors of unemployment and poverty, from racial, national and social oppression. (*Prolonged applause.*)

The defenders of capitalism like to picture the United States as a country of prosperous enterprise, as a model of bourgeois freedom, of bourgeois democracy. One could cite many facts and figures showing what this "model" democracy is really like. I shall not quote such facts and figures, because they are generally known. Allow me to refer only to some statements from a recent speech by an American trade-union leader, George Meany.

An emergency conference, called by the trade unions to consider the economic situation in the United States, opened on March 11. It was convened with the object of drafting proposals to be submitted to the U.S. Administration and Congress which would make it possible to restore the full volume of production and the economic development of the United States. In his speech at the conference George Meany, President of the American Federation of Labour Congress of Industrial Organizations, dwelt on the question of unemployment, which has now spread to all the main U.S. industries. According to the figures cited by George Meany, there are now in the United States 5,250,000 totally unemployed and over three million partially unemployed. During last month alone the number of unemployed in the United States increased by 750,000.

George Meany painted an unattractive picture of the present economic situation in the United States. He said:

"More than 25 per cent of our production capacities are idle. In some industries—for example, steel—production capacities are utilized only 50 per cent.... Freight shipments are 25 per cent below last year. Exports have dropped by 25 per cent compared with March 1957.

"Here are the latest extremely important statistics: In February 170,000 workers exhausted their unemployment compensation," Meany pointed out. "Just think what this means. Every week during February more than 40,000 workers exhausted all the unemployment compensation to which they were entitled. By the middle of February, 7.5 per cent of all those with a right to receive unemployment compensation were getting it."

In his speech George Meany also gave other highly

characteristic data about the burdens the working people of the United States are forced to bear.

"Do you know," he said, "that according to the last survey, in December 1956 13 million families were living in houses not conforming to the accepted standards. Thirteen million families! And the census showed that these figures had remained practically unchanged since 1950.

"We are short of many thousands of classrooms," Meany said. "Many children of our trade-union members today study in buildings which are not much better than mere chicken coops, in old, neglected buildings with a big fire risk ... and then people wonder why we do not have enough scientists, engineers and technicians to equal the Soviet Union.

"We must get America back to work...." George Meany exclaims. "This is the only possible answer to the economic crisis that is confronting our country today."*

Those are some of the facts given by an American trade-union leader.

A small handful of millionaires and billionaires are making fabulous profits out of the sufferings and privations of the people, while the millions of the working masses are compelled for months and years to look in vain for jobs and do not possess the means to feed their children and their aged fathers and mothers. At the same time the American Government is spending thousands of millions of dollars on building military bases.

The arms drive is profitable for the monopolists. They do not worry about the urgent needs of the people. Such is the nature, such is the essence of capitalism. Enrichment, aggrandizement, maximum profits—that is what the rulers of the capitalist countries strive for. Such is the motive force of capitalist society. That is what capitalist prosperity looks like in practice! That is what capitalist freedom means!

* The above quotations are retranslated from the Russian.—*Ed.*

We, of course, do not rejoice over the fact that unemployment, a real scourge for the working people, is growing in the United States. The older generation in our country remember how, before the Revolution, many hundreds of thousands of working-class families suffered hunger and poverty owing to unemployment. Unemployment is an inevitable concomitant of capitalism the ulcers of which were profoundly revealed by Marx and Lenin. They showed the working class and all the working people the road to liberation from the fetters of capitalism, the road for gaining power, the road to socialism.

And if one is to consider which world—the socialist or the capitalist—has a real right to call itself free, then there can be no two opinions on this matter—only socialism brings mankind real, and not fictitious, freedom. And the future belongs precisely to this world. (*Stormy applause.*)

Comrades, allow me to dwell now on some aspects of the international situation.

We can be satisfied with the international position of the Soviet Union. In the past four years, far from losing any friends abroad, we have strengthened still more our friendship with them and have acquired new friends. The international prestige of the Soviet Union has grown immeasurably. The Soviet Union's ties with many peoples of the world have been broadened and strengthened.

As a result of the remarkable successes achieved by the peoples of the Soviet Union and of all the socialist countries, as a result of their co-operation and mutual assistance, the socialist camp has grown immeasurably stronger, the world socialist system has been consolidated and has become a mighty force.

Great successes in building socialism have been achieved in recent years by the People's Democracies.

The imperialists have more than once tried to break the unity and solidarity of the socialist camp, resorting to armed provocations and subversion, to the organization of counter-revolutionary plots and uprisings, as was the case in Hungary in the autumn of 1956. They are trying at all costs to drive a wedge between the socialist countries and to set them at loggerheads.

But the peoples of the socialist countries have repulsed, and will continue to repulse, the forces of reaction. The working people of these countries are well aware that the social gains of the working people and their national independence can be ensured only if all the countries of socialism are united and closely knit together. That is why the further strengthening of the might of the socialist camp and its defence against the encroachments of the imperialists are the vital concern of all the peoples of the socialist countries. (*Prolonged applause.*)

The community of socialist countries is not a closed one, isolated from the non-socialist states and their peoples. Our country has strengthened its friendly ties with India, Indonesia, Burma, the United Arab Republic, and other Asian and African states whose peoples have cast off the colonial yoke and are now working to consolidate the independence of their young states.

The past four years have been years in which the Soviet Union, together with the other peaceful countries, has made persistent efforts to ease international tension, terminate the arms race and prevent a new war.

The most burning, vital question for all mankind today is the question of peace or war. Wars between states have always caused many casualties and much destruction. But a future war, if, contrary to the will of the peoples, it is unleashed, threatens to be the most destructive of all wars—a nuclear war. Apart from direct destruction, the use of nuclear weapons will contaminate the air by radioactive fall-out, and this can lead to the destruction of practically all life, especially in countries with densely populated, small territories. There, literally everything can be swept from the face of the earth.

It is precisely for this reason that in our day the struggle to preserve peace and prevent a new war has become not only the primary, vital concern of those who may be subjected to attack by the imperialists, but also the immediate concern of the people in all countries, regardless of where they may live—in Europe or Asia, America or Africa, irrespective of their class position, religious beliefs or the colour of their skin—it is literally the concern of everyone living on Earth.

The task is to prevent a new war and to ensure peace throughout the world. But this needs more than just appeals, more than the desire alone. Peace must be defended in stubborn struggle against the forces that are trying to unleash a new war.

To live without wars, without fear for the morrow, without slavery and poverty, free from the exploitation of some countries by others, free from social injustices—that is what the best minds of mankind and the working people of the whole world have dreamed of for centuries. But only today can these noble dreams become clothed with reality. This has become possible as a result of the strengthened might of the Soviet Union and the entire world socialist system, that have inaugurated a new epoch in the history of mankind—the epoch of real socialist freedom and the triumph of reason.

Today the decisive requirement for mankind's advance along the path of progress is peace, the prevention of those terrible disasters that a new war would bring.

The Communist Party and the Soviet Government, for whom there is nothing greater than the fulfilment of the aspirations of the people, have done, and are doing, everything necessary to prevent a new war and to direct the development of international relations along the lines of preserving a stable peace. They are doing everything possible to achieve peace and equitable relations and friendship among all peoples in deeds and not in words.

In the four years that have elapsed since the last elections to the Supreme Soviet our Party and the Soviet Government have exerted tremendous efforts to relieve international tension.

Let me remind you of some of the most important steps in foreign policy taken by the Soviet Union. We played an active part in stopping the wars in Korea and Viet-Nam; on the initiative of the Soviet Union the conflict with Yugoslavia was ended and relations were normalized; thanks to the active policy of the Soviet Union, a peace treaty was concluded with Austria; we withdrew our troops from Port Arthur and Dalny and voluntarily gave up the military base in Finland; relations have been normalized with the Federal Republic of Germany and with Japan.

Without waiting for a general agreement on disarmament to be reached, the Soviet Union has repeatedly carried out unilateral reductions of its own Armed Forces—640,000 in 1955; 1,200,000 in 1956-57—and today it is completing another reduction by an additional 300,000 men. Corresponding reductions have been carried out by our country in armaments, military equipment and military allocations for defence purposes.

All honest people see that such measures can be carried out only by a state which wants peace and not war, the normalization and not the worsening of the international situation. Some people accuse us of aggressive intentions. If that were really so, we should not, under any circumstances, have yielded our advantageous positions in Austria, which were won in fierce struggle against fascist Germany. But we did conclude peace with Austria and withdraw our troops from that country. What "conqueror" would have done that? The Soviet Union strove for such a solution of the Austrian problem because it really has the interests of peace at heart and does not interfere in the affairs of other countries, because it is fully resolved to achieve peaceful co-existence with all countries. (*Applause.*)

Or take the question of the military base in Finland.

What state, if it had aggressive intentions, would voluntarily relinquish its rights to military bases provided for by international treaty?

Of course, some Western politicians, who are accustomed to measuring everything with their own yardstick, cannot understand this. But this is well understood by all honest people.

The Soviet Union stands for beneficial good-neighbourly relations with all countries without exception. We are ready to establish such relations with all states that desire it on the basis of reciprocity. (*Applause.*)

We have approached Turkey with good intentions but, unfortunately, have not so far met with the necessary understanding on her part. Nevertheless, notwithstanding unfriendly, anti-Soviet speeches by some political leaders of Turkey, our relations with that country are no longer what they were four years ago. We cannot but mention some signs and tendencies towards an improvement in relations between our countries. We shall spare no effort and shall continue our peaceful policy in the hope that the Turkish people and the Government of Turkey will understand our good and sincere intentions. In the interests of preserving peace for our peoples it is necessary that our countries, which are close neighbours with common frontiers by land and sea, should be friends, not enemies. This will be of benefit to world peace. (*Applause.*)

Another of our neighbours in the South is Iran. During the stay of the Shah of Iran in the U.S.S.R. we had many useful conversations with him. Frontier questions in dispute for hundreds of years have now been settled to mutual satisfaction. Today we are negotiating with Iran on some economic questions: the building of dams, irrigation, the utilization of frontier rivers in the interests of both our countries. The satisfactory solution of these problems will be beneficial for the development of good-neighbourly relations between our countries. We have told the Government of Iran that the Soviet Union did not have, and does not have, any unfriendly intentions with regard to Iran. We think that the Iranian Government has become convinced of this. (*Applause.*)

About our relations with Afghanistan we can say that in recent years they have become still better and sounder than before, and we wish that they continue to develop in a spirit of friendship, mutual understanding and joint concern for the preservation of peace. (*Applause.*)

As has already been pointed out, in recent years friendly relations with the Indonesian Republic have taken shape. Soviet men and women cannot but pay attention to the imperialist machinations in Indonesia. Why are the imperialists trying to interfere in the internal affairs of that country? And why are they organizing plots there? This must not be permitted. The Indonesian people should themselves arrange their life at their own discretion, and no one has any right to impose upon them his will or a way of life they do not want.

One cannot but express regret at the fact that our relations with Pakistan and some other Asian countries that have been drawn by the imperialists into the Baghdad Pact and SEATO, have failed to improve for reasons that do not depend on the Soviet Union.

Good-neighbourly relations are developing between the Soviet Union and Finland, and the other Scandinavian countries. We appreciate the neutrality of Sweden, who wants to keep out of military blocs. The Soviet Union respects the step in foreign policy taken by the Norwegian Government, headed by Mr. Gerhardsen, and the Danish Government, headed by Mr. Hansen, who have displayed an awareness of their duty and a sense of responsibility for the fate of their countries by opposing the basing of atomic and rocket weapons on their territories. (*Applause.*)

Following the conclusion of the State Treaty, our relations with neutral Austria, too, have become normal and are developing in the spirit of good-neighbourliness.

There are great opportunities for better relations with

Italy and Greece. The Soviet people know that the Italian and Greek peoples entertain great sympathy and respect for our country. Similar sentiments of friendship, respect and sympathy are entertained by the Soviet people for the Italian people and the people of Greece. These mutual sentiments have deep-rooted traditions which evolved in past centuries and grew strong in the common struggle against fascism. (*Applause.*)

We cannot, of course, fail to take into account the fact that influential spokesmen of these two countries pay more heed to the voice of NATO generals than to the voice of their peoples, and have already, judging by newspaper reports, begun to prepare for the construction of American rocket bases in their countries. But we believe in the common sense of the Italians and the Greeks. At all events, on our part there is good will and readiness to establish friendly relations with these states. It is now, therefore, up to them.

We can note with satisfaction that there are tangible signs of a certain improvement in the relations between the Soviet Union and the Latin American countries. We are well aware of what is hindering such an improvement even now. But it is not our fault that there are still no broad and mutually advantageous relations between the Soviet Union and these countries. This is being hindered in every way by certain imperialist circles who look upon Latin America as their private domain and who prevent industrialization in these countries and keep them in the position of raw material appendages.

The conscience of mankind cannot tolerate the situation that has developed in Algeria. A bloody war is going on there and the Arab population is being exterminated. Though the Algerian question has been discussed by the United Nations, the complaints of the Algerian people have remained unheeded. The governments of the imperialist states have turned their backs on the tears of millions of Algerians, on the frightful tragedy they are living through.

It is time to put an end to this bloodshed and to facilitate an agreement on the Algerian problem in accordance with the interests of the Algerian population and taking into consideration the interests of France. Cannot the French ruling circles realize that if they do not seek, do not want to seek, a peaceful solution to the Algerian problem, they run the risk of leading their country into an even greater fiasco than was the case in Indo-China?

It is time for the colonialists to realize that each people can and should be the complete master of its own destiny. (*Stormy applause.*)

Our policy with regard to other countries, irrespective of whether they are large or small, is clear. We do not interfere in their internal affairs, for we consider that the political system, the social order, the ideology, or in other words everything that we call the way of life, is the internal, inalienable right of the people of each country. Every nation knows itself how best it should live at a particular time, what views to adhere to, what religion to follow, and nobody, no state, has the right to impose upon other countries and peoples its own way of life. This is the policy bequeathed to us by Lenin, we have been pursuing it unswervingly and shall continue to do so. (*Prolonged applause.*)

We are ready to establish good, friendly relations with all states. Who can deny that this is the only practicable policy, in keeping with the interests of all countries?

I would like to dwell briefly on the problem of relations between the U.S.S.R. and such Western states as France, Britain and the United States, which together with the Soviet Union, the Chinese People's Republic and India, bear great responsibility for maintaining universal peace and safeguarding the security of the nations.

We were allies of Britain, France and the United States during the Second World War and we fought together against Hitler Germany. We respect the peoples of those countries and have a high opinion of the great contribution they have made to the development of world science, technology and culture. Soviet men and women are very well aware that the peoples of those countries, too, are striving for peace. The Soviet Union has exerted, and will continue to exert, every effort to achieve understanding and establish friendly relations with the peoples of those countries and their governments.

The Communist Party and the Soviet Government proceed from the premise that under present conditions all governments who rightly understand their responsibility for the destiny of the world must rise above ideological differences. In international affairs, in settling existing disputes, they should be guided, not by what divides the world today, but by what brings countries closer together in their joint effort to preserve peace.

The only possible foundation for relations between states with different social systems are the well-known Five Principles: mutual respect for territorial integrity and sovereignty; non-aggression; non-interference in one another's internal affairs for economic, political or ideological reasons; equality and mutual benefit; peaceful co-existence.

The principles of peaceful co-existence, recently approved by the United Nations, should actually be made the corner-stone of relations between all states. Unfortunately, such countries as the United States, Britain and France so far show no desire to be guided by these principles in their relations with other countries. And this circumstance has left its mark on the whole of the present situation. It prevents the achieving of a *détente* and the creation of confidence. The result is that the arms race continues; the cold war that is poisoning the international atmosphere is still maintained; the number of controversial international issues is hardly any less, and the danger of war has not been removed. Such a prospect, however, does not suit the peoples at all.

The peoples are tired of the cold war. Fear of the possibility of a devastating war is preventing them from working normally. People cannot live in tranquility if their efforts are senselessly wasted on the production of instruments of annihilation. People are not secure as long as there is the possibility that imperialist provocateurs of some kind will risk starting war. It will not take much in the present tense conditions and with the existing suspicions for the "accidental" appearance of a foreign plane, for a bomb "accidentally" dropped by it, to cause a military conflict which may turn into a general war. Strange as it may seem, there are some persons in official positions in the United States and Britain who are trying to prove that flights of bombers carrying hydrogen bombs are necessary. The more planes with hydrogen weapons are flying in the air, the less the room that is left for the doves of peace and the more for the machinations of the demon of war.

The level of armaments in some countries is now at such a stage that a moment is evidently coming—perhaps it has already come—when these countries themselves, irrespective of whether an agreement on discontinuing the manufacture of atom and hydrogen bombs is reached or not, will have to say: "Enough!"

In the past obsolete weapons and military equipment were replaced as new models were developed, but today, evidently, a stage has been reached in which it is difficult to invent a more powerful weapon than the hydrogen bomb, since there are no limits to its power. It is not by chance that scientists—so far timidly, it is true—are expressing the opinion that if the accumulated stockpiles of nuclear weapons are exploded, this can poison the atmosphere of the entire world.

The appalling consequences of nuclear weapons for all mankind are realized not only by scientists but also by the broadest sections of the public, by hundreds of millions of ordinary people throughout the world. They are increasingly demanding of the governments, and above all of the governments of the countries possessing nuclear weapons, that an end be put to the tests of these weapons. Common sense suggests to the people the only way out of the dead-lock on the disarmament problem. And this way out lies in the complete prohibition of nuclear weapons.

We are apparently approaching a time when governments, if they want to retain their bonds with the people, will no longer be able to turn a deaf ear to this universal demand of our times, and, even if they do not reach an agreement among themselves, they will be compelled unilaterally to discontinue the production of atomic and hydrogen weapons.

The Soviet Union is doing everything in its power to remove the present international tension and to ensure that the people all over the world can breathe freely and live in peace, enjoying the fruits of their labour. The matter is complicated by the fact that the other side does not desire this and is striving to preserve and expand its military blocs Yet, as is well known, the capitalist countries form such blocs not for peace but for war.

The Soviet Union always has been and is against war as an instrument of international policy and against dividing the world into military blocs. We see the way to an easing of international tension not in setting up new military groupings and preserving existing ones, not in the arms race and in stockpiling more and more deadly weapons for the extermination of human beings.

What, indeed, does the stubborn unwillingness of certain Western circles to agree to a relaxation of international tension signify? What is the meaning of their policy of building up military alliances?

Nothing else but preparations for a new war. Already at the present time the stockpiling of instruments of annihilation is doing grave damage to the interests of the peoples. It is leading to the extraction of more and more taxes from the people, to the impoverishment of their material, cultural and spiritual lives, to the subordination of the life of whole nations to the interests of war preparations. The peoples have grown tired of this policy. Their indignation is mounting and social conflicts are becoming sharper. In order to suppress the people's discontent, to fight the workers' movement and resolve their internal contradictions, the ruling circles of the imperialist countries are seeking a way out in military adventures.

We Communists are realists in our policies and we say that peace not only should, but can be preserved. If the peoples acquire a deep understanding of the frightful danger involved in a new world war and the sufferings it can bring to mankind, they will intensify their struggle for peace and will frustrate the machinations of the warmongers. We are decidedly in favour of abolishing the cold war, we are for the greatest possible development of trade relations and cultural ties with all countries, for a relaxation of international tension. In short, we stand for peaceful co-existence, for peaceful competition between all states. (*Applause.*)

It is precisely with this aim in view that the Soviet Government has addressed to the Governments of the Great Powers, and also to the governments of most countries of the world, a proposal for a meeting of representatives of states at the highest level. At such a meeting the representatives of the parties concerned could exchange views on the ways of abolishing the cold war and take the first steps towards solving urgent international problems, the settlement of which is awaited and persistently demanded by the broad masses of the people.

Of course, not all issues can be solved now. The chief task, however, is to make a good beginning for easing international tension. Just as the farmer plants the seed in tilled soil and expects good shoots, a rich harvest, so we can lay the foundation for a better understanding and the solution of major international problems. We can and should promote the growth and strengthening of the tree of friendship and peace, the development of new, healthy relations between peoples, the consolidation of peaceful co-existence, the exclusion of the use of force in solving out-standing issues, observance of the United Nations' principles, prevention of any infringement of the interests of countries and interference in the internal affairs of other states.

In our opinion, the pressing international questions at the present stage are:

immediate discontinuation of atomic and hydrogen weapons tests;

renunciation by the U.S.S.R., the United States and Britain of the use of nuclear weapons;

the establishment of an atom-free zone in Central Europe;

conclusion of a non-aggression agreement between the member-states of the North Atlantic bloc and the Warsaw Treaty Organization;

reduction of the numerical strength of foreign forces on the territory of Germany and other European states;

elaboration of an agreement on questions concerning the prevention of sudden attack;

ways of easing tension in the Middle East;

measures for the expansion of international trade relations;

the cessation of war propaganda.

Who can assert that only the Soviet Union is interested in settling these questions, or that they are of no concern to the peoples of other countries, including the United States, Britain and France? It is life itself that has raised and prepared these questions.

In conformity with the wishes of the United States Government, we are also ready to discuss such questions as:

prohibition of the use of outer space for military purposes and the dismantling of military bases on foreign territories;

conclusion of a German peace treaty;

development of ties and contacts between countries.

Thus, the draft agenda for a summit conference proposed

by us not only takes into account questions raised by our side but also includes proposals by the United States which can be discussed to advantage, striving to improve the international situation and not to worsen it.

We have already said that it is possible and necessary to achieve a settlement also of the questions put forward in the past by President Eisenhower, such as the pooling of efforts to combat malaria and cancer, and the implementation of other measures of a similar nature. On these questions opinions can be exchanged at any level and, if it is found necessary, instruction can be given to the appropriate agencies to work on the solution of these problems. We even think that the respective agencies of both sides can immediately undertake the solution of these problems.

It is well known that we have also agreed to a Foreign Ministers' meeting, suggesting that it be held in April. We have given two variants of the possible composition of its participants. In our opinion it is time to discuss concretely questions of preparing and calling both a Ministers' meeting and a summit conference.

In the reply aide-mémoire of the U.S. State Department and in the message of the President of the United States, the entire question of a summit meeting has been relegated to the starting-point again. These documents say nothing about the substance of our proposals, but again put forward the German question and the question of the situation in the East European countries.

We cannot hide our disappointment with regard to the attitude adopted by the Government of the United States. It was a disappointment not only for us, by the way, but also for the peace forces in every country.

This has been well and convincingly expressed by the President of the Czechoslovak Republic, Comrade Novotny, in the recent interview he gave correspondents of the Czechoslovak News Agency and the newspaper *Rude Pravo*.

"I cannot conceive that any East European country could agree to a discussion on such a question," Comrade Novotný stressed. "Czechoslovakia at any rate rejects it categorically. Our affairs were discussed without us in Munich by Hitler. But 1958 is not 1938." (*Prolonged applause.*)

Indeed, the very fact of the inclusion of the so-called question of the situation in the East European countries in the message of the President of the United States is unheard of in relations between states. Just think, how can a state which maintains normal diplomatic relations with other countries and has its diplomatic representatives in those countries, while those countries have their Embassies in Washington and are members of the United Nations—how can such a state raise with third states the question of the state structure of those countries? Has anyone given this state authority for this? If it has such authority, let it produce it. This is indeed a flagrant breach of elementary rules in relations between states.

We have already repeatedly and resolutely declared that we will not discuss this question. And not because we are so "intransigent," as some people in the Western countries would like to make us out to be; and not because we reject out of hand the proposals of the United States, as they allege. The very raising of this question is insulting to those countries which the President of the United States has in mind, and is contrary to common sense. (*Stormy applause.*)

If anyone wants to discuss the question of the social system of certain socialist countries, why not name such a country as the Soviet Union? Why are the socialist countries of Asia, the Chinese People's Republic, for example, excluded? True, the United States does not recognize China, but China will not cease to exist or suffer any harm because of this. The great People's China exists—and not only exists, but is developing successfully. (*Stormy applause.*)

As we have already had occasion to say, the question of the socialist régime has been subjected to a "discussion," even weapons being used. On this question the peoples of the Soviet Union conducted "negotiations," with the United States as well, when, following the October Revolution, the interventionists invaded our territory in order to abolish the gains of October, destroy Soviet power and restore the capitalist régime. The dispute was already then decided in favour of socialism. (*Stormy applause.*) Why, then, raise such questions again? We reject them, and not only reject them, but declare that in the event of any new attempt from outside to change by force the way of life in socialist countries, we shall not be mere onlookers and shall not leave our friends in the lurch. (*Stormy applause.*) We are true to our obligations and our international duty and we should not like to see anyone try our patience again. (*Prolonged applause.*)

Why, we for our part, too, can put forward similar questions, namely: how long will capitalism exist in the West European countries? Isn't it time for that system to give way to the more progressive, socialist system? (*Prolonged applause.*) Hasn't enough blood been shed in wars instigated by imperialist states? This is a reasonable question, not only from our point of view, but also from the standpoint of all mankind. (*Applause.*) But we are realists. How can we raise this question with representatives of capitalist countries, with whom we intend to conduct negotiations on the abolition of the cold war and the guarantee of peaceful co-existence after these talks? One doesn't have to possess a fertile imagination to realize that such a question cannot be a subject for discussion, either at the highest or at the lowest level. We consider it absurd to raise such questions, and we do not raise them. (*Applause.*)

We tell our Western partners: if you really want to abolish the cold war, of which the people are sick and tired, and ensure the peaceful co-existence of countries, the way to bringing closer together the positions on disputed questions should not be made harder. With two social systems in existence, there can be no other policy than that of reasonable compromise, which does not affect internal régimes, does not place one country or another in a position of advantage, and does not infringe on the security of the states concerned.

I also want to make a few remarks about the so-called German question. At one time we made persistent efforts to settle this question in complete conformity with the Crimean and Potsdam declarations. It is not our fault that this was not achieved. The Western Powers were interested in reviving German militarism instead of creating a united, democratic and peaceful Germany.

The situation has radically changed since then. Two sovereign German states have been formed and they themselves have to find the way to a *rapprochement*. We maintain normal diplomatic relations with these two states—the German Democratic Republic and the Federal Republic of Germany—and we refuse to interfere in their internal affairs.

If there is really a desire to do something useful in this sphere, the question of concluding a peace treaty with Germany should be discussed. If the Western Powers are against that, we shall not insist on including it in the agenda. But we cannot agree to some people tying up European security with the German question, as is done in the State Department's aide-mémoire. Such a tie-up had its history, but those days are gone.

The main thing now is to ensure European security. But a solution to this important problem in the way proposed by the United States and some other Western countries will by no means strengthen peace in Europe and, consequently, will not strengthen world peace either. Need it be said that this will bring neither a more stable peace nor security to the Germans, whether in West Germany or in East Germany.

The German problem is an important one for the German nation. But we must proceed from the interests of ensuring the security of all the European peoples, including the German people. Let us, therefore, begin by settling the problem which concerns all Europe and the entire world, and this will facilitate the solution of the German problem as well.

When Europe stops being a theatre for military competition between the two blocs, when foreign troops go back home, when the threat of war is eliminated, that is to say, when European security is ensured and tension has been eased, all the peoples of Europe, and for that matter not only of Europe, will only gain by that. Would not all this help the German people, who now live in two states with different social conditions, to find a way to contact, to *rapprochement* and to the solution of the issues that cause anxiety to the populations of both those states? Any other way will lead, not to the solution of the German question, but to a worsening of the situation and even to war.

So if the approach to the present international situation is unbiased, it is absolutely clear who is for peace and friendship among the peoples and who aims at sharpening the international situation.

The Soviet Union, the Chinese People's Republic, all the socialist countries are seeking to ease international tension and strengthen confidence among states; they are seeking to stop the arms race, to ban nuclear weapons and to achieve a major settlement of the disarmament problem in general.

Our proposal for a summit conference is fresh proof of the Soviet Union's policy of peace.

As for the Western Powers, and in the first place the United States, in words they declare their allegiance to peace, but in fact they are preventing the ending of international tension and the establishment of confidence among states. The main thing today is that the peoples must not let themselves be fooled by the empty talk of some Western statesmen about peace—talk which is not backed up by concrete deeds.

Let us take, for instance, what the U.S. Secretary of State told a news conference on March 4. The whole of his statement, though well-seasoned with phrases about love of peace, was chiefly aimed at worsening relations and stirring up polemics in order thereby to complicate a summit meeting. We do not want to take this road.

The Soviet Union has stood, and continues to stand for peaceful co-existence, not because it is weak or because it fears threats. If we were not weak before, then today, all the more so, we have everything necessary to protect the peaceful labour of the Soviet people and to smash any aggressor, should he try to attack our country. (*Stormy applause.*) We are sure that the great ideas of communism will triumph, but we have never imposed upon other countries by force of arms the socialist way of life and our ideology, nor do we intend to do so. The Soviet people want to live in peace and friendship with all other peoples.

On the eve of the Supreme Soviet elections we who have leading positions in the Communist Party and the Soviet state, whom the people have put at the helm of the country, declare that we shall spare no effort and shall continue to work perseveringly to accomplish the noble tasks of strengthening peace and preventing another war. (*Prolonged applause.*)

* * *

Comrades, our elections are taking place in an atmosphere of tremendous patriotic enthusiasm, of the further strengthening of the alliance between the workers and the peasants. The Soviet people firmly believe that under the leadership of their Communist Party they will achieve further successes in attaining their cherished goal—the building of communism. (*Stormy applause.*)

The moral and political unity of Soviet society and the friendship between the peoples of our country are growing and becoming stronger. (*Applause.*) Our peoples are still more closely rallying around the Communist Party, which has always considered and continues to consider its aim to be that of faithfully serving the people and protecting their vital interests. This is convincingly borne out by the entire activity of our Party. (*Prolonged applause.*) The people have always regarded the Bolshevik Party as their true defender, expressing their interests. They have rallied round the Party and filled its ranks with their best sons and daughters. So it was half a century ago, when a handful of convinced Bolshevik Leninists fought in the grim conditions of tsarist autocracy for the liberation of the working people from the fetters of capitalism. So it is today, when the Communist Party of the Soviet Union has grown into a mighty army of advanced builders of communism. (*Stormy applause.*)

The lackeys of imperialism babble allegations to the effect that the Communists keep themselves in power by force, that the peoples of the Soviet Union and of the socialist countries are only waiting to free themselves from the "yoke" of the Communists. But everybody knows what these fabrications are worth! The recent claimants to world domination—the Nazis—babbled about the same things when they launched their predatory attack upon our country. By their own experience, however, they learned that the Soviet people and the Communist Party are a united and truly invincible force. (*Stormy applause.*)

The Communist Party, which is the vanguard, the advanced section of the people, is of the flesh and blood of the people.

In these elections to the U.S.S.R. Supreme Soviet, as in previous election campaigns, our Party is in close alliance with non-Party people. This means that the Communists will cast their votes both for Party and non-Party candidates, while the non-Party people will vote both for non-Party and Communist candidates. (*Prolonged applause.*) There is no doubt that the entire electorate will cast their votes unanimously for the candidates of the bloc of Communists and non-Party people and thereby again demonstrate their unbreakable unity and solidarity with the Communist Party and the Soviet Government. (*Stormy applause.*)

Long live our mighty socialist homeland! (*Prolonged, stormy applause.*)

Long live the Communist Party of the Soviet Union—the inspirer and organizer of all the victories of the Soviet people! (*Prolonged, stormy applause.*)

Glory to the Soviet people—the great builder of communism! (*Prolonged, stormy applause. All rise.*)

INTERVIEW GIVEN TO CORRESPONDENT
OF *LE FIGARO*

March 19, 1958

On March 19, N. S. Khrushchov received M. Serge Groussard, correspondent of the French newspaper *Le Figaro*, at the latter's request, and had a talk with him.

Below we publish M. Groussard's questions and N. S. Khrushchov's replies.

Groussard: I have been greatly impressed by the tall buildings and the new blocks which are going up in Moscow. It seems to me you are also exerting great efforts in the countryside, where the collective farms now have large numbers of up-to-date machines.

Khrushchov: You rightly understand our efforts. We rejoice in the successes achieved by our country and rejoice in the favourable prospects for the country's further development.

Groussard: I believe that at the present time the main task of the Soviet Union is of an economic character. It is to overtake and then surpass the most developed capitalist countries in production per head of population.

Khrushchov: You have a correct understanding of the main economic task confronting us. To overtake and then outstrip the economically most developed countries in per capita output—that is the chief task of the Soviet people and our Party. In 1917, when the working class, the working people of Russia, under the leadership of our Party and headed by Lenin, carried through the socialist revolution, Russia was one of the most backward of the capitalist countries. The Soviet people undertook to transform their country. Even very bold people in the West did not believe in Lenin's great plans and projects. You probably remember the pronouncements of H. G. Wells, the famous British writer, who after visiting Soviet Russia and speaking with Lenin, in his book *Russia in the Shadows* called Lenin a great dreamer—"the dreamer in the Kremlin."

Reality, however, corrected H. G. Wells, who was a very great writer but a poor politician. He did not have sufficient imagination to see what Lenin saw when he spoke about our country's future.

The advantages of the socialist over the capitalist system were demonstrated already at the early stages of the Soviet Union's development—the socialist system opens up before all ordinary people, the whole nation, the greatest opportunities to develop and apply their abilities and ensures a steady rise in their material and cultural standards; under socialism the people themselves are the supreme masters of their country. Today the Soviet people are successfully accomplishing a great task—that of overtaking and outstripping in the briefest historical period the most developed capitalist countries, including the United States, in the level of production per head of population.

The Soviet people are building a communist society and are confidently marching towards this great goal. In so doing they are guided by the immortal teaching of Marxism-Leninism. There is no doubt whatsoever that the Soviet people will successfully carry out all the tasks confronting them.

Groussard: The Soviet Union, which already today possesses innumerable political and economic advantages, must be regarded as one of the richest countries in the world. On this basis, don't you think, Mr. Khrushchov, that the Soviet Union, for its part, could render systematic aid to underdeveloped countries?

I know that the U.S.S.R. is already rendering assistance to some economically underdeveloped countries. But has not the time come to conclude an agreement among all the prosperous states of the world so that aid to the poorest peoples may be organized on a wide scale and in a rational way?

Khrushchov: At the Geneva Conference of Heads of Government Edgar Faure put forward the idea that an understanding should be reached to end the arms race and that, out of this, a certain share of the budgets should be contributed to a common fund for assisting underdeveloped countries. At that time, at the Geneva Conference, we regarded this idea with favour. Today, too, we believe that if an easing of international tension is achieved, then by economizing resources now being expended by states on their armaments and armed forces, sums could be allotted sufficient to render real and tangible assistance to the underdeveloped countries.

When underdeveloped countries ask the Soviet Union for help, it meets them half-way and gives them whatever help it can. We shall continue this policy in the future.

Our stand is that the aid given the underdeveloped countries should not place them in a position of dependence on the rich and economically highly developed countries. Many capitalist countries, though, pursue a different policy, and grant credits to underdeveloped countries for military purposes only It is obvious that credits obtained for military purposes do not raise the economic potential of the countries that get them, but, on the contrary, lower this potential. We, on the other hand, are in favour of assisting the underdeveloped countries to build up their own industries, so that they can develop their own productive forces and implement their political and economic plans independently of other countries.

Unfortunately our policy is not meeting with sympathy among ruling circles in the economically highly developed capitalist countries. In granting credits to underdeveloped countries for military purposes or consumer needs, these capitalist countries try to subjugate them and make them still more dependent on the will of the ruling circles of monopolistic states. Take the credits granted for the purchase of consumer goods, for example. The countries obtaining the credits quickly use up the consumer goods and are again obliged to beg fresh credits from the rich countries. Such credits only make those who receive them still more dependent on the rich countries. That is why the rich capitalist countries do not want to grant the under-developed countries credits for industrial development; they do not want these countries to put an end to their economic backwardness. We stand for disinterested and real help to the underdeveloped countries to enable them to overcome their backwardness and grow increasingly more independent from the economic point of view as well.

Groussard: The industrial use of atomic energy in the Soviet Union is becoming increasingly varied and bold. Will not these efforts bring about a transformation of the entire Soviet economy?

Khrushchov: I not only think so—I am sure that the industrial use of atomic energy will promote a still more rapid material and technical transformation and develop-ment of the Soviet economy.

Mastery of the secrets of nuclear energy and its use for peaceful purposes augment mankind's potentialities in the effort to make Nature serve the interests of human well-being. That is precisely why the Soviet people have set about introducing atomic energy in many branches of our country's economy with such vigour and on such a large scale. It is common knowledge that the world's first atomic power plant has been functioning in our country since 1954. We have set ourselves the target of building, in the next few years, atomic power stations with a total capacity of two to two and a half million kilowatts. Last year we launched the world's first atomic ice-breaker, the *Lenin*—a ship which can cruise for two or three years without refuelling. The use of radioactive isotopes in various branches of science, industry and agriculture is also common knowledge. It can be said with conviction that in a communist society atomic energy will be one of the main sources of power.

Groussard: Could you say a word or two about the hopes and achievements emerging from the revolutions of the first artificial satellites around our planet?

Khrushchov: The making and launching of the artificial earth satellites ushered in a new era in scientific and technological development. The sputniks will tremendously enrich our knowledge of the Earth, its atmosphere and outer space. The launching of the sputniks is man's first step into outer space. Scientists are convinced that people will be able to embark upon interplanetary travel in the foreseeable future.

The launching of the Soviet artificial earth satellites is glowing proof of the high level attained by Soviet scientific and technical personnel and of the high level of our industrial development. It is the fruit of successful collective creative effort on the part of the Soviet scientists, engineers, technicians and factory workers who made the sputniks and the intercontinental ballistic rockets which put the satellites into orbit.

Not so long ago the United States also launched an artificial earth satellite. We welcomed this and hope that, like the Soviet sputniks, it will serve the cause of peace and of the progress of all mankind. A few days ago, after a succession of failures, the Americans finally managed to launch their second "Vanguard" satellite, which has now joined Soviet Sputnik II and the American "Explorer" satellite.

Groussard: Will not material achievements lead ultimately to the disappearance of social differences and national barriers, and to a time when political contradictions will lose all meaning?

Khrushchov: Social differences and national barriers

are a result of the class structure of bourgeois society. In that society the means of production are in the hands of a small group of people who live at the expense of the labour of others. Under such conditions the material progress of society, not only fails to eliminate social differences, but, on the contrary, increases social inequality and sharpens the contradictions between the exploited and the exploiters.

The expansion of production, the development of technology, everything that promotes material progress, will not in itself make the worker equal to the capitalist or the small peasant equal to the big landowner. Under the conditions of a class society the dominant classes utilize material progress for their personal enrichment, for concentrating new and ever-increasing material values and riches in their own hands. Can social differences disappear under such conditions? Of course not.

Social differences disappear only under the conditions of socialist society, in which there are no capitalists, landed proprietors, financial tycoons and other groups of exploiters.

In socialist society material progress, far from increasing social inequality, serves to make society still more monolithic, improves the material well-being of the whole of society and raises the standard of living of all those who work. You know that the principle of socialism is paying for work in accordance with the quantity and quality of the labour involved. Socialism is the first phase of communist society, in which the requirements of the people will be satisfied in accordance with their needs and people will work according to their abilities.

As for national barriers, they, too, are a result of the class structure of capitalist society. National discord and enmity are fomented by the ruling classes of the bourgeois states in order that the minority in whose hands the wealth is concentrated may exploit the majority of the people, that is to say, the working classes. The exploiting classes seek to enslave and rob not only their own peoples, but also the peoples of the colonial and dependent countries. Colonialism is a monstrous offspring of the epoch of capitalism. Overlordship in Asia, Africa and South America by the industrially developed countries has brought grave consequences to the peoples in those areas.

Private ownership of the means of production and the capitalist system are inconceivable without the fomenting of enmity between nations. Capitalism has engendered the misanthropic "theories" about the superiority of one nation over another and the inferiority of the so-called coloured peoples. Who doesn't know how the Negro population is treated in the United States? Or remember the notorious "theories" of the German fascists on the necessity of establishing the domination of "Aryans" over all the other nations.

National barriers disappear only under conditions of a socialist society. Only under socialism is the national question properly solved. In old tsarist Russia, for example, there were frequent Jewish pogroms, Armenian-Tatar massacres and other sanguinary manifestations of national enmity, fomented by capitalism. All this has disappeared under Soviet government. Soviet children and young people learn about these abominable occurrences of the past only from the elder people and literature.

National discord and enmity between nations are ruled out under socialism. This is clearly seen from the example of the Soviet Union, the Chinese People's Republic and the other socialist countries. In socialist society man is not an enemy to man but a friend and a brother. People of different nationalities work in one harmonious collective, and here there is no enmity between nation and nation. In socialist society there is complete harmony of the social and national interests of the people.

Thus, it is not a question of the material progress of society, but of the social conditions under which society develops.

Groussard: The Soviet Union is becoming more liberal with regard to travel by foreigners in its territory and with regard to travel by Soviet citizens abroad. If the international situation does not worsen, do you think it will be possible to abolish obstacles to people's movements gradually, within the next few years? Among the concrete measures which could be taken in this direction, would it be Utopian to imagine the possibility of abolishing visas between Russia and the states of Western Europe?

Khrushchov: The Soviet Government has done much to develop foreign tourist travel. Last year we adopted a number of measures facilitating the development of tourism. For example, the cost of services to tourists was revised and a new exchange rate for the ruble, more advantageous to them, was introduced. I think it will be of interest to you to learn that in 1957 about 550,000 foreigners visited the Soviet Union. During that period more than 700,000 people travelled from the U.S.S.R. to various countries of the world. During 1957 about 11,000 Frenchmen came to the U.S.S.R. and about 6,000 Soviet citizens visited France.

You were right in noting that the question of the movement of foreigners is closely linked with the international situation. I think that if we were to agree on disarmament and achieve a decisive relaxation of international tension and the establishment of complete confidence in relations between states, the obstacles to altogether lifting restrictions on the movement of foreigners in the Soviet Union and other European countries, and perhaps on their unrestricted entry into these countries, would similarly disappear.

Groussard: Could you say what you think of France, her civilization, her past, and of what she is doing for the benefit of the world.

Khrushchov: Our people have long had feelings of respect and sincere friendship for France. These feelings have firm roots of long standing. Soviet men and women respect the people of France for their creative genius, for their freedom-loving traditions. Acquaintance with the history of the French people, with their revolutionary past, their struggle for the freedom, democracy and independence of their country has great significance for the Soviet people. As in the past, so today French and Russian culture and art have close relations and exert a beneficial influence on each other.

France is a Great Power that has long played an important part in international affairs. The solution of a number of vital international problems, first and foremost those concerning the preservation of peace and security in Europe, depends to a large extent on her attitude.

We are sincerely interested in seeing a strong and prosperous France. This largely depends on how future international relations will develop and on the course they will take—the course of easing international tension and strengthening peace or the course of continuing the cold war and intensifying the arms race, which means the preparation of another war. One cannot but agree with the good sense of the arguments put forward by those who in France today say that the continuation of the cold war and France's participation in undertakings arising from the "positions of strength" policy imposed upon the members of the North Atlantic bloc, will not bring the French anything except unnecessary and unproductive squandering of France's national resources for military preparations, and unjustified burdens and privations, not to mention the destruction and disasters should France become involved in a new world war contrary to the will and wishes of her people.

I must point out in all honesty that Soviet people find it hard to understand the policy of France's present rulers. When studying France's history we have always been moved by feelings of deep respect for the glorious traditions of that country—the scene of the great French Revolution of 1789, and of the glorious Paris Commune, a wonderful example to all mankind. We Communists have learned from the glorious traditions of the French people's revolutionary struggle.

France's present rulers often impel her to do things that are contrary to her national interests and to common sense. Remember, for instance, the French Government's policy on the eve of the Second World War. If in 1939, when there were French and British delegations in the Soviet Union, the French and the British had had a more serious attitude to the negotiations, there would have been no war. But the French Government merely played at negotiations with us, did not really want to reach agreement with us and in that way encouraged Hitler against us. Thus, at that time France's rulers underestimated the significance of the Soviet Union and failed to show proper concern for their own country's future, though progressive people in your country warned the French Government of that time of what the consequences might be.

I remember 1944, when General de Gaulle was in the Soviet Union. Our countries then had good relations but later the French Government again began to pay more heed to the voice of certain circles in some countries intriguing against the Soviet Union. By worsening her relations with the Soviet Union, France is weakening her positions, too, in her relations with West Germany, Britain and the United States. We very much regret the way the situation has developed; we regret that we are not meeting with proper understanding from France.

When M. Guy Mollet and M. Pineau were in the Soviet Union, we had many conversations with them, and drew attention to the French Government's unwise policy towards Viet-Nam, as a result of which France had lost Viet-Nam completely; North Viet-Nam won independence, with the establishment there of the Democratic Republic of Viet-Nam, while South Viet-Nam is now completely under United States' influence, with the American monopolies today holding sway there. A great deal of energy was wasted on that sterile war for which the French people had to make many sacrifices.

For several years now French ruling circles have been waging a colonial war in Algeria, trying to shore up the colonial system there and to forge stronger chains of colonial bondage. However, France will ultimately lose this war, too, if France's rulers are not wise, and continue to wage a war in which Frenchmen and Algerians alike are dying, and thereby exhaust their own country and do tremendous harm to Algeria. I think it would be far more sensible if the French were to show the same measure of understanding as Britain did towards India and Burma. Now the French in Algeria want to subjugate the Arabs by force of arms. As far as I remember, there are more than eight million Arabs in Algeria and only about one million Europeans, including the French. The Algerian war will be a grim struggle to the point of exhaustion. The Algerian people who have risen up in the struggle for national liberation will not give in.

Groussard: It is my duty to tell you, Mr. Khrushchov, that the overwhelming majority of my fellow-countrymen will be grieved to hear what you say about a drama that my country is taking so much to heart. The French do not want to subjugate the Arabs of Algeria by force of arms. If that was all that was involved it would be so simple. The question is infinitely more complicated. It includes, of course, the fact that 1,200,000 native Frenchmen live in Algeria. But 400,000 Europeans, Jews and people of mixed blood also live there.... There are hundreds of thousands of Moslem servicemen and ex-servicemen who do not want to recognize any flag other than the tricolour. Four hundred thousand Algerian workers live in France. Account must also be taken of the enmity between the Berbers, who comprise the majority of the population, those who belong to the National Liberation Front—and there are many of them, true enough—and those who are in the Algerian National Movement, etc. Let order be restored swiftly so that Algeria may be able freely to decide her destiny. If France and Algeria were able to settle their mutual problems face to face, without open or covert outside interference, a peaceful and harmonious settlement would have been found long ago.

Khrushchov: If a more reasonable approach to the solution of the Algerian problem, in keeping with the spirit of the times, could be found, Algeria would evidently be able to have some kind of state contact with the French Republic in a way that would not weaken Algeria's national economy and political liberties, but would, on the contrary, strengthen them. We stand for a just settlement of the Algerian question and the satisfaction of the aspirations of the Algerian people.

We do not want a weakening of France—we want a strengthening of France's greatness. The greatness of France is no threat to us. On the contrary, the more France displays her independence as a Great Power, the easier it will be, by joint efforts, to achieve a settlement of many European and world problems which have long been demanding a solution. Unfortunately, on a whole number of questions, France is maintaining an attitude which does not increase her prestige, because she is following in the wake of the dollar policy. The impression is created that France's policy on many questions is subordinated to the United States of America. We want to hope that France will rid herself of a policy which leads to the progressive weakening of the country. In our opinion, a change in France's foreign policy would help to increase France's greatness in the international sphere and enhance her role among the Great Powers of the world.

I consider that those people are right who want France, relying on her long-standing peaceful traditions, to initiate proposals to slacken international tension and develop peaceful co-operation among all states. We are convinced that it is precisely along these lines that France can ensure a peaceful life for her people and her future as a Great Power.

I want you to understand me correctly. I am saying this from a friendly standpoint as I am anxious about the none too far-sighted measures of some present-day French statesmen.

Groussard: Do you think the Soviet Union and France could have closer cultural and economic contacts?

Khrushchov: We are deeply convinced of the need to develop fruitful economic and cultural ties between the U.S.S.R. and France. Good trade always leads to better relations. This is also essential for the consolidation of peace; those who think of trade do not think of war. Today certain French commodities have gained currency in the U.S.S.R. The sale of Soviet goods in France has correspondingly increased. But we consider that available opportunities in this field have by no means been exhausted. They would be much more extensive if the bans and the discriminatory lists introduced by the Western countries on trade with the U.S.S.R. and the other socialist countries were abolished. The conclusion in February 1957 of a long-term Franco-Soviet agreement envisaging a threefold increase in trade as compared with 1955, as well as the signing of a protocol in December 1957, are only the beginning of broad and stable economic contacts between our countries.

Economic co-operation should not be confined to commerce alone. As long ago as May 17, 1957, in the Soviet Government's message to the French Prime Minister, we proposed to France a joint discussion on such matters as opening Chambers of Commerce in Moscow and Paris, the periodical organization of industrial and agricultural exhibitions in the U.S.S.R. and France, co-operation in the development of fuel and power resources, co-operation in the peaceful uses of atomic energy, etc. Unfortunately we have not yet received any reply to the Soviet Government's message.

In connection with the latest scientific achievements, in particular achievements in the peaceful uses of atomic energy, new and broad prospects for co-operation are opening up before our countries. I think it would not be a bad idea for our countries to conclude an appropriate agreement on scientific and technical matters, as this would give both states an opportunity to make themselves familiar with the practical experience our countries have accumulated.

The prospects for promoting cultural contacts are equally extensive. Last October there were Franco-Soviet talks in Paris on cultural and scientific contacts. They were concluded with the signing of a protocol and a plan for reciprocal exchanges in the fields of education, science and culture for this year, and with the establishment of a joint Franco-Soviet commission. Under this plan the Bolshoi Theatre Ballet Company is to perform this year in Paris and the ballet company of the Paris National Opera is to perform in Moscow. There will be a wider exchange of concerts, exhibitions, films, radio and television programmes, etc. This, of course, is far from being the limit to what can be achieved. Both sides must help to extend contacts.

Groussard: In your opinion the Soviet Union is now in the last stage separating socialism from communism. Do you think it possible to build communism when the Soviet Union and the People's Democracies are encircled by the so-called capitalist countries?

Khrushchov: I would like to draw your attention to the fact that today the very concept of the "capitalist encirclement" of our country requires serious clarification. With the formation of the world socialist system the situation in the world has changed radically. Moreover, as you know, it has not changed to the advantage of capitalism. Today you cannot tell who is encircling whom—whether the capitalist countries encircle the socialist countries, or vice versa. The socialist countries cannot be regarded as an islet in the middle of a seething capitalist ocean. The socialist countries are inhabited by 1,000 million people out of a world population of 2,500 million. And how many people in other countries adhere to socialist views! Thus, it is now out of the question to speak of capitalist encirclement as it was understood before.

As for the victory of communism in our country, this is beyond all doubt. The Soviet people are confidently marching towards the victory of communism. Those who would like to study the ways and means of building communism in our country in greater detail can address themselves to a host of books and articles that elaborate the subject fully enough. I do not think there is any need for me to explain this matter in detail to the readers of your paper.

Groussard: You were a worker before you devoted yourself to active politics?

Khrushchov: Yes, I worked in the Donets Basin—worked in a mine which was owned by French capitalists in the past.

Groussard: Were they good masters?

Khrushchov: They were just like all the other capitalist masters. I also worked at a plant owned by a German, and at a coke and chemical plant owned by a Belgian. I learned from my own experience that for the working man it makes no difference who owns a factory or mine—a Russian or a German, a Belgian or a Frenchman. All owners wanted us to work more and earn less. The capitalists largely contributed to making a communist internationalist out of me. All capitalists live on the workers' labour and exploit them.

When I read Émile Zola's *Germinal*, I thought that he was writing not about France, but about the mine in which my father and I worked. The worker's lot was the same both in France and in Russia. When, later on, I listened to lectures on political economy and the lecturer spoke about the wage system under capitalism, about the exploitation of the workers, it seemed to me as though Karl Marx had been at the mine where my father and I had worked. It seemed as if it were from observing our life as workers that he had deduced his laws and scientifically proved why and how the workers must liberate themselves from capitalist slavery and build a socialist society.

Groussard: And so, starting as a worker, you advanced step by step. If I am not mistaken, you are the first leader of the Communist Party of the Soviet Union who comes from the midst of the workers. Neither Lenin nor Stalin were workers. Isn't this distinctive feature of yours particularly important for your views, your originality? I have talked about you with Russian people a good deal. They tell me that what they like about you is the fact that you speak a simple language, easily understood by the people.

Khrushchov: This is a somewhat abstract question. I am a member of the Communist Party of the Soviet Union and in this Party there are not only workers. The Communist Party expresses and defends the vital interests of the working class and all the working people of our country.

The working class, the proletariat in the capitalist countries, is the most organized, the most advanced class of society. I myself come from the ranks of the workers. But in our Party there are many people who come from the working peasantry and the intelligentsia. They have been working in our Party for a long time, putting their labour into our common cause, into building communism. Vladimir Ilyich Lenin is the great founder and immortal leader of our Party. And he came from the gentry. But no one understood the interests of the working class, the interests of the people, as well as Lenin did. No one did as much for the working class, for the people, as Lenin did. That is why Lenin is the man who is most highly esteemed in our Party, by our people, by the working class. Lenin is the great leader of all progressive mankind.

I have not ascribed, and do not ascribe, my advancement to the fact that I am a worker. Evidently I have been supported and am being supported in the Party, and elected to leading posts because by my work I justify the trust of my fellow-Communists and carry out the duties entrusted to me. I have always tried to serve the Party, the people and our great cause loyally and faithfully, and I am doing everything I can to justify the confidence of the Party, the people. We Communists are convinced that the only correct path for mankind is the path of socialist development. Socialism expresses the vital interests of the people, of all men and women who live, not by exploiting the working folk, but by their own labour. It brings the peoples deliverance from social and national oppression, from the horrors of unemployment and the arbitrary rule of a handful of monopolists who have usurped a country's entire wealth.

We are convinced that the peoples of all countries will come to socialism, to communism, but when and how— that is the internal affair of each people. Believe me, I do not want to frighten you with communism, since I know that you are an opponent of communism. I am speaking of this only because you have touched on this question.

Groussard: I am not a Communist. But I do not regard a man who is a Communist as my enemy. There are Communists to whom I am openly hostile. Others I respect, in spite of the fact that I seldom share their views. I feel neither hate nor fear. Why should I fear Communists more than they fear me? I had many Communists among my friends in the Resistance Movement and in German camps for deportees. They are still my friends today. The fact that they are Communists, whereas I am not, does not weaken our friendship.

Khrushchov: I have different views on that matter. Friendship is real and strong when people see eye to eye on developments, history and life. If you do not share the philosophy of the Communist Party, since you have your own principles and views, you can only have good, kindly relations with Communists. It would be hard to have deep friendship as we understand it.

Groussard: As far as I know, you have devoted much of your life to combating religion. But I also know that you do not come out openly against religious feelings. I would like to ask you: Does God exist? Is there any Supreme Power?

Khrushchov: Do you think there is?

Groussard: Yes.

Khrushchov: I think there is no God. I have long since rid myself of such a notion. I am a supporter of the scientific world outlook. And science and belief in supernatural forces are incompatible, one excludes the other. That is, of course, if we are to be fully consistent in our scientific views.

Much nonsense is often said about us Communists; it is argued that people who do not believe in God, that even religious people have no clear notion of, cannot be guided by lofty feelings of humanism. The Communists, however, are the most humane of people, because they do not struggle for a good life for themselves alone. It is in the capitalist world that the rich and affluent strive for a good life, caring nothing for others. In America today, for instance, production is sharply falling off and unemployment is inexorably mounting. There, a tiny handful of millionaires and billionaires have piled up immense riches, while many millions of people in that country are now without work. They can die from want and privation or drag out a miserable existence and none of the millionaires or billionaires will be worried about it. Such is the law of capitalism, where private ownership of the means of production predominates. But most of these millionaires and billionaires consider themselves to be believers in God. What, then, is this kind of faith in God worth?

We Communists are against that. We maintain that

every man has a right to work, to the good life which human society can ensure for all. We are for the genuine equality of people and nations. Isn't this an expression of humanity? Concern for the living human being, for the society in which you live, for the life of the people—such are our ideals and such are our convictions. I think this is far better than believing in God and robbing the people who work for you, better than throwing them out of the factories on to the streets, as the capitalists who believe in God do.

The question of who believes in God and who does not isn't a matter for conflicts. It is each person's private affair. So let us not go into details about it.

Groussard: What do you think about the development of the United Nations, Mr. Khrushchov? Perhaps you will say how the Soviet Union plans to promote world peace?

Khrushchov: The United Nations is a useful instrument and is doing something to settle international problems. Yet we cannot blind ourselves to the fact that some influential members of the United Nations are trying to order other countries around and impose upon them a line in foreign policy which has little in common with the noble aims and purposes of the United Nations as inscribed in its Charter. Under such circumstances the United Nations naturally cannot be an organization of international co-operation in the full sense of the term.

We consider it necessary to continue to strengthen the United Nations and to strive to make this organization ultimately a more effective instrument for international co-operation.

As for the Soviet Union's plans for promoting world peace, the Soviet Government has already done much in that direction. That is common knowledge. I believe you, too, know about the latest proposals of the Soviet Government for easing international tension and also about the Soviet Government's messages sent to M. Gaillard, the Prime Minister of France, on December 10, 1957, and on

January 8, 1958. The Soviet Government has suggested calling a summit conference with the participation of the Heads of Government to discuss such questions as: the immediate cessation of hydrogen and atomic weapons tests; renunciation of the use of nuclear weapons; the creation of an atom-free zone in Central Europe; the conclusion of a non-aggression pact between the member-states of the North Atlantic Treaty Organization and the Warsaw Treaty Organization; the reduction of foreign troops in Germany and in other European states; the elaboration of an agreement on the prevention of surprise attacks; measures to extend international commercial contacts; the ending of war propaganda; ways and means of easing tension in the Middle East.

The Soviet Union has adopted a number of unilateral measures to ease international tension which are well known. Prominent among them are the large cuts in the U.S.S.R.'s armed forces. We expect that ultimately the Western Powers will follow the same road.

Those are some views I wanted to express on the questions you have raised.

I would like to take advantage of this opportunity to convey through your paper best wishes to the great French people who have inscribed many a glorious page in the history of mankind.

It is our sincere desire that there should be growing confidence between our peoples and the peoples of the world, that feelings of friendship should become stronger, that the state of cold war should end, and that there should be no possibility of a new war breaking out as a means of settling disputes. Our aim is to have world peace guaranteed by the joint effort of all nations and states. And we are persistently exerting our efforts towards this goal.

Pravda, March 27, 1958

INTERVIEW GIVEN TO ERIC RIDDER,
OWNER AND PUBLISHER OF *JOURNAL OF COMMERCE*,
AND ITS EDITOR HEINZ LUEDICKE

March 22, 1958

Eric Ridder, owner and publisher of the *Journal of Commerce*, and Heinz Luedicke, its editor, asked N. S. Khrushchov, First Secretary of the Central Committee of the Communist Party of the Soviet Union, to reply to a number of questions.

N. S. Khrushchov received Eric Ridder and Heinz Luedicke on March 22. N. S. Khrushchov's replies are published below.*

Ridder: Do you believe that, despite ideological differences, mutually profitable two-way trade can be developed between East and West?

Khrushchov: Our attitude to this question is well known. We considered, and still consider, that ideological differences are in no way an obstacle to the development of mutually profitable trade between socialist and capitalist countries.

I would recall that already in the early twenties many Western countries, because of economic expediency established, despite ideological differences, trade relations with the Soviet Union. Since then trade between the Soviet

---

* All the remarks by Messrs. Ridder and Luedicke are retranslated from the official version of the text of the interview.

Union and capitalist countries, except for certain relatively brief interruptions, has continued to develop steadily.

In 1957, for instance, our trade with capitalist countries increased (at comparable prices) approximately twofold as compared with 1938. But can this growth be considered adequate and corresponding to the interests of the development of world trade? No, it cannot. We are ready for a further extension of trade, but certain circles in the Western countries—those who are interested in the continuation of the cold war—are using the existing ideological differences as a false pretext to justify their unwillingness to develop normal trade relations with the Soviet Union and the other socialist countries.

If the principles of peaceful co-existence are adhered to, then no ideological differences, though they do of course exist, should prevent the development and broadening of mutually profitable economic ties. Peaceful co-existence is a living reality whose significance in international relations is growing. Trade constitutes that sound and stable basis upon which co-existence between countries with different social and economic systems can successfully develop and be consolidated. I think you will agree with me that trade has a more than economic significance. Trade is the most normal way of establishing good relations between countries. Trade and economic ties create a good basis for the consolidation of political relations between states.

I should also like to speak about present-day Soviet-American trade relations.

You will probably remember that a trade agreement was concluded between the U.S.S.R. and the U.S.A. in 1937 and that this agreement laid a good basis for the development of normal trade. Unfortunately, Soviet-American trade did not expand after the war, mainly because the Government of the U.S.A. introduced a number of restrictive measures. In 1951, it denounced the Soviet-American trade agreement.

What can be said on this score? I think that the Soviet Union can exist without the agreement. It is apparently doing so by no means unsuccessfully. Evidently those in the U.S.A. who continue to support the virtually complete severance of the trade relations between our two countries take the view that such a situation causes no harm to the United States. That, of course, is their business. We consider that the successful development of trade between the U.S.S.R. and the U.S.A. on the basis of equality and mutual advantage would not only be in the interests of the Soviet and American peoples and of the strengthening of confidence in U.S.-Soviet relations, but would also contribute to the further relaxation of international tension and would therefore be in the interests of all countries and peoples.

To be more specific, we have a large variety of goods in which your country is interested. For example, we always sold you manganese ore and we are ready to do so now. I don't mean that we can satisfy your needs immediately; if we receive an order we can increase the extraction of this ore. We can also consider the question of selling iron ore. The United States also used to buy some foodstuffs from the U.S.S.R.—crabmeat and caviar; it also bought furs. Today, we can sell you these goods in the same or even greater quantities. Whatever you do not want to buy, don't buy, whatever you do not want to sell, don't sell. But let us exercise the same right: to buy what we need and to sell what we can. It would be in the interests of the United States if it abandoned trade discrimination and adopted a policy directed towards the large-scale development of trade with our country.

Of course, the development of trade is the United States Government's own business, but we believe that not to recognize the Chinese People's Republic is not in the interests of the United States. The Soviet Union, the Chinese People's Republic and other socialist countries could purchase large quantities of American goods. This

215

would be a sure basis for halting the current recession in American industry. Let us recall the thirties. By contemporary standards, we purchased large quantities of goods from you. Today we are able to do much more, our industry is highly developed, we can sell more and buy more, and, consequently, there are prospects for good trade deals.

Ridder: I do not know, Mr. Khrushchov, whether you know that our paper advocates just that—trade with China.

Khrushchov: That is very reasonable. Political dislike of this or that system is a bad counsellor. In business it can only cause harm. Ford was certainly not a Communist, as you very well know. But we had good business relations with him. It was advantageous both to Ford and to us; it was beneficial to our two countries. Colonel Cooper, who was an adviser during the construction of a power plant in Zaporozhye, was not a Communist. But the Soviet Government awarded him the Order of the Red Banner of Labour for the sincere help he gave us. That was a period when our relations with the United States of America were good. And we would be willing to re-establish these relations. Let's agree that you will not sell us armaments and will not buy armaments from us. Let us trade in the products of peaceful labour, that will be to your and to our benefit.

Ridder: But I still suspect that we want to buy your war material, and you want to buy ours. (*Laughter.*)

Khrushchov: You are right, I do not deny, but I think we shall not come to terms on that. I should like to say that the development of trade will bring about the relaxation of international tension and then the sale and purchase of arms will be of much less interest. If countries are not preparing for war, then why should they buy or sell arms or manufacture them at all?

Ridder: I agree. Now we should like to know the following. Are you ready to consider negotiating commercial treaties between the Soviet and the Western countries, as they have long been considered a necessary part of normal international trade relations?

Khrushchov: I do not quite understand what you have in mind. Our trade relations with foreign countries have for a long time been based on commercial treaties which establish the general principles of trade, and also on trade and payments agreements which regulate practical questions of commerce and payment.

The Soviet Union today has trade treaty relations with 45 countries: with all the socialist countries, almost all the countries of Western Europe, including Britain, France, Italy, Austria, Switzerland, Greece, Sweden, etc., with the majority of Asian and African countries, including India, Indonesia, Japan, Iran, Afghanistan, Burma, the United Arab Republic, and many others. We also have trade agreements with two countries of the American continent—Canada and Argentina.

With a number of countries we have agreements which provide for the development of exchange on the basis of agreed lists of commodities for reciprocal deliveries.

Many Western countries are showing an interest in the development of trade with the Soviet Union on the basis of long-term agreements. That is why the Soviet Union has in recent years concluded long-term agreements on reciprocal deliveries with a number of capitalist countries, for instance, a five-year agreement with Finland and long-term agreements with Norway, Iceland and Denmark. In 1957 alone we concluded such long-term agreements with France, Italy, Austria, Afghanistan and Iran. Negotiations are in progress on a long-term agreement between the U.S.S.R. and the Federal Republic of Germany. All these agreements provide for a substantial increase in trade.

The United States of America is now the only Great Power and one of the few countries of the world with which the Soviet Union does not have trade treaty relations. If the Government of the United States expresses a desire to conclude a trade treaty or agreement with the U.S.S.R., I can assure you of a favourable response from the Soviet side.

Ridder: What is your opinion on the development of multilateral trade relations?

Khrushchov: Trade can, of course, be both bilateral and multilateral, like any other ties between countries. If trade develops we agree with anything that will encourage this development.

Ridder: That is a very good statement.

We understand, Mr. Khrushchov, that your policy consists in balancing exports and imports so as to get by without the purchase and sale of gold.

Khrushchov: You won't get very far on gold reserves alone; they are always limited, whereas the development of economic capacity and commodity production is the potential of the nation, the potential of the people, and these are always richer than gold reserves. International economic relations should be developed mainly on the basis of the exchange of commodities—in other words, on the basis of buying and selling. We do not deny that gold plays a part in trade and we are not in favour of just sitting on sacks of it.

Ridder: We would like you to tell us your views regarding price policy in world trade, and particularly on dumping.

Khrushchov: The dumping policy has always been censured not only by us but by other countries too. We believe it to be an unhealthy basis for trade. The subject of dumping has arisen apparently in connection with the recession which has developed in the U.S.A. and in other capitalist countries. The Soviet Union and the other socialist countries will clearly have to do something about preventing the crises which are arising and will continue to arise in the capitalist countries from affecting the economy of the socialist countries.

Luedicke: Let us, for example, take the following case: Germany proposes to sell machines to a country, say, for 100 million rubles, and the Soviet Union proposes exactly the same machines and in the same quantity for 90 million rubles. That is not dumping, because dumping means selling below the cost of production. This is rather a question of undercutting.

Khrushchov: The price depends on the cost of production, and the cost of production depends on many factors, including the level of labour productivity. One manufacturer can ask one price for a certain commodity while another, even in the same country, can ask a different price. This price may be lower, but still be profitable for the manufacturer.

Luedicke: That is quite possible here. But with us, in conditions of competition, prices must be maintained on one level, otherwise the manufacturer will not be able to invest enough money in the development of industry and then he will either go bankrupt or get out of the industry. This is a major difference between our two systems.

Khrushchov: That is true. Take, in particular, the U.S.A., Japan and West Germany. There is now a clear trend showing that West Germany can compete in production with the United States of America. So can Japan. West German and Japanese goods have already penetrated into U.S. markets and thus West Germany and Japan have become America's competitors.

As far as the U.S.S.R. and the U.S.A. are concerned, our countries have no points of conflict (I mean in our economic relations) for we are not your competitors. We manufacture machines and are increasing their production, but basically for our own consumption. We have many useful raw materials, both for industry and for foodstuffs, though I don't suppose you have any need for the latter.

It is strange that business circles in the U.S.A. do not understand that in this sense our countries are not competitors and that the development of trade between our two countries is in the interests of the U.S. economy. It would seem that such trade should be encouraged in every possible way. But some American politicians are so blinded by their hatred of our system that they ignore the interests of their own country and people.

Luedicke: But you do export machines and other types of commodities which we also export?

Khrushchov: We do so not because we need to export machines, but because some countries ask us to assist in their economic development. They cannot get such machines from the United States or Britain, which do not want to trade with them on a mutually profitable commercial basis. But we build our relations with all countries on the basis of mutual advantage, without attaching any political strings. In selling our commodities to these countries, we are not prompted by the profit motive. We try to meet the needs of the people of these countries. We export equipment mainly to friendly countries, to countries which have freed themselves from colonial dependence.

Such a state of affairs cannot be called competition.

Ridder: How would you feel about opening Soviet ports to Western shipping? And which ports would you consider for such treatment?

Khrushchov: This question also surprises me. In this field too some people in the United States still seem to have misconceptions about the Soviet Union, regarding it as a country allegedly fenced off from the outside world. I should like to point out that at present the Soviet Union trades with more than 70 countries of the world (as I said before, with 45 of them we have trade agreements), and that a considerable part of its foreign trade—as much as 40 per cent—is carried by sea. In addition to the Soviet merchant marine, considerable use is made of ships flying foreign flags.

Having in mind only major ports, our foreign trade is carried on through more than 20 Soviet ports, including

Leningrad, Riga, Ventspils, Klaipeda, Odessa, Novoros-siisk, Tuapse, Poti, Murmansk, Arkhangelsk, Igarka, Na-khodka and others. In 1956, about 4,500 foreign ships flying the flags of 37 states called at Soviet ports. It is true that lately United States ships are rare guests at our ports. Well, it's up to you, you know best.

Ridder: Would Russia be willing to permit Western nations to establish direct trade relations with her satellites in Europe and would you grant these satellite nations the right to shape their economic policies to ac-commodate such broadened trade relations?

Khrushchov: You, like some others of your countrymen, have a rather distorted idea about the so-called "satellites of the Soviet Union." If you mean the People's Democ-racies, I must make it clear to you that all of them are sovereign and independent countries. These states draw up and pursue their own home and foreign policies, in-cluding their trade policy, independently. They trade ex-tensively with almost all countries of the world and, as far as I know, are ready to develop such trade in every way on a mutually advantageous basis.

Ridder: Which are the principal trade areas in which closer East-West relations could be built up with mutual benefit? Which products would you like to buy and sell most?

Khrushchov: Opportunities for East-West economic co-operation exist in all parts of the world. International economic co-operation, if developed under normal condi-tions, would enable the nations of the world to make greater use of the benefits and advantages of the interna-tional division of labour.

Forty years have elapsed since the victory of the Great October Socialist Revolution. During these years the Soviet Union has become a major world trading country. Soviet foreign trade turnover for 1957 totalled, in world prices, some 33,000 million rubles (over $8,000 million), approximately one half exports and one half imports. This was 13 per cent more than in 1956, when the Soviet Union already held sixth place among the world's trading nations.

The Soviet Union's biggest trading partners in the capitalist world are Britain, Finland, France, West Germany, Italy, Belgium, Holland and Sweden in Western Europe, and India, Iran, Afghanistan, and the United Arab Republic in Asia and Africa. We expect our trade to continue to expand in the future. We should be only too pleased if the United States of America were to become one of our big trading partners.

The list of Soviet exports today comprises several thousand items, and I should like to point out that the range of our imports and exports has increased considerably in the post-war period as a result of the development of our national economy.

The Soviet Union remains a major importer of many types of machinery and equipment. From capitalist countries we purchase metal-cutting machine tools, forge and press equipment, mining machinery, equipment for the iron and steel industry, hoisting and transport equipment, chemical plant (including equipment for the manufacture of artificial fibres and plastics), power equipment, equipment for the manufacture of building materials and for the light, food and printing industries.

The Soviet Union also imports considerable quantities of raw materials and manufactured goods, as well as some consumer goods. Our purchases include ferrous rolled stock, certain non-ferrous metals, chemical products, rubber, artificial fibres and yarn, hides and other goods.

Soviet exports include several hundred types of metal-cutting machine tools alone. The Soviet Union exports various types of turbines, forge and press equipment, hoisting and transport equipment, road-making and building machinery, equipment for the food and light industries, printing machinery, paper-making machines, agricultural machinery of various types, lorries, cars and tractors.

In addition to machinery and equipment, the Soviet Union exports considerable quantities of manganese and chromium ores, certain non-ferrous metals, ferro-alloys, metals of the platinum group, oil and oil products, coal, asbestos, cellulose and paper products, timber, mineral fertilizers, chemical products, grain, flax, cotton and linter, furs, goat's hair, camel's hair, tobacco, essential oils and medicinal herbs, bristles, horsehair and other animal products, caviar, canned fish and crabmeat, textiles, handicraft goods, etc.

This list, which is far from complete, shows that the Soviet Union has vast opportunities for trade with any country of the world.

Ridder: How would national security requirements have to be handled to satisfy Soviet interests, and what would your attitude be toward the reservations we might feel should be made on national security grounds?

Khrushchov: In asking this question, you apparently proceed from the assumption that to ensure the interests of "national security" the existing restrictions on trade between the capitalist and socialist countries should to some extent be preserved. At the same time, you seem to be in favour of developing East-West trade. These are clearly incompatible positions, for the complete and comprehensive development of trade does not permit of any discriminatory restrictions or bans.

By introducing these bans and restrictions, certain short-sighted people in the West hoped to obstruct the growth of the economic potential of the Soviet Union and the other socialist states, to retard their technical progress and, with the aid of a policy of discrimination and boycott, to hinder the rapid advance of their economies. It was of no avail! History has laughed at the sponsors of this policy. The whole world knows of the achievements of the Soviet Union and of all the socialist countries in the fields of economy, science and technology, including military technology. The Soviet Union developed the hydrogen bomb before the United States. We have developed the intercontinental ballistic missile and were the first to launch earth satellites. We are making gigantic strides in raising the living standards of our people.

The Western Powers, by following this unrealistic and disadvantageous policy, merely aggravate their own economic difficulties. Many prominent Western leaders and also the Western press are with increasing frequency making sharp comments regarding the stupidity of the lists of so-called "strategic goods," the export of which to the socialist countries is either banned or restricted. These lists include many goods which we now export ourselves, and many others which we, perhaps, would not have bought anyway—even if the restrictions on them had been lifted —owing to the development of our own industry.

I should like to recall one fact. You know that the Soviet Government in 1956 allowed the sale to the American Dresser Industries Company of the patent for the Soviet turbo-drill, which American specialists have admitted to be far superior to anything the U.S.A. has in this respect. But the American Government forbade the company to disclose to their Soviet partners certain specifications concerning American oil-drilling equipment.

We advocate the lifting of all restrictions and bans on trade between the capitalist and the socialist countries not only because we hope it would promote the establishment of confidence in the relations between all nations and bring about a relaxation of international tension, but also because discriminatory restrictions lead to uncertainty in commerce and mistrust between the partners in trade. Connected as you are with business circles, you should know full well how much confidence means in commerce and how adversely its absence affects the development of trade.

We are in favour of selling what we can sell and of buying what we want to buy, and we want our partners to be able to sell and buy what they want. And the things which ither you or we cannot sell should not be a subject for reciprocal claims.

Ridder: While there have been a number of studies within the past year or so of the industrial growth of the Soviet economy, the West thus far has had no access to anything comparable to the statistical data available to you on the American economy. Would you be willing to support comparative economic studies to be held strictly outside the propaganda sphere?

Khrushchov: I must point out that your question arises from some misunderstanding. In our country statistical data on industrial development have been very extensively published, particularly after the 20th Congress of the C.P.S.U. at the beginning of 1956.

In the Soviet socialist state the national economy is developing according to plan. You, of course, realize that without statistics it is impossible to draw up a plan, to check its fulfilment, to find reserves for its overfulfilment, etc. Great importance is therefore attached to statistics in our country. Under a socialist system statistics guarantee true data, based on scientific principles, and have access to all reports from industrial undertakings.

Our press regularly publishes the reports of the Central Statistical Board of the U.S.S.R. Council of Ministers on the fulfilment of the state plan for the development of the Soviet national economy for half-yearly and yearly periods. The Central Statistical Board has now begun to issue monthly reports on the fulfilment of the plan in industry. As you probably have already noticed, the report on the fulfilment of the state plan by Soviet industry during February 1958 was published in our central press on March 13.

We publish many statistical surveys. For instance, 10,000 copies of the statistical year-book *The National Economy of the U.S.S.R.* were published in 1956 and 1957. To mark the 40th anniversary of the Great October Socialist Revolution, we published 150,000 copies of a statistical survey *40 Years of Soviet Power in Facts and Figures.* In addition to reference books describing the development of all branches of the Soviet national economy, we also publish surveys dealing with individual branches. Statistical data are also published in the monthly review *Vestnik Statistiki.*

If we take statistical data for industry, I can tell you that last year we published a special statistical survey, *Industry in the U.S.S.R.* In all statistical publications dealing with industry we widely publish the most essential indices showing both the development of industry as a whole and of its various branches: general indices of industrial production, physical volume of industrial output, power indices of industry, technical and economic indices for various branches, the utilization of equipment, increases in productivity of labour, the lowering of costs of production, etc.

I should point out that for a number of indices Soviet statistical publications are more informative than American. For instance, to the best of my knowledge, U.S. statistics, including those in your own paper, publish scant data on the production costs for the principal elements, citing only incomplete and fragmentary information. Soviet statistics systematically publish figures concerning the structure of expenditure for industrial production as a whole and in individual branches, laying particular stress on separate elements. We also periodically publish indices showing the reduction of industrial production costs.

Let us take, for instance, this fact: current American statistics, including—I hope you won't be offended—your newspaper, have in recent years not been publishing complete data on the actual production of metal-cutting machine tools and forge and press equipment, that is, the number produced. They have confined themselves to data concerning the cost of manufactured machine tools and to haphazard data on particular groups of machine tools.

Our statistical publications always contain complete data as to quantity in this respect.

Let us finally consider the stock of metal-cutting and forge and press equipment. Official American statistics do not publish such data, whereas in our statistical returns we periodically publish complete and exhaustive figures.

Of course, the economic conceptions which underlie Soviet statistics and bourgeois statistics are different. Soviet statistics, for example, clearly distinguish between the sphere of material production and that of non-productive branches and between the concepts "production" and "services." In the U.S.S.R. the volume of the total social product does not include the value of "services" in non-productive branches of the national economy, whereas in U.S. statistics the "gross national product" embraces all services irrespective of whether they are connected with production or not. Similarly, while defining the volume and structure of the national income, Soviet statistics treat the national income not as a mere sum of all kinds of income, as is the practice in bourgeois statistics, but as a sum of primary incomes received in the sphere of material production. As far as production costs are concerned, statistics in capitalist countries are obliged, for instance, to take into account the existence of the so-called "commercial secret."

It can therefore be seen that Soviet statistical data provide at least the same opportunities for the study of industrial development in the U.S.S.R. as American statistical data provide for the study of industrial development in the U.S.A., as well as for a comparative study of their development.

Luedicke: How do you determine the costs of production in your plans? True, this is beyond the scope of simple statistics, these are already the fundamentals of economics. Do your prices correspond to the costs of production?

Khrushchov: The cost of production, as you know, consists of many elements. Our domestic prices do not always and in all cases correspond to the costs of production. In our home trade there do not exist the two aspects as you understand them. We sell some goods at prices exceeding their cost of production. But some goods are sold below the cost of production. They are sold at a loss but their production is necessary from the point of view of the development of our country's economic potential. The state uses the funds it receives in the form of extra charges to subsidize the manufacture of goods with a high cost of production. Moreover, they help in the accumulation of funds for the development of our national economy.

Luedicke: But even in these conditions the danger of inflationary tendencies may arise.

Khrushchov: There cannot be any inflation in our country, because in drawing up the budget and production plans we take into account the sums of money to be paid in the form of wages and the necessary quantity of goods to be manufactured in order to maintain the balance between the amount of money and the stock of manufactured goods, etc. Thus, in our socialist economy inflation can only be a result of erroneous calculations in drafting the plans, in other words, it is impossible.

Ridder: Well, that's about all we wanted to ask.

Khrushchov: We were able to meet only on the 22nd of March. This is the day of spring. It would be gratifying if you could become the first swallows of spring in business relations between the Soviet Union and the United States of America, so that trade might develop on a more extensive scale and all the talk of military preparations and about who has more rockets, bombs and other means of annihilating people could stop. The war preparations distress and horrify people. The nations do not want war. It would be much better if we adopted different attitudes in our relations, and talked about the number of machines and other goods you could sell us and the quantity of machines and raw materials you could buy from us. Is that a bad objective?

We are in favour of visits by more American manufacturers and businessmen whom we could acquaint with our production, and of visits to the U.S.A. by our workers in the field of industrial production. This would be useful for the peoples of the Soviet Union and the United States of America. People are indeed tired of reports about rockets, hydrogen and atomic explosions, and bombers.

Our sincere desire is that your visit to our country—a visit by the representatives of the most far-sighted American business circles—should serve as a starting-point for good and friendly relations with the United States of America. We could only welcome this.

Ridder: Mr. Khrushchov, from my very heart I wish to thank you for your courtesy, for having received us, for the wonderful talk we have had. Naturally, we fully agree with you. As to the trade problems, let us hope this interview will serve to improve relations between our countries and to reach the objective of which you spoke with such sincerity.

Khrushchov: I am glad to hear this from you and I hope we shall achieve this, for it is in the interests of both our countries and of both our peoples. I should like only to draw your attention to the fact that our policy is sometimes misinterpreted in the West. When we say that we support peaceful co-existence and that we are for developing trade with Western countries, certain bourgeois spokesmen begin for the sake of their own political purposes to allege that a critical situation has arisen in the Soviet Union which impels it to make declarations of this sort.

I can in all sincerity assure you that the state of affairs in our country is such that we should like to see it continue in the same way; our country is continuously making rapid progress. If we were to picture the economic development of the Soviet Union graphically, the curve would show a steady rise. We want only one thing—to live in peace with all countries, including the U.S.A., and to prevent another war.

You have your political system and we have ours. But that should not prevent our countries from living in peace, coexisting and maintaining good business ties. The question of the internal system of a country, ideological questions—this is a matter of domestic concern for the people of each country, whereas questions of developing normal relations between countries are matters of mutual benefit to all peoples. There is no life without the development of economy, and normal business relations between states contribute to the development of their economy.

We should like you to understand us correctly; we proceed not only from the interests of our country and our people, but also from the interests of all countries and all peoples who want to live in peace and friendship and who want to eliminate the possibility of another war. Trade is the most reliable guarantee for the development and consolidation of business ties between countries.

We are confident that if trade between our countries is expanded it will be followed by a wider exchange of various delegations. If at the first stage of negotiations we fail to agree on the liquidation of military bases and all sorts of installations serving military purposes, then with the development of trade and the expansion of business contacts military bases and airfields will gradually overgrow with grass, for they will lose their significance. And then we shall indeed secure peace throughout the world, we shall secure, as we call it briefly, peaceful co-existence.

Ridder: With those words you have given us the headline for our article on this interview.

Khrushchov: I am very glad to hear that, because it shows that on this point you are of the same opinion.

Ridder: Undoubtedly.

Messrs. Ridder and Luedicke once again thanked N. S. Khrushchov for the interview and took their leave.

International Affairs, No. 5, 1958

REPLIES
TO QUESTIONS PUT BY GIUSEPPE PALOZZI,
IL TEMPO CORRESPONDENT

March 24, 1958

Giuseppe Palozzi, special correspondent of the Italian paper, *Il Tempo,* requested N. S. Khrushchov, First Secretary of the Central Committee of the C.P.S.U., to answer a number of questions. On March 24, N. S. Khrushchov received Giuseppe Palozzi.

Below we print Palozzi's questions and Khrushchov's answers.

Palozzi: I am very glad to meet you, for I have very much wanted to do so. With your permission I should like to ask a number of questions.

Khrushchov: Please do.

Palozzi: In your speech at the Sports Palace on March 14, you stated that there was a possibility of improving relations with my country. What would be the attitude of the U.S.S.R. to Italy if she, like Sweden, for example, were to adopt a position of neutrality between the two blocs, or if, like Switzerland and Austria, she proclaimed her neutrality?

Khrushchov: The policy of a country, its relations with other countries, and its attitude on major international problems are the sovereign affairs of each country. However, nowadays there is not, nor can there be, a single country that is indifferent to the future development of international relations: along the road of easing international tension and strengthening peace, or along the road of increasing tension, continuing the cold war and the arms race that is bringing the world nearer to war. The Italian people, too, it seems to me, are not indifferent to the fate of the world, for they have their strong freedom-loving traditions and a profound interest in preserving peace and normal, healthy relations among all states, irrespective of their social and state systems.

Italy and her Government, of course, know better what line to choose in the present situation, but, as far as one can judge, Italy's membership in the North Atlantic bloc is giving rise to justified apprehension among the broadest sections of the Italian people, because this membership reduces Italy's possibilities and ties her to a definite policy with no favourable prospects for her future. One cannot shut one's eyes to the fact that Italy's membership in NATO is increasingly transforming her from an important factor in international affairs into an object of a policy alien to her.

Is this not shown by the fact that in peacetime, in the absence of any real threat to Italy's security from her neighbours or any other European countries, American nuclear bases have been set up on Italian territory? Italy does not control these bases and they do not help to strengthen Italy's security but to weaken it, since these bases may become a means of attack on other countries without Italy's knowledge. And this will draw Italy into actions imperilling her future. Moreover, the danger to Italy is increased by the fact that in addition to the bases already existing, the attempt is being made to impose upon her the construction of launching sites for ballistic rockets.

Is it surprising that many Italians rightly see in these bases and rocket launching sites a direct threat to their country's security? Recently voices have been raised ever more loudly in Italy, demanding that she be included in a nuclear-free zone, in other words, demanding Italy's atomic neutrality. At he same time, neutral tendencies in the broad sense of the term are developing in Italy, which is evident, among other things, from the way your question was presented.

The experience of history teaches us that some states which in time of war have pursued a policy of neutrality, or a policy of non-participation in military blocs, have thereby helped to safeguard the security of the peoples of their countries and, on the whole, have played a positive peace-making role. Such a policy is in keeping with the national interests of these states, enhances their security and does not draw them into unnecessary useless waste of their productive forces for military purposes. Such countries as Switzerland and Sweden, for example, have already been enjoying the blessings of neutrality for many decades. A major part in the struggle for peace and security is played by such states as India, Indonesia, Burma, the United Arab Republic, Cambodia and other countries which adhere to a policy of non-participation in military blocs. Their attitude evokes understanding and sympathy.

It goes without saying that should Italy choose such a path, the Soviet Union would regard this decision with due understanding and respect.

Palozzi: How, in your opinion, could our neutrality be guaranteed?

Khrushchov: We consider that if a state wants to pursue a policy of neutrality and non-participation in military groupings and raises the question of guarantees of its security, territorial integrity and inviolability, those wishes should be acceded to by the Powers upon which their fulfilment depends. It is a fact that the U.S.S.R., together with the United States, Britain and France, guaranteed the security of Austria, when she proclaimed her neutrality. These guarantees, in our opinion, could be given in the event of a state wanting to join an atom-free zone. Agreement could be reached, for instance, on the Powers possessing atomic weapons undertaking to respect the status of the atom-free zone.

Palozzi: What is your opinion on the question of Italy joining the European Market and Euratom and also of a Europe united politically and economically?

Khrushchov: Italy, like the other countries which have joined the so-called Common Market and Euratom, is hardly likely to reap any tangible benefits from them. An isolated market of six countries, if it functions as a narrow and exclusive economic grouping, will only create additional difficulties for the co-ordination of all-European efforts in the economic field.

Let us consider, for example, the utilization of raw material, water power and fuel resources. We know that the West European countries are greatly in need of fuel and power developments. On an all-European basis there are sufficient potentialities for building powerful thermal power stations and hydroelectric stations in countries which have large fuel and water power resources—naturally with the consent and participation of each of these countries. On an all-European basis it is also possible to build oil and gas pipelines and electric power lines. The same can be said about the utilization of atomic energy for peaceful purposes. That is why the Soviet Union stands for economic co-operation on all-European basis.

It is necessary, in our opinion, to follow precisely along the path of developing extensive and unhampered trade between all European countries and not confining it within the bounds of six countries. It would, for instance, be desirable for all interested European countries to eliminate in trade all kinds of bans and restrictions of a non-economic nature. Vitally important problems of the economic development of the European countries should also be discussed and settled, not in narrow organizations, but, say, at annual conferences of representatives of economic agencies of the European countries.

That is why we regard the establishment of Euratom

and the Common Market of six countries as an artificial restriction of economic co-operation, all the more so since the facts show that the Common Market and Euratom are being used, from the very outset, not so much for economic purposes as for the arms race and for other purposes not of a peaceful nature.

Palozzi: At the Geneva Conference on the peaceful uses of atomic energy in August 1955, the Soviet delegation declared its readiness to give help to all countries needing it to develop the atomic industry and research connected with it. Is the Soviet Union prepared to give this help to Italy, and on what terms? And what terms would be put before us if, for the operation of our industrial reactors, we needed uranium supplied by the Soviet Union?

Khrushchov: The Soviet Union's attitude on international co-operation in the peaceful uses of atomic energy is well known. Our country takes an active part in the work of the International Atomic Energy Agency by supplying other countries with fissionable materials, scientific and technical information, and in training atomic specialists, etc.

In our opinion it would be useful to establish the co-operation of all European countries in the development and use of atomic energy for peaceful purposes. Lastly, we also consider it necessary to develop bilateral co-operation in this field. We already have appropriate agreements with a number of countries. We readily share our experience and our knowledge with these countries, and help them to organize the use of atomic energy for peaceful purposes utilizing their own resources.

Is there any need to say that we give such aid on condition of complete equality between the parties, without infringing on anyone's sovereignty? In short, we are of the opinion that no aid should be used for imposing upon the recipient country military, political, economic or any other conditions.

Co-operation in the peaceful uses of atomic energy opens up broad prospects for improving the well-being of the people and will serve the cause of peace. This cannot be said of the plans now being drawn up for pooling the efforts of certain European states in the production of atomic weapons. Those plans serve to intensify the arms race and increase international tension. Who will benefit, for example, from the co-operation between West Germany, France and Italy in the production of atomic weapons?

The Soviet Union regards with understanding Italy's striving to use atomic energy for peaceful purposes and is ready to conclude with her a bilateral agreement on aid in various fields of the peaceful uses of nuclear energy. As regards practical questions concerning such co-operation, it is obviously too early to talk about them, since the Italian side has not made any such requests.

Palozzi: Assuming that the present state of crisis in U.S. economy were to have an unfavourable effect on the economic and industrial development of my country, especially in our southern provinces which are now in the stage of industrialization, would the Soviet Union assist our economy, and on what terms?

Khrushchov: If necessary, we could share with Italy our experience in reclaiming and developing the economically underdeveloped areas of our country. In the past the Soviet state had had to overcome serious difficulties in solving the problem of developing the former outskirts of tsarist Russia. It is no secret to anyone what those areas were like formerly. Today they are flourishing regions whose economy is developing actively. Their economic and cultural level now compares well with the other economically developed areas of the Soviet Union. We could also give aid in other forms. Take, for instance, the question of power sources. New sources of power, atomic installations in particular, could greatly assist the economic development of Italy's southern provinces.

It goes without saying that when the Soviet Union renders aid, that aid has no political strings attached to infringe upon the interests and national sovereignty of any country.

Palozzi: Do you think that visits and the exchange of views between Italian and Soviet leaders could promote *rapprochement* between our two countries? Do you regard an exchange of visits between the heads of our two states as feasible?

Khrushchov: Contacts and meetings between statesmen on international questions of various kinds are not only useful but also necessary. They undoubtedly help to strengthen mutual understanding and confidence. But meetings of statesmen are beneficial only when both sides have a desire to meet. It goes without saying that the side issuing the invitation has to be confident of its acceptance by the other side. That is how we understand this question.

To put it more concretely, we have already had occasion to express our opinion on the desirability of such a meeting to the Italian Government, but, I repeat, a mutual desire to meet and find acceptable settlement on questions of interest to both sides is necessary. The Italian Government and Italy's leading circles, however, are not ready for a meeting. This can probably be attributed to the fact that Italy has not as yet freed herself from the influence of other, stronger countries. I am convinced that it would be useful for the leaders of Italy to visit the Soviet Union, to see our country, and to establish the necessary business and political contacts. This would be of benefit to both our countries.

Let us wait patiently for better times; events are developing so that these better times will undoubtedly come.

Palozzi: Last year 13 million tourists visited Italy, and among them there were only 3,000 Soviet tourists. What is the reason that the number of Soviet tourists to Italy is so insignificant? Up to now Soviet tourists have come to our country only in groups. Why would it not be possible to increase individual tourist travel, which apart from anything else would help to establish broader contacts between our two peoples? Would you personally like to visit Italy as a tourist?

Khrushchov: There are tourists and tourists. One should not have a stereotyped approach to the tourists of one country or another. In bourgeois society, in capitalist countries, tourists are, as a rule, wealthy people who have capital. They are mostly idle people. It is a fact that Italy is very beautiful and has many picturesque places. The Italian people are a people with a high and ancient culture, famous for their singing. Italy has many remarkable cultural monuments. Therefore, people naturally like to go there.

As for our tourists, tourist travel has developed in our country only in recent years. In our country, the trade unions are the organizers of tourist travel. Group travel abroad is the practice in our country, which does not at all mean that there can be no individual tourist travel.

Moreover, it is necessary to bear in mind that the Soviet Union has almost the same beautiful natural scenery as Italy. Have you been to the Crimea?

Palozzi: No, but I would very much like to.

Khrushchov: And have you been in our Transcaucasia?

Palozzi: No. Only in Moscow.

Khrushchov: There you are—you reproach us on the grounds that our tourists do not travel enough, while you yourself have not been anywhere except Moscow. Do you know that people who have been to Italy and the Crimea, to Sochi, place your beauty spots and ours on a par? All this should be taken into account in considering how many tourists come to you from the Soviet Union.

I myself, it is true, have never been there, but people say that there are places in the Altai Mountains whose beauty is simply enchanting. Or take Uzbekistan, Kirghizia, Kazakhstan, or other Central Asian republics, and their cities. I have been there; I have been to Frunze, Alma-Ata, Tashkent and Stalinabad. They really are places of indescribable beauty. So you see how many places we have where a man can spend his free time with pleasure.

Or take the Black Sea shores of the Georgian Republic—Batumi, Gagra, Sukhumi and other districts. These are delightful places, which have excellent amenities, and the scenery there is exceptionally beautiful. I have not been to Italy, but probably all these places can vie with Italy as regards the beauty of their scenery.

I'll say nothing about the Far East. But what about the northern part of our country? It, too, has many charms of its own. A man's lifetime is not long enough to get to know well all the beauties of the Soviet Union. But we don't want to confine ourselves to our own shell.

That is what can be said about tourist travel. I think that trips by our tourists will go on increasing every year.

As for me visiting Italy as a tourist, my public position does not permit me the free choice of a time for tourist trips, although Italy arouses the very great interest of all cultured people.

Palozzi: The statement issued by the delegation of the Communist Party of the Soviet Union which recently visited Italy contains "approval" of the political and ideological positions of the Italian Communist Party. The fact that representatives of the Communist Party of the Soviet Union have considered it their duty to proclaim their confidence in the Italian Communist Party is regarded by a large section of Italian public opinion as proof that the Italian Communist Party is dependent on the Communist Party of the Soviet Union. How do you assess this matter?

Khrushchov: I look at it in this way. Certain circles in Italy are deliberately distorting the statement made by our delegation that visited Italy. Those circles in Italy cannot claim priority in this respect, because the ruling circles of the United States, which seek to set the Workers' and Communist parties at loggerheads, have long been concocting allegations to the effect that all the Communist parties are subordinate to the Communist Party of the Soviet Union. That is nonsense. But unfortunately there are still people who believe this nonsense.

What does the statement of our delegation speak about? It speaks of a correct understanding of the Marxist-Leninist theory, about questions of an ideological nature. Marxist-Leninist theory is the banner of the international working-class movement. That is why each Communist Party, if it really is a Communist Party, is guided strictly by this theory. And it is, therefore, natural that when representatives of Communist parties meet, they express their loyalty to the revolutionary ideology—to Marxism-Leninism. We do not conceal this.

It is a fact that representatives of Socialist parties of the European countries often meet; the Socialist parties are organizationally united, they jointly elaborate questions of the policy and tactics of the Socialist parties. This, however, does not give rise to any anxiety among bourgeois political leaders. They are disturbed by the ideology of the Communist and Workers' parties and Marxist-Leninist theory. And this is only to our credit, because our parties are real representatives of the working class; they defend the interests of the working class honestly and to the very end—and not only of their own countries, but the interests of the working class of all countries. We are internationalists and must therefore strengthen in every way the ideological bonds between the Workers' and Communist parties, and strengthen and develop proletarian solidarity.

Our political positions are known. We have adhered, and continue to adhere, to positions of non-interference in the internal affairs of other countries.

The Italian Communist Party is a very strong party. It has good, mature cadres who are well versed in questions of the theory of Marxism-Leninism.

Talk about the "dependence" of the Communist and Workers' parties on the Communist Party of the Soviet Union is an old and stupid fable.

Palozzi: Do you consider that a summit meeting could be held within the next two months or, for the sake of the appropriate preparations, would it be necessary to wait until July or August?

Khrushchov: As we see it, a summit meeting could be held within the next two months, in the sense that there exists every reason for a summit meeting and an exchange of views. What is needed is the desire and good will of the governments of the countries that may participate. But this meeting will evidently not take place within the next two months.

Western leaders, and especially those of the United States, would like to put off the summit meeting as long as possible. In general one gets the impression that they do not even want such a meeting. But public opinion in all countries, including the United States, is demanding this meeting, which is really needed.

The opponents of a summit meeting, wishing to bury the very idea of such a meeting, are endeavouring by means of talk about better preparations for it to drag a decision on this question into labyrinths of verbosity from which it would be hard to escape. In words they express their readiness to meet, but actually they are misleading the public; first they want to put off the meeting and then, by some means, to provoke a worsening of the situation so as to find some plausible excuse to prevent the meeting and continue the cold war.

The position of the Soviet Union has been very clearly set forth in our documents. We are guided by the interests of the peoples of all countries—and the peoples want peace, they want an end to the cold war. They desire normal relations to develop between countries. We adhere entirely to such positions and, for our part, are doing, and will do,

. everything in our power to ensure the strengthening of world peace.

Public opinion is now exerting strong pressure on its governments. And the stronger this pressure of public opinion on the governments, the more assurance there will be that a summit meeting will be held. Questions on which a decision can be taken in the interests of universal peace have already become ripe for settlement.

What the questions are on which agreement can be reached has been stated in well-known documents of the Soviet Government. We have also said what questions should not be raised now, as it is clear in advance that no agreement can be reached on them.

Palozzi: One of the questions which caused the failure of the Geneva Foreign Ministers' Conference in November 1955 was the question of the reunification of Germany. It seems that at the present time this same question is an obstacle to a Heads of Government meeting. The Communist Party of Viet-Nam recently declared its readiness to solve the question of Viet-Nam's unification by free elections. What is hindering the application of the same principles to the unification of Germany?

Khrushchov: The point of view of the Soviet Government on these questions has been expressed many times. I can reiterate it briefly. In 1954, at the Geneva Conference, at which the Soviet Union, the Chinese People's Republic, Britain, France, the United States and other countries were represented, it was resolved that two years later, that is in 1956, the population of Viet-Nam should decide the question of their country's unification by free elections. Two years have passed, but South Viet-Nam has not recognized the agreements reached at Geneva. It is apparently not so much a question of the leaders of South Viet-Nam as it is their advisers. It is known that the chief advisers in South Viet-Nam are representatives of certain United States circles.

As regards the German question, the directives to the

Foreign Ministers adopted in 1955 at the Geneva Conference of the Heads of Government of the Four Powers say that the "settlement of the German question and the reunification of Germany by means of free elections shall be carried out in conformity with the national interests of the German people and the interests of European security." And it should be noted that the participants in the conference arrived at that formula after heated debates, because we considered it more correct to solve the question of European security without linking it with the German question, whereas our partners in the talks insisted on the need to solve the German question first.

At the concluding session we made a statement on behalf of the Soviet Union in which we set forth what we considered to be the most rational way of solving the German problem. We stated that this problem should not be solved in the way interpreted by the West. We said that the solution of the German problem should be found through agreement between the two German states, that is, between the German Democratic Republic and the Federal Republic of Germany. We expressed the same view in Berlin as well, when the Soviet delegation was returning to Moscow from Geneva.

Our attitude on the German question is clear and definite. Some prominent Western leaders, however, are distorting it, pursuing their own unsavoury ends. They allege that the Soviet Government does not carry out its commitments. The fact is, however, that at Geneva, the Soviet Union did not commit itself to the unification of Germany by free elections, as Mr. Dulles and others now make out.

Thus the ruling circles of the United States have two approaches: one approach to the question of uniting Viet-Nam by free elections on which agreement was reached, and the other approach to the question of reunifying Germany, on which there is no agreement.

The fact that there are now two sovereign independent German states is indisputable. By what right do those leaders, ignoring the will of these states, want to solve the German problem? That would be a gross violation of the basic principles underlying our relations with all independent states.

Palozzi: I followed with great interest the election campaign in the Soviet Union and visited many polling centres to see how the voting was proceeding. Your electoral system differs from the system in the Western countries, and for that reason I take the liberty of asking you to give me some explanations. In Italy, for example, it is the practice that members of the Government, on the expiry of Parliament's term of office, nominate themselves as candidates for election. In the Soviet Union, on the contrary, I noticed that some of the Ministers in the Government as at present composed did not stand as candidates in the elections to the U.S.S.R. Supreme Soviet, while other Ministers were elected as Deputies to the Supreme Soviet. Does this mean that those Ministers not elected to the Supreme Soviet want to retire from active political life?

Khrushchov: Not at all. The fact that some Ministers were not elected as Deputies to the U.S.S.R. Supreme Soviet does not at all mean that they are retiring from political activity.

You rightly say that our electoral system differs from that of the Western countries. The people elect to the U.S.S.R. Supreme Soviet representatives of all sections of our society—workers, collective farmers and intellectuals—who are capable of worthily expressing the will of the people. When candidates for the Supreme Soviet are nominated at factories, mills, collective farms, state farms, offices, educational establishments and in army units, the question of who will best justify the trust of the people, the trust of their electors in the supreme organ of power of the Soviet Union is widely discussed by the electorate. Our electors nominate to the U.S.S.R. Supreme Soviet as many candidates as possible who work directly in factories, mills, collective farms, state farms and scientific and other institutions, and who are serving in the army and navy. Our society is growing, bringing to the fore its young forces, who are working shoulder to shoulder with the experienced personnel, accomplishing the great tasks confronting our country. All the activities of the Soviet people are guided by the Communist Party of the Soviet Union, which enjoys the tremendous confidence of all our people and is inseparable from them. The Party sees to it that both young and the old personnel work in the various branches of our economy and culture and hold particular posts in accordance with their abilities. And if they work well, the people will always appreciate them highly. Renewal, the promotion of new personnel, is going on constantly in socialist society. The enlistment in state activities of the new, mature forces which our socialist society is continuously producing, is helping us to cope with the most complicated and important tasks in building communism.

Palozzi: During his latest visit to Washington our Foreign Minister Pella put forward a plan for establishing peace in the Middle East. What do you think of this plan?

Khrushchov: As far as can be judged from press reports, Pella's proposal is that a group of West European countries set up some kind of fund for economic aid to Middle Eastern countries. In itself, the idea of giving assistance to Middle Eastern countries merits attention. But won't the implementation of this proposal result in the establishment of an exclusive group of countries with the participation of active supporters of a colonialist policy? It is not difficult to see that with such a composition the activities of this group would be aimed not so much at advancing the economy of the Middle Eastern countries as at further worsening the situation in that area. There are scarcely any grounds for believing that the Powers pursuing a colonialist policy will abandon their old schemes to secure domination in the Middle East if they unite in one group.

The Soviet Union considers it possible and desirable to give assistance to the underdeveloped countries, including the countries of the Middle East. The U.S.S.R. supported the proposal for the establishment of a special United Nations fund to finance the economic development of the underdeveloped countries and is ready to take part in founding this fund by making its contributions.

The United States, however, opposed the foundation of such a fund for the economic development of the underdeveloped countries under the aegis of the United Nations, evidently considering it more advantageous to grant credits to the underdeveloped countries through those financial organizations in which the United States is the complete master, and on terms which it itself dictates. Nor does the U.S.S.R. object to rendering assistance on a regional basis. Why, for example, should not all European countries, the East European countries included, and not a narrow group of states, reach understanding among themselves about rendering aid to the Middle Eastern countries and to other underdeveloped countries, provided, of course, that this assistance is not used to interfere in the domestic affairs of these countries?

Palozzi: What can you say about Soviet "nationalism," that is, about the certain disdain shown by Soviet people to foreigners from "second-rate" countries, and particularly to Italians?

Khrushchov: Frankly speaking, I do not understand the very formulation of such a question. Could such a question seriously arise in your mind? It is generally known that any manifestation of nationalism is alien to Soviet men and women, because we proceed from respect for the rights and dignity of all peoples, both great and small. Soviet men and women do not divide countries and peoples into "first-rate" and "second-rate." The Soviet Union itself is a multi-national state, all of whose peoples, great and small, are equal and united on the basis of fraternal friendship and mutual respect. It is well known that the capitalist world has a division of countries into "first-rate" and "second-rate," but we do not recognize such a division.

As for the Italian people, it is well known that the peoples of the Soviet Union have always entertained for them feelings of deep and sincere respect and sympathy, and continue to do so. Therefore, I think, to speak even in the form of a question about some kind of "disdain" on the part of Soviet men and women towards the Italian people would be a very crude distortion of the real state of affairs.

We should like to have the best relations with Italy, with the Italian people, with the Italian Government. But unfortunately the Italian Government is pursuing a policy which prevents the establishment of friendly relations between our countries. Time, however, marches on, and events are changing. We believe that, if not now, then in the near future, good relations will be established between our countries. This would be beneficial both for the Soviet Union and for Italy.

Pravda, April 2, 1958

SPEECH
AT BUDAPEST AIRPORT ON ARRIVAL OF
SOVIET PARTY AND GOVERNMENT DELEGATION
IN HUNGARY

April 2, 1958

Dear Comrade Kadar,
Dear Comrade Dobi,
Dear Comrade Münnich,
Dear comrades and friends, esteemed citizens of Budapest, splendid capital of the Hungarian People's Republic, it is with deep feeling that we step on your soil today. In these first few minutes of meeting you, our Hungarian friends, we perform the bidding we have received and convey to you and all the working people of Hungary the profound, heartfelt, fraternal greetings of the Soviet people.

The peoples of the Soviet Union are firmly convinced that in the workers, peasants and intellectuals, in all the working people of Hungary, they have loyal fellow-fighters for peace, freedom, happiness and a better future for our peoples.

The Central Committee of the Hungarian Socialist Workers' Party and the Revolutionary Workers' and Peasants' Government have invited the Soviet Party and Government delegation to visit your country. From the bottom of our hearts we say to you, dear comrades: our heartiest thanks for your invitation.

It is always a pleasure to meet friends. But it is particularly gratifying to meet you now, these spring days, when the Hungarian people celebrate an auspicious date in the life of their republic—the thirteenth anniversary of the country's liberation from the yoke of Hitler invaders and the fascist Horthy régime.

We are very happy to join in your celebrations of this signal holiday of the Hungarian people.

We make no secret of the fact that we are deeply moved by this extremely cordial, friendly welcome accorded to us, representatives of the Soviet people. Thank you very much, dear comrades, for your kind hospitality.

Your welcome speaks more eloquently than words of the good friendship which the Hungarian people have for the peoples of the Soviet Union.

We are profoundly grateful for the warmth with which the First Secretary of the Central Committee of the Hungarian Socialist Workers' Party, our dear Comrade János Kadar, referred here to the Soviet Union.

Last year the Soviet people received as their most welcome friends the representatives of the Hungarian people—the Party and Government delegation of the Hungarian People's Republic. At that time we thoroughly discussed with your leaders many questions concerning the further development of friendly relations between our countries and a number of questions related to the international situation. On March 28, 1957, we adopted a Joint Declaration, which was an important milestone along the road to greater friendship between the Soviet and Hungarian people.

Only a year has elapsed since then. But many good and important developments have taken place during these twelve months in our countries. Our friendship has grown stronger still. Our economic, political and cultural connections have expanded greatly. In spite of subversive enemy activity that sought to destroy, or at least weaken, the friendship of our peoples by provocations and conspiracies, the fraternal co-operation between the

Soviet Union and the Hungarian People's Republic has been greatly extended.

The relations between the Soviet Union and the Hungarian People's Republic, and between all the socialist countries, are those of very close friends brought together by identical interests, a single ideology, and a common ultimate goal in the struggle for socialism and communism. Never will anyone succeed in shaking this unity and solidarity of our countries.

Imperialist exertions are opposed by the enduring solidarity and unity of all the countries of the socialist camp. We may say for certain that as long as we are united and of a single mind, we have nothing to fear from enemy intrigues. This is why we shall continue to cherish our unity as the apple of our eye, to rally our ranks closer and strengthen our friendship and fraternal co-operation.

The Soviet people are well aware of the progress made by Hungary's working people under the leadership of the Socialist Workers' Party and the Revolutionary Workers' and Peasants' Government in building the new life. We rejoice with you at these successes and assure you that in the Soviet Union and in the other socialist countries you have your most loyal and reliable friends.

From the bottom of our hearts, dear comrades, we wish you new successes in building a socialist Hungary!

Allow me to express our trust that the stay of our delegation in your country will be a fresh step towards cementing the fraternal friendship of the Soviet Union and the Hungarian People's Republic, and that it will help to consolidate world peace.

Long live the Hungarian People's Republic!

Let the inviolable friendship of the Hungarian and Soviet peoples grow stronger and flourish!

(N. S. Khrushchov's speech was repeatedly interrupted by stormy applause and shouts of welcome.)

SPEECH
AT MEETING IN BUDAPEST IN CELEBRATION OF
13th ANNIVERSARY OF HUNGARY'S LIBERATION

April 3, 1958

Dear Comrade Kadar,
Dear Comrade Dobi,
Dear Comrade Münnich,
Dear Comrades and Friends,

To begin with, allow me to thank you heartily for the opportunity of speaking at this celebration of the 13th anniversary of Hungary's liberation from the Hitler fascists and their Horthy mercenaries.

We, members of the Party and Government delegation, are deeply touched by the warm and friendly words addressed in his report by Comrade Ferenc Münnich to the Soviet Union, our people, and our Communist Party. Permit me to express our heartfelt thanks for your high appreciation of our efforts.

We are well aware that the warm cordiality and hospitality which you have extended to our delegation from the moment it stepped on Hungarian soil are, above all, an expression of the friendly sentiments which the working people of Hungary have for the Soviet people. We assure you that the Soviet people have the same live sentiments of fraternal love and friendship for the people of Hungary.

On behalf and on the instructions of the Central Committee of the C.P.S.U., the Supreme Soviet of the U.S.S.R.

and the Soviet Government, on behalf of the entire Soviet people, I congratulate you heartily, dear comrades, and with you all the Hungarian working people, on this national holiday of the Hungarian People's Republic. The Soviet people sincerely wish you further successes in your grand cause of building socialism, in your struggle for peace and for the security and independence of your fine country.

We have come to your country on a return visit at the kind invitation of the Central Committee of the Hungarian Socialist Workers' Party and the Hungarian Revolutionary Workers' and Peasants' Government to get a better idea of the life and daily labours of the gifted and hard-working Hungarian people. We sincerely hope that our visit will serve to extend and consolidate further the existing friendly relations of our peoples.

Enemies of the Soviet and Hungarian peoples are trying with sinister purpose to persuade the gullible that the history of Russo-Hungarian relations is the history of Austria-Hungary's part in the war of the Triple Alliance against Russia, or the participation of tsarist troops in the suppression of the revolution in Hungary in 1848-49 But that is a stupid and very primitive lie. They resort to fraud in their efforts to pass off relations between the governing exploiter classes of our countries in the past as relations between our peoples. Yet these are different things. Anyone with the slightest knowledge of history, who does not wish to distort it, knows full well what great sympathy our peoples have always had for each other.

When in 1917 the working class, the working people of our country threw off the hated yoke of tsarism and then accomplished the Great October Socialist Revolution, which ushered in a new era for mankind, the working class, the working people of Hungary enthusiastically supported the young Soviet Republic.

The Soviet people will never forget the fraternal assistance of the Hungarian toilers, who fought heroically shoulder to shoulder with the Russian proletariat and toiling peasantry for the triumph of the gains of the October Revolution. Tens of thousands of our Hungarian brothers fought our country's enemies in the Civil War. We are deeply grateful to them, to the Hungarian working class, to your people, for having raised such indomitable and gallant fighters, such true proletarian internationalists, as Tibor Szamuelly, Béla Kun and our frontline comrade and friend Ferenc Münnich, who is with us here today.

Dear comrades, the Hungarian working class, which has known the hard lot of oppression, has always marched in the militant ranks of the international revolutionary movement. Here in Budapest, the Red Banner of workers' and peasants' rule was raised 39 years ago.

We, people of the older generation, remember clearly the enthusiasm roused in Russia and among working people throughout the world by the news that a Soviet Republic had been proclaimed in Hungary. Great Lenin wrote at the time that the news from Hungary "fill us with delight and joy," that they testified to "our moral victory." The example of the Hungarian workers was vivid proof of the all-conquering force of Marxist-Leninist ideas, proof of the international nature of the Great October Socialist Revolution.

In an ardent address to the Hungarian workers, Lenin wrote:

"You are waging the only legitimate, just and truly revolutionary war, a war of the oppressed against the oppressors, a war of the working people against the exploiters, a war for the victory of socialism. All honest members of the working class all over the world are on your side."

The forces of reaction, of international imperialism, succeeded at the time in crushing the Hungarian Soviet Republic. The counter-revolution wreaked brutal vengeance upon the Hungarian freedom fighters: tens of thousands of Hungary's loyal sons were murdered and 70,000 thrown into prison. The oppressors of the Hungarian people expunged with fire and sword its age-long yearning for a free life without capitalists and landlords. The factories and mills were returned to the capitalists, and the land to the landlords. A gloomy period of reactionary fascist rule set in for Hungary.

But the torch of socialist ideas burned on in the hearts of the Hungarian workers, peasants and progressive intellectuals. No fascist brutalities could suppress the Hungarian people's longing for freedom, for liberation from the capitalist yoke and the hateful chains of fascism. The flames of the liberation struggle shot up brightly in April 1945 when, as a result of the victories of the Soviet Army, the Hungarian people won the opportunity of overthrowing the hated Horthy régime and the blood-stained fascist dictatorship—the opportunity of taking power into their own hands, of winning at last their long-awaited freedom and independence.

When the Soviet Army marched westwards, the heroes of Stalingrad remembered the heroes of the Hungarian revolution of 1848-49, the glorious Hungarian revolution of 1919, the working people of Hungary and other countries trampled underfoot by the German-fascist occupationists.

Soviet soldiers did not spare their blood, and life itself, in striking out against the fascist oppressors and hastening to the aid of nations racked by Hitler slavery. One of the biggest battles for the future, for the working man's happiness, unfolded in the Hungarian plains, on the banks of the Danube and Tisza, and here, at the walls of Budapest. Tens of thousands of Soviet people gave their lives for the freedom of the Hungarian people.

The blood shed by our peoples in the joint struggle against fascism has sealed our friendship for all time.

After taking the road of socialist construction, liberated Hungary has in a short time made a giant leap forward both in industrial production and in improving the living and cultural standards of the population, and in the cultural revolution which flung open the door to science and knowledge for the Hungarian worker and peasant.

The enemies of socialism are foaming with rage over the successes of the working people in the socialist countries. They are doing their worst to harm the people and to hinder the people's effort of building a new, socialist life. That they do not even conceal their intentions bares the full extent of their cynicism. You know very well, comrades, that the rulers of some capitalist countries allot huge funds for subversive activities in the socialist countries, announce frankly hostile plans of overthrowing the people's democracies and restoring capitalist régimes.

They had the same insidious designs with regard to the Hungarian People's Republic. Making the most of the mistakes and distortions of the former leadership in Hungary, the imperialists in October-November 1956 set in motion their criminal machine. The domestic reactionary forces in Hungary, inspired and organized from abroad, staged a fascist uprising. They exploited all possible means to deceive the people.

The embittered scum of the defeated exploiter classes swarmed into Hungary like a flock of black crows. Enemies of people's democracy threw off their masks and crept out of their dens. Criminal elements, released from places of confinement, joined hands with the enemy forces.

The socialist gains of the Hungarian working people were in great danger. And in those October and November days of 1956 the Hungarian people demonstrated their high revolutionary maturity and their ability to defend the great achievements of people's democracy under the leadership of the Hungarian Communists.

Naturally, we cannot be blind to the fact that a certain section of the working people, especially among the intellectuals, were taken in by spurious slogans—were deceived and misled. If our enemies were stupid, it would be easier for the people to fight them. But they are crafty and insidious. They do not betray their true intentions at the start. They conceal them. To make their anti-popular handiwork easier, they hide from the people behind high-sounding phrases about "freedom" and "democracy."

But the Hungarian people did not follow the wretched handful of renegades. The conspirators found themselves isolated from the people.

Our antagonists hoped to destroy, or at least weaken, the bonds of close fraternal friendship that hold together the people of the socialist countries. The October-November events in Hungary had been a crucial test of Soviet-Hungarian friendship. It may be said without exaggeration that the whole world had watched tensely what the Soviet Union would do when the forces of international and domestic reaction unleashed their open and brazen attack against one of the links of the united socialist camp.

The Soviet Union, the Soviet people, could not look on indifferently at the fate of a friend in trouble, at the fate of millions of Hungarian working people facing the danger of again falling under the yoke of landlord and capitalist exploitation. Faithful to its fraternal duty and guided by a profound sense of genuine proletarian internationalism, the Soviet Union could not but respond to the appeal of the Hungarian Government and come to the assistance of the Hungarian people.

Soviet-Hungarian friendship has not only withstood the onslaught of the reactionaries; it has been further cemented and strengthened, and now no exertions of the enemy can destroy it, however much imperialist reaction may rave and rant.

By helping the Hungarian people to crush the counter-revolutionary revolt we have prevented the enemy from impairing the unity of the entire socialist camp, rigorously tested during the Hungarian events. We were aware that by helping Hungary to suppress the uprising and eliminate its aftermath as quickly as possible we were also helping all the other countries of the socialist camp. All of you know that the help we gave the Hungarian people in crushing the counter-revolution was approved unanimously by the working people in the socialist countries, by all progressives throughout the world.

The working people of the socialist countries and their Communist and Workers' parties know full well that the social gains of the peoples, their national independence, are guaranteed only as long as the socialist countries stand solid and united.

The Communist Party of the Soviet Union sees its prime obligation and international duty in tirelessly strengthening and extending political, economic and cultural ties with all socialist countries along the Leninist principles of equality, fraternal co-operation and mutual confidence.

Dear comrades, the report of Comrade Ferenc Münnich gives a convincing picture of the recent successes achieved by the Hungarian people. The working people of Hungary have in a short time made striking progress in strengthening their system of people's democracy. This is evidence of the great life-giving force of the political and social system in the Hungarian People's Republic. The political and economic situation inside Hungary is becoming more and more solid. The prestige of the Hungarian People's Republic in the international scene is rising steadily. The Hungarian people are confidently getting into their stride, carrying on firmly along the path of social development, which they have taken 13 years ago.

The achievements of the Hungarian people in socialist construction are the best possible illustration of the mood of Hungary's working masses, of their solidarity with the Hungarian Socialist Workers' Party, the Revolutionary Workers' and Peasants' Government, of their loyalty to the system of people's democracy.

It is primarily to the skilful leadership of the Hungarian Socialist Workers' Party and its Central Committee that the Hungarian people owe all their successes. It is no wonder that the enemy has always directed—and still directs—its main effort against the working-class party. The plan of the reactionaries is obvious. They want to deprive the Hungarian working class, the working people of Hungary, of their vanguard, their advance detachment. Now the Party has been reconstituted and stands unflinchingly at the head of the masses. The skilful leadership of the Hungarian Socialist Workers' Party is a guarantee of successful socialist construction in your country.

In reviving their Party, the Hungarian Communists had to surmount big difficulties springing from the revisionist tendencies within the now reorganized Hungarian Working People's Party and the sectarian, dogmatic mistakes of its former leadership, its loss of due flexibility and ability to properly evaluate the situation, its hesitation and vacillation in enforcing the Party line.

By virtue of the skilful policy of the Hungarian Socialist Workers' Party, of its Central Committee headed by that outstanding leader of the Hungarian working-class movement Comrade János Kadar with his splendid qualities of fighter and leader, the influence of the Party in the people has been restored. Its policy now enjoys the active support of the working people of Hungary.

And that, after all, is the most important thing. The policy of a people's government, the policy of a Marxist-Leninist party, must always conform with the interests of the working class, the interests of the working people; it must always strengthen the system of people's democracy and work for improving the life of the masses. A policy like that will always have the support of the people.

The Patriotic People's Front, a broadly representative

mass organization with a membership of millions of Hungarian working people, is doing much valuable work to rally the country's progressive forces and cement the alliance of the working class and the working peasantry. The solidarity of the Patriotic People's Front embodies the militant unity of Hungary's working people with the Hungarian Socialist Workers' Party, with the Government of People's Hungary.

We wish the Patriotic People's Front of Hungary and its leadership new successes in their activities for the good of the people, and for peace and socialism.

Comrades, we know that you have many difficulties. The survivals of capitalism are known to linger in men's minds, particularly when bearers of capitalist tendencies, representatives of the former ruling classes, are still alive. It is the same in your country, in Hungary.

It is impossible to expect everybody to be pleased with the policy of the Party. Some people, especially those who lost their highly profitable mills and factories and their trading and other establishments when power passed into the hands of the people, are unquestionably at odds with the people's power, with its policy. It is not their government, after all. The days of their reign are over, and for good. Today power in Hungary belongs to the people, the working people, and not to those who rode the people, who exploited them ruthlessly for their own enrichment.

The people in the socialist countries have convinced themselves sufficiently well by their own experience that only the socialist system is capable of providing for the full and all-round advancement of their material and spiritual forces. The achievements of the socialist countries in peaceful creative labour, in raising the living standard of the population, in developing science and culture, are vivid proof that the policy of parties guided in their activities by the immortal ideas of Marxism-Leninism, is the correct policy.

Take our country, for example. People of the older generation here in Hungary probably remember how backward and weak Russia's national economy was on the eve of the First World War.

The First World War, and the imperialist intervention that followed the October Revolution of 1917, brought our country to almost complete ruin. Steel production, for example, amounted to just 200,000 tons in 1920. Today, the Soviet Union produces that much steel in less than two days. In 1917 Russia's share in the world industrial output was just 2 or 3 per cent, while today the Soviet Union produces one-fifth of the total world industrial output.

Thanks to the socialist transformations worked by the Soviet people, our country has now outstripped all, even the most industrially developed countries of Europe, whose economies were formerly incomparably more advanced than the industry and agriculture of tsarist Russia.

The industry and agriculture, the national economy of the Soviet Union, is very much on the upgrade. The whole world knows also of the remarkable progress our country has made in developing science, technology and culture. We have every right to be proud that the world's first artificial earth satellites were made in the Soviet Union. They signalize a new stage in man's knowledge of the Universe.

Today the Soviet people are going well ahead with the task of overtaking and surpassing U.S. output of key industrial items within the shortest possible historical time.

The most important problem of industrial development—that of the rate of growth of production—is long since settled in favour of the U.S.S.R. Between 1929 and 1956, excluding the years of the Second World War, the average annual growth of Soviet industrial production amounted to over 16 per cent. In the United States the average growth of industrial production over the same period was each year less than three per cent.

Furthermore, it should be borne in mind that the Soviet economy, like that of all socialist countries, is rid of crises and mass unemployment, those inevitable companions of capitalism. Soviet industrial development is continuously on the upgrade.

Soviet people never rest on what they have already achieved. They never fail to find fresh resources for the continued expansion of the country's economy. This aim has been well served by last year's reorganization of management in industry and building, the current reorganization of the machine and tractor stations, and by other measures taken by our Party and the Soviet Government for the further advancement of industrial and agricultural production.

The Soviet people are confident that in the very near future our country will not only catch up, but outstrip the United States economically. The new and progressive always triumphs over the old and decadent. Such is the relentless law of social development.

The entire policy of the Communist Party of the Soviet Union, all its practical efforts, are aimed at improving the living conditions of workers, collective farmers and the intelligentsia year after year so our country is immersed in the magnificent flowers of joy, happiness, and confidence in the future. We have no use for wars of conquest, for interference in the affairs of other countries and peoples, nor for the state of cold war, hostility and mistrust.

One need not be a scientist or military man to understand that another war—should any criminal force start it—would be a calamity to all mankind. We share this planet with the capitalist countries, and it is better that there should be no war. We do not say this from weakness. We believe firmly that if there is a military conflict, the socialist system will win out, while the capitalist system will fail to survive the terrible ordeal. But Communists do not want their ideas to triumph at the price of tens of millions of human lives. The socialist countries do not wish to force their system on any nation. We are deeply convinced that the advantages of socialism will unfold most effectively in peaceful competition with capitalism. The Soviet Union offers the capitalist countries to compete in raising living standards rather than in the arms race, in building dwellings and schools rather than military bases and rocket ramps, in extending reciprocal trade and cultural exchanges rather than in the cold war.

In our time there is no other sensible policy but that of peaceful co-existence, of reasonable compromise which does not place any country at an advantage and ensures the security of each state.

Today, the question stands thus: either peaceful co-existence, or war.

The Soviet Union works untiringly for universal disarmament, for the unconditional banning of nuclear weapons, for an immediate discontinuation of atomic and hydrogen bomb tests, for ending the cold war. As part of its peace policy, working for an international *détente* and an atmosphere of confidence, the Soviet Government has in the last three years reduced the country's armed forces by 2,140,000 men.

You know that a few days ago the first session of the Supreme Soviet of the U.S.S.R. has decided upon the unilateral discontinuation by the Soviet Union of tests of all types of atomic and hydrogen weapons.

The Soviet Union has applied, and will continue to apply, every effort to achieve mutual understanding and friendly relations with the peoples of all countries. We act upon the assumption that in present circumstances all governments which appreciate their responsibility for world destinies, must rise above ideological differences. In the past three or four years we have achieved some positive results in that respect.

Regrettably, leading statesmen in a number of Western countries have not as yet shown any desire to adopt the principles of co-existence, non-aggression, mutual respect of territorial integrity and sovereignty, non-interference in domestic affairs, and rejection of the policy "from strength." They take no heed of the people's hatred of cold war, of their urge for peace and action to relieve international tension.

The Soviet Union threatens no one. It has always opposed war as an instrument of international politics. It is against carving the world up into military blocs. It stands for settling international issues by negotiation. This is precisely why the Soviet Government has approached the Governments of the Great Powers and the governments of most countries of the world, with the proposal of convening a summit conference.

At a summit conference statesmen could exchange views on ways and means of ending the cold war. They could take initial steps towards resolving pressing international problems and establishing new, sound relations between the people of all countries.

Heeding the demand of world opinion, sober-minded Western politicians approve the idea of settling urgent problems by peaceful international negotiation. Yet the eye is also drawn to such facts as the series of conferences convened by the military alliances and pacts established by the Western Powers to step up the arms race and bring all the aggressive blocs under a single roof. It should not be left unsaid that in its attempts to obstruct a meeting at the summit, the U.S. Government is again and again raising questions which cannot be discussed at conferences of that sort, such as the German question, for example, or the question about the situation in the countries of Eastern Europe.

The German question is important, but it can only be settled by the Germans themselves—by Germans living in the Federal Republic of Germany and in the German Democratic Republic—without the interference of any other states in their domestic affairs. Any solution of the German problem ignoring the wishes of the whole German people, of the kind suggested by the United States and some other Western countries, will do little to strengthen the peace in Europe. On the contrary, it will lead to a deterioration in the situation, and even to war.

As for the so-called question about the situation in the countries of Eastern Europe, any discussion of it would be a glaring violation of the elementary rules of international relations. No member-country of the United Nations could agree to empowering anyone to discuss questions related to its political system.

It is perfectly clear that no self-respecting government of a sovereign country would ever agree to a discussion of that question. What right have U.S. statesmen to foist their country's way of life on other countries? The people of the East European countries have long since decided what path they should follow, and nobody has the right to interfere in their domestic affairs. The Soviet Government has repeatedly stated, and does so now, that it most emphatically opposes any discussion of that kind.

What moves the men who raise such questions? They know perfectly well that these questions cannot be an object of discussion, because, in effect, they speak of the abolition of the socialist system in the People's Democracies and their return to the capitalist path. To raise these questions is to lose one's reason. The same could also have been said about us if, say, we were to demand that the summit meeting discuss the question of abolishing the capitalist system wherever it is now extant. The system of government is the domestic affair of each nation.

What is the purpose, we ask, for raising these questions? They are not meant, by any means, to end the cold war, but rather to add fuel to it, to cause irritation, to further increase international tension, and thereby to produce an excuse for wrecking the summit talks.

There is every possibility at a meeting of Heads of Government to settle a number of urgent international issues and end the cold war, so as to ensure normal international relations based on the principles of peaceful co-existence.

Normal relations between states would promote greater confidence. With time, they could develop into friendly relations and lead to the establishment of lasting world peace.

All too often Western statesmen speak of their love and allegiance to peace, while in practice they work in every way against discussing urgent international questions, eliminating international tension, and establishing confidence between states. Empty talk about peace, unsupported by concrete deeds, does little honour to the leading Western statesmen and cannot lull the vigilance of the peace-loving nations, particularly the peoples of the Soviet Union and other socialist countries.

Dear comrades, the forces working for peace and international friendship have grown immeasurably, and continue to grow. The Peace Manifesto of the Moscow Meeting of Communist and Workers' Parties met with wide response in all countries. Its call for "peace to the world" is a genuine token of the hopes and wishes of people all over the globe. In their van stand the peoples of the Soviet Union, the Chinese People's Republic, the Hungarian People's Republic and other socialist countries, and also the Communist and Workers' parties in the capitalist countries. We must support this powerful movement for peace in every possible way.

We want all people to live in peace and friendship, without fear for their future. We want the tremendous resources now being expended on armaments to be spent on public welfare, on raising the standard of life, on developing economy, science, culture and art in every country. We must work persistently for this goal, and spare no effort in achieving it. The hard-working Hungarian people doubtless wish the same thing.

The Meeting of Communist and Workers' Parties of Socialist Countries pointed out in its Declaration that the Leninist principle of peaceful co-existence of the two systems is the solid basis of the foreign policy of the socialist states and a reliable basis for peace and friendship among nations.

But to achieve success in this foreign policy, the socialist countries must consolidate their ranks still more, and constantly assist and support one another. At the same time, the socialist countries must work harder to strengthen their economic power and step up the rates of their economic development. We must improve socialist production in every way, co-ordinate our economic plans, raise our productivity of labour, make better use of our resources, of the achievements of science and technology, and improve the living standard. We must help and support each other also in these and other political and economic tasks.

The Soviet people regard it as their sacred obligation, their internationalist duty, to promote in every way the further consolidation of the socialist camp, to help and support all the fraternal socialist countries. You may rest assured, comrades, that the Soviet Union will spare no effort in strengthening the socialist camp. The Soviet people have never failed their internationalist duty.

Dear comrades, this visit of our Party and Government delegation to your fine country comes a year after the Soviet Union was visited by the Party and Government delegation of the Hungarian People's Republic. During their tour of the Soviet Union, your comrades had every opportunity of seeing how warm and sincere is the friendship and sympathy of the Soviet people for the Hungarian people.

Although we have come to your country just a few days ago, the warm and cordial welcome which we receive everywhere from the working people of Hungary adds to our conviction that our return visit, our meetings with the working people of your country, will serve to strengthen our friendly relations still more, and thus to improve greatly the mutual understanding between our nations, to cement world peace.

Long live and flourish the Hungarian People's Republic!

Long live the Hungarian Socialist Workers' Party—the inspirer and organizer of all the victories of the Hungarian people!

Let the unconquerable fraternal friendship of the Hungarian and Soviet peoples live and gain strength all the time!

(N. S. Khrushchov's speech was repeatedly interrupted by stormy and prolonged applause.)

SPEECH
AT MASS MEETING IN BUDAPEST
DURING STAY IN HUNGARY
OF SOVIET PARTY AND GOVERNMENT DELEGATION

April 4, 1958

Dear Comrade Kadar,
Dear Comrade Dobi,
Dear Comrade Münnich,
Dear Comrades Marosan and Pongrac,
Citizens of Budapest,

On behalf of the Central Committee of the Communist Party of the Soviet Union, the Council of Ministers and the Presidium of the Supreme Soviet of the U.S.S.R., I convey to you and to the whole fraternal Hungarian people heartfelt and friendly greetings from the working people of the Soviet Union!

We are very pleased and moved by this meeting today with the working people of Budapest. The Soviet people know well that Budapest occupies a prominent place in the history of your country, the centuries of national-liberation struggle waged by the Hungarian people, the heroic working-class movement.

Forty years ago, a few days after landlord and capitalist rule was smashed in Russia, there were stormy demonstrations and rallies of workers here, in the streets and squares of Budapest, at which people called out such slogans as "Long Live the Socialist Revolution!", "We Want Peace! Down with War!"

Right here, at a city-wide Budapest workers' meeting,

the following moving resolution was adopted forty years ago:

"Workers of Budapest and its suburbs, and with them all the people of the capital, send their fraternal greetings to the Russian revolutionaries who shall with gallant heart, strong mind and firm hand lead mankind out of the inferno of war. All of us who are gathered here are determined to support the Russian revolutionaries in their heroic struggle for peace. We shall also fight with all our strength that the exploitation of one class by another and the oppression of one nation by another should also cease in our country!"

Allow me on behalf of the peoples of the Soviet Union to convey hearty thanks to the workers of Budapest and all the working people of Hungary for their fraternal support and assistance to the Great October Socialist Revolution, to our young Soviet Republic.

Comrades, we have come here on a return visit in connection with your national holiday—the day of Hungary's liberation from the yoke of Hitler fascists and their Horthy henchmen. Thirteen years ago the glorious armed forces of the Soviet Union completed the liberation of the territory of Hungary from German-fascist troops. In stubborn struggle against the forces of home reaction, warding off imperialist attempts to interfere in Hungary's affairs, the working masses won power and established the system of people's democracy. The working man became complete master of Hungary.

Thirteen years is not a very long time. Under the capitalists and landlords nothing would have changed in the country's development in 13 years. There would have been those who would labour to exhaustion, and others who would live in luxury by other people's exploited labour.

But 13 years of people's rule have transformed your country. The life of the people has changed radically. Exploitation of man by man has been wiped out in the main. And this was achieved despite big difficulties, despite the subversive activities of the enemies of People's Hungary. Much may be said about the achievements of People's Hungary. You know them well yourselves.

The antagonists of the Hungarian people do not stop at gross lies and calumny. They try to deny, or at least belittle, the major successes scored by Hungary's working people in 13 years of people's power. But their exertions are futile! Nobody will ever succeed in misleading a people that has won genuine freedom and democracy!

The enemies of socialism lose sleep when a people builds its life by itself, without capitalists and landlords. Just look how many times the imperialists made their vicious onslaughts upon the Soviet Union. But under the leadership of the Communist Party our people have beaten back all their attacks, have built socialism, and are striding forward confidently to their lofty goal—communism.

We must keep in mind that the enemy sometimes takes advantage quite adroitly of the mistakes and shortcomings of one leader or another to deceive and delude individual groups of people and, in the ultimate analysis, to defile the socialist system and undermine the dictatorship of the working class.

This has happened recently in your country. But what was the final outcome? The sound forces of the Hungarian people took the upper hand. They rallied round the Revolutionary Workers' and Peasants' Government and the Hungarian Socialist Workers' Party, and crushed the uprising of forces hostile to the working people. The designs of the reactionaries fell through completely. It was inevitable that they should fall through.

In 1919 international and domestic reaction was still capable of shedding the blood of Hungary's working men and crushing the young Hungarian Soviet Republic. But in an epoch when there exists the mighty socialist camp, the Hungarian working people could count securely on the selfless assistance of the other socialist countries. And at a time of stress they did, indeed, receive such assistance and fraternal support. At the request of your Government, Soviet troops took a hand in smashing the counter-revolutionary uprising. The danger of the fascist régime being restored in Hungary, the danger that a new hotbed of war would arise in the heart of Europe, was squashed by joint effort.

You may recall the hue and cry raised by international reaction. Our enemies ranted about the Soviet Army crushing a "popular revolution." What else could one expect? They had to cover up their tracks, to divert attention from the real instigators of the anti-popular putsch. What kind of a "popular revolution" was it, indeed, if the fascist putschists meant to turn the Hungarian workers into hired slaves and to deprive the peasants of their legitimate rights to land and to the fruits of their labour. But they failed.

The Soviet Army helped the Hungarian working people to defend their gains from the imperialist onslaught and to rout the handful of rebels who had raised their sword against popular rule. All honest people, all people the least bit fair know that the will of the people is sacred to the Soviet Army, which is flesh of the flesh of the people.

By having given a helping hand to the Hungarian working people, the Soviet Union performed a supreme act of proletarian solidarity and done its sacred internationalist duty by a fraternal country. To perform one's internationalist duty means to stand by one's friends in trouble, to come to their assistance if enemy hosts try to raise their arm against the most cherished of all—the power of the workers and peasants.

The imperialists wanted to test the strength of our ranks, the vigour of our solidarity. What came of it? They discovered that it did not pay, that one might get burned, that it is best not to try our patience.

We are confident that the people's power in Hungary, just as in the other socialist countries, stands firm and will stand for all time!

The uprising organized from outside had caused considerable damage to your country. But it could not, naturally, stop—and did not stop—the advance of the Hungarian People's Republic along the path of socialist construction.

The main and decisive thing about the successes scored by the Hungarian People's Republic is that the building of socialism in Hungary is headed by a battle-steeled Marxist-Leninist Party. The Hungarian working class regards it by rights as its very own party—a party bound inviolably to the working men, the people.

The Hungarian Socialist Workers' Party is loyal to Marxism-Leninism, to the idea of fighting for socialism; it blends its love of country with the idea of proletarian internationalism. In this lies its great strength, the source of its achievements.

From the bottom of our hearts we wish the Hungarian Socialist Workers' Party further successes in its vast and manifold endeavour.

The future of the socialist countries is in the hands of the working class, the working people. Having taken power, these are now the sole and complete masters of their countries. Socialism ensures high rates of economic development in the socialist countries. But to attain them, we must always lay stress on raising the productivity of labour on the basis of mechanization and automation and strive for better organization.

Building socialism, comrades, is not the same as promenading along a trodden path. It involves conquering difficulties, which do not end when the working class comes to power. We know this well from our own experience. The new society develops in stubborn struggle with the old world, which has outlived itself.

We know that you, in Hungary, also have your difficulties, although they are much fewer now than, say, a year ago. But the socialist system has everything it takes to conquer these difficulties, to develop all the creative forces of the nation. We are sure that the life of the working people of Hungary will improve year by year.

Comrades, the swift normalization of the situation in Hungary is vivid proof that the development of a country which has taken the socialist path cannot be turned back, that the unity, solidarity and fraternal mutual assistance of the socialist countries is an immense force.

In the community of socialist countries every member strives to help the peoples of the fraternal countries in building socialism and, in turn, takes strength from their assistance and support. Mutual assistance does not mean that some will become stronger at the expense of others. It means that each socialist country individually, and the camp as a whole, will advance steadily and grow stronger.

The consolidation of the socialist camp is having a far-reaching influence on the entire process of mankind's historical development. Our progress and solidarity, comrades, are helping the peaceful democratic forces throughout the world to combat the threat of war and fight for democracy and social progress.

Let us go back to the autumn of 1956. It was not mere chance, at that time, that the imperialists mounted two attacks simultaneously: one against socialist Hungary and the other against Egypt, which had won her independence. They hoped that defeat of the socialist forces in Hungary and confusion in the socialist camp would help them foist their will upon Egypt. We all know the outcome of these imperialist attacks!

The double defeat of the imperialist forces was a turning-point in the development of the entire international situation towards a *détente*. That is the international significance behind the victory of the socialist forces in Hungary and the patriotic forces in Egypt. The fighting alliance of the two greatest forces of our time—the socialist countries and the countries which have recently won their national independence—gained added strength in this joint stand against the imperialist assault.

Comrades, more than 100 years ago the great Hungarian poet, Sándor Petöfi, wrote bitterly· "We have no brother-people in the world whom we could ask for assistance, who could help us; we are alone, like a tree in the desert." Socialism has changed that situation. The Hungarian people is an equal brother in the mighty family of nations of the socialist community.

Hungary's working people know that they can make their social gains secure solely in fraternal alliance with the peoples of the other socialist countries.

The world socialist system is getting bigger and stronger. Yet there was a time when the Soviet Union was the only socialist country. Grim ordeals and hardships fell to the lot of our working class, which was the first in the world to break with capitalism and boldly blaze the trail to a new socialist future.

The Soviet people have conquered all difficulties and scored remarkable successes in industry, agriculture and their country's economy generally.

They follow confidently the path charted by the 20th Party Congress, the path of gradual transition from socialism to communism, the path of strengthening world peace. We assure you, comrades, that the Soviet people will spare no pains in building communism and fighting for peace and international security.

The Soviet Union is applying tremendous efforts in close co-operation with the other socialist countries, shoulder to shoulder with all the peace-loving nations of the world, to avert a new war. But peace does not come of itself. It has to be won in persistent and active struggle against the forces of aggression, war and destruction. Friends of peace in all countries of the world are coming to appreciate this fact more and more.

Loyal to its policy of peace, the Soviet Union has lately made many new constructive proposals and taken a number of steps to relieve world tension, stop the armaments race, and ban nuclear weapons. But our proposals have not had a positive response from the ruling circles of the U.S.A. and the other Western Powers. What is more, they continue to fan the cold war and carry on with their policy "from positions of strength." In order to charge the atmosphere still more, they are stepping up the arms race and preparing a nuclear war against the Soviet Union and the other socialist countries.

Things have gone so far that U.S. aircraft loaded with atomic and hydrogen bombs make daily flights over the territories of many countries. There have even been air accidents involving such aircraft, but this is being carefully concealed from the public. Millions of people live in continuous fear, because some accident or a premeditated provocation by some maniac may plunge mankind into an atomic war. Man's common sense protests against this extremely dangerous situation.

You know that a few days ago the Supreme Soviet of the U.S.S.R. adopted the decision for our country to unilaterally discontinue experimental explosions of atomic and hydrogen weapons. The Supreme Soviet of the U.S.S.R. has called on the United States and Britain to follow suit.

This historic decision was acclaimed by people throughout the world, including America and Britain. Everybody waited to see how the Government of the United States would react to it, how the British Government would react, to see which way the weathercock would turn—towards enduring peace or greater international tension and continuation of the arms race. But the armaments race leads inevitably to a war and not to a peaceful *détente*.

A few days ago the U.S. President, Mr. Eisenhower, held a press conference, at which he made a statement with regard to the unilateral discontinuance of atomic and hydrogen weapons tests by the Soviet Union. Well, what did the President, whom we regard as a realistic statesman, have to say? After all he did make efforts, though weak and hesitant ones, to find ways and means of relieving international tension.

Mr. Eisenhower alleged that this Soviet foreign policy move should not "be taken seriously," that moves of this kind were pure "propaganda."

One might have expected it from other statesmen. But how could a man who understands what this action means call it propaganda? It is understandable, therefore, why Mr. Eisenhower's statement disappointed and chagrined all the peoples of the world.

Before this mass meeting of many thousands of Hungarian working people I want to state the following: If Mr. Eisenhower really thinks that we have discontinued tests of atomic and hydrogen weapons for the sake of propaganda, then why do not he and other Western statesmen engage in the same propaganda and discontinue nuclear weapons tests as well?

As for us, statesmen of the Soviet Union, we are proud of this propaganda, which meets the wishes of all mankind. If the U.S. President and the British Prime Minister were to engage in such propaganda, the people of all countries would be overjoyed!

Some statesmen try to weaken the strong impression which the Supreme Soviet decision to discontinue thermo-nuclear tests unilaterally in the Soviet Union has had on the minds of men by saying that the Soviet Union made a series of test explosions just before announcing its decision. Yes, we did hold tests of thermo-nuclear weapons, but the whole world knows that the United States tested atomic weapons as far back as 1945, and not on some proving ground but in Nagasaki and Hiroshima. And hundreds of thousands of civilians died in these "tests."

The Soviet Union, as you know, started nuclear weapons testing later. And conducted it under conditions which afforded maximum protection to the population *en masse.* Anyone versed in technology will easily say offhand who has made more test blasts of this weapon.

Thus, if we were to count the test explosions made, we should have discontinued testing only after we had drawn level in this respect with the United States. This is why anyone referring to the number of tests made is in fact trying to befog public opinion, to misinform the peoples, and thus to carry on testing and stockpiling thermo-nuclear weapons, to carry on the armaments race.

Some Western statesmen allege also that we announced our unilateral discontinuance of tests to evade international control of testing. But this dodge is easily exposed. You know that not a single explosion of atomic or hydrogen bombs, whether by Britain or the United States, has gone unnoticed. Thus, in fact, international control over explosions already exists.

When the advocates of cold war in the United States claimed that it was possible to make explosions which appliances would fail to register, which could not be controlled, scientists of many countries, the U.S.A. among them, refuted these claims. The U.S. politicians, who had previously said that it was impossible to register all explosions, were compelled to admit that experimental blasts of nuclear weapons could not, indeed, be concealed.

But if some think that the absence of international control over tests of nuclear weapons is an obstacle to the United States and Britain following the Soviet example and voluntarily ceasing tests, the Soviet Union is prepared to agree to international control. We have declared this repeatedly.

We urge our partners to stop testing. Let us, as from today, make no more explosions of hydrogen and atomic bombs, and stop contaminating the atmosphere with radioactive fall-out.

On behalf of the peoples of the Soviet Union, on behalf of the Soviet Government, I address myself to the President of the United States, Mr. Eisenhower, to the Prime Minister of Great Britain, Mr. Macmillan: Follow the example set by the Soviet Union and show your good will by deeds. It would make mankind happy. It would be a noble action that would live down the ages. We regard a stop to nuclear testing as a first step towards complete disarmament, towards creating conditions for lasting world peace, as a step towards peaceful co-existence, peaceful competition between the two systems. The settlement of this vitally important question would facilitate the solution also of other urgent international problems.

Comrades, more than three months have passed since the Soviet Government has made its proposal to convene a conference of leading statesmen, attended by Heads of Government, to settle a series of urgent problems and to frame by joint effort effective ways and means of relieving international tension and terminating the state of cold war.

But they say to us that they want to discuss the situation in the countries of Eastern Europe. What exactly do they want to discuss, and, generally, what right has anyone to discuss the internal development of other countries? No, good sirs, keep your nose out of other people's affairs. The peoples of Eastern Europe have already made up their minds. They are masters of their ship and will let no one meddle in their domestic affairs.

The socialist countries and the world communist movement are on a steep upgrade. The Moscow Meeting of Fraternal Communist and Workers' Parties last autumn has cemented still more their unity and solidarity, and defined the tasks of the working-class and democratic movement.

Our main job is to strengthen peace. The socialist camp is the bulwark of peace. Our camp has the support of all the peace-loving peoples, of the whole of progressive mankind. We are conscious of the responsibility we bear for the historical mission that has fallen to the socialist countries and shall continue firmly, all together, along the path to peace and socialism.

Long live the working people of Budapest, the capital of People's Hungary!

Long live and flourish the Hungarian People's Republic—that reliable link of the powerful socialist camp!

Long live the Revolutionary Workers' and Peasants' Government of the Hungarian People's Republic!

Long live the Hungarian Socialist Workers' Party—the inspirer and organizer of all the victories of the Hungarian people!

Let the inviolable fraternal friendship of the Hungarian and Soviet peoples live and strengthen for ever!

(N. S. Khrushchov's speech was repeatedly interrupted by stormy and prolonged applause.)

SPEECH
AT MEETING IN CEGLÉD DURING STAY IN HUNGARY OF SOVIET PARTY AND GOVERNMENT DELEGATION

April 7, 1958

Dear Comrades, dear class brothers,

We have come to your country on a friendly return visit at the invitation of the Central Committee of the Hungarian Socialist Workers' Party and the Revolutionary Workers' and Peasants' Government.

During our short stay here, when meeting the working people of Hungary, we have everywhere felt and seen that we, representatives of the Soviet Union, were very welcome. And we are happy to express our appreciation and deep gratitude for this kind hospitality and warmth.

We are conscious of the most brotherly feelings that the working people of Hungary have for the Soviet people. We set an especially high value on them. There have been many fine examples of fraternal solidarity between the working people of Hungary and the Soviet Union. Take the time of the October Revolution in our country.

When the working class in alliance with the working peasantry overthrew the authoritarian régime and established Soviet power, the whiteguards and interventionists from many countries assailed the young Soviet Republic. The working class, all the working people of our country, rose to the fight against the enemies of the Revolution. It was a grim struggle, and many Hungarian soldiers who were then war prisoners in Russia took an active part in it on the side of the Revolution. Hungarian and other nationals fought shoulder to shoulder with the workers and peasants of our country against the enemies of the working class and the working people of Russia, against the foreign interventionists. Hungarian working people in soldiers' uniforms knew that by fighting the enemies of the Soviet Republic in Russia they were also striking a blow at the enemies of the Hungarian working people.

We remember the splendid effort of Hungary's working class and working people when in 1919 they overthrew landlord and capitalist rule in their own country and proclaimed Soviet power. We remember the message sent by Béla Kun, the head of the Hungarian Soviet Republic, to our great leader and teacher, V. I. Lenin.

But the Hungarian revolution of 1919 was defeated. It was defeated because the bourgeoisie of the Western imperialist countries came to the assistance of the Hungarian reactionaries. Together, by a joint effort, they crushed the young Hungarian Soviet Republic.

Comrades, the Soviet working people successfully defended Soviet power under Communist Party leadership against domestic counter-revolutionaries and foreign interventionists. However, the imperialists could not reconcile themselves to the existence of the Soviet socialist state. They plotted against us, tried to throttle the young Soviet Republic by economic blockade, and planned an armed attack on our Soviet country. As you know, the war which Hitler started against the Soviet Union ended in a complete rout for fascist Germany. The Soviet Army liberated Hungary from Hitler fascism and wiped out the Horthy régime. In self-devoted struggle the Hungarian working class, the working peasantry and working intellectuals gained the opportunity of building their own socialist state in keeping with the interests of the working people.

The people of Hungary are building their life by themselves along socialist lines, without landlords and capitalists, and have scored big successes. But there is no getting away from the fact that the former leadership in Hungary has in the past committed serious mistakes and distortions. The reactionaries took advantage of them. With the support of external imperialist forces, the enemies of people's democracy in Hungary organized a counter-revolutionary uprising in the autumn of 1956. Reaction tried to destroy the gains of Hungary's working people. The fascist rebels unleashed a reign of terror against the foremost men of the working class.

We, leaders of the Communist Party of the Soviet Union and the Soviet Government, had at the time to make a difficult decision. How should we act? Strength was on our side, and so was truth. Our truth is the truth of the working class—the truth of the working people. The difficulty lay in the fact that a certain, least conscious, part of the Hungarian workers had fallen prey to enemy propaganda and participated in the disturbances caused by the counter-revolution. We had to decide what we were to do. Common sense urged us to help the workers and working people of the Hungarian People's Republic. But it is one thing to help economically—to send metal and grain, and to give advice. It is quite another thing to send troops. We never hesitate when it comes to repelling an enemy attack. But we saw that owing to their lack of political consciousness a certain section of Hungarians had become a tool in the hands of their class enemies.

Comrades, believe us, it was difficult to make our decision, but we thought that we could not look on idly any longer while emboldened fascist elements began their savage massacre of workers, peasants, Communists and other foremost Hungarians in the streets and squares of Budapest and other Hungarian cities, while the counter-revolution sought to drown the socialist gains of Hungary's toilers in the blood of the people. We could not bear with a situation in which a fascist régime would again take ascendancy in your country, and Hungary would become a new hotbed of war.

When we made our decision to come to your assistance in response to the appeal of the Hungarian working people and the Workers' and Peasants' Government, we knew that the enemies of the working class, that imperialist reactionaries throughout the world would use our action to their own ends. But we believed, we were convinced, that the working class and all the working people of Hungary, and progressives all over the world, would eventually appreciate our stand. I repeat, we could not stand idly by when the imperialist reactionaries had drawn their sword against the working people of Hungary. That is why the Soviet Government responded to the request of the Hungarian Revolutionary Workers' and Peasants' Government and decided to assist militarily in suppressing the counter-revolutionary revolt in Hungary. We helped the Hungarian people in their dark hour.

Comrades Hungarians, I think you realize perfectly well that when we sent our soldiers and officers to fight the fascist rebels, we had no other aim than to assist our friends, who were temporarily in trouble. *(Applause.)*

When bourgeois governments send troops to other countries they do so with the intent to conquer, and seek to establish their exploiter rule over the working people of those countries. We helped you, so that you could defend your interests against a handful of fascist conspirators and safeguard the people's right of building its own life without exploiters. By helping the Hungarian people to smash the counter-revolution we performed our internationalist duty.

What is more, after smashing the fascist uprising we gave Hungary considerable economic assistance, so that you could rectify more speedily the damage done to your country by the counter-revolutionary conspirators. The Soviet Union sent Hungary coal, metal and grain. *(Applause.)*

Disinterested assistance was rendered to the Hungarian

working people not only by the Soviet Union, but also by all the other socialist countries, which all wished sincerely to be of help, so that the material losses inflicted upon Hungary's national economy during the 1956 October-November events should not cause any marked drop in the living standard of the Hungarian people. Would a government pursuing aims of conquest act that way? (*Applause.*)

And so, when we went to your country at the suggestion of the Central Committee of the Hungarian Socialist Workers' Party and the Government of your republic, at the suggestion of Comrade Kadar, we did so with the firm belief that we should meet with complete understanding here, knowing that we could look squarely and honestly in the face of Hungary's workers, peasants and working intellectuals. We came to you as to our most loyal friends and brothers. (*Applause.*) And we are happy that we have not been mistaken in our expectations. During our stay in People's Hungary we have encountered everywhere among the working people the most friendly sentiments for the Soviet Union.

Comrades, you remember the hue and cry of international reaction at the time of the Hungarian events of 1956. There was no limit to what our antagonists wrote then. To confuse people, they drew a parallel between 1956 and the Hungarian revolution of 1848. Enemy propaganda raised a howl that the government of tsarist Russia had in 1848 sent troops to Hungary to suppress the revolutionary movement there, and that now, as it were, history was repeating itself and Soviet troops had suppressed the "popular" revolution.

But only enemies of your people, and ours, could draw such a parallel. It is patently clear to all that the Hungarian revolution of 1848 and the counter-revolutionary uprising of fascist elements in October-November 1956, supported as it was by imperialist reaction, were entirely different things. The difference is that in 1848 the Russian tsarist government, that is, Russia's government of exploiters, had come to the assistance of Hungary's government of exploiters. All Hungarians know that in 1848 the Russian tsar sent his troops to help the Austro-Hungarian monarchy because the Hungarian revolution constituted a threat to Russian autocracy. The Russian tsar was an enemy not only of the Hungarian, but also of the Russian, people. *(Applause.)* He persecuted Russian progressives ruthlessly, shot down the Decembrist uprising, and executed its leaders.

But there was also another Russia, comrades. The Russia of Herzen and Chernyshevsky was whole-heartedly with the people of Hungary, who had risen against their oppressors. We are direct heirs of just that Russia.

Comrades, I want to say something here that will doubtless go against the grain with bourgeois nationalists. I suppose some of them are present at this meeting. The Hungarian bourgeois nationalists say that we bear a responsibility for the actions of the tsarist government in the last century. Yet they hush up the fact that Hungarian troops had fought in the territory of the Soviet Union on the side of the Hitler forces, and had gone as far as Stalingrad. This was not so very long ago—just 15 to 17 years. What can the Hungarian bourgeois nationalists say to that? The Soviet people know that the working people of Hungary bear no responsibility for the actions of the fascist Horthy clique. We know that Horthy was an enemy of the Hungarian people as much as he was an enemy of the Soviet people. *(Applause.)* I think that this is clear to the workers, working peasants and working intellectuals *(prolonged applause)*, and it must be explained to those who have not grasped it yet. *(Applause.)*

Comrades, I have already related at the mass meeting in Sztalinvaros that when we announced in the newspapers that our delegation was going to Hungary, but did not say who exactly was going, imperialist reaction wrote in the foreign press that, of all things, Khrushchov would not go to Hungary, for he would be in for a reception there which he would not dare to face. (*Laughter*.) I even had telegrams from non-socialist countries. In one of them a well-wisher wrote: Mr. Khrushchov, don't go to Hungary, and take more guards along if you do. I give you this advice, he wrote on, because I see that you are a good man and work hard for the cause of peace. (*Laughter, applause*.) We have guards, of course, but whatever guards we have, and whatever their number, no guards would help if the people would not support us. The people are a tremendous power. They dethrone kings, perform the greatest revolutions, and it is difficult to impose any idea on them that goes against their class interests.

We came to you without fear, comrade Hungarians, as brother to brother, and we are happy because we proved right. (*Stormy applause*.)

We are pleased to have visited your city, which holds a prominent place in Hungarian history. This is where Kossuth, that splendid son of the Hungarian people, made his first speech, urging Hungarians to fight for their country's freedom and independence. The working people of Hungary and the Soviet Union love him and respect him for his fiery speeches, his love of freedom and devotion to the interests of his homeland. But Kossuth's time was a time of bourgeois revolutions. Today, we all live in a different time—the time of proletarian, socialist revolutions, when the working class is fighting capital.

Comrades, the Soviet Union, Hungary, the Chinese People's Republic, and all the socialist countries, are making fine progress. The economy of the socialist countries is advancing steadily, socialist science and culture are developing at a rapid pace. We rejoice at these successes.

Despite the heavy losses inflicted by the rebels, the Hungarian People's Republic is making consistent and steady progress in developing its socialist economy. But you and we, the Soviet Union, and the other socialist countries, have our difficulties, and these must be conquered. Nobody is going to help us. We have to depend upon ourselves, upon our own labour, our own knowledge. We must continuously raise our productivity of labour, cement labour discipline, produce more with smaller outlays of labour. It is only by increasing our productivity of labour that we can move ahead more rapidly, and achieve fresh victories.

Comrades, the Communist Party of the Soviet Union and the Soviet Government are bending every effort to raise the economy, to improve the living standard in our country, to ensure world peace. We are against war. We do not need war. Yet this does not mean that we renounce the class struggle. The class struggle cannot be stopped as long as there are exploiters and exploited. We have always said, and say now, that the establishment of one state system or another in the various countries is an internal matter for the people of these countries to decide. We do not interfere, nor intend to interfere, in the domestic affairs of other countries. But we have always said, and say now, that the conditions created in the socialist countries will enable us to win the peaceful competition with capitalism in the economic field.

You may recall how our enemies ridiculed us when the great Lenin called on the Russian working class to take power and fight for the triumph of socialism together with the working peasantry. Our class enemies and their agents in the international working-class movement— the diverse revisionists, opportunists, and the like—insisted that this was Utopia. How could the scarcely literate, or totally illiterate, Russian workers and peasants defeat capitalism, they asked. How dare Lenin and the Bolsheviks call on the workers to take power into their hands in so backward a country?

Forty years have passed since then. Where was Rus-

sia at that time? It was then somewhere at the bottom
And where is the Soviet Union now, what heights has i
scaled? It ranks second in the world for economic devel
opment, leaving Britain, France, Germany, and othe
countries far behind. (*Applause.*) What country produces
most specialists with a secondary and university-leve
education? The Soviet Union does. (*Applause*). Whose
artificial earth satellites were the first to soar into oute
space? They were sputniks developed in the socialis
Soviet Union. (*Stormy applause.*) Who is it that now
intends to catch up the Soviet Union in scientific devel
opment? It is the United States that now sets itself the
task of catching up the Soviet Union. (*Applause.*)

I think that I shall not be misunderstood. We are not
bragging, and have no wish to offend the American
people. The Americans are fine people. But the time has
come when capitalism must surrender the right of way
to a new, more progressive system—the socialist system
This does not mean that the socialist countries must interfere in the affairs of the capitalist countries, comrades
They have their own working class, and their own working masses, and these will do their job. Just have patience.
I repeat, the system that exists in one country or
another is the internal affair of the people of that country.

Allow me, dear comrades, again to express our warm
love, our heartfelt gratitude and deep respect. Our Party
and Government delegation has brought you fraternal
greetings from the Soviet people and assurances that
you will not find better friends anywhere than the peoples of the socialist countries. (*Prolonged applause.*)

There is no exploitation and no exploiters under the
system established in the socialist countries. The capitalist system has been abolished there for all time, and
so has the oppression of one people by another. Their
peoples render each other fraternal assistance and respect the labour of their brothers. We must consolidate
our ranks still more—the ranks of workers, peasants and

the intelligentsia of all the socialist countries. We must work persistently for world peace. (*Prolonged applause.*)

Long live the working class of the Hungarian People's Republic! (*Prolonged applause.*)

Long live the working peasantry of Hungary! (*Prolonged applause.*)

Long live the Hungarian intellectuals, who keep step with the working class under the leadership of the Hungarian Socialist Workers' Party! (*Prolonged applause.*)

Long live the Revolutionary Workers' and Peasants' Government of Hungary, headed by Comrade Ferenc Münnich! (*Prolonged applause.*)

Long live the fine son of the Hungarian people—Chairman of the Presidium of the Hungarian People's Republic—our dear friend István Dobi! (*Prolonged applause.*)

Long live the Hungarian Socialist Workers' Party headed by Comrade János Kadar! (*Stormy, prolonged applause.*)

SPEECH
AT MASS MEETING IN TATABANYA DURING STAY IN HUNGARY
OF SOVIET PARTY AND GOVERNMENT DELEGATION

April 8, 1958

Dear Comrades, Dear Friends and Brothers,

Our Party and Government delegation came to you at the invitation of the Central Committee of the Hungarian Socialist Workers' Party and the Hungarian Revolutionary Workers' and Peasants' Government. We are very grateful to Comrades János Kadar and Ferenc Münnich, who have invited us to see how your Party works and how your people live.

Comrades, we are being well received everywhere. Words fail us to describe the warmth and cordiality of the welcome extended to the Soviet Party and Government delegation by the working people of the Hungarian People's Republic. I am particularly pleased to visit you, the miners. After all, it was among miners that I spent my childhood and youth. We wanted to visit you, to see the Hungarian miners, to make their acquaintance, to see whether or not they are like Soviet miners. (*Laughter, applause.*) And we see that the Hungarian miners are just like ours, like Soviet miners. (*Applause.*)

The friendship of the peoples of the Soviet Union and Hungary has a fine history. When the October Revolution broke out in Russia and the whiteguards and interventionists wanted to crush Soviet power, when the French, Japanese, British, American and other interventionists landed their troops in Soviet Russia, when many bourgeois countries sent their soldiers against the young Soviet Republic, and the Soviet people took up arms in response to the great Lenin's call to defend the gains of the October Revolution, the gallant sons of the Hungarian working class, the Hungarian working people—the internationalists of Hungary—joined the young Red Guard, and later the Red Army, together with other nationals to fight against the whiteguards and interventionsts. (*Applause.*)

I know, for example, that Comrade Ferenc Münnich was an active participant in that fight. Here in Tatabanya I was approached by a comrade, one of your miners, who shook hands with me and told me that he had also fought with the Red Army against General Dutov. And, evidently, there is many a dozen old veteran revolutionaries among the Hungarian miners, who have fought in he Civil War along with the workers of the Soviet Union.

Comrades, those days, the early days of the October Revolution, have long since passed. Soviet power is already forty years old in our country. The times when he imperialists thought they could with impunity send heir troops into the Soviet Union, are long over. They ought to know by now that we are impregnable, that the peoples of the entire great socialist camp are with us, and that this camp has sufficient moral and material strength to smash anyone who makes an attempt upon ur freedom and independence, the independence of the peoples of the socialist countries. (*Stormy, prolonged applause, shouts of approval.*)

The path travelled by the Soviet people has been a difficult one. But it is visual evidence of the boundless possibilities that open before the working class, before all working people, if they are led by the Communist Party, devoted as it is to the popular cause, to the cause of Marxism-Leninism. Such a party, created by Lenin, stands at the head of the working class, the working people of the Soviet Union. The great Lenin led the Party, which he had created and tempered, in great undertakings. The Party was followed by the whole working class and the working peasantry of Russia, who went into battle against their class enemies, the landowners and capitalists, and in October 1917 we achieved a great victory.

In forty years of Soviet power our country has made a giant leap in its development. It has moved forward into second place in the world for industrial production. It ranks first today for the training of engineers and technicians. Is not the working class of all countries entitled to be proud of these achievements, scored by the working class, the working people of our country? (*Stormy, prolonged applause.*)

After the October Revolution our country started out along an untrodden path. And it was no promenade by any means. From capitalism we inherited a country with a backward industry and agriculture, a country laid waste in the First World War and the Civil War. The workers and peasants of the Soviet Union had to strain every sinew to rehabilitate industry and agriculture, to build up a powerful heavy industry, a modern agriculture, so as to defend the gains of the October Revolution against the imperialists of all countries.

And the working class of the Soviet Union, the working peasantry, have stood the test of political ripeness, and have made the impossible possible. Where did the working people of our country come by so much strength? What is the source of their all-conquering energy? Under capitalism the working class labours under the whip-lash of poverty, the threat of unemployment, and the peasantry is haunted by hunger and ruin, whereas under the Soviet system the people are conscious that they are the masters of their country, that economic difficulties are to be conquered solely by devoted labour. The working class, the working peasantry, the intelligentsia of the Soviet Union worked tirelessly for a better and happier life.

Under the leadership of their Communist Party, the Soviet people have developed a powerful, steadily growing industry. They have now a developed, mechanized agriculture. Socialism opened up boundless opportunities to the working people. Our great country has made gigantic progress in a historically short time through the heroic labour effort of the Soviet working class, the working peasantry and the people's intelligentsia. When the Hitler host fell treacherously upon the Soviet Union it was repulsed crushingly. The Soviet people and their heroic army not only liberated the enemy-occupied territory of our own country, but smashed the Hitler army and set free the peoples of many countries from fascist slavery.

In heroic struggle against their oppressors, the peoples of a number of countries have won their freedom and are now building their life, developing their economy along socialist lines.

Comrades, no longer is the Soviet Union the world's only socialist country, as it was before the Second World War. Today 13 countries with a population of nearly 1,000 million have taken the path of socialist development, the path illumined by the immortal teaching of Marxism-Leninism. Is it for us, comrades, at a time like this, to hang our heads, to underestimate our strength? (*Prolonged, stormy applause, shouts of approval.*)

But it should be borne in mind that the imperialists have not yet abandoned the struggle against communism, against socialism. We cannot, therefore, sit by idly, and should, as the saying goes, keep our ears cocked and watch the enemy, so that he should not twist us round his little finger.

We have always declared, and declare now, that we do not want war. But we do not renounce the class struggle. The class struggle will continue as long as there is capitalism. (*Stormy, prolonged applause, shouts of approval.*)

Yet this does not go to say that we intend to implant our order and the socialist system in the capitalist countries by force of arms. That is the business of the working class, the working people of each country. It is the internal affair of the people of each country. Naturally, our sympathies have always been, and always will be, with the working class.

We are firmly convinced that socialism will win the peaceful competition of the two systems. And win it will by dint of its great advantages, by dint of its inspiring example. The only right road to victory is through the utmost development of the productive forces. The socialist countries must have the highest productivity of labour to produce a maximum of output at a minimum outlay of labour. That is the mighty source which enables us to steadily raise the living and cultural standards of the peoples of the socialist countries.

There is, comrades, yet another essential condition for our victory. It is the closest possible solidarity and fraternal unity of the socialist countries. We must not give the enemy a chance to cause a quarrel between our peoples. The enemy is trying to stir up trouble, the easier to fish in troubled waters. (*Laughter.*)

Comrades, in November 1957 the Soviet Union celebrated the 40th anniversary of the Great October Socialist Revolution. The representatives of Communist and Workers parties of many countries gathered at that time in Moscow. Suffice it to say that the Peace Manifesto adopted at the meeting of representatives of fraternal parties was signed by representatives of 64 fraternal parties. The historic documents adopted at the Moscow meetings, and the unanimous approval of these documents by all the fraternal parties, show how great is the unity of the Communist and Workers' parties and how serried their ranks in the struggle for the great cause of socialism, the cause of peace!

Dear friends, there is a good line in a revolutionary song of ours. I don't know how it sounds in Hungarian. When the Hungarians sang it, the tune was the same. Evidently, the words are the same, too. It says, "Is it for us to fear the illusory power of the tsars?" Indeed, comrades, is it for us to fear our class enemies? The great camp of socialist countries, the powerful world communist movement make certain the triumph of the immortal ideas of Marxism-Leninism. Is it for us to bow, for us to pander to the enemy? Anyone who not only does this, but even thinks of this, will never be a son of his people, will never be a hero. He will crawl like a snake, not soar like a falcon in the sky. (*Stormy applause, shouts of approval.*)

Dear comrades and brothers, I have spoken in Sztalinvaros and made a few critical remarks. Allow me to repeat them to you, since you are my friends and brother-miners, and since a brother should not take offence at a brother who speaks straightforwardly of failings and mistakes. Bourgeois correspondents wrote that Khrushchov has come to Hungary, that he walks about head up, that he does not excuse himself before the Hungarians for the Soviet troops having participated in suppressing the revolution. They describe the revolt of October-November 1956 as a revolution, but to us, to the working class, it was an outright counter-revolution. (*Shouts of approval, applause.*)

Why can I look fearlessly and squarely in your eyes? Because I am a worker, because I am a Communist and an internationalist. We know very well what revolution is, and what counter-revolution is.

The workers, the working peasantry, all the working people of our country regard their successes not only as successes of the Soviet Union, but also as successes of the entire international working class. (*Applause.*) This is why, comrades, we must support each other like brothers, and criticize each other like brothers, if sometimes we should fall out of step. And in the autumn of 1956 some Hungarian workers, and miners among them, did fall out of step. Some went so far as to call the counter-revolution a revolution. For a revolutionary that is the same as a hen crowing like a cock. (*Laughter, applause.*)

Well then, were we to crow, too? No, we saw that it was not a revolutionary voice, that it was not a revolutionary move.

As for the part played by Soviet troops in suppressing the counter-revolutionary revolt, the matter is absolutely clear. When the Government and Party of the Hungarian working class approached us, we felt that as Communists we were duty-bound to come to the assistance of the workers, the working peasantry, the entire fraternal Hungarian people in their hour of need. (*Stormy applause, shouts of approval.*)

I said in Sztalinvaros, and I repeat now that, after all, having taken power into its hands—and the working class does so at the price of great effort—this power has to be preserved as the apple of one's eye. Once you've taken power into your hands, don't look the enemy in the mouth, but govern firmly. If you do not govern firmly, if you do not strike down the enemy, the enemy will strike you. Whereas you have somewhat broken this commandment.

I said in Sztalinvaros: Comrades Hungarians, can't you, so to say, avoid falling out of step again? You must know how to decipher the designs of the enemy and strike back if he raises his head, so we shall not later have to come to your assistance.

Bourgeois journalists heard what I had to say, but what they wrote was something entirely different. They reported that in his Sztalinvaros speech Khrushchov said that if the forces of counter-revolution would again stage an uprising, the Soviet Union would not come to the assistance of the Hungarian working class.

I have to say to these journalists, pardon me, gentlemen, you have reported an untruth. Firstly, we are sure that the

Hungarian working class will never again give the counter-revolution a chance to raise its head. It will firmly hold the Marxist-Leninist banner, rallying round its party of Communists, and the Party Central Committee headed by Comrade Kadar. (*Stormy applause. The audience scans:* "Long live the Party!")

Secondly, we must warn the devotees of all provocations. We don't advise the enemies of the working class to try our patience and organize new provocations. We declare that if there is a new provocation against any socialist country, the provocateurs will have to deal with all the countries of the socialist camp, and the Soviet Union is always ready to come to the assistance of its friends, to repulse fittingly the enemies of socialism if they should try to disturb the peaceful labours of the people of the socialist countries. (*Stormy, prolonged applause. Shouts of approval.*)

We are realists and must soberly weigh the situation. There exist socialist and capitalist countries in the world today. The working class, the working people in the capitalist countries, tolerate the bourgeois order in these countries for the time being. The working class, the working people of the socialist countries have chosen a different path—the path indicated by Marx, Engels, Lenin. The imperialists have no business sticking their noses into the domestic affairs of the socialist countries, or, as Russians put it, sticking their pigs' snouts into our socialist garden. (*Laughter, applause.*)

We stand for non-interference by states in the domestic affairs of other states. That precisely is peaceful co-existence. (*Applause.*) Every people has the right to the state system that it likes best.

We say that our socialist system is the best, the most progressive. The capitalists say that capitalism is better. But capitalism is already a hard-ridden old hag (*laughter, applause*), while socialism is new, young and brimming with energy. It is the liberation of all popular forces. It is a system under which all working people join in active and creative endeavour, under which all work for themselves, for their popular state in which there are no exploiters and no exploited. Socialism is genuine freedom for all working people, and not the "freedom" of capitalist slavery which the monopolists and their henchmen call the "free world."

Socialism offers ample scope for the development of all the creative forces of the people, for the flowering of popular talents, for the development of science, technology and culture. And it was no accident that socialist rather than capitalist artificial earth satellites soared first into outer space. (*Applause.*)

Dear comrades, allow me to conclude with this and to wish you new successes in your noble labour. You are burdened with a very big responsibility to your homeland, to socialism. You mine coal. Lenin called coal the bread of industry. Without coal, without power, industry is at a standstill. Without industry there is no forward movement. You must remember this.

I repeat, we can win the battle against capitalism for the building of socialism only if we organize our labour better, if the liberated working class has a higher labour productivity.

Long live the miners who produce the coal that is necessary for the development of industry, for the building of socialism! (*Prolonged applause.*)

Long live the working class and the working peasantry of Hungary! (*Prolonged applause.*)

Long live the Hungarian Socialist Workers' Party and its Central Committee headed by Comrade János Kadar! (*Stormy, prolonged applause. The audience scans*: "Long live the Party!")

Long live the Revolutionary Workers' and Peasants' Government headed by Comrade Ferenc Münnich! (*Stormy, prolonged applause.*)

Long live the eternal friendship of the Soviet and Hungarian peoples! (*Stormy, prolonged applause.*)

Long live the friendship of the peoples of the socialist countries! (*Stormy, prolonged applause.*)

Long live world peace! (*Stormy, prolonged applause.*)
The audience sings the "Internationale."

(*N. S. Khrushchov's speech was repeatedly interrupted by ovations, shouts of* "Hear, hear!", *calls of* "Hurrah!")

SPEECH
AT SOVIET EMBASSY RECEPTION
IN BUDAPEST DURING STAY IN HUNGARY
OF SOVIET PARTY AND GOVERNMENT DELEGATION

April 8, 1958

Dear Comrades, Friends,
Esteemed Ladies and Gentlemen,
Our stay in hospitable Hungary is nearing its end. In this brief time we have had the privilege of visiting a number of cities, some villages, factories and plants, and agricultural co-operatives, and have talked to people from all walks of life.

The mass meeting in Budapest on April 4, and all our other meetings, have left a deep, indelible impression. We, representatives of the Soviet people, were given a warm and cordial welcome wherever we went.

These heart-warming meetings were a token of the cordial and friendly sentiments which the Hungarian people have for the Soviet people.

The friendship of our peoples is growing stronger despite the exertions of our enemies, who are trying to sow seeds of discord and ill-feeling between Hungary and the Soviet Union.

The Soviet delegation has received a large number of invitations from various towns and villages of the Hungarian People's Republic, from many collectives of working people, requesting us to visit them. We would gladly visit all our friends, but it would take many weeks if we should accept all the invitations. We thank you heartily for this demonstration of fraternal love and friendship for the Soviet people, whom we represent. Unfortunately, we do not have so much time, because we must return home.

During our stay here we have held talks with the leaders of the Hungarian Socialist Workers' Party and the Hungarian Government. Our conversations concerned further consolidation of friendly relations between our two countries, and some international matters. Our talks passed in an atmosphere of complete unanimity, complete mutual understanding and identity of views in all questions discussed.

We are profoundly gratified with the results of our trip and hope that it will further fortify Soviet-Hungarian friendship, fraternal co-operation between the peoples of our countries and the entire socialist camp. We are also convinced that this trip will serve the interests of world peace.

Allow me to propose a toast to the industrious Hungarian people who, hand in hand with the peoples of the other socialist countries, are confidently building a new society.

To the health of the members of the Political Bureau of the Central Committee of the Hungarian Socialist Workers' Party and the First Secretary of the Central Committee, Comrade János Kadar!

To the health of the members of the Hungarian Revolutionary Workers' and Peasants' Government and its Chairman, Comrade Ferenc Münnich!

To the health of the members of the Presidium of the Hungarian People's Republic and its Chairman, Comrade István Dobi!

To your health, dear comrades and friends!

SPEECH
AT ACADEMY OF SCIENCES OF HUNGARIAN PEOPLE'S REPUBLIC DURING STAY IN HUNGARY OF SOVIET PARTY AND GOVERNMENT DELEGATION

April 9, 1958

Dear Comrade President Rusznyák!

Dear Comrades,

Allow me to thank you, representatives of the Hungarian intelligentsia, for your kind welcome and the fine words spoken here about us, the Soviet Government, the Soviet people. We, emissaries of the Soviet Union, are deeply touched by your warm reception.

Soviet people have a deep respect for the rich and original culture of Hungary, and prize very highly the achievements of Hungarian science. They know and like the works of the leading representatives of Hungarian literature and art. The whole world knows the names of your gifted scientists, writers and men of art.

During our short stay in Hungary we have seen what big successes have been scored in the building of a socialist society in the Hungarian People's Republic. These successes, the fruits of the tremendous labour effort of the Hungarian people, embody the energy and talent of the best representatives of the Hungarian intelligentsia—its scientists, engineers, teachers, doctors, agronomists, and men of art and literature.

But, comrades, you also have your difficulties. It is particularly clear to us, Soviet people, what difficulties some of the Hungarian intellectuals are experiencing. We are well aware of them, because we know the experience of the intelligentsia in our own country.

People's Hungary is building socialism—a new society. Every society produces its own intelligentsia, so as to carry out the tasks it confronts successfully. The socialist system also inevitably produces its own intelligentsia. It produces an intelligentsia bound by all its roots to the people, inseparable from them, serving the vital interests of the people.

At the time of the Great October Revolution, when the Soviet people were carrying out revolutionary changes, people belonging to the old intelligentsia in our country went through the same difficulties of the transition period. The overwhelming majority of the old intelligentsia conquered their doubts and vacillations, took the side of the Soviets, and joined in the great effort of socialist construction with all their talent, creative vigour and tireless labour.

Allow me to illustrate how some of our well-known and respected scientists grappled with these difficulties, and to outline their evolution towards socialism. I think that in this there is much in common between the intelligentsia and scientists of the Soviet Union and the intelligentsia and scientists of Hungary and the other socialist countries.

The workers adjust themselves to revolutionary changes with the least difficulty, because the working class is the bearer of revolutionary ideas, the main force and leader of this social upheaval.

In bourgeois society, the intelligentsia is an intermediate stratum between the main classes. When keen and bitter revolutionary clashes occur, all the links of the old social system naturally begin to crack. Some links break, others show a leaning towards the bourgeoisie, and others still towards the working class. We appreciate your position. It is a difficult one. Not all succeed at once in finding their place, in deciding the question of whom they should follow. And though you are scientists, some of you sometimes resort to unscientific methods—to guesswork on where to go, what camp to join. I do not speak of all, but aren't there people like that? (*Laughter, applause.*) While some make no guesses and take their stand firmly either with the revolutionary class, or go over to the antagonists of revolution, the antagonists of the working class.

We Communists must show especial tact and tolerance towards the old intelligentsia. If sometimes some isolated, or even large, groups of intellectuals do not always understand revolutionary changes, we should never hasten to place them among the enemies of the revolution. Patience, time and persistent effort are needed in our work with the intelligentsia.

All of you know our great scientist, Ivan Petrovich Pavlov. But do you happen to know that in 1935, when a world congress of physiologists convened in the Soviet Union, Pavlov only reluctantly agreed to address members of the Soviet Government as "Comrades People's Commissars"? (*Laughter.*)

When Pavlov went to Ryazan, his hometown, he was accorded a good reception there and given a glimpse of real life. He made a closer acquaintance with ordinary working men and saw what great progress they had achieved under the leadership of the Communists. After all, to put it figuratively, dedicated as he was entirely to science, Pavlov had mostly to deal with experimental monkeys and dogs. (*Laughter.*) He was isolated from social life, knew nothing of revolution. The October Socialist Revolution burst upon him like a bolt from the blue.

And the people of his hometown were witness to an interesting evolution in Pavlov, whose world outlook was changing literally overnight. When he came to Ryazan some of the people of his own age, who had attended the seminary with him and had a touch of anti-Sovietism, decided to bear upon Pavlov, to kindle anti-Soviet feelings in him, to use that distinguished scientist of world renown, to egg him on against the Soviet system.

But when his townsmen showed him his native Ryazan, when he saw how much had changed there in the short spell after the Revolution, he took a different view of things. Pavlov went to the collective farms on the Oka, visited the peasants, chatted with them a lot in the peasant manner of speech. He asked them what harvests they were getting, using the peasant expression for it; do you get *sam-syom*, he asked, meaning whether they got seven times more than they sowed. Speaking to a group of peasants, Pavlov asked how many of them were literate. The chairman told those who had a secondary school education to raise their hands. More than ten young men and girls did so. Pavlov was stunned on learning that among the peasants even at that time there were quite a few people with a secondary school education.

Ivan Petrovich Pavlov was an ardent patriot. During his trip to the United States some individuals there tried to set him against the Soviet system, but he rejected their attempts curtly and declared that he had always served his people, his homeland, and would continue to do so.

Whoever is familiar with Pavlov's letter to the young people of the Soviet Union, comrades, knows that although he did not have a Party card in his pocket, he died a convinced Communist.

"In the team of which I am leader, everything depends on the atmosphere," Pavlov wrote. "All of us are harnessed to a common cause and each pulls his weight. With us it is often impossible to discern what is 'mine' and what is 'yours,' but our common cause only gains thereby.

"... Our country is opening wide vistas before scientists, and—it must be owned—science in our country is being fostered with an extremely generous hand."

In the concluding part of his letter, Pavlov wrote:

"For the young people, just as for us, it is a matter of honour to justify the great expectations that our country puts in science."

Such was the great Soviet scientist Pavlov. He received the socialist revolution in our country with suspicion, but gradually became a convinced protagonist of Soviet power.

I might name Academician Yevgeny Oskarovich Paton, whom I have known well personally. He was a prominent scientist and engineer, and Vice-President of the Ukrainian Academy of Sciences. His father was the tsarist consul in Nice. Paton was a man of abrupt character. I should like to cite the following example on that score. One day a conference was held at the Culture Department of the Central Committee of the Ukrainian Communist Party. Many scientists were invited. Academician Paton was one of them. The conference was a long one. The speeches were of no concern to Paton and held little interest for him. He listened in for a bit, then retired quietly in the English fashion. (*Laughter.*) Some people later tried to interpret his departure as an act of disrespect for the Central Committee, saying that he had been summoned to the C.C. for a conference and had left it demonstratively.

Knowing Paton and his character, I told these comrades that probably he had been invited to a conference dealing with matters of no concern to him at all. And Paton, a purposeful man, a scientist, decided that he had no business being there, that there was no call on his knowledge at such a conference, and hence departed to get on with his own work. (*Laughter, applause.*)

Paton has done very much for the development of Soviet science and technology. The Institute of Electric Welding which he founded shortly before the war with Hitler Germany contributed greatly to the development of the method of automatic continuous welding of tank bodies. In December 1943 I received a letter from Paton, who was then working in the Urals.

The letter was of great interest—a veritable confession of a scientist. He wrote:

"When the Soviets took power in our country I was forty-seven. After working nearly 28 years in the capitalist environment, I had acquired its world outlook. For this reason the Soviet authorities treated me with suspicion. I felt this on more than one occasion. For my part, I thought the undertakings of the new authorities unrealistic. However, I continued to work honestly, because it was in my work that I saw the purpose of my life.

"When I saw the First Five-Year Plan, I did not believe that it was feasible. Time went by. When construction was begun on the Dnieper Power Station, with which the old authorities had had no success, I began to realize that I was wrong.

"As the new projects of the five-year plans, the reconstruction of Moscow, and other prominent Party and Government undertakings were translated into reality, my world outlook gradually changed. I came to appreciate that what brought me closer to Soviet power was that labour, the basis of my life, is placed above everything else by the Soviets. I gained this conviction from the facts.

"I was conscious of the fact that I had been reborn under the impact of the new life. The Patriotic War is vivid proof of the might and stability of the Soviet system. Comparing it with the course of the past two wars—the Japanese and the imperialist—one is amazed at the stamina and heroism shown by the Russian people in the frontlines and in the rear under the firm leadership of the Communist Party and the Soviet Government.

"When the war broke out I found an application for my knowledge and worked in the defence industry in the Urals together with the collective of my Institute. We have done what we could for the defence of our homeland.

"For this work the Party and the Government have rewarded me very generously and have given me to understand that they trusted me.

"This gives me the right to submit this application for membership in the Party. I beg you to allow me to go on with my work and complete it under the banner of the Bolshevik Party.

"Hero of Socialist Labour, Academician Y. Paton."

Thus in his late years Paton turned from an opponent of Soviet power into a Communist, an ardent supporter of socialism. He was admitted to the Communist Party without the usual probationary candidate's period.

I think that there must be people like Paton among you, as well. And probably more than one! *(Animation in the hall, applause.)*

Take the story of the big Soviet writer, Alexei Tolstoi. You probably know that he had been a count. Opposed to the Revolution, Tolstoi emigrated from Soviet Russia after the October Socialist Revolution. He came back to his homeland during the "change of landmarks," when big groups of the old bourgeois intelligentsia changed their anti-Sovietism for pro-Soviet views. All know that this distinguished author became an ardent fighter for socialism. In the last years of his life he was a Deputy to the Supreme Soviet of the U.S.S.R. I could cite thousands of such examples.

If we had the appropriate devices, we would have seen how in some of you your hearts are approaching us, fighting against doubt. Some probably think, there's Khrushchov telling us his Soviet fables. *(Animation in the hall.)*

I am telling you all this, dear comrades, because I would like to do all I can to help those whose hearts have not yet accepted the change which, fundamentally, has already been consummated. After all, when scientists, when intellectuals, have not yet accepted, or do not accept, the new, the socialist, they must be helped, so that the transition to the socialist way is shortened to the utmost, so that anxiety and suffering are reduced to a minimum, in order that the greatest possible number of intellectuals will be put solidly on their feet as quickly as possible. And so that these intellectuals should stand firmly on the socialist foundation!

Our Party has considerable experience in working with the intelligentsia. Having received not a few bruises, we have acquired a proper appreciation of many questions. We are sharing this experience with you, as friends do.

Your situation is more favourable than the situation we had, particularly in the first few years of Soviet power. I remember having to talk with some intellectuals during the Civil War. They were simply aghast at all that was taking place. They looked at us, grimy workers and peasants, and said: all you want is bread and potatoes; what do you care about science, art, the ballet, and other things? You are like goats in a garden—you'll trample everything underfoot, and make everything black.

But now forty years have passed. If we are to speak concretely about the ballet, we can wager that there is no ballet elsewhere in the world like the Soviet ballet! If we are to speak of science, it was our artificial earth satellites that soared first into outer space. And that, you know, is not just physics and mathematics. It requires the development of a set of scientific trends and the solution of a number of most difficult technical problems.

After the October Revolution, the interventionists tried to crush Soviet power by force of arms. When that venture had failed, they began hoping that the Bolsheviks, backed only by illiterate workers and peasants, would fail to restore the economy and to revive culture, and that they would be crushed by the difficulties.

Forty years have passed. And let anyone name a country, other than the Soviet Union, which trains as many specialists as are graduated from Soviet institutions of higher learning. While we annually train over 70,000 engineers and technicians, the United States trains no more than 25 or 26 thousand who, moreover, have nothing to do owing to the economic recession obtaining in America. It is the United States which is now intent on catching up the Soviet Union in the fields of science and the training of specialists.

We are as proud of our successes as a mother is overjoyed when she teaches her child to pronounce its first word, "mama," for we have taught a few blustering American leaders to say quite clearly that they must catch up non other than the Soviet Union, that is, a socialist country, in the field of scientific development and the training of scientists and engineers. (*Stormy applause.*)

But we are absolutely certain that the United States will not catch us up in this field. (*Applause.*) We do not explain that by any special personal qualities of Soviet statesmen, but by the entire pattern of public education in our country. At present, the Americans are studying our system of education in secondary and university-level establishments and give it high marks. Whereas we, Soviet leaders, think that there are still some weak links in that system and are working right now on further improving the training of specialists with a secondary and university-level education, on improving the quality of that training. This will be our next "sputnik," and we shall launch it without fail. (*Applause.*)

Our country has made tremendous achievements in developing science and culture, and secondary and higher education. Now all can see that the Communists and the working class set great store by science and show concern for public education. There can be no progress unless there is education and science. We Communists also set great store by the old intelligentsia, because without it it would be impossible to train new generations of intellectuals. This is the reason why every effort must be made, after the working class wins power, to develop new, young cadres of intellectuals, while preserving the cadres of the old intelligentsia, and to develop them smoothly and flexibly, without losses, so that they would loyally serve the working class, their people, their homeland, in the building of the new life on a socialist basis.

Our stay in your splendid country is coming to an end. The Soviet people have always been very friendly and brotherly to the Hungarian people. During our stay in your country we saw that the Hungarian people have the same feelings for the Soviet people. During these days we have come to respect the working people of Hungary still more deeply. Now I even fear that when we come to the Soviet Union and speak about Hungary, it may cause jealousy. We went to Hungary as representatives of the Soviet Union. I am afraid that we shall return to the Soviet Union as representatives of the Hungarian people. (*Stormy, prolonged applause.*)

There is nothing contradictory in this, because there are no contradictions between our peoples. We have a single goal—to build socialism and communism. One may be a patriot of the Soviet Union and be a patriot of socialist Hungary as well. One may be a patriot of socialist Hungary, and be a patriot of the Soviet Union, a patriot of all the socialist countries. (*Stormy, prolonged applause.*)

Comrades, the whole world knows the peaceful foreign policy of the Soviet Union. We shall carry on with it. We shall do everything in our power to prevent a new war, to ensure peaceful co-existence, to settle controversial issues not by war, but by negotiation. We want to compete with the capitalist countries in peaceful endeavour, rather than in the armaments race. We make our challenge to the capitalist world boldly: let's compete and see who develops the productive forces to a higher level, who produces more per head of population, who provides a higher material and cultural standard for the people, and where better opportunities are created for the development of all of man's abilities. The winner will be the system which provides better conditions for the people.

We are sure that the more progressive socialist system will win. The future belongs to our socialist system. Capitalism is on the downgrade, it is declining, although this does not mean that it is already prostrate and that it has turned up its toes. Much has still to be done to bring it to that state. But it is inevitable, just as inevitable as the death of a living body or plant after a definite period of development. However, it will not come as a result of interference by the socialist countries in the domestic affairs of capitalist countries, but rather as a result of the struggle waged against the exploiters by the working people in each capitalist country. The socialist countries are helping the working people of the capitalist countries in this struggle by their example. If we organize our forces better, we shall make better progress in economic and cultural development, and the advantages of the socialist system will be all the more apparent to everybody. (*Stormy applause.*)

Let me tell you about a talk I had with the representative of a certain country, who visited the Soviet Union. He told me this confidentially, so I shall not mention his name.

"Mr. Khrushchov," he said, "when my friends learned that I was going to your country, they tried to stop me, saying that the Soviet Union was a communist country, that you had communism, and that it was not fitting for me to go to your country. But I did not heed their advice. I came to your country, visited your cities, saw your people and failed to find any trace of communism. I saw that you have good houses, that the people are well dressed, and that, consequently, there is no communism in your country. It is we who have communism, for almost all the people in our country walk around half-naked and hungry." (*Laughter in the hall.*)

Such is the idea some people in the capitalist countries have about the Soviet Union, about communism, under the influence of bourgeois propaganda. But the truth will out, despite the deluge of lies and slander circulated by the imperialists and their lackeys. At present our country is approaching a level of development when our economic achievements will enable us to create an abundance of consumer goods. The ideas of communism will then reach the minds of many people not only through the study of Marxism-Leninism, but also by way of our example. The working people of all countries will see that only communism provides material and spiritual benefits in abundance. That is why victory will be ours. People who now seem unable to pronounce the word "communism" without irony will then join us as well. They will take our path without even being aware of it. And they will go towards the goal, set by Marx, Engels and Lenin, together with the entire people. (*Stormy applause.*)

We shall not foist our socialist system on other countries by force of arms. We are against interference by any country in the domestic affairs of other countries. But we are attacking capitalism from the flanks, from economic positions, from the positions of the advantages of our system. This will make certain the triumph of the working class, the triumph of communism.

Thank you, dear comrades, for your invitation and for the chance you have given me to speak before this venerable gathering. I thank you, I thank your President, Comrade Rusznyák. (*Stormy, prolonged applause. The audience rises and hails the head of the Soviet Government.*)

SPEECH
AT MEETING OF CSEPEL IRON AND STEEL WORKS DURING STAY IN HUNGARY OF SOVIET PARTY AND GOVERNMENT DELEGATION

April 9, 1958

Dear Comrades and Friends,

Allow me to convey to you, the splendid collective of Csepel workers, one of the foremost detachments of the Hungarian working class, the hearty greetings of the Soviet working class, of all our 200-million Soviet people! (*Stormy applause. Cries*: "Hurrah!")

The workers of all countries and nations are brothers, linked by bonds of class solidarity. They are the powerful army of the world proletariat, endowed with the great historic mission of leading mankind to communism.

The working class expresses the age-old aspirations of the popular masses and infuses boundless energy, determination and the ability to overcome all difficulties and hardships into the liberation movement.

The role of the working class is particularly great after it takes power. We all know by our common experience what tremendous effort has to go into building the new life, into building socialism, which is being impeded in every possible manner by the forces of the old world.

In their attempts to perpetuate the capitalist system wherever it still exists and to wrest power from the working class wherever the latter has taken it, the reactionary forces unleash their attacks primarily against working-class rule, against the dictatorship of the proletariat. They are trying to depict the dictatorship of the proletariat as something of a scarecrow. They say it is a brutal power. Indeed, it is by no means a soft power for the exploiters, the enemies of the working people. As for the working people themselves, however, the whole people, to them it is a government of their own, which provides democratic freedoms to the majority. The working people would never have been able to rid themselves of exploiters and to win their freedom without it.

What is the dictatorship of the proletariat? It is working-class leadership in the struggle to overthrow the power of capital, to win and consolidate people's government and build a communist society.

The working class is the most advanced and revolutionary class. Its interests coincide with the vital interests of all the other sections of the toiling population. The victory of the working class releases the peasantry from landlord and kulak slavery, and the petty bourgeoisie from the tyranny of the capitalist monopolies. It furnishes its intellectuals with the happy opportunity of creating cultural values for their people, rather than the exploiters.

It is on this basis that the alliance of the working class with all the non-proletarian sections of the working people under the leadership of the working class takes shape. And this alliance constitutes the substance of the dictatorship of the proletariat.

As repeatedly explained by the great leader and teacher of the working people, V. I. Lenin, the dictatorship of the proletariat is a special form of class alliance between the proletariat and the other sections of the working people, primarily the peasantry, to crush completely the resistance of the exploiters, to thwart all their attempts of restoring capitalism, and to build up and consolidate the socialist system once and for all.

Our enemies' contention that the dictatorship of the proletariat is nothing but violence, is absolutely false.

The capitalists, landlords and their henchmen resist the will of the people and obstruct the efforts of the masses to shape their life on a socialist basis. What to do? Don't the people have a right to crush the resistance of the exploiters, a negligible minority of society, so that the will and the wishes of the toiling majority will triumph?

The workers and the working peasantry in our country overthrew the rule of exploiters back in October 1917. However, the landlords and capitalists tried in concert with international reaction to restore the old regime. They started a civil war, an intervention. What could we do? Could we admonish them with kindly chatter about democracy when they were shooting down thousands of the finest workers and peasants? Or were we to crush enemy resistance in the interests of the people? We preserved our socialist gains solely because the working class, the working people of our country, did not hesitate to crush the resistance of our class enemy.

Or take 1956, when a handful of fascist conspirators and their hangers-on, inspired and guided by imperialist reaction from outside, wanted by force of arms to deprive Hungary's working class, its working people in general, of power and to restore the capitalist system in your country. Could you swallow it? Could your people's democracy—which, as you know, is a variety of proletarian dictatorship—suffer the bloody orgy of the fascist elements when it broke out? Of course, not! The uprising was crushed. The workers and peasants, the working people of Hungary, succeeded in rallying their forces and smashing the counter-revolutionary conspirators with the assistance of Soviet troops. They did not let the counter-revolutionaries divert Hungary from its correct socialist path. (*Stormy, prolonged applause.*)

Bourgeois propaganda picked on the repression of the ringleaders of the anti-popular putsch by the people's authorities in Hungary after the uprising, and described the fascist reign of terror and rebellion as "an outburst of democracy," raising a hue and cry about violence in Hungary. Every honest worker knows that it is better to imprison a dozen ringleaders than to jeopardize the interests of the people. (*Applause.* "Hear, hear!")

When the fascist rebels, the counter-revolutionaries, beat up workers and honest people faithful to the cause of socialist construction, the imperialist reactionaries approvingly looked on and supported them. Yet, when the revolutionary forces of Hungary took determined action against the fascist conspirators and enforced the policy of the Hungarian Revolutionary Workers' and Peasants' Government, imperialist reactionaries the world over howled about violence in Hungary. All this speaks of the foul methods used by the reactionaries in conducting their anti-popular class policy that seeks to perpetuate the rule of the capitalists over the working people.

Permit me, dear comrades, to read you an abstract from V. I. Lenin's article, "Greetings to the Hungarian Workers," written on May 27, 1919. He wrote: "This dictatorship presupposes the ruthlessly severe, swift and resolute use of force to crush the resistance of the exploiters, of the capitalists, landlords and their underlings. Whoever does not understand this is not a revolutionary, and must be removed from the post of leader or adviser of the proletariat."

"But," Lenin went on to say, "the essence of proletarian dictatorship does not lie in force alone, or even mainly in force. Its quintessence is the organization and discipline of the advanced detachment of the working people, of their vanguard, their sole leader, the proletariat, whose object is to build socialism."

The dictatorship of the proletariat has extensive creative functions. It is the instrument of establishing the new, socialist social order, the instrument of building up and developing the socialist economic system, progressive culture, and the material abundance indispensable to man's life and happiness.

Imperialist politicians and ideologists, from whom the modern revisionists take their cue, extol bourgeois democracy. To listen to them, bourgeois democracy gives the people complete power, equality and freedom. But life is a grim teacher. The number of simpletons who believe that there is equality between the workers and the capitalists is shrinking. What "equality" can there be when the owners of mills and factories throw their industrial and office workers into the street by the thousands in defiance of the people's vital interests. According to American press reports, for example, there are more than six million fully unemployed and more than three million partially unemployed in the United States. They are willing to take any job, but cannot find it. Whereas a small handful of monopolists live in luxury and enrich themselves upon the suffering and grief of the people.

Bourgeois democracy is democracy for the rich. The popular masses are kept well away from running production and the state, and deciding social and political matters. Thousands of obstacles are raised to prevent the working class, the working people of the capitalist countries, from electing their best representatives to Parliament or Congress.

Who has been elected to Parliament and who comprises the Government in People's Hungary? It is workers—metal workers, engineering workers, tanners, carpenters and bakers—working peasants and men of science, literature and art. (*Applause.*) All of them are working people. Previous speakers have said here that under people's democracy 5,000 working people from the Csepel industries alone have become ministers, deputy ministers, diplomats, managing directors, officers of the People's Army, etc. (*Applause.*)

In the socialist countries, government is entirely in the hands of the people. The working people here are free from exploitation, unemployment and poverty. They have inalienable rights to labour, recreation and rest, education and old-age security. These are the true freedoms, the true democratic rights. This is true democracy, democracy for the people. (*Applause.*)

Conscious of the weakness of their arguments against the dictatorship of the proletariat, the imperialists resort to all kinds of lies. They kept insisting mulishly, for example, that in the autumn of 1956 it was the workers themselves, rather than counter-revolutionary scoundrels, who allegedly opposed the people's democracy in Hungary. It is easy to see why our enemies stand in need of this vicious slander.

Everybody knows that the overwhelming majority of Hungary's workers were loyal to the people's democracy. Admittedly, there were also workers who, enthralled by enemy propaganda, failed at first to get their bearings and fell into the trap laid by the conspirators. But most of them soon realized that they were being goaded into action against their own interests.

We must not ignore the fact, of course, that in the last few years the Hungarian working class has undergone some changes. Its ranks have swelled considerably in view of the rapid development of industry. Thousands of people from the petty-bourgeois sections of the population, and also from among former Horthy officials, gendarmes and officers, have become workers. While wearing workers' clothes, many of these offspring of the exploiting classes have remained hostile to socialism. It was only natural that when they got their chance these so-called "workers" rose against the people's power.

As for the whole Hungarian working class proper, which has had a severe schooling in the class struggle, it could never side with the counter-revolution. It proved its loyalty to socialism and proletarian internationalism by its revolutionary deeds.

Veteran workers in the Csepel and other industries persistently looked for arms to fight the rebels. But owing to the inefficiency of the authorities and the treachery of some of the officials, the workers failed to get arms. By its foul acts the traitorous group of Imre Nagy disorganized the workers' effort at the Csepel Works and in other districts.

The loyalty of the Hungarian working class to socialism was a decisive factor in the swift suppression of the counter-revolutionary uprising and the elimination of its consequences.

By thwarting the treacherous designs of the enemy and preserving the socialist state, Hungary's masses upheld their vital interests, their future, and did their duty by the international working-class movement.

You were in bad trouble, comrades. The working people of the Soviet Union and the other socialist countries did not abandon you in distress. They came to your assistance when the counter-revolutionaries tried, with the support of imperialist reaction, to drown your people's government in rivers of blood of Hungarian workers, peasants and honest working people. The counter-revolutionaries tried to deprive the working people of Hungary of all their socialist gains.

We had a difficult decision to make then. We saw that the counter-revolutionaries had profited by the mistakes and distortions of the former Hungarian leadership to win over a certain section of the people by underhand means. But we also saw how imperialist reaction was hastily sending in forces from outside to Budapest, and how actively the imperialist agents had begun to operate, trying, as in Guatemala, to overthrow the legal government in your country and to establish their own order. After all, it is not for nothing that the United States openly allots hundreds of millions of dollars from its state budget for subversion in the People's Democracies.

However, there is the difference that Guatemala borders on Honduras, while Hungary's neighbours are socialist countries. (*Applause*. "Hear, hear!") Hence the imperialists did not have the advantages they enjoyed in crushing the resistance of the Guatemalan people who had risen in defence of their legal government.

Comrades, when Soviet troops were withdrawn from Budapest the counter-revolutionaries had their murderous fling. Fascist hoodlums massacred honest workers loyal to socialism, and Communists, with brutal cruelty. They killed people for having taken an active part in the socialist construction of Hungary and for resisting the fascist rebels and defending their people's power.

When we were deciding the question of responding to the Hungarian Socialist Workers' Party and helping the Hungarian Government with our armed forces, we knew that a part of the workers had fallen in with the counter-revolutionary uprising. We knew that we could be accused of allegedly interfering in Hungary's domestic affairs with our armed might. But, conscious of our internationalist duty, we decided that no socialist country with the strength and ability to help another fraternal country could stand by and watch while workers, working peasants, and Communists were being hung and shot by Horthyists and other counter-revolutionary scoundrels. It would have been unpardonable to remain on the side lines and refuse help to Hungary's working class. (*Prolonged applause*. "Hear, hear!")

We knew that the imperialist hydra would raise a mad howl about our "interfering" in Hungarian domestic affairs.

Yet we were sure that after a short time the working class, the working peasantry and the intellectuals of Hungary would acknowledge that we, the Soviet socialist state, had had just one correct choice—to help our Hungarian class brothers. (*Stormy, prolonged applause. Cries:* "Hear, hear!", "Long live Soviet-Hungarian friendship!")

As for the hostile hue and cry about our interfering in the suppression of the Hungarian counter-revolution, we must know its true worth. Think back to 1919, when the Hungarian working class rose up in arms and formed

Soviets. Did the imperialists leave you alone then? No, they sent their troops and crushed the glorious Hungarian revolution of 1919, drowning it in the blood of the people. ("Hear, hear!") They considered it legal, because it was the blood of the Hungarian workers and peasants that was shed for the triumph of the counter-revolution. But when the forces of a fraternal country—the Soviet Union—stepped forward to defend the working class, the working people of Hungary, from the fascist rebels and their imperialist bosses, a howl was raised that, allegedly, we had been ungentlemanly.

No, Messrs. Imperialists, you have failed, and will always fail, to distort the truth with your hysterical howling. Again the money has gone to waste which you have put into the blood-stained cause of the Hungarian counter-revolution in the hope of tearing Hungary out of the camp of socialist countries. (*Stormy, prolonged applause.*) We have told you, and tell you now, good sirs, to abandon your hopes of ever restoring capitalism in the socialist countries. It is a hopeless undertaking to build one's policy on such slippery ground. (*Applause.* "Hear, hear!") By investing your capital in this unsound proposition you will not only fail to get any interest, but are bound also to lose what you have put in.

The people's government in Hungary and in the other socialist countries has stood, and will stand firm. It is a system that has established itself for all time. (*Prolonged applause.* "Hear, hear!")

Comrades, here is our Party and Government delegation, come to visit Hungary. We have gone to many places, spoken to and met many people. We look proudly into your eyes, the honest eyes of workers, peasants and the working intellectuals of Hungary.

We have given you help, disinterested help, which involved sacrificing our soldiers. (*Cries:* "Thank you.") Then we had to help you as brothers to make good the tremendous material losses suffered by Hungary's economy in the counter-revolutionary putsch. The Soviet Union and other socialist countries sent you large amounts of goods and raw materials, so that your mills and factories could operate normally and the workers, all of Hungary's working people, could rapidly heal the wounds inflicted upon the country by the rebels—so that socialist Hungary should grow, strengthen and develop. (*Prolonged applause. Shouts of approval.*)

All this, comrades, is truly disinterested fraternal proletarian assistance. And let our enemies draw the proper conclusions from it. All their exertions are inevitably doomed to failure.

The attempted fascist uprising in Hungary had far-reaching aims. And it was no accident that the counter-revolutionary outbreak in Hungary coincided in time with the Anglo-French-Israeli attack on Egypt. The forces of world reaction, the forces of imperialism, tried to test our determination, our ability to repel their aggressive efforts. And they did receive the rebuff they deserved. They did receive a good object lesson. (*Animation. Applause. Shouts of approval.*)

None should doubt that the Soviet Union will help its friends with all the strength it possesses if the imperialists try a new provocation against the socialist countries. (*Applause. Shouts of approval.*)

Comrades, the forces of socialism are growing throughout the world. The basis of these forces is the mighty socialist camp. Today, one-third of mankind follows the path of socialist development. The socialist countries are steadily increasing their economic power on the basis of mutual assistance and support. The unity and fraternal co-operation of the peoples of the socialist countries make each of them and the camp as a whole strong and impregnable.

Our countries are at different stages in their advance towards their cherished goal—communism. Socialist society has already been built in the Soviet Union. Hungary is still going through socialist transformations. But we march along a single road, illumined by the teaching of Marxism-Leninism. (*Prolonged applause.* "Hear, hear!") We have common interests and aspirations. We rejoice at Hungary's successes in building socialism, and are happy that her working people are rallying closer round their militant vanguard—the Hungarian Socialist Workers' Party and their Revolutionary Workers' and Peasants' Government. This close solidarity of the working people with the Party and Government is a token of popular strength, a guarantee of their invincibility.

One of the chief and decisive advantages of our socialist way of life is the profound daily concern shown by all society for the working man, for improving his living conditions. The striving to satisfy the material and spiritual requirements of the people more and more fully constitutes the substance of the activity of the working class in the socialist countries and of its Marxist-Leninist parties. It is precisely with this aim in view that we should concentrate our efforts on achieving victory in the economic competition with the most developed capitalist countries. And we are certain that in this, too, victory shall be ours. (*Prolonged applause.*)

Comrades, the Csepel Works is well known in our country. The Soviet people know it to be a large modern enterprise—an important centre of Hungarian industry and industrial culture. The many thousands working in Csepel, that industrial hub of Hungary, have rich revolutionary traditions.

Dear comrades, allow me now to share with you some of the impressions I have received on touring your works. (*Applause.*) You have a huge plant, a fine collective, solid and devoted to its cause, the cause of revolution and socialism. (*Applause.*)

Here, among you, we really feel as much at home as in our own proletarian family, as in our Soviet plants among Soviet workers. The only difference is that you speak Hungarian and we speak Russian. As to the rest, I feel that we live upon common thoughts, common aims and common aspirations. (*Stormy applause.*)

The principal task of the working class in the socialist countries today is to make better, more productive use of our forces, so that more is produced per worker than in the capitalist countries. We do not need to work for this by expending greater physical effort, but by stepping up mechanization, improving production and introducing specialization and automation. We must strive to reduce the working day, rather than to prolong it, and to increase output per worker. It is only by raising the productivity of labour that we shall beat capitalist production, demonstrate the superiority of the socialist system, and thereby create the conditions for building a communist society.

In capitalist production automation and automatic lines lead to greater exploitation of the working class and greater unemployment. It is only the monopolists who benefit by it. The unemployed ousted from industry by automation swell the reserve army of labour which gives the monopolists a chance to intensify the exploitation of the working class.

In the socialist countries technical progress serves in the interests of the entire working class, the working people, the state. And do not take it amiss, comrades, if I tell you that looking at your plant from that standpoint, it fails by far to meet the requirements of modern socialist production.

You produce motor cycles, bicycles, pipes, drilling and cutting machines. Perhaps you produce thimbles and pins as well.

Voice: No, not any longer.

There is very little that you don't produce! Some of our plants, it is true, are no better off. I say this, because it is high time to introduce automation in our industry, to convert it to automatic lines. And that is possible only with greater industrial co-operation between the socialist countries, with specialization of our plants. This will enable them to specialize in certain parts, certain units, making more productive use of labour. Yet, this business is going ahead very slowly with us. We Marxist-Leninists have a good grasp of these questions, but at times do too little still to improve specialization and industrial co-operation.

The other socialist countries stand to gain more from specialization and co-operation, because the Soviet Union is so vast that its capacity for production and consumption enables it to specialize and co-operate broadly within its own frontiers. It is the other socialist countries which need co-operation. However, all of them want to co-operate primarily with the Soviet Union. For example, Hungary wants to co-operate with the Soviet Union, and Rumania and Albania also want to co-operate with the Soviet Union alone, and show no particular leaning towards co-operating among themselves.

I think, dear comrades, that this is the key issue, because raising the productivity of labour does not mean giving the worker a bigger spade or a bigger hammer. It is not with the maximum expenditure of muscular strength that we should work, but rather with our heads, because that enables us to produce machines to do a worker's work. The worker must no more than operate these machines. This can only be achieved through mechanization.

Dear comrades, tomorrow we leave for home. We should have liked to stay longer with you, but there is work to be done in Moscow. Speaking today at the Hungarian Academy of Sciences, I said that during our tour of your country we have grown very fond of the Hungarian people. I came to you as a representative of the Soviet Union —to represent my country, the working class, the working peasantry, the working people of the Soviet Union in Hungary. But now, after returning from Hungary to my country, I'm afraid that I shall be rebuked for representing the Hungarian people in the Soviet Union. (*Stormy applause.*)

But, comrades, since the people of the Soviet Union, the people of Hungary and the peoples of all the socialist countries face one and the same task—the task of advancing towards communism under the Marxist-Leninist banner—it seems to me, that there is and can be no antagonism here. Quite the reverse. The intimacy, the unity of our peoples and countries, accords with the interests both of the Soviet Union and Hungary.

Comrades, we are working hand in hand with you to build communism. The Soviet people will come to communism together with you, the working people of Hungary. It is out of the question that we, Communists and internationalists of the Soviet Union, the first to seize power and to engage in the great cause of communist construction, should come to communism alone, and, to use a figure of speech, should eat ham every day while the rest look on and lick their chops. That would be wrong.

Where would the proletarian solidarity, the internationalism, of that socialist country be then? The country with the more developed economy, capable of raising the living standard of its people still higher, must by all means help the other socialist countries to level out their standard of life. The scale of production in the countries of the world socialist system will doubtlessly level out with time. All the countries will rise to the level of the foremost ones, which are also not going to mark time. We must enter the communist world all together.

Good-bye, comrades! We wish you, all those present here and all the working people of socialist Hungary, fresh successes in your work and private life. (*Stormy, prolonged applause. The people scan*: "Long live friendship, long live Khrushchov!")

We wish you, our class brothers, the workers of Red Csepel, that your Csepel should always be the stronghold of Hungary's socialist gains and the terror of all the enemies of socialist Hungary. (*Prolonged applause.*)

We wish ardently that the class consciousness of the Hungarian workers, the true masters of their country, should grow and gain strength, that their intolerance of hostile acts should not weaken, and that the fraternal alliance of the working class and Hungary's working peasantry should constantly solidify.

Long live the working class and the working peasantry of Hungary! (*Prolonged applause.*)

Long live the Hungarian Socialist Workers' Party—the militant leader of the working class and all the working people of the Hungarian People's Republic! Long live the Central Committee of the Hungarian Socialist Workers' Party with Comrade Kadar at its head! (*Prolonged, stormy applause, shouts*: "Long live the Party!")

Long live the Hungarian Revolutionary Workers' and Peasants' Government, headed by Comrade Münnich! (*Stormy approval and applause.*)

Long live the Presidium of the Hungarian People's Republic and its Chairman Comrade Dobi! (*Stormy approval and applause.*)

Long live the friendship of the working class and all the working people of Hungary and the Soviet Union! (*Prolonged stormy applause, cries*: "Long live Soviet-Hungarian friendship!", "Moscow—Budapest!")

Long live the inviolable unity of all the socialist countries! (*Prolonged applause, cries*: "Hurrah!")

Long live the international solidarity of the working class of all countries! Long live proletarian internationalism! (*Stormy applause, ovation, cries*: "Long live Khrushchov!")

(*The ovation continues long after N. S. Khrushchov ends his speech. The workers scan*: "Khrushchov—Kadar!", "Moscow—Budapest!", "Friendship!")

SPEECH
ON DEPARTURE FROM BUDAPEST
OF SOVIET PARTY AND GOVERNMENT DELEGATION

April 10, 1958

Dear Comrade Kadar,
Dear Comrade Dobi,
Dear Comrade Münnich,
Dear Comrades and Friends,

The visit of the Soviet Party and Government delegation to the Hungarian People's Republic has come to an end. Before leaving for home I should like, dear friends, once again to thank you and all the working people of Hungary on behalf of all the members of our delegation for your warm consideration and hearty hospitality.

We are leaving with a store of unforgettable impressions of all we have seen and of what we have had a chance to learn in your wonderful country.

The newspapers today have published the Joint Statement about the successful negotiations conducted between the Soviet Party and Government delegation and the leadership of the Hungarian People's Republic. These negotiations have clearly demonstrated the identity of our views on all questions of international and internal policy pursued by the Soviet Union and Hungary. There were no differences, nor controversial issues between us, and there are none now. During the negotiations both parties reaffirmed their firm resolve to continue developing our friendly relations, based on the sacred principles of equality, respect for the territorial integrity and independence of our countries, and the will to advance further the economy, science and culture of our peoples, and achieve higher living standards through mutual assistance and support.

The impressions we gained in meeting you, dear comrades—the workers, peasants and working intelligentsia of Hungary—will linger long in our memories as a symbol of the profound and heartfelt friendship that has for all time linked the peoples of the Soviet Union and the Hungarian People's Republic. No intrigues of imperialist reaction have been able to destroy our intimate friendship.

Wherever we went—to the steelworkers of Sztalinvaros and Diosgyör, the miners of Tatabánya, the workers of the Csepel Works, the working peasants of Karcag, the textile workers of Szeged, the Hungarian intelligentsia in the Academy of Sciences, or passing Hungarian towns and villages—we invariably enjoyed a hearty reception only to be expected from genuine friends. The mammoth Budapest meeting of many thousands of working people on April 4—the day of your fine holiday, Liberation Day—was a moving demonstration of the inviolability of Soviet-Hungarian friendship.

We are taking home with us the warmest fraternal greetings of the Hungarian people to the peoples of the Soviet Union. On returning to Moscow we shall do what we have been asked to do by the Hungarian working people and tell the Soviet people that in the people of Hungary they have a reliable and loyal ally in the struggle for happiness and a better life, in building socialism and communism, and in their efforts to secure world peace.

We have seen for ourselves what big successes the Hungarian people have scored in all spheres of life in the thirteen years of popular rule in Hungary. Bountiful shoots of socialism are burgeoning everywhere on the fertile Hungarian soil, and no weeds will ever be able to choke them.

We are departing with the firm conviction that the Hungarian working class with its splendid fighting traditions and its wealth of revolutionary experience, will under the leadership of its vanguard—the Hungarian Socialist Workers' Party—bring the construction of socialism and communism to a triumphant end. And we are certain that if anyone should again try to stand in its way, the working class, the working people of Hungary will hurl back the enemy and demonstrate once again that there was, is, and will be a proletarian dictatorship in Hungary.

On behalf of all our Party and Government delegation allow me, dear comrades, to wish you, to wish all the working people of the Hungarian People's Republic, further successes in building socialism for their country's good.

Long live and flourish the people's democratic Hungary!

Long live and flourish the inviolable fraternal friendship of the peoples of the Hungarian People's Republic and the Soviet Union!

Long live the great unity of the countries of the socialist camp!

Long live world peace!

Good-bye, dear comrades and friends!

Good-bye, dear people of Budapest!

(N. S. Khrushchov's speech was repeatedly interrupted by stormy applause, shouts of "Hurrah!", *and cries of greeting.)*

SPEECH
AT MEETING ON RETURN
OF SOVIET PARTY AND GOVERNMENT DELEGATION
FROM HUNGARIAN PEOPLE'S REPUBLIC

April 10, 1958

Dear Comrades Muscovites, allow me on my own behalf and on behalf of my comrades, the members of the Soviet Party and Government delegation that has been to Hungary, to thank you for this warm welcome and for your good wishes. (*Prolonged applause.*)

Allow me to thank Comrade Antonov, a fitter from the Vladimir Ilyich Works, Comrade Trapeznikov, Corresponding Member of the Academy of Sciences of the U.S.S.R., who has spoken here on behalf of the scientists and intellectuals, and Comrade Kolomeitseva, a girl studying at the Moscow Power Institute, who has spoken on behalf of the young people of Moscow, for the kind words they have addressed to us. (*Applause.*)

We have just come from Budapest, the splendid capital of the Hungarian People's Republic. We spent eight days with our Hungarian friends.

The Soviet Party and Government delegation visited many cities, towns and villages, factories and agricultural co-operatives and met representatives of the Hungarian intellectuals. Everywhere the Hungarian working people asked us to convey warm and fraternal greetings and best wishes to the Soviet people. (*Prolonged applause.*)

When the Soviet Party and Government delegation was on its way to Budapest, we were sure that the Hungarian people would give us a cordial and fraternal welcome as ambassadors of the Soviet people. The friendship of our peoples has weathered many trials and tribulations, and in the crucible of the common struggle for the bright future of our countries it has been forged still stronger. For the sake of this friendship thousands of glorious sons of our country, who shed their blood to free the Hungarian people, sacrificed the dearest thing man has—life itself.

Many Hungarian internationalists fell on the battlefields of the Civil War, fighting shoulder to shoulder with the workers and peasants of our country to make the Great October Socialist Revolution triumph, to strengthen the young Soviet Republic.

We regard the results of the visit by the Soviet Party and Government delegation as remarkable. In the Hungarians we met real comrades-in-arms and friends in the struggle for our common cause, for socialism, for communism. (*Stormy applause.*)

Comrades, the meeting held in Budapest on April 4 made a great and unforgettable impression on us, although we Muscovites are accustomed to such huge gatherings and have "seen a thing or two," as the saying goes. About 500,000 people attended the meeting to celebrate the 13th anniversary of Hungary's liberation from the Hitler invaders.

Representatives of foreign states, bourgeois correspondents and photographers were also present. They certainly had a "good time" there (*animation in the hall*), watching the close solidarity of Hungary's working people with the Hungarian Socialist Workers' Party and the Government of People's Hungary.

We have also been to Sztalinvaros, to the Danube Iron and Steel Works, which has been built there since the war. The working people of Hungary take pride in this big industrial establishment, built in accordance with the designs of Soviet specialists and equipped with modern machinery, the greater part of which was made in the Soviet Union. The workers there come from all parts of the country and they work well, and harmoniously. The meeting with the working people of Sztalinvaros also made a great impression on us.

We visited Tatabánya, which is one of the biggest mining towns in Hungary. At the pits there we had frank and friendly conversations with the miners. And I must tell you that the miners there are just like the miners in the Donbas, Moscow, Karaganda or other coal-mining areas. They have the same militant, fighting spirit. They are our brothers. I addressed them on behalf of our delegation.

The Tatabánya miners, when talking to us, expressed their fraternal feelings for our people, for our country. One miner came up to me and said:

"Comrade Khrushchov, (he spoke in Russian) I fought for three years in your country against the whiteguards, I also served in Comrade Frunze's bodyguard."

I shook his hand and thanked him for fighting shoulder to shoulder with our finest sons for Soviet power, against the whiteguards and the interventionists. And, of course, I could not refrain from saying to him:

"Well, dear friend, you fought well in our country against the whiteguards and you guarded Mikhail Frunze praiseworthily, but you poorly guarded your own gains, the gains of your own people. The counter-revolutionary rebels took advantage of the mistakes and distortions committed by the former leaders of People's Hungary and started to perpetrate outrages, and you gave those scoundrels free rein."

To this he replied with an earthy Russian word which required no further interpretation. (*Laughter. Applause.*)

"Yes," he said, "that was just how it was. But we won't let the enemies twist us round their little fingers again." (*Stormy applause.*)

It was the same in Sztalinvaros and in the other towns and villages of Hungary which we managed to visit. We knew that bourgeois correspondents had given a special slant to our visit. Perhaps the Hungarians would give the Soviet delegation the cold shoulder. What a world scandal that would be! Comrades, there was indeed a world scandal, but not for us. It was a scandal for those who plotted their black deeds against the people of Hungary.

We realized, of course, that part of the Hungarian population retained some feelings of dissatisfaction, following the events of the autumn of 1956. In deciding at that time to help the Revolutionary Workers' and Peasants' Government, the working class and the working people of Hungary, we Communists and revolutionaries realized what that signified. But, comrades, we gave our help to the Hungarians, to our brothers. Had we failed to do so, we would have disgraced ourselves in the eyes of the entire working class, we would have covered ourselves with shame in the eyes of the revolutionary forces of the working class. (*Stormy applause.*)

I was told the following story. In one family the father and mother were planning to go out to meet with the Soviet Party and Government delegation. Their little boy remonstrated with them.

"What do you mean by going out and leaving me behind?" he asked.

He was told that a Soviet delegation, led by Khrushchov, had arrived and that, together with other workers, they were going to attend a meeting at which they would see the Soviet Union's representatives. Then the boy asked:

"Tell me, whom did Khrushchov back in the October days in Hungary when the fascists revolted?"

He was told that Khrushchov had done the right thing and had been against the counter-revolution. On hearing this, the little boy said:

"If that's the case, you can go—I'll allow it." (*Animation in the hall. Applause.*)

When we were at Red Csepel, many working men and

women also came up to me, as they did to the other members of the Soviet delegation. I remember how working women came up and began to express their feelings. One of them said to me:

"Thank you, Comrade Khrushchov, and give our thanks to your people. You saved our lives and the lives of our children by your help," she said. (*Applause.*)

Comrades, we also went to some of the villages.

We arrived in Karcag. Many peasants, and also artisans and office workers, had gathered for a meeting there. In that district centre about 80 per cent of the peasants have joined the co-operatives. Our delegation visited the Peace Agricultural Co-operative, where we had some interesting talks with the peasants who belonged to it. In many of the villages the Hungarians are firmly in favour of the co-operatives and are working well. It is true that, taking the country as a whole, there are as yet few peasants in the co-operatives. But one must not hurry too much in this matter. Some really good spade-work has to be done in order to convince the peasants of the advantages of collective farming. The attitude among the peasants is very good. It should be mentioned that at the time of the counter-revolutionary insurrection the Hungarian peasants supported the people's power and did not allow themselves to be provoked.

Today the working peasantry of Hungary continue to give vigorous backing to the policy of the Socialist Workers' Party and the Government.

We also had a meeting with scientists at the Hungarian Academy of Sciences. The impression we got was that Hungary's scientists are a reliable support of the people's democratic system. They correctly understand their tasks and are prepared to serve their people, to take an active part in building the new life. (*Applause.*)

That was a very interesting meeting. The scientists spoke well; they said very many warm words about the Soviet Union and spoke about friendly feelings for the Soviet people and the friendship between Hungarian and Soviet scientists. In addition to this meeting, we had interesting and useful talks with many representatives of the Hungarian intelligentsia.

The intelligentsia is an intermediate stratum between the major classes. In a moment of sharp class struggle it finds itself in a difficult position. In the past we probably made no few mistakes in our work with the intelligentsia. After all, we were the first to carry out a socialist revolution and had no experience whatsoever in building socialism. Forty years of Soviet power have gone by, and now it has become clearer to us that one must be more attentive and understanding with the intelligentsia during a radical change, the breaking up of a social and state system as a result of a revolution, when power passes into the hands of the working class and the exploitation of man by man is abolished. Now the intelligentsia of Hungary has actively joined in the work of building socialism.

Our meeting with the Csepel workers was exceptionally cordial. The Csepel Works is very large. In Hungary it is called the bulwark, the heart of the revolution. And that really is the case.

Many thousands of workers assembled there yesterday for a meeting. They warmly welcomed us representatives of the Soviet people and expressed their sincere sentiments of friendship to our country. It was there that I drew the attention of bourgeois correspondents to the fact that they distort our statements. Let them not take offence, but most of them serve the one who pays the money, and if you don't write the way the boss wishes, he won't pay you for it. (*Animation in the hall. Applause.*) That is how things stand in the capitalist world. I understand their position but, nevertheless, I decided to say to them:

"Look, here are thousands of Csepel workers. Their eyes light up with good will towards us and hatred for the enemies of socialism. You expected that Khrushchov would come to Csepel and be torn limb from limb. See how they welcome the delegation from the Soviet Union!"

Red Csepel is an indestructible bulwark of socialist Hungary and if anyone there were to come out against the friendship that has developed and is growing between the peoples of the Soviet Union and Hungary, he would hardly leave the works alive. *(Applause.)*

In speaking of bourgeois journalists, I do not want to insult them.

But I cannot pass by when they distort the facts. When some people want to kick us, we cannot behave as if we are oblivious to this. No, my fine gentlemen, you should realize that we do not follow the biblical precept: If one smites you on the left cheek, turn the other cheek. No, we prefer to act thus: If we are given one blow, we shall give two in return. (*Animation in the hall. Applause.*)

Comrades,

The meetings our delegation had with the working people of Hungary welled up into a demonstration of the unbreakable friendship between the peoples of Hungary and the Soviet Union. The workers, the working peasantry and the intellectuals of Hungary show a keen interest in everything that is being done in the Soviet Union. The Soviet Union enjoys exceedingly high prestige in Hungary. Today the Hungarians are our staunch friends and brothers. We, comrades, must do everything possible to cement still more strongly this friendship and co-operation between the Soviet and Hungarian peoples. This will benefit our two countries and the entire socialist camp, the entire revolutionary working class.

The Hungarian People's Republic has made great progress in building socialism. The aftermath of the counter-revolutionary insurrection has been eradicated in all spheres of the republic's life, including the national economy as well.

During the talks we saw for ourselves once again that the Hungarians are very understanding and are our good friends. They did not request anything, did not lay claim to anything. They sincerely thanked us for the help given. The Soviet Union, the Chinese People's Republic and all the countries of the socialist camp did indeed render them assistance to the best of their ability. In compliance with the request of our Hungarian friends, I convey to you, to all Soviet people, the gratitude of the Hungarian working people for the fraternal assistance given them. (*Prolonged applause.*)

People's Hungary, of course, needs assistance. We, the Soviet Union, must continue to help not only Hungary but all the fraternal socialist countries so that our camp may always be strong and base itself upon a well-developed industry and a mighty economy. Then our common cause will be even further promoted.

We consider it our duty to tell you that during the talks and our meetings with the members of the Central Committee of the Hungarian Socialist Workers' Party and the members of the Political Bureau of the Central Committee and with the members of the Government of the Hungarian People's Republic, our conversations were frank and amicable. You can see that yourselves from the Joint Soviet-Hungarian Statement published today. Such sincerity, such complete understanding can exist only between the closest friends, between brothers.

We have seen for ourselves that the Hungarian working people are solidly behind the Socialist Workers' Party, whose authority has grown immeasurably. The people of Hungary stand firm on socialist positions and vigorously support their Socialist Workers' Party and its Central Committee, led by Comrade János Kadar. (*Applause.*)

The Hungarian Socialist Workers' Party is successfully making good the mistakes made by the former Party leadership. And, as you know, there were quite a few mistakes.

Comrade Kadar and other friends told me in what a difficult predicament the working people of Hungary had found themselves when the revisionists reared their heads with impunity. Central Committee Secretary Gerö gets up and says one thing; Central Committee member Losonczy, a revisionist, gets up and says something else. The former speaks in the name of the Party and the latter speaks in the name of the Party. "Whom are we to believe? Whom are we to follow?" These were questions that were put not only by non-Party workers and peasants, but by Party members as well.

That was just one aspect characterizing the situation which the counter-revolutionaries took advantage of to stir up rebellion against the people's power. While flagrantly distorting socialist law and undertaking reprisals against honest workers, the old leadership in Hungary at the same time failed to see how the enemies of socialism were weaving a conspiracy against the people.

The counter-revolution utilized all the distortions committed in Hungary in order to fight against the working class and socialism.

Today the Hungarian comrades have taken the course of resolutely rectifying the mistakes and distortions of the former leadership of the Party and the country. At the present time the leading core of the Hungarian Socialist Workers' Party and the Revolutionary Workers' and Peasants' Government consists of staunch revolutionaries, Communists who are devoted to the cause of the working class, to the cause of socialism. They are ready to devote all their energies to serving their people. They are our loyal friends who firmly adhere to the Marxist-Leninist position of internationalism and are waging a struggle against imperialism, against betrayal. They are not glossing over questions of class struggle; they are not currying favour with those who, in seeking to shove off on them goods that have no market, would like to set the Hungarian and Soviet peoples at loggerheads. These people are guided by revolutionary ideas; they are guided by Marxist-Leninist teachings and they know full well that anyone who wants to be a revolutionary must do everything for the victory of the working-class cause, the cause of the working people, for the victory of communism, and must in no case adapt himself to the imperialists. One cannot sit on two stools at the same time, and if one tries to do so he will inevitably fall—and not where he should. (*Applause.*)

During our stay in Hungary we had the opportunity of becoming more closely acquainted with many Hungarian leaders.

Previously I had only a slight acquaintance with Comrade Kadar, the First Secretary of the Central Committee of the Hungarian Socialist Workers' Party. We met only after he had come to the leadership of the Party and the country. Now we have spent eight days together and I have become convinced that he is the kind of a comrade upon whom the Hungarian working class can firmly rely —a comrade who will not let it down, who will always march together with the entire revolutionary working class, with all the Communist parties, and who is fearlessly leading the working class of Hungary to final victory, to the building of communist society. (*Applause.*)

Comrade Ferenc Münnich, Chairman of the Hungarian Revolutionary Workers' and Peasants' Government, is deserving of respect and recognition. He is an old Party member who fought in the ranks of the international Hungarian units against the whiteguards during the Civil War in Soviet Russia. I have known him for a long time. In 1930, when I was studying in the Industrial Academy and he was working in Moscow, the two of us, undergoing military refresher training in the Moscow Proletarian Division, served in the same platoon and even shared the same tent. After the victory of the working class in Hungary, through the fault of the former Hungarian leadership no post corresponding to his knowledge and experience was found for him in the Government. And it is only now that his knowledge and experience have been properly appreciated.

Comrade Münnich is devoted to the cause of the working class, to the cause of his people, and he is truly worthy of full support, both from the Hungarian working class and from us, in his efforts for our common cause. (*Applause.*)

Comrades, we feel that the situation in the Hungarian People's Republic is now very good. The state of affairs at the industrial enterprises we visited is the same as at our own better enterprises; you sense a great uplift, a desire to devote every effort to peaceful construction. The workers and all the Hungarian working people desire peace. The prestige of the Soviet Union, as a country unstintingly striving to do away with the cold war and ensure world peace, is very high among the Hungarian working class, the working peasantry and the intellectuals. The Hungarian people realize full well that peace does not depend only on the efforts of the socialist countries. We must therefore be vigilant.

The Soviet Union has made many constructive moves to ease international tension. But so far we cannot be too hopeful, because the opposite side is twisting and turning all the time and is raising more and more new obstacles to the settlement of the paramount question of the present day—the problem of disarmament.

We have already taken the well-known decision to end unilaterally the testing of nuclear weapons and we have called on the United States and Britain to follow suit. But we are told: Control is needed. All well and good— we agreed. But we are again told in reply: No, something more is still needed. The matter is very simple. The Western Powers do not want to attain agreement and therefore seek to make such conditions as cannot be met. The question is perfectly clear. The scientists of the entire world say that you cannot keep atomic and hydrogen explosions secret and that with existing technical means they are bound to be detected. Yet U.S. statesmen continued to claim that such explosions could be kept secret. However, they were forced by incontestable scientific information to admit that this could not be done. Now they again say that it is possible to carry out nuclear explosions in secret. As you see, they chop and change at every turn.

The disarmament problem is a knotty one. But we shall not lose hope. Our course in the struggle for peace, for disarmament, for a ban on nuclear weapons is crystal clear. All we have to say to the gentlemen who are against abolishing the cold war, is: We have plenty of patience. And it is of no avail to use pressure ₁and intimidation in discussions with us. You will squeeze nothing out of us. We don't want war and we shall do everything to prevent it. But we shall keep prepared for war. (*Applause.*)

You know that American aircraft carrying atom and hydrogen bombs are continuing to patrol the skies above many countries in Europe, and not only in Europe. Is this not a criminal action? The horrible danger of destruction in peacetime hangs over men and women. Common sense protests against such recklessness. But the American monopolists say they are doing this for the sake of security. They seem to think they can do what they like, that no one can stand up to the billionaires, that everyone must quake before them. They have subjugated many capitalist countries, order them around, and would like to boss the whole world.

Only the Soviet Union, People's China and the other countries of the socialist camp do not kowtow to them and conduct an independent policy—a policy of peace. Control is proposed to us. We are in favour of control. But they want the kind of control that would be tantamount to interference in the domestic affairs of our state, infringement of our sovereignty. In short, give them an inch and they'll take a mile. We are in favour of establishing control, but we say: Don't fly where you shouldn't. The holy grave of Gandhi is in India. If you want to visit this grave you must, in deference to the country's traditions, remove your shoes and approach it barefoot.

We were there and respected this tradition. So you, gentlemen, ought to respect not only your own money-bags. Respect the traditions of other peoples and remember that they, too, have their own pride, their own interests, and wish to ensure their own security. (*Applause.*)

The ruling circles of the Western Powers say: Let's agree to have our aircraft fly over your country and your aircraft over ours. But we have no desire to fly over your country and don't want your breath over our country. (*Stormy applause.*)

The Soviet Union has already made proposals which, had they been accepted by the Western Powers, could have led to an easing of international tension, to the establishment of greater confidence between states. We proposed a definite zone for aerial inspection: 800 kilometres on one side and 800 kilometres on the other. But we are told: This is not enough. The imperialists desire that there be no Soviet power. Well, my dear fellows, we would also like there to be no capitalist system in your countries. But this is something quite different; this is the domestic affair of the people of each country. (*Applause.*)

Comrades, the peoples of all countries want peace and we must ensure this peace by all the means at our disposal. But we shall not be intimidated. The ruling circles of the Western countries want to wear us down, to overcome us by hook or by crook. They think: If the Soviet Union proposes to disarm, then, most likely, it is in a predicament that couldn't be worse. For 40 years you have been waiting for such a state of affairs, but it does not materialize, nor will it ever come about. You will never see such a situation in which we prostrate ourselves before you and surrender to your mercy. No, we wish to negotiate on equal terms, maintaining our dignity, and relying on our economic and moral factors. Only on those terms can we converse with you. (*Applause.*)

If you continue to be obstinate and raise obstacles to the settlement of international issues by peaceful means, the peoples will, all the same, demand an end to the cold war and the stopping of the arms race. The cold war advocates are finding the going harder with every year, and every month that goes by. Today not only Labourites in Britain, but even some of the Conservatives say: The Russians do not want war.

They have already become convinced that we do not want war. To make war means killing people. But who has any need of that? What can that provide? War means ruin; we shall kill, and be killed. Other means of struggle against the class enemy exist, and in this struggle the working class will be victorious.

Now everyone sees that our economy is advancing, that labour productivity is rising, and that per capita output is growing. The time will soon come, gentlemen of America, when you yourselves will become convinced of the superiority of the Soviet system. (*Applause.*) We shall achieve a per capita output of consumer goods higher than in the most advanced capitalist countries. On the basis of present calculations we can say that before much time goes by we shall clear the highest hurdle of the capitalist countries—shall exceed the level of production achieved by the United States of America. What will you gentlemen say then? (*Applause.*)

The imperialists are frightening the working people with communism. But when we achieve the very highest level of production and standard of living of the working folk, people from the capitalist countries who visit us will say: So this is communism; so this is the Soviet system. What simpletons we have been, not to have realized it before. This is exactly what the working people need. (*Applause.*)

Allow me, dear comrades, on behalf of our delegation, on behalf of the whole Soviet people, to express deep and heartfelt gratitude to the Central Committee of the Hungarian Socialist Workers' Party and its First Secretary, Comrade Kadar, to the Presidium of the Hungarian People's Republic and its President, Comrade Dobi, to the Government of People's Hungary and its Chairman, Comrade Münnich, to all the working people of Hungary for the hospitable and hearty reception accorded the representatives of the Soviet people. Let us wish the industrious and talented Hungarian people further success in building socialism. (*Stormy applause.*)

May Hungarian-Soviet friendship flourish and grow stronger! (*Stormy applause.*)

Long live the unity and solidarity of the peoples in the countries of the socialist camp! (*Stormy applause.*)

Long live world peace! (*Stormy applause. All rise. Long ovation.*)

SPEECH
AT EMBASSY RECEPTION
OF POLISH PEOPLE'S REPUBLIC ON OCCASION
OF 13th ANNIVERSARY
OF SOVIET-POLISH TREATY OF FRIENDSHIP,
MUTUAL ASSISTANCE AND POST-WAR CO-OPERATION

April 21, 1958

Dear Comrades and Friends,

We rejoice in celebrating this day. It is particularly pleasant for both of us because 13 years ago, on April 21, 1945, a Treaty of Friendship, Mutual Assistance and Post-war Co-operation between the Soviet Union and the Polish People's Republic was signed. Thirteen years have passed, and they have been fruitful years.

There have been various turns in the history of relations between Poland and our country. But let us reiterate that the Polish people are not responsible for the actions of their kings and the Pilsudskis, and our people are not responsible for what the tsars did. (*Applause.*)

Relations between the Polish People's Republic and the Soviet Union are being built on a new, socialist foundation. In October 1917, when the working class of our country triumphed and the workers took power into their own hands, our Party, led by the great Lenin, proclaimed a policy of peace and international friendship. And we have undeviatingly followed this policy.

After the defeat of Nazi Germany, when the Polish people became true masters of their country instead of the handful of capitalists and landed gentry who had ruled Poland in their name, they initiated their own policy which conformed to their vital interests. The policy of the Government of the Polish People's Republic and the policy of the Government of the Soviet Union are directed towards one goal, because our countries are advancing along the road of socialist development and because friendship between the peoples of our two countries is one of the most important prerequisites for our common success in the struggle for the achievement of our lofty aims.

The Polish people produced an outstanding revolutionary like Felix Dzerzhinsky, who was a fiery fighter for the cause of the working people, a remarkable person and friend of our great Lenin. It is not by accident that after the victory of the October Socialist Revolution Lenin proposed that Dzerzhinsky be appointed Chairman of the Extraordinary Commission. Great trust was placed in this son of the Polish people. As a loyal son of his class, and of our Communist Party, Dzerzhinsky served to his last breath the proletarian revolution, the cause of the working class and the cause of the toiling peasantry. (*Applause.*)

Today the President of the Presidium of the U.S.S.R. Supreme Soviet, Voroshilov, and other comrades are visiting the Polish People's Republic. Kliment Yefremovich is old in years, but young in spirit. He telephoned me from Poland and described the stirring welcome given him by the Polish working people. Comrade Voroshilov said that the Polish people gave them such a rousing reception that they were at a loss to find words to describe their emotions. They have been to Nowa Huta, Cracow and other cities, have met miners, foundrymen, peasants and Polish intellectuals. "I am simply amazed," Kliment Yefremovich says, "people lined the roads in pouring rain for scores of kilometres to welcome our delegation."

When the Soviet delegation left for the Polish People's Republic, we did not doubt that it would be accorded a hearty welcome. And we were not mistaken. The Polish people are expressing their sentiments of fraternal friendship for the Soviet people. This is very gratifying.

We must continue to do everything to consolidate the friendship between our two peoples not only because we have a common frontier. We, as all the peoples of the socialist states, have common aims and common interests. We cannot forget that we had a common enemy who attacked Poland, and then, through Polish territory, the Soviet Union.

It is undesirable to invoke "the devil" on such a great day as this. But we must clearly realize the state of affairs and remember that he may appear in different forms.

We must do everything possible to strengthen the friendship between the peoples of all the socialist countries. I subscribe to the words spoken here by Comrade Gede. Being the host, he has spoken first. I shall not repeat what he has already said and shall simply concur in what he said.

The key thing is that we hold the common aim of building socialism and communism. Our friendship is beneficial because it does not threaten anyone. It pursues the noble purpose of safeguarding world peace. Is there anyone who does not desire this? Perhaps a handful of people who are interested in obtaining profits from the arms race. Those people do want war. All those who live by their work want peace and not war. Peace and socialism are inseparable. This applies to all the socialist countries. If a country is socialist, it means that it is peaceful.

The socialist countries do not need war. They need peace to advance their economy, to raise the living standards of the working people. We stand for peaceful co-existence, for peaceful competition between the two systems—socialist and capitalist. And we are convinced that our system will triumph, just as we are sure that the sun will rise, that it will ascend up into the sky again tomorrow to illuminate our planet.

We must say that things are going very well in our country. But we Bolsheviks are avid people. We are not satisfied with what we have achieved today. We want the morrow to be better than today. But what the Soviet people have achieved yesterday, we have no objection to continuing further.

We have planned to increase our industrial production by 7.6 per cent in 1958, and have actually achieved an increment of 11 per cent in the first quarter of this year. During the past three months we have increased retail sales of meat and meat products by 53,000 tons, butter by 16,000 tons, and milk and dairy products by 569,000 tons against the first quarter of last year. Not a bad increase! We are extremely pleased over this because it all makes for higher living standards for the people.

Poland is also striding forward. All the socialist countries are making progress.

Proletarian internationalism does not consist in Platonic friendship and mutual sympathy. We cannot imagine one socialist country making great economic progress, while the other socialist states mark time. The crux and characteristic feature of friendship between the socialist states is that they help one another. If one socialist country makes great progress, it considers that its fraternal duty is to help the other socialist states in their development.

All the socialist countries will achieve communism. This means that socialist states must share their experience, their knowledge and must help one another. Only on this basis can we advance successfully, only on this basis can friendship be unselfish and fraternal.

Socialist countries by their very nature cannot live by exploiting other countries. Are we guided by a desire to derive profit or material advantage when we, as a stronger socialist state, render assistance, grant credit, or supply equipment to other countries? Of course not. Our policy is not geared to deriving profits from helping other countries. Such a policy is characteristic of monopoly capital, the capitalist countries, and not the countries of socialism. By rendering fraternal assistance to the socialist states the

Soviet Union is advancing together with them to the great goal of communism.

Permit me to propose a toast of friendship between the socialist states, to the consolidation of the mighty camp of socialism, to a greater role of the working class in the struggle for the victory of socialism!

To the health of the fraternal Polish people, to the Polish United Workers' Party and the Government of the Polish People's Republic! To the health of the Ambassador of the Polish People's Republic, Comrade Gede, and his wife! To the health of the First Secretary of the Central Committee of the Polish United Workers' Party, Comrade Wladyslaw Gomulka! (*Applause.*)

SPEECH
AT LUNCHEON IN HONOUR
OF GAMAL ABDEL NASSER
PRESIDENT OF UNITED ARAB REPUBLIC

April 30, 1958

Mr. President,
Ladies and Gentlemen,
Dear Friends,

Allow me to express our feelings of friendship to you, Mr. President, and the statesmen of the United Arab Republic who are accompanying you on your good will and friendship visit to the Soviet Union. We are very pleased that you have come to the Soviet Union. We are also happy that your visit to the Soviet Union has coincided with the May Day celebrations.

The discussions we have had during our meetings have again demonstrated a friendly atmosphere and mutual understanding in assessing current international problems, and especially in appraising questions relating to the struggle for peace, for the further development and consolidation of friendship between our countries.

Mr. President, you have participated in the Bandung Conference and taken part in drafting its decisions. If all states had been guided by the principles underlying the decisions of the Bandung Conference, the peace of the world would have been ensured. The Soviet Union has welcomed the Bandung Conference decisions; it also supports the decisions of the Conference of Afro-Asian Countries recently held in Cairo.

Our disinterested foreign policy—a policy based on principle—should be clear to you. It is not a contemplative, but an active policy of struggle against evil forces—the aggressive, monopolistic and colonialist forces which have not renounced their hopes of perpetuating colonial slavery, of continuing to plunder and exploit the peoples of Asia and Africa.

We want peace throughout the world. We desire friendship with all nations; we want disarmament; we want an end to the policy of the cold war.

You know that the Soviet Union has unilaterally halted nuclear weapons tests—an act prompted by our country's sincere desire to make a beginning in normalizing the international situation and achieving a genuine solution to the disarmament problem.

Unfortunately the Western Powers possessing nuclear weapons refuse to follow our example, and now there has come the news that Britain has exploded a hydrogen bomb. But by so doing, Britain has exploded not only a hydrogen bomb—above all she has exploded the faith and hopes of millions of people who have been expecting the ruling circles of Britain and the United States to display sound judgement, to follow the example of the Soviet Union, and thus create the prerequisites for ending the cold war and ensuring world peace. The Western Powers are blasting the hopes of people who have expected that during the conference of Heads of Government the means would be found to settle outstanding issues peacefully, without war.

People in all countries will correctly appreciate the high-minded act of the Soviet Government in unilaterally halting nuclear weapons tests and will condemn the reckless act of the ruling circles of Britain who have sanctioned the explosion of the hydrogen bomb. And it will be especially noted that it was Britain which assumed this unseemly role. By exploding the bomb she has signalled that the United States, too, will follow her example.

The whole world will draw the appropriate conclusions from this circumstance. The Soviet Union is not to be intimidated by such explosions. Our policy remains unchanged and we shall work to reduce international tension, to end the cold war and solve the disarmament problem. But we are duty-bound to be vigilant and not relax our efforts in strengthening our state, so that the Soviet Union should not be caught unawares by aggressors and should be able to give a fitting rebuff to aggressors if they try to push a cold war beyond the brink and convert it into a "hot war."

The President of the United States, in his speeches, has often declared that in his activities he has been guided solely by the interests of safeguarding peace, that the United States has been pursuing only peaceful aims. Such declarations scarcely tally with the deeds. The deeds of the ruling circles of the United States contradict these statements. The explosion of a nuclear weapon by the British has unquestionably been co-ordinated with the United States. The latter is also preparing tests and will evidently carry out explosions of nuclear weapons.

The people judge the policy of political leaders, not by what they say, but by what they do. The deeds and actions of the statesmen of the United States and Britain show up the activities of the American and British governments in a very unattractive light.

We have already drawn the attention of all countries to the provocative flights by American aircraft, loaded with hydrogen weapons, towards the Soviet frontiers. It is clear to everyone that such provocative and dangerous actions in no way correspond with the peaceable statements of the United States Government.

The nuclear explosion carried out by Britain is calculated to charge the cold war atmosphere, to intimidate the faint-hearted. But gone are the times when the British lion roared and everything quaked. Now it can frighten no one. We should not like to recall the failure of the adventurist policy of Britain which, together with France and Israel, committed aggression against Egypt in 1956. But they compel us to bring this matter up because the British authorities have carried out the explosion in order to bring pressure to bear on us. We must tell these gentlemen, however, that they will be disappointed. It does not produce upon us the impression that they expected.

The leading statesmen of the United States and Britain say that they must continue explosions of nuclear weapons because the Soviet Union recently carried out a series of nuclear tests and only afterwards announced the cessation of tests. Yet it is a fact that the United States has carried out considerably more explosions of nuclear weapons than the Soviet Union. If one judges by the number of explosions, then we, having halted tests, remain at a disadvantage. Nevertheless, we have resolved on this course and have urged the countries possessing nuclear weapons to follow our example. We were prepared to perpetuate this disadvantageous position of ours. That did not worry us, however. We believed that our decision would be the initial step towards reaching agreement on disarmament in order to exclude war as a means of settling disputed questions.

Now the Americans, as the American press puts it, are preparing a show. But it is a disgraceful show. They intend to carry out fresh explosions of nuclear weapons and to invite to these tests representatives of other states so that they may see how American monopolists are developing weapons for the mass annihilation of human beings.

The Soviet Government has not yet officially determined its attitude with regard to this show. But I think it will hardly agree to send its representatives there, since that would constitute a form of moral support for those who advocate stepping up the cold war and preparing aggression and support for their allegation that it is possible to develop a "clean" bomb, which would be, so to speak, a "noble" weapon for the vile deed of annihilating human beings.

And the people who are preparing this lethal weapon call themselves Christians, attend church and pray to God. They call us atheists and describe us as people with whom it is impossible to reach agreement and whose word cannot be trusted. It is, nevertheless, precisely these atheists who have been the first to set the example of a noble deed and to unilaterally end tests of the most deadly weapon —the nuclear weapon.

The Soviet Union's peace policy in foreign affairs is clear and understandable to the peoples. They see that the Soviet Government is resolutely and consistently pursuing a policy of peaceful co-existence. At the same time, the peoples see that the ruling circles of the imperialist Powers, who stubbornly cling to the positions of cold war and a continued arms race, do not want to ease international tension and establish greater confidence between states.

We sincerely rejoice that relations between the Soviet Union and the United Arab Republic are not in the least clouded. We have only one desire: the strengthening of the positions gained by the Arab peoples, and above all the United Arab Republic. In this you are backed not only by the Soviet Union, but by all progressive mankind. The peoples of the socialist countries applauded when you were selflessly striving, and they applaud when you now strive so selflessly for your independence, for reinforcing your national economy, for raising the standard of living of your peoples.

Grossly distorting our peace policy, the imperialist circles scream about the Soviet Union's "special" interest in this area. We indignantly deny these utterly false assertions. In our disinterested aid to the Middle Eastern countries we have never pursued any selfish aims. The concepts and methods of the colonialists, who believe that if they do not oppress this or that nation, others must do so, are alien to the Soviet socialist state. We Communists maintain that no one may impose his will on the people. The people themselves are the masters of their land, and only they can and must establish the way of life they prefer to have in their countries.

The imperialists, who are accustomed to oppressing the peoples they have subjugated, at one time established the disgraceful system of colonialism. They are so used to it that they regard the system of colonial oppression as a just and lawful system. We saw this particularly clearly in April 1956, when we visited Britain and had talks with Anthony Eden, Selwyn Lloyd and other statesmen. In one of our talks Sir Anthony Eden bluntly said that if the Arab nations did not supply oil to Britain, then Britain would be ready to go to war.

"We beg your pardon," we said then to the British statesmen, "but the sources of oil belong to the Middle Eastern peoples, and we presume that no one has the right to deprive these peoples of the wealth that belongs to them." It would be much more reasonable, we advised, not to try and seize this wealth by force, but to conduct mutually beneficial trade with those to whom those sources of oil belong. The Arab states would, of course, not sell their oil to those who did not offer a good price for it. The policy of colonial oppression and plunder was now unthinkable; it was doomed to failure.

The British statesmen then told us that the correlation of forces in that area was not in favour of the Arabs and that Israel could defeat the Arab states. We retorted by saying that those who thought so were cherishing vain hopes. The population of Israel amounted to approximately one and a half million, whereas the population of the Arab states was over 70 million. We said that if Israel were to unleash a war against the Arabs, the Arabs would, in our opinion, start a holy war against the invaders. And such a war would inevitably end in the defeat of the aggressors. All progressive mankind would be on the side of the Arab people. In such a case, moral support for the Arab people might entail material support and also the participation of volunteers in the Arab struggle against the invaders.

We advised the British statesmen not to start a war against the Arabs, but they did not heed our counsel, launched aggression against Egypt and suffered a disgraceful failure.

We should like the colonialists to draw the correct conclusion from this and to refrain from using arms to annex foreign territories and subject other peoples to their policy. We want peace throughout the world. Second to Western Europe, where concentrations of large forces are facing each other, the Middle East is one of the most inflammable spots.

The Soviet Government has proposed that a summit conference be held in order jointly to find ways for solving urgent international problems. But the summit meeting and talks must be conducted with due regard for the interests of all countries, on the only acceptable principle of non-interference in the affairs of other states. We must reach mutual agreement, not at the expense of any other countries.

Highly developed countries must render aid to backward states without attaching any political, military or economic strings to it. We must develop mutually beneficial trade so that the Arab lands, for instance, which are rich in oil and cotton, can sell their products at a suitable price to any country.

The foreign policy of the Soviet Union and all the socialist countries is being recognized by an ever-increasing number of states as a policy of peace and disinterestedness. We share—to the extent permitted by our material resources—with the countries which still have an underdeveloped economy. We render assistance to other states and shall continue to do so. Our future aid will obviously grow concomitantly with the expansion of our economy.

My speech has proved to be rather long, but I wished to elucidate certain questions once again so that we may be better understood.

I drink to the health of our dear guest—the President of the United Arab Republic, Gamal Abdel Nasser, to the national hero who boldly raised the banner of struggle against the colonialists, who waged and is waging a struggle for the independence of his republic and the other Arab peoples which have still not thrown off the colonialist yoke!

Our sympathy, dear friends, is on your side, on the side of the peoples waging a struggle for their freedom and independence. I believe that you have the sympathy, not only of the Soviet people, but of the peoples of all the socialist countries as well! This is already about 1,000 million people. In the capitalist countries as well progressive-minded people sympathize with your noble and just struggle.

To your health! To your success!

REPLIES
TO QUESTIONS PUT BY
GREEK NEWSPAPER PUBLISHER
Ch. LAMBRAKIS

Mr. Christos Lambrakis, the publisher of a number of Greek newspapers, including *Vima, Néa* and *Tachydromos,* requested N. S. Khrushchov, Chairman of the Council of Ministers of the U.S.S.R., to answer a number of questions.

N. S. Khrushchov's replies to these questions are given below.

Question: What problems in your opinion could be solved by a summit conference in order to create appropriate conditions for peaceful co-existence?

Answer: The main problem in international politics is to live without war, to co-operate peacefully irrespective of differing social systems and ideologies in the various countries. In short, the point in question is to avoid a new war, the catastrophic consequences of which are beyond human imagination.

The Soviet Union is known to have advanced a proposal for holding a summit conference. This conference could discuss problems whose solution is the basis for the gradual ending of the cold war and an improved international climate in general.

The Soviet Government believes that discussion of such questions as the immediate cessation of atomic and hydrogen weapons tests, the creation of an atom-free zone in

Central Europe, the conclusion of a non-aggression agreement between the NATO and Warsaw Treaty states, the reduction of foreign troops on the territory of Germany and other European states, and the conclusion of an agreement on the prevention of a surprise attack, the relaxation of tension in the Middle East and measures to extend international trade and end war propaganda, as well as other urgent questions would be conducive to achieving favourable results.

If all possible participants in this conference fully realize their supreme responsibility for the destinies of the world and display good will, it will be possible to arrive at positive decisions. The peoples will thus be delivered from the fear of a new war and their faith and hope in the possibility of establishing a lasting peace will be strengthened.

Question: What in your opinion are the ways to curb and end the cold war and how will peaceful co-existence between East and West be achieved?

Answer: The cold war is conducted by those Western circles that are accustomed to living according to outmoded conceptions. They do not comprehend new developments and do not wish to reckon with them. But that which is new in life never asks for permission to be or not to be. It makes its appearance, develops and gains strength. The enemies of the new—and we mean socialism when we say the new—hope to be able to stem the growth and development of new social formations, new relations among the peoples. With this in mind they have invented the cold war and the "positions of strength" policy. However, all now see that socialism is a sound system and one that is triumphing, a system which is ridding the peoples of the wrongs and misfortunes of the past. The best way out is to end the cold war and embark, in deeds, and not merely in words, on the road of peaceful co-existence.

On this basis and provided the desire is mutual, concrete steps could be found for bringing the East and the

West closer together, establishing and strengthening mutual confidence and extending international co-operation in all spheres.

The cold war was conceived in the West and, consequently, it is necessary for only one side to abandon it for it to be eliminated. The socialist states are opponents of the cold war. They have always been for international friendship, for mutual respect and non-intervention in each other's domestic affairs. The entire international situation could easily be normalized on this basis, provided it is observed by the parties concerned.

As for the Soviet Union, we have taken steps and are continuing our efforts to secure a relaxation of international tension and an end to the cold war. These steps are well known to everyone. Only recently the Supreme Soviet of the U.S.S.R. adopted a decision unilaterally to end atomic and hydrogen weapons tests. The Soviet Union hopes that its example will eventually be followed by the other Powers possessing nuclear weapons—the United States and Britain.

Question: Do you have hopes that a way will be found to gradual universal disarmament? Is it possible to establish effective control in the event of it being decided to ban the use of nuclear weapons universally?

Answer: If we were to enumerate all the Soviet proposals on disarmament, this enumeration would, in effect, be an indictment of the Western Powers, which, each time the Soviet Union has made a proposal meeting the Western position half-way, have sought various pretexts for not accepting it.

The Soviet Union is ready at any time to sign an agreement on banning atomic and hydrogen weapons and on disarmament. We are ready to conclude a comprehensive agreement and agreements on individual aspects of the disarmament problem. Yet neither of these two approaches suits the Western Powers. Even their own proposals do not suit them as soon as the Soviet Union agrees to them.

The Soviet Union is known to have proposed at one time the complete banning of atomic and hydrogen weapons, an end to their manufacture, their removal from national armaments and the destruction of all stockpiles of these weapons. Moreover, the Soviet Union's proposal provided for the implementation of these measures under corresponding effective and reasonable controls. However, this proposal did not meet with support from the Western Powers.

We have repeatedly proposed to the Western Powers that unilateral disarmament measures be taken, but they have refused to do this as well. Now we have offered them another opportunity to take a real step towards reaching a disarmament agreement and ensuring international security: to unilaterally end the tests of atomic and hydrogen weapons. The Soviet Union is known to have already taken this step. But we have run up against a blank wall again. The two other Powers possessing nuclear weapons—the United States and Britain—remain stubbornly opposed to this. Nevertheless, we shall continue to be patient and persistent in our efforts to solve the disarmament problem and to achieve a ban on nuclear weapons. We believe that sooner or later the Western Powers will be compelled to agree to a solution of the disarmament problem because all the peoples want this and because it is the only way to save the world from the horrors of a new war.

Question: The Greek people are extremely satisfied with the Soviet Union's attitude on the Cyprus issue and would like to regard this not only as a reflection of the Soviet Union's struggle against colonialism, but also as an action clearly determined by the recognition of the fact that most of the population of Cyprus are of Greek origin. Does this attitude remain unchanged?

Answer: The Soviet Union has stood, and stands now,

for a solution of the Cyprus problem corresponding to the interests of the Cyprus population and the consolidation of peace in this area. We believe that every nation has the right to determine its future, and the sooner the vestiges of the disgraceful colonialist system disappear the better it will be for the peoples, for world peace. The Soviet people sympathize with and respect the desire of the Cypriots to uphold their legitimate rights and get rid of foreign oppression.

The Soviet delegation in the United Nations has actively supported the just demand of the Cypriots and from the rostrum of the United Nations has exposed the intrigues of the colonialists who strive to perpetuate the colonialist system on the island through various plans for "settling" the Cyprus problem by imposing on its population a concocted "constitution," dividing Cyprus and drawing the island into the NATO system and building war bases there, etc.

These plans have nothing in common with the true desires of the Cypriots, who fully realize that their implementation could bring them nothing but new hardships. It is absolutely clear that because of the position taken by Greece's "allies" in the North Atlantic bloc the Cyprus question has not yet been solved as demanded by the Cypriots.

We believe that the United Nations, if it does not want to be tied to the apron-strings of the colonialists, should finally throw its weight in favour of solving the Cyprus problem along lines that are truly democratic and just.

Question: Do you think that the commitments assumed earlier by Greece restrict and hamper her freedom in deciding the question of setting up atomic bases on her territory?

Answer: Here you obviously have in view the commitments undertaken by Greece when joining the military North Atlantic grouping.

The Soviet Union's position with regard to this bloc is

well known. We have not concealed, nor do we now conceal, our opposition to this aggressive military grouping, which is directed against the peace-loving states. Membership in this organization tethers Greece to a one-sided policy which has neither brought her any advantages in the past nor promises any bright prospects for the future. Due to the fact that Greece is a member of an aggressive military grouping, she may, against her will and desire, become involved in a dangerous war gamble started by any other member of this bloc, by the United States or Turkey, for instance.

At present NATO leaders have evolved plans for setting up American atomic and rocket bases on Greek soil. Broad sections of the Greek population are known to be alarmed and disturbed by this circumstance. They are actively coming out against these schemes because their implementation would endanger the future of the Greek people. And this is understandable: the presence of atomic bases on Greek soil could open the country, in the event of a military conflict, to a retaliatory atomic blow with all the attendant tragic consequences.

In spite of their commitments to the North Atlantic bloc, some members of this organization reject the plans for deploying atomic and rocket weapons on their territory. It is not surprising that many Greeks are also proposing that their country should follow this sensible road.

Question: Do you consider the existing economic relations between Greece and the Soviet Union satisfactory? There is a feeling in our country that the vast Soviet market could consume a much greater proportion of Greek products, particularly citrus fruits, whose overproduction has lately been exerting a certain amount of pressure on the Greek economy. Moreover, we are aware that the Soviet Union has almost a centuries-old tradition of importing Greek goods. At present trade between our two countries is conducted on the basis of goods exchange.

Proceeding from this, what goods would the Soviet Union prefer to sell on the Greek market?

Answer: From 1953 on, when a trade and payments agreement was concluded, to this day commercial relations between the Soviet Union and Greece can be regarded as absolutely satisfactory. Trade turnover between the U.S.S.R. and Greece has grown nearly sevenfold during this period. Moreover, it is worth noting that the development of commercial relations between the Soviet Union and Greece has in no way hampered Greek trade with other countries. The Soviet Union is a major buyer of such traditional Greek exports as tobacco and citrus and dried fruits, as well as other agricultural products. At the same time the Soviet Union supplies a number of goods of importance for the Greek economy: oil products, timber, machines and equipment. Trade relations between the U.S.S.R. and Greece are based on equality in reciprocal deliveries, and it is absolutely natural that abidance by this principle will be conducive to the further development of trade between the two countries and will ensure Greece a reliable market for sales.

In spite of the level of trade attained between the U.S.S.R. and Greece, possibilities for the further development of trade between our two countries are far from exhausted. As a highly developed industrial country and a major exporter of goods to many countries, the Soviet Union could considerably increase its deliveries of goods needed by Greece, including machines and equipment, in exchange for Greek agricultural products. The Soviet Union is also ready to consider other forms of economic co-operation with Greece, which could promote the country's industrialization and the development of her independent economy, if the Greek Government displays corresponding interest.

Question: To be absolutely frank, I shall say forthrightly that among the country's political leaders and, consequently, among their followers who constitute the broad masses of the people, apart from the EDA Party, there is widespread mistrust regarding the Soviet Union's ultimate aims with respect to Greece. This mistrust is based on recent events and, in particular, the civil war which followed the liberation of Greece. In their opinion the civil war was actively supported by the Soviet Union and the countries which are its friends. What can you say in order to change this view?

Answer: First of all I wish to say that I do not agree with your assertion regarding the mistrust which broad sections of the Greek population allegedly have towards the Soviet Union's intentions with respect to their country. Various Soviet delegations which have visited Greece in the past few years have been accorded a most cordial, warm and friendly welcome by representatives of the Greek public. Besides, there has not been a single case in which the question of any mistrust for the Soviet Union's intentions arose. Of course, the Greeks are a hospitable nation. But if any deep-rooted mistrust really existed between our two peoples, no hospitality could conceal it and this mistrust would be bound to find expression in one form or another.

Perhaps it would be more correct to assume that the story about "mistrust" is being intentionally exaggerated by those who, for their own selfish interests, would like our two countries to become embroiled in dispute and would like to hamper the development of the traditional friendly relations between the peoples of the U.S.S.R. and Greece.

The Soviet Union has repeatedly declared, and proved in practice, that it bases its relations with all countries, including Greece, on the principles of peaceful co-existence and non-interference in the internal affairs of other countries. The Soviet people have no self-seeking intentions with respect to the Greek people, with whom they have ties of friendship stemming from the distant past. This friendship has been sealed by the blood of the finest sons and daughters of Greece and the Soviet Union, which was shed in the struggle against the sworn enemy of mankind—German fascism.

In recent times the German militarists, who have brought so much suffering to our peoples, are again rearing their heads, arming themselves with all types of modern destructive weapons, including atom and hydrogen bombs. That is why we Soviet people believe that the friendship of the Greek and Soviet peoples, as well as other peace-loving nations, is not simply a matter of history, but an effective factor which can and must play an important part in the present-day international situation.

It is no secret that for some time after the Second World War the cold war left a sinister imprint on relations between the U.S.S.R. and Greece. But is the Soviet Union to blame for that? Who is brazen enough to assert that the events which took place in Greece then were engineered by the Soviet Union? Is it not a fact that the Soviet Union has consistently adhered, and continues to adhere, to the concept that any nation, including the Greek people, can regulate its own internal affairs without foreign supervision?

We are deeply convinced that the socialist system offers unquestionable advantages over the capitalist system, with its crises, mass unemployment, enrichment of a handful of people and ruin for the broad masses of the people. But we are also convinced that there would be nothing more harmful than an attempt to foist any system upon peoples. It is up to the peoples themselves, including the Greek people, to decide which governmental structure and which régime they most prefer.

As is known, relations between the U.S.S.R. and Greece were normalized in 1953 on the initiative of the Soviet Union. Is this not the best proof of the Soviet Union's sincere desire to develop friendly relations with Greece? Almost five years have passed since then. Trade has increased considerably between our two countries during this period, cultural ties have been expanded and mutual contacts strengthened. However, there are still great untapped opportunities for developing all-round relations between the U.S.S.R. and Greece. The Soviet Union stands for the utilization of these opportunities to the utmost, for the broad development of cultural, scientific, sports and other contacts on a regular and durable basis. This will help us to learn still more about one another, to wipe out for ever any shadow of mutual "distrust."

Question: What, in your opinion, should be the role of Greece in the Mediterranean and the Balkans?

Answer: Greece occupies an important position in the Balkans and in the Mediterranean basin. This imposes great responsibilities on her. Further relations in this part of the globe depend largely on the position which Greece takes with regard to the basic problems of the situation in the Balkans and the Mediterranean area.

It should be noted that definite progress has been made recently in developing traditional co-operation between the countries of the Balkan peninsula. Diplomatic relations have been restored between Greece, on the one hand, and Bulgaria and Rumania on the other. Some advances have been made towards normalizing Greco-Albanian relations. The Rumanian Government's initiative in convening a conference of the Heads of Government of the Balkan states to discuss mutual economic and cultural co-operation and the establishment of friendly political relations has called forth a favourable response from the Balkan peoples, because this step was dictated by life itself. Although it is known that the Greek Government has not supported the Rumanian Government's proposal, it goes without saying that the consolidation and development of all-round friendly relations between the Balkan peoples and the transformation of this part of Europe into a genuine "zone of peace" would undoubtedly be of benefit to the peoples both of Greece and of the other Balkan states. Greece can and must play an important part in this noble cause. Naturally, peaceful co-operation between the Balkan peoples is incompatible with any plans to turn Balkan territory into a possible area of atomic and rocket war.

Greece also plays an important role in the Eastern Mediterranean, an area which some Western Powers are seeking to turn into a seat of unrest and conflict. It is enough to recall the dangerous consequences which the British, French and Israeli aggression against Egypt—which is upholding her national independence and freedom— might have had for the cause of peace if this aggression had not been rebuffed in good time by all the peace-loving peoples.

The happiness and prosperity of the Mediterranean countries should be sought in mutual co-operation without any external pressure, and not in forming various war blocs and launching military ventures. It is common knowledge that good relations exist between Greece and the countries of the Arab East adjoining the Mediterranean Sea. The further development and consolidation of these relations and a firm and consistent stand by Greece on questions related to the peaceful co-operation of the Mediterranean countries with all nations will help to raise Greece's international prestige and will be a valuable contribution to establishing an atmosphere of tranquility and friendship in this area.

Respectfully yours,

N. KHRUSHCHOV

Pravda, May 4, 1958

SPEECH
AT RECEPTION AT EMBASSY
OF THE UNITED ARAB REPUBLIC IN HONOUR
OF GAMAL ABDEL NASSER, PRESIDENT OF U.A.R.

May 14, 1958

Dear Mr. President,
Ladies and Gentlemen,
Friends and Comrades,

To begin with, allow me to express our thanks for the kind words and wishes addressed here to the Soviet Union and the peoples of our country.

We are very happy that the President of the United Arab Republic, Mr. Gamal Abdel Nasser, and the statesmen who accompany him, have come to visit our country. We have long waited for this friendly visit, but the armed aggression against Egypt in the autumn of 1956 had prevented Mr. Nasser's trip, which had long been agreed upon.

We have done everything we could to make the stay of the President and his colleagues pleasant and, above all, useful.

Your tour of the Soviet Union has not been a long one. You have seen no more than a bit of our country. But wherever you did go, you had a chance to see the cordial sentiments that the Soviet people have for the people of the United Arab Republic, who are in the front ranks of the fighters against colonialism and imperialism.

Our enemies spread many false stories about the policy of the Soviet Union. Our country's policy of peace is convincingly illustrated by the facts, by life itself.

We do not urge our system or our views on anyone. We want every nation to arrange its life as it wants. And statesmen who come to us on good will visits may observe all the aspects of our country's life. On seeing and appreciating the merits of one phenomenon or another, our visitors may, of course, profit by our experience. But can this be interpreted as urging?

Visitors may find many useful things both in our agricultural development and in our industry, and in the sphere of scientific, technical and cultural development. Hence, there are many things of interest to our visitors, regardless of their own country's social system. They can adopt many useful things from us. And we adopt some of the constructive experience and achievements from the non-socialist countries. There is much that is useful for a mutual exchange of experience in both the socialist and the non-socialist countries and for the better development of economy and culture in each of these countries. And there is nothing unusual about that.

We are gratified that Mr. President has visited Uzbekistan, Azerbaijan, the Georgian Republic and the Ukraine, and that he has acquainted himself with the life and culture of the Soviet people, that he has visited industries and collective farms, and that he has seen what a free nation which has taken its destiny into its own hands can achieve. And all this has been accomplished in the short period that 40 years is in history.

We are gratified that you have visited such of our cities as Moscow, Kiev, Leningrad, Stalingrad, Tashkent, Baku, Zaporozhye, Sochi and Sukhumi, and have gained an idea of what Soviet people have achieved in developing their economy, science and culture. And we regret very much that your stay here, and our friendly meetings and talks which have yielded much to both sides for better mutual understanding, are coming to an end. But our personal acquaintance will, we hope, be very useful for the further development of friendly relations between our countries.

A good beginning has been made in establishing contacts between the statesmen of our countries, and we
hope that this will serve our common cause, that it will
contribute to closer ties between our countries and to more
frequent visits and contacts between the statesmen of
our countries.

The Soviet people received you happily and with an
open heart, Mr. President, the national hero of the Arab
people who rose boldly against colonial oppression, un-
daunted by the fact that Egypt was, and still is, opposed
by fairly large colonialist forces. The imperialists are
bending every effort to crush the resistance of the United
Arab Republic, to subject it again to the will of foreign
monopolies, to deprive it of its political independence.

When troubled times came for your republic and the
colonialists attacked you, we said in no uncertain fashion
that we side with you against the colonialists. We said
this in a way fitting for a freedom-loving and independent state which conducts its policy with due regard not
only for its own interests, but the interests of universal
peace, the interests of the oppressed peoples that have
raised the banner of struggle for liberation.

We have always been, and will remain, on the side of
those who fight for their independence and freedom. We
sympathize with the struggle of the Arabs of Algeria, we
sympathize with Yemen, and Oman, we sympathize
with all the countries that fight against the colonialists
for their independence.

We are well aware that some do not like our policy. It
is to the distaste of those countries, too, with which we
should also like to improve our relations. But we do not
want to improve our relations with them at the price of
ignoring the actions they perform with the aim of enslaving other peoples. That would be not only a deal
against the latter but a compromise with our conscience—
something we have never been prepared to countenance,
and will never countenance. We are a socialist country

whose people is itself fighting for a better future. Such a country can never agree to a deal with anyone at the expense of another country, another people.

We have never concealed our sympathies. Nor do we do so now. I think, Mr. President, that you have already convinced yourself of our disinterested approach, of our devotion to the struggle of the peoples for their liberation and independence. It is our sincere wish that these countries should develop their national economy, their culture, and profit by the latest achievements of science and technology.

Permit me to toast eternal Arab-Soviet friendship, the prosperity of the United Arab Republic, the health of the outstanding statesman of the Arab East, President Gamal Abdel Nasser, the health of our dear guests!

SPEECH
AT MEETING OF FRIENDSHIP
BETWEEN PEOPLES OF THE SOVIET UNION
AND THE UNITED ARAB REPUBLIC

May 15, 1958

Esteemed Mr. President Gamal Abdel Nasser,

Our Esteemed Guests Accompanying the President of the United Arab Republic,

Dear Comrades,

We have gathered here today to express the feelings of friendship which the peoples of the Soviet Union have for the peoples of the United Arab Republic. Allow me once again, from the bottom of my heart, to greet Mr. Nasser, the President of the United Arab Republic, and all our welcome guests accompanying the President. (*Stormy applause.*)

It gives us pleasure to say that the relations between our countries and our peoples are improving with every year and developing in a spirit of sincere friendship and co-operation.

The Soviet Union is an irreconcilable opponent of the shameful system of colonialism and gives support to all peoples who are fighting for their national liberation, for the strengthening of their political independence. We know with what difficulty the new is born. The old forces not only do not want to recognize the new, but do everything possible to nip it in the bud.

The Soviet state was born and grew stronger fighting against the forces of the old world. The United Arab Republic, uniting two independent Arab states, Egypt and Syria, countries with an ancient culture, was born and is growing stronger in the struggle against the forces of imperialism.

The Great October Socialist Revolution struck a powerful blow at the entire system of imperialism and colonialism. The past 40 years have seen tremendous changes throughout the world. The defeat of the aggressors in the Second World War, the victory of the People's Liberation Revolution in China, the formation of a whole group of socialist states in Europe and Asia—all this dealt another crushing blow at imperialism. One colonial empire after another began to tumble down, and more and more independent states are emerging in the world.

When the Government headed by President Nasser took office in Egypt and began to carry out a policy in the interests of its country, the colonialists tried to block the road and to impede the work of the Egyptian Government. They staged conspiracies, hired assassins, and tried to overthrow the Government. The imperialists did everything possible to prevent the consolidation of the Egyptian state. When the plots failed, they decided to restore the colonial régime by force and launched a predatory war against Egypt.

The war gamble against Egypt ended in disgraceful failure for the colonial Powers and a remarkable victory for the Egyptian people. We admire the heroic struggle of the Arab people for their freedom and independence and the courage they displayed when repelling British, French and Israeli intervention against Egypt. (*Stormy applause.*)

The Soviet people rejoice at the liberation of the peoples of Asia and Africa from the yoke of colonialism. We, for our part, are ready to do everything to facilitate the complete liberation of the colonial and dependent countries.

The United Arab Republic follows the road of safeguarding the interests of its state against the intrigues of the colonialists, the road of strengthening co-operation with the peace-loving states.

The friendly relations between our countries took shape on the basis of the recognition and application of the principles of mutual respect for territorial integrity and sovereignty, non-aggression, non-interference in one another's internal affairs, equality and mutual benefit, peaceful co-existence and economic co-operation. These great principles now underlying the relations between many countries fully accord with the peace foreign policy of the Soviet Union which we have been carrying out since the first years of Soviet power. The principles of peaceful co-existence proclaimed by V. I. Lenin, the peace foreign policy of the Soviet state, derive from the very essence of our socialist system.

One of the chief factors making for *rapprochement* between states are mutually beneficial economic relations. Sometimes an incorrect attitude on the part of one side to the economic interests of the other side can lead to serious disappointment. Sometimes it even happens between friends that an incorrect attitude on the part of one country to the economic interests of another can lead to adverse relations between them.

Nothing like this can be expected in relations between our two countries. And we are sincerely glad of it. (*Applause.*)

There are, of course, different notions about friendship. Imperialists like to talk of their "friendship" with the colonial peoples. But what they want in this friendship is that the "friend"—for that is the kindly term they use—should in fact be their slave, that he should work humbly for his "friend," the colonialist, and that the latter should enjoy all the fruits of his work.

It is this sort of "friendship" which the imperialist Powers want. What they change occasionally is only the forms of that "friendship," while seeking to perpetuate its essence—the exploitation of one nation by another.

The colonialists often try to produce the impression that the enslaved peoples are all but dreaming of such "friendship." Their reasoning is roughly as follows:

"Yes, these countries were conquered once. But why were they conquered? It was not as simple as that; educated people came there and brought civilization with them."

But since the people who lived in those countries—Moslems or American Indians, for instance—wanted to live in accordance with the laws and creeds of their forefathers, the colonialists exterminated considerable numbers of them. "Civilization" triumphed in the end, and the colonialists implanted a régime of their own in the countries they had conquered.

The predatory enslavement of peoples has been and is still being carried out under cover of hypocritical claims about the noble mission of the colonialists.

As a result of this practice of installing "civilization," many nations which were once the well-springs of the progress of human culture, came, during the years of foreign domination, to lag far behind the countries which were ruling the subject countries. And now the colonialists maintain that they cannot withdraw from those countries as their peoples have not yet reached the stage in their development which can make them capable of self-government.

How preposterously false such assertions are! Is there, indeed, any need for Dutch, British, French, or any other colonialists, to teach statesmanship or the principles of social structure to the peoples of Indonesia, Egypt, India, Burma or any other similar country where culture developed much earlier than it did in the so-called civilized countries?

We are most determined opponents of such "civilization," opponents of the shameful system of colonialism.

We realize that the countries of Western Europe are interested in the raw materials which they are getting

378

from countries of the East. But this does not in the least mean that the imperialists may impose by force their own predatory terms for the exploitation of the wealth of these countries. The supplies of raw materials for the Western nations must be ensured, not through robbing the countries of the East, but by developing mutually beneficial trade relations, so that those countries may be properly compensated by the Western nations for the raw materials and goods which they supply to them. Far from obstructing such relations, we do everything to encourage them, because we ourselves abide by the principle of developing mutually advantageous relations with all countries.

But we can never, of course, remain indifferent should imperialist circles try to impose their will by force on the nations which have cast off the chains of colonial enslavement, should imperialists persist in their bankrupt policy of colonialism. That is contrary to our understanding of normal international relations. We shall always be on the side of those who are fighting for the freedom and independence of their countries. (*Stormy applause.*)

While establishing friendly relations with other countries, we have never forced on them, nor do we want to force on them, our system of government, nor do we aim to derive privileges or any special material benefits.

What are the Arab countries rich in? They are an exceedingly rich area of the world, possessing vast natural resources and great potentialities for the development of their economies and culture and for improving the well-being of their people. Oil figures largely in the external economic and trade relations of the Arab countries. But nature has not been unkind to our country in this respect. We also have unlimited oil reserves.

The Arab countries are blessed with plenty of sunshine, and favourable climatic conditions enable them to grow cotton—"white gold." We, too, have unlimited possibilities for growing cotton and we grow it in large quantities in our fields.

What else do the Arab countries have? They grow bananas and dates, for instance. We have none of these. So, shall we go to war about it? To please those who are partial to bananas and dates we can buy them, by agreement, from the United Arab Republic or any other country in such a way that they can sell them to us at an acceptable price and buy from us what they have not got. This applies to other things as well: What we do not possess for some reason or other, we can get through a mutually beneficial exchange of goods, that is, by trading, and not by extortion or blackmail. (*Applause.*)

Our people are used to earning their own living; we respect the labour of all peoples and believe that every man and woman and all nations have the right to dispose of the fruits of their work and of the wealth of their country. (*Applause.*)

This is why there are no issues in our relations with the United Arab Republic, or with any other country, that could set us at loggerheads. If every country and every government refrained from creating any artificial causes for conflict, then normal relations between the nations would be developing on a sound and firm basis.

The Soviet Union has concluded agreements with Egypt and Syria, which are now a united Arab state. We shall strictly abide by the terms of these treaties, which will, we hope, promote the development of the United Arab Republic and its economic advancement.

It is well known that political independence alone is not enough. A country's political independence is strong when the country has a firm economic basis. People who are unable to defend their independence can lose it, either as a result of direct enemy attack or of internal subversion through a puppet government.

The imperialists have great "experience" in this matter. They know how to create in dependent countries governments which are national only in form but which, in essence, help to strengthen the domination of colonialism.

With the help of such governments, bought by the colonialists, the imperialists are still virtual masters of the economy of a whole series of states which in form seem to be independent.

We rejoice at the fact that the United Arab Republic, notwithstanding the intrigues of imperialist vultures, is conducting an independent policy, firmly striving for the development of its economy and the utmost strengthening of its national independence, and waging a struggle for peace and international security. (*Prolonged applause.*)

Today the peoples have no greater concern than that of preventing war. The peoples judge the policies of governments according to what they do to improve the international situation, to create normal relations among all states, to eliminate the cold war and to maintain peace.

We stand for the elimination of the cold war. This attitude of ours is well known to all honest people. The Soviet Union has unilaterally stopped nuclear weapons tests. Unfortunately, notwithstanding our persistent appeals and the demand of the peoples that the United States and Britain follow suit, those countries, far from following suit, have demonstratively begun to stage further nuclear weapons tests.

However, we do not give up the hope that common sense will ultimately prevail in world politics.

The Soviet Union stands for an end to the cold war and for peaceful co-existence and competition between the two social systems. We boldly look ahead and firmly believe in the socialist system, in the superiority of its planned development that knows no crises.

The economy, science and technology of our country are steadily advancing. Recently the whole world hailed the launching of two Soviet artificial earth satellites, and today a third Soviet sputnik has been launched into space and has entered its orbit. (*Stormy, prolonged applause.*) The weight of this sputnik is 1,327 kilograms (*applause*), including scientific equipment weighing 968 kilograms. (*Applause.*)

While rejoicing at these achievements of Soviet science and engineering, we do not want in any way to humiliate the United States, and still less to insult it, or to belittle its achievements. Yet we cannot deny ourselves the pleasure of expressing our pride in our country's success. (*Applause.*)

If we take the weight of our third sputnik and, as is done in arithmetic, divide it by the weight of an American earth satellite, one would need a very large basket to accommodate a sufficient number of orange-sized American artificial satellites to equal the weight of the third Soviet sputnik. (*Applause.*)

I should very much like to be correctly understood in the United States. We do not in any way doubt the United States' achievements in industry, science and engineering, but permit us not to deny ourselves our national pride and joy regarding our science and technology, regarding our industry, regarding our socialist system, which has ensured us outstanding success and enabled us to outstrip the technology and science of the United States in this respect. (*Stormy applause.*)

We have said more than once, and we say again, that in no case do we want to use our achievements to harm mankind—neither directly nor indirectly by means of threats and blackmail. We only want to emphasize that attempts by certain circles to surround us by some artificial barrier, to isolate us from other countries, and their effort to impede the development of our economy, to retard the advance of science and engineering in the Soviet Union, which certain U.S. circles have been trying to do for several years, have failed to achieve their objects. On the contrary—they want to isolate us, but in fact, instead of isolating us, they are isolating themselves from our successes. For it has become clear to all that Soviet science and technology have, in a number of fields, surpassed the development of American science and engineering. (*Prolonged applause.*)

Isn't it time for a more realistic approach to things, not to frighten each other, but rather to sit down at one table and talk matters over, about how to go on living, how to improve contacts and extend economic and cultural relations between our countries? The peoples expect this, and not only the peoples of the Soviet Union but also the people of the United States, the peoples of the world. (*Applause.*)

The new and outstanding achievement of Soviet scientists, engineers, technicians and workers who have designed, manufactured and launched such a big artificial satellite into space, shows that scientific and technical thought in the Soviet Union is developing at an exceptionally rapid rate, and that Soviet industry is able to accomplish any task of modern development.

Permit me, from the bottom of my heart, to congratulate our scientists, engineers and workers who took part in the creation of the new artificial earth satellite, to congratulate them on their outstanding victory. (*Stormy, prolonged applause.*)

Everyone knows that we have no call to search for a solution to international problems through aggression and war. Without war, we shall the sooner carry out all the plans for our peaceful construction.

We are sincerely striving for a relaxation of international tension. That is why we are surprised at the fact that the fully substantiated protest by the Soviet Government against the flights by American planes carrying hydrogen bombs towards the frontiers of the Soviet Union has not found support in the Security Council, for it is precisely that body that bears direct responsibility for averting the threat of war and for promoting the maintenance of peace.

Instead of denouncing those responsible for such flights which are dangerous to peace, the U.S. representatives tried to substitute one question for another. Thus, instead of denouncing those who are taking aggressive steps and who may provoke a war, they propose that we should recognize the right to make such flights, only on a smaller scale. The United States Government submitted a proposal to the United Nations for establishing inspection in the Arctic and promised to reduce the number of flights by its planes towards the frontiers of the Soviet Union. To reduce, mark you, and not to discontinue. But how can one accept such proposals?

The Security Council is undermining its own prestige by following in the wake of the sponsors of these dangerous manoeuvres. Such actions are not accidental. The Security Council consists almost entirely of representatives of those countries that are either dependent on the United States or are tied to it through military blocs. Who can take seriously claims that, for instance, the representative of the wretched Chiang Kai-shek clique, installed in the Security Council, can act objectively and contribute to the maintenance of peace? He represents no one and lives by sponging on the United States. And can certain other representatives of the NATO states voice opinions different from those desired by the United States? Of course not, because they are tied hand and foot by various obligations to the United States.

It is high time to understand, however, that arithmetic cannot always be applied in politics.

Sometimes we are blamed for frequently resorting to the veto in the Security Council. We do not exercise this right very often, but we do exercise it. We did not sponsor the inclusion of this rule in the United Nations Charter, but we believe it to be a good rule. It makes it possible to avoid the taking of unjust decisions and compels a search by joint efforts for correct solutions of disputed problems—solutions taking into account the interests of all the Powers concerned, the interests of maintaining peace. The right of veto protects the United Nations from the adoption of tendentious decisions that are sometimes even dangerous to the cause of peace. And we shall exercise this right in order to protect the world from unjust decisions.

At the present time all nations place great hopes in a summit conference. Why do we believe such a meeting might be useful? Because, in our opinion, certain international problems are already ripe for a solution. Agreement on urgent questions at a meeting of the Heads of Government would mark the beginning of an improvement in the international atmosphere, would be an advance towards eliminating the cold war. If we do settle some questions, we shall create a sound foundation for the solution of more complicated problems as well.

A summit meeting is a serious matter and all the possible participants must take it seriously. For our part, we have done and are doing everything possible to bring about an early meeting and to make it a success.

Some Western representatives are putting forward obviously unacceptable conditions and items which a summit conference must allegedly take up. Can such a conference really be a success if it discusses the state system in the East European countries and examines the German question in the way suggested by the Western Powers, ignoring the existence of the two German states? The very presentation of the question lacks justification, as we have said more than once. The German question can be looked into at the summit only in so far as the conclusion of a peace treaty is concerned. The reunification of Germany is the domestic affair of the German people.

Such questions can only be raised if one wants to obstruct the calling of a summit conference, to wreck the improvement that is now to be felt in the international situation.

One of the most vital international problems awaiting solution is the question of disarmament. We have already said that the Soviet Union is willing to settle it, and to settle it immediately. But it must be settled with due regard for the interests of the security of all parties concerned.

The experience of our relations with the Western countries has shown that they do not want to achieve a fundamental solution of the disarmament problem. However, a gradual approach is possible. Why not reach agreement, for instance, on the ending of nuclear weapons tests and the reduction of armed forces, and then try to solve other problems of disarmament and the problems of introducing effective control?

Mr. Eisenhower, the President of the United States of America, recently suggested that technical experts should be instructed to agree on the forms for control to prevent any state from staging secret explosions of nuclear weapons.

Our attitude on this question has always been clear. Far from rejecting it in the past, we ourselves suggested the introduction of appropriate control over the observance of a possible agreement on the ending of atomic and hydrogen bomb tests. But we believed that, above all, agreement had to be reached on the main issue—the prohibition of tests—before taking up technical questions connected with this. However, since the United States Administration believes that positive results can be produced sooner in this way, we have decided to meet them half-way and are ready to nominate our experts without further delay and to instruct them to work out the necessary details on this question. We say to our partners: Let us try this possibility, too.

It is high time to embark upon a realistic road and, proceeding on the basis of the existing situation, on the basis of a sober analysis of the state of affairs, search for a solution to pressing problems on which acceptable agreements can be reached without violating anyone's security. Such an approach would, in our opinion, bring about a reduction of international tension, the ending of the cold war and the creation of conditions for the peaceful co-existence in which all the peoples of the world are so interested.

Comrades and friends!

The visit of friendship to the Soviet Union of President Nasser and his companions is drawing to a close. During these days our guests have been to a number of regions of the country and have seen what warm friendship and sincere sympathy the Soviet people entertain for the United Arab Republic and its freedom-loving people. We are happy about this visit, because we want more and more guests to come to us in order to study our life. Everything that they may consider useful, that suits them, can be used by them in the interests of their peoples. We are ready to share with our friends our experience, the achievements of science and culture, and technical and other knowledge, to share in a disinterested way, as real friends do. (*Applause.*)

During President Nasser's stay in our country meetings and discussions have taken place on questions of interest to the governments of both countries. We have established that there is complete mutual understanding between the governments of our countries on all questions affecting mutual interests.

The results of our conversations are set out in the joint statement.

President Nasser's visit to the U.S.S.R. is of great importance for the strengthening of peace in the Middle East and throughout the world.

We note with satisfaction that the successful development of economic and cultural co-operation between our countries, resting on the principles of equality and friendly co-operation, greatly benefits both the Soviet Union and the United Arab Republic.

In strengthening the friendship between the peace-loving peoples we must always bear in mind that the imperialists have never abandoned and, it seems, will not abandon their attempts to interfere with this friendship. We must display vigilance with regard to the imperialists' intrigues and must not allow them to disrupt the growing co-operation between the United Arab Republic, the Soviet Union and the other peace-loving countries.

We regard the visit to the Soviet Union of President Gamal Abdel Nasser and his companions as a valuable contribution to the strengthening of the friendship between the Soviet Union and the United Arab Republic.

Let us further strengthen and expand the mutually beneficial economic and cultural relations between the Soviet Union and the United Arab Republic, the co-operation between our countries in an effort to ease international tension and strengthen world peace.

We sincerely wish our esteemed and distinguished guest, the national hero of the Arab people, the President of the United Arab Republic, Gamal Abdel Nasser, and his companions good health and success for the good of their country, for the benefit of world peace. (*Stormy applause.*)

Long live Arab-Soviet friendship! (*Stormy, prolonged applause.*)

Long live world peace! (*Stormy, prolonged applause.*)

SPEECH
AT LUNCHEON IN HONOUR OF FINNISH PRESIDENT
DR. URHO KEKKONEN

May 23, 1958

Mr. President,
Ladies and Gentlemen,
Friends,
Allow me on behalf of the Soviet Government and myself personally to welcome the President of the Finnish Republic, Dr. Kekkonen, and the statesmen accompanying
him.

We are very pleased that you have come to our country
on a visit of friendship. We already came to know you and
your country well when we visited you last year. Some of
our comrades who are here have also been to Finland or
met leaders of the Finnish Republic in Moscow.

Very good relations have been established between our
states and our peoples. We shall always have a good word
for that outstanding Finnish statesman, the late President
Paasikivi, who laid the foundations of the good-neighbourly
relations between our countries, which are now becoming
friendly relations. It is a pleasure for us to note that the
policy pursued by the late President Paasikivi was completely in line with our common interests and that in the implementation of that policy a prominent role was played by
the then Prime Minister of Finland who is now our dear
guest, the President of the Finnish Republic, Dr. Kekkonen.
I think there is no need to specify whether it was a Paasi-

kivi-Kekkonen or a Kekkonen-Paasikivi policy—either is good for our peoples and served to strengthen the friendly relations between our states. The initiative in pursuing that policy, I was told by a Finnish Social-Democrat when our delegation visited Finland, belongs to Dr. Kekkonen.

I think that all those present here will agree that we should like this policy to be a policy not only of individual statesmen but also of the peoples of our countries.

Relations between our countries are developing in the right direction. This can best be traced in the development of Soviet-Finnish relations over the past five years. The strengthening of friendly Soviet-Finnish relations pleases the peoples of the Soviet Union as well as the people of Finland. In its foreign policy the Soviet Union wishes only friendship and peace with all countries and all peoples. Above all we want friendship with our neighbours, with countries that border on us.

Unfortunately, there are still people who enjoy raking in the dustbin of history to find something to spoil our relations. Some Finnish papers sought notoriety in this thankless business. It is no good work they are doing and our peoples will not praise them for it. Such raking in the past and the search for facts which do not help to improve relations between our countries run counter to the policy pursued by the Government of Finland and the Government of our country. Both our states stand for peaceful co-existence and co-operation. Consequently, they stand for ensuring world peace, which is in line with the interests of the Soviet and Finnish peoples and all peace-loving countries.

We should like to see Soviet-Finnish relations continue to grow stronger and develop: For this there is no need to rake up the past or return to questions solved by time and events.

I should have liked not to have to touch upon such questions today in such splendid friendly company, but I am constrained to do so by statements in some Finnish papers which do not take a sober enough view of the situation. and rake up the past in order to spoil our current relations.

You know our policy. We have repeatedly set out its basic principles in our documents.

In order to establish stability in the world and avert a new war it is necessary to recognize the *status quo*, that is, the situation which has now taken shape, and not to try to change that situation by force, otherwise the inevitability of war will have to be recognized. The experience of history reminds us that state frontiers have never been changed without wars. Let us therefore proceed from the realities of the situation and on that basis develop our cooperation and the relations between our countries. Let us develop economic ties, let us trade, let us help each other to develop industry. Your country can do much that is useful to us and probably you will find in our country much that is of interest to you and that can be used to raise and develop your economy.

Our policy is clear. We are interested not only in developing our economy and raising the prosperity of our country. We are also interested in seeing your economy flourish and your country develop, and the welfare of the Finnish people enhanced. Our growing orders placed with Finnish industry obviously play a definite role in ensuring fuller employment to the Finnish population.

We are able to supply you with the necessary equipment to build a metallurgical plant and to develop other industries. We are prepared to examine concrete proposals in order, taking account of your circumstances, to do everything possible in that respect. This will be conducive to the development of Finland's economy, to fuller employment and to a further rise in the living standards of the people.

In order to solve the problem of employment, in my opinion, an agreement could be concluded, for example, on the construction in Finland of a metallurgical plant by Finnish labour with Soviet blueprints and equipment. I think that this would be well received by the peoples and would benefit Finland's economy. It would be pleasant for us to render this friendly service to our neighbour.

The technical level of Soviet plant and equipment is fully in line with modern requirements. Our country has entered the international arena of economic competition. We are currently building a very big metallurgical plant in India. West Germany and Britain are also building similar plants. Soon it will become clear whose plant is better. We do not underrate the abilities and potentialities of German and British industry. The Germans and the British are good metallurgists. But today Soviet metallurgists do not lag behind and, as our people say, they will not fall down on the job, they will be equal to the task.

A few words about the Saima Canal. We understand that the exploitation of the canal is of great economic importance to Finland. We are prepared to negotiate and find mutually acceptable solutions in order to give the Finnish Republic the opportunity of using the canal on a treaty basis. International practice provides many examples of a similar use of canals on the territory of other states. Why should our countries not come to an agreement about the use of that canal for the transit shipment of Finnish goods? The solution of this problem is in line with our desire to live in friendship and help each other to develop the economies of our respective countries.

I propose a toast to the health of our dear guest, the esteemed President of the Finnish Republic, Dr. Kekkonen, and to the health of his colleagues who are accompanying him and whom we have met. We regard them as our friends who are doing everything to develop and strengthen friendly relations between our countries. And this can only be beneficial both to Finland and to the Soviet Union.

We sincerely desire that mutually advantageous economic relations should continue to develop between our countries as successfully as they have been developing up to now, because that is the very basis for the development and strengthening of friendly relations. I should like to say:

Let us resist those who wish to cool and poison the atmosphere of our good relations with Finland. We shall struggle against such people at home, while you could undertake a moral obligation to struggle in your country against the forces who wish to poison the atmosphere of friendship with the Soviet Union and who are hindering the strengthening of friendly relations between our states. To all those who wish the best for their native country it is clear that good-neighbourly relations between our countries are very advantageous to our peoples, and not only to our peoples, but also to the peoples of all countries who stand for world peace.

We hope that all those present here join us in this desire and we do not in the least doubt that our dear guest, Dr. Kekkonen, will exert his efforts in that direction.

To friendship between the peoples of the Soviet Union and Finland!

To our dear guests!

To the President of the Finnish Republic, to our dear guest, the esteemed Dr. Kekkonen!

SPEECH
AT MEETING OF POLITICAL CONSULTATIVE
COMMITTEE OF WARSAW TREATY

May 24, 1958

Dear Comrades,

More than two years have passed since the last meeting of the Political Consultative Committee of the member-states of the Warsaw Treaty, held in Prague in 1956. This period has been packed with many important international events.

In summing up briefly the meaning and significance of these events, we may say with confidence that the principal result of the last two years is the further growth of the strength of the countries of the socialist camp and their increased cohesion, and the growth of the forces of peace throughout the world. These factors are having an ever-increasing effect on the international situation, tending to remove the danger of a new war and to consolidate world peace.

It would be a mistake, however, to ignore the fact that influential circles of the imperialist Powers, in spite of the obvious failures of their "positions of strength" policy, are intensifying their military preparations, openly banking on preparing a war with the use of nuclear and rocket weapons.

In these conditions the principal task today, just as was the case at our 1956 meeting in Prague, is to wage a persistent struggle for peace, for the removal of the threat of a new war breaking out, for relations among states to be based on the principles of peaceful co-existence and business-like co-operation. The efforts of all peace-loving states and peace supporters in all countries must be aimed at ending the arms race, putting an end to the cold war and establishing an atmosphere of confidence in international relations.

Wars between states have always brought grievous distress to the people. But a future war, if the aggressors should succeed in unleashing it, threatens to become the most devastating war in the history of mankind, because there is no guarantee that it would not become a nuclear war, with all its catastrophic consequences. In the conflagration of such a war millions of people would perish; great cities and industrial centres would be razed from the face of the earth; unique cultural monuments created by mankind throughout the ages would be irrevocably destroyed, and vast territories would be poisoned with radioactive fall-out.

Therefore there is not, nor can there be, any task more important or noble than that of barring the road to a new war, of relieving the peoples of our planet of the grave danger that is looming over them. This is what the supreme interests of mankind demand.

Overcoming the Resistance of Forces Hindering Normalization of the International Situation and Peaceful Co-existence

The peoples refuse to reconcile themselves to the growing danger of an outbreak of nuclear war and with ever-increasing determination they are opposing the aggressive policy of certain influential Western circles. The resistance of broad masses of the people to the adventurist policy of "balancing on the brink of war" has assumed unprecedented scope.

Mass public organizations, trade unions, prominent figures in culture and science, members of the clergy, millions of ordinary men and women in all countries of the world are coming out in favour of the peaceful co-existence of states, irrespective of their social systems, in favour of settling outstanding international problems by peaceful negotiation, and in favour of a radical relaxation of international tension.

Now not only the governments of the countries of the socialist camp but also many governments of other peace-loving states, and in particular those which have recently freed themselves from colonial oppression, are supporting the idea of negotiations for the purpose of easing international tension.

One should bear in mind, however, that along with the steady growth of the forces striving to strengthen peace and to rid mankind of the danger of a devastating nuclear war, those circles in imperialist states who pin their hopes on continuing the "positions of strength" policy and preparing a new war, are also intensifying their activity.

These circles were alarmed by the fact that after the Geneva Conference of the Heads of Government of the Four Powers in 1955 there appeared signs of a relaxation of international tension. They feared lest the extension of business-like co-operation between socialist and capitalist states result in an easing of international tension, in the ending of the cold war, which would provide the prerequisites for solving the disarmament problem.

Certain influential circles regard such a course of events as a threat to their own selfish interests. They fear that the solution of the disarmament problem, and consequently a drastic cut in military spending, might result in a considerable reduction of the super-profits which monopolies are making out of military orders. For this reason the monopolies are interested in preventing the relaxation of international tension, in preserving the state of cold war, in again aggravating relations among countries.

A clear example of the efforts of international reactionary forces to worsen the international atmosphere and create a dangerous hotbed of war in Europe was the counter-revolutionary uprising staged in Hungary. That gamble fell through, however. The Hungarian people, with the assistance of countries of the socialist camp, upheld their own people's power and gave a fitting rebuff to the international reactionary forces and the Hungarian counter-revolution.

The smashing of the counter-revolutionary uprising in Hungary convincingly demonstrated the strength of the people's democratic system, the might and cohesion of the socialist camp.

The events in the Middle East, when certain Western circles launched an open military attack on Egypt, are still fresh in everyone's memory. By organizing the British, French and Israeli aggression against Egypt, those circles planned, under cover of the hue and cry raised over the Hungarian events, to suppress the national-liberation movement in the Middle East, to restore their colonial domination both in Egypt and in the other countries in that area.

The heroic resistance of the Egyptian people, and also the firm stand and assistance of the Soviet Union, the Chinese People's Republic and the other countries of the socialist camp, had a sobering effect on the bellicose circles of Britain, France and Israel and made them end the aggression and withdraw their armed forces from Egyptian territory.

The successful struggle of the Egyptian people against the foreign invaders resulted in the consolidation of the freedom and independence, not only of Egypt, but of other Arab states as well. Seeing in this a threat to the domination of the American monopolies in the Middle Eastern countries, the United States put forward the so-called Dulles-Eisenhower doctrine. This doctrine has the aim of facilitating—under the pretext of filling the "vacuum" allegedly formed following the defeat of Britain and France—the American monopolies' task of replacing Britain and France in the Arab East and putting down the national-liberation movement in Africa and the Middle East.

It is common knowledge that the Dulles-Eisenhower Doctrine met with resistance in the Middle Eastern countries, whose peoples have learned sufficiently well from their own experience what colonial oppression is like.

Having suffered a defeat in this fresh attempt to establish their domination in the Middle East, the initiators of this colonialist doctrine began to hatch plots against Syria. By conspiring against the lawful Syrian Government they counted on creating a military conflict between the countries of this area, on aggravating the situation in the entire Middle East, on strangling Syria's independence and thus attaining their own selfish ends.

At this difficult moment the Syrian people received the help and support of the Soviet Union and other peace-loving countries, which prevented the aggressive circles from carrying out their plans.

The war against the Algerian people, who are upholding their lawful right to self-determination and independence, is still continuing. A peaceful settlement of the Algerian question through the satisfaction of these just demands of the Algerian people and with due consideration for the historical relations between France and Algeria would be in line with the interests of world peace. We are deeply convinced that such a settlement will be in keeping with the interests of the peoples both of Algeria and France.

By ending the war against Algeria and thereby eliminating the possible danger of its growing into a large-scale military conflict, which cannot but alarm the Soviet people, France would contribute greatly to the strengthening of world peace.

The systematic raids by British troops on the peaceful towns and villages of Yemen are also continuing.

These actions of Britain, inflicting numerous losses among the peaceful Yemeni population, are arousing the just anger of all decent people.

An object of foreign intrigues and dangerous provocations at the present time is the Lebanon, where the Western Powers are openly meddling in the internal affairs of that state with a view to establishing a colonial régime there and dealing a blow at the national-liberation movement of the peoples of the Arab East in general.

Some states which are members of the aggressive SEATO bloc have embarked upon the path of military interference in the internal affairs of the Indonesian Republic where they are rallying together the local reactionary forces, supplying them with arms, and even smuggling armed hirelings into the country to fight against the lawful Government of Indonesia.

Recent events show that the ruling circles of the Western Powers continue to do everything to step up the arms race, from which a handful of monopolists are enriching themselves at the expense of millions of ordinary workers, and continue to oppose the easing of international tension and to cling to the cold war policy. This is seen particularly clearly from the attitude of the Western Powers toward the question of calling a summit conference with the participation of the Heads of Government, as proposed by the Soviet Union. Striving to delay the summit meeting, they repeat incessantly the necessity for "making thorough preparations for it," although the entire world knows that the preparations are not the point at issue.

In the interests of the early convocation of this meeting, the Soviet Government has met half-way the wishes of the Western Powers on several questions. It agreed to preparatory work being carried out through diplomatic channels and through Foreign Ministers, and also to the holding, in the course of these preliminary conferences, if need be and by mutual consent, of an exchange of views on the problems which the parties suggest for inclusion in the agenda of the summit meeting, for the purpose of ascertaining the desirability of including a particular question and the possibility of making mutually acceptable decisions on it.

The Governments of the Western Powers, however, are now apparently looking for fresh excuses for avoiding a meeting with the participation of the Heads of Government.

Indeed, although more than five months have gone by since the Soviet Union proposed a summit meeting, the Governments of the United States, Britain and France have still given no answer either with regard to the questions involved in organizing the conference, namely concerning its date, place and composition, or with regard to the range of problems which are to be considered at the conference.

Thus, when it is a question of preparations for a top-level conference to settle pressing international problems, the Western Powers and their diplomatic departments certainly move at a snail's pace.

There has been more than enough time to prepare the conference. But the fact is that the leaders who now stand at the helm of the leading NATO member-states refuse to take the road of peaceful co-existence, refuse to renounce the policy of cold war. This is why the so greatly needed turning-point in the development of international events towards the normalization of the international atmosphere has not as yet been reached.

However, we are now living, not in the 18th, and not even in the 19th century, when some rulers or other could ignore the will of the peoples, although it must be said that even in those times it was far from safe to do so. In our days hundreds of millions of people in all countries have found their way to active political life and hardly anyone would be able to ignore indefinitely the will of the peoples for peace.

Already at the present time the more far-sighted political leaders of the capitalist world have realized the need for radical changes in method and approach to the solution of international problems. True, assurances of their peaceable intentions and readiness to settle international problems by negotiation are not rarely heard from those leaders of the Western Powers who shape the policy of military blocs. But real intentions are gauged, not by words, but by deeds. If we look at the policy of the Western Powers from this angle, we shall obtain a totally different picture.

It is a fact, comrades, that while dragging out negotiations on a summit meeting, the Western Powers are intensifying their military preparations and for this purpose have already held a series of conferences of various military blocs—NATO, SEATO, the Baghdad Pact.

The feverish haste with which this activity is being developed indicates that the opponents of a relaxation of international tension, sensing the indomitable force of the popular demand for a summit meeting, want to confront the peoples with accomplished facts, to worsen the atmosphere, to prevent the calling of such a meeting or to doom it to failure.

The Western Powers are now trying hard to draw more states into military blocs, to unite the existing aggressive groupings—NATO, SEATO and the Baghdad Pact—in a single bloc under the leadership of the United States of America, and to create new military blocs directed against the Soviet Union and the People's Democracies. In this connection one might mention, for instance, the plans for the so-called Mediterranean bloc.

However, try as the imperialists may to camouflage the real purpose of the aggressive blocs, the latest sessions of NATO, SEATO and the Baghdad Pact show that those taking part in them intend to foment the cold war, to carry on their "positions of strength" policy, which has been condemned by the peoples, and to continue the arms race. The establishment of rocket and nuclear bases, the arming of other participants in the blocs with American nuclear weapons—such are the principal items on the agendas of sessions of these aggressive groupings.

Let us take, for instance, the session of the NATO Council of December 1957 and the session of the SEATO Council held in Manila early this year. They show that the United States, Britain and certain other Western countries are carrying out at a forced pace military preparations which tend to worsen the international climate.

The meeting of NATO War Ministers held in April and the NATO Council session held early this month in Copenhagen had the same aims.

The plans of American ruling circles with regard to the Federal Republic of Germany are especially dangerous to the cause of peace. Ignoring the lessons of the recent past, the rulers of the U.S.A. close their eyes to the fact that the arming with atomic weapons of the Federal Republic of Germany, whose ruling circles openly disagree with the existing European frontiers, can have consequences the gravity of which is, possibly, not realized even by some of West Germany's NATO allies, not to mention the fact that it inevitably leads to a dangerous nuclear weapons race between the European states.

When the Western Powers concluded the Paris Agreements, the Soviet Government and the governments of the other countries in the socialist camp gave warning that the drawing of the Federal Republic of Germany into NATO would result in the absolutely unrestricted remilitarization of West Germany and in strengthening the circles seeking revenge. The Western politicians tried to present this warning of ours as "communist propaganda."

Moreover, in order to justify West Germany's inclusion in NATO, the ruling circles of the Western Powers loudly claimed that this would permit them to exercise effective control over the quantitative and qualitative arming of Germany. In those days Western propaganda insisted that the Federal Republic of Germany would under no circumstances be allowed to have nuclear weapons.

However, the ruling circles of the Western Powers no longer speak about this at present. On the contrary, the Western Powers, and above all the United States, are striving to arm West Germany with atomic weapons. This policy made possible the Bundestag decision to equip the West German armed forces with nuclear weapons—a decision approved by NATO allies of the Federal Republic of Germany—and also the United States decision to set up nuclear weapons depots and American rocket bases on the territory of West Germany.

Thus, the ruling circles of West Germany have set foot on the road to preparing a nuclear war—a road fraught with serious consequences. In its Appeal of March 31 to the Bundestag of the Federal Republic of Germany, the Supreme Soviet of the U.S.S.R. justifiably emphasized that the implementation of the decision to equip the West German army with nuclear and rocket weapons, like the establishment of foreign atomic and rocket bases on West German territory, was leading to a situation in Europe very much similar to the time when Hitler Germany launched preparations for the Second World War. It is not without reason, therefore, that the plans for delivering nuclear weapons into the hands of the West German military clique have caused serious alarm and anxiety in many states and among the peoples, including the population of West Germany.

One must be blind not to see that the decision of the Bundestag to arm West Germany with atomic weapons does more than merely widen the split in Germany. The nuclear arming of West Germany would shut the only remaining door to the restoration of the German people's national unity through *rapprochement* and agreement between the German Democratic Republic and the Federal Republic of Germany.

Using the system of military blocs—NATO, SEATO and the Baghdad Pact—the United States is stationing on the territories of their member-countries special task units equipped with nuclear weapons. What is more, officials in the United States and other Western countries do not even consider it necessary to conceal their plans to employ atomic and hydrogen weapons against the Soviet Union and the other peace-loving states.

In one of his numerous statements made in 1957, for instance, the Supreme Commander of the NATO Armed Forces, General Norstad of the United States, said that NATO strategy was based on nuclear weapons. Distorting the foreign policy of the Soviet Union and ascribing all kinds of intrigue to it, Norstad said that in the event of "Russian aggression" the NATO armed forces were ready to use atomic weapons first, even if the Soviet Union declared that it would not employ nuclear weapons. The same idea was reiterated in the British Government's recently published White Paper, which openly proclaims Britain's intention of using nuclear weapons against the Soviet Union first.

The question suggests itself: Did the authors of the White Paper consider where this policy will lead? Did they ponder over the consequences of an atomic war to their country?

Ruling circles of the United States now attach particular importance to the creation of a network of nuclear and rocket bases in Europe and other areas of the world, directed against the countries of the socialist camp. It is easy to understand that the very idea of establishing such bases many thousands of kilometres away from American territory proper has nothing in common either with the interests of U.S. defence or the security of the countries where these bases are situated, but is from beginning to end an expression of an aggressive policy.

As is well known, the signing of an Anglo-American agreement on establishing rocket launching sites in Britain was announced in February of this year. Such an act, which is unpopular in Western countries, and especially in Britain herself, cannot, of course, be regarded as an expression of a desire on the part of the Governments of the United States and Britain to help to ease international tension.

The leaders of the North Atlantic bloc are spreading fabrications of all kinds in order to somehow justify in the eyes of the peoples the establishment of rocket bases on the territories of West European states. An example of these fabrications can be found in the false reports alleging that the Soviet Union has bases for intermediate-range rockets on the territories of the German Democratic Republic, Poland and Czechoslovakia. It can easily be seen that such reports are aimed at aggravating international tension for the purpose of continuing the arms race. Is not the intention of the United States to continue the arms race confirmed by President Eisenhower's statement on May 6 that the United States plans to spend more than $40,000 million a year on armaments for the next 10, 15, and perhaps even 40 years? It undoubtedly is.

However, such a policy on the part of the United States and other NATO countries naturally compels the Warsaw Treaty member-states to draw the appropriate conclusions. However unwilling to do so, they might be compelled by circumstances to consider the question of stationing rocket weapons in the German Democratic Republic, Poland and Czechoslovakia. What would this mean for the situation in Europe? It would mean that the distance between rocket installations aimed at one another would become smaller and smaller, which would inevitably increase the danger of an outbreak of war, of a terrible war of extermination. It is well known that rocket weapons are area weapons, striking at enormous areas and objectives. They are weapons for the mass extermination of human beings and for the destruction of immense material wealth.

We should like to hope that NATO leaders will display sound judgement and not compel the Warsaw Treaty states to take reciprocal measures with regard to the stationing of rocket weapons.

Leaders of the United States responsible for American foreign policy obviously hope that the presence of American bases on the territory of European states will ensure that those states automatically become involved in a war which might be unleashed by the United States. These plans which envisage the use of territories of other states for establishing bases, atomic and thermo-nuclear weapons depots and sites for launching rockets with nuclear war-heads, show that the American politicians, at the cost of sacrificing their allies, hope to divert a retaliatory blow and to protect the territory of the United States of America from the fatal consequences of a nuclear war, or at least to mitigate those consequences.

Some of the military leaders of the United States do not even consider it necessary to conceal the real purpose of American overseas bases. At the end of last year the NATO Chief of Staff, U.S. General Schuyler, spoke at a press conference in Oslo. The gist of his statement was that the principal advantage of American bases in Europe consisted in their being far removed from U.S. vital centres.

As for the European countries on whose territories the American bases are situated, Schuyler said that those countries should be prepared for the possible use of nuclear weapons against them. Such is the prospect which American atomic strategists hold out for the peoples of Europe!

No wonder that in these conditions the policy of the ruling circles of the United States is arousing increasing anxiety and mistrust among its NATO partners and in other countries on whose territories American bases are being established. It is not by chance that the Governments of such countries as Norway and Denmark, displaying a sense of duty and responsibility for the future of their countries, have opposed the establishment of American nuclear and rocket weapon launching sites on their territories.

One cannot help feeling surprised at the short-sightedness of American ruling circles who hope to divert a retaliatory blow from themselves to their allies in the event of the United States unleashing a nuclear war. Some people should not forget that intercontinental ballistic rockets and other modern means of warfare can now hit targets at any point on the globe.

If there is talk of American bases brought forward close to the frontiers of the states against which these bases are aimed, it would be naive to suppose that only the American side possesses modern means of warfare. The progress of science and technology now offers equal opportunities for highly developed industrial countries to manufacture weapons of the most up-to-date types. Every intelligent person who has some understanding of the progress of science and technology realizes clearly that the Soviet Union and the other Warsaw Treaty countries can have, and do have, everything necessary to avoid being placed in a strategically disadvantageous position.

A very convincing proof of the technical potential of the Warsaw Treaty states is the creation in the U.S.S.R. of intercontinental rockets and the launching of Soviet artificial earth satellites. It is not advisable, therefore, for anyone to proceed from positions of strength, or for either side to threaten the other. The end product of all this is only an arms race, and an arms race, as everyone knows, has eventually always led to war.

Every statesman who is conscious of his responsibility must make a sober appraisal of the situation and, far from doing anything, for his part, that might be likely to make the atmosphere more charged and promote the arms race—and thus tend to bring war nearer, he must make it his concern to bring about an end to the cold war and work in earnest towards creating conditions for good-neighbourly relations between all states. We have never failed, nor shall we ever fail, to pursue this goal.

An atmosphere of war hysteria is being maintained by regular flights of American planes loaded with atomic and hydrogen bombs, both over the territory of the United States itself and over that of a number of other countries. Is much needed under such circumstances for a nuclear war to break out?

Anyone whose mind is not afflicted by war psychosis shares the feeling of grave alarm and righteous anger with which world opinion reacted to the news that a nuclear bomb "accidentally" dropped from an American bomber on a small town in the American State of South Carolina, and although the bomb failed to explode, the peoples of the world are posing this legitimate question: What will happen if an incident like that repeats itself and if this time a nuclear explosion, with all its horrible consequences, does occur? What guarantees do we have against an accidental explosion of an American atomic or hydrogen bomb on American territory or on that of some other state over which American bombers loaded with atomic weapons are flying, being taken for a surprise attack? There is nothing to guarantee that this will not happen. Thus, an accidental atom bomb explosion may well trigger off another world war.

A wave of indignation has swept all countries at the news that the United States is systematically dispatching its military aircraft with atomic' and hydrogen bombs flying towards the frontiers of the Soviet Union. Such actions on the part of the American military command, which are unprecedented in peacetime, are indeed bringing the world to the brink of a nuclear war.

As is known the Soviet Government has .emphatically protested against these flights and has brought the matter before the United Nations Security Council. Nevertheless, the United States, far from calling a halt to the provocative flights of its aircraft, attempted to distract the attention of world public opinion from the essence of the question raised by the Soviet Union. It proposed that an international inspection system to forestall a sudden attack should be established in the Arctic region over which American planes are flying.

The Soviet Government has had occasion to point out that this proposal of the United States does not in any way reduce the threat to world peace represented by the flights of American bombers loaded with atomic and hydrogen weapons towards the frontiers of the Soviet Union.

The shortest air route between the Soviet Union and the United States is through the Arctic region. For this reason it is of great strategic importance, and the flights of American military aircraft with atom and hydrogen bombs over that region are, undoubtedly, a grave threat to peace. It is precisely for this reason that the United States must put an end to such flights of American aircraft towards the Soviet frontiers. Yet the Government of the United States is stubbornly refusing to comply with this just demand and to heed the voice of reason.

In addition, the Soviet Union's security is being jeopardized by the flights of American aircraft not only across the Arctic region, but also over those areas of Europe, Africa and Asia where the United States maintains an extensive network of air bases.

Under these conditions, the American proposal for an Arctic inspection system cannot be of any value to the security of the Soviet Union because, in the first place, the United States, in proposing such a system, is not even promising to end such flights altogether, but only to reduce their number; secondly, this proposal concerns only one stretch of the Soviet Union's frontier; and lastly, the system of inspection under the American proposal is to cover a substantial portion of the territory of the Soviet Union and not one inch of that of the United States proper.

Consequently, the purpose behind the United States proposal is to gain certain military and strategic advantages for the United States at the expense of weakening the security of the Soviet Union. It is obvious that no self-respecting state can agree to such a proposal.

These proposals can only indicate that the United States of America is persisting in its "policy of strength," for only a state banking on such policy can put forward such proposals. But it is making a mistake, for to every force there is always a counter-force. It is only natural, therefore, that no state, and still less a state possessing all the necessary means of defence, can accept proposals which are advantageous to one side only, like those which have been made by the United States.

In an effort to counter in one way or another the popular pressure for an end to the arms drive being carried on by the Western Powers, the statesmen of the United States, Britain and France often declare that they are compelled to follow this policy because of a threat to the West from the Soviet Union.

Yet, have any of these statesmen been able to adduce even a single fact to indicate any activity on the part of the U.S.S.R. which jeopardizes the security of any state? No one has ever adduced such facts and, indeed, no one can do so, for no such facts exist.

Definite efforts are now being made in the West to justify the policy of speeding up war preparations, including the installation of American atomic bases and rocket launching sites on other people's territory, by pointing to the Soviet Union's development of an intercontinental missile. But it is well known that the United States had begun to set up its military bases outside its own territory long before modern rockets, and especially intercontinental missiles, had been created.

It must be recalled in this connection that after the end of the Second World War, the Soviet Union advanced the proposal to withdraw all foreign troops from the territories of other countries and to eliminate all foreign bases set up on the territories of other states. The Governments of the United States, Britain and France not only flatly refused to accept that proposal of the Soviet Union but also continued to set up more and more military bases in the vicinity of our frontiers.

Could the Soviet Government be expected, under the circumstances, not to display due concern for the security of its own country and not to think of creating reliable means of ensuring that security? No, it could not.

Yet even today, when the Soviet Union is in possession of the intercontinental weapon, we are prepared to come to an agreement to ban the use of outer space for military purposes if the Western Powers, for their part, agree to dismantle their military bases on foreign territories. It is common knowledge that the Soviet Government has proposed the inclusion of that question in the agenda of a summit meeting. It is now up to the Western Powers, and in the first place the United States.

In stepping up the arms race, the ruling circles of the United States and the other Western Powers are demanding ever new sacrifices from their peoples for the sake of expanding war preparations. All this cannot but affect the economic conditions of the working people, who are forced to bear the heavy burden of military expenditures.

The militarization of the economy of the Western Powers has led to a serious disruption of the economy, to a growth of unemployment in those countries and to distress for millions of people. The supporters of the "positions of strength" policy and the stepping up of the cold war spare no pains to inculcate in the minds of the working people that such a policy is in their own interests because it is connected with a rise in military production and therefore, so they allege, leads to greater employment in industry.

They go so far as to frighten the working class with the assertion that if the cold war were to be terminated and the need for an arms race ceased to exist, this would lead to a drop in production, a growth in the army of unemployed and a fall in the working people's living standards.

Are these arguments which are used by the opponents of ending the cold war and the flunkeys of monopoly capital sound? No, these arguments are unsound. First and foremost, they contradict the essence of human life. They are profoundly anti-humanistic, because they are used to convince man, whose function is to engage in creative labour, that he can live only when creating the means of his own destruction.

These arguments also fall to the ground when analyzed from the scientific standpoint. Is it not true that the possibility now exists for organizing on a large scale the production of the means of consumption and the means of production rather than the manufacture of means of destruction? The market for this—both internal and external—is veritably limitless. If the United States, for example, were to cut prices for consumer goods and raise the working people's wages, the purchasing power of the population would sharply increase and this would create the conditions for expanding the production of the means of consumption.

Is it not clear that if the United States were to follow a policy of peaceful co-existence and business-like co-operation, this would open up vast possibilities for developing the productive forces of the United States? Such countries, for example, as India, People's China, Pakistan, Indonesia, Iran, the countries of the Arab East and the Soviet Union could alone become vast markets consuming enormous quantities of American goods

This would lead to greater employment and consequently to higher living standards for the American people and would at the same time help to realize the desire of the peoples of other countries to develop and expand their economy, raise their living standards and promote their national culture.

Under the present "positions of strength" policy, the Powers participating in NATO have spent a total of more than $400,000 million for military purposes in the period from 1950 to 1957. However, these vast military expenditures have not helped them to evade the mounting difficulties in the economy which is clearly evident in the United States, now undergoing an economic crisis, as the Americans themselves admit.

Nor has this policy of the United States benefited the countries which support the cold war policy and the arms drive. Quite the contrary, by fettering themselves with the "positions of strength" policy, these countries are forced to shoulder unbearable military expenditures. Their economy is being undermined and civilian production is being curtailed—a fact which allows the American monopolies to reduce these countries to a position of ever greater dependence, in the economic as well as the political sense.

All this shows that the real interests of all countries are not served by the cold war policy, but by a policy of peaceful co-existence, of developing mutually advantageous trade and business-like co-operation.

Needless to say, all the peoples would heave a sigh of relief if the threat of war were eliminated and people everywhere could devote their efforts to creative labour, to raising their living standards and developing their culture.

That is precisely what the interests of mankind demand. Every day the peoples are realizing ever more clearly the ruinous effects of the arms drive and the cold war policy, and it may be said with confidence that the demands of the peoples will triumph and they will compel their governments to end the arms race.

It should be noted that even at the present time the policy-makers of the Western Powers cannot fail to reckon with these demands. That is why they pay lip service to peace, although they systematically work to step up the pace of preparations for a new war.

Socialist Countries Stand for Ending Arms Race, for Eliminating Cold War

Comrades, the peoples represented by those taking part in our conference know what war is. They were spared neither by the First World War nor by the Second. In both these wars the peoples of the Soviet Union, the Germans, the Poles, the peoples of Czechoslovakia and other countries party to the Warsaw Treaty suffered the greatest sacrifices. And we are justified in saying that there are no other states on earth whose governments so insistently and unflinchingly follow a policy of preventing the unleashing of a new war as do the governments of the social-ist states, expressing the cherished desires and vital interests of their peoples.

In our time war has ceased to be fatally inevitable. The profoundly abnormal international tension which now prevails can and must be overcome. Peace can and must be preserved.

Like the other governments of the socialist countries, the Soviet Government is far from believing that the prevailing situation cannot be changed for the better. It will be recalled that in the period of the Second World War, relations of close co-operation existed between the Soviet Union, the United States of America, Britain and the other Powers of the anti-Hitler coalition. If this co-operation gave way to relations of mistrust, estrangement and even a certain hostility, that has occurred in spite of the wishes of the Soviet Union.

Friendship with states having social and economic system differing from that of the United States evidently was not to the liking of the Government of the United States, and not only to that Government. In the post-war years, politicians have come to power in the United States of America who have taken it into their heads that the United States can succeed in tilting the balance of forces in its favour and eliminating the socialist system in the People's Democracies, a system established by the peoples of these countries. Not daring to attack the Soviet Union directly, these politicians have concentrated their efforts against the East European countries, as they call them, trying to make the peoples of these countries swerve off the road they have chosen and accept the way of life favoured by certain circles in the United States of America. It is obvious that such calculations are not the result of sound reasoning or a correct evaluation of the situation and correlation of forces in the international arena.

Having set before themselves the fantastic task of eradicating socialism all over the world, these politicians would like to solve that problem in stages because they lack the means even to dare to hope for more. At the same time they continue to act against the world's first socialist state, the Soviet Union, pouring hundreds of millions of dollars into subversive activities against the Soviet Union.

Today the failure of the originators of the "positions of strength" policy is patent. The socialist camp has become even more united and powerful, while the United States of America, in pursuing such a policy, has largely lost its international prestige by assuming the role of leader of the cold war and organizer of military blocs hostile to the cause of peace.

If we turn to considerations of a military nature, it will be found that the American leaders in that sphere have also made considerable miscalculations. This is particularly evident since the launching into outer space of the three Soviet artificial earth satellites, which have demonstrated the high level of industrialization and development of science and engineering in the Soviet Union. Far be it from us, of course, to deny that the United States and other countries with a high level of development in industry, science and technology are able to achieve similar results.

We should like to hope that the leaders of the United States of America, for their part, might take a more sober view of things. A solution of the contradictions dividing the states of the East and the West does not lie in an arms race, but in negotiations between them. It is not sabre-rattling but meetings between responsible statesmen that will lead to a solution of controversial issues.

In the present circumstances, with the cold war outgrowths that have accumulated over the years making themselves felt literally at every point, a daring search and a concerted and determined effort are needed to secure a turn in international relations which the peoples desire, and to spare the world a war catastrophe.

It can hardly be disputed that only a conference of the most authoritative and plenipotentiary representatives of states can tackle this task. This is precisely why the Soviet Union, upon consulting all the socialist countries, made a proposal last December for a top-level East-West conference.

The Soviet Government has done everything in its power to clear the way to a conference at the summit and to create an atmosphere of confidence and business-like co-operation. It is enough to mention the Soviet Union's reduction in its armed forces and its unilateral suspension of all atomic and thermo-nuclear weapons tests. This conference is also considering further steps to be taken by the Warsaw Treaty countries towards relaxing international tension and safeguarding peace in Europe. We have concrete deeds to back our good will for agreement and mutual understanding.

The Soviet Union and the other socialist countries will steadfastly and perseveringly continue to pursue a policy aimed at easing international tension and ending the cold war. Every day the peoples will increasingly support this peace policy and duly appreciate it. We are confident that through hard work we shall eventually bring about a situation in which the peoples of the states whose governments pursue a "positions of strength" policy and the arms race will compel their governments to take the road of peaceful co-existence.

The Soviet Union and the other Warsaw Treaty countries are prepared for a summit conference and have forwarded to our partners proposals to this effect. The Minister of Foreign Affairs of the U.S.S.R. is holding preparatory discussions to this end with the Ambassadors of the United States, Great Britain and France in Moscow. But we are finding it increasingly difficult to overcome the conviction that lying behind the talk of the Western leaders about the need for careful preparations for a summit conference is the unwillingness of the Western Powers to talk business, although the governments of these Powers must have as much ground for being concerned about easing international tension and removing the rocket and nuclear war danger as the countries of the socialist camp have.

The questions we suggest for discussion at a summit meeting are well known. They have been raised and made urgent by life itself. Every one of these proposals, whether it deals with ending nuclear tests, the creation of a zone free of atomic, hydrogen or rocket weapons in Europe, measures for the prevention of a surprise attack, the conclusion of a non-aggression pact between the Warsaw Treaty Organization and NATO, or anything else suggested for discussion, has the purpose of contributing to a relaxation of tension in international relations. At the same time every one of them could be put into effect even today, provided only that our partners at the talks are guided

417

by the same striving as we are; namely, to put an end to the cold war and reduce international tension.

We cannot, however, fail to note that the present tac tics of the United States and the countries supporting it boil down to an attempt to lull the vigilance of the peoples by declarations and by talk about thorough preparations for a summit conference and to bury the very idea for ever. Nor can one fail to see that what lies behind the talk of the need for careful preparations for a summit meeting is, in point of fact, the intention of certain circles in the West to go ahead with their "positions of strength" policy in order to try to compel the Soviet Union and the other Warsaw Treaty countries to accept the U.S. demands without the least objection, something these circles openly declare.

But who, indeed, can take seriously the calculation that as a result of some careful preparations for a summit conference the Soviet Union and the other Warsaw Treaty countries will agree to an international conference considering such issues as the situation in the East European countries, designed to interfere in the internal affairs of these countries in order to force a change in the socialist system established by the peoples of these countries?

Or take the question of German reunification, as treated by the Western Powers. Can one consider as serious the statements that Germany can be reunited, while ignoring the existence of the two sovereign German states, the German Democratic Republic and the Federal Republic of Germany, and that this can be done without them, behind their backs and in the interests of certain groups in one of these states alone, the Federal Republic of Germany?

If the Western representatives, in pleading the need for thorough preparations for the meeting have in mind to compel the Soviet Union to agree to a discussion of such questions, we must say openly that the time needed for such "preparations" would be endless, for never, under no circumstances, will the Soviet Union agree to such a solution.

The Soviet Union has submitted very concrete proposals for discussion at a summit meeting. These proposals have been dictated by life itself. If the Western Powers are not yet prepared to settle all these questions, it might be possible to select some of them, to reach agreement on them and thereby lay the foundation on which a solid edifice of peace could then be built.

We consider that, in preparing for a summit meeting and in preparing questions for discussion there, such questions should be selected as could be resolved now, at this stage. This can be successfully accomplished only if countries with different internal systems, that is, capitalist countries and socialist countries, approach the matter realistically, proceeding from the indisputable fact that at present two world systems—capitalism and socialism—exist on the globe and if they recognize the principle of peaceful co-existence of the two systems and tackle questions that would promote this peaceful co-existence.

That is why the Soviet Union and the other socialist countries propose that a summit meeting should consider questions that in no way affect the foundations of the capitalist countries and at the same time do not prejudice the socialist countries. This is the principal thing, and it is precisely this approach that can make a summit meeting successful.

We propose to the United States of America, Britain and our other partners to try the way of partial disarmament measures. We are by no means doing this because we consider radical, all-embracing disarmament to be less desirable. On the contrary, the Soviet Union is prepared to come to an agreement on this even today. But the experience of years of long negotiation in the United Nations shows that the Western Powers refuse to reach a radical solution of the disarmament problem.

It appears that not the least of the fears of the Governments of the U.S.A. and other Western Powers is that curtailment of military production would lead to an economic recession in their countries. Our proposals for partial disarmament measures, as a start, take these fears into account, enabling the Western Powers to convert their war industry to peaceful production gradually and painlessly.

The Soviet Union has always considered that its sacred duty to mankind is to bring about a ban on the means of mass destruction—atomic and hydrogen weapons.

How can this problem be most speedily approached? Since the Western Powers say that they cannot agree at present to the complete prohibition of nuclear weapons and their removal from national armaments, we suggest that they take—as a beginning—merely the first step in this direction, and halt these weapons tests, for the continuation of atomic and hydrogen bomb tests poisons the atmosphere with radioactive fall-out and leads to the development of even more powerful nuclear weapons which are increasingly frightful in their consequences.

Considering that the Western Powers have turned the question of control into the main stumbling-block in the course of disarmament talks, the Soviet Union proposed the organization of a system of control over the suspension of tests through the establishment of control posts in the U.S.S.R., the U.S.A., Britain and the Pacific. We agreed to this even though we knew that the existing national scientific institutions are themselves able to detect all nuclear explosions, anywhere in the world, without the aid of any international control system.

But this did not induce the Western Powers to agree to a universal suspension of atomic and hydrogen weapons tests. So far, all our proposals have met with a blank wall of Western objections.

Guided by a desire to make a start on the universal suspension of nuclear weapons tests and thereby take the first step towards a complete ban on these weapons, the

Supreme Soviet of the U.S.S.R. passed a decision on the unilateral suspension of atomic and hydrogen weapons tests by the Soviet Union and called on the other countries to follow suit.

It is now obvious that the Western Powers will not respond to the initiative of the Soviet Union. Towards the end of April the United States and Britain started another series of atomic and hydrogen weapons tests. These nuclear tests show that the ruling circles of the U.S.A. and Britain are sabotaging the solution of the question of an immediate, universal suspension of atomic and hydrogen weapons tests and thereby assume a heavy responsibility for the continuation of the nuclear arms race.

To evade the cessation of nuclear weapons tests, the Western Powers insist on preliminary work by experts on the technical details of controlling the suspension of tests.

The Soviet Government holds, as it always has held, that it is necessary to agree in principle on the suspension of nuclear tests first and then to take up the matter of control. However, wishing to hasten agreement with the Western Powers on the suspension of nuclear tests, the Soviet Government has agreed to the assigning of experts who would start work immediately, studying the means of detecting possible violations of an agreement on the suspension of nuclear weapons tests. We stressed, however, that this work should be completed in a short period, to be specified in advance.

These steps of the Soviet Government have cleared the way fully for agreement on the immediate suspension of tests of all types of nuclear weapons. All peoples agree in demanding that the suspension of nuclear weapons tests be the first item discussed at the summit, and they will not forgive the Governments of the United States and Britain should they impede the cessation of nuclear tests, a problem tackled so vigorously by the Soviet Union.

Rejection of the use of atomic and hydrogen weapons with which the Powers are armed would be of great importance for easing international tension and ending the arms race. That this measure is perfectly realistic is obvious to all. It requires neither lengthy talks nor any control or material expenditures. But such moral condemnation of nuclear arms would be of truly inestimable value to the cause of peace, besides creating conditions for further steps towards resolving the disarmament problem.

A moral pledge by states not to use atomic and hydrogen weapons would be especially significant today when it is no longer possible to establish foolproof control over the observance of an agreement banning nuclear weapons, and when it is easy for either side to begin, should it so desire, the secret manufacture of nuclear weapons.

We now have to reckon with the fact that the process of nuclear materials manufacture is the same, whether for military or peaceful purposes. The very same nuclear materials can be used both in peaceful branches of production and for the manufacture of nuclear weapons. This means that the manufacture of nuclear energy for peaceful purposes, which is becoming increasingly developed and widespread, can be used, simultaneously, to secretly stockpile explosive nuclear materials in circumvention of control. And once enough materials have been stockpiled, it would not be too difficult to conceal the designing and manufacture of nuclear bombs and atomic rocket warheads. This can be done by any industrially developed country.

Today, when nuclear arms have ceased to be the monopoly of one state, as was the case 13 years ago, it is very, very dangerous to use these weapons of mass destruction without risking massive retaliation. Things must be viewed realistically. Under the present circumstances, the way to eliminate the threat of atomic war is moral condemnation of the use of atomic and hydrogen weapons.

Anyone who seeks to evade agreement on renunciation

of the use of nuclear arms is hypocritical in stating that it would possess no force but would remain an uncontrolled moral commitment.

Moral condemnation by the peoples is a great force It will represent a means of rigid control and a containing factor against those planning to use nuclear weapons, those barbaric weapons for the mass annihilation of people and the destruction of material values. The experience of the recent past confirms the significance and effectiveness of international agreements imposing moral obligations on states.

It is common knowledge that the Geneva Protocol of 1925, banning chemical and bacteriological means of warfare, played a positive role, preventing the use of these weapons of mass destruction during the Second World War. The aggressors dared not use these weapons, morally condemned by an international treaty and by world public opinion.

A ban on the use of atomic and hydrogen weapons would be a good beginning. Later, when the relations between states are developed and consolidated, when these relations become relations of friendship, favourable conditions will arise for broader control and greater international confidence, and this will make it possible to exclude war altogether as a means of settling disputed issues.

A summit meeting should also give the closest consideration to the proposal of the Polish People's Republic for the establishment in Europe of a zone free of atomic, hydrogen and rocket weapons. The Soviet Union, like the other members of the Warsaw Treaty Organization, does not seek any military advantages in supporting this proposal. It wishes only one thing—to achieve a relaxation of tension in Central Europe and to reduce the likelihood of atomic war in the area and, consequently, help eliminate the threat of such a war in general.

Those who allege that only one side stands to gain from the establishment of such a zone are chopping logic. They are deliberately obscuring facts which run counter to their contentions.

In what circumstances could the establishment of an atom-free zone—composed, as is proposed, of four countries: Poland, Czechoslovakia, the German Democratic Republic and the Federal Republic of Germany—be said to give definite military advantages to the Soviet Union and its Warsaw Treaty allies? Only if NATO's contribution to the establishment of such a zone will be greater than that of the Warsaw Treaty countries. In reality, this is far from being the case.

Naturally, simple arithmetical calculations are inapplicable in comparing military and economic factors. But some figures are indisputable.

A comparison of the territories of the states to make up this zone shows that the combined territory of the German Democratic Republic, Czechoslovakia and Poland is more than twice that of the fourth proposed member of the zone, West Germany. Moreover, the combined population of the Warsaw Treaty countries in the zone is also greater than the population of the sole NATO country in it.

It is known that neither the German Democratic Republic, nor Czechoslovakia, nor Poland, nor the Federal Republic of Germany manufactures its own nuclear weapons. What is more, the Government of the Federal Republic of Germany at one time assumed an international commitment not to manufacture such weapons in the future. All this shows that there are no grounds for supposing that the establishment of a zone free of atomic, hydrogen and rocket weapons would give any military advantages to the Warsaw Treaty countries to the detriment of the interests of the NATO countries.

If the Western Powers fear that following the establishment of such a zone the Soviet Union would retain superiority in conventional arms in this territory, one might ask why they reject the Soviet proposals for reducing the strength of foreign troops on the territory of Germany and other European states.

To our mind, it would be scarcely correct to preclude in advance the possibility that the establishment of a zone free of nuclear and rocket weapons would be accompanied by measures for the reduction and mutually acceptable regulation of the strength of foreign troops now maintained on the territory of states which may form the proposed zone.

The establishment of a zone free of nuclear and rocket weapons would not only be of great international significance, but would also go a long way towards ensuring the security of the states which would belong to it. We find it difficult, therefore, to understand the position of the Government of the Federal Republic of Germany, whose attitude to the Polish proposal has been negative thus far.

The Soviet Government has already announced its readiness to undertake to respect the status of the zone free of nuclear and rocket weapons and to regard the territory of the countries within it as excluded from the sphere of employment of nuclear and rocket weapons, if the Governments of the U.S.A., Britain and France do likewise.

The Soviet Government has recently made another concession to the Western Powers by proposing the conclusion of a broad international agreement on banning the use of outer space for military purposes and closing down military bases on foreign territories, and on international co-operation in the study of outer space.

The rapid scientific and technical progress in the development of rockets capable of reaching out into cosmic space places a grave responsibility on the states. Their duty is to channel progress in this field to peaceful uses, so that intercontinental and all other rockets may be used for peaceful research, for conquering the great expanses of the universe and not for killing people.

The Soviet Union has proposed the establishment of a United Nations agency on international co-operation in the study of outer space with a view toward making the new scientific discoveries serve the peaceful needs of mankind. The Soviet proposals, serving as they do the security interests of all states in equal measure, make it possible to provide a really solid foundation for international cooperation. They are, at the same time, a major step towards solving the problem of disarmament in general.

The United States approaches the question of outer space from a different position. It limits its proposals to control over intercontinental missiles, disregarding the question of other rockets which may carry nuclear war-heads, and also the question of overseas bases adapted to the launching of such rockets and to accommodating warplanes carrying atom and hydrogen bombs.

One cannot fail to see that the United States, in limiting its proposals to a ban on intercontinental ballistic missiles, wants to safeguard itself against nuclear retaliation through outer space in case of atomic war, at the same time retaining its numerous military bases on foreign territories which are intended for an attack on the Soviet Union and the peaceable countries friendly to it.

It goes without saying that the Soviet Government cannot agree to the jeopardizing of the security of the Soviet Union and the countries friendly to it.

The task of ensuring the maximum security of all states requires that a ban on the military use of outer space be accompanied by measures for the closing down of military bases on the territory of other states, primarily in Europe, the Middle East and North Africa.

Discussion at the summit of other questions listed in the well-known Soviet proposals would also be of great significance for the relaxation of international tension. However, the Western reaction to them cannot be regarded so far as encouraging.

In their efforts to prevent the holding of a summit conference, certain circles in the West would like to do some bargaining, as it were, depicting the Soviet Union as having some special interest in the questions submitted by the Soviet Government for consideration at the summit. Therefore, they argue, if we drive a hard bargain with the Soviet Union, in exchange for our consent to take part in the meeting, we can wrest some advantages at the expense of unilateral concessions by the socialist states.

The Western demands for a discussion of matters which signify interference in the internal affairs of the socialist states cannot be regarded in any way other than as provocations designed to stir up enmity between states.

It is time for the Governments of the Western Powers to realize that the question of the system of government of the People's Democracies, as well as that of any other sovereign state, is not a matter for discussion at international conferences, for it has long been settled by the peoples of these countries, who have firmly and unequivocally embarked upon the course of building socialism.

Conclusion of Non-Aggression Pact
Between Member-Countries of Warsaw Treaty
and NATO Countries
Is Effective Step Towards Consolidation of Peace

Comrades, the efforts made by the Soviet Union and other countries of the socialist camp to achieve a relaxation in international tension, to take the first steps in disarmament, to halt the tests of atomic and hydrogen weapons, and to reduce armed forces and conventional armaments have been warmly received, as you know, by all the peoples of the world.

The Soviet Union has demonstrated by deeds its peacefulness and its sincere desire to provide conditions for a firm and lasting peace. The Soviet Government, without awaiting an international agreement on disarmament, has unilaterally reduced its armed forces repeatedly in recent years. In 1955, it reduced them by 640,000 men and in

1956-57 by another 1,200,000. At present, a further reduction, by 300,000, is nearing completion, with considerable cuts effected in our troops temporarily stationed abroad under existing agreements—in the German Democratic Republic and Hungary.

Our country's armaments, military equipment and expenditures for defence have been reduced accordingly.

The other member-countries of the Warsaw Treaty Organization reduced their armed forces by a total of over 337,000 in the course of 1955-57.

We all give due recognition to the great contribution made to the maintenance of peace by the great Chinese People's Republic, which recently decided to withdraw the Chinese Volunteers from Korea. If the United States following the example of People's China withdrew its troops from South Korea and dismantled all its bases there, this would unquestionably help to strengthen peace in the Far East and to solve the Korean problem.

In discussing the convening of the Political Consultative Committee, the parties to the Warsaw Treaty agreed on the questions to be considered by our meeting.

The Soviet Government considers it expedient for our meeting to go on record for the further unilateral reduction of the armed forces of the Warsaw Treaty member-countries and to call on the NATO countries to effect a similar reduction.

Following consultations with the Government of the Rumanian People's Republic, the Soviet Government submits to the meeting the question of withdrawing the Soviet troops stationed on the territory of the Rumanian People's Republic under the terms of the Warsaw Treaty, as another measure designed to ease international tension.

The Soviet Union favours the withdrawal of all foreign troops from the territories of other states and the closing down of all military bases on foreign territories. Considering Western objections to the proposal for the complete withdrawal of troops from foreign territories, the Soviet

Government has proposed to the Western Powers as a first step to agree at least to a reduction of their troops on these territories. But this proposal, too, is opposed by the United States and its NATO partners.

Recognizing the importance that the withdrawal of foreign troops from European states would have for improving the international climate, the Soviet Government considers it necessary, in the present situation, to make new efforts, to do everything to induce the Western Powers to effect such a measure. The withdrawal of Soviet troops from the Rumanian People's Republic conforms to this aim. This step of the Soviet Union could represent a practical start toward withdrawal of foreign troops from the territories of other states and clear the way for agreement on this matter between all countries concerned.

The Soviet Union's peace policy in foreign affairs like that of the other socialist states, meets growing support of all the peoples of the world with each passing day.

In the opinion of the Soviet Government, the easing of tension in the relations between those countries party to the Warsaw Treaty and those countries belonging to NATO would be of paramount importance under the present circumstances. No one can deny that the friction and mistrust engendered by membership in NATO and the Warsaw Treaty of the 23 economically and militarily most developed countries is having a deleterious effect on the entire gamut of international relations.

The conclusion of a non-aggression pact between these two groupings would help remove the existing strained relations between them. After all, it is clear to everyone that a new major war can only result from a conflict between the Warsaw Treaty Organization and NATO. If, on the other hand, their military machines are not set into motion, then such a war would not take place.

Very important also is the fact that a non-aggression pledge is an effective antidote to aggression, since violation of it, as shown historically, leads to the isolation of the aggressor internationally, facilitating the rallying of forces opposed to aggression and, thereby, to the aggressor's defeat.

The Soviet Government takes a positive view of the pronouncements by some statesmen of the NATO countries that a non-aggression pact could be useful and could serve the interests of peace. In this connection, mention should be made of the well-known statement made on the subject by the Prime Minister of Britain, Mr. Macmillan.

The Soviet Government considers that it would be useful for those taking part in the present meeting to propose to the NATO countries the conclusion of a pact of non-aggression between members of that bloc and the countries belonging to the Warsaw Treaty Organization.

In so doing, the NATO member-states could be informed that the Warsaw Treaty Organization is willing at any time to delegate representatives for an exchange of opinion on questions arising from the proposal concerning the conclusion of a non-aggression pact. Such an exchange of opinion between representatives of the Warsaw Treaty Organization and the North Atlantic Alliance could take place immediately.

Many Western statesmen cannot stomach the fact that the socialist countries hold the initiative in international affairs, that they are making proposals which are popular with the people. One might ask why should our countries not take such initiative if it accords with the vital interests of all peoples, including those of the member-states of the Western Powers' military blocs, and why should we worry if our peace initiative deprives of sleep those who are interested in the arms race and are haunted by the fear of losing their profits!

Quite the contrary, the negative attitude and impotent rage of the opponents of our proposals reinforces the belief that the governments of the socialist countries are acting correctly and are on the right road. Every peace offer by the Soviet Union, the Chinese People's Republic and other socialist countries wins new friends for us abroad, gives fresh vigour to the powerful peace movement.

In our era international development is determined by the progress and results of the competition between two differing social systems—socialism and capitalism. The greater the successes achieved by the working people of the Soviet Union, the Chinese People's Republic and the other socialist countries in expanding industry, improving technology, raising the productivity of agriculture and advancing material and cultural standards, the stronger become the forces of peace, the more remote becomes the danger of another war. We sincerely rejoice in the tremendous successes of our friends, the peoples building socialism.

It has been proved conclusively that socialism, in emancipating labour, sets free the inexhaustible forces of the broad masses, offers unbounded scope for their creative endeavour, for a renaissance of science and culture, for the realization of man's most daring plans. The practical experience of the peoples bears out that socialism as a social system is superior to capitalism. It ensures the development of the productive forces at a pace which is unprecedented and unattainable for capitalism, ensures the steady advance of the material and cultural standards of the working people.

We say to the capitalist countries: Let us compete in the manufacture of goods and articles which the peoples need to make their life fuller and happier, let us compete in advancing the living standards and well-being of the peoples. And let the peoples themselves decide during this competition for the benefit of man which road coincides more with their interests.

The socialist states do not fear peaceful competition with the capitalist countries, for they are deeply confident of its outcome.

A firm guarantee of the national independence and sovereignty of each socialist country is the close cohesion of socialist states, united ' a single camp on the basis of the principles of fraternal mutual assistance and proletarian internationalism, full equality, respect for one another's territorial integrity, national independence and sovereignty, non-interference in one another's internal affairs. The solidarity of the socialist states is not directed against any other countries but serves the interests of all peoples by containing the aggressive tendency of the imperialist circles and supporting the steadily growing forces of peace and progress.

Comrades, the questions under discussion at our meeting make it quite clear that we have assembled here not to draft new plans for intensifying the arms race. Unlike NATO and other aggressive military blocs of the Western Powers, the Warsaw Treaty has been concluded exclusively for the purpose of safeguarding the security of our countries and serves the interests of consolidating peace. The states which are party to this treaty have never intended, nor do they intend, to attack anyone.

At the same time, we must draw correct conclusions from the fact that the NATO countries reply to our measures for reducing armed forces and arms expenditures, to our proposals for easing international tension, by increasing their forces and their military budgets and by stockpiling armaments.

All this is being done to prevent a relaxation in international tension and the achievement of agreement between the states that would ensure their peaceful co-existence, thus impelling the Warsaw Treaty countries to take part in the arms race and in the cold war in order to retard our peaceful construction.

In taking new steps in this situation to end the cold war, to reduce armed forces and to provide conditions for peaceful co-existence, we must display a sober attitude and a sense of responsibility for the security of our socialist countries.

The governments of the countries which are party to

the Warsaw Treaty could not allow a situation in which the vigilance of our peoples might be lulled and conditions arise in which the advocates of "positions of strength" policy might be tempted to use force against the socialist countries. This means that in fighting consistently for the easing of international tension we should in no way forget the necessity for safeguarding the peaceful labour of the peoples of the socialist countries against any encroachment by aggressive forces.

Let the governments of the countries relying on "the policy of strength" always bear in mind that war against the socialist countries can end in only one way—in the destruction of the aggressor.

The Soviet Government is confident that our conference will successfully accomplish the task before it, that it will make decisions that will promote peace and contribute to an early settlement of the pressing international problems which are troubling mankind.

MESSAGE
TO CENTRAL COMMITTEE
OF ITALIAN COMMUNIST PARTY

The Central Committee of the Communist Party of the Soviet Union sends the Central Committee and all the members of your Party heartfelt fraternal congratulations on your outstanding political and moral victory in the parliamentary elections.

The glorious Italian Communist Party has stood a grim test and has overcome the attacks of reaction and revisionism. It has again convincingly demonstrated that it has the very deepest roots in the people—the working class, the peasant masses, and the middle strata of the population. Its brilliant success at the elections proves convincingly once again that all the talk by imperialist reaction about a so-called "crisis of communism" is utterly false. The victory of your Party in the elections and the weighty achievements of the Socialist comrades are an important phase in the development and consolidation of the democratic forces of the Italian people, in their struggle for peace and social progress.

We wish the fraternal Italian Communist Party new successes in its heroic struggle and tireless efforts for the good of the working class and all the working people of Italy.

On instructions of the Central Committee of the C.P.S.U.
N. KHRUSHCHOV, First Secretary of the C.C., C.P.S.U.

Moscow, May 31, 1958
Pravda, June 1, 1958

SPEECH
AT 7th CONGRESS
OF BULGARIAN COMMUNIST PARTY

June 3, 1958

Dear Comrades and Friends!

Allow me, on behalf of the Central Committee of the Communist Party of the Soviet Union and of our entire Party, and on behalf of the Soviet people, to convey to the 7th Congress of the Bulgarian Communist Party, to the Bulgarian Communists and all the Bulgarian people warm fraternal greetings and good wishes for success in the work of your congress. (*Stormy, prolonged applause. All rise.*)

Our Party and the peoples of the Soviet Union, like all the peoples of all the socialist countries, together with you sincerely rejoice over the outstanding successes with which the Bulgarian Communist Party has come to its 7th Congress.

The Bulgarian people, under the leadership of their Communist Party, have taken a big step forward in building socialist society. The working people of the Soviet Union whole-heartedly congratulate the Bulgarian people on the historic victories that have been achieved. (*Prolonged applause.*)

The rapid development of the economy of the People's Republic of Bulgaria, the steady improvement in material well-being and the rise in the cultural level of the people, strikingly shown by Comrade Zhivkov in the report of the Central Committee of the Bulgarian Communist Party, provide one more convincing proof of the superiority of socialism over capitalism. (*Prolonged applause.*)

The lackeys of the bourgeoisie love to boast about the alleged advantages of the so-called system of free enterprise. If you listen to them, the picture you get is that this system is the limit of man's dreams, that there is nothing better, nor could there be. But why is it that they cannot name a single capitalist country which, within such a short period of time, has made such progress in the development of its economy as the countries which have taken the road of socialism? Take, for example, countries that are neighbours of Bulgaria—Greece and Turkey. Statistics objectively reflect the fact that People's Bulgaria, who has embarked on the road of socialist development, has achieved much greater successes in promoting her economy and culture than her capitalist neighbours. *(Applause.)*

In the socialist countries industrial output as a whole has increased more than 300 per cent as compared with the pre-war level, whereas in the capitalist countries, notwithstanding the frenzied arms race and other methods of "stimulating business activity," it has risen less than 100 per cent.

We are firmly convinced that the time is not far distant when the socialist countries will outstrip the most developed capitalist countries, not only as regards the rate of industrial production but also as regards the volume. *(Applause.)* Our conviction is based on hard facts. The Soviet Union has already drawn considerably nearer to the most powerful capitalist country, the United States, both as regards total industrial output and per capita output. *(Applause.)* Our successes in the development of science and technology are common knowledge. The Soviet Union now has everything necessary for accomplishing, within a historically brief period, the main economic task: to overtake and surpass the most developed capitalist countries in the output per head of population. *(Prolonged applause.)* The Chinese People's Republic is now working to overtake and surpass Britain within the next 15 years in the output of steel and other major industrial products. (*Applause.*) The Czechoslovak Republic has already outstripped Sweden, France and West Germany as regards per capita steel production, and France and Italy as regards production of electric power. (*Applause.*)

With the emergence of socialism beyond the bounds of a single country and with the formation of the world socialist camp, new and exceptionally important possibilities have arisen for speeding up the pace of development of the socialist economy. It is necessary to make use of these possibilities in a rational and business-like way.

In this connection I should like to discuss some questions concerning the economic co-operation of the socialist countries.

A meeting of representatives of the Communist and Workers' parties of member-countries of the Council for Economic Mutual Assistance was held in Moscow recently. The meeting was also attended by representatives of the Communist Party of China, the Korean Party of Labour, the Working People's Party of Viet-Nam and the Mongolian People's Revolutionary Party. The meeting arrived at the unanimous conclusion that today, when the economic ties between the socialist countries have grown considerably in scope and strength, the further improvement of the forms of economic co-operation and more thorough specialization and co-operation of interconnected branches of the national economy in the countries of the socialist camp acquire major significance. Consistent implementation of the measures for the further development and deepening of the international division of labour of the socialist countries, worked out by the meeting, will ensure the most expedient use of natural and economic resources, higher labour productivity, and a further rise in the standard of living of the people in each of our countries. The rational organization of economic co-operation among the socialist countries will undoubtedly speed up the development of national productive forces and strengthen the economic might of the socialist camp as a whole.

Like the November meetings of representatives of the Communist and Workers' parties, the recent Moscow meeting demonstrated the unbreakable unity of the peoples of the socialist countries and their deep interest in continuing to strengthen their commonwealth and to develop and improve co-operation among the countries of the socialist camp. (*Prolonged applause.*)

Bourgeois ideologists assert that the formation and strengthening of the socialist camp restricts the independence and national sovereignty of the countries that belong to it. The entire practice of the development of co-operation among the socialist countries since the world socialist system was formed convincingly shows that it is precisely socialism that brings to the peoples genuine state independence. The socialist camp is a voluntary union of equal and sovereign states in which no one seeks or strives for any special rights, privileges or advantages for himself. It goes without saying that each socialist country independently decides the question of the forms of its co-operation with the other socialist countries. There is not and cannot be any compulsion in this matter.

But is it possible for the sake of the victory of socialism, to make full use of the rich possibilities possessed by the socialist countries, if each of them acts alone and "stews in its own juice," so to speak? Is it possible, in the present international conditions, to ensure the reliable defence of the gains of socialism, if the socialist countries act in an un-coordinated way? Of course not.

It is only the unity of the socialist countries that ensures the maximum utilization of the advantages of the world socialist system and enhances its strength and might in the struggle to prevent a new war, and in the economic competition with capitalism. Life has convincingly demonstrated that the strengthening of the unity of the countries of the socialist camp, far from infringing on the national interests of any of these countries, is a reliable guarantee of their national independence and sovereignty. (*Stormy applause.*)

The Communist and Workers' parties unanimously agree that only the unity of the socialist countries and the strengthening of all-round co-operation and fraternal mutual assistance based on the great principles of proletarian internationalism ensure the common advance of the socialist economy and the raising of the formerly backward countries to the level of the advanced ones, and make it possible to abolish the existing inequality in economic and cultural development which they have inherited from the past.

The cohesion of the countries of the socialist camp is ensured, above all, by the unity of the Communist and Workers' parties—a unity based on the unshakable principles of Marxism-Leninism, tried and tested by the experience of history. By creatively applying the general principles of Marxism-Leninism, each party works out the most expedient concrete forms for embodying these principles in the conditions of its own country, and thereby makes its contribution to the theory and practice of socialist construction, to the development of Marxism-Leninism. (*Applause.*)

Our great teacher, Vladimir Ilyich Lenin, attached tremendous importance to the revolutionary creative endeavour of the masses in producing, developing and perfecting concrete forms and methods of struggle for the triumph of the socialist revolution and the new social system. "Marxism," wrote Lenin, "differs from all other socialist theories in the remarkable way it combines complete scientific sobriety in the analysis of the objective state of affairs and the objective course of evolution with the most definite recognition of the importance of the revolutionary energy, the revolutionary creative genius and the revolutionary initiative of the masses. . . ." (*Works,* 4th Russ. ed., Vol. 13, pp. 21-22.)

The creative development of Marxist-Leninist theory is the concern of the entire international communist movement, of all the revolutionary parties of the working class. (*Applause.*) It is well known, for example, what an immense contribution to the theory and practice of socialist revolution and the building of socialism is being made by the Communist Party of China, which skilfully combines the universal truth of Marxism-Leninism with the concrete practice of the revolution and socialist construction in its own country. Also of great value for the development of Marxist-Leninist theory is the creative elaboration of the problems of the transition period by the Communist and Workers' parties of the socialist countries of Europe and Asia, and notably the experience of the Bulgarian Communist Party in the reconstruction of agriculture on socialist lines. (*Applause.*)

The forms of agricultural producers' co-operation worked out and applied in the People's Republic of Bulgaria are one of the examples of the correct combination of the general laws of the socialist transformation of agriculture with the concrete conditions and special features of Bulgaria. (*Applause.*) The experience of your Party has once again confirmed the fact that, whatever the special national features, there is no way of attracting the broad masses of the peasants to socialism other than that of the Lenin's co-operative plan, which has been tried and tested by life itself. (*Prolonged applause.*)

The fraternal Communist and Workers' parties greatly value the importance of the decisions of the 20th Congress of the Communist Party of the Soviet Union in the development of Marxism-Leninism. They have pointed out that these decisions initiated a new stage in the international communist movement and have facilitated its further development.

The Communist and Workers' parties of the capitalist countries, in working out forms and methods of working-class struggle in the present situation for gaining politi-

cal power, are enriching the Leninist theory of the socialist revolution.

The Declaration of the Meeting of Representatives of
the Communist and Workers' Parties of the Socialist Countries rightly says: "Creative application of the general
laws of socialist construction, tried and tested by experience, and the variety of forms and methods of building socialism used in different countries, represent a collective
contribution to Marxist-Leninist theory." This collective
contribution contains a part from each Communist Party,
a part of the experience of all countries that are building
socialism. (*Applause.*)

The force and significance of the Declaration consist in
the fact that it summarizes the vast experience of socialist
construction in the U.S.S.R. and the People's Democracies,
the experience of the international working-class and communist movement, the experience of the world movement for national liberation. This historic document
further develops, in a creative way, the basic principles
of Marxism-Leninism as applied to the conditions of our
era.

In speaking of the creative development of the theory
of Marxism-Leninism in present-day conditions, we cannot remain silent about the assertions—assertions which
are wrong in principle—contained in the draft programme
of the League of Communists of Yugoslavia. This draft
alleges that "in recent decades Marxist thought has lagged
behind the development of contemporary society" and
that as a result of this "many vacuums have arisen in the
further scientific, Marxist elucidation of contemporary social problems, and particularly in the elucidation of the
laws and contradictions of the period of transition from
capitalism to socialism."

How is it possible to assert that in recent decades the
development of Marxist-Leninist thought, particularly in
elaborating the laws governing the transition period, has
lagged behind, when it is precisely during these years

441

that the Communist Party of the Soviet Union and the entire international communist movement have introduced so much that is new in Marxist-Leninist theory!

During these years socialism was built in the Soviet Union for the first time in the history of mankind. (*Stormy applause.*) In a number of countries in Europe and Asia the revolutionary transfer of power into the hands of the working class was carried out under the guidance of the Communist parties and a new form of the dictatorship of the proletariat—people's democracy—has arisen and developed. Socialism has emerged beyond the bounds of a single country and has become a world system. The Communist Party of China and the other fraternal parties of the People's Democracies have carried out on a large scale the transformation of capitalist industry and trade and have found specific forms for applying Lenin's co-operative plan. The Patriotic and National Front headed by the Marxist-Leninist parties, a form of uniting the working masses to fight for socialism, has developed in all the People's Democracies.

Isn't it clear that the assertions about the so-called "vacuums" in the development of Marxist-Leninist theory are contrary to reality and, in our opinion, show that the Yugoslav leaders are ignoring the practice of socialist construction in other countries and the experience of the fraternal Communist and Workers' parties?

Attempts have been made in the draft programme of the League of Communists of Yugoslavia and in speeches by Yugoslav leaders at the 7th Congress of the League to accuse other Communist parties of the socialist countries of "practicism."

What the Yugoslav comrades seem to mean by "practicism" is that the Communist and Workers' parties of the socialist countries are concentrating their main efforts on working out and applying practical measures which ensure the development of the economy and culture and an improvement in the people's standards of living. We maintain that such "practicism" is in keeping with the fundamental interests of the masses, with the interests of socialism. The masses of the working people judge of the advantages of the socialist system and its superiority over the capitalist system first and foremost by such matters as who wields political power, who owns the means of production; they judge by the results of economic development, by the successes of science and technology, by the advance in the cultural and material standards of the working people in the socialist countries. (*Stormy applause.*) It is precisely the elaboration of the questions of the theory and practice of building socialism and communism which, in our opinion, constitutes a genuinely creative development of Marxism-Leninism.

We Communists attach great importance to revolutionary theory and we are achieving all our successes precisely because we are always guided by Marxist-Leninist teaching. The theory of Marxism-Leninism is our compass, our guiding star. The strength of Marxism-Leninism lies in its unbreakable bonds with life, with the processes of social development. (*Applause.*)

It is well known that socialism appeals to the working people even if they do not have a complete grasp of the theory of scientific socialism. The working people want to get rid of capitalism and of its incurable evils and vices. They are looking for a way out of the hopelessness of capitalism, and only when a revolutionary party, armed with the scientific theory of communism, organizes the workers, peasants and intelligentsia in the right way and leads them to fight for the building of a new life—only then does Marxist-Leninist theory become comprehensible and accessible to the broadest mass of the working people.

In drawing the working masses into revolutionary struggle and in concentrating their energies on the accomplishment of the concrete tasks of transforming society, a Marxist party thereby creates conditions in which the workers and peasants are able, not only to grasp with their minds, but also to learn from their own experience the correctness and vitality of the victorious teaching of Marxism-Leninism. The further development of the theoretical principles proceeds on the basis of the practice of the revolutionary struggle and socialist construction.

The working class of Russia, in alliance with the working peasantry and under the leadership of the Communist Party, which creatively applied and developed Marxist theory, took power into its own hands in October 1917, in order to refashion the economy and the entire life of the country along socialist lines.

The great Lenin, in the very first years of Soviet rule, working out the plans for the building of socialism, set the paramount task of developing heavy industry—the cornerstone for promoting the advance of all branches of the national economy. A concrete plan for our country's electrification was worked out under the guidance of Lenin, who called this plan the "second programme of the Party." Doesn't this show that Lenin examined questions of the theory and practice of the building of socialism in their inseparable unity?

After the working class takes power, the socialist state has to tackle many questions of economic and cultural development. The theory of Marxism-Leninism is embodied and further developed in the course of building socialism.

In the 40 years the Soviet state has been in existence our Party has done an immense job of work, directing the creative efforts of the Soviet people towards the building of socialist society.

Take, for example, some of the questions which the Communist Party of the Soviet Union has tackled recently. The Party has done a great job in reorganizing the management of industry and construction, which is having a tremendous economic effect. Now it can be asked: "Is this a theoretical or a practical question?" It is a question which has both tremendous practical and tremendous theoretical significance.

Our Party has carried out a number of important measures in agriculture, which have resulted in the opening up of tremendous reserves and possibilities in our country. Agriculture in the Soviet Union is now making rapid progress. At the beginning of 1955, a six-year programme for the development of livestock farming was worked out. As a result of implementing the measures worked out by our Party on the basis of the Marxist-Leninist principles of socialist economic management, and of the profound understanding by the masses of the necessity for these measures, the six-year plan for the production of milk and dairy produce has been fulfilled ahead of schedule, in three years. (*Applause.*)

A year ago leading collective and state farms of the Soviet Union, supported by the Central Committee of the Party, put forward the task of catching up with, and surpassing, the United States in the per capita production of meat, milk and butter within the next few years. We are sure that this task will be successfully accomplished. (*Applause.*)

Are these practical or theoretical questions? We consider that they are first of all practical questions. But if the national economy of a socialist country is forging ahead, if social wealth is increasing every year, if the labour of the people is being better remunerated and if the well-being of the working people is improving, this means that the positions of socialism are growing stronger, that the principles of Marxist-Leninist theory are being realized. As you see, these questions are major theoretical questions. (*Applause.*)

On the initiative of the Central Committee of the C.P.S.U., a law was adopted recently on the further development of the collective-farm system and the reorganization of the machine and tractor stations. Now machines are sold directly to the collective farms, and the machine and tractor stations have been reorganized into maintenance and repair stations. The spring field work carried out on the collective farms has demonstrated that this measure has been fully justified. The tractors and other agricultural machines are being used on the collective farms, not worse, but better than in the machine and tractor stations. Now, is this only a practical question or only a theoretical one? It is a question of both the theory and practice of the building of socialism. ("Hear! Hear!" *Applause.*)

The May Plenary Meeting of the Central Committee of the C.P.S.U. adopted a big programme for the development of the chemical industry of the Soviet Union. Fulfilment of this programme will ensure further technical progress in many branches of the national economy of our country and will make it possible to accomplish more quickly the task of increasing the production of consumer goods.

At first glance all these are strictly practical questions but at the same time they are also theoretical. Here we have two sides of a single whole: theory and practice. By our achievements in developing industry, farming and culture, we are demonstrating in a striking way the superiority of our theoretical thought, the strength and viability of Marxist-Leninist theory, on the basis of which socialist society is being built. By applying this theory in practice, by developing the socialist economy, by blazing new trails into the future, we affirm and develop revolutionary theory, enriching it with the experience of the millions. (*Stormy, prolonged applause.*)

Every practical question of the building of socialism is at the same time also a theoretical question, directly related to the creative development of Marxism-Leninism. The one cannot be separated from the other.

Theory without practice is sterile. Sometimes, as you know, an orchard blossoms and a man rejoices when he looks at the blossoming trees. He expects that in the autumn the orchard will yield an abundant crop of fruit and reward his labour. But blossom time passes and the man sees that after the blossoms have fallen off no ovary has been formed. So there will be no fruit, and this is a great disappointment. The man feels that his high hopes and expectations have been deceived. When the orchard blossomed and was full of fragrance, he rejoiced and expected plenty of fruit. But the orchard didn't provide him with that fruit and the work he had put in turned out to have been in vain. The orchard which the man had cultivated didn't reward him for his efforts.

People are also equally badly disappointed in theoreticians who are fruitless. (*Laughter.*) Listening to the flowery speeches and to the reasoning of certain theoretical phrase-mongers, people are sometimes enraptured and begin to believe the high-sounding phrases of such men. But then they see that in practice nothing comes of the beautiful words. (*Animation. Applause.*) The beautiful words remain empty promises, without any connection with life. And when people see that the grandiloquent phrases of such "theoreticians" are blossoms without fruit, are empty prattle, are sterile, they turn away from such "theoreticians" and from their "theories." ("Hear! Hear!" *Prolonged applause.*)

The revolutionary theory of Marxism-Leninism has great and all-conquering power precisely because it is inseparably bound up with life, with the processes of social development, and undergoes its historic test in life itself. (*Applause.*)

Practice that is not illumined by an advanced revolutionary theory is doomed to grope in the dark. Marxist-Leninist theory lights up for the working class, the working people, the ways to the solution of practical problems in building socialism and communism. (*Applause.*) But theory alone, without practice, is dead and barren. Lenin, in ridiculing people divorced from life and steeped in abstract theoretical arguments, said: "We are of the opinion that the practice of the **mass** working-class movement is in no way less important than theory and that only this practice can subject our principles to a serious **test**. 'Theory, my friend, is grey, but green is the eternal tree of life!' " (*Applause.*) (*Works*, 4th Russ. ed., Vol. 20, pp. 495-96.)

Theoretical propositions which seemed infallible were repeatedly put forward in the history of human society, but they did not stem from life itself and were not confirmed by practice. Such theoretical postulate soon died, without being of any benefit to mankind.

The vitality of Marxist-Leninist theory lies in that, having arisen in the course of the struggle of the working class, it develops in inseparable unity with practice, furnishing mankind with answers to the most urgent questions. The correctness of the Marxist-Leninist theoretical propositions is confirmed and proved by the practice of the struggle to build communist society. It is confirmed by the wealth of experience of our Party and all the fraternal parties of the socialist countries. It is confirmed by the experience of the Communist parties in the capitalist countries which, guided by revolutionary theory, are leading the struggle of the working class and of all working people for liberation from capitalist slavery, for the building of a socialist society.

Communism is not an abstract philosophical concept. It has a definite content: the need to abolish the exploiting classes and the exploitation of man by man, to establish a social system in which all the material and spiritual values created are social property and the people who create these values dispose of them themselves at their own discretion and enjoy all the fruits of their labour, working according to their abilities and receiving according to their needs.

Communism is the radiant future, and mankind is striving for it. (*Stormy applause.*)

Some "theoreticians" try in every way to belittle the practical activities of the Communist and Workers' parties in building socialism, scornfully dubbing them "practicism," but they themselves do not want to analyze, either from the standpoint of theory or of practice, the question of why they themselves are getting hand-outs from the imperialist countries. (*Animation.* "Hear! Hear!" *Stormy applause.*)

It is clear, however, to every conscious working man that the advance of the socialist economy cannot be promoted by that method. A fine method, indeed, to promote socialism, to develop Marxist-Leninist theory!

While such ill-starred theoreticians are sometimes not aware of what harm can be done to the cause of the working class by the "theories" they put forward, the imperialist circles know very well what they want and are doing everything in their power to support and encourage the things that help them in the struggle against communism.

I don't want to offend anyone, but at the same time I cannot help asking a question which is worrying honest Communists everywhere. Why do the imperialist leaders, who seek to wipe the socialist states from the face of the earth and to crush the communist movement, at the same time finance one of the socialist countries, give it credits on easy terms and hand-outs? (*Laughter, applause.*) No one will believe that there are two socialisms in the world: one that is viciously hated by world reaction, and another acceptable to the imperialists, to which they render assistance and support. (*Laughter, applause.*)

Everyone knows that the imperialists have never given anyone money for nothing, simply because they like his "beautiful eyes." They invest their capital only in enterprises from which they hope to get good profits. (*Animation, applause.*)

If the imperialists agree to render "aid" to a socialist state they do so, of course, not in order to strengthen it. The monopoly circles of the United States can by no means be suspected of being interested in strengthening socialism and developing Marxist-Leninist theory. (*Laugh-*

ier, applause.) Representatives of this particular country allege that we are deviating from Marxism-Leninism, but claim that they themselves are taking a correct stand. We get quite a curious situation—the imperialists want to "develop" Marxism-Leninism through this country. (*Laughter.*) It is appropriate to recall. Bebel's apt words: "If the enemy praises you, think what stupid thing you have done." (*Laughter. Prolonged applause.*)

While the imperialists are uniting their efforts in their attacks on socialism, on the working class, some leaders who call themselves fighters for socialism are trying to weaken the determination of the working class in the struggle against capitalism, to weaken the vanguard of the working class, the Communist and Workers' parties, to blunt their vigilance, to weaken the unity of the socialist countries.

With such "allies," the aggressive circles of the bourgeoisie may really cherish certain hopes and rejoice that their attempts to undermine the socialist states from within may prove successful. But I must tell you in confidence that these illusory hopes of the imperialists are also doomed to failure, and the capital invested in this "business" will be wasted, as has happened every time the imperialists have tried to base their calculations on a weakening of the unity of the Communist and Workers' parties. (*Stormy, prolonged applause.* "Hear! Hear!" *Delegates and guests rise and scan*: "C.P.S.U.!")

The Communist parties safeguard and preserve the unity of their ranks like the apple of their eye. They wage an irreconcilable struggle against revisionism and dogmatism. In this struggle the main fire of the Communist parties is, naturally, directed against the revisionists, as scouts of the imperialist camp. The ancient legend of the Trojan horse is widely known. When its enemies could not take the city of Troy by siege and storm, they "presented" a wooden horse to the Trojans, in which they concealed their own men so that they could open the city gates at night.

Modern revisionism is a kind of Trojan horse. ("Hear! Hear!" *Applause.*) The revisionists are trying to undermine the revolutionary parties from within, to undermine their unity, to sow disorder and confusion in Marxist-Leninist ideology. (*Cries of* "They will fail!" *Applause.*)

Comrades, the Communist and Workers' parties in their historic Declaration unanimously and sharply condemned revisionism, when they said that under present conditions it is the main danger in the international communist movement. Revisionism is Right-wing opportunism, a manifestation of bourgeois ideology which paralyzes the revolutionary energy of the working class and demands the preservation or the restoration of capitalism. The Declaration most correctly stresses that "the existence of bourgeois influence is an internal source of revisionism, while surrender to imperialist pressure is its external source."

The Communists of all countries have warmly endorsed the Declaration adopted by the meeting of the fraternal parties of the socialist countries and have acknowledged it to be an all-important programme document of the international communist movement giving a profound Marxst-Leninist analysis of the basic objective laws of social levelopment in the present epoch and defining the tasks of he world communist movement with exceptional clarity.

Of all the Communist and Workers' parties, only one. the League of Communists of Yugoslavia, announced its disagreement with the Declaration and thereby set itself up against all the Marxist-Leninist parties of the world. This position of the Yugoslav leaders is most clearly expressed in the draft programme of the League of Communists of Yugoslavia and in the work of the League's 7th Congress. All the Communist and Workers' parties have shown complete unanimity in resolutely condemning the evisionist postulates contrary to Marxism-Leninism contained in the League's programme and the wrong attitude of the Yugoslav leaders.

In this connection, allow me, Comrades Delegates, to express certain views regarding the relations between the Communist Party of the Soviet Union and the League of Communists of Yugoslavia. I consider it desirable to express these views at your congress, because they not only concern the relations between the Communist Party of the Soviet Union and the League of Communists of Yugoslavia, but they also affect the relations of all the fraternal parties with the League of Communists of Yugoslavia.

As I have already pointed out, the Declaration of the fraternal parties expressed their common viewpoint and defined, on the basis of Marxist-Leninist principles, their common views on the major questions of our time.

Marx, Engels and Lenin always attached primary importance to the struggle for the purity of the ideological principles of scientific communism. They were irreconcilable to each and every attempt to deprive the militant theory of the working class of its revolutionary soul. They have taught us that the theory of scientific communism is the chief ideological weapon of the working class in its struggle for its emancipation and for the transformation of society on communist lines. They have taught us that without revolutionary theory there can be no revolutionary movement.

We all know what a tremendous struggle Lenin waged against international revisionism and against the opportunism of Bernstein, Kautsky and their like, in upholding revolutionary creative Marxism. In this irreconcilable ideological struggle the Marxist-Leninist parties of the working class, which have now become a mighty organizing and inspiring force of the international working-class movement, have grown, have been strengthened and have become steeled.

True to the behests of our teachers and leaders, the Communist and Workers' parties are vigilantly guarding the purity of Marxist-Leninist principles and are very sensitive to any distortions of these principles and deviations from them. The Marxist-Leninist parties consistently and resolutely oppose those who seek to weaken the unity of the fraternal Communist parties, to undermine the international unity of the working class of all countries, to disorganize their revolutionary struggle. Those who call themselves Marxist-Leninists but who in practice, whether they want to or not, play the part of agents of the class enemy in the working-class movement are particularly dangerous to the revolutionary struggle. The Communist and Workers' parties are therefore very particular about questions of theory and are irreconcilable with regard to any attempts to revise Marxism-Leninism. (*Applause.*)

The relations of our parties with the League of Communists of Yugoslavia have their history. Some important moments in this history should be recalled at the present time.

You know that prior to 1948, good relations had existed between Yugoslavia and the Soviet Union—relations formed in the joint struggle against the fascist invaders during the Second World War and the first post-war years. In September 1947, when imperialist reaction began intensive attacks against the socialist countries, the Communist Parties of the Soviet Union and the European People's Democracies and also certain Communist parties in capitalist countries of Europe established the Information Bureau of Communist and Workers' Parties (the *Informburo*), whose working bodies were in the initial period in Belgrade.

Looking back, it should be said that at a definite stage the Information Bureau played a positive part in the history of the revolutionary Marxist-Leninist movement, in the consolidation of the forces of the Communist and Workers' parties on the basis of the principles of proletarian internationalism and in the struggle for lasting peace, democracy and socialism. (*Prolonged applause.*)

The Communist Party of Yugoslavia, together with the Communist Party of the Soviet Union and a number of other fraternal parties, was one of the organizers of the Information Bureau and was an energetic participant in its activities during the initial period. That is how matters stood prior to 1948. Then came the worsening of relations between the Communist Party of Yugoslavia and the other fraternal parties.

In 1948, a meeting of the Information Bureau adopted a resolution on "The Situation in the Communist Party of Yugoslavia," which contained just criticism of the activities of the Communist Party of Yugoslavia on a number of questions of principle. This resolution was correct in the main and corresponded to the interests of the revolutionary movement. Subsequently, in the period from 1949 to 1953, a conflict arose between the Communist Party of Yugoslavia and the other fraternal parties, when in the course of the struggle mistakes were made and one thing piled up on another, which did harm to our common cause.

With full awareness of its responsibility to our countries and peoples, to the international communist movement, the Communist Party of the Soviet Union took the initiative in order to end this conflict, to achieve a normalization of relations between our countries, to establish contact and co-operation between the Communist Party of the Soviet Union and the League of Communists of Yugoslavia on a Marxist-Leninist basis. With this aim in view, talks were held on our initiative in May and June 1955 between representatives of the Soviet Union and Yugoslavia and these talks ended in the signing of the Belgrade Declaration. It is very important to note that during the talks in Belgrade, Comrade Tito was in favour of not raking up the past, of starting our relations on a new basis. We readily agreed to this and for our part did everything possible to strengthen friendly relations. In so doing we were aware that there remained ideological differences between our parties on a number of important questions. For our part, we showed a great deal of restraint and patience in order to achieve a unity of views on the basis of principle, on the basis of Marxism-Leninism.

Life has shown, however, that the burden of the past has weighed too heavily on the Yugoslav leaders and they have proved incapable of abandoning their wrong positions and firmly adopting the positions of Marxism-Leninism. The Yugoslav leaders, even after relations had been normalized continued to make anti-Soviet statements and made attacks on the socialist camp and the fraternal Communist parties. The Yugoslav leaders did particularly great harm to the cause of socialism by their public pronouncements and their actions during the Hungarian events. During the counter-revolutionary putsch in Budapest, the Yugoslav Embassy, in effect, became a centre for those who had started the struggle against the people's democratic system in Hungary, a refuge for the treacherous and capitulator Nagy-Losonczy group. Remember the unprecedented speech made by Comrade Tito in Pulj, in which he took the rebels in Hungary under his protection, while describing the fraternal assistance of the U.S.S.R. to the Hungarian people as "Soviet intervention"—a speech which contained direct calls to certain forces in other socialist countries to follow the so-called "Yugoslav road."

We know very well what that road is, comrades. Let him who wants to, follow that road. But parties which really adhere to Marxism-Leninism will not follow it. (*Applause.*) Our socialist countries, with the compass of Marxism-Leninism, are firmly following the road to communism. (*Prolonged applause.*)

In view of this attitude on the part of the Yugoslav leaders we have been compelled to come out with open criticism of their views and actions. Our position has been fully supported by all the Communist and Workers' parties. Thus it is not the fraternal parties, standing as they do on Marxist-Leninist positions of principle, but the

Yugoslav leaders, who by their splitting activities against the socialist countries and the fraternal parties have isolated Yugoslavia and the League of Communists of Yugoslavia from the socialist countries and the international communist movement.

Subsequently, on the initiative of the Yugoslav leaders the well-known meeting of delegations of the Soviet Union and Yugoslavia took place in Bucharest in August 1957. During that meeting we frankly outlined to the Yugoslav leaders our views concerning the policy of the League of Communists of Yugoslavia, both on the Hungarian question and on other questions. As a result of the talks, accord was reached on the main problems of the present international situation, although it was recognized that there were certain differences between us on ideological questions.

During the meeting in Bucharest we hoped to find a common language and to pave the way for further friendly co-operation. At the same time we frankly told the Yugoslav leaders that if they continued to make attacks on the countries of the socialist camp and fraternal parties, not a single one of those attacks would remain unanswered by us. I say this with all responsibility before the fraternal Communist Party of Bulgaria, which we respect for its courage and devotion to the great ideas of Marxism-Leninism. (*Stormy, prolonged applause.*)

At the Bucharest meeting it was agreed that a delegation of the League of Communists of Yugoslavia would take part in the planned meeting of the fraternal parties of the socialist countries and in drafting a declaration of that meeting. Subsequent events showed, however, that the Yugoslav leaders retreated from the positions agreed upon. They refused to sign the Declaration of the Communist and Workers' Parties of the Socialist Countries, and decided to come out with their own platform, the draft programme of the League of Communists of Yugoslavia, which is opposed to the common views of the Marxist-Leninist parties and which claims to be a programme document for the international communist and working-class movement.

The programme of the League of Communists of Yugoslavia is, of course, an internal affair of the Yugoslav Communists. But since the draft of that programme contains tendentious and insulting appraisals of other parties and socialist countries, and revises the foundations of the revolutionary theory of Marxism-Leninism, our Party considered it its direct duty to criticize the anti-Marxist propositions of that document. The position of our Party—a position based on principle and set out in the letters of the Central Committee of the C.P.S.U. and in our Party press —has been unanimously supported and approved by all the Communist and Workers' parties.

Rejecting the comradely criticism, based on principle, from the fraternal parties, the Yugoslav leaders have again found themselves in isolation, continuing stubbornly to uphold their erroneous anti-Marxist views. Instead of seriously analyzing the reasons that have placed the League of Communists of Yugoslavia in a difficult position, the Yugoslav leaders are trying to accuse the fraternal parties of not being objective with regard to them and of interfering in the internal affairs of the League of Communists of Yugoslavia. This is indeed a case of putting the blame on someone else! (*Animation.*)

Some Yugoslav comrades are trying to find differences in the assessment of their mistakes by individual Communist and Workers' parties. They attack the Communist Party of the Soviet Union and they would like in some way to single out the Communist Party of China, claiming that it criticizes their mistakes in some special manner. But attempts to find different shades in the criticism of present-day revisionism by the fraternal parties are vain. All the fraternal parties are at one on this matter. We consider that the Chinese comrades and also the other fraternal parties are rightly and profoundly criticizing the revisionist propositions of the draft programme of the

457

League of Communists of Yugoslavia and are consistently upholding the principles of Marxism-Leninism. We fully agree with this criticism based on principle. The forces of socialism and the unity of the Communist and Workers' parties can grow stronger only in the struggle against revisionism, in the struggle for the purity of Marxist-Leninist theory. (*Prolonged applause.*)

The weekly journal *Komunist*, organ of the League of Communists of Yugoslavia, the other day published an article on the third anniversary of the signing of the Belgrade Declaration. It may seem at first glance that the article is written in calm tones and aims at easing tension that has arisen in the League's relations with the other fraternal parties. But in fact this article is utterly wrong and tries to justify the erroneous position of the Yugoslav leaders. Thus, for example, the article contains an assertion that the struggle for peace is, so it claims, the chief content of the struggle for socialism. One cannot agree with such an assertion.

It is an indisputable fact that those who fight for socialism consistently fight for the cause of peace. But peace is also upheld by many personalities who do not support the principles of socialism. Even some Conservatives, members of the clergy and various bourgeois public and political leaders fight for peace. Of course, we join forces with them in the struggle for peace. Thus, people and organizations of different views and political convictions can and do unite in the struggle for peace.

Matters, however, are altogether different with regard to the struggle for the victory of socialism. Here one cannot count on pooling the efforts of the working class and capitalists, of Communist parties and bourgeois parties. The struggle for the victory of socialism demands unity of views and unity of action by the parties of the working class which adhere to Marxism-Leninism. It demands consistent adherence to the principles of proletarian internationalism and the fraternal mutual assistance of the peoples building socialism. (*Applause.*)

We have adhered, and continue to adhere to the view that it is necessary to strengthen in every way co-operation with all states in the struggle for peace and international security. We want to maintain such relations with the Federal People's Republic of Yugoslavia as well. But as Communists, we would like to have more: we would like to reach an understanding and co-operation on Party lines. The Yugoslav Communists have rich revolutionary experience and have done great service in the struggle against our common class enemies. The working class and the entire working people of Yugoslavia made a notable contribution to the struggle against fascism in the Second World War. Of course, if co-operation on Party lines is not achieved, we shall maintain and develop normal relations with Yugoslavia along state lines. At the same time we frankly declare that we shall not tolerate distortions in questions of ideology; we shall safeguard the unity of the Marxist-Leninist parties and shall fight for the purity of revolutionary theory.

Comrades, I recall a conversation I had with the Yugoslav leaders in 1956, when we were exchanging views in a friendly talk. Speaking of our disagreements, I drew Comrade Tito's attention to the need for a deeper analysis of the events and our mutual relations, for a correct appraisal of the situation that had developed, in order the more rapidly to secure unity of views on a basis of principle. In this conversation I reminded them of the well-known popular saying: "The whole company is marching in step, and only one soldier is out of step," and I asked who must get into step—the company or the soldier. (*Animation.*) Koča Popović, who was present during the conversation, asked:

"And who is the company, and who is the soldier?"

To that retort I replied:

459

"Ask yourself who is the company and who is the soldier."

"At any rate," I said, "every soldier knows that a company is a company and that a soldier is only part of the company, and therefore it is not the company that must get into step with the soldier, but the other way round. (*Animation. Applause.*) If you take a different attitude, then say plainly that you are not a soldier of this communist company which is marching together in step, guided by Marxism-Leninism." (*Prolonged applause.*)

We shall always guard as sacred the unity of our great Marxist-Leninist international army of fighters for communism. The fraternal Communist Parties of the Soviet Union, China, Bulgaria and other socialist countries, the Communist parties of the world are united and monolithic and they resolutely oppose contemporary revisionism. The Communists of all countries are holding high the victorious banner of Marxism-Leninism and under this glorious banner they are confidently marching to their great goal. (*Prolonged applause.*)

Comrades, the 7th Congress of the Bulgarian Communist Party is summing up the results of an important period in the building of socialism in Bulgaria and is charting the ways for a further advance to socialism. There is no doubt that the new tasks put forward by you will be successfully accomplished by the Bulgarian people, closely rallied round their militant Party of Communists.

The Bulgarian working class and all the Bulgarian people can be justly proud of their Communist Party. (*Stormy applause.*) For decades it was tempered in fierce battles against imperialist reaction, against the forces of fascism, and it aroused the working class and the working peasantry to struggle for a free socialist Bulgaria. Many of the finest sons of your Party gave their lives for the great cause of the working class.

Your Party was reared by Dimitr Blagoyev and Georgi Dimitrov in the spirit of profound loyalty to Marxism-

Leninism and irreconcilability towards any deviations from it. These splendid qualities are manifested with fresh force in the staunch struggle of the Bulgarian Communists for the building of socialism, for unbreakable friendship and unity among all the socialist countries and the Communist and Workers' parties. By its Leninist internationalist policy and its loyalty to our common cause, the Bulgarian Communist Party has won profound respect in the international communist movement, in the ranks of all the fraternal parties. (*Prolonged applause.*)

For us, the Communist Party of the Soviet Union, a fraternal party always closely linked with the Bulgarian Communist Party, it is pleasant to note that the correct line and policy of the Bulgarian Communist Party, both on questions concerning socialist construction in the People's Republic of Bulgaria and on questions of the international communist and working-class movement, are proof of the Marxist-Leninist maturity of its leadership, of the ability of its Central Committee to develop the principles of Marxism-Leninism creatively and apply them in practice. (*Prolonged applause.*)

We are firmly convinced that, rallying its ranks still closer round this tried and tested leadership, the Bulgarian Communist Party will achieve new and still greater victories in building socialism in the People's Republic of Bulgaria and will always march in the front ranks of the international communist movement. (*Stormy applause.*)

The relations between the Communist Party of the Soviet Union and the Bulgarian Communist Party have always been, and continue to be the best, genuinely fraternal relations. They were so at the time when the leadership of the Bulgarian Communist Party was headed by a great son of the Bulgarian people, Georgi Dimitrov, and they remain so after his death, when in the leadership of the Bulgarian Communist Party and the People's Republic of Bulgaria there are loyal followers of Dimitrov, true

Marxist Leninists, headed by the Political Bureau of the Central Committee of the Bulgarian Communist Party (*Stormy, prolonged applause.*)

Allow me, on behalf of the Central Committee of the Communist Party of the Soviet Union, to express our pleasure at the fact that complete understanding and fraternal alliance have always existed on all questions between our parties, just as they have existed between our states. Whatever questions we have discussed with each other, we have always seen that the representatives of the fraternal Communist Party of Bulgaria have approached these questions from the same standpoint as the Communist Party of the Soviet Union, from the positions of Marxism-Leninism. (*Stormy, prolonged applause. Shouts of approval. All rise.*)

That understanding of our common tasks is founded on the unswerving application of the principles of Marxism-Leninism by which we are guided, and which are being consistently implemented by the Central Committee of the Bulgarian Communist Party, headed by its Political Bureau and the First Secretary of the Central Committee, Comrade Zhivkov. (*Stormy applause.*)

Our relations with the People's Republic of Bulgaria along state lines are developing exceptionally favourably. Between our countries, just as between our parties, there have never been any divergencies, nor even a trace of divergencies. The Government of the People's Republic of Bulgaria, headed by Comrade Yugov, guided by the vital interests of its people and its state, by the interests of world peace, is pursuing this line consistently on all questions concerning the country's internal development and international relations. (*Applause.*) We and the Bulgarian comrades have never had different points of view; our views and appraisals have always coincided. And this is understandable, because our countries are led by parties which firmly adhere to Marxism-Leninism, to the positions of strengthening fraternal bonds between all Communist and Workers' parties, between all socialist states, to the positions of proletarian internationalism. (*Stormy applause.*)

Our unity, our solidarity are not only a slogan, not only an appeal. The unity and solidarity of the Communist and Workers' parties are a force which really exists and is constantly growing stronger. They have become an organic need for all our parties. Each Communist and Workers' Party is doing everything possible for the further consolidation of the unity of the parties adhering to Marxism-Leninism, because this furthers the attainment of our great goal—the building of communist society. This is how we understand and apply in practice the great slogan put forward more than a hundred years ago by the founders of scientific communism: "Workers of all countries, unite!" (*Prolonged applause.*)

Drawing our ranks closer together, strengthening the mighty camp of socialism and persistently striving for world peace, we indignantly reject the slander concocted by representatives of a certain party, who call themselves Communists but who in practice pursue a policy alien to communist principles. These people reason something like this: If there are no disagreements between fraternal Communist parties, this means that some one party is imposing its will upon the others, that these parties are, as it were, dependent upon that party.

To agree with such a point of view would mean splitting —in order to please the imperialists—the unity of the Communist and Workers' parties, organizing their relations in such a way that each would be acting alone, in an un-coordinated way, ignoring the experience accumulated by the other parties. All this would lead the Communist and Workers' parties to contradictory actions and, in the last analysis, to disagreements. This is precisely what is desired by certain imperialist circles who spare no efforts to win, by all kinds of hand-outs, allies of theirs in the socialist countries, people who will spread their ideology alien to Marxism-Leninism.

There is no need to say that such a policy would, of course, bring joy to our enemies, in the same way as it would do immense and truly irreparable harm to the communist and working-class movement, to the entire great cause of building socialism and communism.

But we shall never give our enemies cause for joy. We are Communists, and this means that we are consistent and true internationalists. The Communist parties resolutely condemn any policy which runs counter to the strengthening of friendship among the Communist parties, which departs from Marxist-Leninist principles.

Communists have always been and always will be faithful to the Marxist-Leninist teaching; they have always fought and always will fight against those who by their actions weaken the unity of the Communist and Workers' parties and the unity of the camp of the socialist countries, which is growing and becoming stronger. (*Applause*).

Leninist Communists differ from the so-called "Communists" precisely by the fact that they are able correctly to discern any manoeuvres by enemies designed to weaken the forces of the communist and working-class movement, to weaken the vanguard of the working masses—their Communist and Workers' parties.

We are confident that the fraternal relations, relations on a genuinely equal footing, between all the Communist and Workers' parties will continue to grow stronger and flourish for the good of the great cause we serve, for the success of which we fight—the building of communist society, the most just society on earth. (*Prolonged applause.*)

Allow me, comrades, to read this message of greetings from the Central Committee of the Communist Party of the Soviet Union to the 7th Congress of the Bulgarian Communist Party:

TO THE 7th CONGRESS OF THE BULGARIAN
COMMUNIST PARTY

The Central Committee of the Communist Party of the Soviet Union warmly greets the delegates to the 7th Congress of the Bulgarian Communist Party, the Bulgarian Communists, and all the working people of Bulgaria, and wishes them further successes in the building of socialism. (*Stormy applause.*)

Unswervingly following Marxist-Leninist principles and creatively applying them in the conditions of its own country, the Bulgarian Communist Party has achieved outstanding successes in building a socialist society. In the People's Republic of Bulgaria socialism has won a decisive victory, not only in the town, but also in the countryside. The rich experience of your Party in the socialist reorganization of agriculture is a valuable contribution to the theory and practice of the building of socialism.

In the struggle to build up the new life the alliance between the working class and the labouring peasantry has become still stronger, the moral and political unity of the Bulgarian people has been consolidated still more, and their labour activity has risen to a higher level, which is evidence of the further strengthening of the socialist state as a powerful instrument for building a new society.

The Bulgarian Communist Party bears aloft the victorious banner of Marxism-Leninism and fights irreconcilably for the purity of revolutionary theory, against any and every attempt to revise it. The Bulgarian Communists, led by their Central Committee, faithful to the behests of Georgi Dimitrov, the outstanding leader of the Bulgarian and international communist movement, guarding as sacred, and adding to, the glorious revolutionary traditions of the Bulgarian working class, displayed a high degree of loyalty to principle and staunchness in the struggle for the great ideas of proletarian internationalism, for the unity of the mighty socialist camp and the world communist movement.

The Central Committee of the Communist Party of the Soviet Union whole-heartedly wishes the Bulgarian Communists and all the working people of Bulgaria fresh victories in the building of socialism, in the struggle for the prosperity of their happy and free homeland, for the strengthening of the unity and friendship among all the socialist countries, in the struggle for world peace.

May the fraternal People's Republic of Bulgaria and its heroic people, who are building socialism, live long and flourish! (*Stormy, prolonged applause. Cheers. All rise.*)

Long live the Bulgarian Communist Party—the tried and tested guide and leader of the Bulgarian people! (*Stormy, prolonged applause. Cheers.*)

May the eternal and unbreakable friendship between the Soviet and Bulgarian peoples and the unity and solidarity of the peoples of all the socialist countries develop and go from strength to strength! (*Stormy, prolonged applause. Cheers.*)

CENTRAL COMMITTEE
OF THE COMMUNIST PARTY
OF THE SOVIET UNION

(*Stormy, prolonged ovation. Audience, standing, shouts* "Eternal friendship!", "C.P.S.U.!", "C.P.S.U.!", "C.P.S.U.!")

REPLY
TO Mr. CYRUS S. EATON

On the initiative of Mr. Cyrus S. Eaton, an industrialist well known in American public affairs, the Second Pugwash Conference of Atomic Scientists was held at Lake Beauport, Canada, from March 31 to April 11, 1958. It was attended by prominent scientists from Australia, Britain, Denmark, India, Canada, the Chinese People's Republic, the U.S.S.R., the United States, France, the Federal Republic of Germany and Japan. The conference discussed the danger of the atomic arms race.

On April 11, Mr. Eaton sent a letter to N. S. Khrushchov, Chairman of the U.S.S.R. Council of Ministers.

It reads:

Dear Mr. Khrushchov:

I have the honour to associate myself with the enclosed communication from Lord Russell and the group of scientists who have participated in the Second Pugwash Conference.

I have followed the initiative they have taken with the deepest interest, and am glad to have been able to assist them with their arrangements. I believe their deliberations may be of value in contributing to the solution of the urgent problems now facing the statesmen of the world.

Sincerely yours,

CYRUS EATON

N. S. KHRUSHCHOV'S REPLY TO CYRUS S. EATON

On June 4, the Soviet Embassy in the United States handed Mr. Eaton the following reply from N. S. Khrushchov:

Dear Mr. Eaton,

Thank you for your letter and the appended main reports of the Second Pugwash International Conference of Atomic Scientists, held in Canada in April with your active assistance and co-operation.

Having read the interesting materials of the conference, I wish to draw attention to the great importance of the efforts being made by scientists of different countries to remove the horrible danger of nuclear war that is hanging over mankind. The competent opinion of scientists on this major problem of our age is undoubtedly of considerable interest to the governments of the different countries.

In this connection I would like to point out that the Soviet Government, well aware of its responsibilities for the destinies of the world and striving to help remove the threat of atomic war and strengthen peace, has decided unilaterally to discontinue tests of all nuclear weapons as a first practical step in this direction, in the hope that other states possessing atomic weapons will also follow this example. Unfortunately, other Powers have so far not joined in this initiative.

I also wish to note the important part which you personally are playing in assisting the efforts of scientists of the world in their struggle against the atomic danger and in the establishment of mutual understanding and confidence between our countries.

With sincere respect,

N. KHRUSHCHOV

Pravda, June 6, 1958

SPEECH
AT MEETING OF SOFIA WORKING PEOPLE
TO MARK CONCLUSION OF 7th CONGRESS
OF BULGARIAN COMMUNIST PARTY

June 7, 1958

Dear Comrades and Friends,
Citizens of Sofia,

Allow me to convey to you, the working people of the glorious capital of socialist Bulgaria and through you to the entire Bulgarian people warm fraternal greetings from the Communist Party of the Soviet Union, from all the peoples of our country. (*Stormy, prolonged applause. Cheers. The audience scans,* "Eternal friendship!")

Allow me to thank with all my heart the working people of Bulgaria for the exceptionally cordial welcome which we, the representatives of the Soviet people, have received in your beautiful country. (*Prolonged applause.*)

At the invitation of the Central Committee of the Bulgarian Communist Party our delegation attended the 7th Congress, which has just concluded its work.

Like the other delegations we greatly rejoice and take pride in your Party and its glorious deeds. We have been greatly impressed by the high level of political activity and the complete unanimity that prevailed at the congress from beginning to end. (*Stormy applause.*) This atmosphere reflects the great labour enthusiasm and creative upsurge which now embraces the entire Bulgarian people, who are building the new, socialist society.

The proceedings of the Congress of the Bulgarian Communist Party have demonstrated once again the unbreakable unity of the ranks of all the Communist and Workers' parties, their loyalty to the great and victorious banner of Marxism-Leninism, to the principles of proletarian internationalism, their determination to continue to strengthen this unity, to uphold the revolutionary theory of scientific communism in the struggle against all kinds of manifestations of revisionism and opportunism. (*Applause.*) The fact that the Congress of the Bulgarian Communist Party was attended by delegations from 36 fraternal parties is conclusive proof of the cohesion of the Communist and Workers' parties, an expression of the high appreciation of the great services of your Party as one of the militant detachments of the international communist movement. (*Stormy, prolonged applause.*)

By its devoted struggle for the triumph of the great ideas of Marxism-Leninism, for the interests of the people, the party of the Bulgarian Communists has earned the love of its people and universal esteem and authority among the fraternal parties. It gives us pleasure and joy to see that our fraternal Bulgarian Communist Party is monolithic, strong, loyal to Marxism-Leninism and the principles of proletarian internationalism. The glorious Bulgarian working class, all the Bulgarian working people can take legitimate pride in their Communist Party. (*Stormy, prolonged applause. The audience scans,* "BCP!")

The decisions of the 7th Congress sum up the remarkable results of the building of socialism in Bulgaria. In a brief period tremendous changes have taken place in your country. Bulgaria, once an agrarian country with a backward agriculture and semi-artisan industry, has become a socialist industrial and agrarian Power with a flourishing economy and culture. In the post-war years socialist Bulgaria has achieved successes such as she could not have achieved in the course of many decades under the bourgeois system.

Bulgaria has existed for almost 1,500 years, but it is only in the last one and a half decades that the Bulgarian people have been the real masters of their destiny, the builders of their happiness. The victorious socialist revolution opened up to the Bulgarian workers and peasants, to the entire people, the road to a new and happy life.

We Soviet people whole-heartedly rejoice with you in the flourishing of socialist Bulgaria, before which bright new prospects are opening up. The directives of the 7th Congress for the development of the Bulgarian People's Republic show at what a swift pace your country's economy and culture will develop in the third five-year plan period.

New factories and mills will be built, all branches of industry will be further expanded. The republic's industry will turn out still greater quantities of the most varied goods. Bulgaria's agriculture has great prospects for development. You have everything needed to make your country a blossoming orchard in the next few years. (*Stormy applause.*)

Bulgaria has splendid climatic conditions, an abundance of sunshine and a fertile soil, which makes it possible to raise bumper crops of a variety of fruits and vegetables. But her main wealth is her people, the outstanding fruit and vegetable growers who are famous throughout Europe as masters of their craft. Socialist Bulgaria, covered with orchards and vineyards, will blossom and become even more beautiful. We wish from the bottom of our hearts that your orchard may be in full flower, may grow and bear its abundant fruit! (*Stormy, prolonged applause. Cheers.*)

The fulfilment of the magnificent programme for the building of socialism in Bulgaria mapped out by the 7th Party Congress depends on the efforts of the people, on their labour. By their devoted labour the people are consolidating the gains of socialism, are accomplishing the great tasks confronting socialist Bulgaria. The higher the labour productivity, the lower the production costs, i.e., the less labour will be expended per unit of goods produced, the richer the country will be, the more goods will be produced to satisfy the needs of man, both material and spiritual. And people, comrades, are the main thing. It is they who create values and give an impetus to life; in our socialist countries they are the sovereign masters of life, the builders of their happiness. (*Applause.*)

The working class, all the working people in the socialist countries, are the masters of their country. The people and the people alone are the owners of the means of production, the owners of all the wealth created by their labour. Hence, the people themselves, by their entire life and activity, test and confirm in the socialist countries the principles of the theory of Marxism-Leninism on the building of communist society.

The brilliant founders of scientific communism and our great teachers, Marx, Engels and Lenin, created the immortal teaching of the working class, demonstrated the inevitability of the victory of the working class, the working people, over the exploiting classes and showed the laws governing historical progress and the inevitability of the victory of socialism over the capitalist system, which is living out its day.

Marxism-Leninism, which has conquered the minds and the hearts of millions upon millions of people, has become a great material force. This teaching is now being developed not in the quiet of scientists' and theoreticians' studies—it has emerged into the wide expanses of life, and the working class, the labouring peasantry, all the working people have become the most active fighters for this teaching, building on the basis of the theoretical principles of Marxism-Leninism a new communist society whose construction is illumined by the unfading beacon of the theory of Marxism-Leninism. The working class, all the labouring people of our socialist countries, guided by their Communist and Workers' parties, are carrying out the theoretical principles of Marxism-Leninism in practice.

The working man in socialist society, no matter how small his sector, is making a useful contribution to society, provided he works honestly, and by his work is confirming and developing the theory of Marxism-Leninism. Guided by this theory, the working class, the working people of our countries took power into their hands and rid themselves for all time of capitalist slavery and all the calamities of capitalism. Guided by this theory, the peoples will build a communist society, the most just society on earth.

That is why we say that the further development of theoretical, social thinking is no longer the realm of individual theoreticians or a handful of people who sit in their studies and develop theory. No, today the entire people take part in this great work, because the shortening of the transition period from socialism to communism depends on their labour, on their efforts. And this is the main thing. Life itself, the activity of the Communist and Workers' parties, the practical activity of the people building socialism and communism, reaffirm the theoretical postulates of Marxism-Leninism, give rise to the new that helps develop these theoretical principles.

Whereas in the past the revolutionary theory of social development was accessible only to a certain group of people who studied theoretical problems, in our concrete socialist conditions this theory has now become accessible to the broadest masses of the people. And the masses of the working people of socialist society who take part in the noblest cause—the building of communism—have become the creators of this theory, the participants in the materialization of this theory in practice, in the development of theoretical thought. The theory of Marxism-Leninism has merged with the practice of the building of communism and therein, comrades, lies its irresistible, vital force. A people whose ideology is Marxism-Leninism is invincible. (*Stormy applause.*)

Dear comrades, the socialist camp, gaining in strength and scope, is a source of great happiness for all the peoples of the socialist countries, including the Bulgarian people. This camp ensures their freedom and independence, reliably guarantees the defence of the gains of socialism and provides fraternal mutual assistance in building socialism. (*Prolonged applause.*)

The peoples of our countries are vitally interested in a lasting and stable peace. They threaten no one. They are fighting for peace, against war and the danger of war. War is alien to the very nature of the socialist countries, who are coming out as the champions of the security of the peoples, as the standard-bearers of peace. (*Applause.*)

Let us look, for instance, at the Balkans. It is well known that the Balkan peninsula was called for many years the powder barrel of Europe, a breeding ground of constant conflicts and armed clashes. The tenser the relations between the imperialist states were, the more dangerous the situation in the Balkans became. The peoples of the Balkan countries still remember the immeasurable calamities which they experienced as a result of military clashes.

After the Second World War, when a large proportion of the Balkan countries took the socialist road, the situation in that part of the world changed fundamentally. The Balkan socialist countries not only live in fraternal friendship among themselves, but are also consistently carrying through a policy of peace and co-operation with their neighbours. This has created a completely new situation in the Balkans.

The Soviet Union, though not a Balkan country, lies in immediate proximity to them. That is why our people cannot remain indifferent to what is going on in that part

of the world. Our country, like the other socialist countries, is vitally interested in seeing that the cause of peace
in the Balkans, just as in the rest of the world, continues
to grow stronger, that all peoples of the Balkan countries,
all peoples of the world live in peace and concord. (*Stormy applause.*)

Dear comrades, we have spent only a week in your
wonderful country, but even this brief space of time has
enabled us to feel with all our hearts the depth and sincerity of the sentiments the fraternal Bulgarian people
entertain for the peoples of the Soviet Union. (*Stormy applause. Cheers. The audience scans,* "Eternal friendship!")

The close friendship between the peoples of our countries is of long standing and has great and glorious traditions. Our peoples have more than once fought shoulder
to shoulder against foreign enslavers. The progressives of
our countries had always been ideologically linked in the
common struggle for progress and the happiness of the
people. But the friendship between our peoples has become especially cordial since the time when Bulgaria took
the road of socialism.

As brothers, as true comrades in the common cause, we
are marching towards our bright future—communism.
There is no force in the world which could separate our
peoples. (*Stormy, prolonged applause. Cheers. The audience scans,* ' Eternal friendship!")

Let me assure you, our dear comrades and brothers,
that the Bulgarian people have in the Soviet people a true
and dependable friend on whom they can rely always and
in all respects. (*Stormy, prolonged applause. Cheers.*)

We wish the Bulgarian people, the Bulgarian Communist Party further big successes in the struggle for socialism, for world peace! (*Stormy, prolonged applause.
Cheers.*)

Long live the Bulgarian people, our true friends and
brothers! (*Stormy, prolonged applause. Cheers. The
audience scans,* "Eternal friendship!")

Long live the leader of the Bulgarian people—the heroic Bulgarian Communist Party and its Central Committee! (*Stormy, prolonged applause. Cheers. The audience scans,* "BCP!")

Long live unbreakable Soviet-Bulgarian friendship! (*Stormy, prolonged applause. Cheers and cries of* "Eternal friendship!")

Long live the unity of the countries of the mighty socialist camp—a reliable guarantee of the peace and security of the peoples of the world! (*Stormy, prolonged applause. Cheers.*)

Long live the victorious banner of Marxism-Leninism! (*Stormy, prolonged applause. Cheers. Cries of* "Friendship!" *The audience scans,* "C.P.S.U.", "BCP.")

REPLIES
TO QUESTIONS PUT BY EDITOR
OF MELBOURNE *HERALD*, JOHN WATERS

June 11, 1958

Mr. John Waters, editor of the Melbourne *Herald*, recently submitted a number of questions to N. S. Khrushchov, First Secretary of the Central Committee of the C.P.S.U. and Chairman of the Council of Ministers of the U.S.S.R.

Below we publish N. S. Khrushchov's replies to the questions of Mr. Waters.

Question: Your constant appeals for co-existence between the communist world and the Western world are undoubtedly arousing wide interest everywhere. Would you like to explain your conception of co-existence, which, in the view of many people, is not quite clear?

Answer: Our point of view regarding the nature of interstate relations between the socialist and capitalist countries has been set forth a number of times. The gist of it, in brief, is, first, that the form of state organization and the form of social organization of any particular country must be decided by the people of that country themselves; secondly, that no state or any external forces can or should impose on other nations their way of life or their political or social system; thirdly, since man's social development takes place along an ascending line, it inevitably gives rise to new forms of life for society. Consequently, the appearance of states with a socialist system, as a result of the operation of the objective laws of social development, is just as natural as was, in its day, the appearance of bourgeois states; and lastly, in order to rid mankind of devastating wars and, in particular, of the threat of the most destructive war ever known by humanity—nuclear war—we feel that the principle of peaceful co-existence and co-operation must prevail in relations between the socialist and capitalist states.

What does this principle mean in practice? It does not demand that the capitalist states renounce their existing system or ideology. Naturally, acceptance of this principle will not lead to the immediate elimination of disputes and contradictions that are inevitable under conditions in which different states exist. But this principle demands that the states, in settling outstanding issues between them, should renounce the use of force in any form, including military force, and seek the peaceful settlement of possible conflicts with an eye to the mutual interests of the parties concerned. Peaceful co-existence also presupposes the complete and unqualified non-interference of states in the internal affairs of one another with a view to changing their system or way of life, or for any other reason.

I think that the meaning imparted to the term peaceful coexistence will now be clearer to you. As you see, we stand for a healthy and realistic basis for relations between states with different social systems. The principle of peaceful co-existence does not place any individual state or any group of states at an advantage over other states and does not infringe on anyone's interests; it is of benefit to all who desire peace, not in words, but in deeds.

When Vladimir Ilyich Lenin, the great founder of the Soviet state, put forward for the first time the idea of peaceful co-existence, there were "wiseacres" in the West who regarded this as a display of weakness on the part of socialism. Forty years have gone by since then. The whole history of development of the Soviet socialist state has proved its great strength and viability. I don't think there is any need for me to remind you that in the Second World War the Soviet Union not only withstood Hitler Germany, which had enslaved practically the whole of Europe, but also completely routed all its enemies.

And it was not by chance that after the Second World War the peoples of a series of countries in Europe and Asia resolutely took the road of socialist development. In following this course they have achieved great success—unknown under capitalism—in developing their countries.

No one now has the temerity to talk about socialism being weak. But we continue, as in the past, to firmly advocate peaceful co-existence between countries, regardless of their social or state systems. Our stand is that no single country should intervene in the internal affairs of any other country.

In circumstances in which two systems exist on our planet—the socialist system and the capitalist system—no one has yet figured out another way of sparing mankind from wars other than peaceful co-existence.

The Bandung Conference of Afro-Asian countries, and later the United Nations, recognized the principles of peaceful co-existence. In this we see the triumph of good sense. Now all that is required is for the peoples of all countries to insist that their governments—in deeds, and not merely in words—apply the principles of peaceful co-existence.

Question: Could you dwell in greater detail on your hopes for a relaxation of international tension as a result of summit talks?

Answer: All nations desire to live in peace and friendship and wish to be delivered, once and for all, from fears preying upon the minds of people for their future and that of their dear ones. They wish to bring about a situation in which the vast sums now being spent on armaments could be used for the good of mankind, to raise living standards, to develop the national economy and culture, and so on. Such conditions can be secured only by gradually achieving normal relations between states, and this requires, above all, the settlement of those questions which hinder an understanding between states.

What are these issues? Frankly speaking, this involves problems resulting from the Western Powers' pursuance of the policy of cold war and "positions of strength." At the present time the best way to deal with questions which are ripe for settlement is through a conference of leading statesmen, that is to say, a summit conference. We are convinced that, given the desire on the part of both sides, such a conference could discover ways of solving urgent international problems.

A beginning should be made with what is realistically possible, so as to solve the problems by stages, that is, to proceed from the simpler to the more complex questions. It is precisely for this reason, therefore, that we suggested that talks be held with the Western Powers first of all on the questions which, in our view, are already ripe for solution. These questions are well known and so I shall not repeat them. Naturally, in addition to these, we are also ready to discuss other urgent questions regarding which the attitudes of the parties involved have already come so close that there are prospects of reaching agreed decisions on them, provided their discussion helps to ease and not intensify international tension.

It has to be noted that so far the Western Powers have shown no real desire to hasten a meeting at the summit.

It is more than five months since the Soviet Union put forward the proposal for a summit conference. How far have preparations advanced during this period? The Western Powers, albeit with considerable reluctance, consented in principle to holding a conference. But how many preliminary conditions and provisions and restrictions of every description did they advance! The impression is created that while proclaiming in words the desirability of a conference, they are simultaneously doing their utmost to delay it as long as possible or not to hold it at all. Moreover, they are forcing the pace of the arms race, trying to establish rocket launching sites on the territories of European countries, and trying as much as possible to extend existing military blocs.

As far as the Soviet Union is concerned, it has exerted and will continue to exert, every effort to bring about a summit conference. We believe that if the conference settles even a few of the questions which are ready for solution, this will provide a good basis for further steps in easing world tension. The settlement of even a few important international problems could produce a chain reaction for an over-all normalization of international relations. And this in turn would help to strengthen confidence between states—confidence which with time would grow into strong friendly relations based on the principles of peaceful co-existence.

Question: Assuming that the Western Powers were to agree to the cessation of tests could you indicate what the U.S.S.R. proposes as the next steps in solving the problem of prohibiting the production of nuclear weapons, destroying stockpiles of such weapons, and securing the complete banning of the use of fissile material for military purposes?

Answer: As yet there is no sign that the United States and Britain are agreed to the ending of tests. On the contrary, Britain and the United States are already carrying out new nuclear weapons tests, and declare that they intend to continue to do so.

However, we have not lost hope that under pressure from the peoples they may revise their present attitude.

Although the facts indicate that there are no grounds as yet for believing that the Western Powers will agree to the ending of nuclear tests, nevertheless, I should like to say a few words about possible subsequent steps by the Soviet Government.

Following the ending of nuclear weapons tests, it would be possible to raise the question of the Powers assuming a solemn undertaking not to use atomic or hydrogen weapons, and subsequently to make a decision on the total outlawing of atomic and thermo-nuclear weapons, ending their production, destroying all stockpiles, and establishing an appropriate effective system of control and inspection. The cessation of tests would make it possible, with the simultaneous solution of the nuclear weapon aspects of the disarmament problem, to settle in a radical way problems relating to conventional armaments I assume that you are already aware that the Soviet Union, in the recent past alone, has carried out a unilateral reduction in its armed forces by 1,840,000 men, and is now carrying out a further reduction by 300,000 men Needless to say, a corresponding reduction is being carried out in the armaments and war materiel at the disposal of the Soviet Army and Navy.

As you see, the Soviet Union has by its deeds set an example for a real settlement of this most important question. It is now the turn of the United States and British governments.

Question: The Western point of view has been repeatedly set forth as demanding an all-round agreement on disarmament, to cover all types of nuclear weapons, conventional armaments and military personnel, on the ground that the total abolition of nuclear weapons without a corresponding reduction in conventional armed forces would result in the West finding itself faced with overwhelming Soviet superiority. Could you indicate how you propose to answer this viewpoint which the Western Powers have never relinquished?

Answer: I cannot agree to the way in which the question is posed. Please don't be offended, but the many years of discussion of disarmament have shown that the representatives of the Western Powers, to put it mildly, have n burning desire to reach agreement, whether complete or partial, on that problem.

The Western press has recently written much about the U.S.S.R. not wanting a comprehensive settlement of the disarmament problem and the prohibition of atomic weapons, and only calling for a partial settlement of individual aspects of the problem. Is that really the case? Let me recall a few facts.

From the very first days of the discussion on the disarmament problem in the United Nations and at various international conferences and meetings, the Soviet Government put forward, and has insistently upheld, a comprehensive plan for radically solving the disarmament problem as a whole, that is to say, a solution which would ensure the total prohibition of atomic and hydrogen weapons, the withdrawal of these weapons from the armaments of the states and the destruction of all stockpiles, a substantial reduction in armed forces, conventional armaments and the military appropriations of the states, the dismantling of foreign military bases on alien territories, and also the establishment of the strictest international control over the observance of any agreement reached on these questions.

Only such a solution would make it possible to free the peoples completely from the danger of a devastating atomic war.

The United States and its Western partners base their calculations in foreign policy and their military plans primarily on the use of nuclear weapons. That is why they refuse to prohibit atomic and hydrogen weapons on the grounds, so they claim, that they need them to counterbalance the Soviet Union's preponderant strength in conventional armaments and armed forces. At one time they declared that the Western Powers would agree to the prohibition of nuclear weapons if the Soviet Union agreed to accept their proposal establishing limits for armed forces at 1,000,000-1,500,000 men for the United States and the U.S.S.R. and at 650,000 men for Britain and France.

However, no sooner did the Soviet Union, in May 1955, accept the level proposed by the Western Powers, than those Powers immediately backed out, refusing to prohibit atomic and thermo-nuclear weapons. Furthermore, on the pretext that in the existing circumstances it was impossible to reach agreement on comprehensive disarmament, they called for an agreement to be worked out on certain individual aspects of disarmament.

The Soviet Union met the Western Powers half-way, and expressed its readiness to solve the disarmament problem piecemeal. What was the Western Powers' reply to this? In 1957, they came out with fresh proposals, amounting in fact to merely a reduction of the armed forces of the U.S.S.R. and the United States to the level of two and a half million men, since the Western Powers made all the subsequent reductions in two stages to 1,700,000 men conditional upon the settlement of international political problems, including the solution of the German question on their own terms. In the same way the Western Powers refused to accept the Soviet Union's proposal for a reduction of 15 per cent in the military appropriations of the states, and tried to reduce the whole matter to one of providing information on military expenditures. They opposed the Soviet Union's proposals for the dismantling of foreign military bases on alien territory and for a reduction in foreign armed forces on German territory by one-third or by any other agreed amount, and they also opposed the Soviet Union's proposal for the reduction of foreign armed forces on the territories of other European states.

Thus, the Soviet Union has displayed its readiness to solve the disarmament problem and the prohibition of atomic weapons both as a whole, as well as piecemeal. But no sooner had the Soviet Union agreed to the Western Powers' proposals on the need to solve the disarmament problem in parts than the Western press forthwith began to write about the Soviet Union opposing a cardinal, comprehensive solution of this important problem. As for the United States and the other Western countries, they have come out not only as opponents of banning atomic weapons but also as opponents of a substantial reduction in the armed forces and the armaments of states. All this has been done to the accompaniment of solemn assurances to their devotion to peace and their sincere desire to solve the disarmament problem.

Now regarding talk of the Soviet Union's so-called numerical superiority over the NATO forces. The leaders of the North Atlantic bloc countries require such talk for the exclusive purpose of justifying their own feverish thermo-nuclear armaments race. I have already pointed out that in the period from 1955 to 1958 the strength of the Soviet armed forces, taking into account the unilateral reduction now being carried out, has been lowered by 2,140,000 men. We have adopted a decision to end nuclear weapons tests unilaterally. The Soviet Government has also repeatedly declared its readiness to examine the question of the withdrawal of the armed forces of foreign Powers from the territory of Germany and other member-countries of NATO and of the Warsaw Treaty and of dismantling foreign military bases on alien territories or, as a first step, to discuss the question of a reduction of the strength of foreign troops stationed on these territories.

You are no doubt aware that a conference of the Political Consultative Committee of the Warsaw Treaty was held recently in Moscow. This conference adopted the Declaration of the States Party to the Warsaw Treaty and other important decisions which are indicative of the peaceable nature of the socialist states. A decision was adopted for a further reduction in the armed forces of the Warsaw Treaty member-states and the conference approved the Soviet Government's proposal, in agreement with the Government of Rumania, for the early withdrawal from that country of troops stationed there under the Warsaw Treaty. By agreement with the Hungarian Government, the Government of the U.S.S.R. has also decided to reduce this year the number of Soviet troops stationed in Hungary.

In addition, the Political Consultative Committee decided to invite the member-states of the North Atlantic Treaty Organization to conclude a non-aggression pact between the states party to the Warsaw Treaty, and the NATO member-states.

However, the Soviet Union's peaceable efforts have so far not met with proper understanding and support from the Western Powers. Furthermore, the strange situation has arisen in which concrete steps by the Soviet Union in reducing its armed forces and armaments, and even as humane an act as its unilateral ending of nuclear weapons tests, are portrayed in the West as propaganda, while the activity so dangerous to peace of certain circles in the Western countries, who are pursuing the armaments race, the policy of strength, and conduct nuclear weapons tests—all this is portrayed as beneficial.

It must be stated with complete frankness that the ruling circles of certain countries, pursuing the "positions of strength" policy, have so completely turned their backs on the logic of facts, and their subservient press depicts matters in such a way, that the peoples of these countries are finding it increasingly difficult to understand the events now taking place. We must note with regret that the militarists are deliberately poisoning the minds of the people and fomenting war hysteria.

The Soviet Government is of the opinion that the question of disarmament will have to be one of the major questions discussed at a Heads of Government conference. In view of the fact that it has not been possible so far to reach agreement on the disarmament problem as a whole, and since the Western Powers oppose this, the Soviet

Union suggests the gradual solution of the disarmament problem, as the method most realistic and warranted in the present circumstances. In particular, the Soviet Government proposes that the conference should discuss the following urgent disarmament questions: the immediate ending of atomic and hydrogen weapons tests; renunciation by the U.S.S.R., the United States and Great Britain of the use of nuclear weapons; the establishment in Central Europe of an atom-free zone; the reduction of the number of foreign troops stationed on the territory of Germany and within the frontiers of other European states; the drawing up of an agreement on questions connected with the prevention of a surprise attack.

In deference to the wishes of the United States, the Soviet Union has also agreed to discuss at the conference the prohibition of the use of outer space for military purposes, but not as an issue considered in isolation, and not on such conditions as would be advantageous to the United States alone inasmuch as it does not yet possess the intercontinental ballistic missile, but linked with the question of dismantling foreign military bases on alien territories—bases which are springing up like poisonous toadstools after the rain around the entire perimeter of the state frontiers of the Soviet Union and the other socialist countries.

Thus, you can see, the Soviet Union is prepared to conclude both a comprehensive agreement on the disarmament problem as well as an agreement on individual aspects of that problem. Matters now rest with the Western Powers.

Question: Does the launching of the Soviet sputniks indicate that the U.S.S.R. has achieved permanent superiority over the West in the field of technology, or do you consider that uninterrupted invention by both sides of new types of atomic weapons has resulted in a deadlock, in which neither side can ever hope to achieve decisive military superiority?

Answer: First of all I should like to stress that the launching of artificial earth satellites is one of the most important landmarks in the history of the development of mankind, of science, technology and culture. Scientists in many fields are now being given vast opportunities to make fuller study of outer space, the solar system and the structure of our Earth. They are being given great opportunities not only for posing new theoretical problems, but also for their practical solution.

Of course, in order to launch such sputniks as Soviet scientists and engineers have sent into outer space—particularly the third sputnik, which weighs almost a ton and a half—it is necessary to possess exceptionally highly developed, large-scale technology. But the Soviet people do not consider that what they have accomplished is unattainable, in the final analysis, by other peoples as well. The important thing is that the fruits of human activity should be used not to the detriment but for the benefit of mankind.

Today precisely the opposite picture is being created. Although the Soviet Union is prepared to renounce the military use of rockets, with the help of which the sputniks were launched, it may be said that Britain and the United States are also concentrating every effort on developing intercontinental ballistic missiles, but with the sole purpose of making them a weapon for the mass destruction of human beings and material values. And they proceed from the strange philosophy that the possession of this terrible weapon by both sides will create the necessary prerequisites for maintaining peace.

The arms race has its logical conclusion—it leads in the long run to war. The talk about atom and other deadlocks serves a purpose—to justify the arms race, particularly the nuclear and thermo-nuclear arms race. When the advocates of this philosophy are asked why peace has to be secured by brandishing atom and hydrogen bombs, they can give no convincing reply.

We firmly believe that in present conditions there is only one way to maintain peace and security—general disarmament, the prohibition of weapons of mass destruction, peaceful co-existence, and creative, constructive effort aimed at establishing lasting confidence among all nations.

Question: Could you explain in greater detail why the Soviet Union objects to German reunification, and indicate on what conditions the U.S.S.R. would agree to reunification?

Answer: Your question, in the form you have posed it, testifies, unfortunately, to a most deplorable ignorance of the facts concerning the Soviet Union's position on the German problem, or else you have become—wittingly or unwittingly—the victim of fabrications on this question which for more than ten years have been circulated in the West.

In view of this, permit me to recall certain facts which prove incontestably that it is precisely the Soviet Union, in contrast to the Western countries, which has always advocated and consistently continues to advocate restoring the national unity of the German people. This is due not only to our fundamental recognition of the right of all nations to self-determination and the establishment of independent national states, but also to the realization that the split created in Germany by the Western states and the policy of resurrecting German militarism are fraught with a serious threat to European peace and security.

The Soviet Union has repeatedly submitted concrete proposals for the reunification of Germany as a peaceful and democratic state. Let me just recall the Soviet Union's proposals of March 10 and April 9, 1952, to the Governments of the United States, Britain and France, to initiate discussions on the questions of a German peace treaty, German reunification and the creation of an all-German government. We submitted a draft of the fundamentals of a peace treaty with Germany and proposed that the question of holding free all-German elections should be discussed. These provided realistic opportunities for solving the German problem, but they were not made use of through no fault of ours.

The conclusion of the Paris Agreements, West Germany's inclusion in the aggressive NATO bloc, the perpetuation of the occupation of West Germany and the establishment of foreign military bases on her territory, the Bundestag decision to give the West German Bundeswehr atomic and rocket weapons—all these and similar measures have greatly aggravated the situation in Europe. The Soviet Union has repeatedly warned of the danger of this policy for the German people and other European peoples, as it erects insurmountable barriers to German reunification and creates a hotbed of new war in Europe. Responsibility for this must be borne by the Western Powers and the ruling circles of West Germany who follow in their wake, and in no way by the Soviet Union.

Today two sovereign German states exist and are developing on the territory of Germany, each possessing a different social and economic system. The question of German reunification in practice has become a question of *rapprochement* and the reaching of understanding between these two German states. Without doubt, this is only possible provided West Germany renounces the policy of reviving German militarism and *revanche*. I am stressing this because I fear that in your country, Australia, there is apparently insufficient appreciation of the well-founded apprehensions aroused among European peoples by a policy aimed at reviving German militarism and *revanche*.

Thus, the reunification of Germany today depends on appropriate actions by the German people themselves. The Germans themselves, on the basis of mutual agreement between the two existing German states—the German Democratic Republic and the Federal Republic of Germany —must first and foremost resolve the problems of German reunification. As before, the Soviet Union is ready to help the German people actively in creating a single peaceful and democratic Germany, and to support such proposals as the creation of a confederation of the two German states, the establishment of an atom-free zone in Europe, the reduction of foreign troops stationed on German territory, and any other proposals which facilitate this purpose.

Question: What in your opinion are the main factors determining relations between the East and West since the death of Stalin?

Answer: In speaking of relations between the East and West you apparently have in mind the development of relations between the socialist and capitalist states over the past five years. We Communists think it is incorrect to divide history into periods according to the life and work of any given statesman, however outstanding he may have been. The basic and decisive factor determining relations between the East and West for more than forty years has been the existence of two social and political systems.

The imperialists have never abandoned their hopes of destroying the first socialist state in the world, and later the socialist camp as well. They have tried every means to accomplish this, including war—and nothing has come of it—but they have not drawn the necessary historical conclusions from this.

The socialist countries by their very nature have no need of war, are not interested in enslaving other peoples. It is precisely for this reason that the foreign policy of the Soviet Union, from the very day of its birth, has been the policy of peaceful co-existence. I repeat: always, for more than forty years now. Soviet foreign policy has continuity of character: it has always been, it is and it will continue to be, the Leninist policy of peaceful co-existence.

During the past five years we have particularly clearly seen a struggle between two opposing trends in international relations. One trend is the determined and consistent struggle of the countries in the "peace zone"—the countries of the socialist camp and the Asian and African countries which have recently cast off the fetters of colonialism—for peace, for a relaxation of tension in relations between states, for ending the cold war, for settling outstanding international issues by means of negotiations. The other trend is the stubborn unwillingness of certain Western circles to put an end to the cold war, their desire to solve international problems from a "position of strength," which, without doubt, only sharpens tension in international relations.

Characteristic of this period is the tremendous growth of the forces standing for peace, for the relaxation of international tension. It is precisely thanks to this that the wars in Korea and Viet-Nam were ended, that the peace treaty was signed with Austria and that the well-known Four-Power Conference of Heads of Government was held in Geneva in 1955.

I should also like to draw attention to another feature typical of this period. No sooner is a slight easing in international tension observed, than certain circles in the West resort to artificial means to prevent an improvement in the international situation, with a view to electrifying the atmosphere once more and making the situation more acute.

The struggle of these two opposing trends is to be seen most clearly at the present time over the question of convening a summit conference, of which I have already spoken.

Question: Do you consider it vitally important for the success of summit talks to invite communist China to take part in the talks or to join an agreement later?

Answer: I think there is hardly anyone with the slightest understanding of international relations who would deny the outstanding role played by People's China, with her 600 million inhabitants, in international affairs. The

People's Republic of China is exerting a most beneficial influence on the development of the international situation, not only in the Far East but also throughout the world.

The most important point is not whether the People's Republic of China will or will not be invited to a summit conference, but whether the legitimate interests of one of the Great Powers, whose foreign policy, like that of the Soviet Union, is based on the principle of peaceful co-existence, the desire to establish good-neighbourly and friendly relations with all countries, will be taken into account. It must be borne in mind that there can be no decisions taken that harm the interests of the People's Republic of China.

Question: Australians, who want friendship with our Asian neighbours, are showing particular interest in the statements by Mao Tse-tung on contradictions which may exist in communist society and on the existence of "different roads to socialism." Are there any differences between the Russian and Chinese communist doctrines?

Answer: This question can only arise through lack of knowledge of Marxism. The Communist Party of the Soviet Union and the Communist Party of China neither have had, nor now have, different views on fundamental questions, for they proceed from the monolithic teachings of Marxism-Leninism, which they follow loyally.

If you study the Declaration of the Meeting of Representatives of Communist and Workers' Parties of the Socialist Countries, held in Moscow November 14-16, 1957, you will note that it reflects the unity of views of the Communist parties on all the major problems of international relations, the international labour movement and socialism. The Declaration was signed, together with the other parties, by representatives of the Communist parties of the Soviet Union and the People's Republic of China.

I can assure you that to seek "differences between the

Russian and Chinese communist doctrines" is to labour in vain.

Question: If there is a new interpretation of Marxism, which admits "defferent roads to socialism," how in your opinion will this affect the future role of those non-Communist parties in the West which are devoted to socialism?

Answer: In the first place, the way you have raised the question is in itself incorrect. There is absolutely no "new interpretation" of Marxism regarding different roads to socialism. It was V. I. Lenin who developed the concept that, provided such fundamental principles of the socialist transformation of society as the dictatorship of the proletariat and the leading role of the Communist Party were observed, each country would make its own contribution to the establishment of the socialist system, in accordance with the specific conditions of the given country. The 20th Congress of our Party only gave concrete form to this proposition of Lenin's as applied to the situation today, pointing out in particular the possibility of making use of peaceful forms, including parliamentary methods, for the transition to socialism.

Concerning the role and place of non-Communist parties, it should first of all be stressed that, in the present situation, co-operation between the Communist Party and other parties is not only possible but essential for the socialist transformation of society. Socialism today has become a world system. In every country it is gaining more and more supporters, and not only among the working class. This gives rise to the realistic prospect of forming broad alliances between the working class and its vanguard, the Communist Party, and other social strata, and consequently, other parties, in the struggle for socialism.

Naturally, alliances of this kind can only take place with such parties which, not in words, but in deeds, have as their purpose the building of socialist society or, as you put it, are devoted to the ideal of socialism. What is meant by being devoted to the ideal of socialism? This means to have as one's aim the creation of socialist society, that is, to give the working people control of the instruments and means of production, either by expropriation or, in individual instances, by buying them from the capitalists; it means the abolition of the exploitation of man by man. The party which genuinely sets itself these ideals, and is ready to fight for them, naturally can and should be an ally of the Communist Party in the socialist transformation of society. In alliance with such parties, the Communist parties will be able to unite the forces of the working class and then, through joint efforts, achieve unification of its allies—the working peasantry, handicraftsmen, intelligentsia—around the working class. This unification is an essential condition for the conquest of power by the working class and the establishment of the socialist system, among others by peaceful, parliamentary means.

At the present time, views can be heard in the West alleging that co-operation between the Communists and other parties—first and foremost the Socialists—can only be of a temporary nature, that after they have won power "the Communists will swallow up the Socialists." This fabrication is needed by the Right-wing leaders of the Socialist parties in certain Western countries in order to frighten the rank and file of their parties and alienate them from the idea of unity of action with the Communists. In actual fact, Communists consider it not only possible but desirable to maintain co-operation with non-Communist parties after coming to power, if these parties prove their desire for building socialism in practice.

There are numerous examples to prove that this is actually the case. For instance, the experience of many countries in the West and the East, in particular, the experience of the German Democratic Republic, Czechoslovakia and the People's Republic of China, shows that political leadership by the working class and the Communist parties is exercised in these countries with the continued existence of parties expressing the interests of the middle strata of town and countryside. Furthermore, co-operation with these parties, when they sincerely sympathize with the ideals of socialism, is of great assistance, capable of hastening the advance to socialism.

Question: Could you give me your views regarding the apprehensions of Australians lest the Russian request to prolong the stay of Russian scientists in the Antarctic after the end of the International Geophysical Year represents a threat to Australian claims to sovereignty in the area?

Answer: Your statement about "the Russian request to prolong the stay of their scientists in the Antarctic" seems to be based on a misunderstanding. We have never made any such request to anyone. The decision to prolong the International Geophysical Year in the Antarctic was taken, as is known, at a meeting of the Special Committee for Antarctic Research under the International Council of Scientific Unions, held at the Hague in February, this year, and the proposal to prolong scientific research in the Antarctic was submitted by the representative of the United States, not of the U.S.S.R. Soviet scientists simply supported this proposal.

As far as our position on the question of jurisdiction over the Antarctic is concerned, we consider the Antarctic to be of international importance inasmuch as its territory and the adjacent waters are of great economic value to many states, including the Soviet Union. Therefore, according to international practice, all interested countries should take part in discussing the question of the status of any area of international importance. The Soviet Government feels that this international practice should also be followed in deciding the question of jurisdiction over the Antarctic.

Question: In view of the fact that the severance of diplomatic relations between Moscow and Canberra was caused by circumstances arising in the Stalin era, are you of the opinion that the time has now come for the complete resumption of diplomatic relations between our two countries?

Answer: Yes, I do think so. Incidentally, the "Stalin era" has nothing to do with the matter. The fact that diplomatic relations do not exist between Australia and the U.S.S.R. is not the fault of the Soviet Union, but the result of a notorious anti-Soviet campaign which did great harm to relations between our two countries. The Soviet Union has always advocated, and advocates today, the maintenance of normal relations with every country, irrespective of its political or social system. This applies equally to Australia.

If the Australian Government, on its part, wishes diplomatic relations between our countries to be normalized, we on our part are ready to do so. Incidentally, talks have already taken place between the Australian and Soviet Ambassadors in Washington on the question of establishing normal diplomatic relations between our two countries; as a result of this in the autumn of 1956 they agreed upon the text, submitted by the Australian side, of a joint communiqué on the resumption of activity of their diplomatic representations in both countries. However, the Australian Government up to now has not indicated its readiness to have the text of this communiqué published and, consequently, it is up to Australia to give the word.

Question: What proof has the Soviet Union to justify the criticism of Australia's methods of administering New Guinea, as a trustee of the United Nations? Is there any connection between this criticism and the Soviet Union's support for Indonesia's claims to Western New Guinea?

Answer: As a member of the Trusteeship Council, the Soviet Union has advocated, and will continue to advocate, the consistent application of the principles set out in the United Nations Charter in respect of trust territories. The Soviet Union is doing all it can in order, as laid down in the United Nations Charter, to promote the political, economic and social advancement of the inhabitants of the trust territories, to encourage respect for human rights and for fundamental freedoms for all, without distinction as to race, sex, language or religion, and to promote the development of trust territories towards self-government and complete independence. And this is what determines the attitude of the Soviet representative on the Trusteeship Council.

The Indonesian Government's justified demands for the return of Western Irian, ancient territory of Indonesia, which was wrested from her by the colonialists, is an entirely separate question. The Soviet Union fully supports this legitimate demand of the Indonesian people.

Question: What are the prospects of trade between Australia and the U.S.S.R., taking into account that the bulk of Australian exports comprises wool and other raw materials?

Answer: As you know, up till 1954 there were normal trade relations between the Soviet Union and Australia. The Soviet Union favours the development of trade with every country on the basis of equality and mutual benefit. Therefore, if our relations with Australia are normalized, trade between the Soviet Union and Australia could undoubtedly be given considerable impetus. In 1957 the Soviet Union's foreign trade reached 33,000 million rubles (over $8,000 million). The foreign trade of the Soviet Union today is the sixth largest in the world, and is conducted with more than seventy countries. It exports a wide range of goods. Some of these are goods Australia normally imports, in particular oil and petroleum products, ferro-alloys, asbestos, sawn timber, products of the paper and timber industries, potassium salts, tinned salmon and crab, and also machinery and equipment. On the other hand, certain goods which are among Australia's regular exports, such as wool, which you have mentioned, could be of interest to the Soviet Union.

Question: What are the prospects for improving contacts

between Australia and the U.S.S.R. in the cultural field? For instance, is there any hope of a visit by the Russian ballet? Which Australian artistes, scientific experts or sportsmen would be most popular and welcome in Moscow?

Answer: We regard cultural ties as an important means of improving understanding and bringing peoples closer together. We would therefore welcome the development of contacts between the Soviet Union and Australia in the field of culture.

We are aware that interest is shown in Australia in the cultural, scientific and sports life of the Soviet Union. Thus, for instance, we have received invitations from a number of Australian organizations to send to Australia a Russian ballet group, a song and dance ensemble, and individual artistes.

There is great interest in the Soviet Union in the cultural, scientific and sports life of Australia. We would be most happy to offer hospitality in the Soviet Union to Australian artistes, scientists and sportsmen.

There is no obstacle to the development of cultural exchanges between our countries, whether officially sponsored or through sports, cultural, scientific and other organizations. Naturally, the re-establishment of diplomatic relations would create more normal conditions for such contacts, in which both our countries are interested.

June 11, 1958.

Pravda, June 25, 1958

SPEECH
AT LUNCHEON OF AMBASSADORS
OF BANDUNG CONFERENCE COUNTRIES
IN HONOUR OF THE KING AND QUEEN OF NEPAL

June 23, 1958

Your Majesties,
Ladies and Gentlemen,
Comrades,

It has become a splendid tradition to welcome eminent guests from Asia and Africa who visit our country at a special reception arranged by the Ambassadors of the countries which took part in the historical Bandung Conference.

We whole-heartedly support this tradition and are happy today together with you all Messrs. Ambassadors, once again to welcome on behalf of the Soviet Government our dear guests, Their Majesties the King and Queen of Nepal.

Your Majesty,

We are very happy that you have come to our country on a friendly visit and have personally become acquainted with the life of the Soviet people and with our accomplishments in industry, agriculture and culture.

We regard your visit as proof of the further development and strengthening of friendship and co-operation between our countries. In this connection I should like to note that our Government greatly values your personal efforts, which have been largely instrumental in establishing and developing Soviet-Nepalese friendship and co-operation.

The relations between our countries are built on the sound foundation of the well-known Five Principles of

Peaceful Co-existence and International Co-operation—the *Panch Shila*—which were supported by and proclaimed at the Bandung Conference and which are now winning increasingly wide recognition as the basis for relations between countries with different social systems. It may be said without exaggeration that today the Five Principles are becoming the universally recognized standard for international relations.

The Soviet Union's foreign policy is clear. We stand for stable and lasting peace and for broad co-operation with all countries of the world, regardless of their social and economic systems. And it is with a feeling of friendship that we regard all states and peoples who are working for the great cause of peace.

The Soviet people have been following with great sympathy the efforts of the Nepalese people in fulfilling plans for the economic and cultural development of their country and also for the strengthening of Nepal's ties with other countries.

The Soviet Government regards the strengthening of relations with the Kingdom of Nepal as yet another step forward in the development and extension of its ties with the Bandung Conference countries. This is a healthy and natural process which is leading to an extension of the peace zone.

I would like to hope that the visit of Your Majesties to the Soviet Union will be conducive to the further development of friendly ties between the U.S.S.R. and Nepal, which is entirely in the interests of the Soviet and Nepalese peoples.

To the health of Your Majesties, of all our esteemed Nepalese guests, and of the Ambassadors, whom I thank for the invitation to attend this very pleasant gathering! To the prosperity and happiness of the Nepalese people, to Soviet-Nepalese friendship, and to the strengthening of the solidarity of the Asian and African countries and to world peace!

SPEECH
WELCOMING ANTONIN NOVOTNÝ,
FIRST SECRETARY OF CENTRAL COMMITTEE OF COMMUNIST PARTY OF CZECHOSLOVAKIA AND PRESIDENT OF CZECHOSLOVAK REPUBLIC

July 2, 1958

Dear Comrade Novotný,

Dear Comrades and Friends,

Allow me on behalf of the Central Committee of the C.P.S.U., the Presidium of the Supreme Soviet of the U.S.S.R. and the Soviet Government, on behalf of the entire Soviet people, to welcome you heartily in our capital—Moscow.

The visit to the Soviet Union of Comrade Novotný, First Secretary of the Central Committee of the Communist Party of Czechoslovakia and President of the Czechoslovak Republic, is a big and joyous event for our Party and all the Soviet people. The Soviet people know you well and respect you deeply, dear Comrade Novotný, as an outstanding leader of the revolutionary working-class movement and tireless fighter for socialism, for peace.

We also heartily welcome the prominent leaders of the Communist Party of Czechoslovakia and the Czechoslovak Government who have come with you—Comrade Václav Kopecký, member of the Political Bureau of the Central Committee of the Czechoslovak Communist Party and Deputy Chairman of the Government, Comrade Rudolf Barák, member of the Political Bureau and Minister of Interior, Comrade Jiři Hendrych, member of the Political Bureau and Secretary of the C.C., Comrade Rudolf Strehai, candidate to the Political Bureau of the C.C., Chairman of the Corps of Representatives of Slovakia, and Comrade Václav David, member of the C.C. and Minister of Foreign Affairs.

Dear comrades, in your persons we greet the glorious Communist Party of Czechoslovakia, which holds high the victorious banner of Marxism-Leninism, and the fraternal peoples of socialist Czechoslovakia who have enduring bonds of long-standing inviolable friendship with the Soviet people.

You have come to our country at an auspicious moment in Czechoslovak history. The 11th Congress of the Communist Party of Czechoslovakia, which has drawn up a programme of completing the building of socialism in your country in the next few years, closed a few days ago. The Soviet people received the results of your congress with a sense of profound satisfaction. The completion of socialist construction in Czechoslovakia will have a tremendous international impact. Your successes in building socialism go to strengthen the might of the socialist camp and cement the forces of peace and democracy throughout the world.

This is not the first time we meet as close friends and brothers brought together by the great ideas of communism, the ideas of peace and people's happiness. It is good to know that your present visit, just as our frequent meetings in the past, is not bound up with the need of settling any controversial questions and misunderstandings, because such controversial questions have never existed and do not exist now.

The friendship between our countries, based on principles of proletarian internationalism and all-round mutual support, accords with the basic vital interests of our peoples, the interests of the socialist camp as a whole. At the same time, this cordial and inviolable friendship helps to strengthen the peace in Europe and the world.

We do not doubt that during your stay in the Soviet

Union you will again see how profound and sincere are the sentiments of love and friendship which the Soviet people have for the peoples of Czechoslovakia.

Allow me, dear friends, to express the trust that your arrival in the Soviet Union will contribute to a still greater strengthening of fraternal relations and co-operation between our Communist parties, between the peoples of the Soviet Union and Czechoslovakia.

For our part, we shall do our best for you to feel at home in our country.

Welcome, dear friends!

(Stormy applause. Cheers for inviolable Soviet-Czechoslovak friendship.)

SPEECH
AT GRAND KREMLIN PALACE DINNER IN HONOUR OF COMRADE ANTONIN NOVOTNÝ, PRESIDENT OF CZECHOSLOVAKIA

July 2, 1958

Dear Comrade Novotný,
Comrades and Friends,

Permit me, dear guests from fraternal Czechoslovakia, again to bid you a hearty welcome.

It is good and heartening to meet genuine friends. Such meetings are always imbued with great human warmth and deep cordiality. We, representatives of the peoples of socialist countries, are brought together by our common goals and the identity of our views, by our joint struggle for socialism and peace. We meet as fellow-Communists. We are proud of the outstanding successes achieved by the fraternal family of socialist nations in building our new society.

The rulers of the imperialist camp also have some views in common. Their minds work in a single direction: how to wipe the socialist states off the face of the earth, destroy communism as the ideal of hundreds of millions of working people, and perpetuate exploitation and oppression of the working man. But just as a pig is not endowed by Nature to see the sky, so the imperialist designs of destroying the socialist countries are not destined to be realized.

Whenever it comes to dealings between capitalist states, between monopoly combines, the imperialists no longer tread common ground. Anyone who feels strong enough tries to grab more than the others, to bear down upon them, to dictate his will to them.

The friendship and unity of the socialist countries have a different foundation. The peoples of our countries have set themselves the goal of building a classless society that rules out exploitation of man by man, where men are not divided into rich and poor and there is an abundance of everything man needs—a society in which science and technology, literature and art, will climb to unheard-of heights.

And the closer our countries stand together, the more concerted our efforts, and the more we help each other, the quicker communism will triumph. Along the path to this, man's happy morrow, there can be no competition, no struggle between us of whatever form. On the contrary, we march along this path in a united front and the success of one socialist country can only cause joy to the peoples of the other countries, for it brings them nearer to our common goal.

The Soviet people, who were the first in man's history to blaze the highroad to socialism, heartily welcome the decision of the 11th Congress of the Communist Party of Czechoslovakia to complete the building of socialism in that country in the next few years. From the bottom of their hearts, the Soviet people wish their blood-brothers, the working people of Czechoslovakia, every success in this great and noble undertaking.

There can be no doubt that the hard-working and gifted people of Czechoslovakia will, under the guidance of their militant Communist Party, honourably fulfil the programme charted by the Communist Party.

Permit me to make a toast to the successes of Czechoslovakia's working people in building the new life, to their completing the building of socialism in the Czechoslovak Republic, to its further progress!

To the heroic Communist Party of Czechoslovakia and its Central Committee!

To the Government of the Czechoslovak Republic!

To the health of the First Secretary of the Central Committee of the Czechoslovak Communist Party, President of the Czechoslovak Republic, Comrade Antonin Novotný!

To the health of our Czechoslovak friends who have come here with Comrade Novotný!

To the health of all those present here!

To the everlasting and inviolable friendship of our peoples!

SPEECH
AT U.S.S.R.-CZECHOSLOVAKIA
FRIENDSHIP MEETING IN LENINGRAD

July 4, 1958

Dear Leningrad Comrades,

We are gathered here today in Leningrad's historic Palace Square to extend a brotherly welcome to our dear guests, the leaders of fraternal socialist Czechoslovakia. (*Prolonged applause.*)

We heartily welcome Comrade Antonin Novotný, the First Secretary of the Central Committee of the Communist Party of Czechoslovakia, President of the Czechoslovak Republic, an outstanding leader of the communist movement and our true friend, who has come to the Soviet Union on a friendly visit. (*Stormy applause.*)

We are happy to greet heartily the prominent Party and Government leaders of Czechoslovakia who have come with Comrade Novotny—our dear friends Comrade Václav Kopecky (*applause*), Comrade Rudolf Barák (*applause*), Comrade Jiři Hendrych (*applause*), Comrade Rudolf Strehaj (*applause*), Comrade Václav David (*applause*), and the other comrades. (*Applause.*)

The Soviet people are fond of Leningrad. We know that our foreign friends also deeply respect this fine city. And not just because it is a beautiful city and has a wealth of striking architectural ensembles, historical monuments and institutions of art. People want to see it above all because Leningrad is the cradle of the Great October Socialist Revolution, the greatest revolution of all times and all nations. (*Prolonged applause.*)

This city, which bears the great Lenin's name, is the city of one of the foremost detachments of the Soviet working class. Throughout the history of the Soviet state the fine people of Leningrad have always stood in the front ranks of the builders of socialism in our country. The feats of Leningrad working people—staunch defenders of our Soviet homeland in the Civil War and the Great Patriotic War of the Soviet people against the fascist oppressors—will never fade from our memory.

Today, when our Czechoslovak friends are in Leningrad, I should like to speak again about the tremendous development of the socialist forces, whose triumph and advance began here in October 1917. Just a bit over 40 years have passed since the October Revolution. That is not a very long time. It fits into the life of a single generation. But what striking changes have taken place in the Soviet Union in this time, just as in the whole world! Socialism has been established in our country for the first time in man's history, and it has become a mighty socialist Power.

The history of this period is the history of the emergence and rapid growth of socialism as a social and government system, first in one country, the Soviet Union, and then in a number of other countries comprising the now powerful socialist camp.

It is a joy to know that we live in a wonderful time, and that a wide and remarkable road—the road to happiness, prosperity and a bright future—has been opened to the working people by socialism.

What grand prospects confront us! Our Party and the Soviet Government are taking important measures to accelerate the development of the key industries and steeply raise agriculture, to perfect the management of industry and building, and to further improve the living and cultural standards of the people. The impact of these measures goes far beyond the frontiers of our country, because they help very greatly to consolidate the forces and the international prestige of the entire socialist camp, to cement the forces of socialism and peace throughout the world.

The fact that the Soviet Union has considerably outstripped the capitalist countries in the rates of growth of total industrial and agricultural production, that it has forged ahead into second place in the world for industrial output, and that it is steadily catching up the most developed capitalist country, the United States—all this is adding to the confidence of the peoples of the socialist camp and of the world working-class movement in the inevitable triumph of socialism and communism. Small wonder that these successes are causing consternation in the West!

Hostile propaganda is obviously in a tight spot, one absurdity succeeding another in its evaluation of socialist economic developments. It either howls about "crisis" in some economic branch of our country or, compelled to speak about Soviet economic successes, the achievements of Soviet science and technology, switches to warnings about the "danger" to the West of the rapid growth of Soviet economy and culture.

And people in the capitalist countries are coming to see the falsehood of bourgeois information about the Soviet Union and the other socialist countries. They are coming to realize how far these countries have advanced in their development.

It is not just radio-signals and reflected sunbeams that the Soviet artificial earth satellites send to earth. They have proclaimed to all men the heights achieved by the world of socialism, liberated from the bonds of capitalism. To see these achievements there is no need for the powerful telescopes without which you cannot see the space "oranges." You need simply to look up into the sky at the hour when the Soviet sputnik or its carrier-rocket hurtle past in the atmospheric ocean above our planet. (*Stormy applause.*)

Comrades, our dear Czechoslovak friends have come to us soon after the closing of the 11th Congress of the Communist Party of Czechoslovakia, which summed up the creative endeavour of Czechoslovakia's working people and the organizational effort of the Communist Party. The congress has unanimously drawn the historic conclusion that the foundations of socialism have essentially been laid in Czechoslovakia and that the country has all it needs to complete the building of socialism in the next few years.

The Soviet people congratulate their Czechoslovak friends, the Communist Party of Czechoslovakia, the fraternal peoples of Czechoslovakia, on this great victory from the bottom of their hearts. (*Stormy applause.*)

One can scarcely exaggerate the tremendous importance of socialist successes in Czechoslovakia. All the People's Democracies have made such great progress in socialist construction that now the time is not far distant when, on completing the building of socialism, they will follow the Soviet Union in the gradual transition from socialism to communism, to man's bright future dreamed of for centuries by the leading minds of humanity.

The successes of the working people of the Chinese People's Republic, Czechoslovakia and the other People's Democracies striding confidently along the path of socialist development, are vivid testimony to the all-conquering power of Marxist-Leninist ideas.

A proper understanding and application of the basic principles of Marxism-Leninism, the general laws of socialist revolution and the experience of fraternal Communist parties in the concrete conditions of their country—that is the reliable compass, using which the Communist Party of Czechoslovakia and the other fraternal parties lead their peoples to brilliant triumphs.

We are firmly convinced that under the leadership of their glorious Communist Party, the peoples of Czechoslovakia will in a short time achieve new progress in industry, agriculture and culture, and solve the historic task of completing socialist construction in their country in the next few years.

From the bottom of our hearts we wish our Czechoslovak brothers success in this great undertaking. (*Prolonged applause.*)

Relations of genuinely fraternal inviolable friendship exist between the peoples of the Soviet Union and the Czechoslovak Republic. The friendship of our peoples, of our Communist parties, is based on the immortal ideas of Leninism, which illumine mankind's path to a happy future, to communism.

We are the pupils and successors of the great Lenin. Everything Vladimir Ilyich Lenin had ever done served the interests of the working people, those ordinary people whose hands have created all the good things on earth. Lenin's profound and consistent internationalism was a characteristic feature of his entire activity.

We never forget the profoundly creative nature of Lenin's work. Nobody knew better than Lenin how to apply the lessons of practical experience, to spot the new that is nurtured by life. And he always did his best to help this new to make headway. Lenin always showed the maximum of flexibility and skill in carrying out Party policy, but he could not be budged when it came to the basic principles of revolutionary theory, any deviation from which could inflict irremediable damage to the working-class cause.

All Lenin's activities were imbued with trust in the strength of the working class, the working masses. It is solely with the conscious support of the bulk of the working people, making the best of their experience and initiative, that the ideas of socialism can triumph.

Loyalty to Lenin's teachings is a guarantee of our success. The Communist and Workers' parties are successfully solving complex problems of socialist construction by skilfully and creatively applying the Marxist-Leninist teaching to the concrete circumstances of their countries. That the peoples of Czechoslovakia have achieved great successes is to be explained principally by the fact that the Communist Party of Czechoslovakia has adhered consistently to Lenin's teachings in its daily practical activities.

Comrades, the fraternal contacts and co-operation of the socialist countries, the unity of the international communist movement, are gaining new strength every day. The fraternal Communist and Workers' parties are putting up a determined stand against all attempts—whoever may make them—to undermine this Leninist unity and weaken the forces of world socialism.

It is to be deplored that the leaders of the League of Communists of Yugoslavia, a country whose people have shed much blood for the triumph of socialist ideas and the friendship and brotherhood of nations, should have undertaken the unseemly role of splitters.

Everybody knows how much was done by our Party and other fraternal parties in recent years to find a principled solution to the differences and to establish co-operation with the Yugoslav League of Communists on the basis of Marxist-Leninist principles. It was this purpose that we and other fraternal parties had in mind when we made our principled criticism of the draft programme of the Yugoslav League of Communists. We have told the leaders of the Yugoslav League of Communists in all frankness that they have taken the dangerous path of revising the basic propositions of Marxism-Leninism and undermining the unity of the international communist movement. But how did the leaders of the Yugoslav League of Communists react to this criticism? They raised a howl about the Communist and Workers' parties "interfering" in Yugoslavia's internal affairs and applying pressure to the Yugoslav League of Communists.

The Yugoslav leaders are manoeuvring clumsily and trying to prove that the Soviet Union and the other countries of the socialist camp are allegedly conducting "an organized campaign against Yugoslavia," acting against the Yugoslav people. Only he who, after a Russian proverb, wants to "becloud a clear day" could claim anything of this sort.

We have said repeatedly, and say again, that no one has ever conducted, or intends to conduct, any "campaign" against Yugoslavia and her peoples. But we have waged, and shall continue to wage, a consistent and principled struggle against all individuals and groups preaching anti-Marxist, revisionist views under the guise of "developing" the theory and practice of scientific socialism. That is our duty, our sacred duty. The great Lenin has taught us to do so.

Comrades, more than 40 years have passed since the Great October Socialist Revolution. And throughout this time the imperialists have not for a moment ceased their efforts to destroy the socialist world. The cold war against the socialist countries, launched by aggressive groups in some Western states, is now more than 10 years old. The makers of the policy "from strength" are not giving up their hopes of splitting the ranks of the socialist countries and of intimidating them with their atomic weapons, their military economic potential, their military bases.

Yet it is high time for them to realize, at long last, how futile their efforts are! (*Applause.*)

Lately, spokesmen of ruling circles in the Western countries have made statements to the effect that the only way out of the present situation is to step up the armaments race still more, which, they claim, may lead to an economic upturn. Reasoning of this kind is extremely dangerous. Some Western statesmen apparently fail to take account of the possible consequences of their political game.

The behaviour of the proponents of the armaments race is reminiscent of the man who set fire to his neighbour's flat to warm his hands, forgetting that he himself lived in the same house. (*Laughter, applause.*)

It is to be hoped that sooner or later Western ruling circles will be compelled to understand this fact and to assess realistically the situation and balance of forces in the world. (*Applause.*)

The only way to preserve peace is by peaceful co-existence. The forces of the socialist camp, all people of good will in all countries, stand guard over peace. And however much the imperialists may rave and rant, the cause we stand for is unconquerable. (*Stormy applause.*)

We are happy that in this struggle for socialism, peace and democracy, the peoples of Czechoslovakia, whose representatives we welcome here today so joyously and heartily, are standing by us. (*Prolonged applause.*) No friendship is stronger than the friendship of the socialist peoples, the friendship sealed with the blood shed by our peoples in joint battles against fascism, the friendship sealed with the great ideas of communism. (*Stormy applause.*)

Let us then tirelessly cement our friendship and co-operation with the peoples of fraternal Czechoslovakia, the unity and solidarity of all the countries of the mighty socialist camp! (*Stormy applause.*)

Long live and flourish the peoples of the socialist Czechoslovak Republic! (*Stormy applause. Cries*: "Hurrah!")

Long live the Communist Party of Czechoslovakia and its Leninist Central Committee headed by Comrade Antonin Novotný! (*Stormy applause. Cries*: "Hurrah!")

Long live Leninism! (*Stormy applause. Cries*: "Hurrah!")

Long live world peace! (*Stormy, prolonged applause. Cries*: "Hurrah!", "Long live Soviet-Czechoslovak friendship!")

ON ARRIVAL IN BERLIN OF C.P.S.U. DELEGATION
TO 5th CONGRESS OF SOCIALIST UNITY PARTY
OF GERMANY

July 8, 1958

Dear Comrade Ulbricht,
Dear Comrade Grotewohl,
Dear Comrades and Friends,
Allow me to convey to you and all the working people
of the German Democratic Republic the hearty fraternal
greetings of the Communist Party and the workers,
peasants and intelligentsia of the Soviet Union, and to
thank you from the bottom of our hearts for your warm
welcome.

We express our profound thanks to the Central Committee of the Socialist Unity Party of Germany for inviting a delegation of the C.P.S.U. to the 5th Congress of
the Socialist Unity Party of Germany. The Central Committee of our Party was very happy to accept this invitation. As we step on German soil today, we know that we
have come to our friends and fellow-fighters for peace, democracy and socialism.

We have come to the 5th Congress of the Socialist Unity Party of Germany eager to strengthen still further the
fraternal relations between our Marxist-Leninist parties
and between our peoples, who are building socialism and
communism.

There exist good, friendly relations, complete understanding and confidence between our parties. The Soviet

people are aware of the warm sentiments and sympathies that the working people of the German Democratic Republic have for the Soviet people. You, too, have unquestionably had occasion many times to see that in the common struggle for socialism and the preservation and consolidation of world peace the German working people have a loyal friend and fellow-fighter in the Soviet people.

Our Party and the peoples of the Soviet Union show a lively interest in the changes taking place in Germany. They rejoice at every new achievement of the workers, peasants and intellectuals of the German Democratic Republic in building a new state—the first workers' and peasants' state in the history of Germany.

There is deep satisfaction over the growing international ties of your republic, its increasing friendship with all the countries of the socialist camp, in whose fraternal family the German Democratic Republic occupies a fitting place.

We are sincerely happy that the working people of the German Democratic Republic, all the progressive forces brought together in the National Front of democratic Germany under the leadership of the working class and its militant vanguard—the Socialist Unity Party—are fighting confidently and persistently against the militarization of West Germany and the arming of the Bundeswehr with atomic and rocket weapons, for the country's peaceful reunification on a democratic basis, for safeguarding and strengthening peace and friendship among the peoples.

Allow me, dear comrades, to wish you new labour successes in building socialism in the German Democratic Republic.

Long live peace, friendship and co-operation between the Soviet and German peoples!

Long live the German Democratic Republic and its working people!

Long live the Socialist Unity Party of Germany—the leader of the working people of the German Democratic Republic!

(N. S. Khrushchov's speech was repeatedly interrupted by stormy applause, shouts of "Hurrah!" and wishes of long life to Soviet-German friendship, the Communist Party of the Soviet Union and the Socialist Unity Party of Germany.)

AT MASS MEETING IN HALLE DURING STAY
OF C.P.S.U. DELEGATION TO 5th CONGRESS
OF SOCIALIST UNITY PARTY OF GERMANY
IN GERMAN DEMOCRATIC REPUBLIC

July 8, 1958

Dear Comrades,
We are extremely pleased to attend your mass meeting
and to meet the workers, intellectuals and working people
of Halle—one of the biggest industrial centres of the German Democratic Republic. Permit me on behalf of the
delegation of the Communist Party of the Soviet Union,
the Central Committee of our Party, to greet you warmly
as our loyal friends and allies. (*Stormy, prolonged applause.*)

Permit me to thank you for the kind sentiments addressed here to the working class, the working people of
the Soviet Union and to our Communist Party. (*Prolonged
applause.*)

Comrades, you know that our Party and Government
are doing their best to ensure world peace. (*Applause.*)
We have made many good proposals to that end. If these
proposals had been accepted, they would unquestionably
have helped to ease international tension and achieve lasting peace. (*Stormy applause.*) But, as you know, every
time we make such proposals, the enemies of peace, like
pettifoggers, look for a pretext to reject them. When
we say that relations between the socialist and capitalist
countries should be built upon the principles of peaceful
co-existence, highly placed leaders in the capitalist coun-

tries not infrequently declare that they do not want to co-exist with the socialist states. But what does that imply? After all, we live on the same planet. It implies that some of the states should remove elsewhere from this planet. (*Laughter, applause*). We say that since there are states with different systems on our planet, they can and must co-exist, that is, they must live without war and not attack each other. (*Stormy applause, shouts of approval.*)

We do not interfere, and have no wish to interfere, in the affairs of other countries. Let us by all means have a trial of strength, but rather in peaceful competition than in war. Let the young, burgeoning, rising socialist countries compete with the old, senile capitalist world, and let us see who takes the upper hand, who wins. (*Animation, stormy applause.*)

Capitalist propaganda insisted that if the workers and peasants took power they would not know how to govern, how to organize production. If that is so, Messrs. Capitalists, you need not fear peaceful competition with socialism. You know how, and we do not. Hence, you will have an easier time. (*Laughter.*)

Admittedly, people who used to say that the working people are incapable of running a state are dying out in the capitalist countries. They kept expecting all the time that Soviet power would soon collapse, and claiming that communism was going through a crisis. But now the whole world knows where the crisis is, and where prosperity. (*Applause.*)

The Soviet Union, for example, is going to build seven blast furnaces this year and thereby alone increase the output of pig iron by more than four and a half million tons. (*Applause.*) We shall see by how much the capitalist countries increase their pig iron output! Where is the crisis then? (*Stormy applause.*)

We pick our words with care and do not speak of the capitalist countries the way imperialist propaganda babbles about our socialist system. We do not underestimate the powers of capitalism for we know that it is still strong. This is why we must rally the forces of the working class. But we know equally well that victory will rest with the working class, that the working class will win. (*Stormy applause, shouts of approval.*)

Comrades, we are raising the rates of socialist construction from year to year. The socialist countries are getting stronger each year and the friendship between them is growing and hardening. Yugoslavia alone stands apart. We have done, and continue to do, a lot for it to fall in step with all the socialist countries. But the Yugoslav leaders are against it and speak of some road of their own, while seeking support in American hand-outs. That road is not for us, however. We are accustomed to building socialism by combating capitalism. (*Stormy applause.*)

Take the Soviet Union, for example. In the 40 years of its development it has travelled a long way. Yet what did people say about us in the past? The exploiters stated, for instance, that if the working class took power, science stood to lose by it. However, whose earth satellites does the world see today? They are Soviet earth satellites! (*Stormy applause.*) The Americans launched three of their orange-size sputniks. (*Laughter.*) But their sputniks are a hundred times smaller than the third Soviet sputnik.

And what does that imply? It implies that Soviet science has surpassed American achievements. That is a big victory for us, comrades! It is an expression of the will of the working class and the wisdom of the communist movement. (*Stormy applause, shouts of* "Hurrah!")

Herr Adenauer knows that I have come to you, to your republic. He and I met when we negotiated in Moscow. He is still doting on his policy "from positions of strength." But that strength exists solely in his imagination. We do not recognize strength, but the right of the working class, of the working people, the right of nations to fashion their life after their own pattern. It is he who creates values, he who works, that must have at his disposal the fruits of his labours. (*Stormy applause.*)

Herr Adenauer does not recognize the existence of the German Democratic Republic. Well, we can't help that! (*Laughter.*) The U.S.A. does not recognize the existence of the Chinese People's Republic. But People's China has not ceased to exist on account of that. The United States had for a long time failed to recognize the Soviet Union as well. But for all that the Soviet Union did not cease to exist, and ultimately the United States was compelled to recognize the Union of Soviet Socialist Republics.

If a blind man who has never seen the sun is told about sunshine, he will not appreciate it anyway, and will say that there is no such thing as the sun's light. Likewise the hangers-on of capital do not want to concede that socialism has come to replace capitalism. They stubbornly refuse to concede that.

But they are finding it more and more difficult to deny the achievements of socialism. The socialist countries are raising their economy higher and higher every day.

Naturally, our countries also have the necessary armed forces to guard the socialist countries which are well able to defend their freedom and independence, their gains, from any enemy attack. Our countries maintain armies not for attack, but for defence. We are prepared to disarm at any time and, as you know, are taking steps towards disarmament. We shall defeat capitalism without war. We shall defeat it in peaceful competition, by our labour. (*Stormy applause.*)

I want to console Herr Adenauer: we believe that if today it is only the German Democratic Republic that is socialist, the time will come when all Germany will follow the socialist path, and not just Germany, but the entire world. Socialism will not conquer its positions by war. The working class, the working people of Germany and other countries, will ultimately triumph. Our sympathies are with the working class, with the working people, in their struggle for the future, for socialism and communism. (*Prolonged applause.*)

Comrades, the 5th Congress of the Socialist Unity Party of Germany is opening on July 10. Our delegation has come to it at the invitation of your Central Committee. We believe that your 5th Congress is going to be very fruitful and that after it the working class will rally still closer round the Socialist Unity Party, which represents the vital interests of the working class, the working peasantry, and the intellectuals of Germany. (*Applause.*)

Long live the German working class!

Long live the working people of Germany!

Long live the friendship between the peoples of the Soviet Union and Germany!

Long live world peace!

I wish you success, dear friends! (*Stormy, prolonged applause. The people scan*: "Friendship!" *Cries*: "Hurrah!")

SPEECH
AT MEETING HELD IN PALACE OF CULTURE OF BITTERFELD ELECTRO-CHEMICAL WORKS DURING STAY IN G.D.R. OF C.P.S.U. DELEGATION TO 5th CONGRESS OF SOCIALIST UNITY PARTY OF GERMANY

July 9, 1958

Dear Comrades and Friends,

Allow me, on behalf of our delegation, to express our sincere gratitude for the hearty welcome you have given us.

Comrade Schirmer, the director of the works, in his splendid report has said many flattering things about the Soviet Union. We are particularly pleased to note that he correctly understands the need for uniting the efforts of the German people with those of the peoples of the Soviet Union and the other socialist countries for the achievement of the speediest economic development of our countries and the attainment of a high standard of living for our working people.

I would like to outline some of my views on a number of specific questions. Let us take, if you will, the development of the chemical industry in the Soviet Union and the German Democratic Republic.

In order to co-ordinate our efforts in making more rational use of the material resources of our countries for the rapid development of the chemical industry, we must, in the first place, give thought to such a very important matter as co-operation and specialization in production processes. The German Democratic Republic possesses no large power resources and has scarcely any water

524

power. You have brown coal, of which you are making good use.

Other socialist countries, however, have power resources richer than brown coal. The Soviet Union, for example, has tremendous, still untapped resources of water power. Moreover, we have great potentialities for using coal for the production of power. In the Krasnoyarsk area, for instance, coal deposits have been discovered which extend for nearly 1,000 kilometres, with seams up to 100 metres in thickness. Coal can be strip-mined there by excavators. Experts say that if thermal power plants are built there, the electricity will be almost as cheap as that generated by hydroelectric power stations.

The question therefore arises: Should we not give thought to developing the chemical industry in our countries on the basis of a division of labour? Chemical enterprises with processes which consume most power should be situated in places where power is cheaper, so that raw materials may be produced there, while factories for the manufacture of finished goods should be developed in places where skilled manpower, engineering and technical personnel and chemists are available. This will enable our fraternal countries to make better use of human labour, raw material and power resources, and to ensure the production of high-quality goods at a lower cost.

I am not an engineer and consequently I cannot tell you precisely how this can be done. Let chemical experts, scientists, engineers and economists work out the most advantageous way of organizing this and then we shall, by taking into account the interests of our two countries, find the most correct solution to this problem. In any case, we can definitely say that the accomplishment of this task will be of tremendous significance and will be of great economic advantage, both for the German Democratic Republic and for the Soviet Union, as well as for all our fraternal countries.

I should like to offer one more consideration. It is a fact

that the Germans have made a remarkable contribution to the development of chemistry. They accomplished ahead of all others the task of industrially producing from coal a liquid fuel which is not inferior in quality to the petrol obtained from oil. At the time the rapid accomplishment of this task was dictated by strategic considerations, because Germany was then preparing for war. In our age of motors, war could not be waged without petrol—the motors would be still. That is why attention and effort in Germany were concentrated on carrying out this task. It must be said that it was done well.

The situation has now changed, and we should examine how economically expedient it is to produce liquid fuel from coal. It may be economically more profitable to switch over your plants producing liquid fuel to oil refining and thus obtain petrol for the economy at a considerably lower cost. Is it not possible to reduce the cost of producing liquid fuel and, furthermore, to obtain by-products for the development of the chemical industry at a lower cost? It would seem that this too should be given thought.

The reserves of oil in the Soviet Union are almost limitless and output is increasing every year. Our specialists are discovering more and more new oil deposits which makes possible a substantial increase in oil production. This means that we can supply the German Democratic Republic with the necessary quantities of oil.

Today the socialist countries cannot operate their economies in isolation, within the framework of each individual country alone. It is necessary to develop and improve co-operation so as to most rationally utilize the natural wealth and economic resources that are available in the socialist countries.

Even within the limits of a single country, co-operation and specialization are of huge importance. Let us take coal mining, for instance. If we take production costs per ton of coal mined in the Donbas, they will probably be three to five times greater than in Kemerovo or Krasnoyarsk. That is why we are now emphasizing the development of power-consuming industries in the eastern areas, where coal is mined at lower cost.

In the Donbas, coal is mined by combines and coal-cutting machines, and the seams there are often only half a metre in thickness, whereas in the Krasnoyarsk area, as I have already said, the seams measure up to 100 metres. The coal there lies on the surface, and it can be scooped up by excavators and loaded directly into railway wagons. Naturally this is more advantageous.

That is how matters stand in the Soviet Union. But today our country is not alone. The camp of socialist countries is growing and becoming stronger. And we should take into account not only the interests of one country but the interests of all the socialist countries. When I was speaking about co-operation between the chemical industries of the Soviet Union and the German Democratic Republic, I had in mind the interests not only of our country, but also those of the German Democratic Republic and the other socialist countries. Such co-operation will be mutually advantageous for our countries.

Naturally we understand mutual benefit differently from Comrade Tito. We have rendered, and shall continue to render, assistance to the socialist countries in developing their economies so that all can go forward together more quickly, giving each other support. (*Stormy applause.*)

Allow me to dwell on the question of pooling our efforts in developing science and technology, in the fields of engineering and technological work and designing. Professor Schirmer spoke well about this in his report. We have to unite and to concentrate our efforts in these fields as well. You possess a highly developed chemical science and chemical industry. I mean no offence, dear comrades, but we shall certainly catch up with you. (*Stormy applause.*)

I am glad you approve of this intention of ours. This is understandable enough, for there are no antagonistic contradictions between our countries. We have common aims and tasks: to build socialism and communism. Therefore let us apply our forces, as they say in physics, to a single point, so that they may act in one direction and not cancel each other out, but grow. Then, with smaller outlays we shall obtain better results and ensure a still higher rate of development in the chemical industry and in the whole of the national economy.

The appropriate agencies of our states, after making a careful preliminary study of these questions, should come to an understanding on how to practically organize cooperation between the enterprises of the chemical industries of our countries. We should give thought to defining the problems which the German comrades will undertake to work out, the questions which are to be worked out by the Soviet side, and those which should be tackled jointly.

Comrades, the development of the chemical industry calls for experienced personnel—scientists and engineers. We have such personnel. But we would gladly enlist the services of German chemical engineers and scientists and other specialists, including experts from West Germany, for work in our chemical industry. West German specialists may say that their political convictions and views differ from ours. But let them set aside questions of political conviction. If a scientist or engineer does not share communist views and communist convictions, let him keep his own convictions and come to us simply as a chemist or scientist. If he really wants to achieve the best results from the application of his labour, we shall offer him every opportunity for doing so. We shall pay him more than the richest concerns and firms are paying. We shall provide such scientists, engineers and technicians with the finest equipment for the tackling of scientific and technical problems.

We shall do this for those persons who wish to stay out of politics and to act only on the basis of material considerations. But if one bears in mind political considerations as well, it must be said quite categorically that the most profitable "undertaking" in which material resources may be invested is in the building of communism. This "undertaking" is developing without crises and to it belongs the future. (*Applause.*)

The main thing to be borne in mind is the noble aims and principles of communism. Under capitalism man is to man a wolf. Every capitalist wants to snatch more for himself, caring nothing about the interests of other people or the interests of society, and he spies upon his neighbour in order to steal his secret and use it for his own ends. Such are the laws of capitalist competition. Nothing like this exists under socialism. Under socialism there are no oppressors or oppressed; all men and women live by their own labour, and all have equal rights and duties to society. At the highest stage, under communism, the full satisfaction of man's needs will be ensured. And these are not idle words. Under socialism man is to man, a friend regardless of the language he speaks and the God to whom he prays. Religion is a matter for each person to decide for himself.

Socialism is the most just and noble social system, under which the efforts of the whole of society are aimed at promoting the welfare of the people and the constant development of the economy, science, culture and art, at ensuring that the people live better and better. It is well worth working for these lofty aims, sparing neither effort nor knowledge. In the language of Western businessmen, one can figuratively describe the firm of communist construction as sound and upright. (*Stormy applause.*)

However, in speaking now about co-operation with West German specialists in developing the chemical industry we are digressing, as it were, from this political aspect of the question. It is, of course, good to deal with people who are devoted, heart and soul, to building communism. If, however, a person still has certain bacilli meandering about in his head, which do not allow him to take a firm stand and recognize the need to rebuild society on communist lines, then let him continue with his ailment for a while. Let us pay him well, give him a good salary, a house in the country, and so on.

If a man works well and confers great benefits on society, let him enjoy what he deserves. In a socialist society such people are valued and properly remunerated.

The Soviet atomic experts and specialists who have created the intercontinental rocket and the sputniks have no complaint against their socialist country. They live so well that God grant you a life like theirs, as the saying goes! (*Stormy applause.*) The Soviet Government has rewarded them and many of them have received Lenin Prizes and the title of Hero of Socialist Labour. They are also well provided for from the material point of view. They "suffer" somewhat only in one respect—they are as yet anonymous as far as the outside world is concerned. They live, as it were, under the general designation of "scientists and engineers working on atomics and rocketry." But so far it is not widely known exactly who these people are. We shall erect a monument in honour of those who have created the rocket and the sputniks and shall inscribe their glorious names in letters of gold, so that they may be known to future generations throughout the ages. (*Prolonged applause.*)

Yes, when the time comes, the photographs and names of these illustrious people will be made public and they will become widely known to all men. We greatly value these people; we treasure them and protect them from enemy agents who might be sent in to destroy such outstanding men—our treasured personnel. But today, in order to ensure the country's security and the lives of these scientists, engineers, technicians and other specialists, we cannot as yet make known their names or publish their photographs. This, however, applies only to specialists who work in branches of technology and science which are at present classed as state secrets. In all other spheres scientists, engineers and specialists enjoy the widest renown in our society. The Soviet state and our society know how to highly appreciate our scientists, engineers, technicians and other specialists and fittingly reward them for their work, which is of great social benefit.

I think that German specialists, too, could work in our country under similarly good conditions. It is not necessary for them to share our views in order to do so.

It is a fact that there are still scientists and specialists in your republic who have not yet completely defined their political attitude. In the past there were also people like that in our country—the Soviet Union. This state of affairs was very aptly described in a humorous story relating how a check-up of office employees was made in the first years of the revolution in our country. Each employee had to fill in a questionnaire which, among other things, contained the following question: "Do you believe in God?"

One employee replied: "At work no, at home yes." (*Laughter, animation in the hall.*)

My dear specialists, please don't be offended if I frankly say that in your country, the German Democratic Republic, too, there are evidently still a certain number of such office employees, scientists and engineers—people who, if asked: "Are you for socialism or against it?" would say, if they wished to be frank: "In the German Democratic Republic we are for socialism, in Bonn we are against it." (*Burst of laughter. Applause.*)

And so a man of that kind goes from Berlin to Bonn and from Bonn to Berlin. He will continue shuttling back and forth as long as he does not acquire a more accurate and true compass. At present he is like a tiny boat on the high seas. Without rudder or sail, it is tossed about by the waves.

Such people, however, although at present without a political compass, are of value and a struggle for them is being waged between the socialist and the capitalist countries. Many of these people are not attracted to political ideas; they are more attracted, as the Americans say, to business. So let us pay them well, pay them more than the Americans pay, more than Bonn pays. And when they work with us they will learn that we are not enemies. Working together with us, such people will in action become convinced that socialism is the most progressive social system and that communism is mankind's radiant dream of the future.

The majority of those people who will at first march, or who are marching, together with us because their work is well remunerated in our socialist countries, will themselves not notice how, subsequently, they will come to stand firmly on their own feet, acquire a political compass, and, together with their own people, follow the road along which the nation is being led by the Communist parties— the road to communism! (*Prolonged applause.*)

Perhaps I am putting all this too baldly and perhaps some of you are now applauding with everyone else only for the sake of appearances, while thinking, deep down, as the Russian saying has it: "No, brother, an old bird isn't caught with chaff!" (*Laughter in the hall.*)

Believe me, I don't wish to "catch" or mislead anyone. I am telling you what is urged by life itself. That is why, in the interests of the men and women who are now living without a political compass, I advise obtaining this compass in order to steer a straight course and go forward, together with their people, to a better future for mankind —to communism. (*Stormy applause.*)

Our Government has recently received many offers from large firms in Western countries to deliver equipment for the Soviet Union's chemical industry. Such proposals, for instance, have been received from industrialists in West Germany, Britain, France and the United States. We are now studying all these offers with a view to concluding satisfactory contracts. Here we are really acting on the basis of mutual benefit. The capitalists enter into business contacts only when it is to their advantage. We, for our part, want to do business with capitalist firms, which is advantageous to our country. So it is necessary to find a basis which is beneficial to both parties and then sign business contracts. The capitalist businessman must be ensured a legitimate percentage of profit. Here we cannot count on friendly, unselfish assistance. There is no capitalist who would not strive to obtain bigger returns, to profit from any business transaction.

We have proposed to the Government of the United States that an agreement be concluded for the delivery of chemical equipment to our country and that appropriate credits be granted in this connection. But so far we have received no reply from the United States. It is apparently very difficult for the United States Government to reply to our proposals. But we are in no hurry about this—we shall wait. Furthermore, if we do wait, that does not mean we are doing nothing. We are waiting for an answer, but at the same time we ourselves are working on the problem of speeding up the development of our chemical industry with our own resources.

The Central Committee of the Communist Party of the Soviet Union and the Soviet Government, in deciding to speed up the development of the chemical industry, and especially the production of synthetic materials and their products to meet the requirements of the population and those of the national economy, took as their main point of departure the internal potentialities of our country, bearing in mind the achievements of our own industry, the discoveries of Soviet scientists and specialists in the field of chemistry, and the successes of research institutes and designing organizations. We relied on the creative forces of the Soviet people, on the tremendous experience accumulated by the working class, by the engineering and technical personnel, and on the inexhaustible natural wealth of our country. Of course, we are also relying on your assistance, on the assistance of German chemists, engineers, technicians and economists, on the assistance of the workers of the German Democratic Republic, and we are relying on the help of expert chemists in other socialist countries.

At the same time we are sure that we shall also be dealing with businessmen from capitalist countries, with all who want to earn by taking part in the development of our chemical industry. If they don't want to make money, that is their own affair. The Soviet Union offers them orders, and it is up to them to accept or reject those orders. We do not intend to quarrel with anyone about this.

Comrades, today we have been to your works. Earlier, in 1946, I had occasion to visit one of your plants producing artificial fibre. Today—as then—we saw many interesting things at your works. Thank you for showing us your plant. I have not often had the opportunity of visiting chemical enterprises. I am better acquainted with the mining industry. My father was a miner and I, too, worked in the mines for quite a time, and have still not forgotten the conditions in which miners work and mining equipment. Though mines are now provided with new equipment and have new working conditions, I try, from force of old occupational habit, to keep in touch with the mining industry. I have a fairly good idea about metallurgy and the building industry; and now fate has linked me with maize. (*Animation in the hall. Applause.*) Maize offers great opportunities for the development of agriculture, in your republic as well. Maize means sausage, and a German, you know, can't live without sausage and beer. (*Laughter in the hall.*)

You have shown us your chemical production. Now it is a question of concluding agreements on co-operation in developing the chemical industries in our countries— agreements that will benefit our peoples.

Allow me now to say a few words about the important and acute problem of the reunification of Germany. Herr Adenauer and his colleagues are pursuing a "policy of strength" and want to intimidate the Soviet Union, to make us exert pressure on the Government of the German Democratic Republic so that it will agree to the reunification of Germany at the price of abolishing the G.D.R., that is to say, by abolishing the social gains of the working people of the German Democratic Republic. They want you to agree to the factories and mills being returned to the German capitalists, to capitalism being restored in your republic.

And that is what Herr Adenauer calls the reunification of Germany! He thinks that the Soviet Union will help him in this. (*Laughter.*) If any leader in the Soviet Union were so much as to think that way, people in our country and in our Party would say that such a leader be placed in a lunatic asylum and have his head examined. (*Stormy applause.*) I do not know how to describe such ideas, but it certainly reflects a failure to understand the real state of affairs.

We have said, and we continue to say, that the reunification of Germany is an internal matter for the Germans themselves, for the German workers, for the whole people of the German Democratic Republic and the Federal Republic of Germany. No one but they can decide this question or has any right to do so. (*Stormy applause.*)

As a means of exerting pressure West German militarists wish to use such levers as the arming of the Bundeswehr with nuclear weapons and the establishment of rocket launching sites on the territory of the Federal Republic of Germany. But this is sheer madness. It should not be forgotten that rocket sites and atomic bases have a reverse power of attraction for rockets from other sites and bases. Only those who are insane can play with the lives of millions of men and women. It is high time that this was understood by Herr Adenauer, and above all by the War Minister of the Federal Republic of Germany, Herr Strauss, as well as by those who stand behind them.

As for the Soviet Union, we shall not be intimidated

by threats and blackmail. The attempts to intimidate us are foolish and futile, and it is high time they were abandoned.

There is only one way to reunify Germany, and that is to have representatives of the governments of the two German states meet, sit down at a round table and come to an understanding—all the more so since the talks will be conducted in a single language—the German language—and no interpreter will be needed.

If West German militarists continue to employ blackmail and intimidation with the threat of war, we shall have to tell them that blackmail against the German Democratic Republic is blackmail against the Soviet Union, and against all the socialist countries. And therefore all the forces of the socialist countries will be used to defend the German Democratic Republic. (*Stormy, prolonged applause.*)

The German people are a very talented and industrious people. They have given mankind many remarkable discoveries and inventions. The German people do not need aggressive campaigns for *Lebensraum.* It will be remembered that Hitler, Göbbels and others urged the Germans to conquer foreign territories. They dreamed of Ukrainian sausage. But how did it all end? Now neither Hitler nor Göbbels has any desire for Ukrainian or German sausage, or the conquest of foreign territories.

What prospects have the German people then with their relatively small territory? They have the broadest and brightest prospects. Today, when one-third of mankind is building its life under the banner of Marxism-Leninism, the question of territories has been eliminated.

We do not regard the wealth of the Soviet Union as being solely our own wealth—it is the wealth of all the socialist countries. That, too, is the view of real Communists, Marxist-Leninists, of other socialist countries, who look upon their countries' wealth as our common wealth, serving the common interests of the peoples of all socialist states. And this wealth is so great that it amply provides for the requirements of the peoples of all our countries. (*Stormy applause.*)

Under socialism the products of labour are distributed in accordance with the quantity and quality of work contributed by each member of society, i.e., according to the principle: From each according to his ability, to each according to his work. Under communism distribution will take place according to the principle: From each according to his ability, to each according to his needs. In order to speed the advance of all the socialist countries to communism, we must do everything possible for each socialist country to develop its economy and increase its labour productivity more rapidly. Each of our countries must render genuinely fraternal aid to the other socialist countries. By uniting our efforts, by promoting co-operation and collaboration, our countries are achieving greater successes in economic development. At the same time each socialist country must make the best possible use of its internal potentialities for developing its national economy.

In the process of building communism, all socialist countries will equalize their economies, eliminate differences in level of development, without taking the relatively underdeveloped countries as their criterion. This equalization will not take place by lowering the level of the countries that are economically highly developed. By no means. The equalization should and will proceed through the more rapid advance of the countries that are relatively less developed economically by bringing them up to the level of the most developed countries. Thus, all the socialist countries will march in a common united front along the road of socialism, along the road of building communist society.

Comrades, capitalism and socialism are antagonistic social systems. The imperialists want to ensure their own interests, not only at the expense of the working people of their own countries, but also at the expense of the peoples

of other countries, ignoring their vital interests. Statesmen of capitalist countries frequently speak openly about
this. For example, in 1956, during our visit to Britain, Sir
Anthony Eden and Mr. Selwyn Lloyd told us that if something were to happen in the Middle East and the supply of
oil from that area would be cut off, they would not stop
short of war. We told them at that time: It is easy to start
a war but it is difficult to end it. Even a fool can start a
war, and it would more likely be a stupid man who would
start a war, but it is difficult even for a wise man to end it.
Please do not forget this.

At that time we frankly warned Sir Anthony and Mr.
Lloyd: If you start a war in that area, we shall not be
able to remain as onlookers. We have no special interests
in the Middle East. But the Middle East is not so far away
from the Soviet Union and a war there would threaten the
security of our country. However, the British Government
of that day did not heed our advice.

You know how the Soviet Government reacted when the
imperialists unleashed aggression in the Middle East. It
is also well known that this ended in ignominy for the aggressors.

No one can violate foreign frontiers with impunity.
State frontiers have scarcely ever been changed without
war. We stand for non-interference by states in the domestic affairs of other states, for the peaceful co-existence of
states, irrespective of their existing systems. We say: It
is necessary, as the diplomats put it, to recognize the
status quo, to establish good relations between states, to
recognize the necessity for peaceful co-existence of states,
with everything that entails, to end the cold war, to create
conditions for all-round contacts and trade among all
countries. Only on this basis will each country be able to
develop its economy and culture and raise the standard
of living of the people.

There is an abundance of wealth for everyone in the
world—it must simply be rationally and economically

538

used. Marxism-Leninism teaches us that only under socialism can this wealth be most rationally used for the good
of all people. That is why we advise people who are living without a compass or with a faulty one: Throw
your bad compass into the sea, equip yourself with
our communist compass and take the road of building
a new social system—the socialist system. You may
be confident that the Marxist-Leninist compass will
unerringly lead mankind to a radiant future. (*Stormy
applause.*)

Comrades and friends, we are doing everything possible
to strengthen the friendship among socialist countries,
friendship among all nations, and to ensure world peace.
We do not confine ourselves within the boundaries of the
socialist countries, but strive to establish contacts and
develop ties with all countries, irrespective of social system. But first of all we must strengthen the friendship
among peoples of the socialist countries. So long as this
friendship is strong and indestructible, no enemy can
daunt us. The friendship of the peoples of the Soviet
Union, the German Democratic Republic, and the peoples
of all socialist countries is one of the inexhaustible sources
of our titanic strength.

You are building socialism in your country under the
leadership of the Socialist Unity Party of Germany, which
is in the forefront of the bloc of democratic parties united
in the National Front of democratic Germany.

We have very good relations with your Government,
with the Central Committee of the Socialist Unity Party of
Germany and its leadership. We knew Comrade Thälmann
well, and we know Comrade Pieck—men utterly devoted
to the cause of the working class, to the cause of the working people. We know Comrade Ulbricht well—a man on
whom the enemies of socialism are concentrating their
fire, inventing all kinds of fables. Why are they doing this?
Because the enemies always choose important targets on
which to concentrate their fire in order to put them out of

action and weaken our positions. But the more the enemies of socialism fume and rage, the more they scream against Comrade Ulbricht, the more he is supported by the Party and the people. (*Stormy applause.*)

August Bebel put it very well in his day: If an enemy praises you, ask yourself what stupidity you have committed and for what he is praising you. And that is correct. Consequently, if an enemy censures you, that means you are on the right path and are faithfully serving the working class and your people.

At meetings with Comrade Tito I said to him time and again: What are the American imperialists praising you for? Why are they giving you wheat? What is this Yugoslav socialism which Mr. Dulles likes? Think about it. If you are really in favour of socialism, it is something the American imperialists cannot like. They apparently detect in your country an odour that is not quite socialist, and that is precisely what they like. Such is the law of the class struggle.

The leaders of the Socialist Unity Party of Germany are resolutely and unswervingly following the path charted by the great teachers of the working class—Marx, Engels and Lenin, and that is why we have such fraternal relations with them.

We know your other leaders—such as Comrades Rau, Matern, and the other members of the Political Bureau of the Socialist Unity Party of Germany, who spare no efforts to serve the interests of their people and their Party—and we hold them in high esteem.

I would like to draw attention to the outstanding role of our dear friend Comrade Grotewohl. He took the Marxist-Leninist path a little later than his comrades in the Political Bureau, but having great practical experience, he is devotedly serving his Party and his people, sparing no effort, waging an irreconcilable struggle against the enemies of Marxism-Leninism and resolutely upholding the great cause of building socialism. (*Applause.*)

Such is the situation, comrades. It must be said that the general situation in your country is now good.

As regards the German question, the wind is blowing, not in your faces, but against Herr Adenauer. The time will come when people will come to you, knock at your door, and say: "We are from Bonn and we have come to you for talks." (*Applause.*) I do not know when they will come, but I am certain that they will come to you. You can well afford to wait. Every day works in your favour and at the same time every day works against Adenauer. So let us wait.

Comrades, I want to say a few words about the state of affairs in the Soviet Union. In many parts of our country harvesting has already begun and it appears that it will be a very good one. It is rather rare that over a territory as vast as that of the Soviet Union, a good harvest is expected in almost all regions. A good crop is anticipated in the Northern Caucasus; good crops are ripening in the Ukraine, in the Volga area, and in Kazakhstan. Good yields are also expected in Siberia, although it is a little early as yet to speak about Siberia. In short, this year we shall apparently procure no less grain—and even more—than in 1956, when we procured 3,300 million poods, so that we shall be able to eat both bread and sausage, and have enough to spare for beer. (*Laughter.*) Our socialist camp has everything it needs. We are not dependent on the capitalist world. They organized a blockade and sought to reduce our opportunities for developing technology and science. But our sputnik rose earlier than the small American satellite. And, incidentally, even that little American satellite was made with the participation of such German specialists as Dr. von Braun. (*Stormy applause.*)

Our industry is working well. The reorganization of the management of industry has been a huge success. Many people have been drawn into the management of industry and the rights of the local bodies have been extended, while centralized planning has been preserved. And this is a good combination: enlisting the masses in management, and preserving centralized leadership so as to avoid anarchy. Now our plans are being overfulfilled and we are going forward with confidence. While there is a recession in American industry, and signs of a recession can be observed in other capitalist countries as well, the economy in the socialist countries is doing well and developing like a healthy organism with a good appetite. We are confidently marching forward.

We have now charted a far-reaching plan for the development of the chemical industry. And we are sure that this plan will not only be fulfilled, but overfulfilled.

Comrades, the working class and all the working people of our country are rallied more closely than ever around the Communist Party and are unanimously supporting its policy.

Friendship and co-operation among the peoples of all the socialist countries have grown stronger. The cementing force of this friendship is the unity of views of the Communist and Workers' parties, based on the great principles of Marxism-Leninism.

When the leaders of the League of Communists of Yugoslavia took to revising Marxism-Leninism and tried to shake the unity of the international communist movement, they met with a vigorous rebuff from all the Marxist-Leninist parties. This once again convincingly demonstrates the unshakable firmness and unity of the forces of world communism. There is no force on earth that could bar the road to the working class, and all mankind, or hold back the inexorable forward march of the peoples to communism! (*Stormy applause.*)

Long live the working men and women, engineers and scientists of your chemical works! (*Prolonged applause.*)

Long live the working men and women, peasants, office employees and scientists of the German Democratic Republic! (*Prolonged applause.*)

Long live the everlasting and indestructible friendship between the peoples of the Soviet Union and the German people! (*Prolonged applause.*)

Long live the fraternal friendship between the peoples of the socialist countries! (*Prolonged applause.*)

Long live world peace! (*Stormy, prolonged applause. All rise.*)

SPEECH
AT 5th CONGRESS
OF SOCIALIST UNITY PARTY OF GERMANY

July 11, 1958

Dear Comrades and Friends,

Allow me on behalf of the Central Committee of the Communist Party of the Soviet Union, on behalf of our Party and all the Soviet people, to convey to the 5th Congress of the Socialist Unity Party of Germany, to the members of your Party, to the working class and all the working people of the German Democratic Republic warm fraternal greetings and good wishes for success in the work of your congress. (*Stormy, prolonged applause.*)

Your Party has come to its 5th Congress with great successes. Looking back, we can see how the positions of socialism have been strengthened in the German Democratic Republic during the brief period it has been in existence.

The German Democratic Republic has translated into reality the dreams of the founders of scientific communism—Karl Marx and Frederick Engels, and of courageous fighters for the freedom and happiness of the German people, outstanding leaders of the German and international working-class movement—August Bebel and Franz Mehring, Karl Liebknecht and Rosa Luxemburg, Ernst Thälmann, Klara Zetkin and many others.

The fact that Germany has taken the road to socialism is of epoch-making significance. It is now clear to every sensible person that the imperialists' hopes of undermining the building of socialism in the German Democratic Republic have been completely dashed. The working people of your republic, under the leadership of the Socialist Unity Party, have come through the test with honour and have overcome many difficulties on their road.

As is shown in the report of your Party's Central Committee and in Comrade Walter Ulbricht's report, your republic, in a relatively brief space of time, has grown stronger, has stood firmly on its own feet and has laid a solid foundation on which the magnificent edifice of socialist society can be confidently and rapidly built. The socialist sector in industry is contributing 88.7 per cent of the total output and in agriculture already one-third of the land is being cultivated by enterprises of a socialist type.

With all our hearts, dear comrades, we congratulate you on these remarkable victories. (*Prolonged applause.*)

Up to now the building of socialism has been completed in only one country—in the Soviet Union. Now we are entering an era in which it is to be completed in many countries.

The 7th Congress of the Bulgarian Communist Party, which was held recently, summed up the results of the great work done by the Party and noted that socialist transformations in Bulgaria had been completed in the main. The 11th Congress of the Communist Party of Czechoslovakia also pointed out that socialism had won a decisive victory in that country and that the task of completing the building of socialism within the next few years was on the order of the day. The Second Session of the 8th Congress of the Communist Party of China, held in May, drew attention to the tremendous successes achieved by the Chinese People's Republic in building socialism. The Communist Party of China has worked out its general policy for building socialism. The implementation of this policy will enable the Chinese people to turn their country into a great industrial socialist Power.

The Chinese, Bulgarian, Czechoslovak and other free

peoples will complete the building of socialism before long. The day is not far off when by their untiring and glorious efforts the workers, peasants and intellectuals—all the working people of the German Democratic Republic will also build the radiant edifice of socialism. All friends of the talented and industrious German people, all progressive mankind will sincerely and warmly rejoice in your victory. (*Stormy applause.*)

Socialism is winning ever new historic victories. Let the ideologists of the bourgeoisie hunt for "evils" and shortcomings in the socialist system and shout about a "crisis of communism." They have been doing this ever since the first days of Soviet power in Russia. Yet in spite of all the intrigues of our enemies, we have built socialism and are now advancing successfully to a communist society. (*Applause.*) As regards industrial output our country has already outstripped all the capitalist countries with the exception of the United States, and is now rapidly overtaking that economically most developed country. (*Applause.*)

Not long ago there were many vociferous cries in the West that the new form of the dictatorship of the proletariat, people's democracy, which had arisen after the Second World War in a number of East European countries, has been artificially imposed by the Communists on the peoples of these countries and had no future. Today, too, there are quite a few people who delude themselves with assertions of that kind.

But a number of People's Democracies are already directly tackling the task of completing the building of socialism. During the years of socialist development these countries have expanded their productive forces several times and now have a bigger industrial output than they even had under capitalism. The peoples themselves, who have become the owners of all their countries' wealth, have proved in practice that they are more zealous owners than were the capitalists. This means that the system of people's democracy has withstood the test of time and has proved its vitality as a system in conformity with the fundamental interests of the working people. (*Prolonged applause.*)

This is a great victory, comrades, a victory of truly historic significance.

The fact that the rates of socialist economic development are much faster than those of capitalism is of decisive importance. Less than a year has gone by since we pointed out that the countries of the world socialist system, embracing 35 per cent of the world's population, were producing about one-third of the world's total industrial output. Since that time the economy of the socialist countries has been steadily advancing, while the economy of the capitalist countries has been in a feverish state as a result of crisis phenomena in the principal capitalist country— the United States of America.

Whereas in the Soviet Union total industrial output in the first quarter of this year was 11 per cent **higher** than in the corresponding period of 1957, in the United States, according to official American statistics, total industrial output in the first quarter of this year was 11 per cent **lower** than in the corresponding period last year. Output dropped particularly sharply in the decisive branches of U.S. heavy industry. For example, oil output dropped during this period by 12 per cent; production of coal dropped by 21 per cent and that of steel by 40 per cent. The output of durable consumer goods fell by 20 per cent and that of motor vehicles dropped by 26 per cent.

In the Soviet Union's peaceful competition with the main capitalist country, the United States, we have obtained results which cannot fail to gladden the hearts of all friends of socialism. (*Applause.*) The Soviet Union is moving ahead of the United States as regards both the rates of growth and the increase in production of iron ore, coal, oil, pig iron, steel, cement and woollen fabrics. In the case of a number of agricultural products, the Soviet Union is approaching the volume of output in the United States, and with respect to some products it has already overtaken and even surpassed America's present level of production. (*Applause.*) The Soviet Union produces more than twice as much wheat as the United States and about three times as much sugar-beet. In 1957 the output of milk in the Soviet Union already amounted to about 95 per cent of U.S. output, and the production of butter was somewhat higher than in the U.S.A.

Our victories in peaceful competition with capitalism are indisputable, but this does not give us any grounds for self-satisfaction, conceit or complacency. Not for one moment must we forget that in a number of branches of industry and agriculture we are still lagging behind capitalist countries and are not as yet meeting in full the constantly growing requirements of the population of our countries.

The ordinary person, of course, judges the merits of this or that system first of all by who is in power, who owns the factories and mills, the land, all the country's wealth, what political rights the people have in this or that country, and so on. But it is also important to him how he, the worker, eats and clothes himself, what access he has to science and culture and what his position is with regard to public education.

We should not be Marxist-Leninists if we were to ignore this. Today we can say with confidence that a worker or peasant in any of the socialist countries fares much better than he did in the past under the system of exploitation. And this is so, in spite of the fact that the socialist countries, while surmounting tremendous difficulties, had to begin building the new life by overcoming the consequences of the war and by laying the foundation for an independent socialist economy. In these conditions the working people consciously had to accept certain restrictions in the fulfilment of their essential needs.

You are well aware how the Soviet people acted in building their socialist economy. We denied ourselves a great deal and restricted ourselves with regard to food, clothing and production of consumer goods, and each ruble saved was invested in the construction of factories and mills for heavy industry, in erecting power stations. We made great haste in this matter, because we knew that if, within a brief historical period, we did not create our own powerful industry, our own large-scale mechanized agriculture, our own skilled personnel, or if we lagged behind in the development of science and technology, the imperialists would crush us and would destroy the country in which, for the first time, workers and peasants, the working people, had come to power. And we emerged victorious. (*Stormy applause.*)

When the imperialists unloosed on our country the fascist beast which they had reared, the Soviet people, fully armed, met this deadly enemy. Everyone knows how the Hitler adventure ended. Our country, having routed the enemy, emerged from the war still stronger and more steeled. After healing the grievous wounds of war, the Soviet Union rapidly began to develop its economy, science and culture, and made enormous progress of which we are justly proud, for such successes are only possible on the basis of socialism. (*Applause.*)

Today the situation is such that the Soviet Union, relying on the extensive production base of socialism, is in a position to step up sharply the production of consumer goods within the next few years, to increase the output of foodstuffs and radically to improve the housing conditions of the working people, without reducing the rate of development of the basic branches of the national economy. For socialism and communism mean a better, more cultured and more prosperous life for the working people than they had under capitalism.

Our Party is making strenuous efforts to uncover and more fully utilize internal reserves, to give still greater impetus to the initiative of the working masses and to ensure the maximum satisfaction of the needs of the working people within the next few years. The Communist Party of the Soviet Union has recently carried out the big task of reorganizing the management of industry and construction. These measures are already yielding tremendous economic results. In recent years the Soviet Union has also carried out a number of important measures for the further development of agriculture.

We have adopted an extensive programme for the development of the chemical industry. The fulfilment of this programme will ensure further technical progress in the country's national economy and will enable us to solve quickly the problem of increasing the output of consumer goods.

The successes achieved by the socialist countries in developing industry, agriculture, science and culture graphically demonstrate the strength and vitality of the new social system, of the new forms of relations between the peoples. (*Applause.*)

Comrades, the Meeting of Representatives of the Communist and Workers' Parties of the Socialist Countries, which was held in Moscow last November, and the recent Moscow meeting on economic questions were of great significance for strengthening the socialist camp. The documents approved by these meetings sum up the vast experience accumulated in the building of socialism in the U.S.S.R. and the People's Democracies. The Declaration contained a further development of the fundamental principles of Marxism-Leninism as applied to the conditions of our era.

These meetings demonstrated the indestructible unity of the peoples of the socialist countries, their all-round interest in the further consolidation of their friendship, in the improvement and development of co-operation between the socialist countries.

Much is being done to strengthen this co-operation on the part of the Socialist Unity Party of Germany and the President of your republic, an outstanding veteran leader of the German and international working-class movement, the companion-in-arms of Karl Liebknecht and Ernst Thälmann, our dear friend and comrade Wilhelm Pieck (*Stormy, prolonged applause.*)

The ranks of the Socialist Unity Party of Germany are being untiringly welded together by its glorious Central Committee and by the First Secretary of the Central Committee of the Socialist Unity Party of Germany, our dear friend and comrade Walter Ulbricht. (*Stormy applause.*)

Under the leadership of the Socialist Unity Party the Government of the German Democratic Republic, headed by our dear friend and comrade Otto Grotewohl, is persistently and steadfastly working for the building of socialism in the German Democratic Republic, for the consolidation of peace and the establishment of a united democratic and peace-loving German state. (*Stormy applause.*)

In the struggle for the building of a new social system, the Socialist Unity Party has rallied together all the democratic and political forces in the National Front of democratic Germany. The co-operation of the parties of the democratic bloc in the National Front, in which the Socialist Unity Party has the leading role, is a reliable guarantee of success in building the new society, in striving for a better future for the German people. With all our hearts we wish the parties co-operating in the National Front of democratic Germany further successes in building the new life, in strengthening peace, in striving to accomplish the vitally important task—the establishment of a united, democratic and peace-loving German state. (*Prolonged applause.*)

Comrades, the unity and solidarity of the socialist camp presupposes the broad independence and national sovereignty of the countries belonging to it. The development of co-operation among the socialist states, ever since the world socialist system came into existence, has clearly shown that it is precisely the socialist system which ensures genuine national independence for the peoples. The socialist camp is a voluntary alliance of equal and sovereign states, in which no one strives to gain special rights for himself and no one seeks for privileges or advantages.

Experience has shown that the socialist countries cannot act disconnectedly in face of the imperialist camp. If any country marches singly and apart, it will not be able to fully utilize the rich possibilities afforded by the socialist system for the victory of socialism. Acting singly, it will not be able in the present international conditions to maintain a reliable defence of the socialist gains or to guarantee them against encroachments by the imperialists.

That is why the Communist and Workers' parties unanimously maintain that only the unity of the socialist countries, based on the principles of proletarian internationalism, ensures the maximum use of the advantages of the world socialist system and increases its strength in the struggle to prevent a new war and in the economic competition with capitalism. Experience has conclusively shown that the consolidation of the unity of the socialist countries is a reliable guarantee of their defensive capacity, national independence and sovereignty. (*Applause.*)

Comrades, recently reactionary circles of the Western Powers have again been intensifying their campaign against the socialist countries, using as a pretext the sentence passed by the Supreme Court of the Hungarian People's Republic in the case of the traitors to the Hungarian people—Imre Nagy and his associates.

What can be said about these provocative activities of the reactionaries aimed at increasing international tension? The tactics of the imperialist forces have recently borne an increasingly close resemblance to those they employed in the autumn of 1956, when imperialist reactionaries raising a hysterical clamour about the events in Hungary which they themselves had engineered, unloosed British, French and Israeli aggression in Egypt, against that country's national independence. Now too, the situation in the Arab East is extremely tense. The leading imperialist

Powers are preparing for intervention in the Lebanon, whose people are fighting for their independence, against the notorious Dulles-Eisenhower Doctrine.

For their own selfish ends aggressive circles in the West are ready to use anything and everything in order to aggravate the international situation, to intensify the cold war and to wreck the summit talks.

The Soviet Union, all the countries of the socialist camp, have exposed, and will continue to expose, the enemies of peace—those who, resorting to slander and the hypocritical slogan of "anti-communism," are trying to intervene in the affairs of other countries and to sow enmity and hatred among the nations. Loyal to the principles of the Leninist policy of peace, the Soviet Union, together with all the other socialist countries, will continue to do everything in its power to strengthen international security, to ease international tension and to ensure peace throughout the world. (*Applause.*)

The Soviet Government has recently published its proposals on the questions being put forward for consideration by a conference of Heads of Government. The Soviet Government is again proposing a discussion on the more important international problems which are ripe for solution and which, given the good will of all parties, can already be settled at the present time.

But how are the Western Powers responding to the peace moves of the Soviet Union? What practical contribution have they made to ease international tension?

Unfortunately it must be said that the attitude adopted by the Western Powers by no means provides evidence of their readiness to help create a favourable atmosphere for a summit meeting. The flights of American planes, loaded with hydrogen bombs, towards the frontiers of the Soviet Union, the policy of nuclear arms race, the arming of the West German Bundeswehr with atomic weapons, the stubborn refusal to follow the U.S.S.R.'s example in ending tests of atomic and hydrogen bombs, the creation of atomic and rocket bases aimed against the socialist countries—all this hinders the preparation of a summit conference and prevents the easing of international tension. The Western Powers are dragging out such issues as cannot be settled, because the conditions are not yet ripe, or such as do not at all come within the competence of a summit meeting. It is clear what they are aiming at. They want to shout from the house-tops at some future date that they were right in predicting that the summit meeting would fail.

Among these questions is the reunification of Germany. The Western Powers insist that the summit conference should take up this internal affair of the German people. It is perfectly clear, however, that this question is an internal matter for the German people and does not come within the competence of an international conference. To put forward this question for the conference agenda is to wreck the calling of such a conference.

The West German press has lately been boosting the project, put forward recently in the Bundestag, for setting up a so-called "Four-Power committee," that is to say, a permanent body consisting of representatives of France, Britain, the United States and the Soviet Union, which according to the authors of the project, should prepare agreed proposals on the German question. Quite a fuss has been raised about this project. It is being presented as practically a "new approach" to German reunification. In practice, however, there is nothing new about it. The plan for setting up a "Four-Power committee" is yet another attempt to make the German people accept the illusion of a possible Four-Power solution to the German problem or, in other words, to deceive the German people and divert them from realistic ways of reunifying the country on a peaceful and democratic basis.

The Soviet people deeply respect and support the German people's efforts to create a united, peace-loving and democratic German state. The Soviet Government is convinced that the only road offering prospects for ending the splitting of Germany lies through negotiations, agreement and closer relations between the two German states —the German Democratic Republic and the Federal Republic of Germany. Only the Germans themselves, the two German states, can solve the problem of Germany's national reunification. (*Applause.*) Let representatives of Berlin and Bonn meet and find a reasonable solution to this problem.

The Government of the German Democratic Republic, in its proposals, has pointed out a perfectly concrete way of peacefully restoring Germany's unity, one which is entirely practicable, even under present complex conditions. This way is through the establishment of a German confederation. The Western Powers, not wishing to take into account the national interests of the German people, fear to recognize the right of the German Democratic Republic and the Federal Republic of Germany independently and without external interference to come to an agreement on ways to reunify Germany.

In the Western Powers' proposals the question of the unity of Germany is tied to the question of European security. The purpose behind this is to ensure, under the guise of "reunifying" Germany, the abolition of the people's democratic system in the German Democratic Republic and the inclusion of a Germany, thus reunified, in the North Atlantic alliance. That is what the imperialists want, and they are even inviting us to have a hand in it. (*Laughter.*)

Pursuing their provocative aims, the Bonn ruling circles present the case as though the Soviet Union might at some stage agree to this—agree to the abolition of the German Democratic Republic. The imperialist gentlemen, accustomed to regard peoples and entire states as so much small change in bargaining among themselves, evidently apply their own standards to us as well, and because of this, they even name the price which West Germany could pay the Soviet Union if the latter were to agree to the reunification of Germany on the Western countries' terms, that is, contrary to the will of the working people of the German Democratic Republic and without taking into account the vital interests of the German people.

But how can Communists assist in abolishing the socialist system? Could we be parties to turning the entire German people into cannon fodder for American generals? (*Prolonged applause.*)

After all, how can there be any question of European security, if it is planned to turn the whole of Germany into a bridgehead for an attack on the socialist countries? It should also be remembered that the population of Europe is over 500 million, whereas about 70 million are living in the two German states. This alone shows that European security is a much broader and more all-embracing question than the German problem.

No one can deny that the adherence of West Germany to NATO, the introduction of universal conscription in West Germany and now, too, the decision to equip the Bundeswehr with nuclear and rocket weapons are exacerbating international relations still more, and particularly the relations between the two German states. In this way the Bonn Government is itself building up, brick by brick, a wall separating the two parts of Germany.

We can only be astonished at the ease with which the ruling circles of the Federal Republic of Germany are venturing to take such a step as equipping the country with nuclear weapons. To listen to them one might think that it was not a question of the fate of Germany but merely of standardizing armaments for the armies belonging to the North Atlantic bloc.

The Soviet Union has opposed, and continues to oppose, aggressive blocs whose existence is a source of constant tension in the relations between states. It is also well known that the member-countries of the Warsaw Treaty Organization have been proposing for a long time that agreement be reached on the abolition of the existing military groupings. Neither the Soviet Union nor the other signatory countries of the Warsaw Treaty have any intention of using their military strength to the detriment of the security of any other state. We have put forward a proposal for the conclusion of a non-aggression pact between NATO and the Warsaw Treaty Organization.

Remember the Federal Chancellor's statement that he could not welcome the arming of new Powers with nuclear weapons. A little more than a year has elapsed since then. It is said that Herr Adenauer now feels uncomfortable when he is reminded about that statement of his. In order to "justify" himself somehow, he now attributes his change in attitude to the Soviet Union's development of intercontinental rockets.

Yet what do these arguments have in common with the task of safeguarding the security of West Germany, if one takes into account the fact that the military bases and rocket installations on the territory of West Germany can be rendered harmless by a state defending itself with the help of short-range weapons and that no intercontinental ballistic missiles at all are needed for this purpose?

We can only regard it as bitterly ironical that the cult of atomic weapons in West Germany is being created by a party which calls itself Christian. (*Animation in the hall.*) This is indeed the situation described in the popular saying: "The Devil jumps out of his skin, trying to make you sin." (*Laughter in the hall. Applause.*) And this Devil, although he comes from overseas, is evidently strong, since his spell cannot be broken even by the Pope of Rome who, as we know, has denounced nuclear weapons. (*Laughter in the hall. Applause.*)

The Soviet people are glad that understanding of the advantages of good-neighbourly relations between our peoples is also increasing among both the working people and wide sections of the bourgeoisie in West Germany. In West Germany, however, the anti-Soviet propaganda in which the most highly placed government leaders are taking part casts a shadow on the young shoots of improved relations between the U.S.S.R. and the Federal Republic of Germany and prevents them from growing. Every time responsible spokesmen of the Federal Republic of Germany, such as Defence Minister Strauss, call the Soviet Union their potential adversary and enemy, one must draw the conclusion that forces seeking to throw relations with the Soviet Union back many years are gaining the upper hand in the Federal Republic of Germany. It is not difficult to imagine the situation which would arise if the Soviet Government, on its part, were to take similar steps and bring up its people, who have not forgotten the horrors of the Hitler invasion, in a spirit hostile to West Germany.

In the pre-war period all of Germany's domestic and foreign policy was permeated with anti-communism. Everyone knows that this policy led the German people to an unprecedented national catastrophe.

And if today there are again politicians in West Germany who take up anti-Soviet slogans, the question naturally arises: For what are they preparing their state—peaceful co-operation with the Soviet Union and the other peace-loving countries, or a repetition of the road along which Hitler led Germany—a road which proved disastrous to the destiny of Germany?

Herr Strauss and those who think like him should remember the high price Germany paid for Hitler's adventurism.

We are well aware, comrades, that the working people of Germany do not want war, and we do not equate the handful of bellicose revenge-seekers with the people, who want peace and reject "atomic death." (*Prolonged applause.*) We thoroughly understand the anxiety of the working people of Germany over the policy of the militarization and fascization of West Germany, and from the bottom of our heart we wish them success in the struggle for a united, peace-loving ar' democratic Germany (*Stormy applause.*)

The cause of strengthening peace in Europe and throughout the world is served by the decisions of the recent Berlin Conference of European Communist Parties—decisions with which our Party fully agrees.

Our people desire to live in peace and friendship with the entire German people. Enmity between our countries has always brought untold misfortune and suffering. The Soviet Union and the German Democratic Republic—this bulwark of the peace-loving forces of the entire German people—are linked by ties of close friendship and fraternal co-operation. (*Stormy applause.*)

To assist in the more rapid economic development and further advancement of the material well-being of the people of the friendly German Democratic Republic, the Soviet Government has decided to forego, as of January 1, 1959, the sums which the German Democratic Republic was to pay annually to cover part of the costs of maintaining Soviet troops temporarily stationed on its territory. We are confident that this measure will help strengthen still more the friendship between our countries and peoples. (*Stormy, prolonged applause. All rise.*)

The Soviet people, like the other peoples of Europe, see in the German Democratic Republic a state which has decisively broken with the policy of imperialism and militarization and has resolutely taken the road of peace and friendship among the nations. It is precisely this that explains the growing influence and prestige of the German Democratic Republic in international affairs and the confidence in its peace policy.

Comrades, present here at the congress of the Socialist Unity Party of Germany are delegations from 46 fraternal Communist and Workers' parties. This is a very significant fact which bears witness to the monolithic cohesion of our revolutionary forces and to the unshakable proletarian solidarity of the Marxist-Leninist parties. (*Stormy applause.*)

True to the principles of Marxism-Leninism, the revolutionary workers' parties see in the unity of their efforts and in their united action the mighty source of their strength and a guarantee of success in achieving their aims. The enemies of socialism are infuriated by our revolutionary unity, by our fraternal solidarity. And they spare no effort in their attempts to undermine or shake the unity of the Marxist-Leninist parties, to weaken the cohesion of the socialist countries.

That is why we greatly regret that the leadership of the League of Communists of Yugoslavia views its role in relation to our united family of Communist and Workers' parties from certain particular positions. I have already had occasion to speak about certain actions of the Yugoslav leaders which cannot but arouse in us—the Communists of the Soviet Union and the Communists of all other fraternal parties—a feeling of protest and condemnation.

Allow me to express certain views on this matter.

The Yugoslav leadership is now persistently trying to instil in the Yugoslav people and the members of the Yugoslav League of Communists the idea that the present worsening of relations between the League of Communists of Yugoslavia and all the Communist and Workers' parties is a continuation of the events of 1948, that is, a continuation of the previous conflict.

But what happened in 1948? At that time our parties criticized the opportunist and nationalist mistakes of the leadership of the Communist Party of Yugoslavia. It was not our criticism—which we have never renounced—that was wrong, but the call to replace the leadership of the Communist Party of Yugoslavia, contained in the resolution of the Information Bureau. That is all that pertains to 1948. Mistakes were made by both sides—I emphasize, by both sides—in the sense that the disputes and bad relations between the parties were extended to the relations between the governments. The Yugoslavs place the blame on the Information Bureau, in whose establishment and work they took an active part until June 1948, for all the mistakes of the past.

We subjected the mistakes made by our side to honest and open criticism. Nothing of the kind was done by the Yugoslav leaders when relations were re-established, although they had no little grounds for self-criticism, for subjecting their mistakes to criticism. Suffice it to recall, for instance, the slanderous decisions of the 6th Congress of the Communist Party of Yugoslavia in 1952, in which it was asserted that the U.S.S.R. was not a socialist country but an imperialist Power pursuing an expansionist policy. For such ranting the Western imperialists lavishly subsidized them at the time with hundreds of millions of dollars. But the Yugoslav leaders never came out with self-criticism. Furthermore, they even concealed from the members of the League of Communists of Yugoslavia the fact that from the very beginning of the talks in Belgrade in 1955 we told them that we considered our criticism of their mistakes in 1948 and the 1948 resolution of the Information Bureau to be basically correct.

The assertions of the Yugoslav leaders that the present worsening of relations between the League of Communists of Yugoslavia and all the Communist parties is a continuation of the conflict which began in 1948 will not bear examination. It is a fact that this conflict was settled in 1955, when the Soviet-Yugoslav Declaration was signed. Relations with Yugoslavia along governmental lines were normalized and, it may be said, became good. At the same time contacts were also established along Party lines and they, too, were developed to a considerable extent. Thus, the conflict which began in 1948 could already be regarded as a past stage.

In 1955, we agreed with the Yugoslav leaders when they said that they considered it desirable to open a new chapter and not rake up the past, so that relations between our parties could be improved gradually, step by step. The leaders of the League of Communists of Yugoslavia, as we know, have now broken this agreement as well.

During the Hungarian events in the autumn of 1956 the

Yugoslav leadership again intensified its activities aimed at undermining the unity of the countries in the socialist camp. At that time our parties energetically rebuffed those splitting activities. But following the well-known Soviet-Yugoslav meeting in Bucharest, the situation was again restored to normal. Even the decision of the Yugoslavs not to take part in the Meeting of the Communist and Workers' Parties of the Socialist Countries in Moscow in the autumn of 1957 and not to sign the Declaration of those parties did not cause an open exacerbation of relations.

Our parties refrained at that time from any open reaction to the acts of the Yugoslav comrades, such as might upset the relations that had been developed by that time, although each of the fraternal Communist parties undoubtedly drew its own conclusions from what had happened. The attitude adopted by the Yugoslav leaders could not fail to put us on our guard; their actions were a serious warning to all of us. Although it had been well-known before this, too, that on a number of questions the Yugoslavs had their own particular views, which contradicted the spirit of Marxist-Leninist ideology, nevertheless our parties considered it possible to maintain relations and contacts with the Yugoslav comrades on those questions on which we had a certain identity of views.

But this was not enough for the Yugoslav comrades. They evidently wanted something more. Deliberately setting themselves up in opposition to the other Communist and Workers' parties and speculating on differences with them, they tried to boost their stock in the international arena. It may be assumed that when our parties did not react openly to the Yugoslav leadership's decision not to take part in the meeting of the Communist and Workers' parties and when we merely limited ourselves to drawing our own appropriate conclusions from this—precisely at that time the Yugoslav leaders decided to adopt the course of openly attacking the C.P.S.U., the

Communist Party of China, and all the Communist and Workers' parties. This created a situation in which our parties had to refuse to send delegations to the 7th Congress of the League of Communists of Yugoslavia.

So, if we are to speak of the causes of the present worsening of relations it becomes clear that 1948 has nothing to do with the matter and it is wrong to say that present relations are a continuation of the old policy. The Yugoslav leaders are spreading these absurd inventions and are trying to lay the blame for everything on the past, on Stalin, on "Stalinism," because otherwise they would be unable to explain the causes of the present conflict to the League of Communists of Yugoslavia and to their people; while they lack the courage to accept responsibility for the conflict.

Our line is clear. It is the line of struggle for the purity of the ideas of Marxism-Leninism and for the utmost consolidation of the ranks of the communist movement. Guided by these considerations of principle, we came out vigorously against the revisionist propositions formulated in the programme of the League of Communists of Yugoslavia. The anti-Marxist, anti-Leninist views of the Yugoslav leaders were subjected to thorough-going principled criticism by the Communist Party of China, the Socialist Unity Party of Germany and all the other fraternal parties. (*Applause.*) In decisions taken by their leading bodies and in articles in the Party press, all the parties took a clear-cut position and condemned those views, paying considerable attention to a critical analysis of them. And this was correct.

How did the Yugoslav leaders take this comradely criticism? They completely rejected our criticism, avoided discussion on the substance of the ideological questions raised and adopted the course of making unprincipled, crude attacks on the Communist and Workers' parties. The leaders and the "theoreticians" of the League of Communists of Yugoslavia evidently cannot make their own views tally, are weak in their own "theories," and therefore are unable to defend them against criticism.

The Yugoslav leaders were offended by the criticism and presented it to the Yugoslav Communists in a very distorted way. It turned out to be not a criticism of the ideological mistakes of the authors of the programme of the Yugoslav League of Communists, but rather an application of the "policy of strength," "unscrupulous attacks on Yugoslavia, on the policy she is pursuing and on the building of socialism in Yugoslavia," as *Borba* wrote and as Yugoslav propaganda is daily insisting. This propaganda is aimed at smearing and disparaging in every way the Soviet Union, the Chinese People's Republic and the other socialist countries and their parties, and at seeking to arouse in the Yugoslav people a feeling of estrangement, offence, and even hatred for our countries and parties. It is significant that the word "comrades" has begun to be used more and more rarely when they write and speak about our parties, which have proved in practice their loyalty to the ideals of socialism and which are successfully building socialism in their countries.

In *Borba, Komunist, Politika* and other organs of the Yugoslav press there have appeared again, as in the past, unseemly articles and objectionable cartoons. In the Yugoslav press and on the radio, those who in the past built up their careers on anti-Soviet and anti-communist concoctions are again speaking and writing. In giving them an entirely free hand, the leadership of the League of Communists of Yugoslavia obviously approves of their views which are quite compatible with the most rabid propagandists of imperialism.

At the beginning one might have believed that the slanderous concoctions in the Yugoslav press did not meet with the approval of the leaders of the League of Communists of Yugoslavia, that they would take advantage of the first opportunity and, in a business-like way, would objectively consider our criticism and show alarm at the dangerous way in which relations between our parties were developing. But after Comrade Tito's speech in Labin, it became perfectly clear who was really organizing and inspiring this campaign against the Communist parties and the socialist countries.

A feeling of indignation and protest is aroused by the unworthy and insulting attacks made by Comrade Tito and Yugoslav propaganda on the Chinese People's Republic, on the glorious Communist Party of China and on its leaders, who administered a vigorous rebuff to the splitting activities of the Yugoslav revisionists.

Now the Yugoslav leaders seek to disparage our system and our methods of building socialism. They allege that we are distorting Marxist-Leninist teachings and that they themselves are the real custodians of Marxism-Leninism. We have read and heard this before, on more than one occasion. Yet how is it that the Soviet Union has achieved, and continues to achieve with every new year, results which are recognized by the whole world? How is the one to be reconciled with the other?

Yugoslav propaganda reiterates that Marxism-Leninism is being distorted in the Soviet Union and is being incorrectly applied, that the Soviet Union is a bureaucratic state, and so on, whereas in actual fact our rate and level of development, especially in science, culture and a number of branches of the economy, have surpassed the most highly developed capitalist countries. Today, when the Soviet Union has been the first in the world successfully to launch three big artificial earth satellites, it has become clear to everyone what a high level of development the Soviet Union has achieved. (*Prolonged applause.*) The actual facts show convincingly that the statements of the Yugoslav revisionists on the Soviet Union will not hold water, as the saying goes.

Now, what successes have been achieved by Yugoslavia, whose leaders consider themselves to be the champions of true Marxist-Leninist teachings? After all,

Comrade Tito boasted at the meeting in Labin that he can build socialism even with the help of free American wheat. (*Laughter in the hall.*)

Let us compare the conditions in Yugoslavia with those of her neighbour, Bulgaria. We know in the past their level of development was approximately the same. Since Bulgaria, throughout the post-war years, has been steadily carrying out a socialist transformation and has developed her national economy, relying on the mutual support of the other socialist countries, she has achieved considerably better results than Yugoslavia in the major indices of economic development. For example, industrial output in Yugoslavia rose in 1957 to 3.1 times that of 1939, and in Bulgaria to 7.7 times its 1939 level. In the period from 1948 to 1957 industrial output in Yugoslavia rose 2.1 times and in Bulgaria—3.8 times.

Or let us take such a very important question of socialist transformation of society as co-operation among the peasantry. It is well known that without co-operation in the village, it is, as Lenin said, impossible to wrest the peasant from barbarism; it is impossible to make him cultured; it is impossible to switch his farmstead on to socialist lines and to organize his labour on the basis of the most modern mechanized production. "If we remain, as of old, on small farmsteads, even though as free citizens in a free land," Lenin pointed out, "we shall all the same face the threat of inevitable ruin. . . ."

Guided by the Lenin's co-operative plan, the People's Democracies have won remarkable successes in the socialist transformation of agriculture. It is a fact that the Chinese People's Republic has already completed co-operation in agriculture. In the Korean People's Democratic Republic more than 95 per cent of all peasant households had been united in co-operatives by the end of 1957. In the Bulgarian People's Republic the socialist sector accounts for more than 92 per cent of the cultivated area. In Czechoslovakia the socialist sector embraces over

70 per cent of the total area of farmland, in Albania, nearly 70 per cent of the entire cultivated area, and so on.

Yet in Yugoslavia only about 2 per cent of the peasant households are united in producers' co-operatives and no consistent work is being conducted to transform agriculture on socialist lines. It transpires that on the peasant question, too, the Yugoslav comrades are clearly at loggerheads with Marxism-Leninism.

In Yugoslavia, there is much said about Marxism-Leninism, but there is much done which is contrary to Marxist-Leninist teachings.

Recently Yugoslav propaganda has been misleading the population with the allegation that the low standard of living of the population is to be explained by the economic blockade of Yugoslavia. If it is a question of a blockade, we must say most definitely that it did not exist in the past and most certainly does not exist now. We Soviet people know full well what a blockade is. Yugoslavia, far from being subjected to a blockade, enjoyed special patronage and received large sums when the United States of America, in appraising the situation, decided that the Yugoslav brand of national communism deserved special support. It should also be recalled that Yugoslavia received substantial aid from the Soviet Union in the first four post-war years and afterwards from the United States, Britain, France and West Germany. What kind of blockade is this?

In recent years, after the conflict with Yugoslavia had been ended and her economic ties with the socialist countries had begun to develop, there followed such events as the appearance of the anti-Marxist draft programme of the League of Communists of Yugoslavia, the slanderous attacks on the Communist and Workers' parties made at the 7th Congress of the Yugoslav League of Communists, and so on. One cannot but ask whether all that has not been prompted by a desire to recreate the "blockade" situation or by nostalgic feelings for it. Evidently this alleged "blockade" was to the liking of some people in Yugoslavia.

According to reports the United States is already making a new "contribution" to the cause of "building Yugoslav socialism." (*Laughter in the hall.*) But the leaders of Yugoslavia bashfully say nothing about this new handout, because the peoples know well the price of American generosity. The capitalists do not give away something for nothing, and if they do give something, they take one's soul in return. A high price must subsequently be paid for their aid.

The Yugoslav leaders claim that they are staying outside any blocs; they denounce the policy of blocs, and so on. This claim of theirs does not accord with reality, for Yugoslavia, herself, together with Turkey and Greece, belongs to the Balkan Pact and, through her allies in that bloc, is in some measure tied to NATO and the Baghdad Pact.

As for the socialist camp, which the Yugoslav leaders persistently equate with a "bloc," it by no means constitutes a grouping of that kind. Incidentally, they are well aware that a number of socialist countries do not belong to the military organization of the Warsaw Treaty, set up by a group of countries for defence against the aggressive machinations of the imperialists united in NATO. The prattle about a policy of "no blocs" has evidently been needed by the Yugoslav leaders for the purpose of misleading the people and obtaining their approval for their policy of ignoring the socialist camp, a policy of maintaining neutrality with regard to the struggle of the socialist forces in the international arena.

But what is the significance of holding aloof and ignoring the community of socialist countries in our day, when a fierce class struggle is being waged on a world scale? To real Communists, neutrality in conditions of sharp class struggle means weakening the forces of the revolutionary movement, the forces of socialism; it means helping the enemies of the working class.

The Yugoslav leaders are shouting themselves hoarse, declaring that someone is encroaching on their independence. But what kind of independence is in question? Loyalty to Marxism-Leninism is obviously a burden to them, and they want to rid themselves of it. So let them say so plainly; then everything will fall into place, and all will become clear. (*Applause.*)

In the struggle for peace, we are prepared to pool our efforts with all honest people, whether they are members of the Labour Party, liberals, reformists or nationalists. On this ground we establish relations of co-operation with all peace-loving forces. But when the Yugoslav leaders declare they are Marxist-Leninists and use Marxism-Leninism only as a cover to mislead gullible people and divert them from the path of revolutionary class struggle charted by Marx and Lenin, they want to wrest from the hands of the working class its sharpest class weapon. Whether they wish to or not, they are helping the class enemy of the working people, and in return for this they are given loans; in return for this the imperialists praise their "independent" policy of "no blocs," which the reactionary forces make use of in an attempt to undermine our socialist camp. But we most vigorously and firmly declare: "Nothing will come of it, Messrs. Imperialists—your arms are too short." (*Stormy, prolonged applause.*)

The imperialists are fighting against us with might and main, and there is nothing surprising in that. The world of capitalism is striving to uphold the old and is fighting for it with every means available. But when people call themselves Marxist-Leninists and actually help the imperialists, we consider it our duty resolutely to expose such people.

In the course of the class struggle the imperialists make every endeavour to use all kinds of opportunists and revisionists in their own interests in order to undermine the unity of the ranks of the international communist movement. It is a very dangerous phenomenon and a relentless struggle should be waged against it; the monolithic unity of the ranks of the Marxist-Leninist parties must be strengthened.

The more united our movement is, the greater will be the successes of every party, of the working class, of all the socialist states and of the entire international communist and working-class movement. We have such unity now; it is unbreakable, because it is based on unshakable loyalty to Marxism-Leninism. (*Prolonged applause.*)

The Yugoslav leaders allege that the Soviet Union and the Communist Party of the Soviet Union lay claim to some special role, to hegemony, and wish to give orders, while they, the Yugoslavs, are not in agreement with this. Such statements are completely false. It would be understandable if the propagandists of the imperialist camp were trumpeting it, but when such things are said by people who call themselves Communists, the question involuntarily arises: How could they sink to such base slander?

And this slander is not directed solely against the Soviet Union. The authors of these lying assertions are trying to smear the essence of our revolutionary struggle, to besmirch communist comradeship, and socialist cooperation. They distort the concept of united action by the working class of all countries in the interests of struggle against the yoke of capital, in the interests of the working people. Unity for the working class does not mean the sacrifice of its interests or its submission to someone. The working class of one country unites with the working class of another in order to do away with capitalism which engenders the policy of dictation, pressure and national oppression. (*Applause.*)

The Yugoslav leaders have chosen as a target for their attacks the section in the Declaration of the Meeting of Representatives of the Communist and Workers' Parties of the Socialist Countries in which the leading role of the

Soviet Union and its Communist Party is noted. But the Yugoslav leaders know perfectly well that there was no such point in the draft Declaration which they had before the meeting. The addition about the role of the U.S.S.R. and the C.P.S.U. was proposed and substantiated at the meeting itself, not by the C.P.S.U. delegation, but by representatives of other fraternal parties. (*Applause.*)

Where do we, the Communists of the Soviet Union, stand on this question?

I wish to dwell on this because enemies often use the fabrication of "Soviet hegemony" for their own vile purposes, and the Yugoslav leaders play up to the enemy by stirring up passions. They stretch their nets out to ensnare naive people, playing on feelings of national pride and seeking to inculcate into people's minds the monstrous allegation that all Communist parties fall under the rule and command of one party. We have already grown accustomed to these slanderous inventions, because one cannot expect anything else from enemies. But if these things are said by people who call themselves Communists, we cannot fail to rebuff such allegations. (*Applause.*)

The role of our Leninist Party of Communists and of the peoples of the Soviet Union in the revolutionary movement is expressed in the fact that the working class, the working people of Russia, guided by the Party of the Bolsheviks, were the first to crush their class enemy, the first to win the revolutionary battle in October 1917 and to create a state of the working people. (*Stormy applause.*) Overcoming famine and economic dislocation, they routed the imperialist invaders and the forces of counter-revolution, created a socialist industry and mechanized agriculture, and built socialism. The peoples of the Soviet Union bore the brunt of the war against Hitler fascism and defeated it. That victory was a gain for the whole world, and for the peoples of many countries, who were given the opportunity to build socialism. (*Prolonged applause.*) These included the peoples of Yugoslavia, who had waged a prolonged struggle to secure the conditions for building socialism in their country. If all this is our "special role," then this role has been won by the working class, the peoples of the Soviet Union and our Communist Party through suffering and sacrifice, through their great constructive labour, through their heroic struggle for the cause of communism. (*Stormy applause.*) They have not imposed this special role upon anyone; it has been recognized by the working class of the whole world, for everything that has been accomplished by our people has not only corresponded with their own national interests but has also been a worthy contribution to the common cause of the proletariat of all countries. (*Stormy applause.*)

In what does our country's role consist, now that the Soviet Union has achieved great successes in its development, in its economy, science, culture and in the continuous improvement of the well-being of the working people? It consists in that our country is paving the way to communism. It consists in that the Soviet Union, as the strongest and economically most developed state, gives other states the most unselfish assistance, and considers the cause of building socialism in each country as its own cause and the successes of all the peoples building socialism as its own success. (*Applause.*) The imperialist rulers are now no longer able to isolate socialist countries and establish an economic and political blockade around them. And we take pride in the fact that the Soviet people by their labour have contributed much to the growth of the forces of the world socialist camp. (*Prolonged applause.*)

Our state is giving assistance to other countries, because we Communists, Marxist-Leninists, do not isolate ourselves within our own frontiers. We regard the cause of building socialism and communism as a great international cause.

It is not by accident that enemies are concentrating the main fire of their propaganda machine against the Soviet

Union. They know that the working people of all countries, the oppressed peoples, associate the Soviet Union and our Communist Party with all the great transformations that the working class is bringing to mankind. The enemies of communism not only want to destroy the unity of the forces of the international working class, but also intend to strike a blow at the very heart of the revolutionary movement. That is why they are slandering the Soviet Union and showering praise on the so-called "national communism," which the imperialists of the United States often identify with "Yugoslav communism." For at the present stage "Yugoslav communism" is not dangerous to them; what is dangerous to them is the Communist Party of the Soviet Union and the successes of the Land of Soviets, the strength of the socialist camp, the unity and solidarity of the international communist movement. The imperialists realize that the Soviet Union is the blazing torch which is seen by the working people of the whole world and which lights up their road in the struggle for a radiant future. (*Stormy, prolonged applause.*)

The imperialists calculate that if they succeed in minimizing the role of the Soviet Union, they will be able in that way to disorganize the international working-class and communist movement, and then to undermine in general the faith of the working class and the Communist parties of other countries in the Communist Party of the Soviet Union as the vanguard of the international communist movement, and in the Soviet Union as a stronghold of world peace. Afterwards they would concentrate their fire on other parties, and apparently in the first place on the Communist Party of China. As long as the Soviet Union, the Chinese People's Republic and other socialist countries remain strong and their unity remains firm, the imperialists will give every possible material encouragement to all subversive actions directed against the unity of the socialist countries.

The conclusion formulated by the fraternal Communist parties concerning the role of the Soviet Union reflects the objective progress of the epoch-making struggle for the victory of socialism, for the triumph of the ideas of Marxism-Leninism. At the same time it serves as a vivid testimonial to the solidarity of the Communist parties of all countries. The enemies of communism and the slanderers have been given battle on an important issue, and they should take care to remember that the international communist movement will not permit any attempt to discredit the Soviet Union and will respond to any slanderous anti-communist campaign with still greater solidarity of the revolutionary forces. (*Prolonged applause.*)

In the camp of the socialist countries, in the international communist movement, there can be no question of orders being given to anyone or the subordination of one party or country to another. There is neither the need for this, nor is there any organization which could issue such orders.

We are grateful to the fraternal Communist and Workers' parties for their high assessment of the role and efforts of the Soviet Union and our Communist Party. This high appraisal obligates the Communists and all the Soviet people to strive still more perseveringly to build communism in order to justify the hopes placed by the fraternal parties in our Party and the Soviet Union. We are helping our friends in the socialist countries not only with advice and experience, but are also giving them material assistance in the building of socialism. (*Applause.*) We have always said and we continue to say: We shall share everything fraternally with the Communist parties and the socialist countries—joy in our successes and victories, and the hardships of struggle for our common and great cause. (*Prolonged applause.*) We realize that it is impossible to advance to communism alone, separated from our brothers, the peoples of the socialist countries; it is necessary to help one another, in order by joint efforts to bring those who are lagging behind up to the level of the most advanced. We shall go forward and reach communism on a broad front. (*Applause.*) Our course is clear. It is lighted up by the teachings of Marxism-Leninism. It is the straight highway by which the free peoples will come to communism. The peoples of the non-socialist countries, following the example of the socialist states, will carry through social and political transformations in their lands, will eliminate the system under which the exploitation of man by man predominates, and will join in the general movement of the peoples towards a bright future. (*Applause.*)

At the present time all the Communist and Workers' parties are rallied in solidarity as never before; there is no divergence among us in our assessment of Right-wing opportunism and revisionism within the communist movement as the Trojan horse of the imperialists on which they are now banking. However, we ought to say, comrades, that we see things as follows: Although the Trojan horse is still dangerous today, it was more dangerous for Troy. (*Animation in the hall.*) In the time of Homer, the people withstanding the siege shut themselves up in a fortress. In our times such fortresses are unnecessary. At the present time, therefore, the Trojan horse can obviously no longer play the role it once did. (*Laughter in the hall. Applause.*)

The Russians have a popular saying about a horse not being worth the fodder it eats. (*Laughter in the hall.*) A peasant goes on feeding a horse, but the animal, instead of filling out, grows thinner. Then the peasant says that it doesn't pay to feed that horse well, because it cannot even wag its tail. (*Laughter in the hall.*) The imperialists are wasting their money in the same way. No matter what fodder they give their horse, it will be unable to drag the chariot of revolution away from the course traced by Marxism-Leninism. (*Stormy, prolonged applause.* "Hear! Hear!" With the monolithic unity of Marxist-Leninist forces, this horse is essentially doomed, and consequently disappointment awaits those who are feeding it, because the revolutionary movement is advancing and cannot be held back. (*Prolonged applause.*)

More and more people are marching under the banner of Marxism-Leninism, and we can already see our ultimate goal appearing on the horizon—the victory of the working class throughout the whole world, the victory of the ideas of communism. (*Stormy applause.*)

The Communist Party of the Soviet Union will resolutely continue to repulse the attacks of opportunists and revisionists. We shall do this, not by interfering in the internal affairs of this or that party, but by means of comradely criticism, by means of the comradely influence of the world revolutionary movement and Marxist-Leninist parties upon erroneous attitudes which may arise in this or that party. We are not in favour of interference by any parties in the internal affairs of other parties; and even less are we in favour of interference by some states in the internal matters of other states. We are for comradely criticism, which is at the same time comradely support for those who make mistakes, who are still able to realize those mistakes and understand where they may lead, who are still capable of rectifying mistakes. As regards the leadership of this or that party, the leadership of this or that country—all this is wholly within the competence of each party, within the competence of the government and the people of each country.

We cannot leave unanswered statements which are aimed at revising the ideological foundation of our parties—the theory of Marxism-Leninism—and at undermining the unity of the Communist parties.

In their speeches and official documents the Yugoslav leaders have outlined openly revisionist views that are contrary to the revolutionary essence of Marxism-Leninism. They have taken a clearly schismatic, revisionist line and by so doing are helping the enemies of the working class in the fight against Communism, in the imperialists' fight against the Communist parties and against the unity of the international revolutionary working-class movement.

Of course, the fact that revisionist views have gained the upper hand in the leadership of one of the Communist parties is bad. But, as the popular saying goes, "It's an ill wind that blows nobody good." At the 7th Congress of the League of Communists of Yugoslavia its leaders did in fact expose themselves. Their true face, which they assiduously mask behind noisy and demagogic phrases about loyalty to Marxism-Leninism, has been revealed to the entire international communist movement. If previously some comrades might have thought that not everything possible had been done to improve relations between the socialist countries and Yugoslavia and to ensure that Yugoslavia would keep in step with all the socialist countries, then the 7th Congress of the League of Communists of Yugoslavia has shown that it was not a question of improving relations, but of the fact that the leaders of the League of Communists of Yugoslavia had adopted a line that was incorrect in principle and was alien to Marxism-Leninism.

In essence, the programme of the Yugoslav leadership is a worse version of a whole series of revisionist platforms held by Right-wing Social-Democrats. Consequently the Yugoslav leaders have not been drawn to the path of revolutionary Marxist-Leninist teachings; they have followed the path laid down by revisionists and opportunists of the Second International—Bernstein, Kautsky and other renegades. In actual fact they have now joined forces with Karl Kautsky's offspring—his son Benedict, who acted as one of the authors of the Right-wing opportunist programme of the Austrian Socialists.

But whereas Kautsky openly declares that Marxism is obsolete, the Yugoslav revisionists, on the contrary, are trying to conceal, in phrases, their corrupt position under the banner of Marxism-Leninism.

Communists have been and will continue to be implacable in the struggle against distortions of Marxism-Leninism, the struggle to keep the Marxist-Leninist banner unsullied, and they will not allow revisionists and those who have betrayed revolutionary principles to hide under the banner of Marxism-Leninism. (*Applause.*)

To us and to the international communist movement, the ideas of the Yugoslav revisionists are not new; examples of such sallies have been known more than once in history. And all of them have been exposed and rejected by history. The Yugoslav leaders are harping on propositions that are old, obsolete and rejected.

In our struggle for our common cause we should not pay more attention to the Yugoslav revisionists than they actually deserve. The more attention we pay to them, the more they will think that they are a force playing an important role. They want their reputation to be enhanced, so that others may think that the Yugoslav revisionists are very important. As was the case in the recent past, so now, too, they are evidently hoping to curry fresh favour with the imperialists in this way.

The leadership of the Communist Party of the Soviet Union is of the opinion that we should not meet the wishes of the Yugoslav leaders who are trying to exaggerate the present conflict between us. We are not going to assist in working up passions or in making relations more strained. Even in the existing state of our relations with the League of Communists of Yugoslavia it will be good to preserve some spark of hope and to search for acceptable forms of contact on certain questions.

The assertion that we are rejecting all that is positive in the work of the League of Communists of Yugoslavia and are bringing pressure of some kind to bear on the Yugoslav state is absolutely untrue and is a slander against us. The people of our countries and our parties have a deep respect for the freedom-loving peoples of Yugoslavia and appreciate the contribution the Yugoslav

Communists made to the common struggle against fascism. Both they and we have a common enemy and we believe that in spite of the conditions which have arisen, we shall continue in the future to wage a joint struggle against that enemy and shall jointly defend peace and the cause of socialism.

In general, comrades, it should be said that no matter how unpleasant are the results of the revisionist kinks of the leaders of the League of Communists of Yugoslavia, this is still not an earthquake that might shake our building of socialism. (*Animation in the hall.*) On the contrary, by our common efforts we have recently strengthened our building still more. An unshakable foundation for the building of communism has already been laid. We are firmly marching along our road and shall continue to do so, and as for those who are not going along the same way, that is, with the Communist and Workers' parties which take their stand on the positions of Marxism-Leninism and spare no efforts in the struggle for the triumph of communism—let them find other partners for themselves.

Comrades, in the Socialist Unity Party of Germany the German working class has a militant leader, inspirer and organizer of socialist construction, a worthy continuer of the best traditions of the German labour movement. Your Party has succeeded, in alliance with the anti-fascist democratic parties, in bringing about a revolution in the minds of the broad masses of the working people, in awakening their creative forces and directing the people's energy to building up a new socialist society.

Thanks to the activities of your Party, the working people of the German Democratic Republic have won the confidence of all peace-loving peoples. Consistently carrying out the ideas of Marxism-Leninism, the ideas of peace and friendship among the nations, the Socialist Unity Party of Germany has won sympathy and respect in the friendly family of the Communist parties of the whole world. They see in your Party a faithful friend, a militant detachment of the international communist movement.

Your congress is convincing proof of the militant unity of the Party, of the fact that it is tightly knit around its Central Committee, and has close ties with the broad masses of the working people. A manifestation of the fighting efficiency of your Party is the fact that it is waging an implacable struggle for the purity of Marxist-Leninist theory, against revisionism and dogmatism.

Communists are consistent and loyal internationalists. All the Communist parties resolutely condemn any actions that run counter to the strengthening of friendship among nations. Holding high the banner of proletarian internationalism, the Communist and Workers' parties are rallying the masses of working people, millions strong, for the struggle for peace and socialism, for a better future for all mankind. (*Prolonged applause.*)

The cordiality and warmth with which we have been received at your congress speak louder than any words of the profound friendship that has been established between our parties and peoples. The Soviet people cherish sincere feelings of friendship for the working people of the German Democratic Republic. The friendship between the working people of the German Democratic Republic and the Soviet people rests on the firm and unshakable foundations of proletarian internationalism; it is inspired by the noble ideas of the struggle for a brighter future for mankind. (*Applause.*)

The Communist Party of the Soviet Union has always considered, and will continue to consider, that its highest international duty is to develop and strengthen all-round co-operation among all the socialist countries, to strengthen steadily the unity and might of the great socialist camp. In unity lies the strength and invincibility of the growing world socialist system, of the entire international communist movement. And the Communist parties will continue to strengthen this unity in spite of all the machinations of our class enemies. (*Applause.*)

Comrades, permit me to read the text of a message of greetings from the Central Committee of the Communist Party of the Soviet Union to the 5th Congress of the Socialist Unity Party of Germany.

MESSAGE TO THE 5th CONGRESS
OF THE SOCIALIST UNITY PARTY OF GERMANY

Dear Comrades,

The Central Committee of the Communist Party of the Soviet Union sends heartfelt fraternal greetings to the delegates of the 5th Congress of the Socialist Unity Party of Germany and warmly wishes you success in the work of your congress. (*Stormy applause.*)

The Socialist Unity Party of Germany is a militant and tested leader of the working class and of all the working people of the German Democratic Republic, staunchly guarding the interests of the German working people and consistently applying to life the great ideas of Marxism-Leninism. In its selfless struggle for the creation and consolidation of the German Democratic Republic, for the peaceful development and prosperity of its homeland, for the reunification of Germany on a peaceful, democratic basis, your Party has shown itself to be the spokesman of the fundamental national interests of the entire German people and is utterly devoted to them.

The establishment of the German Democratic Republic— the first peaceable, democratic state of workers and peasants on German territory—has proved to be a turning-point in the history of the German people, opening up for them splendid prospects for peaceful development and the building of a new life. The working people of the G.D.R. have steadfastly pursued the course of building socialism, and by surmounting great obstacles caused by the splitting of Germany, have achieved remarkable success in consolidating their workers' and peasants' state and in developing their socialist economy and culture. The consolidation of the German Democratic Republic and its progress in laying the foundations of socialism are of tremendous significance for the fate of the German people and the development of the world socialist system.

The German Democratic Republic represents the bulwark of all the progressive forces of the German people fighting against the ruinous anti-popular policy of the West German militarists and revanchists, and it is invaluably contributing to strengthening peace in Europe and throughout the world.

The Socialist Unity Party of Germany is the worthy successor and continuer of the glorious traditions of the German revolutionary working-class movement forged under the direct leadership of the great founders of scientific socialism—Karl Marx and Frederick Engels. It struggles implacably to maintain the purity of Marxist-Leninist teachings. It fights resolutely against present-day revisionism, to cement the unity of the countries in the socialist camp and knit together the world communist movement in keeping with the principles of proletarian internationalism.

The Central Committee of the Communist Party of the Soviet Union, in the name of our Party and the Soviet people, warmly wishes the Socialist Unity Party of Germany and all the working people of the German Democratic Republic new successes in the further development of their socialist economy and culture, in improving the well-being of their working people, in the struggle for peace and the reunification of Germany on a peaceful and democratic basis. (*Prolonged applause.*)

Long live and prosper the peaceful German Democratic Republic and its working people, the builders of social-ism! (*Stormy, prolonged applause.*)

Long live the Socialist Unity Party of Germany, the well-tried leader of the working people of the German Democratic Republic! (*Stormy, prolonged applause.*)

Long live the friendship and co-operation between the Soviet and German peoples, the indestructible unity of the countries of the socialist camp and the international communist movement! (*Stormy, prolonged applause.*)

CENTRAL COMMITTEE
OF THE COMMUNIST PARTY
OF THE SOVIET UNION

(*Stormy, prolonged ovation. The delegates at the congress rise to greet the delegation of the C.P.S.U. Cries:* "Long live the C.P.S.U.!", "Hurrah!" *The delegates and guests join in singing "Internationale."*)

SPEECH
AT SOVIET-CZECHOSLOVAK FRIENDSHIP MEETING
OF MOSCOW WORKING PEOPLE

July 12, 1958

Dear Comrade Novotný,

Dear Czechoslovak Friends,

Dear Comrades,

The working people of Moscow, the capital of our country, have come to this meeting today to voice their sentiments of fraternal love and to bid hearty welcome to our dear guests—the First Secretary of the Central Committee of the Communist Party of Czechoslovakia and the President of the Czechoslovak Republic, Comrade Antonin Novotný, and the leading statesmen of the Czechoslovak Republic who have arrived with him, Comrade Václav Kopecký, Comrade Rudolf Barák, Comrade Jiří Hendrych, Comrade Rudolf Strehaj, Comrade Václav David, and other comrades. (*Prolonged applause.*) In their persons, we greet the glorious Communist Party and all the working people of Czechoslovakia. (*Stormy applause.*)

Dear comrades, permit me at this gathering in honour of our dear Czechoslovak friends to fulfil the request of the 5th Congress of the Socialist Unity Party of Germany and convey hearty greetings to the Communist Party of the Soviet Union and the entire Soviet people from its delegates. (*Stormy applause.*)

To our deep regret, the stay in the Soviet Union of our dear friends is coming to an end. The Soviet people would have been only too happy to have our Czechoslovak friends prolong their stay in our country. (*Prolonged applause.*)

The tour of our country made by Comrade Novotny and the other Czechoslovak comrades developed into a manifestation of inviolable Soviet-Czechoslovak friendship. The splendid speeches made by Comrade Novotný at friendship meetings in Leningrad, Tbilisi, Kiev and Stalingrad were heard with great attention by millions of Soviet people. They will never forget all the moving and warm meetings they had with the representatives of the fraternal peoples of Czechoslovakia. (*Prolonged applause.*)

The enthusiasm with which Soviet people everywhere met the leaders of socialist Czechoslovakia is a token of their sincere sympathy and inviolable friendship, of their joy and pride for Czechoslovakia's splendid successes in building socialism. The Soviet people rejoice at the historic pronouncement of the 11th Congress of the Communist Party of Czechoslovakia to the effect that the foundations of socialist society have already been essentially laid in Czechoslovakia and that she was solving the grand tasks of completing the building of socialism. (*Applause.*)

The peoples of the Soviet Union, of all the socialist countries, prize highly the outstanding labour achievements of our Czechoslovak brothers and the big contribution made by the Czechoslovak Republic to the struggle for world peace. Czechoslovakia is known in all, even the most remote, corners of our country as one of our closest friends—a reliable unit in the socialist camp. (*Prolonged applause.*)

We Soviet people are proud of our friendship with the peoples of Czechoslovakia. We value this friendship sincerely and shall always do all we can to strengthen and extend it further. (*Stormy applause.*)

The Soviet people regard the successes of the fraternal countries in building socialism as being successes of our common cause. For the socialist countries mutual assistance and support is a cardinal condition for good progress towards socialism. International proletarian solidarity, socialist internationalism—which has come to be the basis of state policy in the relations between the countries of the socialist camp—is an integral element in the spiritual pattern of the builders of the new society. (*Applause.*)

Under the socialist system the friendship of our peoples has become the concern of literally all working people. Fraternal friendship, mutual assistance and support shape every aspect of the relations between socialist countries. There is no facet or field in the life of our peoples that fails to benefit by the friendship and co-operation of the socialist countries, their mutual assistance and support. (*Applause.*)

The alliance of socialist countries in a fraternal community of equal states is a vital necessity. The peoples combine their efforts to support and help each other in building the new world, to jointly defend the gains of socialism against imperialist plotting.

It is only natural that this community based on the identity of the social, economic and political system in the socialist countries, the identity of their Marxist-Leninist ideology and of their goals in the struggle for socialism and peace, has nothing in common with the aggressive imperialist blocs aimed against the freedom and independence of the peoples, against peace and socialism.

The lessons of history show that **political** co-operation between countries of the socialist camp is a reliable safeguard for their national independence and sovereignty, and that it creates the necessary conditions in each of them for successfully realizing their plans of peaceful socialist construction.

Life also shows that the **economic** co-operation of these countries, based as it is on principles of complete equality and mutual assistance, enables each of them to utilize, most rationally and fully, its natural resources and to develop its productive forces. On the other hand, it enables them to co-ordinate and combine their effort in the interests of all and to make the best of the tremendous advantages of the world socialist system in order to consolidate the economic might of the socialist camp as a whole.

The **cultural** co-operation of the socialist countries reciprocally enriches the spiritual life of the peoples of each of them and helps tremendously in the rapid and all-round advancement of their national culture, science and technology.

All this taken together speaks convincingly of the vast advantages which each socialist country derives from its close co-operation and unity with all the other socialist countries.

It is obvious that, while depending entirely on its own strength, no country of the socialist camp could, if deprived of fraternal mutual assistance and support, achieve the impressive successes in evidence today in so short a historical time.

It is solely on the basis of unity, solidarity and all-round co-operation that the countries of the socialist camp can really achieve the complete triumph of socialism and communism. Anyone unable or unwilling to understand this, anyone acting differently, does damage to the vital interests of his own people and of socialism!

The peoples of all the socialist countries consider it their sacred duty to cement the might of the socialist camp, whose common interests each of them regards also as its own. (*Applause.*)

For its part, the Soviet Union is doing its best to strengthen the socialist camp. It has always rendered disinterested assistance and support to all the socialist countries, and continues to do so. Our people are perfectly well aware that by strengthening their own country, by developing its economy, science and technology, they serve not only their own interests, but also those of all the peoples of the socialist camp. The greater the might of the Soviet Union, the more successful its advance to its cherished goal of communism, the stronger and more solid the entire camp of peace and socialism, the more convincing the impact which socialist ideas have on the working people of the capitalist world. (*Prolonged applause.*)

Take the facts. The launching of the Soviet artificial earth satellites opened the eyes of new tens of millions of people to the true state of affairs in the U.S.S.R. and the entire socialist camp. It has served to raise still higher the international prestige of the Soviet Union and the socialist camp as a whole. In recent years the Communist Party of the Soviet Union has done much to accelerate the development of key industries and steeply raise agriculture, and to advance still more the living and cultural standards of the working people.

Is this just a domestic affair of the Soviet people? Of course, not. The impact of these developments reaches far beyond the frontiers of our country, for they help tremendously to consolidate the forces and the international prestige of the entire socialist camp—to cement the forces of socialism and world peace. (*Prolonged applause.*)

Comrades, permit me to deal with a few questions concerning the contemporary international situation and the foreign policy of our Party and the Soviet Government.

The question uppermost in the minds of men today, regardless of their political convictions, social status, religion and colour, is the question of peace, the question of what direction international developments will take. This question is extremely important to us, Soviet people. We approach it from the standpoint of the Leninist postulate on peaceful co-existence.

The socialist and capitalist systems have now been co-existing for more than forty years. There have undeniably been, and will be, irreconcilable political and ideological contradictions between these two systems, and there has been, and will be, a definite struggle between them on these grounds. But it is not unavoidable by any means that this struggle should take the form of armed conflicts. Controversial issues between states may and must be resolved peacefully, by negotiation and mutually acceptable agreements based on the principles of peaceful co-existence.

What does peaceful co-existence of capitalist and socialist states connote? It connotes mutual respect of territorial integrity and sovereignty, non-aggression, non-interference in each other's domestic affairs for economic, political or ideological reasons, equality and mutual advantage and co-existence. The principles of peaceful co-existence have already won broad international recognition.

The governing circles of the imperialist Powers aim their policy against peaceful co-existence. There are statesmen in the capitalist countries who deny the need of peaceful co-existence. But what does that mean? It means going to war. There is no other alternative.

We do not need war. The socialist countries are growing, rapidly developing countries. They are young, sound and strong, and the future inevitably belongs to the young, the growing. We need peace to build the new society. Our countries have all the requisites for it. Our Chinese friends have put it very aptly thus: "Socialism is the morning sun rising in the East, and capitalism is the evening sun sinking in the West." (*Stormy applause.*)

Like a grievously sick man prepared to do anything to prolong his life, capitalism, too, fatally ill as it is, seeks salvation in such things as the armaments race, war preparations, hydrogen bombs, and military blocs, hoping thereby to check-rein the development of socialism and prolong its own existence.

Certain in the triumph of socialism, certain that the future belongs to it, we resolutely oppose the cold war. Socialism does not need atomic or hydrogen bombs to assert itself. Like sound seed thrown on good earth, socialism is yielding abundant fruit. And this causes joy to millions of people all over the world. (*Prolonged applause.*)

Acting upon the compelling need of improving the international situation, the Soviet Government last December approached the Western Powers with the proposal of calling a conference of Heads of Government, so as to end the cold war by joint effort and pave the way for peaceful co-existence between states.

We also suggested concrete questions for inclusion in the agenda of the conference. These were questions which, in our opinion, have long become ripe for settlement. Indeed, if we take any one of them—be it immediate discontinuation of nuclear tests, complete rejection of the use of nuclear weapons, the proposal of a non-aggression pact for NATO countries and the signatories to the Warsaw Treaty, or any of our other proposals—and hold a poll on them among the population, they are sure to be backed by an absolute majority. This is beyond doubt, because settling these questions would pave the way to lasting peace. It would end the cold war and lead to a more sensible use of material resources in all countries with the object of raising living standards. (*Applause.*)

The Western governments were compelled to declare in favour of a conference of Heads of Government. But they proposed that it should be prepared through diplomatic channels. We were aware from the start that this proposal was made with the purpose of burying the matter of a summit meeting in a maze of diplomatic procedure.

Developments confirmed our fears. While diplomatic spade-work has bogged down, fables are being spread in the Western countries about the "intractable" and "uncompromising" attitude of the Soviet Union, about the Soviet Union wanting to act by *diktat*, and the like. And lately much is being said about us allegedly having lost all interest in a summit conference. That is a vicious lie. The Soviet Union has not lost interest, nor could lose interest, in a summit conference. It is not interested in a summit conference *per se.* It views such a conference as a step towards relieving international tension.

What makes us interested in negotiations with the Western Powers?

It would be futile to look for reasons in the situation within the socialist camp. Our camp is homogeneous and united as never before. We discuss our internal matters in our own fraternal circle, without outsiders. We are well able to solve all matters helping to consolidate further the socialist states and to expedite the development of their economy and culture. We have no difficulties in that domain, nor do we foresee any. (*Prolonged applause.*)

It would also be futile to look for reasons for our interest in negotiations with the Western Powers in the internal situation of the Soviet Union. That is simply absurd. The stability of our international position is based on the close solidarity of our peoples, the steady development of our economy, science, technology and culture. (*Applause.*) The weight of the three artificial earth satellites placed in orbit by the Soviet Union is a symbol of our country's weight in international affairs. (*Prolonged applause.*) Yet this is only a beginning. The Soviet giant circling our planet is only a pathfinder blazing the trail for still greater successes of Soviet science and technology. (*Stormy, prolonged applause.*)

The Soviet Union's interest in negotiating with the Western Powers is not to be explained by internal reasons or our international position, but by human, universal considerations, by the fact that we stand firmly for the peaceful co-existence of states with different social and political systems. We want to remove the danger of a destructive war, to deliver the people from constant fear of a new military conflict, and to win them a peaceful and tranquil life. (*Applause.*)

The United States and its partners have set forth their items for the agenda of a top-level conference. But, comrades, let us examine these items. For example, they want to discuss the so-called question of the situation in the European People's Democracies.

Everyone, even a person unfamiliar with politics, realizes that raising questions of that kind for discussion at the Heads of Government conference means torpedoing the conference. You should know, gentlemen, whom you are going to meet. How can anyone think that we, Communists, shall agree to join representatives of capitalist countries in a discussion of how to abolish the socialist system in any country. (*Animation. Applause.*)

Who do you take us for, and who do you think you are to put things that way? (*Applause.*)

Let us ask our Czechoslovak friends present here what the peoples of Czechoslovakia think of these proposals? The Czechoslovak Government, like the governments of the other socialist countries of Europe, has replied firmly on behalf of its people to the imperialists concerning their "proposal." Translated from the Czech their reply goes something like this: Gentlemen, keep your nose out of other people's affairs! (*Stormy, prolonged applause.*)

If the conference is going to be made conditional upon questions of that sort, it is evidently better not to meet at all, because our views are well known on that score, and we are not going to change them. (*Prolonged applause.*)

Lately the imperialists have been trying to use the just sentence passed by the Hungarian people on a handful of traitors to whip up a storm and wreck the summit meeting. Is it not clear that the judgement passed on Imre Nagy and his accomplices is a purely internal affair of the Hungarian people? Like every other country, the Hungarian People's Republic is entitled to prosecute the enemies of its people.

Why were there no protests from the West when the counter-revolutionaries in Budapest and other Hungarian cities were killing hundreds of people and hanging Communists and non-Communists on lamp-posts? Quite the reverse; the imperialists were rejoicing then, because it was mostly Communists and progressives who were being beaten and killed, and because the outrages organized by Nagy and his accomplices were aimed against the social-ist system. But when in self-defence the Hungarian Peo-ple's Republic applied its rights on lawful grounds—through the court and not by lynching—against the ene-mies of the Hungarian working people, the imperialists went into hysterics.

There you see imperialist morals. They want to obscure the issue and delude public opinion.

Why are the imperialists reluctant to negotiate with us and reach an agreement? They fear that an agreement with the Soviet Union and other socialist countries would knock the bottom out of the imperialist propaganda about the Soviet Union and the countries of the socialist camp wanting to conquer the whole world by force of arms. If they should acknowledge that the so-called "communist threat" is non-existent, they will have to acknowledge the principle of peaceful co-existence of the two systems, and to accept the existence of the socialist countries. In that case the entire system of aggressive pacts which they built up—NATO, SEATO, the Baghdad Pact, etc.—will begin to crumble. The fable of a "communist threat" is something like a main thread knitting together the system of military pacts. Speaking figuratively, that system is reminiscent of a knitted article. Pull a single thread out of it and it runs until it becomes a shapeless mass of thread. (*Applause.*)

The other reason why agreement with the Soviet Union does not suit the monopolists is that any slackening of the arms race costs them their profits. The monopolists are not too squeamish about producing means of annihi-lation—hydrogen bombs, aircraft and rockets; in a word, all things in current demand. Arms are in great demand when a cold war is in progress and international tension has risen to boiling-point. Whereas a *détente* would reduce the demand in means of annihilation and, consequently, reduce the profits derived from producing armaments.

Moreover, the cold war gives the American monopolists an opportunity of subjugating their allies politically and economically, of exploiting them and saddling them with unequal treaties and agreements. By limiting world trade and hindering their allies from developing commercial relations with the socialist countries, the U.S. monopolists keep them in a subject state and prevent them from developing industries which would compete with their own.

And yet, in spite of these and other factors impeding an international *détente*, we trust that sooner or later there will be a summit meeting, that tension will slacken in the relations between socialist and capitalist countries, and the principle of peaceful co-existence will triumph. (*Stormy applause.*) Present capitalist rulers may be shirking an agreement, but the men who succeed them will have no choice but to agree to a *détente*, and to recognize the principle of peaceful co-existence of two different systems. (*Prolonged applause.*)

We are sure that Western governing circles will sooner or later have to take this path, because of the obvious failure of the policy "of strength." The people who want enduring peace and confidence in the future are exerting pressure on Western governments by urging clear-cut steps to relieve international tension. And this pressure will keep mounting. At present it is evidently the British Government which is being subjected to the greatest public pressure. Quite a number of British Labour Party members, for example, are critical of British Government policy and duly appreciate the peaceful nature of the Soviet foreign policy. It may be added that more and more people from among the followers of the Conservative Party are also displeased with the present British foreign policy.

A battle for peace and an international *détente* is unfolding in all the countries of the Western bloc—from

Norway in the north to Italy and Greece in the south. And increasing numbers of Americans are calling attention to the failure of Mr. Dulles' present foreign policy and urging a new, more realistic approach to international affairs.

One of the key issues now troubling world opinion is that of disarmament.

As before, the Soviet Union is consistenly calling for decisive steps in that sphere. As you know, all our efforts have until now unfortunately failed to yield the desired results. Western spokesmen are resorting to a multitude of diverse manoeuvres to check disarmament, to lead it into a blind alley, and to torpedo it. What they like most is to talk about control. They seek to replace disarmament talk with talk about control and insist that control should precede disarmament. First control—then disarmament. First control—then easing international tension. First control—then mutual confidence. Such, in a nutshell, are their tactics.

But it is an absurd approach, because mutual control is an act of great trust. What does control mean? To permit one state to exercise all-round control within another means opening all one's doors to the other party, to admit its inspectors and controllers to places considered sacred by one's people.

In every church, at least in every Orthodox church, there is a place before the altar which only a priest may tread. Others, even pious people, are not supposed to go there. Each country likewise has its altar, its sacred places which it does not even show to all its friends, or shows just to its closest friends—those who have won its trust. (*Applause.*) I am deliberately using clerical terms here, because our Western partners like to refer to the Bible and to seek cover behind the Scriptures. (*Animation. Applause.*)

It would seem clear that we should first establish at least a modicum of mutual trust and then proceed gradually to control and inspection. That would be the natural approach. While our partners are setting the question on its head. No, they say, admit us first to your communist altar, and with time we'll see whether or not you ought to be trusted, and whether or not it is worth while reducing armaments.

Is it possible in present international circumstances, when even a modicum of trust is lacking, to speak in earnest about installing all-round control and inspection as a first step? Those who put matters that way only reveal themselves in their true colours and show that they have no intention of speaking in earnest about disarmament, or confidence, or control. (*Applause*.)

If the attempt is made to establish control without confidence, it will not be control but an act of intelligence with the object of locating the adversary's vulnerable points for an aggression. Since we have no thought of aggression, we have no need of such "control." (*Applause*.)

We shall never relinquish the right to guard our security. Nor do we deny this right to others. That is why we say: Let us not begin with control. Keep out of other countries' altars until you have first proved that you may be trusted, that you will not desecrate their sanctity and will not strive to violate the laws of the country which you want to inspect.

But when many politicians in the United States speak openly of war against the Soviet Union, when they pronounce spiteful speeches against our country, and follow this up with proposals about inspecting Soviet territory, it sounds, in effect, like a provocation.

We declare once again that the Soviet Union favours control and inspection. Our proposals about establishing control posts to prevent sudden attack, primarily at railway junctions, highways and ports, are well known. Furthermore, we have proposed air inspection 800 kilometres both sides of the line dividing our troops and Western troops in Germany and over a part of Soviet territory in the Far East and a corresponding part of U.S. territory. The Soviet Government has proposed to the U.S. Government that experts should work out practical measures to eliminate all possibilities of sudden attack.

As confidence gradually develops between states, we shall be ready to agree to further measures of control. And as soon as there is complete trust between ourselves and the Western Powers, as soon as we see that nothing is being conspired against our country and against world peace, we shall be ready to open all doors and to show everything we have. But as long as these conditions are lacking, we do not intend, and have no right, risking the security of the socialist countries. (*Stormy, prolonged applause.*)

That is our attitude on the disarmament question and control.

Comrades, every possible development of economic contacts with all countries is part and parcel of the effort to strengthen peace and peaceful co-existence by the Soviet Union, the Chinese People's Republic, the Republic of Czechoslovakia and the entire socialist camp. Allow me briefly to present our conception of the nature of interstate economic relations.

Economic contacts, and above all barter trade, is an enduring basis for international intercourse. Commodity exchange is the well-trodden path followed by all nations since ancient times. We favour the broadest possible reciprocal trade with all who want to buy our commodities and want our markets for their own goods.

Economic relations between the Soviet Union and other countries develop in different ways, depending upon the policy of a country towards us. There are countries with an unfriendly policy towards us and the socialist camp, which, for all that, think it useful to trade with us. In dealing with them, we follow the policy of establishing relations based on mutually advantageous commercial operations. In this case both parties approach the negotiation of trade agreements from the standpoint of commercial advantage. If such an advantage is on hand, they sign the agreement, pay in cash or in kind, and the deal is settled. That is one form of relations.

The other form applies to dealings with underdeveloped countries in need of economic assistance. Owing to centuries of the imperialists' colonialist policy the economy of many Asian and African countries which recently won their independence is very backward. The Soviet Union and other socialist countries consider it their duty to help them and to extend trade and all other forms of economic relations with them in every way.

Naturally, in their case we cannot say that our economic relations are based on mutual advantage. Generally speaking, from the commercial standpoint, our economic and technical assistance to underdeveloped countries is even disadvantageous to us. However, we consider it a good proposition from the standpoint of humanity, of human solidarity. (*Applause.*)

What is more, as our economic power grows, we shall each year increase our assistance to the peoples of underdeveloped countries. We give them credits if they ask for them, deliver equipment against these credits, and send them our scientists, engineers, agronomists, doctors, etc. This is done to help their people lay a stable foundation for their economy, to advance their national science and culture. We call this disinterested assistance and, indeed, there is no interest in it for us. (*Applause.*) There is, of course, a kind of "interest" (I put the word in quotes), but it has nothing to do with material interest, with exploitation and profit. By giving them economic, technical and other assistance, we give these countries, which have shaken off the colonial yoke, a chance to keep clear of unequal transactions with the colonialists, to avoid begging for their favours and surrendering their economy to them; we thereby give them a chance to resist all attempts of restoring the old-time colonial relations even in modified form. By helping these countries to rehabilitate their industry, to develop their economy, to improve their living standard, we help them to strengthen their independence, won in struggle against the imperialist colonialists.

India, Afghanistan, Burma, the United Arab Republic and some other countries are building industrial plants, power stations, ports, canals and roads on Soviet credits and with Soviet equipment, technical consultations, etc. All this accelerates their economic development and reflects beneficially on the material and cultural standards of their population.

The peoples receiving help from the socialist countries appreciate its genuine character. And it is only natural that this should infuriate the imperialists.

The capitalist countries also "help" underdeveloped countries, but in doses and on terms that prevent the recipient country from building up its own industry, its economy, leaving it in continued political and economic dependence upon one capitalist country or another, and, more often than not, upon many of them at once. Furthermore, this help is used chiefly to build military bases, and to increase the armed forces.

The economic assistance rendered by the Soviet Union and the other socialist countries to the underdeveloped countries of Asia and Africa is causing mounting alarm in the colonialist camp. The colonialists are fussing about in these countries, scaring timid people with claptrap about the dangers of our assistance. In this they now have zealous helpers in the Yugoslav leadership, who try to cast doubts upon the Soviet Union observing its economic aid commitments.

Lately, Yugoslav statesmen have been cutting loose about the question of Soviet credits to Yugoslavia. The attitude and concrete proposals of the Soviet Government on this score are set forth in documents published in the Soviet press.

The Yugoslav leadership put their own construction upon our proposals. They say that we are violating an equal agreement. Yet if one of the signatories wants to revise an agreement this means that the treaty does not satisfy it. By virtue of changed circumstances each signatory is entitled to raise the question of revising an agreement. We want our agreements with Yugoslavia to be based on equality and mutual benefit. In other words, we want them to follow, rather than contradict, the formula defined by Comrade Tito in his speech at the 7th Congress of the Yugoslav League of Communists.

We want the terms of our economic relations to be really reciprocal. Who would reject such terms? No one has ever rejected advantageous terms.

Today the Yugoslav leaders are trying to exert pressure upon us and insist on credit benefits. They go so far as to appeal on this score to Western opinion. The Yugoslavs know very well that the terms on which they have been receiving credits from the Soviet Union are very favourable to them and unfavourable to us. Do not, therefore, try to force us. Nothing will come of it, because we do not want agreements whose terms are damaging to our socialist economy and favourable only to the other side. Yet we are being required to withdraw resources from our own economy and thereby to reduce the means of developing it. In other words, we are being required to cause damage to our own economy in the interests of the other side. Where do you see a reciprocal basis in that?

We are surprised to hear that our proposals are allegedly illegal, and that we must pay a kind of forfeit. I ask you: Why are they illegal? After all, even laws are revised and amended when necessary. Even a marriage contract, which is considered sacred, has to be broken sometimes. (*Animation.*) If one party produces evidence that the other party has not lived up to its marital duties, even the church recognizes the right of annulling such a marriage. (*Animation. Applause.*) Some people, it is true, act as follows: After first accepting the bonds of matrimony, they later break these bonds without even informing the other party about it and pay no forfeit whatsoever. (*Laughter.*)

We are ready to trade, and shall trade, on a mutually advantageous basis. But the Yugoslav leaders evidently wish to be given things without giving in return, rather than deal on a basis of give-and-take. Our view is that relations between socialist countries should be based on the principle of mutual assistance. What the Yugoslav leaders want, however, is for the socialist countries to give them all they need, and they may then be expected to say that their economy is outstripping that of other countries by virtue of the so-called special "Yugoslav road" in developing socialism. (*Animation. Applause.*)

Yugoslav leaders, and Comrade Tito in person in his recent Labin speech, are trying to prove that we are contradicting ourselves, and putting a different definition upon the use of credits given by capitalist countries. Look, they try to say, how Moscow flays them, the Yugoslavs, for taking U.S. credits, while it is no less eager to receive Western credits, for has not Khrushchov recently approached Eisenhower on this score.

Rest assured, Comrade Tito, that Khrushchov did not ask for hand-outs. He spoke as equal to equal and proposed mutually advantageous terms. We do not ask anyone for alms. We do not need alms. We do not accept them. (*Stormy, prolonged applause.*)

We are building up the might of our country by ourselves, and are paving the way for even more successful progress in the future.

We have approached the Government of the United States because we want to normalize and develop economic relations between our two countries. We are able to sell our raw materials and goods, and to buy from any country, and that country will benefit from it. The people of America, France, Britain, West Germany and Italy stand to benefit from developing trade with the Soviet Union. It is beneficial for all nations to develop their trade.

The broader trade becomes, the more remote the chance of a military conflict between nations. (*Prolonged applause.*)

U.S. politicians often shed crocodile tears about the Soviet Government allegedly doing too little to develop the consumer industries. So we have decided to put their attitude to a practical test and to demonstrate what the U.S. imperialists are really concerned about: the welfare of the Soviet people—that the Soviet people should consume more—or undermining our country's economic potential, crippling its defence, and thereby getting a chance of carrying on their cold war policy and dictating terms from "positions of strength"?

If American business circles want to accept our proposals and to make a profit from our orders, that is their affair. In either case our country has always been, and remains, a truly independent country and will develop its economy, will follow its own path. (*Stormy applause.*)

If the United States fails to understand that, if it refuses to do business with us, we shall carry out our plans just as well without it, because our economic development programme is drawn up irrespective of outside assistance and the participation of capitalist countries.

The Yugoslav leadership shape their relations with the capitalist countries quite differently. However, those Yugoslav leaders who still have a vestige of proletarian conscience are likewise aware of this. They are unable to make ends meet in their speeches, and substitute rhetoric for proofs. They cannot explain why the imperialist countries, which hate socialism and strain every sinew to crush the revolutionary movement, give such "generous" aid and credits to a socialist country. Yet the explanation is very simple, and clear to anyone, even if he may be unfamiliar with theory, as long as he is endowed with class intuition.

The imperialists do not by any means help Yugoslavia with the object of cementing the socialist system and supporting the communist movement. They do it to fatten, to bribe those forces which, though they style themselves as Marxist-Leninist forces, are willing to oppose the socialist countries, and primarily the Soviet Union. This aid is a tribute for the policy of splitting the socialist camp. The American senators themselves make no secret of that. This, Comrade Tito, is where the difference lies in the question of credits, and surely you know it.

In this connection I recall our talks with Comrade Tito in Bucharest, in Yugoslavia, and also in the Crimea, where we did not spend our time hunting at all, as was reported, but where we talked politics. The hunting was meant to reassure certain people in the West who follow the policy of Yugoslavia with a jealous eye. Comrade Tito said at the time that soon they would no longer need Western economic assistance, that they were already in lesser need of it, and that we had ostensibly failed to grasp that. I voiced my personal opinion and the opinion of other Soviet comrades that when capitalist countries give credits to a socialist country and the recipient country keeps in step with all the socialist countries, we see nothing wrong in taking credits. We are not against credits in principle. The important thing is what their terms are, and for what purposes they are given. The capitalists help Yugoslavia, they give credits to it, because they want to inject a germ of decay into our camp with the object of splitting the socialist countries and the Communist parties. We oppose credits on these terms and condemn anyone willing to abandon revolutionary principles for a mess of pottage. (*Prolonged applause.*)

Anyone with class intuition, may he be ever so weak in theory, will see why the imperialist countries hate us so, and why they carry on their fight against the socialist camp. But there is a tremendous distance between the imperialist wish to destroy the socialist camp—the stronghold of peace and socialism—and its realization. We are strong and are not to be intimidated by threats.

When we speak of our strength it is not because we wish to threaten anyone. Leave us alone, for we have no intention of touching anyone. Together with our Czechoslovak friends, together with all the other socialist countries, together with people of good will the world over, we shall do everything in our power for the triumph of the great cause of world peace. (*Stormy applause.*)

We are well aware that the stronger we make our socialist camp and the more closely we work together for the victory of our common cause, the harder it will be for the enemies of peace to start a military adventure.

Comrade Novotný has put it splendidly in his report to the 11th Congress of the Communist Party of Czechoslovakia:

"We shall not reach our goal, unless we think every minute not only of the benefit of our republic, but also of the benefit of all the fraternal countries and of socialism throughout the world, unless we always see our own strength in the growing strength of the whole socialist camp, and render each other all-round disinterested support. It is only along this path of close international co-operation that all the historic victories of socialism have been scored in the past, and along this path alone shall we score new victories in the future." (*Stormy applause.*)

We are very happy that you have come, our dear Czechoslovak friends and brothers. For this visit will serve to further our friendship and to extend our all-round co-operation, and to cement still more the forces of our entire socialist camp. We can proudly say that the fraternal relations between our peoples are an example of the new, socialist relations. No force on earth will ever be able to destroy the friendship of our peoples. (*Stormy, prolonged applause.*)

Long live and flourish the peoples of the socialist Czechoslovak Republic! (*Stormy, prolonged applause.*)

Long live the Communist Party of Czechoslovakia—the organizer and inspirer of the victories of the Czechoslovak peoples! (*Stormy, prolonged applause.*)

Long live the eternal inviolable friendship of the peoples of the Czechoslovak Republic and the Soviet Union, of all the peoples of the socialist camp! (*Stormy, prolonged applause.*)

Long live world peace! (*Stormy, prolonged applause, ovation. All rise.*)

SPEECH
AT LUNCHEON IN HONOUR
OF GOVERNMENT DELEGATION OF AUSTRIAN
REPUBLIC

July 22, 1958

Mr. Federal Chancellor,
Mr. Vice-Chancellor,
Ladies and Gentlemen,
Friends,

Permit me· on behalf of the Soviet Government, and on my own behalf, to welcome the Federal Chancellor of Austria, Mr. Julius Raab, Vice-Chancellor Mr. Bruno Pittermann, the Foreign Minister of Austria, Mr. Leopold Figl, the State Secretary of the Austrian Foreign Ministry, Mr. Bruno Kreisky and their party.

We welcome the friendly visit of the Austrian government delegation to our country.

It is more than three years since the Austrian State Treaty was concluded. We are happy to note that in these years friendly relations have developed between the U.S.S.R. and Austria, and that the political, economic and cultural contacts between our two countries have expanded. Both sides have come to see that such relations are beneficial and accord with the basic interests of the peoples of our countries.

We shall continue basing our relations with Austria on friendship and equality, non-interference in internal affairs, and respect of sovereignty and national independence. The Soviet Union develops its economic and cultural relations with Austria without any political strings whatsoever, on a basis of complete equality and mutual advantage. I should like to stress that the U.S.S.R. wants to improve and develop its relations with Austria without prejudicing Austria's relations with other countries.

Austrian leaders take a sober view of the dangerous situation obtaining in the world in connection with the events in the Middle East.

I should like to say that we have taken satisfaction from the statement made by Federal Chancellor Mr. Julius Raab before his departure for Moscow, to the effect that in these circumstances of great international strain Austria would seek to co-operate in good faith and within her powers to relieve political tension.

The facts show that some imperialist countries spurn the sovereign rights of other countries. In unfolding their aggression in the Middle East, for example, the U.S. air force is known to have violated Austrian air space. This lawless act of the U.S. Government obviously contradicts the principles of international law and grossly violates the Austrian State Treaty, under which the United States, together with Britain, France and the U.S.S.R., has undertaken to respect the independence and territorial integrity of Austria. As you know, our country has condemned the acts of American top brass. The Soviet Union refuses to reconcile itself with this attitude towards international treaties.

The policy of permanent neutrality guarantees Austria's security and provides the Austrian people with the benefits of peaceful development. In the present circumstances the position of neutral Austria is unquestionably much more stable than that of any of the minor states which have been drawn into NATO. The Austrian people, who have gone through the terrors of many wars and have been deprived of their statehood by the *Anschluss*, are benefiting more and more from the advantages of neutrality, which guarantees them peaceful labour and independence.

We all know that there are forces within and outside your country which are trying to push Austria off its neutralist path and to make it dependent upon other states. Under the pretext of discussing the nature of Austria's neutrality certain Austrians speak out against its permanence by declaring that "Austrian neutrality is a transient affair" and that "it is not a commitment made by Austria under international law." It is hard to understand why politicians who consider themselves Austrians make such statements. Apparently, they take their cue from someone else.

The statements of the Austrian Government that Austria would adhere strictly to her voluntarily adopted principles of permanent neutrality and resist efforts to violate it, are to be welcomed.

In our opinion, neutral Austria could be a big force in the efforts to preserve peace if she would adhere firmly to the policy of neutrality and would as a neutral country promote mutual understanding between peoples.

The Soviet Union has due regard for Austria's neutrality, and will support all efforts of the Austrian Government to strengthen their country's neutrality and independence.

We hope that the visit of the Austrian government delegation to the U.S.S.R. and a frank exchange of opinions between the Austrian and Soviet leaders will serve to promote the further development of friendly relations between the U.S.S.R. and Austria and to achieve better mutual understanding and confidence between our peoples.

Permit me to propose a toast to the health of Federal Chancellor Mr. Raab, to the health of Vice-Chancellor Mr. Pittermann, Foreign Minister Mr. Figl, State Secretary Mr. Kreisky, and to the health of all our Austrian guests!

To friendship and all-round co-operation between the peoples of the Soviet Union and Austria!

SPEECH
AT RECEPTION AT EMBASSY OF POLISH PEOPLE'S REPUBLIC ON 14th ANNIVERSARY OF DAY OF NATIONAL RENASCENCE

July 22, 1958

In the first place allow me to thank the esteemed Ambassador, Comrade Tadeusz Gede, for the invitation to attend the reception on the occasion of the national holiday of the Polish People's Republic—the 14th anniversary of Poland's Day of National Renascence.

We are very glad that our friend, the Polish People's Republic, is confidently advancing along the road of socialist construction. We can see and hear its firm steps as we feel our own heartbeat.

The friendship between our countries is growing and gaining in strength. And that is very good, because the stronger our friendly relations become, and the closer the countries of the socialist camp rally together, the more confidently do we all advance to our great goal and so much greater are the successes scored by the peoples of our countries. The peoples of all the socialist countries, including the people of the Polish People's Republic and those of the Soviet Union, are interested in strengthening our fraternal friendship. The friendship between the socialist countries is one of the potent sources of our strength, one of the inexhaustible reservoirs for the successes of each of our countries.

These are good times in which we are living. As during a great spring flood, the ice is now breaking up, everything is on the move, everything is forging ahead in its historical development. The age-old ice of the colonial régime also has cracked and is breaking up before our eyes in quite a number of countries. The peoples are casting off and breaking the chains of colonialism. In vain are the efforts of those who would like to curb the liberation struggle of the peoples who have risen against age-old colonial oppression. As the spring waters break the winter ice on frozen rivers, so the peoples of the colonial countries and imperialist dependencies are breaking the hateful order established in their countries by alien enslavers. The colonialist policy of the imperialists is tottering and breaking up and this drives them to violent fury.

We revolutionaries, followers of Marx, Engels and Lenin, rejoice that the colonial peoples have risen in resolute struggle against their oppressors, against the colonialists, and that they wish to be masters of their own destiny. We hail their movement, sympathize with them in their liberation struggle and want to do everything to help them achieve their legitimate and noble aim—the liberation of their countries and national independence. We wish the peoples of these countries to be masters of their own national wealth, to ensure for themselves a state structure in their own countries that is dictated by their national interests.

Great changes are taking place in our days. Few expected that the Baghdad Pact would so soon cease to exist. The situation that existed only yesterday is today completely different. Baghdad was only recently a mainstay of the imperialist camp but with the coming of July 14 the very same Baghdad became odious to the imperialist Powers, and they wish to strangle the Iraq Republic, and to halt the national movement of the Arab world. But they won't succeed; it is beyond their powers.

We acclaim the Government of the Iraq Republic, we acclaim the Prime Minister of the Iraq Republic, Abdel Karim Kassem, for his courage and determination, for his devotion to his people and fine character—he does not fear the imperialists.

That is fine. I think that the representatives of the imperialist camp present here, the journalists, also will understand me correctly. We want peace throughout the world, we do not need war. The sooner you understand us, the better for you, as journalists, and at the same time the better and more useful will it be in general for the cause of peace.

War is the last recourse of desperate men. Just as a man stricken by an incurable disease is ready to do anything, ready to undergo any operation in the hope of saving his life, so the imperialists, too, are ready to go to war as a last resort. But even this recourse and this operation will not save the capitalist system. Karl Marx proved that mankind can get rid of all the misfortunes engendered by capitalism only by taking the road of socialist development. The Soviet Union was the first to embark on this road; it was followed by other countries of the socialist camp.

The Arab peoples who have risen in resolute struggle against imperialism are waging this struggle not under the Marxist banner, but under the colours of the national-liberation movement. How they will order their life afterwards is their own affair. We greet them as they are today—fighters against colonialism, against imperialism, who demand that the jackboots of the alien invader should not trample upon their soil.

Recently Mr. Nasser, President of the United Arab Republic, paid a visit here. Our talk was pleasant and useful. I am a Communist and he is the leader of the Arab national-liberation movement. He does not share our political views. But when we exchanged opinions on the situation in the Middle East there was understanding between us. I understood him and he understood me. What did we talk about? We discussed how to stop the imperialists, how to prevent them from unleashing a war.

You may rest assured that we shall do everything to avert war in the Middle East. We shall do everything possible for the newly born Iraq Republic to grow stronger. The future social system in that republic is the business of the people of Iraq. The Soviet Union has only one desire: it wants the Iraq Republic to be independent, to grow stronger, to develop its economy and prosper.

Mikoyan: You have given away all the "secrets."

Khrushchov: These are the "secrets" about which we talked with President Nasser. I know the correspondents will ask about that, so I am meeting them half-way and telling them what we discussed with the President of the United Arab Republic, Mr. Nasser. The Ambassador of the United Arab Republic, Mr. el-Kouni, is here. He was present at our talks. If you are not satisfied with my answer, you can ask him.

We would like the leaders of the United States and Britain to show wisdom, to display an understanding of the changed conditions in the world, and of the spirit of the times, and to withdraw their troops from the Lebanon and Jordan.

One can imagine how Jordan "rejoices" at the entry of British troops which two years ago were driven from that country by the people. The question arises: Who asked for British troops to be brought back to Jordan? It is said that King Hussein requested this. But it is high time to realize that kings who lose the confidence of their people will not be able to retain their power with the help of foreign bayonets. Russia, too, had a tsar but what happened? The people overthrew him.

I shall be betraying no secrets if I declare that all kings and tsars who in their policy ignore the interests of their peoples, who depend on foreign bayonets, will not be tolerated by the people and will be overthrown by them.

Why did American armed forces invade the Lebanon? It is said that this was done at the request of President Chamoun. The ground has slipped from under the feet of President Chamoun, he has lost the confidence of his people. He wants to prolong his stay in power with the help of American bayonets. It is not for us to wish him success in this. We wish the Lebanese people success in their struggle for their freedom and independence, we wish them to be masters of their own country and of their destiny, and to dispose of the wealth of their homeland themselves.

As for the situation in the socialist camp, our affairs are progressing quite well—better than ever before. He for whom this is glad news may rejoice, and he for whom these are unpleasant tidings may be chagrined, our situation will not be affected. Industry in the Soviet Union is on a steep upgrade, a very good crop of grain and other produce has been grown on the fields of our country.

We rejoice in the unity of the peoples in each socialist country, the solidarity of the peoples of the entire socialist camp.

What else do we need? We need peace.

We say to the representatives of capitalist countries: If you capitalist gentlemen are confident that your system is strong, that it is unshakable, let us compete peacefully. Demonstrate in action the advantages of your capitalist system and we shall demonstrate the advantages of the socialist system. The system which ensures better living conditions for man is the system that will win. If you are confident of winning this "battle," let us match our strength in peaceful competition.

Our socialist system is young, fresh and strong. Socialism is confidently advancing—to it belongs the future.

Allow me to propose a toast to our friends, the friendly Polish People's Republic, the Polish United Workers' Party, its Central Committee, our very close friend Wladyslaw Gomulka, the State Council of the Polish People's Republic and its President Alexander Zawadski, the Government of the Polish People's Republic, and Chairman of the Council of Ministers Jozef Cyrankiewicz. I toast our friend, the Ambassador of the Polish People's Republic in Moscow, Tadeusz Gede, and the entire staff of the Embassy who have so kindly invited us here.

(N. S. Khrushchov's speech was repeatedly interrupted by enthusiastic applause.)

REPLIES
TO QUESTIONS PUT BY KINGSBURY SMITH, VICE-PRESIDENT AND GENERAL DIRECTOR OF UNITED PRESS INTERNATIONAL AGENCY

July 22, 1958

On July 22, Kingsbury Smith, Vice-President and General Director of the United Press International Agency, posed some questions to N. S. Khrushchov, Chairman of the U.S.S.R. Council of Ministers. Below we publish N. S. Khrushchov's replies to the questions of Kingsbury Smith.

Question: Would you agree to expand the composition of the top-level conference, which you proposed, so that this conference takes the form of a U.N. Security Council meeting in accordance with Article 28 of the Charter and under the conditions that the Council would appoint a subcommittee consisting of the Heads of Government of the United Kingdom, France, the U.S.S.R., the U.S.A., and would also invite the head of the Indian Government to participate in the discussion of the situation in the Middle East as an interested party?

Answer: Your considerations concerning the method of discussing the question of the situation in the Middle East are interesting. At present a tense situation resulting from U.S. and British intervention has arisen in this area creating a real threat to peace and security. Under these conditions further procrastination in considering the question of measures to avert a world conflict would be criminal.

Guided by these considerations, the Soviet Government in its Message of July 19 proposed the immediate calling of a conference of the Heads of Government of the U.S.S.R., the U.S.A., Great Britain, France, and India, with the participation of the U.N. Secretary-General. This proposal has won wide support in all countries of the world.

You express the thought that the meeting of the Heads of Government should be held within the framework of the U.N. Security Council. This is not contrary to our views. The Soviet Government, as implied in its Message of July 19, considers that no action should be taken circumventing the United Nations, which is called upon to safeguard the peace and security of the peoples. We consider that at present the issue is not one concerning the form of a conference of Heads of Government, but rather one concerning the immediate measures to be taken to remove the danger of war and to give the peoples of the Arab countries an opportunity to build their life without foreign interference. In this respect your considerations are useful and constructive. I would like to stress particularly that the participation of Mr. Nehru, Head of the Government of India, in this conference would undoubtedly facilitate the achievement of decisions in the interest of peace.

Question: If the reply to the first question is a positive one, then would you agree to the meeting of such a subcommittee being held in the U.N. building in Geneva not later than the end of the current month?

Answer: The matter concerning a place of meeting of the Heads of Government is not an essential one and does not play a major role. As for the Soviet side, we are prepared to meet immediately at any place, including Geneva and New York.

Question: Will you personally participate in such a meeting if the other Heads of Government are present?

Answer: If Prime Minister Macmillan, President of the Council of Ministers de Gaulle, and President Eisenhower participate in the conference, then the Soviet Union will be represented at this conference by the Chairman of the Council of Ministers of the U.S.S.R. It stands to reason that the Soviet Government firmly hopes that Mr. Nehru, Prime Minister of India, will also participate in the conference.

July 22, 1958
Pravda, July 24, 1958

SPEECH
AT DINNER GIVEN
BY EMBASSY OF AUSTRIAN REPUBLIC

July 23, 1958

Esteemed Mr. Federal Chancellor,

Esteemed Mr. Vice-Chancellor,

Ladies and Gentlemen,

The experience of the last few years shows that meetings between Soviet and Austrian statesmen have invariably benefited the peoples of both countries. We are sure that the present visit of the Austrian government delegation to Moscow will serve further to develop and strengthen the friendly relations obtaining between our countries.

The Soviet people have the very best of sentiments for the people of Austria. They are sincerely eager to further develop and strengthen Soviet-Austrian relations. Our country has always consistently given its support to the integrity and independence of the Austrian state. It did so in 1938, when our Government firmly condemned Hitler Germany's aggression against Austria. It did so during the grim years of war against Hitlerism. It did so after your country was liberated, when the Soviet Union urged a just settlement of the Austrian question. You may rest assured, ladies and gentlemen, that the Soviet Union will maintain this attitude in the future as well.

Today, we can all state with satisfaction that Austria did right when she adopted neutrality. It benefited your people and your state. The Soviet people sincerely wish that you may live in peace and friendship with all nations, that you may conduct an independent foreign policy and assist in relieving international tension.

It is gratifying to note that our governments are in agreement concerning the need to preserve and strengthen peace, and avert a destructive atomic war. In our time everybody is deeply concerned over the course international developments will take in the future—whether it will be a course of slackening tension and cementing peace or of exacerbating the international situation, leading to the terrors of a new war.

Both the Soviet people and the Austrian people do not want war. They want a stronger peace throughout the world. That is a splendid foundation for close co-operation between us in the struggle for preserving and cementing peace.

Allow me to propose a toast to the further development and strengthening of the friendship between our peoples, to our co-operation in the struggle for world peace.

To the health of Federal Chancellor Mr. Raab, to the health of Vice-Chancellor Mr. Pittermann, Foreign Minister Mr. Figl, State Secretary of the Foreign Ministry Mr. Kreisky, to the health of our Austrian guests!

SPEECH
AT KREMLIN RECEPTION IN HONOUR
OF GOVERNMENT DELEGATION
OF AUSTRIAN REPUBLIC

July 24, 1958

Esteemed Mr. Chancellor,
Esteemed Mr. Vice-Chancellor,
Ladies and Gentlemen,
Friends,

We have had a useful and fruitful exchange of opinions with our esteemed guests from Austria. The outcome of our negotiations is recorded in the Joint Soviet-Austrian Communique just signed by us, which testifies to the further strengthening of friendship and mutual confidence between our countries. In our frank and friendly conversations we touched upon a number of important questions concerning Soviet-Austrian relations and to the international situation, and can note with satisfaction that our views coincide in the matters discussed. As far as we, Soviet representatives, are concerned, we are pleased with the outcome of our talks. I think that our guests, too, are pleased with the results of their trip to Moscow.

The Soviet Union and Austria have different social and political systems. But does this prevent our peoples from living in peace, developing their economic relations and strengthening contacts in science, culture and sport? Our relations are an object lesson that differing social systems are no obstacle to friendship and co-operation. The relations between the Soviet Union and Austria are a concrete practical example of the application of the principles of peaceful co-existence, when two countries with different social and political systems live in peace and friendship and do not interfere in each other's domestic affairs.

An alarming international situation has arisen at present. The Soviet Union pursues its peace policy consistently and works unremittingly with other peaceful countries to avert the outbreak of a new war. We are deeply convinced that the peoples will uphold the cause of peace if they actively combat all attempts to start a new war. The forces of peace have grown and have gained strength so much that they are capable of curbing any aggressor, of preventing war. But this is not easy, because alongside active friends of peace there are still reckless people who not only dream of a new war, but are preparing one. Unfortunately, these reckless men occupy posts of prominence in some countries. For this reason, the nations must be vigilant

The neutral countries are called upon to play a big part in preserving peace and improving the international situation. They cannot keep aloof when other peaceful nations are working to prevent war and achieve lasting peace.

The Soviet people welcome the contribution which Austria is making and, we hope, will continue to make to the cause of preserving and consolidating peace. Co-operation of the Soviet Union and Austria in the struggle for peace and a further development of economic and cultural relations between them are a good and reliable basis on which to build Soviet-Austrian friendship with benefit to both peoples.

I raise a toast to the active consolidation of all peaceful forces the world over in the struggle against war, for peace, to peaceful co-existence of states, to friendship and co-operation between peoples, to still greater friendship between the Soviet and Austrian peoples!

To the health of Federal Chancellor Mr. Raab, to the health of Vice-Chancellor Mr. Pittermann, Foreign Minister

Mr. Figl and State Secretary Mr. Kreisky; to the health of
our Austrian guests; to the health of the esteemed Austrian
Ambassador to the Soviet Union, Mr. Bischoff!

To the health of the President of the Austrian Republic,
Mr. Adolf Schärf!

*(N. S. Khrushchov's speech was enthusiastically ap-
plauded.)*

SPEECH
ON DEPARTURE FROM MOSCOW OF GOVERNMENT
DELEGATION OF AUSTRIAN REPUBLIC

July 28, 1958

Esteemed Mr. Raab,
Esteemed Mr. Pittermann,
Esteemed Mr. Figl, Mr. Kreisky and all our Austrian guests,

Today you are leaving the Soviet Union and returning home. We were gratified at meeting you and holding conversations which have led to a further improvement in Austro-Soviet relations, and to still better mutual understanding.

The agreement reached between us on economic questions will give fresh impetus to an all-round development of business contacts between our countries. It is good to note that in the course of our conversations we discovered that our points of view coincide on quite a number of international issues directly related to the struggle for peace and the relaxation of international tension.

Thus, the development of economic relations and the identity of our interests in questions of preserving and strengthening peace and international security are a point of departure for a further development of relations between our countries based on the principles of peaceful coexistence, based on Austria's declared neutrality.

Our meetings and talks have again confirmed the usefulness of personal contacts between the leading statesmen of Austria and the Soviet Union. They showed that the questions that arise between us can be successfully settled in the atmosphere of confidence and mutual understanding which has been established between us. Future personal contacts between us will unquestionably be as useful and fruitful.

In this connection I should like to express our sincere gratitude to Mr. Raab and Mr. Pittermann for their kind invitation to visit Austria. You have asked us, Mr. Federal Chancellor, not to "leave behind" Comrade Mikoyan when we go to Austria. I think that you will not object if, apart from not "leaving him behind", there are a few other leading statesmen we shall not "leave behind"; lest they be jealous of Comrade Mikoyan for being the only one to visit your wonderful country.

Allow me to wish you good health and a happy journey! Until we meet again, gentlemen! *Auf Wiedersehen*!

INTERVIEW
WITH INDIAN JOURNALISTS

July 29, 1958

N. S. Khrushchov, Chairman of the U.S.S.R. Council of Ministers, on July 29 received a group of editors and correspondents of Indian newspapers and magazines who had attended the Stockholm World Congress for Disarmament and International Co-operation.

In the course of their talk N. S. Khrushchov replied to questions put by the Indian journalists. Published below is a record of the interview.

Khrushchov: I am happy to welcome you to Soviet soil.

Jagjeet Singh Anand: We are grateful to you for finding the time to receive us, in spite of the tense international situation, which is no doubt taking up a great deal of your time.

Our people remember you very well as a good friend of our country ever since you visited India in 1955. They particularly remember your saying that should we even be in trouble, we could appeal to you across the mountains and help would be forthcoming from the Soviet Union.

Khrushchov: Our trip to India on a friendship visit was very pleasant. The Indian people, the Central Government of the Republic of India and the governments of the provinces extended friendly hospitality to us. As envoys of the Soviet Union we were received by the peace-loving Indian people with exceptional cordiality and genuine sincerity. We shall always remember our stay in India. In our country envoys from India are invariably accorded a most cordial reception and friendly hospitality and attention; they are welcomed as honoured guests.

Anand: The people of India greatly appreciate the present attitude of the Soviet Union with regard to the situation in the Middle East and they are also grateful that the Soviet Union is displaying firmness, on the one hand, and on the other hand, is not succumbing to provocations. Moreover, the people of India greatly appreciate the Soviet Government's initiative in proposing a summit conference and especially the Soviet Union's initiative in inviting Prime Minister Nehru to that conference. But now, when the Western Powers have shown that they evidently do not want India to take part in such a meeting and when, it seems, they are trying to prevent the holding of this meeting, what, in your opinion, are the prospects for the development of international relations?

Khrushchov: At present, it is better to wait before defining the prospects because relations between countries are in a state of crisis. The following example will make it clear. When a state of crisis occurs in a sick organism, the doctors who are taking steps to cure the patient have to wait for a certain period of time in order to get a clearer picture. Will the bacilli that are undermining the patient's health win the day, or will the organism overcome the disease, counteract the deleterious effect of the bacilli that are ravaging it? Similarly, it would appear that at the present time we political leaders also need a certain amount of time in order to determine the direction which the development of international relations will take—for better or for worse. I am convinced, however, that the organism is so strong—I mean the forces fighting for peace—that it will vanquish the colonialist bacilli. The peace-loving peoples will rebuff the bellicose colonialists and the aggressors will be compelled to reckon with the forces fighting for peace, against war and colonialism.

Anand S. Jain: When President Nasser returned recently from Moscow, he said at a press conference in Damascus that certain decisions had been made during the meeting with you in Moscow. We know nothing about the nature of those decisions, however. Would it be possible for you to elaborate on this subject?

Khrushchov: He did not say that decisions had been made. The adoption of decisions is the function of governments. During the visit of Gamal Abdel Nasser, President of the United Arab Republic, to Moscow, views were exchanged on the situation that has arisen in the Middle East. There were no differences in our assessment of this situation which has resulted from the aggression of the United States and Britain in the Middle East; we shared the same views. We exchanged opinions on the type of measures to be taken against the aggression by the colonialists in order to prevent it from spreading, to curb it and to compel the aggressor countries to recall their troops in order to create normal conditions in the countries of the Middle East. The peoples of these countries should govern their countries themselves and use their wealth as they desire, without foreign interference in their internal affairs. We agreed that it was necessary to take all measures to safeguard peace, to guarantee the independence of the Arab countries.

Anand: Our people adhere to the principles of non-violence. Our civilization is an ancient one and we attach great importance to moral principles. We consider that the Soviet Union's decision on the unilateral ending of nuclear weapons tests confirms the adherence of the Soviet Union to high moral principles. This is also confirmed by the fact that the Soviet Union, even after the Western Powers have continued with their nuclear weapons tests, has not undertaken another series of tests of its own.

We also consider that the Soviet Union's attitude with regard to the present international crisis is likewise distinguished by high moral qualities and constitutes support

627

for the ideals of non-violence and the ideals of the struggle for peace.

In this connection we would like to ask Mr. Khrushchov what forms, in his opinion, could be assumed by joint actions of the Soviet people, the people of India and the peoples of other Eastern countries for the purpose of maintaining world peace.

Khrushchov: I would like to express my most sincere gratitude for your kind and friendly assessment of the Soviet Union's policy, which is a policy of ensuring peace and peaceful international co-operation in the interests of the peoples. Soviet policy is based on high moral principles. These principles have been substantiated by our great teacher Lenin, the founder of the Soviet state. We have always been, and shall continue to be, loyal to the Leninist principles of friendship and brotherhood among the peoples, and we shall work tirelessly for world peace.

What, then, are the measures which should be taken now to prevent war? The main thing now is for public opinion, for the peoples in all countries, not to allow themselves to be lulled by some manoeuvre or other on the part of the colonialists, and for the peoples to condemn with still greater vigour the aggressive actions of certain Western states against the countries of the Middle East. The peoples must urgently press for the withdrawal of the troops of the interventionists and must spare no effort in striving to put an end for all time to the imperialist methods of settling international problems. To put it briefly, it is necessary to strive for relations between all states, whatever their internal régimes, to be based on the principles of *Panch Shila.* Those are splendid words which contain the broad idea of ensuring peace and friendship among nations. It is necessary to assert the right of all peoples to live as they desire, and to deliver mankind from the policy of strength, with the help of which some persons in the West still intend to impose their rule on other peoples. It is necessary to deliver mankind from the methods of the last century, when the imperialists decided the fate of peoples and divided and redivided the world into spheres of influence for themselves. There is no going back to a past when a small handful of countries exploited the Asian and African peoples and waxed fat at their expense.

In our day anyone who is not willing to take into account the aspirations of the peoples for peace and freedom, anyone who still seeks to continue the policy of colonialism and imperialism, in accordance with the "divide and rule" principle—such a person will inevitably be cast aside by history. We hope that common sense will finally triumph over the adventurist political line of certain Western leaders.

Anand: We have just come from the Stockholm Congress. We were in Stockholm at a time when serious events occurred in the Middle East. In addition to a large delegation from India, the Congress was attended by delegations from many Asian and African countries, Arab countries, by big delegations from South America and other countries. In the past, at such assemblies, there have been certain differences of opinion about the relation between the struggle for national liberation and the struggle for peace. Some leaders from Western countries, even among the peace supporters, in the past argued that the struggle against colonialism not infrequently interferes, and comes into conflict, with the struggle for peace. This time we saw that now there is a high degree of understanding within the peace movement that lasting peace cannot be achieved while the shameful colonial system remains. This has greatly encouraged us.

In this connection, allow me to ask you what, in your opinion, could be done to achieve better mutual understanding between the socialist countries and the countries which have recently gained their national independence, so that both the former and the latter may jointly lay a still firmer foundation upon which the edifice of peace can be erected.

Khrushchov: You have rightly noted the distinctions

which still exist between the views of representatives of the colonial or former colonial countries and some representatives of the Western countries. This is not a chance phenomenon. It is a product of the historical conditions of the past.

The struggle for liberation from colonial dependence is a matter of life and death for the colonial peoples. But those who are accustomed to being colonialists do not want to understand that at all. Moreover, at times it is not understood even by people who consider themselves progressive and free thinking, and who condemn violence. They seem to have become accustomed to a situation in which the imperialists of this or that Western state lord it over a number of countries of Asia, Africa and South America by virtue of being more "developed and highly civilized," as if destined to fulfil a "noble mission," to "bring civilization and culture" to the peoples of underdeveloped countries. Such explanations are untenable. There are no arguments, nor can there be, to justify the preservation and continuation of the policy of colonialism.

It is sufficient to consider the example of India, which was a colonial country for many years. Did India prior to being subjugated by the colonialists have a low culture? On the contrary, if we compare Indian culture with that of the colonialists, we find that the high culture of India has deeper roots which reach far back into the centuries. This is borne out by the many monuments of India's ancient culture, created by the talented and industrious people of India.

The colonialists, however, did not take into account the right of the people of India to order their lives in accordance with their own interests. As a result of the domination of the foreign colonialists they were condemned to bear the colonial yoke for a long time. India was oppressed and ruthlessly plundered. For a long time the colonialists retarded the development of the Indian economy and culture and condemned the people to poverty and starvation.

And today, when people boast that in Britain and in some other Western countries the standard of living is higher than in other countries, we must not forget at whose expense this has been achieved. It became possible at the expense of the millions of people who were sacrificed to attain that high level. How many millions have died and are still dying today in colonial countries so that colonialists may be able to make huge fortunes out of the blood, poverty and suffering of the peoples. It is not civilization and culture that the colonialists bring to the countries dependent upon them, but oppression, violence, poverty, backwardness and enslavement.

I have already said that even among democratic sections of the public there are people infected with the bacillus of colonialism. Take, for example, some Labourites in Britain. They consider themselves Socialists and should, therefore, be more progressive than Conservatives on questions of colonial policy. But they include individuals who are indistinguishable from Conservatives on questions of colonial policy.

And it was not by chance that during the attack on Egypt in 1956, some Labourites did not oppose that aggression.

Or take the French Socialists. Was not the French Government, which at the time was headed by the Socialist Guy Mollet, an accomplice in the aggressive attack on Egypt, together with Britain and Israel?

It is not surprising, therefore, that even among those who are taking part in the struggle for peace, there are still people who are beset with doubts as to the possibility of combining the peoples' struggle against colonialism with the peoples' struggle for peace. They regard the existence of colonialism as unjust, but when a situation arises that threatens to deprive certain Powers of one colony or another, they are assailed with doubts and vacillations. Some of them find various justifications for the colonialists having to obtain oil from dependent countries for a mere song.

In so doing they apparently fail to realize that this means robbing the peoples of those countries.

The imperialists who extract oil and other wealth, practically for nothing, from the colonial and dependent countries, ignore the fact that owing to this, millions upon millions of people—children and adults—perish in those countries. This does not disturb them in the least. They say that the Asian and African peoples have always lived in greater poverty, and fared worse than the population in the Western countries.

Can the peoples of Asia and Africa reconcile themselves to such prospects? They are fighting, and will continue to fight, for their independence, for the right to dispose of their countries' wealth themselves. The peoples of Asia and Africa are waging a determined struggle for the national independence of their countries. The colonialists will not be able to halt this struggle. It began despite the wishes of the colonialists and it will reach a successful conclusion.

It is necessary, therefore, to differentiate here between colonialists who want to rule over other peoples in order to rob them and grow rich at their expense, and deluded people who desire peace and regard colonialism as unjust, but who do not know whether it is possible to combine the struggle for peace with the struggle for the abolition of colonialism.

As for relations between the socialist countries, on the one hand, and the former colonial countries and the colonial countries which are liberating themselves, on the other, here there is complete clarity. It is necessary to strengthen in every way the relations between these countries, both along governmental lines and along social lines: to exchange delegations, to render each other assistance in economic and cultural matters and in the development of industry.

Economically highly developed countries should help the underdeveloped countries to enable the peoples of those countries to utilize the available possibilities for promoting their economy, culture and science and for raising the standard of living of the population. I think that relations of just such a kind are developing at the present time. In the future, too, they should develop in the same direction. I believe that all socialist countries understand their role precisely in the following way: to help one another, to help the socialist countries, and at the same time also to help the countries which are throwing off, or have already thrown off, the colonial yoke; not to interfere in the internal affairs of those countries, but to help them in their development, in the consolidation of national independence and sovereignty. Accordingly, it is always necessary to be guided by the well-known Five Principles which are now recognized by many countries: mutual respect for territorial integrity and sovereignty, non-aggression, non-interference in one another's internal affairs, equality and mutual benefit, peaceful co-existence and economic co-operation. Such a development of relations provides the only correct way. It will promote the strengthening of tne forces of progress, the strengthening of friendly relations between countries and, consequently, it will help to ensure lasting peace.

S. R. Tikekar: The Americans in the Lebanon and the British in Jordan, having occupied those two countries, now seem to be marking time there. Does this mean that the forces of peace have succeeded in frustrating the further plans of the British and Americans in the Middle East? It must be assumed that they had far-reaching plans which did not envisage only the occupation of those two countries.

Khrushchov: I think you are right in your assumptions. The landing of troops there envisaged not only what had already taken place, but also a subsequent attack on the Republic of Iraq and its liquidation, the unleashing of war in that area in order to destroy the United Arab Republic and thereby create conditions for a return to the old colonial system which formerly existed in those countries. Times have changed, however. All this proved to be not so easy to accomplish as the initiators of those plans had imagined. The people of Iraq have successfully carried out a revolution. Complete order has been established in the Republic of Iraq. The people are supporting the new Government and the republican system that has been established in the country. A wave of popular protest has swept all countries, including those whose governments have sent troops into the Middle East, especially Britain. The aggressors are therefore compelled to camouflage their predatory actions. But the danger has not as yet been removed. The interventionists have so far been stopped— they have now put a halt to their active operations in carrying out the task they had set themselves. But the build-up of forces is continuing. In these conditions the peaceful countries must be exceptionally vigilant. All peoples must raise their voices still louder and vigorously press for the withdrawal of the troops of the United States and Britain from the Lebanon and Jordan, and must put an end to the intervention of the colonialists in the internal affairs of the Arab countries.

It should be noted that the fact that nearly 1,000 million people are now building their life in accordance with socialist principles is of great importance in strengthening peace, in the struggle for peace. This is a great force that is restraining the aggressors and all who have not given up attempts to unleash war.

Nor should it be forgotten that the peoples of the countries which have liberated themselves from the colonial yoke are determined to defend the cause of peace, since only in an atmosphere of peace can they ensure the economic development of their countries, which have won their national independence. Among them we have such a great country as India, whose lofty moral principles are known to the whole world and deserve great respect.

Needless to say, the Soviet Union is playing a great role in the defence of peace. The very existence of such a peaceful and powerful state as our country has an exceptionally beneficial significance for mankind and acts as a powerful deterrent to aggressors. I would like to stress that the existence of such a mighty state as the Soviet Union instils in the hearts of all people, who are longing for peace, the hope of preserving and strengthening world peace.

Colonialists are people with rather low morals. In their public statements they very often appeal to God, and at the same time hold a concealed dagger which they are ready to use against the weak in order to seize their wealth—their oil or other assets. The colonialists are now raving especially against the Soviet Union, trying to discredit it in the eyes of the peoples. Why are they doing this? Because they see that the Soviet Union has won great respect among the peoples, since it bases its policy on high moral principles.

The Soviet state and all the socialist countries desire peace and not war, peaceful co-operation and not enmity. All the more do they oppose the subjugation of one people by another. The Soviet Union, the Chinese People's Republic and all socialist countries are resolutely opposed to colonialism. The Soviet Union has the proper means available for dealing with colonialists if they do not come to their senses. Colonialists should not be allowed to endanger peace and subjugate small nations with impunity. The voice of the Soviet Union in defence of colonial peoples and its possibilities of exerting influence on the aggressors are bringing the latter to their senses. Sometimes the colonialists are compelled to sing and serenade in order to lull the vigilance of the peoples and to make a verbal show of their peaceful disposition.

The forces standing for peace are growing increasingly stronger. The advocates of colonialism are losing more and more strength, as they pursue aims that are unjust and do not have, and cannot have, the support of the peoples.

Tikekar: Just a few words, by the way, about moral actions. The American actions in the Lebanon were entirely immoral, because the Americans were not invited there by any legal authority. The same is true with regard to the

British actions in Jordan. The treaty between Jordan and Britain was abrogated, and nevertheless British troops have now entered Jordan. Evidently these immoral actions on the part of the British in Jordan are resulting in King Hussein becoming less and less popular among the people of Jordan. Could not this circumstance provide the grounds for an uprising of the people of Jordan against the King and the British?

Khrushchov: King Hussein has no influence at all among the people. It was this that made the British send their forces into Jordan to maintain him on the throne. The press has even reported that Hussein has already consulted the British and the Americans about whether he should abdicate. But he was advised to remain, and he did. King Hussein holds his throne, not because the people want him to be king, but because the colonialists wish to have such a king, to use him as a screen for ensuring their domination in Jordan and, with the help of an "invitation" from the King, to disguise the intervention of their forces in Jordan.

The people of Jordan will drive the British forces out of their country all the same. As you know, the British have already been there but they were forced to get out. So the intervention of British forces in Jordan is not something new. They were driven out at one time and they will be seen off now with the same "honours" from foreign soil. What is new is that whereas in the past statesmen of the U.S.A. did not openly admit their role as colonialists, now they can no longer conceal it from the peoples. The peoples now see more clearly that in essence there is no difference at all between the imperialists of Britain and the United States, because both of them use armed force against the vital interests of all countries struggling for their national independence against the colonialists.

Jagat Narayan: We would like to know what, in your opinion, are the prospects for a summit conference, now that American and British forces have gone into the Lebanon and Jordan.

Khrushchov: The American leaders have done, and are doing, their best to prevent the meeting. They still maintain the same attitude. But owing to great pressure from the peoples and to the growing trend in favour of a summit conference in the United States itself, U.S. statesmen do not talk openly about their desire to prevent a summit meeting. They disguise their efforts in that direction by inventing various complicated procedural problems which allegedly hinder such a meeting.

Narayan: What is the role of the British in this situation?

Khrushchov: It is about the same as that of the United States. However, the position of the British Government is more difficult, because the Labour Party members in that country are strong and are exerting great pressure on the Government. That is why the British Government has to pursue a more astute policy. Besides, British policy is in general more subtle and flexible, because the British are more skilful diplomats than the Americans and they do not act as crudely as their American colleagues.

H. P. Desai: In view of the fact that the attitude of the member-countries of the Baghdad Pact continues to be aggressive, what are the prospects for peace in the light of this?

Khrushchov: To a certain extent I have already answered this question. The Baghdad Pact has now been left without Baghdad. The fact is also not without significance. (*Laughter.*)

Now too the prospects for maintaining peace are very considerable. The countries which stand for peace should make skilful use of their forces and should not give way to the colonialists. Peace can be maintained if the peoples display greater vigilance with regard to the intrigues of the imperialists.

As for the British and the Americans, they will eventually withdraw their troops from Jordan and the Lebanon, for the peoples of those countries will not rest until they have achieved their aims, and the troops of the colonialists will ignominiously depart.

M. G. Desai: Today we visited the Institute of Oriental Studies. We were very pleased to learn that this institute recently published a book devoted to our national uprising of 1857, and then a book about Tilak, our great leader and Gandhi's predecessor, and very soon it expects to publish a book about Gandhi and his contribution to the national-liberation movement of the Indian people. We have no doubt that the thorough study of our national movement will strengthen the ties between our two countries, as certain imprudent remarks made by individual Soviet authors in the past gave the enemies of Soviet-Indian friendship an opportunity to exploit their statements to the detriment of this friendship. Such misunderstandings are now evidently out of the question with the scale which the study of our national movement has acquired in the Soviet Union.

Khrushchov: It is gratifying that you understand our policy so well. Indeed, we are seeking in every possible way to broaden and strengthen the friendship between our countries. In the past some inaccurate views on several Indian personalities did appear in certain works by Soviet authors. We are trying to put this right so as to pay tribute to everyone who played a truly great role in his country and made a big contribution to the liberation of his native India from the colonialists. We are filled with admiration for their outstanding activities and their splendid records, and we are doing everything possible to enable our people to obtain an accurate picture of the forces which fought for India's freedom and independence and rallied their people in the fight against foreign colonialists. The Soviet people show great interest in the history of India and want to know more about this friendly, great and peaceful country.

You know that it was not only about your leading personalities that our press published incorrect allegations. At one time mistakes were made regarding a number of very prominent personalities in the sphere of our own Soviet culture, for instance, regarding such an eminent figure in Soviet music as the composer Dmitry Shostakovich, or regarding Alexander Korneichuk and Wanda Wasilewska. Their names are widely known throughout the world, not only as prominent representatives of Soviet culture, but also as active fighters for the cause of peace—they take part in the work of the World Peace Council.

You evidently know that not so long ago a special decision was made here on this question, in which we swept overboard everything that had been wrongly brought up against these and other comrades, and in that way we developed a correct attitude to the understanding of their work and created for them, as for all our other artists, even better opportunities for the more fruitful application of their creative endeavours. Unfortunately, at one time the mistakes to which you have referred were also made in evaluating and characterizing certain Indian personalities.

Jain: Some time ago a Lebanese opposition leader said that if American troops landed in the Lebanon, it would lead to volunteers being sent to the Lebanon by the forces which stand for peace.

Now that the landing of American troops has taken place, but further military developments have been suspended, what opinion is held on the question of volunteers?

Khrushchov: The participation of volunteers from other countries in events in the Middle East would mean a real war! It would be better if there was no such war, if in that country there were neither volunteers nor soldiers sent in on the orders of certain governments. I believe it would be far better for the Lebanese to be in the Lebanon, for the Jordanians to be in Jordan, and for the peoples of those countries to live without uninvited outsiders.

Tikekar: Today we were told in the Institute of Oriental Studies that on your initiative the study of Indian languages is being expanded and that, in particular there is talk of establishing an institute for the study of Indian languages. In this connection I would like to express the following wish. It is, of course, worth while developing the study of contemporary Indian languages, but it is worth while developing the study of Sanskrit as well. I would like to express the hope that in the immediate future there will appear a new edition of the very good Sanskrit dictionary which, in the past, was published in St. Petersburg.

Khrushchov: In the Soviet Union there is very great interest in studying the languages of the peoples of the East, including the peoples of India. We want more people in our country to know these languages so as to make it easier to develop cultural relations between our countries. I would prefer, however, to refrain from making any sweeping statement on this question and would like to give the specialists in this field an opportunity to make a detailed study of these matters so as to take the necessary steps afterwards.

O. Paliwal: In concluding our interview, I would like to say that there can be no doubt that among the forces standing for peace a great role is being played by the Soviet Union and by the Soviet Union's strength. A big part is also being played by the countries of Asia and Africa which have achieved their independence or are now striving for their independence. We feel that the movement of the former colonial peoples can be a great factor in the struggle against foreign exploitation and aggression, in the struggle for peace. We would like to express the hope that these two factors—the Soviet Union and the community of Asian and African countries which took shape at Bandung and was further developed at the Cairo Conference—will jointly play a great role in the fight for peace.

Khrushchov: I agree with you and can assure you that the Soviet Union is a state which is strong enough to make a worthy stand for the cause of peace, and that is a fortunate thing for all the peoples who wish to preserve peace throughout the world. Why is that so? It is so because the national economy of our country, our strength—both moral and material strength in the shape of our army—will never be used to the detriment of any neighbour state or to the detriment of any nation whatsoever. The Armed Forces of the Soviet Union have been created and exist for the purpose of worthily defending the freedom and independence of our people, our country, for the purpose of maintaining peace throughout the world.

We are sure that in further pursuing our peace policy we shall be able to achieve even greater results in strengthening peace throughout the world and maintain such conditions that aggressors will not dare to unleash war. But if, in defiance of common sense, they venture to unleash a new war, that war will be fatal for them. We have said, however, and we reiterate, that it is better not to have any war; it is better to nip in the bud any attempt to start a war. We have done and are doing our best towards this end, and for the sake of this we are ready for complete disarmament. You are probably aware of the concrete steps we have taken towards this end. Recently, for instance, we forwarded to the Governments of European states and to the United States Government a proposal for the conclusion of a treaty of friendship and co-operation among European states. The Soviet Government does not spare its efforts for the strengthening of peace throughout the world.

It is very gratifying to see that you understand our policy and assess it correctly. I should like to express my thankfulness and appreciation for this.

Narayan: Could you express any wish to the people of India so that we might convey it to them?

Anand (adds): During your visit to India you succeeded in winning the hearts of the people of our country and a new message from you at the present time would be very favourably received.

Khrushchov: As for my wishes for the Indian people,

they have always been, and they remain, most sincere and open-hearted. First of all I heartily wish that the people of India may enjoy all the fruits of the independence India has won in her struggle against the colonialists. It is our wish that India may develop her economy, because independence can only be retained when the national economy is developed to a high level, making it possible to provide abundantly for the needs of the people.

If we do not achieve a solution to the problem of universal disarmament, a country must possess the means to defend its freedom and independence.

If colonialists were to attempt to re-establish their colonial domination in your country, you would not tolerate that, would you? In order to retain the national independence which many countries have now achieved, after having driven out the colonialists, they should develop their national economy in every possible way.

What the peoples need is material well-being, the opportunity to satisfy their spiritual requirements and to develop education—primary, secondary and higher education—so that people can bring out and develop their talents and use them in the interests of the economic and cultural development of their country and their people, so that the people of every country can be prosperous and can enjoy all the fruits of their labour.

It is our wish that friendly relations may develop between all nations and states, that good relations may develop still further between the Republic of India and the Soviet Union in the direction in which they are developing now, when such good relations exist between our governments and the peoples of our countries. I wholeheartedly wish the Republic of India happiness and prosperity.

We greatly appreciate the peace policy that is being pursued by the Indian Government and the peoples of India. We note in particular the distinguished role of your Prime Minister Jawaharlal Nehru in this connection. We sincerely wish that India may continue steadily to pursue her peace policy in the struggle for world peace. We heartily wish the Indian people success and your Prime Minister, Mr. Nehru, good health.

M. G. Desai: At present when the international situation is in a state of crisis, it is an exceedingly great honour for us that you have been able to spare an hour and a half of your precious time for this talk with us.

Khrushchov: I deeply respect the representatives of India, the representatives of the Indian press, and I think that correct understanding of our policy by Indian public opinion depends to a great extent on a true presentation of that policy in the Indian press. And if ever wider sections of the Indian public understand the policy of the Soviet Union correctly, that will contribute to an even greater strengthening of friendly relations between our countries. That is why I not only do not regret the time spent on our talk, but I am glad to have had the opportunity to answer your questions. And if my answers have satisfied you and can promote and further consolidate friendly relations between our states, I shall be very pleased and satisfied.

I wish you every success in your work. Good-bye.

Pravda, August 5, 1958

REPLIES
TO QUESTIONS OF *PRAVDA* CORRESPONDENT
ON ENDING OF NUCLEAR WEAPONS TESTS

Question: How do you regard the position of the Governments of the U.S.A. and Great Britain on the suspension of nuclear weapons tests in the light of statements by President Eisenhower and the British Government, made public on August 22?

Answer: Unfortunately, these statements do not show that the Governments of the U.S.A. and Great Britain are prepared to follow the Soviet Union's example and halt nuclear weapons tests immediately. They are in effect proceeding with their old policy of evading—under various pretexts—a commitment to halt at once the tests of nuclear weapons. They have been doing so for several years now, beginning with May 1955, when the Soviet Government proposed an agreement on immediate suspension of tests of atomic and hydrogen weapons.

The Supreme Soviet of the U.S.S.R., sharing the wishes of the peoples to put an end to test explosions and guided by the desire to make a practical move towards universal suspension of nuclear tests, decided on March 31, this year, to cease unilaterally tests of all types of atomic and hydrogen weapons in the Soviet Union. We took this step for the sake of achieving general agreement on the universal suspension of nuclear tests, even though we realized that it could place the Soviet Union in an unfavourable position as compared with the NATO countries. Having stopped its nuclear tests, the Soviet Union called upon the U.S.A.

and Great Britain to follow its example so that atom and hydrogen bomb tests could be ended everywhere and for all time.

However, the Governments of the U.S.A. and Great Britain refused to follow the Soviet Union's example. They continued, and are still continuing, to hold tests, showing thereby their real attitude to the cessation of tests of atomic and hydrogen weapons.

Can it be said that the statements by the Governments of the U.S.A. and Great Britain of August 22 show any change in their position on this matter? No. If the Governments of the U.S.A. and Britain really wanted atomic and hydrogen tests to be ended completely, they should have discontinued them immediately. The statements by the Governments of the U.S.A. and Great Britain, however, show that these governments are still looking for loopholes to evade the immediate suspension of nuclear tests. The reservations and the obviously contrived conditions with which the Governments of the Western Powers are hedging their proposals make this especially clear.

Indeed, what do the Governments of the U.S.A. and Great Britain propose?

To begin with, instead of announcing the immediate discontinuation of tests, the Governments of the U.S.A. and Great Britain speak of a temporary suspension of nuclear tests for one year. It is obvious, however, that the suspension of tests for so short a period is of no importance whatsoever, for a year is precisely the period necessary for preparing another series of nuclear tests.

Does this speak of a serious approach to the subject or of a sincere desire of the Governments of the Western Powers to end the tests of atomic and hydrogen weapons? By no means. It looks more like mockery of the aspirations of the peoples, who demand that test explosions be ended at once and for all.

True, the Governments of the U.S.A. and Great Britain say that they will be prepared to extend the period of suspending tests by one year at a time, but they hedge this agreement with such reservations and conditions that it becomes clear that they have no real intention of discontinuing further tests of nuclear weapons.

One of the conditions they put forward is the establishment of an effective system of control over the cessation of tests. This "condition" is of course artificial, for it has long been known that present-day science guarantees detection of any nuclear explosions and, consequently, the control of an agreement to stop tests is easily realized. If any proof of the utterly artificial nature of this condition were needed, it would be enough to recall the results of the recent Geneva meeting of experts of eight countries.

The Governments of the U.S.A. and Great Britain state further that they will be prepared to prolong the one-year agreement on the suspension of nuclear tests only if "satisfactory progress" is made in the solution of the general problem of disarmament. Who does not know, however, that it is the Western governments, and they alone, that are thwarting agreement on disarmament, year after year, by clinging to the policy of armaments race and atomic blackmail? The question arises: With things as they are, how can one believe that they really want a cessation of tests, if they put forward such a condition? Is there any surer way of sabotaging the halting of nuclear tests than making such conditions?

Some people in the West are ready to go into raptures about the statements by the Governments of the U.S.A. and Great Britain concerning a possible suspension of nuclear tests by them, and lavishly praise these statements as a peaceful act. It should be frankly said that those who want the tests to be really ended cannot wax enthusiastic over these statements.

A curious situation arises. First we were told for a long time that the question of the discontinuation of nuclear tests could be settled only as an integral part of a broad disarmament agreement. When the incongruity of the

Western position became clear to all, the Western Powers, under public pressure, retreated from that position, stating that they were prepared to consider the cessation of tests independently, as a separate problem. At the same time, however, they began to play up the question of control over the ending of tests, grossly exaggerating the difficulties of such control—contrary to the facts—and even alleging control to be impossible. Now, when it has become clear to all that control is quite feasible, Washington and London are again saying that the solution of the question of the cessation of tests is possible only concomitantly with the solution of other disarmament problems.

Thus, the opponents of the universal halting of nuclear tests have come full circle—a vicious circle.

After all this, how can one put any faith in the professions of the Governments of the U.S.A. and Great Britain to the effect that they desire a cessation of tests? Would it not be more correct to suppose that this is still another attempt to lull the vigilance of the peoples who manifest legitimate concern over the continuing nuclear tests carried out by the U.S.A. and Great Britain on an increasingly larger scale?

Question: What importance do the results of the recent Geneva meeting of experts of eight countries concerning the methods of detecting nuclear explosions have, in your opinion, for the solution of the question of the universal halting of tests of atomic and hydrogen weapons?

Answer: The significance of the Geneva conference of experts lies first of all in that it finally buried the legend concerning the alleged impossibility of control over the observance of an agreement to end nuclear tests. This legend, as is known, was circulated by certain circles of the Western Powers, particularly the United States, in order to prevent the ending of tests. The experts who met in Geneva, including those of the Western Powers, have reached the unanimous conclusion that any nuclear explosion can be detected and that effective control over the ending of nuclear tests is quite practicable. We note with satisfaction that the findings of the conference of experts fully confirm the correctness of the Soviet Government's viewpoint, which it has continually maintained, and show up the falseness of the position of the Western Powers. The results of the Geneva conference compel those who oppose the universal ending of tests to acknowledge the completely untenable and unscientific nature of their arguments.

The Soviet Government has carefully examined the results of the work of the Geneva meeting of experts and considers it necessary to state that it agrees with all the conclusions and recommendations regarding the system of control over the universal ending of nuclear tests which are contained in the report of the conference.

In the light of the results of this conference, there can now be no excuse or justification for the refusal to desist at once from experiments with nuclear weapons everywhere, even on the part of those who previously used such excuses to dupe the credulous.

Question: The Soviet public is alarmed by the fact that the Governments of the United States and Great Britain not only failed to follow the example of the Soviet Union, which has unilaterally halted all nuclear tests, but, on the contrary, began to conduct such tests even more intensively. What can be said regarding the position of the Soviet Government in connection with such actions of the Western Powers?

Answer: Yes, the Governments of the United States and Great Britain actually did refuse to follow the example of the Soviet Union and are continuing to conduct more intensively test explosions of atom and hydrogen bombs. Even after the unilateral halting of tests by the Soviet Union and after the Soviet Government's proposal to the Governments of the United States and Great Britain to discontinue all tests immediately and everywhere, the United States undertook its biggest series of tests, in the Pacific. Between April 28 and July 26 alone, it carried out over 30 nuclear explosions. The British Government also conducted several nuclear tests. Moreover, on the very day of August 22, when the Government of Great Britain announced to all the world its readiness to start negotiations to end nuclear tests, it proceeded with a fresh series of explosions of nuclear weapons. The Governments of the United States and Great Britain are clearly using the cessation of nuclear tests by the Soviet Union in order to gain unilateral military advantages for themselves.

The Soviet Government, which has done everything possible on its part to assure a positive solution of the problem of the ending of nuclear tests everywhere, naturally cannot allow the security interests of the Soviet Union to be jeopardized by such actions of the Western Powers. In this respect we are guided by the well-known decision of the Supreme Soviet of the U.S.S.R. of March 31, this year, which stated that if other Powers possessing atomic and hydrogen weapons continued tests of these weapons, the Government of the U.S.S.R. would be free to act as it saw fit with regard to the question of the Soviet Union conducting tests of atomic and hydrogen weapons, in order to ensure the security of the country. We, the leaders of the Soviet state, would cut fine figures if, in the face of such actions of the Western Powers, we were to ignore the vital and legitimate security interests of our country.

The actions of the United States and Great Britain, actions which run counter to the will of the peoples, relieve the Soviet Union of the obligation it had assumed unilaterally, counting as it did on the good will of the Western Powers with regard to the question of the immediate and universal ending of nuclear tests.

Question: What is the Soviet Government's attitude towards the proposal of the Governments of the United States and Great Britain to initiate three-Power negotiations on October 31 on the ending of nuclear tests?

Answer: The Soviet Union has repeatedly suggested to the United States and Great Britain that negotiations be held on the immediate ending of tests of nuclear weapons by all Powers possessing such weapons. Now the Governments of these Powers have announced their readiness to start negotiations on October 31, this year. This date is acceptable to the Soviet Government. We consider that the most suitable place for the negotiations would be Geneva, where the experts who worked out the technical methods of control over the observance of an agreement to end nuclear tests have recently successfully completed their work. However, our idea is that the purpose of such talks must be to conclude an agreement to end tests of atomic and hydrogen weapons of all kinds and by all states once and for all. Only under such circumstances will the talks conform to the interests of the peoples and avoid being used as a screen to cover reluctance to seek agreement.

We can by no means agree with those reservations and conditions with which the Western Powers hedge their statement concerning their readiness to participate in negotiations, since agreement with them would mean foredooming the negotiations to failure. We also believe that in order to avoid any delay it would be useful to agree beforehand on the duration of these negotiations. In view of the positive results of the Geneva conference of experts, it is our opinion that these negotiations could be brought to a conclusion within two or three weeks.

But it would of course be wrong if the preparations for such negotiations resulted in less attention being paid to the importance of an urgent solution of the task of ending nuclear tests by all states. In particular, it would be a great error if less attention were paid to this question on the part of the United Nations, including the forthcoming 13th Session of the General Assembly, which, in our opinion, must say an authoritative word on this question which so deeply concerns all mankind.

Pravda, August 30, 1958

REPLIES
TO QUESTIONS SUBMITTED BY A. E. JOHANN,
WEST GERMAN WRITER AND JOURNALIST

September 20, 1958

During his recent visit to the U.S.S.R., Herr Johann submitted a series of questions to N. S. Khrushchov.

Khrushchov's replies are published below.

Question: Everywhere in the Soviet Union both ordinary Soviet citizens and prominent people assured me that they sincerely desired peaceful co-operation and even friendship not only with the German Democratic Republic, but also with the Federal Republic of Germany. Is this just the personal desire of individual Soviet citizens or is it also the political aim of the Soviet Government?

Answer: The warm wishes voiced by the Soviet people for peaceful co-operation and friendship between the Soviet Union and the two German states reflect the policy of the Soviet Government. There is the widespread belief in the Soviet Union that co-operation and friendship between the peoples of our country and the entire German people constitute the shortest road to strengthening peace in Europe.

While strengthening its fraternal friendship with the German Democratic Republic, the Soviet Union builds its relations with the Federal Republic of Germany on a basis of peaceful co-operation and strives to infuse a spirit of mutual confidence and friendship into these relations. In our opinion, this accords with the interests of both the Soviet Union and the Federal Republic of Germany. We would also like to see less attention paid in West

Germany to those who still try to raise doubts among the public in Federal Germany about the usefulness of further efforts to develop Soviet-West German relations.

We do not intend to force our opinion on anyone, but we do consider it unpardonable that West Germany is deliberately neglecting the existing possibilities for *rapprochement* between the Soviet Union and the Federal Republic of Germany. We have time and again told those who have a sober understanding of the importance of good relations between the U.S.S.R. and the Federal Republic of Germany that they would always find due support in Moscow and that we shall welcome any proposal aimed at improving relations between our two countries.

Question: During my tour of the Soviet Union I was often assured that as far as the Russian side was concerned peaceful co-existence with the Federal Republic was quite possible in spite of the latter's different political views. Can the population of the Federal Republic be sure that in the event of peaceful co-operation between the two nations the Soviet Union would not attempt to influence the political development of the Federal Republic in line with its own political principles?

Answer: We not only accept peaceful co-existence, but strive to build our relations with your country along the principles of peaceful co-existence. It is just these principles that require the recognition of the fact that the social and state system is the internal affair of a state, of the people inhabiting it, and that they alone are entitled to determine the political structure of the country. In its relations with the Federal Republic the Soviet Union has always unswervingly abided by the principles of peaceful co-existence, which rule out interference in other nations' domestic affairs, and will continue to do so.

Can it be said that the Federal Government is also building its policy along the principles of peaceful co-existence? Unfortunately, not.

It is well known that the Federal Government never misses an opportunity to reiterate its loyalty to the "Atlantic Community." But no one has ever heard it speak in favour of the policy of peaceful co-existence of states with differing social systems. Yet that is not all. As a resident of West Germany you should know better than anyone living outside your country that in its practical activity the Federal Government has repeatedly shown blind hostility towards the socialist countries. Can one ignore the fact, for instance, that the statements of highly placed West German leaders are full of gross, inadmissible attacks against the Soviet Union. It looks very much as if these people have set themselves the task of fomenting animosity in the Federal Republic towards the Soviet people and of hampering in every possible way the development of relations between the two states.

No less significant, too, is the fact that for several years the Federal Government has been stubbornly refusing to establish normal relations with the East European countries. And it does not appear to care in the least that in its animosity towards countries with a different social system it has gone much farther than such of its NATO partners as the United States, Britain and France, who have long since established diplomatic relations with these countries.

In the light of these facts it is not at all surprising that the Government of the Federal Republic of Germany seeks to establish contact and achieve understanding with governments which on their part also intend to follow an anti-communist policy.

It is not difficult to see what is behind the recent meeting between Chancellor Adenauer and French Premier de Gaulle, which took place in days anxious for France, at a time when she is going through an acute political crisis.

It is well known that France is now the scene of a bitter struggle between the supporters of the republican system, who are defending the democratic rights and interests of the people, and the extremist imperialist groups, who are trying to push the country on to the path of fascism. Just where the French reactionaries are dragging the country is evident from the fact that they are making heroes out of such fascist-type leaders as Soustelle, one of the organizers of the military putsch in Algeria. Chancellor Adenauer is naturally also well informed about the situation in France. Since the Federal Government thought fit to announce the establishment of close co-operation with the French Government at a time when France is deciding whether or not to remain a republic, this can pursue just one aim—to encourage and spur on the forces of French reaction to an anti-democratic coup. And this can scarcely be a surprise to anyone, because for years now the Federal Republic itself has been following a policy of suppressing the democratic forces and curtailing civil liberties.

As far as one can judge from the communiqué and press reports, Chancellor Adenauer and Premier de Gaulle were concerned at their first meeting not only with co-ordinating their actions at home, but also with the ways and means of drawing the countries of Eastern Europe into the so-called European Community, which is nothing but an affiliation of the aggressive North Atlantic bloc.

The press of certain countries spoke on this score of the possible establishment of a sort of "Bonn-Paris axis." The question arises: on what basis is it planned to set up this axis? Even from the brief and deliberately vague communiqué on the Adenauer-de Gaulle meeting and from the explanatory statements of the Federal and French Foreign Ministers, one can see that it is a policy of hostility towards the socialist countries in Eastern Europe, of attempts at interfering in their domestic affairs which will serve as the basis of co-operation of the French and West German governments.

One cannot help recalling other meetings of the Heads of Government of certain West European countries, which took place before the war, for the recent Adenauer-de Gaulle meeting definitely resembles them. We remember the meeting between Hitler and Mussolini in 1934, which led to a deal between the two dictators against the democratic freedoms of the European nations, against the interests of peace. The establishment of the Rome-Berlin axis, which followed this meeting, brought Europe to the brink of the Second World War.

Those who again want to raise the tattered banner of struggle against communism would do well to remember the fiasco suffered in the recent past by all kinds of anti-communist "axes" and "triangles." It is all the more advisable to bear this in mind, since the correlation of forces in the international arena has changed radically since the pre-war years in favour of the forces of peace and progress. Under the circumstances, it is clear that any government which allows itself to be blinded by its hatred of the peoples who are building a new society would take an extremely dangerous path, at the end of which it is doomed to inevitable catastrophe. And no axes and blocs would help it.

Question: Is the Soviet Union prepared to open the Russian market to the industry and trade of the Federal Republic widely enough for long-term participation in the economic development of the Soviet Union?

Answer: The Soviet Union favours broad, all-round development of economic and, especially, commercial ties with all nations. We want to establish stable, mutually beneficial and lasting relations with our trading partners. It is precisely this type of relations that best suits the Soviet economy, which is developing successfully according to plan, without recessions and crises. The Soviet Union has long-term trade agreements with many European countries, including France, Italy, Finland, Austria and others countries.

Recently we signed a Long-Term Agreement on Commodity Exchange and Payments and an Agreement on General Questions of Trade and Navigation with the Federal Republic of Germany. These agreements create a more solid basis for economic relations between our two countries than existed before. They provide for a considerable increase in the volume of trade between the two states—more than twofold within the next three years. But these agreements, in our opinion, do not by far exhaust the economic possibilities available for an expansion of Soviet-West German trade. Being economically highly developed countries, the Soviet Union and West Germany could trade on a much broader scale.

As you know, the Soviet Union has launched a large-scale programme of increasing the output of consumer goods, and that includes a considerable increase in the production of synthetic materials, fibres, plastics, artificial leather, furs, and articles made of them. To speed up this programme, the Soviet Union could make large purchases of appropriate equipment in the Federal Republic of Germany. We would expect its industry to offer us equipment that accords with the present level of technology, and at reasonable prices. The Federal Republic could also take part in the development of this branch of Soviet industry by sending its experts to work as advisers in Soviet enterprises, by selling licences, and in other appropriate ways. Trade between the U.S.S.R. and West Germany could also be expanded beyond the volume provided for in the agreements in other branches of industry. The Soviet Union is prepared to pay for its purchases with Soviet goods of interest to the Federal Republic.

Question: Wherever he goes in the Soviet Union, an observant traveller encounters astonishing plans of economic and cultural development. He is everywhere assured that these tasks can be fulfilled only if peace is maintained on earth. It appears to me that the Soviet Government through this peace propaganda has undertaken before its citizens to do everything humanly possible to preserve peace. Is that right?

Answer: The Soviet Union can fulfil its far-reaching plans of national economic development within the terms set only if there is peace in the world. You will agree with me, I think, that past wars also caused tremendous damage to the economy, ruined it, and thereby subjected the people to great hardships and calamities. Who can deny that any new war unleashed by the aggressive forces, involving as it would modern weapons of mass annihilation and destruction, would cause an incalculable sacrifice of human lives and tremendous, unprecedented economic disruption, the destruction of towns, industrial and agricultural centres, and of huge material values created by the efforts of many generations.

As regards the consequences suffered by the Soviet economy in the last war, it may be recalled that Nazi Germany's treacherous attack on the Soviet Union caused our national economy a loss of 2,569,000 million rubles, counting military expenditures and the temporary loss of the industrial and agricultural profits in the occupied areas. If this colossal sum had been used for the nation's economic needs, the tasks we now have to solve would unquestionably have been solved long ago. It should not be forgotten that of the forty years that the Soviet state exists, almost twenty were taken up by wars that were forced upon us and the subsequent rehabilitation of the national economy.

The Soviet Government's desire to preserve peace is, naturally, not motivated by propaganda. Peace is a vital necessity for the Soviet state. If you care to call that propaganda, you may; we shan't object. It is a kind of propaganda one can be proud of. We would welcome the same propaganda from the Governments of the Western Powers.

Question: Would the Soviet Union be prepared to believe in the Federal Republic's sincere desire for peace, would it co-operate with the Federal Republic in the future as with a friendly nation and, in particular, would it assist in Germany's reunification, if the Federal Republic carried out the following conditions: a) not to arm the Bundeswehr with atomic weapons; b) to limit the numerical strength and armaments of the Bundeswehr to a size which would eliminate all doubts about its purely defensive purposes?

Answer: I would like to think that you put the matter in this way because you are concerned about the destinies of the German people. As I understand it, you want to stress the hopeful opportunities that would open to West Germany, if she were to carry out the conditions you have outlined. Your question is frank, and I shall try to answer it just as frankly.

There can be no doubt that if the Bundeswehr were not being armed with atomic weapons and its strength and armaments were limited to a size required by defence, this would be a peace action of considerable significance and would contribute to close co-operation between our countries on a basis of trust and friendship. The Soviet Union would naturally be prepared, as before, to do everything in its power to dissipate whatever doubts there may be about the security of West Germany. In so doing, we could examine not only the proposals already made, but think about new ones.

A halt to the equipment of the Bundeswehr with atomic arms and the limiting of its strength and armaments to the size required by defence would, at the same time, have a beneficial effect on the situation in Europe, would turn its course towards eliminating the existing tension in that area, and creating an atmosphere of trust among the European states. It would unquestionably serve as a powerful stimulus to German reunification and would bring it out of the stalemate caused by the policy of militarizing West Germany and her participation in the aggressive blocs of the Western Powers, whose aims, we are deeply convinced, have nothing in common with the national interests of the German people.

By switching resolutely from war preparations to a policy of consolidating peace in Europe, the Federal Government would contribute decisively to an agreement between the two German states on practical steps towards the national reunification of the German people. As for the Soviet Union, it will naturally do everything it can to help achieve this goal.

Question: The Federal Republic would like to live in peace and friendship not only with the Soviet Union, but with the whole world and especially with the United States. Would the Soviet Union regard the continued good relations of the Federal Republic and the United States as an obstacle to better Soviet-West German understanding?

Answer: If the Federal Republic of Germany, as you say, wants to live in peace and friendship not only with the Soviet Union, but with the whole world and especially with the United States, we can only welcome this wish, for the Soviet Union also wants to live in peace and friendship not only with the Federal Republic of Germany, but with all countries, big and small, the United States included. In stressing the necessity and benefit of good relations between our countries, we proceed from the fact that such relations cannot and should not be developed to the detriment of the relations of the Soviet Union and the Federal Republic with other states. Good, friendly relations between the U.S.S.R. and the Federal Republic of Germany can only further their international ties in the interests of peace. This is why there is no reason to fear that the Soviet Union will make any demands on the Federal Republic or urge it to spoil its relations with other states.

We assume for our part that the Federal Republic will not nurture the hope of a deterioration of relations between the Soviet Union and states that are friendly to it. We address this wish first and foremost to those who hope to get the Soviet Union to exert pressure on the German Democratic Government in the interests of the ruling circles in the Federal Republic. I stress once again that we make no secret of our interest in good relations with the Federal Republic and openly declare that it depends on these relations which way Europe goes: towards a stronger peace or towards military upheavals and the attendant grievous consequences.

Question: Is the Soviet Government prepared to invite, say, 12 well-known West German publicists and journalists, assign each of them a good interpreter and give them a chance to tour Russia on their own, as I have done on my own responsibility, so that they form their own opinion about the conditions existing in Russia, acquaint themselves with the true sentiments of the Russian people and inform the West German public about it?

Answer: As you have seen, our doors are open to all foreign journalists who sincerely desire to acquaint themselves with the economic and cultural achievements of the Soviet Union and the life and work of the Soviet people, and who report objectively to the public of their countries on the Soviet Union.

Since the establishment of diplomatic relations our country has been visited by many representatives of various sections of the West German public. There have been about 200 journalists among them. In the same period, Federal Germany has been visited by about 30 Soviet journalists. In my opinion, the exchange of journalists should be continued, with the aim in view that it should help promote mutual understanding between the U.S.S.R. and Federal Germany. We have some experience in exchanging groups of journalists with other countries. I think that your suggestion could be examined and put into practice on a reciprocal basis.

N. KHRUSHCHOV

September 20, 1958
Pravda, September 24, 1958

REPLIES
TO QUESTIONS PUT BY *PRAVDA* EDITORIAL BOARD CONCERNING EVENTS IN FRANCE

The editors of *Pravda* have received many letters in-quiring about the substance of the developments in France. In the last few days many also ask how to assess the de Gaulle-Adenauer meeting. The editorial board of *Pravda* requested N. S. Khrushchov to state his opinion on these matters.

N. S. Khrushchov's replies are given below.

The events in France cannot but interest the Soviet people. History shows that the destiny of this Western Power is most closely related to the destiny of Europe as a whole. Now that twenty years have passed since the dis-graceful Munich deal with Hitler, which opened the door to the Second World War, the manoeuvres of the French reactionaries, who are traversing the old road, are attract-ing the close attention of all those who value peace. It is natural therefore that the Soviet people, adhering fully to its principled stand of strict non-interference in the inter-nal affairs of other countries, is following most closely the developments in France which most directly bear on prob-lems of European security.

Pravda readers are perfectly right in expressing concern in their letters over the developments in France since the fascist rebellion in Algeria last May.

Three or four months ago some people in Europe could still entertain the hope that the new Government, headed by General de Gaulle, would wish to, and be able to, curb the fascist rebels, put an end to the unjust colonial war against the Algerian people, and preserve the republic in France. True, already then the progressive forces were warning that all these were just empty and harmful illusions, and that a most direct connection existed between the events in Algeria and the rise to power of the new Government in Paris.

Soon life itself ruthlessly shattered such illusions. Already on July 14, the day of the French national holiday, the rebel generals and colonels were showered with decorations and promotions. Paratroopers, rushed by air from Algeria to participate in a military parade, marched in triumph through Paris as through a conquered city. On viewing this, many of those who had sincerely entertained illusions began to see the truth. The lie about the new Government's imaginary mission of salvation became even more apparent when a feverish race began to prepare the new constitution, which invests the head of the state with sweeping dictatorial powers.

Now, on the threshold of the referendum of the new draft constitution, redoubled efforts are being made to give a veneer of legality to the change of régime which is being prepared in France. This is being done in order to facilitate the realization of the extremely far-reaching plans of those who gave the signal for the mutiny in Algeria on May 13.

The events in France cannot be viewed in isolation from the general situation in Western Europe. All through the post-war period the forces of imperialist reaction, which suffered a fiasco as a result of the Second World War when German and Italian fascism was smashed, have persistently sought to strengthen their shaken positions. During these thirteen years repeated attempts have been made to restore fascism in a new form, under a new guise.

Now in one, now in another West European country the ruling circles have gone over from parliamentary tactics of compromise to those of open dictatorship and the crude suppression of democratic forces. Everywhere these attempts encountered determined resistance by the people, who had grown wiser through their experience of struggle against Nazi fascism. In some places, however, the reactionary forces have won temporary success, as in West Germany where the militarists have been able to have the activities of progressive organizations banned. Now the same strategic line of the reactionaries is taking shape in France.

The plans for establishing a personal dictatorship underlying the new constitution; the reduction to naught of the role of Parliament; the régime of brutal police repression and, in some places, for instance, in Algeria, a régime of terror modelled on Hitler's methods; the appointment of the military to commanding positions in the state; the gradual repeal of even those liberties which are granted under bourgeois democracy; the threat to deprive the working class of its social gains and the encroachment on its democratic organizations; all this involuntarily brings back to memory the events of 1933 in Germany. This is why today we have every reason to speak of the danger of fascism looming over France.

It is no accident that French monopoly capital has now put in the forefront of the country's political life thugs who are twins of those who were active in Germany in 1932-33. Soustelle, a former spy, General Massu, the butcher of Algeria, de Serigny, Hitler's collaborator in the Vichy Government, Georges Bonnet, former Foreign Minister in the Government of the traitor Pétain, and their like —these are the people who now call the tune in French ruling circles by advocating the new constitution which establishes a régime of personal dictatorship.

Nor is it an accident that the threat of fascism began to spread to France from Algeria where the French colonialists are trying to strangle the national-liberation movement of the Algerian people. One of the founders of the

French Socialist Party, Jules Guesde, wrote: "Colonial wars have always been a school for civil war. Butchers of the Cavaignac type were trained in Algeria in wars against the Arabs and the Kabyles." Guesde had in mind General Cavaignac who staged a brutal massacre of Paris workers in June 1848; he further recalled that the executioners of the Paris Commune were also trained in colonial expeditions. Now one who aspires to the role of the Cavaignac of our times—General Massu—who also went through a school of colonial war in Algeria, declares unceremoniously that after the adoption of the new constitution the French progressive forces will be "outlawed" and threatens "shootings in conformity with official decrees."

The fact that the French ruling circles are switching over to methods of undisguised violence, throwing overboard bourgeois democracy, bears witness to their increasing weakness. Mindful of the fate which befell Hitler, the most adroit politicians of the French ruling circles are trying to drown the revelations of General Massu by falsely claiming that the new constitution guarantees the preservation of the republican system and legality. At the same time they indulge in social demagogy. In his time Hitler tried to corrupt the German working class by prattle about "national socialism." The Soustelles are trying to invent their own methods of duping the masses and it is not by mere chance that chauvinism is being fanned now, as never before, in France under the flag of patriotism. At the same time the working people are served a new version of the American theory of "people's capitalism" in an effort to convince them that it is possible to "abolish hired labour" while leaving untouched the system of private property and exploitation. . . .

The French reactionaries would like to establish a fascist order under a legal veneer, relying on General de Gaulle's authority. But in this respect, too, they are not original. The "steel barons" of the Ruhr acted in the same way when they used the Reichstag and the then President,

General Hindenburg, who also enjoyed a certain measure of popularity in his country, to hand over full power to the fascists.

This is realized by many Frenchmen who have gone through a hard schooling of struggle against fascism. And it is not by chance that, in the course of preparations for the referendum, representatives of the most diverse sections of the French people are becoming evermore active in their opposition to the new draft constitution. They regard the referendum as "legalization of a *coup d'état*," as one French public figure put it a few days ago.

The position of the leadership of the French Socialist Party and, above all, that of its General Secretary Guy Mollet, appears particularly unseemly against this background. He is following in the footsteps of the Right-wing Social-Democratic Party leaders of Germany, who committed the shameful act of splitting the German working class in the tragic days of 1933 when Hitler was in the act of seizing power. Rejecting the idea of a common front with the Communists, those leaders displayed short-sightedness, expecting Hitler to make short work only of the Communists while leaving alone the Social-Democrats. That was why the Social-Democratic group of the Reichstag invariably backed Hitler until May 1933. The end of it is well known; when Hitler no longer needed the Social-Democrats he issued a decree stating that "the Social-Democratic Party should be considered a party hostile to the German people, a party against which the same measures should be applied as those applied against the Communist Party." Then, thousands upon thousands of upright German Social-Democrats went to concentration camps and to the gallows in the wake of the Communists.

This historical lesson is recalled today by sober-minded leaders in the French Socialist Party. The Party's former General Secretary, Daniel Mayer, declared on September

18: "Their first step is to make preparations for banning the Communist Party. But I submit that the disbanding of the Communist Party would be a prelude to the disbanding of other parties, the Socialist Party, for example."

As to Guy Mollet and his followers, who are eager to hang on at any cost to the running-boards of the General's carriage, they have long since forfeited the right to call themselves Socialists. It is a matter of common knowledge, for instance, that it is Guy Mollet who, as former Prime Minister, is responsible for the launching of the criminal Suez adventure against the Arab peoples. It is equally well known that Guy Mollet set up a nest of fascist conspirators in Algeria. Finally it is generally known that it is Guy Mollet who played a particularly unsavoury role in clearing the way for the forces of reaction last May.

There has now been a rift in the French Socialist Party, with the result that the Socialist leaders who have broken with Guy Mollet are launching a new party under the banner of struggle against the forces of reaction. This is a sign of the times. It shows once more that things are no longer going on as they did in 1933 and that today the forces of democracy and progress have grown immeasurably stronger and have steeled themselves in battle.

In their attempt to install a régime of ruthless political reaction, French ruling circles wish to weaken and suppress the democratic forces. But the only effect this policy can have in the present conditions is to sharpen the internal struggle in France still further. This struggle will keep mounting as the smoke-screen of demagogic promises to preserve republican liberties begins to be dispelled.

The Soviet people are openly declaring their sympathy for the working people of France who are fighting a hard battle to defend the democratic rights they have won over a number of decades. The Soviet people believe in the strength of the valiant working class of France, headed by the battle-steeled French Communist Party. The Soviet people can easily understand the aspirations of the working class of France, of her working peasants, middle classes and progressive-minded intellectuals, who remain loyal to the traditions of free thought and of courageous struggle against tyranny. The healthy elements of France today will, beyond all doubt, find a way to consolidate and rally their forces to beat off the onslaught of reaction.

The present international situation is also not conducive to the success of any attempts at reviving fascism. Gone are the days when Hitler and Mussolini could unceremoniously force political upheavals in certain European countries. The powerful camp of peace and democracy is exerting an ever-growing influence on the international situation today, and the forces of reaction are finding it more and more difficult to carry through their plans, including plans for establishing hotbeds of aggression and war in Europe.

One cannot fail to note in this connection the attempts being made by French ruling circles to find a common language and a common line in foreign policy with the West German militarists. These circles seem inclined to lean on the support of one of the most reactionary régimes in Europe as is that of West Germany. In so doing, they are prepared to sacrifice the vital national interests of France, which faces a mortal danger in the emergence of an increasingly powerful militarist state across her eastern frontier. This threat was at one time repeatedly emphasized with great persuasiveness by General de Gaulle.

But just at the height of preparations for the referendum, it is Chancellor Adenauer of the Federal Republic of Germany who came to France scenting there the breath of fascism. He had long tête-à-têtes with General de Gaulle. These have led to his rapturous statement:

"The General has changed his views on the German question as compared with the early post-war years."

It is indicative that the final communiqué of the Adenauer-de Gaulle meeting contained a vague provision for the integration of "as many European states as possible" in the "European Community." The Foreign Minister of France has explained that this "integration" is to include the countries of Eastern Europe as well. Thus, twenty years after Munich, another attempt is being made to take France in tow behind a German tank and drag her off to the East. One has to lose all sense of reality, however, to place any real hopes on the success of any adventure in Eastern Europe.

One cannot fail to note that Paris has lately been the scene of an intense anti-Soviet campaign, whipped up with the knowledge and approval of the French authorities and fully in line with the usual American pattern. West German and Hollywood anti-Soviet films are flooding the screen and heaps of foul, slanderous literature are piled up in the bookshop windows. Some papers have gone to the length of calling the Soviet Union "enemy No. 1." For what purpose is all this being done? Have not the French authorities lost all sense of proportion?

Older people in France remember that all these are the same tricks that were used to flirt with German militarists on the eve of the Second World War. But what did all that add up to? The Soviet people had to shed their blood to help deliver France from the yoke of those before whom her rulers had bowed.

It is being clamoured in France today that the de Gaulle-Adenauer meeting has put an end once and for all to Franco-German contradictions. This is no more than a blind. Only a democratic France and a democratic Germany could really find common language and the way to peaceful co-operation. The friendship of French reactionary circles with the West German revenge-seekers leads to war, not to peace.

It scarcely needs to be emphasized that these plans, carried out to the detriment of French national interests, are contrary also to the interests of the German people and all the nations of Europe.

Let us hope that the common sense which is typical of the French nation will prevail.

As for the Soviet people, they are, as they have always been, the true friends of the peace-loving French people. They wish them all success in emerging with honour from the stern trials which confront France. The Soviet people wish to see France occupy a deserving place as a great democratic Power in the international arena, pursuing her own independent policy of promoting peace and international co-operation.

Pravda, September 22, 1958

REPLIES
TO QUESTIONS PUT BY
MURILO MARROQUIM DE SOUZA,
BRAZILIAN JOURNALIST

October 3, 1958

The Brazilian journalist and participant in the Stockholm Congress for Disarmament and International Cooperation, Murilo Marroquim de Souza, addressed a number of questions to N. S. Khrushchov, Chairman of the Council of Ministers of the U.S.S.R.

N. S. Khrushchov's replies are published below.

Question: Do you consider that peace is in danger? If so, then what, in your opinion, are the best means of achieving so-called peaceful co-existence? Can we, in your opinion, look forward to a favourable outcome in the clash of the opinions and interests of the two political blocs existing in the world?

Answer: I shall not be revealing any secret when I say that in recent years some lovers of adventure have several times brought mankind to the brink of war. The policy from "positions of strength" pursued by the United States and its partners in military blocs with the aim of imposing their domination on other countries has already more than once threatened to hurl the world into the catastrophe of war. Let me recall, for example, the events of the last two years in the Middle East: the attack upon Egypt by Britain, France and Israel, encouraged by the United States, the threatened attack upon Syria, the brazen invasion of the Lebanon by U.S. forces and the occupation of Jordan by the British. As a result of the decisive action taken by the peace-loving forces, the Anglo-American aggression in the Arab East has been halted. But the situation in the area will continue to remain extremely dangerous, until the U.S. and British forces leave the Lebanon and Jordan.

Today we see yet another deterioration in the world situation—this time in the Far East. Encouraging the reckless intentions of Chiang Kai-shek and his supporters, the United States is interfering in the internal affairs of the Chinese People's Republic. At the same time, the United States wants to mislead world opinion by talk about a "cease fire" and to give a semblance of legality to its aggressive moves against People's China. U.S. aggression creates a serious threat not only to the security of the great Chinese people, but also to the peoples of Asia and the whole world. To prevent the further exacerbation of the international situation and to put an end to tension, the United States must stop interfering in the internal affairs of the Chinese People's Republic and withdraw all its forces from the Taiwan area.

The aggressions in the Middle East and in the Far East are all links in a single chain—and the direct outcome of Dulles' policy of balancing "on the brink of war."

The Soviet Union stands for the establishment of friendly relations with all countries regardless of their social and political systems, and we see no obstacle to the broadest development of all types of contact between the socialist and capitalist countries. We do not, however, close our eyes to the fact that there are bound to be points of difference or, as you term them, clashes of opinions and interests, between the socialist and capitalist countries. But we consider that these differences and clashes should not lead to war. It must not be forgotten that in our age, the age of atomic energy and intercontinental rockets, any country which attempts to settle international disputes by force of arms hazards its own existence by so doing. Those in the West who do not want to understand this and who still console themselves with hopes about the power of aircraft carriers and bombs are thinking in terms of the last century. Only political maniacs and suicides can consider war as a means of settling international disputes and differences. The only rational way of settling international differences and disagreements is through negotiations and mutually acceptable agreements which take into account the interests of all the parties concerned.

As I have already said, the socialist countries consistently adhere to the principles of peaceful co-existence. But for peace to triumph, the policy of peaceful co-existence should be recognized and pursued, if not by all, then at least by the majority of countries, and above all by those upon whose policy the question of peace or war depends. The rulers of the United States, Britain and their partners must renounce their policy from "positions of strength" and their claims for domination over other countries. The sooner the illusions and emotions of the Western Powers give place in politics to reality and common sense, the better it will be for everybody, and for world peace.

As regards the ideological differences between the capitalist and socialist countries, it is today nothing short of madness to attempt to impose one's own ideological opinions on others by force of arms. We are firmly convinced that in life's disputes those views and conceptions will triumph which most faithfully reflect the objective laws of mankind's social development and the requirements not of the minority, but of the majority of people. In our opinion, Marxism-Leninism is such an ideology. Reality day by day and hour by hour continues to confirm its correctness.

Question: Do you consider that the pursuance by the stronger states of a policy of non-interference in the internal affairs of weaker countries supporting the policy of the former is a necessary condition for peaceful co-existence?

672

Answer: Undoubtedly. Non-interference in the internal affairs of other countries is one of the basic principles to which our country adheres in its foreign policy. Every people is master in its own house, and it and it alone has the right to decide what shall be its internal system.

But the imperialist Powers support a diametrically opposite point of view on this question. They consider interference in the internal affairs of other, weaker countries to be perfectly normal. We do not have to go far to find examples. Consider the history of the Latin American countries. It is in its entirety an example of unceremonious interference by foreign monopolies in the affairs of the Latin American peoples. All remember the tragic fate of Guatemala, while the heroic but unequal struggle of the people of Cuba for their freedom profoundly moves all honest people everywhere in the world.

We resolutely condemn the use of the *dıktat* in international relations. The principle of non-interference in the affairs of other countries must be observed by all countries, not only in words but in deeds.

Question: In the latest joint communiqué signed by the Governments of the Soviet Union and the People's Republic of China direct reference is made to Latin America for the first time. What can you say in this connection?

Answer: You apparently have in mind the communiqué regarding the meeting in Peking between the Chairman of the Central Committee of the Communist Party of China and the Chairman of the Chinese People's Republic Mao Tse-tung and myself early in August. The communiqué, it will be recalled, stated that the Soviet Union and People's China firmly support the just struggle of the peoples of the United Arab Republic, the Republic of Iraq and of the other Arab countries, and also the national-liberation movement of the peoples of Asia, Africa and Latin America.

A great historical transformation is taking place before our eyes: more and more nations are taking the path of just struggle against colonialism and against exploitation by foreign monopolies. It is not only the peoples of the colonies and dependent countries of Asia and Africa who are taking this path: so, too, are the peoples of Latin America. This is, of course, understandable. For many decades American, British and other foreign monopolies have like giant leeches attached themselves to the living body of Latin America and are draining her natural wealth, ruthlessly exploiting her peoples and distorting the economies of the Latin American countries, and thus obstructing their independent development. Can the peoples of Latin America accept such a state of affairs?

The age of colonialists, the days when they ruled over the fates of countries and peoples, making and remaking the map of the world in accordance with their own desires, everywhere installing reactionary régimes detested by the people, have gone for ever. The national-liberation struggle of the peoples of Asia and Africa, and also of the peoples of Latin America, is the unconquerable movement of our time. The forces of colonialism and aggression cannot hold back this mighty irresistible flood. The glorious traditions of the struggle of the Latin American peoples for democracy and national independence are well known to the Soviet people. The Soviet Union, People's China and other socialist countries firmly oppose the enslavement and exploitation of some countries by others. Our sympathies have always been and will always be on the side of the just cause, on the side of those who are fighting to consolidate the independence and sovereignty of their countries.

Question: Do you consider that the establishment of diplomatic relations between our countries is a necessary preliminary condition for trade between the Soviet Union and Brazil?

Answer: I have already had occasion to state the Soviet point of view regarding the normalization of relations between the Soviet Union and Brazil to the Brazilian journalists Martorelli and Fleuri last November. I can state again that the absence of normal diplomatic relations between two such countries as the Soviet Union and Brazil, which throughout their whole existence have never had any conflicts or clashes, is altogether unjustifiable. The lack of normal diplomatic relations does not, of course, facilitate the development of economic relations, trade and cultural contacts, but makes them more difficult.

Question: Do you consider that the Soviet Union could at the present time assist the industrialization of Brazil by supplying her with engineering equipment and specialists?

Answer: We Soviet people understand and sympathize with the desire of other peoples to develop their own economies independent of foreign capital. The Soviet Union has acquired great experience in its own industrialization and willingly shares it with countries wishing to take advantage of it in their own economic development.

The Soviet Government would certainly consider an appropriate request from the Brazilian Government and render such assistance as lies within its power in the industrial development of Brazil. Representatives of the two countries could discuss this question and find suitable mutually acceptable forms of co-operation. It would be possible to reach agreement on the delivery of Soviet machinery and plant, on the sending of Soviet experts to Brazil and on the training and education of Brazilian specialists in the Soviet Union.

In conclusion, I would like to point out that the improvement and normalization of relations between our two countries would be in the interests of our peoples and of peace throughout the world.

Respectfully,

N. KHRUSHCHOV

October 3, 1958
International Affairs, No. 11, 1958

REPLY
TO QUESTION OF TASS CORRESPONDENT

In connection with some statements made by Dwight D. Eisenhower, President of the United States, at his press conference on October 1, a TASS correspondent asked N. S. Khrushchov, Chairman of the Council of Ministers of the U.S.S.R., the following question:

At his press conference on October 1, U.S. President Dwight D. Eisenhower asserted that the actions of the Chinese People's Republic in the Taiwan Straits, aimed at liberating age-old Chinese territory from the Chiang Kai-shek clique, could not be regarded as civil war, that is, as an internal affair of the Chinese people. In substantiation of his assertion, the President stated: "If it is a civil war, why is Russia already saying, through Mr. Khrushchov in his letters, that they are ready to participate in this war! If that is a civil war, I am quite ignorant as to what the term really means."

How can this statement of the U.S. President be regarded? As far as it is known, none of the statements made by the Soviet Government has given any grounds for such assertions.

The following is N. S. Khrushchov's reply to the TASS correspondent's question:

I fully agree that at the aforementioned press conference President Eisenhower gave an absolutely incorrect interpretation of the statements made by the Soviet Government on the developments in the Taiwan area. One can only express surprise at the cavalier fashion in which the Soviet Union's stand has been distorted. I would never have believed that such methods would be employed. I am still convinced that the President of the United States correctly understands our statements pertaining to the situation in the Taiwan Straits. And if distortions are nonetheless made of the Soviet Government's statements which are dictated by a desire to preserve peace in the Far East, this merely proves that those who resort to such methods are guided, not by the interests of peace, but by the interests of a certain exclusive group in the United States which, for the sake of enrichment, is pursuing a policy of increasingly aggravating international tension and preparing for a new war.

But the assertions—patently at variance with the facts —with the aid of which certain people seek to represent the Soviet Government's stand in a distorted light cannot yield the results expected by their authors. The Soviet Union's stand is clear-cut, consistent and well defined. The Soviet Government has unequivocally stated, in its messages to President Eisenhower in particular, that if the United States should unleash war against our friend and ally, the Chinese People's Republic, the Soviet Union would fully carry out its obligations under the Treaty of Friendship, Alliance and Mutual Assistance with the Chinese People's Republic, and that an attack on the Chinese People's Republic represents an attack on the Soviet Union.

Is there the slightest hint in this that the Soviet Union, as President Eisenhower insists, is prepared to take part in the civil war in China? We have declared, and declare once again, something entirely different—the Soviet Union will come to the assistance of the Chinese People's Republic if it is attacked from without—to

677

put it more concretely, if the United States attacks the Chinese People's Republic.

The Soviet Government has found it necessary to issue this warning because the situation in the Far East has been developing in such a manner that interference by the United States in China's domestic affairs has brought the U.S.A. to the very brink of direct military conflict with the Chinese People's Republic. And if the United States goes over the brink, the Soviet Union will not remain on the side lines. But we have never interfered, and do not intend to interfere, in the civil war which the Chinese people are waging against the Chiang Kai-shek clique.

It is the inalienable right of every people to arrange their domestic affairs as they see fit. The intention of regaining their islands of Chinmentao and Matsutao and liberating Taiwan and Penghuletao is an internal affair of the Chinese people. It is common knowledge that these lands belonged to China long before Columbus discovered America. And the U.S. Government's attempts to prevent the Chinese people from completing their struggle against the Chiang Kai-shek clique expelled from the mainland, and from liberating age-old Chinese territory constitute gross and open interference by the United States in the civil war in China.

This President Eisenhower prefers to ignore.

In conclusion, I consider it necessary once again to underline that the U.S. Government is assuming an exceptionally grave responsibility in the face of the peoples and of history for all the consequences which may result from the intolerable interference by the U.S.A. in China's internal affairs and the aggressive actions of the American armed forces in the Taiwan Strait area.

Pravda, October 6, 1958

SPEECH
AT RECEPTION BY VICE-PRESIDENT
OF UNITED ARAB REPUBLIC,
MARSHAL ABDUL HAKIM AMER

October 21, 1958

Dear Mr. Vice-President,

Dear Guests, accompanying Marshal Abdul Hakim Amer,

Dear Comrades and Friends,

Permit me to express profound appreciation for the kind words which you, Mr. Vice-President, have addressed to our people and to our Government. We have been very pleased to hear in your speech an appreciation and correct understanding of the Soviet Government's policy.

The Soviet Government stands firmly for a policy of struggle for peace, for peaceful co-existence, for the creation of a situation in which no state may intervene in the internal affairs of other countries. We want to live in peace and friendship with all peoples. A splendid manifestation of these good relations is the friendly relations which have developed between our land and the United Arab Republic and other countries. There are very many such countries and I shall not undertake to enumerate them.

The friendly relations established between our countries show convincingly that states with different political and economic systems can live in harmony and friendship. The difference in social systems does not prevent us from conducting mutually advantageous trade, from exchang ing experience and achievements in the fields of economics, science and the arts.

You have spoken correctly of the Soviet Union's policy concerning economic assistance to underdeveloped countries. Disinterested aid to those countries is characteristic of the policy of the Soviet Government and of the governments of the other socialist countries. Such a policy is being carried out only by the Soviet Union and the other socialist countries, which want to consolidate friendly relations with all peoples, and help to strengthen the economy of the peaceful countries, irrespective of their political systems. We have concluded agreements with you on economic assistance and are conscientiously fulfilling them. This is the foundation of our friendly economic relations.

The strengthening of the economy of the United Arab Republic and other independent countries, the advance of their industry not only do not frighten us, as their successes frighten the imperialists, but give us instead sincere joy. Why? Because the higher the development of your economy and the higher the living standards of your people, the stronger will be your state and the more successfully will you uphold your independence.

The imperialist states give "aid" to other countries, above all, by setting up military bases on their territories, dispatching their troops there and supplying them with rocket weapons. It turns out that for every dollar they spend on this, they compel these countries to expend five dollars for armaments. Such "aid" leads to exhausting the economy of these countries and placing them in jeopardy, since rocket bases may attract the fire of other rockets. Such a policy does not promote the cause of peace but only complicates the international situation and endangers those countries in which foreign military bases are set up.

The press in Western states devotes much space to the need for rendering economic aid to underdeveloped countries. We are in favour of such assistance. Let us compete in this field. But such aid must be rendered as to enable the country assisted to really develop its economy and to rid itself of dependence on economically stronger countries, actually ensuring its independence. It is precisely such assistance that the underdeveloped countries need.

The imperialist states, however, will never accept this. The Rockefellers cannot afford to help underdeveloped countries build up their own industry so that this industry could compete with them or the country in question could do without purchasing the goods manufactured by the capitalist monopolies. I have referred to the Rockefellers, but all the monopolists are alike in this.

Here is the way the imperialists would like to render assistance: to ship to countries in need some wheat, butter and other goods which cannot be sold and by this "gesture of good will" show the whole world that they are helping the hungry. They are advertising that they are rendering disinterested assistance to people in need, but in fact they wish to make the poor permanently dependent on the rich. And they themselves do not conceal that if they do not render such aid this will still further impel the peoples of the colonial countries and those who have cast off the colonial yoke to fight for their genuine independence in all respects.

If underdeveloped countries are to be helped, this must be done in a way to enable them to increase their economic potential, in order to strengthen these states, and help them stand on their own feet. But the imperialists cannot accept this because it contradicts the essence of imperialism.

There is no friction in relations between the Soviet Union and the Arab countries. Relations of sincere friendship and co-operation have been established between our countries. We are not interested in your wealth. Everything you possess we have at home, and what we have not enough of we can buy from you on a mutually advantageous basis. But for a pennyworth of assistance the imperialists want to rob you of pounds. They need your oil, they need the diamonds of Africa, they need other minerals and products. They want to keep these countries in subjection, and to ruthlessly exploit the peoples of the colonial and dependent countries.

In a conversation a representative of a big imperialist Power told me that the Soviet Union and the Western Powers should pool their efforts in rendering assistance to underdeveloped countries. On what terms, I asked, and on what basis? The terms, he said, are such that for every dollar of assistance that you give, we shall give three. I told this representative that we cannot agree to cover up the imperialist policy, because the imperialists offer assistance to these countries on the condition of keeping them dependent on imperialist states. Thus they offer the three dollars, not because they wish to help such countries acquire independence, but because they fear the colonial peoples rising in struggle for their independence.

The imperialists have reduced those countries to poverty, their peoples are rising in rebellion, and now the imperialists would like us to help them pacify the insurgent peoples for the sake of maintaining the old order and to give our money for this purpose. We would get nothing from this, whereas the imperialists would continue to obtain oil, uranium and other resources for a song, virtually for nothing.

The imperialists have been plundering the peoples of Asia and Africa for centuries. They do not mind boasting that high living standards have been attained in their countries. But this is largely due to the exploitation of the Afro-Asian peoples, to the fact that millions of people have died of poverty and starvation.

The imperialists have pumped tremendous wealth out of the colonial and dependent countries. Let them return at least a portion of what they have plundered. They are under obligation to do this.

Our country has taken no hand in colonial plunder. From the moment Soviet power was proclaimed Lenin declared that our state was vigorously opposed to the imperialist colonial policy, the enslavement and oppression of some countries by others. And our state has undeviatingly carried out and will continue to carry out such a policy.

The imperialists talk a great deal about assistance to underdeveloped countries. But if they indeed want to render assistance, why not introduce the following procedure: They are pumping out, for instance, Middle East oil. Then let them earmark a definite proportion of their profits obtained by exploiting the natural resources of those countries to a fund for assisting underdeveloped countries. That would be a just solution. The capitalist countries are obligated to return their plunder to the exploited peoples of the Afro-Asian countries. They have amassed tremendous wealth out of it. And it would be only just if they set up their assistance fund for underdeveloped countries in proportion to the profits they have derived from exploiting them. As for the Soviet Union, it has helped and will continue to help underdeveloped countries disinterestedly, by lending direct assistance. We come to terms on an honest basis with those countries which need such assistance. Everyone can see that our assistance differs fundamentally from that "aid" which the imperialists are rendering underdeveloped countries.

It would be a different matter if an international fund for helping underdeveloped countries were to be set up from the savings made by reducing armed forces and cutting military budgets. All of us, the Soviet Union included, bear these expenditures. And if we succeeded in halting the cold war, reducing armed forces and cutting military budgets it would be fair to earmark the means thus released to an international fund of economic assistance to underdeveloped countries.

We would recommend to the imperialist countries that instead of spending money on dispatching their troops for intervention, as was the case in the Lebanon and Jordan, they transfer these means to countries in need of assistance. For they have moved troops, tanks and other military equipment to the Lebanon and Jordan and now they must move them back. This is unwise economically and politically.

The purpose of the intervention in the Lebanon and Jordan was to frighten the peoples. But it is high time to realize that lions can no longer frighten peoples by their roaring, and that it is a thing of the past for other countries to be seized with impunity and nations plundered. New forces have appeared: the Soviet Union, the Chinese People's Republic and the other socialist countries. And these countries have all that is needed to bar the road to the imperialists and not permit them to frighten those peoples who are still weak today but fully determined to fight for their freedom and independence.

The imperialists want to build up a kind of international police force which would virtually be under the control of the United States and be used to suppress the peoples who have risen against colonial slavery. This will not succeed! The peace-loving peoples are strong enough to counter intrigues of the imperialists, to frustrate their perfidious designs. There is no force on earth which could halt the movement of the peoples fighting for their independence, for their liberation.

We salute the Arab people, the United Arab Republic! We salute the revolution in Iraq, we salute the Government of the Republic of Iraq headed by Premier Kassem! We salute all the peoples who are fighting for the liberation of their countries from colonial dependence.

Permit me to propose a toast to the friendship between the peoples of the Soviet Union and the United Arab Republic, to the friendship between all peace-loving peoples, to world peace, to the successes of the peoples fighting against colonial oppression and striving to strengthen their independence, to the prosperity of the peoples of the United Arab Republic, to the good health of our friend, esteemed President Gamal Abdel Nasser, to the good health of all our guests, to your good health, Mr. Abdul Hakim Amer!

(N. S. Khrushchov's speech was listened to with great attention and was repeatedly interrupted by bursts of applause.)

SPEECH
AT GRAND KREMLIN PALACE RECEPTION IN HONOUR OF PARTICIPANTS OF AFRO-ASIAN WRITERS' CONFERENCE IN TASHKENT

October 22, 1958

Dear Comrades and Friends,

On behalf of the Soviet Government, I am very pleased to welcome you, the leading representatives of literature in the Asian and African countries, to the capital of our country, Moscow.

All of us have followed the work of your conference with great interest. This interest is fully understandable, for all progressive people in the world know and highly appreciate the active role played by writers in developing the national awareness of the peoples of Asia and Africa, who are fighting for liberation from the shameful chains of colonialism and imperialist oppression. But the role of the writers is even greater in those countries which have won their freedom and independence. There, literature becomes a mighty force in building a new life.

All those who sincerely sympathize with the fate of your peoples could not but rejoice that the meeting of Asian and African writers in Tashkent was so large and so representative.

The Tashkent Conference was attended by many well-known writers and poets of whom the peoples are proud. A writer is a mighty force, because his words carry great weight. It is not for nothing that the people say: A word is not an arrow but it strikes home.

Asia and Africa are continents of ancient cultures, but they have never witnessed so impressive an assembly of men of letters as the one you have attended. This is the first time that a meeting has been held of writers and poets of so many countries and nationalities, both large and small: People's China, India, the United Arab Republic, our own Central Asian Republics, Ghana, the Ivory Coast, and other countries. In addition to delegates from countries which have already won their freedom and independence, it was attended by writers from countries which are still languishing under colonial oppression, from countries fighting for their liberation.

Comrades and friends, you are people of various political convictions, you profess different religions. But you are all made kith and kin by a great love for your peoples, a respect for their original national traditions and their literary treasures, and by common hatred of imperialism, colonialism and racial discrimination. And the mighty voice of your conference has been heard all over the five continents.

It can safely be said that your unanimity of views on the paramount questions of developing literatures and friendly exchanges between them will be another thorn in the flesh of the imperialists and the colonialists.

It is probable that in some places the imperialists and colonialists will unloose their hounds against you with the command to smear the unity which you have demonstrated so forcefully and which is so hateful to them. But, as an Eastern saying goes, an enemy's anger is the highest approbation.

Men of good will, all those who believe that reason will prevail over obscurantism, all those who are open to understanding, who want peace on earth, will approve your declaration as a document of good will. The Soviet people whole-heartedly welcome the decision of your conference. (*Applause.*)

Your fine aspirations are especially understandable to us

Soviet people. The Soviet people have erected on the ruins of tsarist Russia—which was a prison-house of nations—a mighty multi-national socialist state, a union of equal socialist republics in each of which new, impressive cultures, national in form and socialist in content, have developed and flourished in the years of Soviet power.

In travelling through our country, all of you have had every opportunity to become acquainted with the cultures of the Soviet republics. Our achievements cannot help bringing satisfaction to all upright people. But we ourselves regard them as only the beginning of a great advance and flowering of the national cultures of our peoples. The Soviet people understand full well your keen desire for flourishing cultures in all Asian and African countries, and share and welcome it with all their hearts.

I was told that a new expression—the spirit of Tashkent—was born in the course of your conference in the speeches made there. You imply by this the friendly mutual understanding and co-operation between creative artists of different peoples in the struggle for the great objectives of mankind, strong ties between writers and the life of their peoples, and active participation of literature in the fight for the freedom and independence of your countries and in building a new life where freedom and independence have already been won.

All my colleagues and I want the spirit of friendship and understanding which united you at the conference to mature and develop. In our time, a writer—provided, of course, he is a good one—a writer linked with the people, breathing their thoughts and aspirations, is not merely a chronicler of life but a fighter and a standard-bearer of progress.

Is there any doubt that what united you at the conference will not only promote the development of fruitful contacts between the literatures of Asia and Africa, these two great continents, but will also contribute to the successful development of world culture and to the consolidation of ties between the progressive culture of the East and the progressive culture of the West?

In cordially greeting you on behalf of the Soviet Government, I would also like to thank you for the kind sentiments for the Soviet people spoken in appreciation of their hospitality and cordiality, to thank you for what you have said with such warmth and enthusiasm about the achievements of our country.

In conclusion, I would like to wish each one of you success in your work and your art which helps the peoples of your countries to achieve their vital goals and assists them in the struggle for the happy future of mankind. Love and respect from the people is the writers' greatest reward.

I wish you to add by your fruitful work to the treasury of world culture, and to make a worthy contribution to the common efforts of the peoples fighting for peace on earth. (*Applause.*)

Allow me to propose a toast to your health, and to your creative achievements for the good of the peoples. (*Applause.*)

To happiness and peace between all peoples, to peace throughout the world. (*Stormy applause.*)

SPEECH
AT KREMLIN RECEPTION IN HONOUR
OF VICE-PRESIDENT OF UNITED ARAB REPUBLIC,
MARSHAL ABDUL HAKIM AMER

October 23, 1958

Dear Mr. Vice-President,

Dear Guests, accompanying Marshal Adbul Hakim Amer,

Dear Comrades and Friends,

We note with great satisfaction, our dear guests, that your visit to the Soviet Union represents a new contribution to the development of co-operation between the Soviet Union and the United Arab Republic and will help strengthen the ties of our friendship in the interests of peace in the Middle East and the world over. This visit is fresh confirmation of the fact that the friendly contacts between the leaders of the Soviet Union and the United Arab Republic are, to an ever-increasing extent, developing into a good tradition. Such contacts correspond to the mutual interests of the Soviet and Arab peoples and promote economic and cultural ties between our countries.

Now, as before, we declare that we wish to develop our relations with all countries of the Middle East, without exception, and also with all other countries, strictly in accordance with the policy of equality, peaceful co-existence and non-interference in the internal affairs of other states.

Now the people of your country, having cast off colonial oppression, are enthusiastically working for the regeneration of their country. Under the leadership of their Government, the Egyptians and Syrians, having united in one state, are working heart and soul to build the edifice of their independent state. New industrial plants, schools, clinics and institutes are rising in different parts of your country. The defence potential of the United Arab Republic—a token of its independence—is increasing. These achievements of your country on the road of national renascence meet with a warm response and sympathy from all the peoples of the Soviet Union. An expression of these sentiments is the Soviet Union's fraternal support for the noble cause of your country's national development and its disinterested aid in the construction of mutually agreed industrial plants within the framework of a general plan aimed at consolidating the political and economic independence of the United Arab Republic. The Soviet Union has rendered, and will continue to render, aid in economic planning, in the construction of new plants, in the utilization of water resources and the reclamation of arid lands.

The Soviet Government has considered the request you have conveyed from the Government of the United Arab Republic for assistance in the construction of the first section of the Aswân Dam.

Acting upon the friendly relations between our two countries and in the interests of strengthening them, the Soviet Government has undertaken to participate in the construction of the first section of the Aswân Dam, a project which is of such great importance to the national economy of the United Arab Republic and to the consolidation of its national independence.

The Soviet Government is willing to send the necessary number of specialists to the United Arab Republic, to supply the United Arab Republic with the necessary machinery and equipment and with the materials it lacks for the accomplishment of this project, and to grant a loan of up to 400 million rubles to cover the expenses involved.

The repayment of the Soviet Union's investment in this project is to begin on the completion of the first section of the construction.

In conformity with the wishes of the Government of the United Arab Republic, we agree to send our specialists to Cairo in the near future to discuss with your competent representatives the details of this project and to draft an appropriate agreement between our two countries.

Mr. Vice-President, our meetings with you and the frank exchange of opinion we have had on a number of international problems, which have taken place in a cordial and friendly atmosphere, are bound to promote and cement the bonds of friendship between our two countries.

As in previous discussions between the government leaders of the Soviet Union and the United Arab Republic, we have ascertained that our views coincide on current international problems of decisive importance for the preservation and consolidation of world peace. This identity of views is not a matter of mere coincidence. It follows from the entire course of historical development of our peoples and rests on the principles of sincere friendship and unselfish co-operation, in the name of peace and the prosperity of the peoples of our countries.

At the United Nations, the Soviet Union and the United Arab Republic maintain a common stand on disarmament, the banning of nuclear weapons, the ending of nuclear tests and on other important questions connected with safeguarding international peace and security.

We are unanimous in recognizing that the main task before the peace forces in the Middle East at present is to secure the earliest possible withdrawal of American troops from the Lebanon and of British troops from Jordan and to ensure the peace and tranquility essential for the creative work of the population of the Arab countries in developing their national economy and raising their cultural and living standards.

With all our hearts we wish further success to the friendly peoples of the United Arab Republic in strengthening peace and national independence and in working for economic prosperity and for the unity of the Arab nations.

May the edifice of our friendship stand as firm and as eternal as the ancient pyramids on the banks of the Nile— the majestic witnesses to the glorious centuries-old history of your peoples.

Permit me to propose a toast to the courageous people of the United Arab Republic, whose heroic struggle for their independence has evoked the admiration of all throughout the world and in whose successes all honest people rejoice.

To the health of our friend, President Gamal Abdel Nasser!

To the health of the members of the United Arab Republic's Government!

To our friendship!

To your health, Mr. Vice-President!

To your health, dear friends!

Long live the friendship of the peoples of the Soviet Union and the United Arab Republic!

(N. S. Khrushchov's speech was met with hearty applause.)

SPEECH
WELCOMING POLISH PEOPLE'S REPUBLIC
DELEGATION IN MOSCOW

October 25, 1958

Dear Comrade Gomulka,

Dear Comrade Zawadski,

Dear Comrade Cyrankiewicz,

Dear Comrades, Members of the Delegation of the Polish People's Republic,

On behalf of the Central Committee of the Communist Party of the Soviet Union, the Presidium of the Supreme Soviet of the U.S.S.R. and the Soviet Government, I welcome you heartily in the Soviet capital—Moscow. All Soviet people welcome you, the representatives of the fraternal Polish people, who advance along the path of building a new, socialist life under the tested leadership of the Polish United Workers' Party.

Your present visit to the Soviet Union, dear comrades, is a new token of the continuously developing inviolable friendship of the Soviet and Polish peoples. Just two years have passed since the delegation of the Polish People's Republic headed by our friend Comrade Gomulka came to our country in the autumn of 1956. It is gratifying to note that the friendship of the Polish and Soviet peoples has taken new strength and the fraternal co-operation between our countries has been cemented. Enemy attempts have failed to undermine, and even to weaken, our friendship, to divert the peoples of Poland and the

Soviet Union from the right path of fraternal friendship, co-operation and mutual assistance, which they are following hand in hand. The present visit of the delegation of the Polish People's Republic to the Soviet Union will unquestionably be a new, most important step forward along this path.

The facts of life confirm convincingly that the friendship between our countries, based as it is on the principles of proletarian internationalism and all-round mutual support, accords with the basic interests of our peoples, the interests of the socialist camp as a whole. It is in strengthening this friendship in every way that we have a guarantee of the successful accomplishment of the historical task of building socialism and communism in our countries. At the same time our fraternal co-operation is an important factor strengthening peace and security in Europe and the world.

Dear friends, during your stay in the Soviet Union you will see again that the peoples of the Soviet Union have profound feelings of love and friendship for the fraternal Polish people.

You have come to us on the eve of the 41st anniversary of the Great October Socialist Revolution. We are happy that you will be our guests at this time and that together with our people you will take part in celebrating that glorious anniversary.

Welcome, our dear friends!

SPEECH
AT KREMLIN DINNER IN HONOUR
OF POLISH PEOPLE'S REPUBLIC DELEGATION

October 25, 1958

Dear Polish Friends,

We are happy to welcome you again, leaders of the Polish People's Democracy.

We bid hearty welcome to the First Secretary of the Central Committee of the Polish United Workers' Party, Comrade Gomulka, loyal son of the Polish people, tireless fighter for peace and socialism, our friend who is well known and deeply respected in this country.

We bid hearty welcome to the Chairman of the State Council of the Polish People's Republic, our friend Comrade Zawadski.

We extend cordial greetings to the Chairman of the Council of Ministers of the Polish People's Republic, our friend Comrade Cyrankiewicz.

We bid cordial welcome to all members of the delegation of the Polish People's Republic.

The arrival from Poland of this representative delegation is a new token of growing Soviet-Polish friendship and an expression of ideological kinship between our Communist parties.

Fraternal friendship and inviolable unity are the chief elements characterizing the relations between the peoples of Poland and the Soviet Union, the peoples of all the socialist countries. The very nature of the social system in our countries gives impetus to mutual assistance and support among free peoples. The unity of countries of the socialist camp does not in the least detract from their national independence. Quite the reverse. It is the best guarantee of the sovereignty and security of each individual socialist country and all the socialist countries as a whole.

The lessons of history show that the building of socialism and communism makes better progress when all the socialist countries unite their efforts in that great cause. Socialism and communism cannot be successfully built on one's own, in isolation from one's fellow-fighters in other countries.

By advancing in a broad and united front we achieve higher rates of progress in the fraternal countries towards socialism and communism, a higher standard of living for our peoples. Thereby we cement world peace and infuse greater confidence in the triumph of our just cause into all democratic, progressive, peace-loving forces.

Hundreds of millions of ordinary people throughout the world support the socialist camp and are proud of the successes scored by the socialist countries. At the same time, our successes cause irritation and hatred among the imperialists, who are trying in every way to check-rein our advance. But all the exertions of the imperialists are doomed to failure, because the socialist camp is powerful and strong as never before.

Allow me to propose a toast to new successes of the fraternal Polish people in building socialism!

To inviolable Polish-Soviet friendship!

To the further strengthening of friendship and solidarity among all the countries of the socialist camp!

To world peace!

To your health, dear Comrade Gomulka!

To your health, dear Comrade Zawadski!

To your health, dear Comrade Cyrankiewicz!

To your health, dear Polish friends!

SPEECH
AT LUNCHEON GIVEN
BY COMRADE WLADYSLAW GOMULKA, CHAIRMAN
OF POLISH PEOPLE'S REPUBLIC DELEGATION

October 27, 1958

Dear Comrade Gomulka,
Dear Comrade Zawadski,
Dear Comrade Cyrankiewicz,
Dear Comrades and Friends,

To begin with, allow me on behalf of the Central Committee of the C.P.S.U. and the Soviet Government, on behalf of all the Soviet comrades present here, and on my own behalf, to convey hearty thanks to Comrade Gomulka, the First Secretary of the Central Committee of the Polish United Workers' Party, and Comrade Cyrankiewicz, the Chairman of the Council of Ministers of the P.P.R., for the warm sentiments and kind wishes addressed by them to the Soviet people, the Communist Party and the Government of the Soviet Union on behalf of the Polish United Workers' Party, the Government of the Polish People's Republic and the people of Poland.

The Soviet people derive deep satisfaction from the thought that the relations of enduring and inviolable friendship between our peoples and states are becoming more intimate and cordial every day.

We have always prized this fraternal friendship and, for our part, shall do everything to strengthen it still more.

The friendship of the peoples of the Soviet Union and Poland, like that of all the peoples of the socialist countries, works for the triumph of socialism and communism. Socialism and international friendship are inseparably connected. The closer the friendship of our peoples, the closer their solidarity and fraternal co-operation, the greater the scale and the impact of the achievements of socialist construction. This is an objective law of historical development. For this reason, we must cherish our friendship and preserve it lovingly from all the intrigues of the enemies of socialism.

The friendship and unity of our countries serves the best interests not only of the socialist camp, but of all progressive mankind. By helping each other in their economic development our peoples add to the power of the whole socialist camp, that unconquerable stronghold of socialism and insuperable obstacle to warmongers. The socialist camp is a reliable bulwark of world peace. All people of good will, all who want peace and hate war, have a vested interest in strengthening it and its solidarity.

The forces inimical to peace are forever seeking to shake the unity of the socialist camp, to split it. Your exertions are in vain, Messrs. Imperialists! The unity of the socialist countries is now durable as never before. A big part in cementing this unity is played by the friendship and co-operation of the Polish People's Republic and the Soviet Union. Comrade Gomulka was absolutely right when he said at the 12th Plenary Meeting of the Central Committee of the Polish United Workers' Party that any attempt of the reactionaries, of the various imperialist groups, to drive in a wedge between Poland and the Soviet Union, to undermine our friendship, to breach the unity of the socialist camp, will fail inevitably.

Permit me to propose a toast to further successes of the Polish people in building socialism, in developing their economy and culture, in improving the living standard of the working people!

To the Polish United Workers' Party, to its Central Committee, to the health of the First Secretary of the Central Committee, Comrade Gomulka!

To the State Council of the Polish People's Republic, to the health of its Chairman, Comrade Zawadski!

To the Council of Ministers of the Polish People's Republic and the head of the Polish Government, Comrade Cyrankiewicz!

To the health of all the members of the delegation of the Polish People's Republic!

To inviolable fraternal Soviet-Polish friendship, to world peace!

SPEECH
AT BALTIC WORKS MEETING DURING STAY
IN LENINGRAD
OF POLISH PEOPLE'S REPUBLIC DELEGATION

November 3, 1958

Dear Leningrad comrades, dear comrades of the Baltic Works,

Allow me to greet you heartily on behalf of the Central Committee of the Communist Party of the Soviet Union and the Council of Ministers of the U.S.S.R. (*Applause.*)

Spokesmen of your works, and of your Party and Young Communist League organizations have spoken well about meeting our dear friends, the Polish People's Republic delegation headed by Comrade Gomulka. This visit of the delegation from People's Poland is very important.

The vital interests of our two countries have become interwoven historically. The fundamental interests of the Soviet and Polish peoples are so close and inseparable that it is not enough for us merely to live in peace. To build the new life successfully, to defend the gains of socialism in our countries, in the entire socialist camp, the peoples of our countries must live in solid friendship. The fraternal friendship of the peoples of the socialist countries is that tremendous force which is capable of preventing war in Europe and the world.

After all, we and the Polish people have common enemies, since any armed attack on Poland would bring the theatre of war directly to the frontiers of the Soviet Union. On the other hand, an attack on the U.S.S.R. from the West is most likely to occur somewhere across Polish territory, and would thus inevitably also affect her interests. This is why we must see to it that our power grows and the friendship between our countries, between the peoples of the Soviet Union and Poland, takes new strength.

The peoples of the Soviet Union and the toilers of People's Poland are highly conscious of the need to strengthen their friendship. The relations which now exist between our countries are good friendly relations. There are no questions to disunite us, on which we have our own special opinion, distinct from the viewpoint of our Polish comrades. Nor do I expect any particular snags, hitches or skids to arise in the future along the path of greater friendship between the peoples of our countries.

Our Polish brothers are building socialism. The Soviet people are advancing successfully towards communism. We rejoice at each other's successes, because we have a single great goal. (*Stormy applause.*)

Our Polish friends, I must say, hold an advantage, for they are not building socialism alone. Today many countries are making good progress in building socialism. The great socialist camp is growing and gaining strength. We, the Soviet people, had a harder time. When the workers and soldiers of Petrograd rose against the rule of the bourgeoisie, against capitalism, and this uprising, supported by the working class, the working peasantry of all Russia, was crowned with a great victory—the establishment of Soviet power—our country was the only working people's state in a turbulent capitalist ocean. There were so many Kersons and other antagonists of all kinds after the victory of the Great October Socialist Revolution who opposed us and did all they could to crush us. We did not have a trained army then, nor experience in governing a country. We did not have our own intelligentsia. What is more, many people of the old intelligentsia followed the events then unfolding in Russia with a wolf's eye, as the saying goes.

The workers, the working people of our country who

had taken power, did not flinch in face of difficulties, and did not surrender to the enemy. They surmounted all hardships with courage—survived hunger and the Civil War and defended their homeland against the interventionists. The imperialists calculated literally the days when, in their opinion, Soviet power in Russia would crumble. They expected the Soviet Republic, that giant on "feet of clay," as they called it, to topple any minute under the joint onslaught of domestic and external counter-revolutionary forces. But, thank God, here we are. Days, months and years came and went, and our Soviet country took new strength, steeled itself, crushing its enemies. It has become a great socialist Power—the glory and pride of working people throughout the world. (*Stormy applause. Cries*: "Hurrah!")

Now all can see that the "feet of clay" described by our class enemies were really stronger than the hardest granite. The Soviet Union has emerged from all the storms and ordeals a mighty world socialist Power.

Today a number of European and Asian countries whose peoples have also overthrown bourgeois rule, are following our country steadfastly along the path of socialist construction. They have taken power into their hands and confidently proceed along the road charted by Marxism-Leninism.

The imperialists have frequently tried to intimidate us with threats of war, with their military power. But we are not easily frightened. We have firmly and steadfastly followed our path and achieved historic victories. It is not we who tremble, but the capitalist world, confronted as it is by the new, growing and developing socialist world, by those hundreds of millions of working people who have taken power for good and shown all mankind how to live without exploiters and exploitation. (*Stormy applause.*)

The gentlemen from bourgeois countries will never be able to overthrow the power of the working people, which has firmly established itself in the socialist countries. They will never be able to recover what they have lost. Now it is becoming increasingly clear that capitalist rule is approaching its end in other countries as well, and that capitalism, a system which has outlived its time, is doomed. The future is ours. The future, comrades, belongs to Marxism-Leninism, to communism! (*Stormy applause.*)

We are doing very well. We now have all we need to advance rapidly to our goal. The alliance of the working class and the working peasantry, which has successfully withstood all trials in forty years of socialist development, is now strong as never before. The new intelligentsia, an intelligentsia of the people, has grown up in the years of Soviet power and is working heart and soul for the socialist cause, adding glory to Soviet science by its labour. Only recently our enemies described our gifted people haughtily as ignorant "muzhiks." They could not countenance the thought, you see, that workers and peasants could govern their country without landlords and capitalists and to develop science and culture. Yet now these "muzhiks" have launched the world's first artificial earth satellites, while they, the antagonists of the Soviet Union, the antagonists of socialism, are petrified and their jaws have dropped from astonishment at our successes. (*Laughter, prolonged applause.*)

Comrades, now many people come to us from the bourgeois countries, and there are some among them who come to snoop how soon Soviet power will topple. (*Laughter.*) People known in the capitalist world as businessmen—industrialists and capitalists—visit us as well. When honest people see how much has been done in the forty-one years of Soviet power, they acknowledge the grandeur of what our people have created. Others slander our country viciously. But already they are much fewer. The majority are unable to escape the facts and cannot help saying on their return home that the Soviet Union they saw was not something backward, but a country of vigorous and hard-working people, a foremost technology, powerful plants, a rising culture and a mounting living standard.

The Soviet people have worked with a will and are reaping rich harvests from their great creative effort. The difficult times when our country was poor and technically backward are long over. You may recall that at one time we looked upon the United States with envy, as if it were something almost unattainable. Yet now the day is near when we shall say: "Step aside, we are taking the lead, and you can get behind and follow in our wake." (*Laughter. Stormy applause.*)

And that, comrades, is no empty boast, but our immediate future, our tomorrow. Already now, our economists are calculating pencil in hand when that day will come. And our calculations are always very accurate and hardly ever let us down. The first Land of the Soviets will be first in per capita production. We shall have the highest living standard. Our working class, our working people, are sure to achieve it! (*Loud cries:* "Hurrah!" *Stormy, prolonged applause.*)

Even today bourgeois propaganda is trying to frighten the man in the street with communism. In doing so it resorts, as is its custom, to shameless deceit and all sorts of provocations. Sometimes it succeeds. There are still those, even among honest men in the capitalist countries, who fear communism. However, this is not surprising. The older generation may recall that in the early years of Soviet power in our country, the working people's enemies also made up quite a few absurd fairy-tales about the Bolsheviks and the proletarian revolution. Their object was to scare and confuse the ordinary people. But our Bolshevik truth has conquered the hearts of men, and has won their sympathies. The same will happen also in the other countries of the world.

After we raise our economy, culture, and the standard of living to still higher levels, the ordinary people all over the world will see for themselves that communism is a social system embodying all mankind's finest dreams for a happy life. We live at a time when new millions and millions take their stand under the great banner of Marxism-Leninism. (*Applause.*)

Our principal weapon is Marxism-Leninism. We shall defeat the capitalist world by using this powerful ideological weapon rather than the hydrogen bomb. We produce the hydrogen bomb with the sole object of cooling the ambitions of some excessively zealous politicians and generals in the capitalist countries. (*Laughter, applause.*) After all, living among wolves one must have the means to let them know how dangerous it is for them to show their fangs. (*Laughter, applause.*) We have no wish to attack anyone. But we do not want to be simpletons who can be taken barehanded. Now we cannot be taken with gloved hands, let alone barehanded! (*Laughter. Stormy applause.*)

The Soviet state, like all socialist countries, is a peaceful state. We adhere steadfastly to the Leninist principles of foreign policy. We stand firmly for peace, for the prohibition of atomic weapons, for disarmament. We are ready today to sign a treaty and end nuclear tests for all time, but this must be done in good faith, with our Western partners displaying as conscientious an approach as we are to solving this problem.

However, the ruling circles of the Western Powers, particularly the United States, do not agree to that. Everybody knows that the Soviet Government has unilaterally discontinued nuclear tests and urged the Governments of the United States and Britain to follow suit. When we declared that we would do no more testing, they did not accept our proposal and stepped up their tests. Months went by, but the United States and Britain gave no thought to discontinuing tests of atomic and hydrogen bombs. Not to be at a disadvantage, in an unequal position, we had no other alternative but to resume our tests. And that was what we did, attaining more powerful nuclear weapons. If they go on making their tests, they better not think that we shall be caught napping and wait until the imperialists boost their strength against us. (*Laughter, applause.*)

Now there is talk about suspending nuclear tests for a year, that is, for the time required by the United States and Britain to sum up the results of their recent tests. A year later they will again hold a series of nuclear weapons tests. Is that an adequate solution to the issue? Of course, not. We stand for ending tests of atomic and hydrogen weapons for all time, for establishing appropriate control, but the ruling circles of the United States and Britain do not want that.

We have stated repeatedly that the controversy over which system is better, socialism or capitalism, should be settled by competition in peaceful endeavour rather than by armed conflict. There always have been, are, and will be ideological, class differences between socialism and capitalism. But the socialist and capitalist countries exist on the same planet and have to co-exist peacefully. We say: Let us settle the existing differences between socialism and capitalism by peaceful competition rather than by unleashing war. If you, gentlemen, the adherents of capitalism, say that your system is good and strong, let that system reveal its superiority in peaceful competition with the socialist system.

The ruling circles of countries which have enriched themselves, and still enrich themselves, at the expense of colonies, are not loath to brag about their countries having a high standard of life. But their high standard of life was achieved at the cost of millions of human lives, by prostrating entire nations, and doing in millions and millions in the colonies by starvation.

Capitalism cannot exist without plundering the masses, without oppression and exploitation. A handful of men appropriate tremendous riches belonging to the people. The imperialists have always enriched themselves, and still enrich themselves, by plundering not only the peoples of their own countries, but also the peoples of the colonies.

Now, as before, imperialism continues to plunder many peoples of Africa and Asia. But in recent times the peoples in many countries have cast off the chains of colonialism and won their national independence. Colonialism is today splitting at the seams.

Under socialism the oppression of one people by another is unthinkable. Socialism has brought equality to all nations. We in the Soviet Union have achieved striking successes not on any funds received from abroad. It was the working class, the working people of the Soviet Union, who have created everything that is now the pride of our people, that today amazes people abroad, with their own labour, their own intellect. People abroad wonder how a country could turn from a backward into an advanced state in so short a time, and assume a leading place in the world. Comrades, we owe this to our socialist system, our Marxist-Leninist teaching. (*Stormy applause.*)

While capitalism plunges people into the slavery of exploitation, into poverty, and deprives them of their rights, socialism brings a free, happy life to the people, ensuring their all-round and rapid development. I have said already that as a result of the triumphant October Revolution the face of our country has changed. All countries that have taken the socialist path are developing along the same lines. This may be seen from the Polish example. During Pilsudski's reign Poland was one of Europe's backward countries. Today the Polish People's Republic has a highly developed industry, and has scored big successes in public education and the development of science and culture. The Pilsudski clique is known to have brought the Polish people to the brink of a national catastrophe by its inane policy of "sabre-rattling." The present workers' and peasants' government of Poland conducts a peaceful foreign policy in the interests of the broad masses.

Our dear guests, Comrade Gomulka, the First Secretary of the Central Committee of the Polish United Workers'

Party, Comrade Zawadski, Chairman of the State Council, and Comrade Cyrankiewicz, Chairman of the Council of Ministers, are our brothers. They think as we do, and do everything in their power to strengthen their working people's state and to further the friendship between our countries, between our peoples and between the peoples of all socialist countries and fight for world peace.

Comrades, our Polish friends are visiting us at a time when the Soviet country is approaching the 41st anniversary of the October Revolution, which we shall celebrate in a few days. It is a big and good holiday! (*Applause.*)

We are summing up the results of the economic development of the U.S.S.R. in 1958. In agriculture these results have been exceedingly good. We have already procured 1,300 million poods more grain than last year. This means that now we shall have grain enough to bake brown bread, and white bread, and make pancakes, and dumplings, and still have much left over for stock. (*Laughter. Stormy applause.*)

N. S. Khrushchov goes on to say that the harvest of sugar-beet has been very good in the current year, and that this ensures a considerable increase in sugar output. Marked successes have also been achieved in the production of milk and meat.

"Do you have milk in Leningrad?" Khrushchov asked.

Voices: We do!

Khrushchov: Perhaps you don't want to let down your leadership, or do you really have milk?

Voices: We do! We do! (*Laughter, applause.*)

Khrushchov: Our industry is also doing much better work. Considerable emphasis is being laid on developing the chemical industry, which offers most excellent opportunities of increasing the output of consumer goods, so as to satisfy in full the requirements of the population in high-quality and cheap commodities:

709

There are also appreciable advances in housing construction. More dwellings are going up. Are they now building more in your city than before, comrades?

Voices: They are!

Khrushchov: I think that the task set by the Central Committee—to solve the housing problem in ten to twelve years—will be successfully accomplished!

Voices: Couldn't this term be reduced?

Khrushchov: That depends on you, on all our people. What does it mean to reduce the fixed schedule of solving the housing question? It means that as much as possible steel, bricks, cement, reinforced concrete, and other materials indispensable in building are to be produced in the shortest possible time. And it is you, the workers, who produce them. It isn't I who makes bricks and cement. (*Laughter.*)

To reduce the schedule of solving the housing problem fixed by the Party and the Government, we must work better, raise the productivity of labour and produce more cement, metal, timber, and other materials. This is what has to be done, comrades! (*Prolonged applause.*)

N. S. Khrushchov turns to questions of international politics and the struggle for peace. He replies at length to questions asked by the workers. Then Comrade Khrushchov says:

Allow me, comrades, to conclude my speech by wishing you new successes. I visited your plant some three years ago. Now you have advanced far ahead. Three years ago you were only making your first experiments of introducing automatic shielding powder welding. While now this progressive method has been broadly introduced at your plant. Automatic welding has a big future. You have mastered the job begun by that remarkable scientist, a representative of the old, pre-revolutionary intelligentsia, Academician Paton. Automatic welding will enable us to achieve still greater successes in raising the productivity of labour.

We must continue to improve the technology of production; we must not be content with what we have today and pick up new and progressive methods more boldly, so that labour of Soviet workers becomes still more productive.

The Soviet people are carrying out the task of overtaking the United States in per capita production. And what does that mean? It means that we must produce products needed by man in greater quantities than any capitalist country. This is possible only if our workers, our engineers and technicians, and our farmers attain the very highest productivity of labour.

So we urge you, comrades, to raise still higher the level of production, to raise still higher the productivity of labour, so as to give our people the highest standard of life. It is this that will enable us to draw near to communist society.

Long live the workers of the Baltic Works, the workers of fighting Petrograd, the workers of glorious Leningrad!

Long live the great Soviet people!

Long live the fraternal friendship of the peoples of the socialist countries!

Long live the fraternal friendship of the peoples of the Soviet Union and the Polish People's Republic! (*Stormy, prolonged applause. Cries*: "Hurrah!")

SPEECH
AT SOVIET-POLISH FRIENDSHIP MEETING
OF LENINGRAD WORKING PEOPLE

November 4, 1958

Dear Comrades,

We have with great attention heard the splendid speech of our dear friend Comrade Gomulka, who spoke well about the friendship of the peoples of our countries, about strengthening the unity of the socialist countries in the fight for socialism and communism, for securing the great gains of the working class, the working people of our countries, and for ensuring and strengthening world peace.

It may be said in all sincerity that the thoughts and sentiments voiced by Comrade Gomulka are also our thoughts and sentiments. We are entirely of a single mind with him both in assessing international developments and in questions concerning the further development of our countries, which advance confidently along the road to socialism and communism.

We have gathered here today to welcome heartily the emissaries of the fraternal Polish people, the leaders of socialist Poland.

This meeting of our dear Polish guests with you, the citizens of Leningrad, has special significance. Leningrad was the cradle of the Great October Socialist Revolution. It was in Leningrad that the first historic decrees of the young Soviet state were adopted, which have a tremendous impact not only on the peoples of the Soviet Union, but also on Poland, on all mankind.

In November 1917 the Soviet Government published the Declaration of Rights of the Peoples of Russia, which proclaimed the right of the peoples of Russia to free self-determination. The declaration applied equally to the Polish people as well.

In August 1918 the Soviet Government reaffirmed by special decree the inalienable right of the Polish people to independent statehood. This historic act signed by Lenin, said: "All treaties and agreements concluded by the government of the former Russian empire ... concerning partitions of Poland are hereby r e v o k e d for all time, because they contradict the principle of the self-determination of nations and the revolutionary sense of justice of the Russian people, which recognizes the inalienable right of the Polish people to independence and unity."

Fifteen treaties by which tsarism sought to perpetuate the division of Poland were annulled at that time. It was then that enduring foundations were laid for the re-emergence of Polish statehood.

As far back as the eve of the first Russian revolution the great Lenin pointed out that the Polish proletariat would win its freedom only in close alliance with the Russian working class. In his article, "The National Question in Our Programme," he stressed that only the most complete and closest alliance with the Russian proletariat would meet the requirements of the then current political struggle against autocracy and that only such an alliance would guarantee the full political and economic liberation of the working people of Poland. Lenin repeatedly elaborated upon this proposition later too, particularly when in the summer of 1912 he moved from Paris to Poland to be nearer to Russia and guide the revolution which was then maturing there.

The Polish working people have seen by their own experience how very right Lenin had been, who saw the guarantee of complete liberation for the Polish people in a close alliance of the Polish working people with the Russian working class. Under the impact of the Great October Socialist Revolution, the working people of Poland, headed by the working class, waged a stubborn struggle for a democratic Polish state. Soviets of Workers' Deputies sprang up in Warsaw, Lodz, the Dombrowski coal basin and other districts of Poland after Soviet Russia's example.

However, the forces of democracy in Poland were then still weak and the working class insufficiently organized. The Polish bourgeoisie and landlords took advantage of this and with the support of the imperialist countries seized power and established their own reactionary dictatorship.

But no brutalities, no exertions of the Polish reactionaries, could destroy what the Great October Socialist Revolution had given Poland's working people. It inspired the Polish working class to wage a determined revolutionary struggle; it furnished experience, and showed the proper road to liberation.

Comrades, forty-one years ago the salvoes of the *Aurora* resounded here, in Leningrad. They served the entire Russian proletariat as a signal to storm the bourgeois-landlord system. They were heard throughout the world by our class brothers, who perceived the beginning of the end of capitalist slavery—the resplendent dawn of the new life— in the triumph of Russia's working people.

Here, on the banks of the Neva, Soviet power was born. Here the dictatorship of the proletariat triumphed and took root for the first time in world history. In the years of Soviet power our country developed into a mighty socialist Power, blazing the trail to a new world—the world of socialism. Today, a group of countries is already following this path. They are benefiting extensively by the accumulated experience, and concurrently contribute much of their own to socialist construction. But for all the great abundance and diversity of political forms emerging in the transition from capitalism to socialism, their substance, as Marx and Lenin had foreseen, is inevitably one— the dictatorship of the proletariat. This dictatorship alone can provide working-class political guidance to society. It alone can ensure the steady advance of productive forces, the burgeoning of real democracy for all working people and a rise of living standards for the masses.

It is only natural that contemporary revisionists concentrate their main attacks against the dictatorship of the proletariat, of which the alliance of the working class and the peasantry under the leadership of the working class is the supreme principle. They want thereby to strike at the very heart of the working-class liberation movement. With this in view, they vilify the dictatorship of the proletariat in every possible way and contrast it with democracy. To hear them, it appears that the dictatorship of the proletariat is ultra-violence, suppression of all and every freedom, oppression of the individual.

The dictatorship of the proletariat, it is true, involves a certain amount of compulsion. But who is that compulsion aimed at? It is aimed at those who have for centuries oppressed the people, who are reluctant to abandon their privilege of plundering the toiler, who advocate restoration of the old régime. Can the working people really allow these idlers to recapture the mills and factories, the best fields and forestlands, and to harness the people into the yoke of exploitation?

Suppressing the resistance of the exploiters is not the only, and not even the main, function of the dictatorship of the proletariat, the power of the working people. The dictatorship of the proletariat performs a tremendous organizational, educational and constructive job. This facet of the functions of the socialist state is particularly prominent today, when hundreds of millions of people participate actively in the building of socialism and communism. To the working people the dictatorship of the proletariat in all its stages provides genuine democracy, genuine popular rule.

The closer the people approach socialism, and then communism, the more broadly and fully the advantages of socialist democracy come to light. This is recognized not only by our friends abroad, but also by those of our enemies who are still able to look the truth squarely in the face.

Not infrequently, the revisionists mask their acts against the dictatorship of the proletariat with talk about the specific features of one country or another. Yet they do not, nor can they, cite a single example of successful socialist construction without the dictatorship of the proletariat. It is on the basis of proletarian dictatorship that all the countries of the socialist camp are making splendid progress in building the new life.

The experience of some countries, the Polish People's Republic among them, shows that in the new historical circumstances the functions of the dictatorship of the proletariat are adequately performed by state of people's democracy. The Polish United Workers' Party, its Central Committee headed by Comrade Gomulka, have firmly rebuffed the revisionist elements who demanded that people's democracy be supplanted as a form of proletarian dictatorship by so-called "pure" democracy. But what is "pure" democracy? Lenin said that "pure democracy" was a spurious phrase used by liberals to fool the workers. Behind a smoke-screen of high-sounding phrases about "pure democracy" and "democratic socialism" modern revisionists urge a return to bourgeois democracy which, as you know, is nothing but a dictatorship of the exploiting classes.

By preaching these views the revisionists want to disarm the working class ideologically, and to sow in its ranks the poisonous seeds of disbelief in its strength. It is not accidental that international imperialist reaction is extolling the revisionists to the skies and supporting them. The Communist and Workers' parties have firmly repelled the attacks of the modern revisionists and revealed them in their true colours as traitors to the interests of the working class. The Communist and Workers' parties will carry on their uncompromising struggle for the purity of Marxist-Leninist theory and will cement the unity of their revolutionary ranks.

Comrades, the October Revolution has aroused the millions. It has wakened them to conscious creative effort. By participating actively in the building of the new social system, the masses mature politically and spiritually at an unbelievably rapid rate.

Take our country, for example. The Soviet people display a model sense of duty and a selfless devotion to building socialism and communism. This is universally recognized. The achievements of the Soviet Union have a magnetizing appeal for working people abroad. The Soviet people have won the admiration of toilers in all countries for their creative labour, their revolutionary scope, their high sense of duty, unmatched tenacity and self-sacrifice.

The Polish people are on the crest of a creative upsurge. What they have done in their country in less than 15 years of free labour would have been impossible to achieve under capitalism even in a hundred years.

The conscious creative effort of the masses, their high devotion, is unusually strong in all the People's Democracies—the Chinese People's Republic, Czechoslovakia, Bulgaria, Rumania, Hungary, the German Democratic Republic, Albania, the Mongolian People's Republic, the Korean People's Democratic Republic and the Democratic Republic of Viet-Nam. We live at a time, comrades, when for the first time in history working people in vast territories have become free creators and masters of life. Labour in a non-exploiter society elevates and transforms man.

Socialism and communism is being built by the entire mass of working people. It is the daily labour at the mills and factories, in the fields and the laboratories, that advances history and brings our countries nearer to socialism and communism.

Comrades, for centuries capitalism has sown discord and enmity among nations. Socialism breeds so powerful a force as fraternal international friendship. The fraternal family of peoples who have taken the road of socialist construction, has emerged and taken strength in a very short historical time. A mighty socialist camp has emerged. The Communist and Workers' parties have had their work cut out clearing the ground for this community, rooting out feelings of national discord and mistrust, nurtured down the centuries by the exploiters.

There have been in the past many misunderstandings and much unfriendliness, and even military conflicts, between Russia and Poland. Yet, even in the past, this was not the principal feature of the relations between the peoples of our countries. Indeed, what was there to quarrel over for our peoples at the time of the tsarist autocracy? Nothing at all. They were oppressed and rightless. On the contrary, they had much in common, and chiefly the joint struggle for social liberation. We all know that the Polish working class actively supported the revolutionary struggle of the proletariat and all the working people of Russia both in the 1905 revolution and 1917. The great Lenin thought highly of the revolutionary manifestations of Warsaw and Lodz workers in 1905. The Soviet people remember very well how resolutely the working people of Poland supported the young Soviet Republic, how they fought against the Polish capitalists and landlords, who had plunged Poland into a war against Soviet Russia at the bidding of Western imperialists. The glorious "Red Regiment" formed by Polish revolutionary soldiers, greeted heartily by Lenin before departing to the front, is remembered in our country.

The Soviet people gratefully received and highly valued the mass manifestations of the Polish proletariat in support of the Soviet Union whenever the imperialists tried to obstruct the peaceful socialist development of our country and threatened it with armed provocations. For their part, the Soviet people have always enthusiastically supported the revolutionary struggle of the Polish working class, headed by the Communist Party of Poland.

During the Second World War the peoples of our countries fought together against the Nazi invaders. Crushing the fascist armies and advancing westward, the heroic Soviet Army, hand in hand with units of the Polish Army and with Polish partisans, drove the enemy out of Polish territory.

After the triumph of people's democracy in Poland relations of close friendship and fraternal co-operation have developed between our countries. Helping each other, our peoples are working confidently for their great and cherished goal—socialism and communism.

Fraternal relations between Poland and the Soviet Union, and between all the socialist countries, develop on the basis of the immortal ideas of Leninism, the principles of proletarian internationalism. The Polish and Soviet peoples know full well that if there is no friendship between Poland and the Soviet Union, it is our common enemies alone who stand to gain therefrom. I said so this spring in replying to questions put by the editors of *Trybuna Ludu*, and I say so now. The peoples of Poland and the Soviet Union realize that the closer and stronger their friendship and that of all the socialist countries, the more impregnable they will be in the face of any enemy, and the more enduring world peace will be. The alliance and friendship of Poland and the Soviet Union accords with the vital interests of our fraternal peoples, the interests of all the peoples of the socialist camp.

Our Party does its best to further and strengthen Polish-Soviet friendship. We note with deep satisfaction that the Polish United Workers' Party is giving a fitting rebuff to the attempts to sow discord and mistrust between the peoples of our countries.

In his report to the 12th Plenary Meeting of the Central Committee of the PUWP, Comrade Gomulka said that the Polish United Workers' Party "has prevented Poland from being led along a fatal path, which the revisionist 'correctors' and all enemies of socialism tried so hard to do. Their attempts to drive a wedge into the alliance and into Polish-Soviet friendship have failed."

The friendship of People's Poland and the Soviet Union is a powerful factor of peace in Europe and the entire world. In the past the imperialists made Poland a pawn in their political gambles and sought to turn her into a beach-head for an attack upon the Soviet Union. People's Poland has become a genuinely independent, sovereign state. Together with the Soviet Union and the other socialist countries it holds high the banner of peace.

Comrades, the Soviet people rejoice at the successes of socialist Poland, of her gifted and hard-working people. The gains of socialism in Poland add very greatly to the might of the entire socialist camp, the forces of peace and progress. From the bottom of their heart, all Soviet people wish Poland's working people new outstanding successes in building socialism.

This meeting with our Polish friends takes place on the eve of the 41st anniversary of the Great October Socialist Revolution. Permit me, comrades, citizens of Leningrad, on behalf of the Central Committee of the Communist Party of the Soviet Union and the Soviet Government to congratulate you on the coming holiday and to wish you fresh successes in labour and life.

We live in a remarkable time when historical development leads inevitably to the final triumph of socialism and communism throughout the world. From a dream socialism has turned in our day into a great and unconquerable world force which astonishes mankind with its magnificent victories.

Long live the great socialist camp!

Long live the fraternal Polish people!

Long live the Polish United Workers' Party and its Central Committee headed by Comrade Gomulka!

Long live Marxism-Leninism!

Long live world peace!

(N. S. Khrushchov's speech was repeatedly interrupted by prolonged applause.)

November 7, 1958

Dear Comrades and Friends,
Our dear Guests from abroad,
Ladies and Gentlemen,

We are gathered here to mark a national holiday of
the Soviet Union—the 41st anniversary of the Great October Socialist Revolution. Permit me, in the name of the
Central Committee of the Communist Party of the Soviet
Union, the Council of Ministers of the U.S.S.R., the Presidium of the Supreme Soviet of the U.S.S.R., to greet
all those assembled in this hall—representatives of the
Soviet public as well as foreign guests who have come
to celebrate the 41st anniversary of the October Revolution.

We warmly greet the representatives of the fraternal
Polish people—the delegation of the Polish People's Republic headed by Comrade Gomulka who are celebrating
with us in Moscow the anniversary of the October Socialist Revolution.

November 7 is the brightest and most joyful holiday in
the history of the Soviet people. Forty-one years ago, the
working class of Russia in alliance with the working peasants under the leadership of the Communist Party headed
by our leader and teacher Vladimir Ilyich Lenin carried
out the great revolution. The power of the bourgeoisie and

landowners was overthrown, and Soviet power, the rule of the workers and peasants, was firmly established in our country.

There has never been an event in world history that has exerted as great an influence on the destinies of nations as the October Revolution. It marked the transition from the capitalist system of exploitation to a new, socialist system. The ideas of the Great October Socialist Revolution inspire the working people of the entire world to struggle against social and national oppression, for peace, democracy and socialism.

Our country has travelled a great and glorious path in the 41 years of Soviet power. The Soviet people, rallied round the Communist Party, have built socialism, have made tremendous economic and cultural progress, have effected magnificent transformations. The standard of living of the working people is rising year by year.

The Soviet Union's achievements are well known. Comrade Mikoyan spoke of them in detail in his report yesterday.

The camp of the socialist states, which is growing and becoming stronger, is an embodiment of the ideas of the October Socialist Revolution. Today the Soviet Union, the Chinese People's Republic, Czechoslovakia, Poland, Bulgaria, Rumania, Hungary, the German Democratic Republic, Albania, the Mongolian People's Republic, the Korean People's Democratic Republic and the Democratic Republic of Viet-Nam are advancing in a united front towards the great aim—communism. The co-operation and mutual assistance between our countries are steadily gaining in strength and scope.

Even our outspoken ill-wishers, who earlier did not believe in the forces of socialism and ridiculed our plans, are now no longer able to deny the gigantic successes of the Soviet Union and all the countries of the socialist camp.

The advance in the economy of the Soviet Union and all socialist countries and the rise in the standard of living of our peoples provide conclusive proof of the advantages of socialism over capitalism. The successes of the Soviet Union and the other socialist countries strengthen the influence of the ideas of socialism on the working people of the capitalist, dependent and colonial countries.

The imperialists are afraid of the growing strength of the Soviet Union, of the world socialist camp. In speeches by many politicians and statesmen of the West and in the bourgeois press one comes more and more often across expressions of open fear that the Soviet Union is capable of economically outstripping the most highly developed capitalist countries.

We firmly believe that the time is not far distant when the Soviet Union will take first place in the world both in total output as well as per capita production, which will secure for our peoples the highest standard of living in the world.

We do not need war. Peace is indispensable for the building of communist society. The general line of our foreign policy is the line of peaceful co-existence, of establishing friendly relations among all peoples. That is why the Soviet Government is steadily striving to further improve relations with all countries and is persistently working to consolidate world peace.

The imperialists are trying hard to turn back the wheel of history, they are seeking to preserve and extend the sphere of capitalist exploitation and colonial oppression, to reimpose their yoke upon the peoples who have achieved national liberation. That is precisely why the ruling circles of the United States and some other countries are pursuing a "positions of strength" policy in international relations, and are meeting with hostility any Soviet proposal aimed at easing international tension and strengthening peace.

Such a policy, however, arouses increasing dissatisfaction among the peoples of all countries, including the American people. Surely this is borne out by the elections

724

to the Senate and the House of Representatives just held in the United States. Of course, elections are an internal affair of each state, of each people, and no one may interfere in such matters. But the American electors have already had their say. We are pleased that the people of the United States condemn the policy of "brinkmanship" and "positions of strength," carried out by the Secretary of State, Mr. Dulles, and supported by the President, Mr. Eisenhower.

The peoples of the Soviet Union are championing peace. The Soviet Government, in its relations with non-socialist countries, firmly adheres to the well-known Five Principles: mutual respect for territorial integrity and sovereignty, non-aggression, non-intervention in one another's internal affairs, equality and mutual, benefit, peaceful co-existence and economic co-operation.

The ruling circles of the United States obstinately reject all the peace efforts of the Soviet Union, they do not want peaceful co-existence among states.

And although we understand that the Republican and the Democratic parties differ little in their foreign policy, we regard the United States election returns from the viewpoint of the possibility of improving relations between our countries.

We hope that the results of the elections, which showed the dissatisfaction of the American electorate with the present foreign policy of the U.S. Administration, will lead to essential changes, to an end of the cold war and the discontinuance of the short-sighted policy of "brinkmanship."

It is high time for all to recognize that the Soviet Union, the Chinese People's Republic and all the other countries of socialism are a reality. This reality must be recognized and a policy must be pursued which takes into account the existence of the socialist countries.

In our time the forces of peace have developed and strengthened. The instigators of international conflicts and military provocations are opposed by the front of the peaceful socialist states and the other independent countries standing for peace. All the peoples are striving for the maintenance of peace and are working for it. The forces of peace, provided they are organized and vigilant, are capable of curbing the imperialist aggressors.

Comrades, we are celebrating our holiday at the time of a fresh powerful upsurge when all Soviet people are preparing worthily to meet the 21st Congress of the Communist Party of the Soviet Union, the congress of builders of communism. This congress will outline a new programme for the large-scale building of communist society, to ensure a further sharp rise in all branches of the economy and on this basis to bring about another substantial advance in the standard of living of the people.

Long live our great socialist homeland, confidently advancing towards communism!

Long live the 41st anniversary of the October Socialist Revolution, whose great ideas are inspiring all progressive mankind!

Glory to our great Soviet people!

Allow me to propose a toast to lasting peace and friendship among all the peoples of the world.

To the good health of our esteemed guests!

(*N. S. Khrushchov's speech was heard with great attention and was repeatedly greeted with hearty applause.*)

SPEECH
AT FRIENDSHIP MEETING
OF POLISH PEOPLE'S REPUBLIC
AND THE SOVIET UNION

November 10, 1958

Dear Polish Friends,

Dear Comrades,

We have gathered here today to welcome cordially our dear guests: Wladyslaw Gomulka, First Secretary of the Central Committee of the Polish United Workers' Party (*applause*), Alexander Zawadski, member of the Political Bureau of the Central Committee of the Party and Chairman of the State Council of the Polish People's Republic (*applause*), Jozef Cyrankiewicz, member of the Political Bureau and Chairman of the Council of Ministers of the Polish People's Republic (*applause*), Jerzy Morawski, member of the Political Bureau and Secretary of the Central Committee (*applause*); representatives of the parties of the People's Unity Front—Stefan Ignar, Chairman of the Chief Committee of the United Peasant Party and Vice-Chairman of the Council of Ministers (*applause*), Stanislaw Kulczynski, Chairman of the Central Committee of the Democratic Party and Vice-President of the State Council (*applause*), Edward Gierek, Secretary of the Central Committee and First Secretary of the Katowice Voivodoship Committee of the Polish United Workers' Party (*applause*), Tadeusz Galinski, Minister of Culture and Arts (*applause*), Marian Naszkowski, member of the Central Committee of the Polish United Workers' Party and

Deputy Foreign Minister (*applause*), Michalina Tatar-kówna, member of the Central Committee and First Secretary of the Lodz City Committee of the Polish United Workers' Party (*applause*), and Tadeusz Gede, member of the Central Committee of the Polish United Workers' Party and Polish Ambassador to the U.S.S.R.

The visit of the delegation of the Polish People's Republic to the Soviet Union, your tour of our country, dear friends, turned into a moving demonstration of fraternal Soviet-Polish friendship.

You visited Moscow, Leningrad, Tbilisi, Kiev and Minsk, and met workers and collective farmers, and people engaged in science and cultural work, Party and government workers. Everywhere you were received as true friends. During your tour of our country you were able to see for yourselves once more the sincere and profound fraternal feelings which the Soviet people have for the Polish people. (*Prolonged applause.*)

The roots of our people's friendship go far into the past. The ruling classes of Russia and Poland—the landed gentry and capitalists—tried hard to sow discord between our peoples, to incite mutual enmity among them. The tsarist policy of oppressing and subjugating Poland has left bitter memories among the Polish people. No less bitter are the memories of Ukrainians and Byelorussians of the dark years under the rule of Polish barons. In the past there was strife and misunderstanding, conflicts and clashes between our countries.

But against all barriers and obstacles, the great idea of friendship was making its way into the hearts of our peoples. It was born and grew stronger in the joint uprisings of the Polish and Russian peasants, it found expression in the creative friendship of the great poets of our peoples—Pushkin and Mickiewicz. It found expression in the utterances of Revolutionary Democrats. The working class, the most progressive, the most revolutionary class of our epoch, the consistent champion of the

728

concepts of internationalism and brotherhood of peoples, became the true standard-bearer of this friendship. (*Applause.*)

Soviet-Polish friendship is illumined by the immortal ideas of the great leader of the working people of the world, Vladimir Ilyich Lenin, who also conducted his titanic revolutionary work on the territory of Poland, eloquently evidenced by the places associated with the memory of Lenin in Cracow and Poronino which are sacredly revered and preserved by the working people of People's Poland. (*Applause.*)

The proletarian revolutionaries of Russia and Poland always advocated the united struggle of the Polish and Russian proletariat, realizing that the independence of Poland was impossible without the freedom of Russia. Many Polish workers, peasants and soldiers took an active part in the Great October Socialist Revolution, in the struggle against the enemies of Soviet power.

A vivid personification of collaboration in the fight of the Polish and Russian working-class movement was the outstanding revolutionary, Felix Dzerzhinsky, who was one of Lenin's closest companions in arms. (*Prolonged applause.*) The Soviet people will always remember with love and admiration this great son of the Polish people who combined a passionate love for the working people with hatred for the oppressors.

The revolutionary traditions of the Polish labour movement were inherited and continued by the glorious Communist Party of Poland, the 40th anniversary of which falls due in December, this year. (*Applause.*) In the most difficult conditions of the fascist régime established by Pilsudski's supporters, the Communist Party of Poland led the struggle of the Polish workers and peasants against the exploiters, defended the principles of proletarian internationalism, educated the mass of the working people in the spirit of utmost support for the heroic struggle of the peoples of the Soviet Union.

Our Party highly appreciates the revolutionary services of the Communist Party of Poland, its selfless struggle for the victory of the great Marxist-Leninist ideas in the Polish labour movement. In the difficult years of the Second World War, the Polish Workers' Party became the continuer of the revolutionary struggle of the Communist Party of Poland. (*Applause.*) It was the leading force of the Polish working people in the struggle for the liberation of the country from the Nazi yoke, for the victory of the people's democratic system, for radical social and economic reforms in the country.

The leading role of the Polish working class has become even greater since the closing of the rift in the labour movement in the country, a fact which was of paramount significance for the further development of People's Poland. As a result of the merger of the Polish Workers' Party and the Polish Socialist Party on the basis of the ideological and organizational principles of Marxism-Leninism, a single party of the working class was formed —the Polish United Workers' Party, which rallied the people for the accomplishment of the great tasks of building a new, socialist society. (*Prolonged applause.*)

The achievements of People's Poland are great, and all her friends rejoice sincerely in them. In place of the old, economically weak bourgeois-landlord Poland which was a pawn in the hands of the big imperialist Powers, a new, truly independent state, a People's Democracy, has been established. Poland's socialist economy is growing and the well-being and cultural standards of her people are improving.

The Polish people have regained their ancient western lands and have obtained broad access to the Baltic. For the first time in history Poland has friendly states for neighbours—the Soviet Union, the Czechoslovak Republic and the German Democratic Republic. (*Applause.*)

The achievements of People's Poland are all the more significant in that they have been secured despite grave hardships. To build a socialist society is a noble, but also a difficult and complicated task. It is only natural for difficulties to arise in the process of a radical break-up of old relations and the building of a new society, in the course of socialist construction, and mistakes are bound to be made. But we Communists, as builders of a new life, should be able to see the main, the most essential, feature in every phenomenon. And the main thing in Poland's development in the years of people's power is undeniably the big achievements in the Polish people's economic and cultural life.

Friendship and fraternal co-operation have become the foundation of our relations since the establishment of the system of people's democracy in Poland. It is known that the imperialists gambled in staking their hopes on various nationalists and revisionists. They cherished the hope of setting our countries at loggerheads and wresting People's Poland away from the socialist camp. But these insidious designs have failed ingloriously. (*Stormy applause.*)

And it could not be otherwise, comrades. The experience of the Soviet Union's relations with Poland and other socialist states offers convincing evidence that there are no issues between our countries, nor can there be any, that cannot be settled amicably. (*Applause.*)

The nearer our cherished goal, communism, the firmer becomes the co-operation of the socialist countries. With the triumph of socialist relations in the economic sphere and with the growth of communist consciousness national mistrust is being increasingly overcome and the bonds of international friendship are growing stronger. Moreover, the unity of the socialist camp is one of the basic and decisive conditions for the successful advancement of every socialist country along the road to building a new life.

Comrades, a new balance of forces has developed in the world today. The mighty socialist camp is growing and gaining in strength and nothing can arrest the peoples' advance toward socialism and communism. (*Stormy applause.*) Therefore, the attempts of the forces of reaction to prevent the building of socialism in the People's Democracies are doomed to failure.

It is high time for Messrs. Imperialists to realize that the remnants of the reactionary forces in the People's Democracies have no genuine support among the people. In all the People's Democracies the leading role of the working class has become more prominent. The labouring peasantry is in close alliance with it. The intelligentsia is working for the welfare of the people and serves them honestly.

The fact that the balance of forces in the world today is in favour of socialism reduces to hopelessness the imperialist ambitions of restoring the old order of things in the socialist countries. Only incorrigible adventurists can dream of this today. The social gains of the working people in every socialist country are guarded by the might of the entire socialist camp. (*Prolonged applause.*)

Fortunately for mankind, the course of international developments today does not depend entirely on the will of the ruling circles of the imperialist Powers. Experience shows that the international prestige of the countries of the socialist camp, and its influence on the entire flow of world history and the destinies of mankind are growing year by year. In recent years the world has time and again been spared from catastrophic explosions that threatened to touch off a new world conflagration. This has been made possible primarily by the solidarity of the socialist countries, the consistency of their peace policy, and the determination of all the peoples to uphold world peace.

Why are the political and military leaders of certain Western Powers subject to paroxysms of war hysteria? It is because big capital, the monopoly owners, need a tense international situation constantly to intensify the arms race and to enrich themselves at the expense of the working people. Therein lies the main reason for the ever new gambles which the imperialist circles, disregarding realities, undertake. They are hoping thereby to keep mankind constantly on the brink of war, to receive huge super-profits, to subjugate countries which have committed themselves to aggressive military blocs.

The imperialists have turned the German question into an abiding source of international tension. The ruling circles of West Germany are doing everything to whip up military passions against the German Democratic Republic, against the Polish People's Republic, against all the socialist countries. Speeches by Chancellor Adenauer and Defence Minister Strauss, the arming of the Bundeswehr with nuclear weapons and various military manoeuvres all bespeak a definite trend in the policy of the ruling circles of West Germany.

We wish to warn the leaders of the Federal Republic of Germany: The road followed by West Germany today is a road dangerous to peace in Europe and fatal to West Germany herself. Indeed, can realistic politicians today hope for success in a new "march to the East"? Hitler in his time also did everything to fan war hysteria, in order to prepare the ground for an attack on the Soviet Union. However, it is well known how this all ended. It is not hard to imagine the fate of those who would try to unleash new aggression against the socialist states. No speeches by Chancellor Adenauer or his Minister Strauss can change the balance of forces in favour of imperialism. To march against the East would mean marching to death for West Germany. (*Stormy applause.*)

It is high time to realize that the times when imperialists could act from "positions of strength" with impunity have gone never to return, and try as they may, the imperialists will not be able to change the balance of forces in their favour. Nor should they forget the geographical position of West Germany which—with means of warfare what they are today—would not survive a single day of modern warfare. (*Prolonged applause.*)

We do not desire another military conflict. It would be fatal to West Germany and would bring untold disaster to the peoples of other countries. The Soviet Union and the other socialist countries are doing everything to keep the adventurists who are dreaming of new wars from making a fatal step. The West German policy-makers would do well to appraise the existing situation more soberly and desist from whipping up war passions.

The Western press today says much about the Government of the Federal Republic of Germany planning to approach the Soviet Union, the United States of America, Britain and France with a proposal to call a new Four-Power meeting to settle for the Germans, and without the participation of the Germans, the question of unifying their country. But this is nothing but a continuation of the old, unrealistic policy which is contrary to common sense and devoid of legal justification. No Powers have the right to interfere in the internal affairs of the German Democratic Republic and to dictate their will to it. (*Applause.*)

We quite understand the German people's natural yearning for the restoration of their national unity. But German militarists and their American patrons are using these profound national sentiments for purposes that have nothing to do either with the reunification of Germany or with ensuring a lasting peace in Europe. West German militaristic circles are in fact following a course of deepening the cleavage of the country and preparing military adventures.

If the West German Government really wanted reunification, it would have followed the only way leading to this, the way of establishing contacts with the Government of the German Democratic Republic, the way of agreement that would suit both the German Democratic Republic and the Federal Republic of Germany.

The German question, in the sense of reunification of the two German states now in existence, can only be settled by the German people themselves along the lines of *rapprochement* between these states. The conclusion of a peace treaty with Germany is an entirely different matter which, indeed, should be settled primarily by the Four Powers which formed the anti-Hitler coalition, in co-operation with representatives of Germany. The signing of a peace treaty with Germany would help to normalize the entire situation in Germany and in Europe generally. The Soviet Union has proposed, and is proposing, that this measure should be tackled without delay.

If one is to discuss the Four Powers' undertakings with regard to Germany, one must consider the obligations springing from the Potsdam Agreement.

Let us recall the main obligations assumed by the parties to the Potsdam Agreement with regard to their policy in Germany, what course of development for Germany was determined in Potsdam.

At that time, the members of the anti-Hitler coalition assumed clear-cut and definite obligations: to extirpate German militarism, to prevent its resurgence once and for all, to do everything to prevent Germany from ever again threatening her neighbours or world peace.

The parties to the Potsdam Agreement also recognized the necessity for putting an end to German fascism, blocking its revival in Germany, and curbing all fascist activities and propaganda.

Another important integral part of the Potsdam Agreement was the commitment to liquidate the rule of the cartels, syndicates and other monopolies in the German economy, that is, forces that had brought Hitler to power and had encouraged and financed his military ventures. Such is the substance of the agreements concluded in Potsdam in 1945.

And what do we have today, more than 13 years after the Potsdam Conference?

No one can deny that the Soviet Union, on its part, has scrupulously observed all these agreements and that they have been carried out in full in the eastern part of Germany, the German Democratic Republic. Let us see how the Potsdam Agreement is being carried out in the western part of Germany, in the Federal Republic of Germany, the responsibility for whose development rests with the three Western Powers—the United States, Britain and France.

It should be openly said that militarism, far from having been eradicated, is rearing its head ever higher in West Germany. The Powers which should have fought against the resurgence of German militarism have drawn West Germany into the aggressive military bloc of NATO that they have created. They are doing everything to promote the growth of German militarism and the establishment in West Germany of a mass army equipped with the latest weapons.

By decision of the Government of the Federal Republic of Germany, and, of course, with the approval of the NATO Powers, West Germany is building an army which the German militarists envisage as stronger than the armies of Britain and France. It is, perhaps, already stronger than the French army, in view of the fact that a substantial part of the French army is maintained outside the country in the colonies, where the liberation movement against the French colonialists is at the boiling point.

The armed forces that are being re-created in West Germany are again headed by Nazi generals and admirals. The West German army is being trained in the predatory spirit of the Nazi Wehrmacht, in the spirit of *revanche* and hatred for the Soviet Union and other peaceful states.

Moreover, the German militarists—with the blessing of the Western Powers, and primarily the United States—are receiving nuclear weapons. The Federal Republic already has American rockets which can be fitted with nuclear war-heads.

Economically, West Germany is literally grasping her West European allies by the throat. It is enough to note, for the sake of comparison, that in 1957, for instance, the Federal Republic produced 24,500,000 tons of steel, as against 22,000,000 in Britain and little more than 14,000,000 in France.

West Germany is today also financially stronger than either Britain or France. Consider their gold and currency reserves, for instance. According to official figures, West Germany's reserves amounted to over $5,600 million at the end of 1957, as compared with Britain's $2,370 million and France's $775 million. All these economic resources of West Germany are being placed at the service of reviving German imperialism.

No matter which basic provisions of the Potsdam Agreement concerning the demilitarization of Germany and prevention of the resurgence of fascism we may consider, we shall inevitably arrive at the conclusion that these provisions, bearing the signatures of the United States, Britain and France, have been violated by them.

What then is left of the Potsdam Agreement?

One thing, in effect: The so-called Four-Power status of Berlin, that is, a position providing the three Western Powers—the United States, Britain and France—with the possibility of lording it in West Berlin, turning that part of the city, which is the capital of the German Democratic Republic, into a kind of state within a state and profiting by this to conduct subversive activities from West Berlin against the German Democratic Republic, the Soviet Union and the other Warsaw Treaty countries. On top of all this, they make use of the right of unrestricted communication between West Berlin and West Germany via the air space, railways, highways and waterways of the German Democratic Republic, a state which they do not even deign to recognize.

The question arises: Who stands to benefit from this situation and why have the United States, France and Britain not violated this part of the quadripartite agreement as well? The answer is clear: They have no intention of violating this part of the Potsdam Agreement. On the contrary, they cling to it, for the agreement on Berlin is advantageous to the Western Powers, and only them. The Western Powers, of course, would not be averse to perpetuating such "interallied" privileges for ever, even though they have long destroyed the legal basis for their presence in Berlin. (*Applause.*)

Is it not time for us to draw appropriate conclusions from the fact that the key items of the Potsdam Agreement concerning the maintenance of peace in Europe and, consequently, throughout the world, have been violated and that certain forces continue to nurture German militarism, strongly encouraging it in the direction in which it was pushed before the Second World War, that is, towards the East? Is it not time for us to reconsider our attitude to this part of the Potsdam Agreement and to repudiate it? (*Prolonged applause.*)

The time has obviously arrived for the signatories of the Potsdam Agreement to discard the remnants of the occupation régime in Berlin and thereby make it possible to create a normal situation in the capital of the German Democratic Republic. The Soviet Union, on its part, would hand over to the sovereign German Democratic Republic the functions in Berlin that are still exercised by Soviet agencies. This, I think, would be the correct thing to do. (*Applause.*)

Let the United States, France and Britain themselves build their relations with the German Democratic Republic, let them reach agreement with it themselves if they are interested in any questions concerning Berlin. As for the Soviet Union, we shall sacredly honour our obligations as an ally of the German Democratic Republic—obligations which stem from the Warsaw Treaty and which we have repeatedly reaffirmed to the German Democratic Republic. (*Prolonged applause.*)

If any forces of aggression attack the German Democratic Republic, which is a full-fledged member of the Warsaw Treaty, we shall regard this as an attack on the Soviet Union, on all the Warsaw Treaty countries. (*Stormy, prolonged applause.*) We shall then rise to the defence of the German Democratic Republic, and this will signify the defence of the vital security interests of the Soviet Union, of the entire socialist camp, and of the cause of world peace. (*Stormy, prolonged applause.*)

The Western Powers which, at one time, signed the Potsdam Agreement are today working to aggravate the international situation, to encourage the growing militarist tendencies of German revenge-seekers, that is, they support all that the Potsdam Agreement denounced. They have long since been guided by the aggressive North Atlantic Treaty and not by the Potsdam Agreement.

They have violated the Potsdam Agreement repeatedly and with impunity, while we remain faithful to it as if nothing had changed. We have every reason to free ourselves from such outlived obligations under the Potsdam Agreement which the Western Powers are clinging to, and to pursue a policy with regard to Berlin that would spring from the interests of the Warsaw Treaty.

The leaders of West Germany say that good relations between the Soviet Union and the Federal Republic of Germany can only be established if the Soviet Union ceases to support the German Democratic Republic and if it brings pressure to bear on it along lines required by the West. Bonn does not, apparently, desire good relations with the Soviet Union if it entertains such absurd hopes. If the Government of the Federal Republic really wants to have good relations with the Soviet Union it should abandon, once and for all, the hope that we shall cease to support the German Democratic Republic. (*Prolonged applause.*)

The Government of the Polish People's Republic has shown valuable initiative in proposing the establishment in Central Europe of a zone where atomic, hydrogen and rocket weapons would not be manufactured or stockpiled. This constructive proposal has been supported by the Governments of the Soviet Union, Czechoslovakia, the German Democratic Republic and other socialist and non-socialist countries which firmly stand for the preservation of peace. The ruling circles of West Germany, however, have turned down the Polish proposal and have taken to equipping the Bundeswehr with atomic and rocket weapons. German militarism today is more dangerous to the world than before. German militarists hope to swallow the German Democratic Republic and to take away from Poland her ancient western lands. They lay claims to the territory of Czechoslovakia and other socialist countries.

But they are playing with fire. The Oder-Neisse frontier is a frontier of peace. (*Prolonged applause.*) Any encroachment by German revenge-seekers on the German Democratic Republic would be regarded as an encroachment on the Oder-Neisse frontier, as a threat to the security of our peoples. (*Stormy applause.*)

The Polish people can rest assured that in the Soviet Union they have a reliable friend and ally in the struggle against German militarism and imperialist aggression. (*Stormy, prolonged applause.*)

I would like to say a few words about our relations with some of our neighbours. You have read the Soviet Government's statement to the Government of Iran, published several days ago. We made this statement because Iran is being increasingly drawn into the aggressive NATO bloc and because the threat has arisen lately of her territory being turned into an actual *place d'armes* of the American military.

We would not like to believe that the Iranian Government and the Shah of Iran personally would take this dangerous road. We hope that a sober appraisal of all the dangers involved for Iran in such a foreign policy will prevail, and that the Iranian leaders will not follow in the wake of outside forces to which the interests of Iranian security are really foreign.

It is well known that the Soviet Union has not threatened and does not threaten anyone. This applies in full to our neighbours, including Iran, whose independence we respect and shall continue to respect. We do not seek to maintain military bases on her territory and, indeed, we would not agree to this even if we were invited to have such bases on the territory of Iran.

One may ask: How, under these circumstances, should one regard the actions designed to turn Iran into an American spring-board, in particular through the conclusion of a new military treaty with the United States —the aims of which, by the way, those who press for the conclusion of the treaty make no effort to conceal? We regard it, and shall regard it, as an act hostile to our country, with all the attendant consequences.

No neighbour of the Soviet Union, whether Iran or any other country, would place its territory at the disposal of the aggressive NATO grouping if it had the good intention of strengthening good-neighbour co-operation with the Soviet Union. If it does take such a step, it means that it will be committing an aggressive act against the U.S.S.R.

We sincerely hope that the Iranian Government will not nullify everything good done in the recent past by both countries to adjust relations between them and will not invite calamity upon its country.

Comrades, the socialist camp is a mighty stronghold of world peace. Its peace policy, the policy of friendship and co-operation, conforms to the fundamental interests of all peoples. The source of strength and power of the socialist camp is the unity and solidarity of the countries belonging to it. (*Applause.*) Any attempts to weaken and

741

undermine this unity play into the hands of the enemies of peace and socialism.

Our enemies spare no efforts to weaken the influence of the Communist and Workers' parties among the broad masses of the working people, to undermine the international communist movement. All the attempts of imperialist reaction, however, invariably suffer shipwreck.

A most striking demonstration of the increased might of the world communist movement, of its greater unity and solidarity were the meetings of representatives of the Communist and Workers' parties held a year ago in Moscow during the celebration of the 40th anniversary of the Great October Socialist Revolution. The Declaration and the Peace Manifesto summed up in a creative way the collective experience of the Communist and Workers' parties, formulated the tasks of the communist movement in the struggle for peace, democracy and socialism at the present stage.

The most important result of the year since the November meetings has been the still greater unity of the international communist movement. Evidence of the solidarity of the world communist movement is the unanimous stand taken by all Communist and Workers' parties against present-day revisionism, which found its fullest expression in the programme of the League of Communists of Yugoslavia.

There was not a single Marxist party in the world or any sizable group within such a party which would share the anti-Marxist views set forth in the programme of the Yugoslav League of Communists or would defend the position of the Yugoslav leadership. All the revolutionary parties of the working class assessed the Yugoslav programme as revisionist and severely condemned the subversive, splitting actions of the leaders of the Yugoslav League of Communists.

I should like to stress the great significance of a number of statements by Comrade Gomulka, who pointed out that the leadership of the League of Communists of Yugoslavia, owing to its fallacious revisionist theories, is isolating Yugoslavia from the community of socialist countries and is thereby causing harm to the international labour movement, and that the attitude of the leaders of the Yugoslav League of Communists towards the camp of socialist states corresponds objectively to the wishes and aspirations of international reactionary forces, whose support for Yugoslavia is not accidental.

We fully and entirely subscribe to the assessment of Yugoslav revisionism made by Comrade Gomulka. (*Stormy applause.*)

The unanimous condemnation of revisionism by the revolutionary parties of the working class is a remarkable fact, comrades. It indicates how mature our parties have become ideologically, how great is their unity on the basis of the principles of Marxism-Leninism, what an invincible and ever-increasing force is the international communist movement. (*Stormy applause.*)

We have reiterated how highly we value the past services of the Communist Party and the people of Yugoslavia, who have made such great sacrifices in the struggle against German and Italian fascism. In that struggle our peoples fought shoulder to shoulder against a common enemy.

Unfortunately the leaders of Yugoslavia, the individuals who head the party, are backsliding from a working-class position to the position of its enemies. Therefore, one can hardly expect mutual understanding now in our relations with the League of Communists of Yugoslavia on a Party level, although we should not like to give up hope in this respect.

On a state level we shall strive to promote friendly relations with Yugoslavia, to extend trade and cultural intercourse. In the future, too, we are ready to maintain trade with Yugoslavia on a mutually profitable basis.

What does this mean? It means that we shall sell to Yugoslavia what she needs if we have such goods available for sale, and purchase from her what we need and what Yugoslavia finds it possible to sell. This is what is called trade on a mutually advantageous basis. (*Applause.*)

We stand for a broad interchange of various delegations with Yugoslavia—delegations of persons engaged in cultural activities, delegations of collective farmers, workers and others. It would be extremely beneficial, for instance, for our collective farmers to visit Yugoslavia and for Yugoslav peasants to come to our country, or for workers of the Soviet Union to be able to visit Yugoslavia and for Yugoslav workers to visit our country more often. Let the working people of our countries familiarize themselves with each other's life. Let them see that no one bears any enmity for Yugoslavia, that our peoples have only one desire—closer friendship. (*Applause.*)

After the normalization of relations with Yugoslavia, after the elimination of all extraneous elements which existed in the relations between our countries, after the clearing up of absurd accusations, quite a few positive results have been achieved both in the relations between our countries and with regard to problems of co-operation in the struggle for peace. We may note with satisfaction that on many major international issues our positions often coincide, and we hope that in the future, too, our countries will join their efforts in an active struggle for the preservation and consolidation of peace. (*Applause.*)

As for our differences on ideological problems, we shall continue to wage an irreconcilable struggle against all distortions of Marxism-Leninism. All fraternal Communist and Workers' parties are united in this. They regard revisionism as the main danger at the present stage. The struggle against revisionism is the struggle for the purity of our ideas, for the monolithic unity and solidarity of the international communist movement. (*Prolonged applause.*)

Comrades, majestic perspectives, perspectives of building a communist society are opening before us. We rejoice in the fact that the vanguard detachments of the working class, the ranks of those who are rallied under the banner of Marxism-Leninism, are multiplying. (*Prolonged applause.*)

The working class, the collective-farm peasantry, the intellectuals in the Soviet Union are confidently advancing onward to communism. (*Applause.*) The 20th Congress of the C.P.S.U. was a historic landmark on this road. Now our country is preparing for the 21st Congress of the C.P.S.U., the congress of the builders of communism. (*Applause.*) This congress will outline a programme for a further great advance in the Soviet economy, in the material and cultural standard of life of the entire Soviet people. (*Applause.*)

There is no doubt that these majestic tasks will be fulfilled with credit. The Soviet Union, within a historically short time, will overtake and forge ahead of the most highly developed capitalist countries in per capita production. This will be a great contribution to the victory of communism over capitalism, a system which is moribund. (*Stormy applause.*)

The achievements of the Soviet Union, the Chinese People's Republic, the Polish People's Republic and all the socialist countries, the radical changes in the world balance of forces in favour of socialism, instil confidence in many millions of working people in the ultimate triumph of the great ideas of Marxism-Leninism. The victorious banner of communism rises ever higher above our planet. (*Prolonged applause.*)

Allow me, on behalf of all the working people of our country, to wish the fraternal Polish people fresh successes in building a socialist Poland. (*Stormy applause.*)

Allow me to express confidence that the bonds of fraternal friendship between the peoples of the Soviet Union and the Polish People's Republic will become ever closer and stronger day by day. (*Stormy applause.*)

Long live the indestructible Soviet-Polish friendship! (*Stormy applause.*)

Long live the parties of the Polish People's Unity Front, of which the Polish United Workers' Party is the leading force! (*Stormy applause.*)

Long live the militant vanguard of the working people of the Polish People's Republic—the Polish United Workers' Party and its Central Committee headed by Comrade Gomulka! (*Stormy applause.*)

Long live the unity of the countries of the great socialist camp! (*Stormy applause.*)

Long live world peace! (*Stormy, prolonged applause All rise.*)

SPEECH
ON DEPARTURE FROM MOSCOW OF POLISH PEOPLE'S REPUBLIC DELEGATION

November 11, 1958

Dear Comrade Gomulka,
Dear Comrade Zawadski,
Dear Comrade Cyrankiewicz,
Dear Friends—members of the delegation of the Polish People's Republic,
Dear Comrades,

Today we are seeing off our guests, the delegation of the Polish People's Republic, which is returning home after a visit of friendship to our country.

The stay of our Polish friends in the Soviet Union developed into a moving demonstration of inviolable friendship and solidarity between the Soviet and Polish peoples.

The Joint Polish-Soviet Statement signed yesterday reveals the identity of our views on all questions discussed. This applies both to questions of Soviet-Polish relations, and to international problems and the tasks of the peace-loving peoples in the fight for preserving and strengthening peace. The Statement indicates that both sides are resolved to continue extending in every way the political, economic and cultural co-operation of the Soviet Union and Poland on the basis of Marxist-Leninist principles of proletarian internationalism. Together with the entire socialist camp, our peoples will continue to march in the van of progressive mankind fighting for peace and for a relaxation of international tension.

Allow me, comrades, on behalf of the Central Committee of the Communist Party of the Soviet Union, the Presidium of the Supreme Soviet of the U.S.S.R. and the Council of Ministers of the U.S.S.R., on behalf of the entire Soviet people, to thank the delegation of the Polish People's Republic heartily for the warm words addressed to the peoples of the Soviet Union and our Communist Party at numerous meetings with the working people of our country by Comrade Gomulka, Comrade Zawadski, Comrade Cyrankiewicz and other members of the delegation of the Polish People's Republic.

From the bottom of our hearts we wish fresh successes to the glorious vanguard of the Polish people—the Polish United Workers' Party and its Central Committee headed by Comrade Gomulka. We also send our best wishes to the parties of the Polish People's Unity Front—the United Peasants' Party headed by the Chairman of the Central Committee of that party, Comrade Ignar, and the Democratic Party headed by the Chairman of the Central Committee of that party, Comrade Kulczynski. Rallied round the Polish United Workers' Party, the leading party of the People's Unity Front, these parties contribute greatly to the building of the new life in Poland.

Allow me also to thank the delegation of the Polish People's Republic for inviting Soviet Party and Government leaders to visit fraternal Poland. We have accepted this kind invitation with satisfaction.

On behalf of the entire Soviet people, we ask you, dear Polish friends, to convey to the Polish people our warm and sincere greetings and our heartiest wishes of new successes in the building of socialism.

Happy journey, dear comrades!

Long live the Polish people—builder of socialism and fighter for international peace!

Long live inviolable Soviet-Polish friendship!

(N. S. Khrushchov's speech was warmly applauded.)

SOME QUESTIONS
CONCERNING INTERNATIONAL SITUATION

From Speech at Reception of Graduates
of Military Academies

November 14, 1958

Comrades,

The Communist Party and the Soviet Government, all our people, are doing everything to maintain the Armed Forces of the Soviet Union at the necessary standard and to equip them with the latest weapons. But we are not doing it to prepare our Army for any wars of conquest, as the imperialists try to insinuate. By attributing aggressive aims to the Soviet Union, our enemies betray their own ambition of organizing military campaigns against peaceful countries and gaining predatory imperialist domination over the world.

We have no aggressive aims whatsoever. The Soviet people have been brought up on the grand ideas of Marxism-Leninism, in the spirit of respect for the freedom and independence of all countries, the spirit of international friendship. We proceed from the fact that there are no unpopulated countries, and that for this reason conquering a country or territory is tantamount to enslaving its people and exploiting them and their wealth. This goes entirely against our ideology, the great teaching of Marxism-Leninism, and the policy of the Soviet Union and all the socialist countries.

We know our strength very well. The socialist camp is now strong and powerful as never before. Yet we cannot disregard the strength of the imperialist camp. The ruling circles in the imperialist countries see what formidable economic and cultural progress has been made in the Soviet Union, the Chinese People's Republic, and all the socialist countries.

The imperialists would like to halt the development of the socialist countries by means of war. They would like thereby to check or completely destroy the socialist trend in social development, so as to preserve their domination, to preserve the capitalist system.

Not to be caught by surprise, to keep the aggressive forces at arm's length from the Soviet Union and all the socialist countries, to discourage the imperialists from using war as a means of settling the ideological controversy between socialism and capitalism, we must see to it that our Armed Forces are always ready to repel the aggressor, and to rout him. (*Prolonged applause.*)

We have said before, and say now, that our Armed Forces will at no time or place ever be used for aggressive purposes, which conflict with the very nature of our socialist system. We shall never seek to settle controversial issues in international relations by means of war and shall always strive to settle them peacefully through negotiation.

Comrades, we live at the wonderful time when the scientific foresight of our great teachers, Marx and Lenin, about the triumph of socialism over moribund capitalism is coming true and the disgraceful colonial system is in the act of collapsing. The peoples in the colonial countries are emerging from centuries of colonial oppression and fighting stubbornly to become masters of their destiny, their national wealth.

The imperialists are going to all lengths to preserve their domination and keep the colonial countries in a state of dependence. They are looking for new forms of keeping the peoples of economically underdeveloped countries dependent upon them. They are building up aggressive pacts and alliances, such as NATO, the Baghdad Pact, SEATO, and others. With this object U.S. and British imperialists conclude diverse bilateral treaties and military agreements with a number of countries.

But all these pacts, blocs and agreements are nothing but an artfully camouflaged form of the same old imperialist policy of keeping these countries in complete subjection to the principal imperialist Powers under the pretext of defending them from the "communist threat," and paralyzing the struggle of their peoples for liberation from colonialists, from these dyed-in-the-wool imperialist exploiters.

The imperialists stop at nothing to appropriate the resources of the peoples of colonial and dependent countries. Aided by venal men occupying high government posts in some of the dependent countries, the imperialists try to drag these countries into their own camp so they should themselves help the imperialists in shoring up rotten and corrupt régimes and keep the peoples in the dependencies in colonial slavery. The most prominent part in this belongs to the imperialists of the United States, Britain and France.

But the peoples are carrying on their fight against imperialism and colonialism. Take the recent revolution in Iraq. Iraq was considered a staunch support for the imperialist countries in the Middle East. Yet the Iraqis managed to break out of the imperialist trap, into which their country had been lured by the reactionaries headed by a traitor king and a corrupt government obedient to the will and directives of foreign monopolists to the detriment of the interests of their country and people.

It was in this Iraq, thought by the imperialists to be a reliable Baghdad Pact bastion, that the revolutionary events broke out, which left the Baghdad Pact without Baghdad. (*Applause.*) Today Iraq is an independent republic conducting a policy of peace.

This has greatly frightened the imperialist Powers and Iraq's neighbours, who are members of aggressive imperialist blocs. The kings and rulers of these countries are trembling in their boots. And it is not communism, not the Soviet Union, which has put fear into them. It is their own people whom they fear. In each of these countries each king and ruler now imagines events that occurred in Iraq. For this reason they fear and tremble before their people and rush from extreme to extreme, soliciting support for their tottering thrones and corrupt cliques. It is not in their own people that they seek support. They make no effort to get a better understanding of their people's needs, to satisfy their wishes, to give them democratic freedoms and an opportunity of stamping out social injustice, to find better forms of government, and to improve social conditions. The kings and rulers seek support in those who install colonial régimes, who oppress and plunder the peoples, who are intent on playing the part of modern international policeman.

The United States and Britain willingly assume the functions of international policeman. During the revolutionary developments in Iraq they sent their troops to the Lebanon, and to Jordan. Their agents roam about in other countries, offering their police services at what would appear a trifling price. But in reality the price of their services turns out to be very high.

At present the rulers of some capitalist countries agree to unequal treaties with the United States. But to conceal this in some way, they claim that these treaties are allegedly defensive and a safeguard against the Soviet threat, although it is common knowledge that the Soviet Union has never threatened anyone, and does not threaten anyone now. Our enemies harp on some Soviet "threat," while the kings and rulers of certain states have something else in mind. What they fear is their own peoples, and they want the United States to back them, to protect them from the righteous wrath of the people.

U.S. ruling circles undertake police functions against the peoples of many countries where poverty reigns and millions die of starvation and disease as a result of colonial domination. These peoples wage a gallant struggle for freedom, for their rights, for a better life. And no police force—neither internal, nor external—will save the kings and rulers who do not heed the interests of their countries, but seek the support of external imperialist forces.

In hammering together their military blocs, the imperialists do not conceal their aggressive designs. Generals in countries that are party to these aggressive blocs often make provocative statements against the peaceful nations. Recently, Field Marshal Montgomery, known for his inflammatory statements and attacks upon the Soviet Union, retired from the post of Deputy Supreme Commander of NATO Armed Forces in Europe. Now he has been replaced by another Englishman, General Gale. No sooner had he assumed his duties than he adopted the methods of his predecessor and made a provocative speech. He bragged brazenly about the possibilities of military adventures against the Soviet Union and other peaceful countries. Among other things, he extolled in every way the modern means of communication and the air power of the NATO countries. In the past, Gale declared, it took eight hours to connect Paris and Oslo, whereas now it takes just a few seconds. In the past the Western armed forces had just so many airfields, he said, whereas now they have so and so many bases. General Gale advertised the armed forces of the North Atlantic bloc in every way.

I should like to say in this connection that the sabre-rattling speeches of this general are inept and naive. He obviously lacks wisdom in understanding the contemporary situation and making a sober estimate of the balance of forces that has taken shape in the latest period.

With modern means of annihilation what they are, when there are atomic and hydrogen weapons, and intercontinental ballistic missiles, and winged rockets, and submarines armed with ballistic and winged missiles, it matters little that NATO forces can connect Paris and Oslo in a few seconds. Today, one only needs to press a button to blow up not only airfields and means of communication of diverse headquarters, but to lay waste entire cities, and entire countries. Such is the tremendous destructive force of modern man-made weapons.

We have said repeatedly that it is best to cease these inflammatory speeches, which cause alarm and fear in people. It would be far more sensible to work for a settlement of controversial issues by negotiation, barring threats, let alone the use of weapons, so that people could live peacefully and enjoy the fruits of their labour.

But statesmen of the more aggressive imperialist groups carry on their notorious policy "from positions of strength." Recently Mr. Dulles declared again in a speech that the Western Powers were prepared to use armed force to retain control of West Berlin.

The Soviet Government is preparing an appropriate document concerning the status of Berlin. We intend to approach the countries which participated in the war against Hitler Germany and fascist Italy with certain proposals, of which I have already spoken at the meeting of Polish-Soviet friendship.

As for Mr. Dulles' attempts to intimidate us, we can say categorically that threats and intimidations carry no weight with us, and all the more so since the Soviet Union, as everybody knows, has the means to bring any aggressor to his senses. (*Stormy applause.*)

Speaking of Berlin, we do not say that we shall go to war against the West. There was nothing of the kind in our speeches. We never said anything of the kind. But we did say, and we say now, that if the aggressors attack the Soviet Union, the socialist countries, they will encounter a crushing rebuff. (*Prolonged applause.*)

Mr. Dulles likes to refer to God in his speeches. If he is really a pious man, we should recommend under the circumstances that he go to church and pray that God give him, a man in a high post, the patience and intelligence to get his proper bearings in the international situation and not to abuse his standing, not to frighten people, but to strive for a **sensible** settlement of controversial issues without resort to threats of war. (*Applause.*)

High-ranking statesmen such as Mr. Dulles must not liken themselves to a duellist who reaches instantly for his sword or pistol in an argument. They would do well to bear in mind that the partner whom they want to attack, apparently has the same, and perhaps an even more powerful and dangerous weapon. (*Prolonged applause.*)

They say that before making important decisions, the ancient Romans were in the habit of taking a cold shower. Perhaps this should also be recommended to some excessively zealous proponents of the policy of "brinkmanship."

Today, when there are modern weapons of mass annihilation, methods of intimidation are absolutely inadmissible. With the modern intercontinental ballistic missiles and medium- and short-range rockets there is no country on Earth and, what is more, no corner of the globe, which would be safe if a third world war were to break out. Today everybody knows what destructive and disastrous consequences an atomic war can bring about.

While encircling the Soviet Union with their military bases, the American imperialists like to use the language of chess players. They often say that they want to check us, that is, to put us in a difficult position. But it must be borne in mind that if one side wants to check, the other side might, for its part, also declare check, and even checkmate. (*Stormy applause.*)

In our day one cannot indulge in blackmail and intimidation with impunity as the imperialists like to do.

The Soviet Union, all the socialist countries, for their part, are doing everything to secure world peace.

Comrades, the Theses on Control Figures for the Economic Development of the Soviet Union for 1959-65 testify to the formidable achievements and the grand prospects our country faces in the future. We need no war. We need peace. Nor is it our country alone that needs peace. The peoples of all the world are vitally interested in preserving and consolidating peace. We shall compete peacefully with capitalism in the economic sphere, where our controversy will be decided through economic development rather than atomic and hydrogen weapons. Naturally, the ideological, the class struggle will continue. But the socialist countries have no wish whatsoever to foist their ideology on other countries by force of arms.

Some spokesmen of the American capitalists say that the word "competition" should not be used and that it should be replaced by the term: economic collaboration. We have no objections to that. We stand for economic collaboration on mutually beneficial terms. The main thing is to banish war as a means of solving controversial questions, to give the peoples a chance to choose their path of development by themselves.

Our seven-year plan has set grand tasks. The time is not far distant when we shall catch up the United States in per capita production of key industrial items. Our country will achieve the highest living standard and have the world's shortest working day.

To use a figure of speech, we are putting everything projected in our seven-year plan on the scales. Let the capitalists give the working people all that has been, and soon will be, achieved in the socialist countries. But the capitalist system cannot give the working people, the whole nation, what the socialist system can give.

We want the people to choose for themselves what suits them best, what system accords with the fundamental interests of the toilers and what system gives some the opportunity of enriching themselves by exploiting and plundering others. We are sure that the peoples will make the right choice. All peoples will choose the path charted by Marxism-Leninism. (*Stormy applause.*)

The future is with us, with socialism, with communism! We have created all the conditions we need to advance with giant strides along the road shown us by Marx and Lenin—the road to communism. And no hostile forces will stop our advance! (*Stormy, prolonged applause. All rise.*)

PROPOSALS OF THE SOVIET GOVERNMENT
ON THE BERLIN QUESTION

Press Conference in Kremlin Held by N. S. Khrushchov, Chairman of the U.S.S.R. Council of Ministers

November 27, 1958

A. A. Gromyko: Allow me to declare the press conference open. N. S. Khrushchov, Chairman of the Council
of Ministers of the U.S.S.R., has the floor.

Khrushchov: I asked the Minister of Foreign Affairs of
the U.S.S.R., before handing over for publication the texts
of our Notes on the Berlin question—which were forwarded earlier today to the Governments of the United States
of America, Britain, France, the German Democratic Republic and the Federal Republic of Germany—to acquaint
the correspondents with these documents so that, after
reading the Soviet Government's Notes, they could prepare the questions they would like to put.

P. Naumov, "Pravda": Why has the Soviet Government
chosen this particular moment to suggest the ending of
the occupation status of Berlin? What is the purpose of
the Soviet Government's step towards changing the status
of West Berlin?

Khrushchov: I shall try to answer this question. You in-
quire why the question of ending the occupation status
of Berlin has arisen, and why it has become necessary to
settle this question at this particular time? This is explained by the particular relations which have developed
between the Great Powers or, as the press would say,
between the West and the East.

We have taken many steps towards relieving the tension in international relations, paving the way for a *détente*, for developing normal relations between states, ensuring peaceful co-existence and solving whatever differences may arise by peaceful means, without allowing matters to lead to conflict. We have undertaken no few measures to find methods of approach to this problem, that is to say, towards the establishment of a normal situation throughout the world and, above all, in Europe, towards ensuring understanding and peace among the states which fought against Nazi Germany. And enough time—more than 13 years—has elapsed since the war.

The obstacle to the conclusion of a peace treaty with Germany, as the representatives of the Western Powers explain and upon which West Germany particularly insists, is their unwillingness to recognize reality. And the actual reality is that there are two German states in existence—the Federal Republic of Germany, which bases its existence on the principle of private capitalist ownership, and the German Democratic Republic, which is growing and developing on a socialist basis and moving in the direction of socialism.

If we accept this reasoning which is often regarded in the West as valid, then it is necessary to perpetuate this situation. Indeed, the German Democratic Republic would hardly be able to persuade Herr Adenauer and his Government that West Germany should adopt a socialist trend in her state activity. That would, of course, be desirable both for the Germans of the German Democratic Republic and for many of the Germans in West Germany, as well as for all progressive mankind, and we, as Communists, would welcome this very much.

But to think that Herr Adenauer and the ruling circles of West Germany will agree to it would mean indulging in wishful thinking.

On the other hand, certain circles in West Germany and, to my regret, Chancellor Adenauer and others, do indulge in this sort of wishful thinking, as they are hoping, for some reason or other, to get the German Democratic Republic to renounce its socialist system and to adopt a capitalist system. This, they say, would be the basis for the "reunification" of Germany, that is to say, for the monopoly circles of West Germany to absorb the German Democratic Republic and thus create a united Germany on the same social basis prevailing in West Germany. And only after this will it become possible, in their opinion, to conclude a peace treaty. Are these hopes realistic? Of course not. They must be described as fantastic, since the working people of the German Democratic Republic will never agree to give up their social and political gains in favour of exploiters and monopolists.

So what is to be done?

One must proceed from the real facts. There exists a divided Berlin where the occupation régime is still maintained. The war was ended more than 13 years ago. I feel that every normal person finds such a situation abnormal. It is necessary, therefore, to find a solution that will end this abnormality, because the present existence of the occupation régime serves no positive purpose at all. The perpetuation of such a situation would be to the advantage only of a party pursuing aggressive aims.

West Berlin is a convenient place for the Western Powers to conduct an aggressive policy against the German Democratic Republic, and against the Soviet Union and other countries of the socialist camp. In view of a definite policy of the Western Powers to whip up revengeful sentiments in West Germany and to encourage the revival of reactionary fascist organizations and forces there, West Berlin has been turned into a kind of cancerous tumour. And if it is not eliminated this threatens to become a danger that may lead to quite undesirable consequences. It is precisely because of this that we have decided to perform a surgical operation, i.e., to terminate the occupation status of Berlin and to create conditions that will help to normalize relations between the Great Powers of the former anti-Hitler coalition. We wish to establish a normal atmosphere, normal conditions, in which the relations between our countries will become what they were during the war against Hitler Germany.

We are convinced that all peoples who stand for ending the cold war, for establishing normal conditions in the mutual relations between countries, for ensuring the peaceful co-existence of countries, irrespective of their systems and for ruling out friction and conflicts between countries—all these people will welcome the Soviet Union's proposals for the solution of the Berlin problem.

At the same time, we realize perfectly well that certain circles who are in favour of continuing the cold war, stand for utilizing West Berlin as a hotbed of discord for kindling a hot war. These circles will naturally be displeased with our peace proposals and will oppose them. But we are convinced that such people constitute a minority in the world. The overwhelming majority of people want peace in the world and therefore we count on the support of these people.

H. Shapiro, United Press International: Would it be correct to infer from the Soviet Note that for half a year the Soviet Union would not take any steps changing the régime existing in Berlin at the present time?

Khrushchov: I think that you are right in your conclusion that in the course of the period announced, that is to say, for six months, we shall not alter the conditions which have already taken shape in Berlin, although we regard them as abnormal. But we should like to eliminate even these abnormal conditions in a normal way, that is to say, by means of agreement. In eliminating the abnormal situation we do not wish to worsen in any way the relations between the peoples. By means of an agreement we wish to create normal conditions which would help to promote a friendly atmosphere in the relations among all states.

I am saying this, naturally, with one reservation: Throughout the period stated, we shall observe the norms established by the occupation régime, on condition that other countries do not take provocative steps endangering the cause of peace.

I believe there is nothing left to say on this question.

K. Sarneko, Agence France-Presse: Berlin is known to be the capital of the German Democratic Republic. Why then, in spite of this fact, is it proposed to give the western part of Berlin the status of a free and demilitarized city?

Khrushchov: The question is put correctly. Indeed, if we are to proceed from the provisions which stem from the Potsdam Agreement, it is clear to everyone that Berlin is situated within the territory of that part of Germany where the German Democratic Republic has been created and is developing. Therefore the most correct decision would be one in accordance with which, the western part of Berlin, now actually torn away from the German Democratic Republic, would be reunified with its eastern part. Then the city of Berlin would become a single entity within the composition of the state on whose soil it is situated.

Thirteen years have elapsed since the end of the war and the signing of the Potsdam Agreement. During this time different directions have been taken in the economic development and in the state systems of West Berlin and of East Berlin, and of the German Democratic Republic as a whole. If liquids of entirely different composition are mixed in one vessel, then, as chemists say, a certain reaction takes place. But we want the Berlin problem to be solved on a basis that will not cause a turbulent reaction.

We want to approach the solution of this question taking into consideration the actual conditions that exist. And the best, most realistic approach to the solution of the Berlin problem is to recognize the fact that there exist two German states and to recognize the different systems existing within these states. In view of this it would be best to establish for the western part of Berlin the status of a free city with its own government and with its own social and governmental systems.

We believe that in the present situation, only on the basis of such a realistic approach is it possible to find a correct solution of the Berlin problem and painlessly to remove the cancerous tumour into which West Berlin has now been converted. We wish to provide normal conditions for the solution of this problem, so that people residing in West Berlin and having different views and convictions, should not be forced against their will to accept a system which they do not like.

We greatly appreciate the position of the German Democratic Republic, the Government of which has understood our proposals correctly and supports them. We highly value such a position because it is evidence of the deep understanding by the Government of the German Democratic Republic of the interests of strengthening peace and reunifying their country. The Government of the German Democratic Republic supports this measure with regard to West Berlin in the interests of ensuring peace and solving the German problem, in the hope that this step may set a good precedent for solving other outstanding problems as well. I believe that all who support the interests of peace will understand this step correctly and approve it. This step may help to solve the questions involved in the signing of a peace treaty with Germany, in establishing contacts between the two German states— the German Democratic Republic and the Federal Republic of Germany.

M. Gerasimov, TASS: The Western press claims that the steps envisaged by the Soviet Government for eliminating the vestiges of the occupation régime in Berlin might aggravate the economic position of the city and its residents. Are there any grounds for such assertions?

Khrushchov: In my opinion our proposals contain the

763

answer to this question. We have stated that the Soviet Union, by the orders it places, will ensure that West Berlin's industrial enterprises operate at full capacity. The Soviet Union also undertakes to fully supply West Berlin with food. Naturally, we intend to do both these things on a commercial basis. I think that no one questions the possibilities at the disposal of the Soviet Union. West Berlin workers and employers can engage in activities useful to the Berlin population. Far from resulting in a deterioration of the standard of living, this will ensure a higher level of employment and provide the conditions for raising the standard of living.

Thus, should anyone be in doubt or uneasy about this matter, it must be said that these doubts have no grounds whatsoever.

V. Kudryavtsev, "Izvestia": How is one to interpret the statements of certain political leaders of the Federal Republic of Germany insisting on the preservation of the existing situation in Berlin?

Khrushchov: I think I have already partly replied to this question. The political leaders and the statesmen who are insisting on maintaining the old status of Berlin are also insisting on maintaining the abnormal conditions which have arisen in Europe and in the rest of the world. There is tension in international relations at the present time. To insist on retaining the source of this tension means perpetuating it, rather than eliminating it. However, all tension in relations can generate over-tension and this, in view of the present development of armaments, may entail rather grievous consequences for the human race.

It is necessary, therefore, to stamp out the source of tension and to create normal conditions so that people may sleep undisturbed without the danger of an outbreak of a new war involving atomic and hydrogen weapons hanging over them. One may legitimately question the sanity of those who insist on the preservation of an abnormal situation.

V. Buist, Reuters: What guarantees will the Soviet Government give with respect to West Berlin as a free city? Will there be any change in the Soviet Government's policy on Berlin should West Germany give up her rearmament programme?

Khrushchov: The statements of the Soviet Government and all of our documents provide a full guarantee in this respect. We shall do everything to safeguard and support the free city and ensure non-interference in its internal affairs, so that it can develop in keeping with the wishes of its population.

Should other countries recognize this situation or should they agree to sign a joint document and, if necessary, to have this recorded in a resolution of the United Nations, we would be willing to do so.

You ask whether there will be any change in the Soviet Government's policy on Berlin should West Germany give up her rearmament programme? No, there will be none. It must be borne in mind that Germany is not supposed to be armed under the Potsdam Agreement. Therefore one cannot regard West Germany's renunciation of her rearmament programme as being a concession for a concession. These are two different things and of different value. Should West Germany declare that she will not arm herself, with the occupation régime of Berlin still maintained, the source of tension and conflict will not be stamped out, but it will remain as before. It is necessary, therefore, to do away with this abnormal situation. It would be very wise if West Germany did not arm herself, and it would be still wiser if the other states with forces in East and West Germany withdrew their troops, which we have suggested repeatedly. The ending of the occupation régime in Berlin and the establishment of a free city in the western part of Berlin would contribute to solving the problem of withdrawing the troops from Germany and would also be helpful in solving the problem of disarmament.

H. Leonhardt, ADN (German Democratic Republic): What steps and measures would be desirable, in your judgement, to ensure that changes in the status of Berlin could be made normally and without any difficulties?

Khrushchov: We desire that these measures involve no difficulties. If all the states whom we are addressing were to reply to our proposals by welcoming them and stating their willingness to meet, if necessary, to sign appropriate documents, that would be most reasonable. I am convinced that such a position would be welcomed by all people who stand for safeguarding world peace. We do not expect acclaim, but we do believe that our proposal will be properly understood and received as one corresponding to the interests of international peace and security.

The Berlin question will take time to settle, and for this reason we have fixed a time limit of six months in which to think over carefully every aspect of this question, and to solve it radically and eliminate this seat of danger.

C. Kiss, I. Szabo and I. Kulcsàr, correspondents of the Hungarian Telegraph Agency, the newspaper "Népszabadság" and the Hungarian Radio: What steps does the Soviet Government propose to take should the Western Powers decline to accept a free-city status for Berlin?

Khrushchov: It would be highly undesirable if the governments concerned whom we are addressing were to disagree with our proposals. But even if things did take such an unwelcome turn, that would not stop us. When the time limit expires, we shall carry into effect our proposals as stated in our documents. I am not going to enlarge on the reasons why we have taken this decision, since these have been set out in great detail in the documents of the Soviet Government.

B. Nielsen-Stokkeby, DPA Agency (Federal Republic of Germany): What will the Soviet Government's position be should the Government of the United States decline the proposal for a free-city status for Berlin and should it also refuse to withdraw its troops from Berlin or to hold any talks with the Government of the German Democratic Republic?

Khrushchov: If the United States rejects our proposal, we would certainly regret it. But this, as I have said, would not stop us from carrying out our proposals. We have no other way out. When the Western Powers, that is to say, the United States, Britain and France, violated the most important provisions of the Potsdam Agreement with respect to German demilitarization and began to arm the Federal Republic of Germany, we protested against it. But our protests passed unheeded and the process of reviving militarism in West Germany goes on. Therefore, if our proposal for West Berlin is not accepted, we shall have to do just what the Western Powers did when they cast aside the commitments they had assumed at Potsdam and other obligations resulting from the defeat of Nazi Germany.

S. Russel, "Daily Worker" (Britain): In view of the fact that various spy organizations and radio stations carrying on subversive activity in West Berlin provide employment for many people, what does the Soviet Government propose to do to prevent these people from becoming unemployed? (*Laughter.*)

Khrushchov: Evidently, the only thing to recommend to these people in this case is to change their trade (*laughter*), that is, to stop lying and spying and get down to work which is useful to the peoples. And if some of them still remain unemployed, I can offer them no sympathy. (*Animation in the hall.*)

M. Tatu, "Le Monde" (France): Mr. Chairman, you have said that West Berlin belongs to the German Democratic Republic. Does this mean that, in the opinion of the Soviet Government, this status of West Berlin will be temporary and at a later stage the Soviet Government will propose the inclusion of West Berlin in the German Democratic Republic?

Khrushchov: I have understood your question and shall give you my answer. No, we do not consider that this is temporary recognition or temporary sacrifice on the part of the German Democratic Republic. We believe that the free-city status of West Berlin will continue as long as the citizens of the free city of Berlin so desire it—that is to say, they will establish the order they may choose.

H. Schewe, "Die Welt" (West Germany): If West Berlin is given the status of a free city, will a corridor be provided in that case for access to the city from West Germany, such as the one which was once provided for the free city of Danzig?

Khrushchov: These are details about which it is difficult for me to speak at present. But I think that the free city of Berlin certainly should be given a guarantee of free communication, both in the eastern and western directions. This is provided for in our proposals.

M. Frankel, "New York Times": The Soviet Government's Note to the U.S. Government states that if the proposals put forward in the document should not be acceptable to the U.S. Government, there would remain no subject for negotiations on the Berlin problem between the former occupying Powers. Does this mean that if the Government of the United States disagrees with the specific proposals put forward in the Soviet document, the Soviet Government will not be interested in considering any other proposals on the Berlin question?

Khrushchov: You see, it depends on exactly what the United States will not be in agreement with. If it rejects as a whole the question posed in our document, then indeed there will remain no subject for talks about the Berlin question. If, however, the need arises to specify and discuss our proposals, that, in my opinion, is quite permissible and even necessary. For this reason we put this question, not in the nature of an ultimatum, but suggest a six-month time limit for a comprehensive discussion on it, for meetings with representatives of Western

Powers, to discuss the Soviet Government's proposals if the Western Powers display readiness to discuss this question.

J. Steinmayr, "Süddeutsche Zeitung" (West Germany): It has been said that the Soviet proposals regarding Berlin are planned on a long-term basis. Are they envisaged approximately for the period of the existence of the two German states?

Khrushchov: If the two German states agree on reunification, this in itself obviously will settle the question of the discontinuation of the existence of the free city, because Germany would be united and by the will of the German people Berlin would obviously become the capital of the single German state.

T. Lambert, "New York Herald Tribune": Should the Soviet Note be regarded as a denunciation of the Potsdam Agreement?

Khrushchov: And do you believe the Potsdam Agreement is being observed now? (*Laughter.*)

Lambert: Some people believe that it is. (*Animation in the hall.*)

Khrushchov: The Governments of the United States, Britain and France have grossly violated the Potsdam Agreement and sabotaged its fulfilment. At the same time they cling to one part of this agreement to prolong somehow the occupation of Berlin. Other participants in the war against Hitler Germany consider that by having sabotaged the observance of a number of the major provisions of the Potsdam Agreement, the Western Powers have forfeited the right to stay in Berlin. As you know, we adhere to this point of view.

Khrushchov (addressing the correspondents):

Have you any other questions you wish me to answer? No? I hope that I have been able to satisfy the requests of the correspondents present. I should like the Soviet Government's step with regard to Berlin to be understood correctly. It has already been said before that this step is aimed at eliminating a source of tension, at ensuring a world *détente*, and providing normal conditions for peaceful co-existence and competition. This is an interesting sphere offering wide scope for activities for the benefit of the peoples. It is this aim that has been pursued by the Soviet Government in putting forward its proposals on the Berlin question. I urge you to contribute to this noble cause.

I have read today the speech of U.S. Vice-President Nixon, in London. For the first time, perhaps, I can say that I agree with the concluding part of his speech which mentioned peaceful competition. This is a rare event. In the closing of his London speech, Mr. Nixon stated that we must at last pass over to economic competition. He said: Let our main aim be, "not the defeat of communism, but the victory of plenty over want, of health over disease, of freedom over tyranny."

I welcome this statement. If Mr. Nixon adopts such a tone in his speeches in future and if other statesmen of the United States, Britain, France and West Germany follow suit, we shall welcome it.

One cannot help noting the new ring in the voice of Mr. Nixon, the final portion of whose speech in this case did not breathe fall-out from the fission of atomic explosions with which the peoples are threatened. We are against the arms race, against the threat of a new war. We stand for peaceful competition in the economic sphere. Let us compete on such a basis—who will beat whom?

Mr. Nixon speaks about a readiness to compete in the peaceful sphere to see who will ensure a higher standard of living for the people, who will provide the people with better conditions for enjoying the benefits of culture, who will guarantee more freedoms for the people. He expresses a readiness to compete in providing better conditions in order to "eliminate tyranny." We differ with Mr. Nixon with regard to our conception of tyranny: What he regards as freedom for the rich to exploit the poor, we regard as

770

tyranny; we forbid exploitation but he regards our measures against exploiters as tyranny. These are different conceptions.

Let there even be different interpretations of some conceptions and terms. What is important is that our efforts should be directed towards peaceful competition.

In conclusion Khrushchov thanked the correspondents for their attention and said good-bye.

Pravda, November 28, 1958

Hans Ulrich Kempski, chief correspondent of the West German *Süddeutsche Zeitung,* requested N. S. Khrushchov to reply to a number of questions. Below are published N. S. Khrushchov's replies to the correspondent's questions.

Question: Could you describe in greater detail the status of the free city of West Berlin?

Answer: The Soviet Government's proposals for doing away with the vestiges of the occupation régime in Berlin and for turning West Berlin into an independent political entity—a demilitarized free city—give one an idea of what West Berlin would be like. In our view West Berlin must be a free city in whose economic and political life no country, including the existing German states, would be able to interfere. The free city of West Berlin will have its own constitution, based on democratic principles. The constitution should guarantee all the citizens of West Berlin, regardless of political or religious convictions, the fundamental human rights and principal freedoms, including freedom of speech and of the press, freedom of assembly and of association, and freedom of conscience. Legislative power will be vested in a freely elected Parliament, and executive power in the government appointed by the Parliament. The city will also have its own independent judicature.

As regards the economic aspect, the free city of West Berlin will be a single entity with its own budget, its bank, currency circulation and taxation system. The revenues will all go to the city budget, and will not be pumped out of West Berlin taxpayers' pockets for the military preparations of the Federal Republic of Germany and the upkeep of foreign occupation troops in West Berlin. Given appropriate agreements, the industrial output of the West Berlin undertakings would be exported both to Federal Republic of Germany and the German Democratic Republic, as well as to all other countries with which the free city establishes business contacts, without any restrictions. The stability and advancement of the city's economy also would be ensured by the development of all-round, mutually beneficial economic relations with the countries of the East and West. The Soviet Union, on its part, is ready to provide the industry of the free city with orders and raw materials, thereby ensuring full employment for the population and a sound, well-balanced economy.

The Soviet Government proposes that West Berlin be demilitarized and have no foreign armed forces on its territory. It goes without saying that the free city will have the necessary police formations to maintain law and order in the city. Some advocates of perpetuating the occupation regime in Berlin are now trying to assert that if the troops of the three Western Powers leave the city, West Berlin, so they allege, will be deprived of all protection. We are confident that the opposite is the case: precisely the absence of American tanks and British guns in the streets of West Berlin, and its transformation into a free city, will create an atmosphere of tranquility and will guarantee the appropriate security. It is hardly possible to imagine better guarantees for the security of West Berlin than the commitments of the four Great Powers and the two German states.

These commitment-guarantees may, if necessary, be recorded with the United Nations. The Soviet Union and the German Democratic Republic are ready to take part in these guarantees with a view to observing the status of the free city. Only the Western Powers are still refusing to do so.

It is appropriate to ask: Where would the threat to the status of the future free city come from—the East or West? In this connection one cannot fail to note the absurdity of some statements about mythical plans of the German Democratic Republic to seize West Berlin. Is it not clear that if such plans actually existed, the Soviet Union, as an ally of the German Democratic Republic under the Warsaw Treaty, would not be advancing a proposal to grant West Berlin the status of a free city and would not be expressing its readiness to take part in guaranteeing its security? Moreover, for the sake of easing tension in Germany and Europe, the German Democratic Republic is making no small sacrifice by agreeing to the existence of a free city in the heart of the republic and by guaranteeing this city's unobstructed communications with the East and the West.

Those who insist that it is necessary that a certain number of Western troops stay in Berlin in order to safeguard the present situation there, should learn to assess realistically the existing situation. Indeed, if there were reasons for solving the Berlin question by force, would the presence of some troops in West Berlin constitute an insurmountable obstacle, with the modern means of warfare available? On the contrary, the stay of these troops in Berlin is precisely what creates the "cancerous tumour" which all the peace-loving peoples, and above all the German people themselves, fear may grow to such dimensions that conflicts, and then open military clashes, may break out. Precisely for this reason we propose to do away with this malignant tumour, in order to create conditions which, instead of increasing tension in Europe, would, on the contrary, reduce it to naught and create a favourable climate for peaceful co-existence. The implementation of our proposal will lay the foundation for easing and improving the atmosphere in Europe and eliminating such a hotbed in Berlin.

Given the requisite understanding and good relations, favourable preconditions would be created for solving other still more complicated questions, and particularly the question of withdrawing troops, so that the armed forces of the two opposing military groupings would not be in direct contact, as a result of which there would be created a kind of disengagement zone. We are ready, on our part, to reduce the number of troops stationed in the German Democratic Republic, on condition that the Western Powers as well agree to cut down their own forces stationed in West Germany. We are even prepared to withdraw all our troops from the territories of the European countries where they are now temporarily stationed to our national frontiers, if the Western Powers do likewise. If these proposals of ours were accepted, we would be ready to establish a control over the reduction and withdrawal of foreign troops from both German states. There is hardly any need to demonstrate the advantages arising from the withdrawal of foreign troops from German territory. I am sure that this step would bring substantial alleviation to the German people.

I should like to reply, in this connection, to certain windbags who concoct fabrications about the Soviet Union intending to seize West Berlin. Their speculations on this subject are merely stupid. Such an allegation can only be made by people who desire, at whatever cost, to perpetuate the present tension, while we are striving to create conditions for the ending of the cold war, to create an atmosphere which would not poison relations among the Great Powers, and, for that matter, not solely among them. We are sincerely striving to dispel the sinister clouds of a third world war that is now being prepared by certain people. Who else, if not the Germans in the two German states, who have paid a toll of many human lives and colossal material wealth in wars, and particularly during the last war, should know what war is really like? They are fed up with wars and, I have no doubt, are opposed to the preparation of a third world war. The implementation of the Soviet proposals would create favourable conditions for a more rational use of material and monetary resources, would prevent the draining of national budgets to meet military needs, and would make them available for raising the peoples' standard of living.

The status of a free city does not impose any onerous obligations on West Berlin or its residents. We propose only one thing: West Berlin must not permit any hostile, subversive activity or propaganda on its territory against any other state, and above all against the German Democratic Republic. And furthermore, the residents of this city will be the first to gain from this—residents who are now becoming enmeshed, against their will, in the webs of various espionage and subversive organizations, and thereby exposing their own lives to grave danger.

These are some of the considerations which, in our opinion, could be taken into account in preparing a free-city status for West Berlin. Of course, this question must be thoroughly thrashed out, and the Germans themselves could make a big contribution to this effort. In the discussion of the question of turning West Berlin into a demilitarized free city, the Soviet Union is ready, of course, to set forth a more detailed definition of its status.

Question: What questions connected with the status of West Berlin does the Soviet Government believe could be the subject of talks between the four Great Powers, and what questions are not subjects for such a discussion?

Answer: In its Notes to the Governments of the three Western Powers the Soviet Government has declared the best solution to the Berlin question to be that based on the fulfilment of the Potsdam Agreement on Germany.

This would stipulate the return of the Western Powers to the Potsdam principles, to a joint policy with the Soviet Union on the German question. In that case, the question would arise of annulling the decisions taken in violation of the Potsdam Agreement, and above all of its military injunctions. It goes without saying that these questions should be the subject of a quadripartite discussion. It is true that all indications are that the Western Powers do not wish to give up their policy of turning West Germany into NATO's main atomic and rocket base, into a militarist state whose entire life, even now, is being directed along the road to war and revenge, although that road spells disaster for the Federal Republic of Germany.

In an effort to put an end to the abnormal situation in Berlin, the Soviet Union has proposed to the Western Powers that talks be initiated on granting West Berlin the status of a demilitarized free city. Besides the propositions I have set forth—propositions determining the status of the free city—all the technical questions relating to the final elimination of the vestiges of the occupation of Berlin could be the subject of talks. We would be ready to consider any possible proposals and amendments by the Western Powers.

I take the second part of your question to mean that you allow for possible Western attempts to prevent the elimination of the vestiges of the occupation régime in Berlin and to question the right of the Soviet Union to transfer to the German Democratic Republic the functions temporarily discharged by the Soviet side. In the event that the Western Powers refuse to grant the status of a free city to West Berlin, there will be no basis left for talks with the Western Powers on the Berlin question. We declare once again that we do not need the consent of the Western Powers in order to implement the steps we plan with regard to Berlin, and no claims of theirs to this effect will stop us. It is also absolutely clear that the Soviet Government will not abandon the principles of non-interference in the internal affairs of other states and will not discuss with the three Western Powers those aspects of the German problem which can and must be solved by the Germans themselves, and only by them. We would like to tell those who are trying to inveigle us into such interference that their efforts are futile and only demonstrate how far those making these attempts are from understanding the actual situation in Germany, and what a thick mist shrouds their eyes.

Question: What actions by the Western Powers would you regard as a frustration of the Soviet proposals?

Answer: The best thing for the Western Powers to do, if they really desire to ease tension in Europe and do away with potential danger points, would be to accept the Soviet proposals to turn West Berlin into a demilitarized free city. If the Western Powers refuse to accept the Soviet proposals on the Berlin question, and this is the most they can do, they will be unable, all the same, to prevent steps —which depend on the Soviet Union—from being taken to eliminate the vestiges of occupation in Berlin, because these vestiges must and shall be done away with. I shall say nothing of the fact that in the event the Western Powers refuse to seek, together with the Soviet Union, for a reasonable basis for doing away with the occupation régime in West Berlin, they will expose themselves before the German people—and, for that matter, not merely before them—as advocating the maintenance of an occupation régime for an indefinitely long period.

To continue the occupation of West Berlin means to contribute toward carrying on and even stepping up the cold war. The preservation of such a régime is explicable only by a desire on the part of the Western Powers to prepare for a hot war. There is, and there can be, no other explanation because, if statesmen of the countries on which this depends really want to create normal conditions and eliminate all that is fraught with the danger of war, then nothing better than our proposals is conceivable. If some other ways and means for eliminating tension were indicated, we would gladly consider and accept them. But it seems to us that in our proposals we have exhausted all possibilities and we hope that tomorrow, if not today, those responsible for the destiny of the world will realize the timely and reasonable nature of our proposals.

The Western Powers have violated the obligations they assumed towards the end of the war to destroy aggressive German militarism. The Soviet Union is not bound by the commitments of the Western Powers to equip West Germany with atomic weapons. If the Western Powers do not accept our proposals for eliminating the danger spot in West Berlin, it will confirm that their actions point to an early completion of the arming of West Germany and preparation for a third world war. Therefore we shall press with increasing insistence for ending the present situation in West Berlin.

Some hot-headed Western military leaders take the liberty of making irresponsible statements concerning armed forces and tanks to be used in clearing the way to Berlin. But is it not clear that this would mean war, because the other side also has tanks and other more powerful weapons which would not remain inactive. We do not believe that the West wishes to unleash war in connection with the Soviet Union's proposal to abolish the last vestiges of the occupation régime in Berlin and in connection with the fact that the German Democratic Republic will gain complete sovereignty after taking over the functions temporarily discharged by the Soviet side. But if, to our regret, this does happen, and if the frontier along the Elbe is violated and aggression against the German Democratic Republic is committed, then the Soviet Union, as a loyal ally of the German Democratic Republic under the Warsaw Treaty, will fulfil its commitments and, together with the German Democratic Republic, will safeguard the inviolability of the republic's land, water and air frontiers. The entire responsibility for the consequences will be borne by those who try to secure by force their domination over territory belonging to another state, that is to say, to violate the sovereignty of the German Democratic Republic. Therefore the best solution to the problem would be to stop playing with war and settle the Berlin question with due consideration for the interests of our peoples and our future.

Question: What is your attitude to the arming of the Federal Republic of Germany with atomic weapons?

Answer: Those who advocate arming the Bundeswehr with nuclear and rocket weapons are trying to present matters as if the measures they are taking in this direction are necessary to protect the Federal Republic of Germany from some "threat" coming from the East, and as if these might ensure the security of the Federal Republic. It is not difficult to see that these allegations, to say the least, have nothing in common with the truth. The talk about a "threat" from the Soviet Union is deception, and its purpose is to justify measures aimed at drawing the Federal Republic into the atomic and rocket race and to stir up hatred against the Soviet Union among the West German population.

The Soviet Union has never waged any aggressive wars—such wars are foreign to the very nature of our state. The U.S.S.R. does not intend, and never has intended, to attack either the Federal Republic of Germany or any other state. The threat of "local attacks" on the Federal Republic by the Soviet Union, with which the Federal Republic's Defence Minister Strauss recently tried to scare the West German population, is an absurd fabrication invented to meet the needs of revenge-seekers and militarists. West Germany as a state would undoubtedly stand to gain and would earn the confidence of neighbouring peoples if it called to order the ill-starred strategists in the Federal Republic who continue to slander peace-loving nations and foment revanchist passions among the German population.

The Soviet Government fully shares the opinion of those West German circles who maintain that nuclear weapons cannot serve as a means of ensuring the security of the Federal Republic of Germany, and that arming the Bundeswehr with these weapons, and stationing these weapons on West German territory, threaten to destroy the Federal Republic of Germany and spell death for millions upon millions of Germans, since all these measures are pushing West Germany further and further along the road of war preparations. Only politically blind and ignorant people can fail to see the horrible prospects which are being prepared for the Federal Republic of Germany by those who are shaping the present military and political course of this state.

We get the impression that those who advocate the nuclear arming of the Federal Republic either do not realize to the full the danger to which they are exposing the West German population or are doing this deliberately. In either case they are committing a crime by pushing the Federal Republic of Germany along a fatal course.

Question: Do you continue to support the proposal for a confederation of the German states?

Answer: The Soviet Government has repeatedly stated that the reunification of Germany is an internal matter concerning the two German states. The solution of this question can be effected only by the Germans themselves; it cannot be introduced or imposed by someone from outside.

One can only be astonished by the statements of responsible officials of the Western Powers and the Federal Republic of Germany to the effect that the Americans and the British are better qualified to solve the task of restoring Germany's unity than the Germans themselves. This by no means signifies that the Great Powers could not play a definite part in restoring the unity of Germany by facilitating a *rapprochement* of the two German states. But the Western Powers do not wish to promote this; they prefer to prescribe formulas to the Germans. This attitude of the Western Powers and the Federal Republic with regard to reunification is unrealistic.

Let us be frank. The people in the German Democratic Republic are building socialism, while the capitalist system still exists in the western part of the country. Only people who are completely divorced from reality can suggest a mechanical merger of two different states. Given such an attitude, the impasse reached on reunification cannot be resolved.

Proceeding on the basis of the situation that actually prevails—the existence of two sovereign German states with different social and economic systems—the Government of the German Democratic Republic has put forward a constructive plan for the reunification of Germany through the creation of a confederation. This idea is gaining ground every day. Increasingly broad sections of the German population approve of this proposal of the Government of the German Democratic Republic.

You are well aware that the Soviet Government fully supports the initiative of the German Democratic Republic. In the present situation the formation of a confederation is a reliable and practical way of establishing a united democratic German state. No doubt you also know that in spite of the favourable prospects opened up by the proposal for confederation, Chancellor Adenauer rejects this way—the only realistic way—of reuniting Germany. This shows once again that the ruling circles of the Federal Republic of Germany are using the talk about German unity merely as a smoke-screen and that in actual fact they are enemies of this unity. They do not want the reunification of the country, but only talk about reunification. In actual fact Adenauer and his followers fear the reunification of Germany, since the establishment of a united, peaceful, democratic Germany would mean the collapse of their plans for making West Germany the main striking force of the aggressive NATO military bloc and the collapse of their plans for aggression and revenge.

If the Federal Chancellor were really concerned about the restoration of the country's unity would he then emerge as the leader of a campaign for continuing the occupation of West Berlin indefinitely? Why is he doing this? In any case, it is not being done in the interests of the West Berlin population, who have to put up with the occupation régime. Nor is it being done, of course, in the interests of a *détente* and the establishment of normal relations between neighbouring countries.

Or let us take the question of a peace treaty with Germany. It is indeed unbelievable that the Head of the Government of one of the existing German states does not want to conclude a peace treaty through negotiations with the Soviet Union and the three Western Powers—the leading participants in the anti-Hitler coalition—and with the participation of the two sovereign German states which have emerged on the territory of Germany. Chancellor Adenauer, like his NATO partners, is apparently striving for some other peace treaty which would actually abolish the German Democratic Republic. But no sober-minded person can expect this to be accepted. What grounds are there for raising the question of abolishing the German Democratic Republic—the first workers' and peasants' state in the history of Germany? For that matter, the Germans in the German Democratic Republic could suggest the abolition of the Federal Republic of Germany and reunify the country on the basis of the socialist principles on which the German Democratic Republic is based. But it is obvious that neither of these two approaches to the question is realistic. The only practical possibility of solving the German question once and for all is through a peaceful settlement with Germany. In concluding a peace treaty with Germany, the existence of the two German states must undoubtedly be taken into consideration and they must be invited to take part in the negotiations of the four Great Powers. This would be the most reasonable solution to the problem and would be welcomed by the people of all countries, who yearn for the relaxation of tension and for peace to be secured. But if the Federal Chancellor insists on something else, it signifies that he is pursuing other aims but not those which guarantee peace. It means that he is pursuing a dangerous "positions of strength" policy. He wishes to create an army and to arm it with atomic weapons; he wishes to pursue a policy of force. Thus it follows that Chancellor Adenauer is pursuing a policy which may lead to disaster, to the collapse of West Germany, since under present conditions, with the existence of modern weapons of mass destruction, war would be of a devastating nature. This is monstrous, of course, but it is a fact, and we must not shut our eyes to it. We would like to believe that the sound patriotic forces which exist in West Germany and are concerned for the destiny of their people, will correctly understand this in good time and do everything in their power to prevent the unleashing of a third world war.

Pravda, December 13, 1958